The Elementary School Teacher

The Elementary School Teacher

DOROTHY G. PETERSEN
Chairman, Graduate Study
TRENTON STATE COLLEGE

New York: APPLETON-CENTURY-CROFTS
Division of Meredith Publishing Company

To My Husband

Preface

A SHORT TIME ago, the author visited one of the most magnificent elementary school buildings in the country. It was obvious at a glance that the city taxpayers had spared no expense in providing for their children a physical plant which was designed to implement the best of educational theory and knowledge. The spacious and flexible classrooms which could be adapted to a variety of purposes were a joy to behold. The science laboratory, creative arts studio, audio-visual department, medical-dental suite, and the outdoor education facilities were only some of the outstanding features of this impressive plant. A little overawed by such magnificence, the author paused for a few minutes in a third grade classroom to chat with the children. She told them how much she admired their new school and asked them if they also liked it. Every third grade head nodded enthusiastically. She then commented, "There are so many wonderful things about your school, I don't know which one I like the best. Will you tell me what you like most about your school?" The answer came back immediately: "We like our teacher!"

The incident is significant because it points up a fact long recognized by most, but unfortunately forgotten by some, namely, that the most important factor in the education of children is, and always will be, *the classroom teacher*. Good teachers make good schools. Poor teachers make poor schools. This fact in no way contradicts the importance of physical facilities, organizational patterns, administrative plans, experimental instructional devices, and other factors receiving much attention in current literature. Research and experimentation on the contributions these may make to the total educational program are undoubtedly commendable and should be encouraged. But preoccupation with these should never obscure the basic fact that the quality of education in any school or nation is directly proportionate to the competence of its teachers.

This book focuses upon the roles and responsibilities of the classroom teacher as the central feature of a quality educational program. Part I examines both the position and the person. The social, professional, and economic status of the elementary teacher, together with basic requirements and conditions of service, are examined in historical perspective. In this section, also, is included a discussion of the personal qualities and professional competencies usually associated with teaching effectiveness in the elementary school.

One of the most important and demanding aspects of the elementary teacher's task is the establishment of harmonious interpersonal and intergroup relationships. Part II discusses the relationships of the teacher with his pupils, their parents, and his professional colleagues.

The teacher's major duties and responsibilities in guiding the learning process are examined in Part III. His duties in providing a desirable learning environment, organizing and planning the teaching-learning situation, improving the curriculum, providing for a wide range of pupil abilities, securing and using to best advantage the many worthwhile instructional materials available today, and appraising the growth of pupils constitute the major emphases in this section of the book.

One of the major characteristics of the effective elementary teacher is his continuing professional and personal growth. The last section discusses the teacher's continuing growth through participation in a structured in-service education program, self-directed improvement activities, and the identification and solution of certain persistent problems associated with elementary school teaching.

The book is designed as a text for an introductory course in elementary school teaching. It should be helpful to college students, on any level, who seek a thorough understanding of the basic principles, techniques, and procedures of effective elementary school teaching. It should also be of interest to in-service teachers who are attempting to refine the quality of their classroom performance. Supervisors and principals should find it of value in guiding elementary teachers toward improved classroom practices.

The author is indebted to many friends and colleagues who have offered valuable advice, assistance, and criticism. She wishes to acknowledge especially the contributions of the following people at Trenton State College: Mr. Jay Mills of the staff of the Antheil Demonstration School; Dr. Robert Worthington, Chairman of the Industrial Arts Department; Dr. George Krablin, Chairman of the Health and Physical Education Department; Dr. Robert Price, Associate Professor of Mathematics; Mr. John McIlroy, Associate Professor of Mathematics; Mr. Warren Nutt, Assistant Professor of Education; and Mr. James Silver, Associate Professor of Education.

The photographs of classroom activities were taken at the Joseph Stokes Memorial School in Trenton, New Jersey, and the author is grateful to the principal, Miss F. Myrtle Goetz, and to the faculty of that school for their very willing cooperation and assistance.

The author's indebtedness to Dr. William H. Burton, Consulting Editor of textbooks in Education for her publishers, for his helpful editing of the entire text is equaled only by her respect for him as an educator.

Above all, the author is indebted to her husband and parents who have been a constant source of encouragement and inspiration to her in this project, as in all others.

D.G.P.

Contents

PART **I**

THE POSITION AND THE PERSON

THE BEST should teach. Teaching beckons to those with the brightest minds, the finest personalities, and the soundest moral and spiritual commitments. It holds before them a life packed with excitement and satisfaction. It appeals to them to make the mature choice to put service to humanity above self.

Although teaching promises little material rewards, the invitation is extended without apology. It is a call to join the ranks of the truly great of the ages. Teachers are the curators of all our yesterdays and the architects of our tomorrows. Always they accomplish their mission through the minds and talents of others.

To do is noteworthy; but to be able to do and to devote one's knowledge and energies to helping others learn is man's noblest work.

The world seldom notices who teachers are; but civilization depends on what they do.

Lindley J. Stiles, "The Best Should Teach," *Wisconsin Journal of Education,* Vol. 90 (March, 1958), p. 7.

CHAPTER **1**

The Position—Then and Now

Eunice, why does not thee open a school? Thee knows the verbs
and the articles and I will come once a week and do the whipping.[1]

THE PASSING YEARS have produced a far different concept of the elementary school teacher than that held by the Nantucket Quakeress who gave
this advice to her daughter. From a fairly humble origin, the position of
the elementary teacher has risen steadily to one of increasing stature,
importance, and respect. Many factors have contributed to this change,
most of which are discussed in the present chapter. However, none are
more important than the character, ability, and personality of the countless number of men and women who have held the position over the past
many years. Of course there have been some, perhaps more than we like
to admit, who have been incompetent, poorly prepared, and unsuccessful.
This is true in all fields. But in teaching, these have been overshadowed
by the many great and inspired teachers who have devoted their lives to
the education of young children. There was, for instance, the incom-
parable Anne Sullivan about whom her gifted pupil, Helen Keller, said,
"The most important day I remember in all my life is the one on which
my teacher, Anne Mansfield Sullivan, came to me."[2]

There was also a Miss Williams whose kindness earned the undying gratitude of a poor, friendless, itinerant waif who later became a prominent
writer and lecturer.

There was Miss Williams, kind and motherly, who let me stay in at recess and
water her plants. She had found me hiding in the fire escape. It was a big
round pipe on the outside of the building, through which pupils could slide to
the ground in case of fire. Many of the school buildings used to have them. I
would crawl up inside them at recess to hide, so the children on the playground

---

[1] Christopher Coffin Hussey, *Talks about Old Nantucket* (n. p., 1901), p. 20.
[2] Helen Keller, "Out of the Dark," in Houston Peterson, ed., *Great Teachers* (New
Brunswick, N. J., Rutgers University Press, 1946), p. 5.

3

could not tease me. Miss Williams saw me through her window and let me climb in over the window sill as though we were playing a game. She did not scold, but rather laughed with me about it. She did not ask a question, but always, after that, she had some work for me to do at recess. I understood her motive, and yet it did not crush my spirit to accept her favor. I felt that she knew I understood and we shared a plot together. The whole situation was simply a temporary inconvenience which a camper kid had to put up with until she could get enough schooling to catch up with the people who lived in houses.[3]

When Miss Emma Belle Sweet received the Golden Key Award of the American Association of School Administrators, her distinguished pupil, Dr. Ralph J. Bunche, paid the following tribute to her. "I imagine that there is no greater happiness that can come to a boy in a classroom, particularly if that boy has been bruised with rebuffs and humiliation elsewhere, than to be given to understand by his teacher that he belongs, that he is wanted and respected and even liked, that he counts as all the others count."[4]

One could go on and on in a discussion of outstanding elementary school teachers. There is, for instance, Mary Field Schwarz, housewife, mother, and third-grade teacher who, when nominated a few years ago by a board of educators as the "teacher of the year," had managed to create a wonderfully exciting place for children to learn in a substandard, temporary classroom converted from a once-condemned church.[5] Still another is Elda Mae Childers who explains her success at working with fifth-graders in the modest statement, "I don't really know. The youngsters just work like Trojans and they learn."[6]

Then there is Carol Eldridge who, when asked what she likes about teaching, replies, "Things like the thrill you get when the child who's been a word-reader starts making the characters in the story talk . . . the way the light will break on a child's face when he really understands . . . that sudden unexpected proof that one of your private talks about right human conduct has paid off."[7]

Another "teacher of the year" is Jean Listebarger whose popularity with children and parents may be explained by the fact that, "She possesses a rare insight into the emotional needs of children, and under her

---

[3] Billie Davis, "I Was a Hobo Kid," *The Saturday Evening Post*, Vol. 225 (December 13, 1952), p. 107. Reprinted by special permission of *The Saturday Evening Post*. Copyright 1952 The Curtis Publishing Company.

[4] "Emma Belle Sweet," *NEA Journal*, Vol. 51 (May, 1962), p. 39.

[5] "McCall's Teacher of the Year," *McCall's*, Vol. 84 (June, 1957), pp. 62, 67-68.

[6] H. E. Philby, "Today's Teacher Series," *NEA Journal*, Vol. 48 (May, 1959), p. 41.

[7] Ed Ritter, "Today's Teacher Series: *I Love Teaching Children*," *NEA Journal*, Vol. 48 (September, 1959), p. 42.

skillful management they acquire an unmistakable inner contentment and calmness which contribute importantly to their success in the classroom."[8]

Each of these, and hundreds of thousands of others—great or mediocre, famous or unknown, capable or inept, past or present, young or old, man or woman—has contributed a part of the composite of the position of the elementary school teacher as we know it today. The developing concept of the position according to its (1) social and professional status, (2) economic status, (3) requirements of educational preparation and certification, and (4) conditions of service is examined in this chapter.

SOCIAL AND PROFESSIONAL STATUS

In this new, raw, bustling land of a few centuries ago, it was perhaps natural that recognition was given to the man of action, the doer. Homes needed to be built; land had to be plowed; dangers threatened survival; crops had to be harvested. In such a culture the teacher was frequently on the periphery. He was accepted but was rarely considered essential to the existence of these hardy, busy people.

Moreover, of no one was this more true than of the teacher of young children. In some communities, the teacher of the grammar school was occasionally a well-educated, cultured individual who enjoyed a certain prestige among his fellow colonists. This was usually not true of the "lower school" teacher, particularly in the rural areas. Our worthy forefathers reasoned, with dubious logic, that since the knowledge of young children was very limited, any adult was capable of teaching them. For more than two hundred years this absurd assumption dominated the educational scene of the country. It accounted for the fact that the colonial teacher of the lower school was often, at his best, a well-meaning but inpecunious, poorly educated, and incompetent individual. Occasionally, he was an indentured servant serving out in labor his passage to the new world. Or he may have been physically incapacitated, unable to perform in more important occupations such as wig-making or rail-splitting. At his worst, he was a drunkard, a scoundrel, a rogue, or a fugitive from justice.

Throughout the nineteenth century and the early years of the twentieth century, many educational leaders fought long and hard to raise the caliber of teachers and the level of the profession. Today, there is considerable evidence that these efforts were not in vain and, for the first time in our history, we are perhaps nearing a breakthrough that will place teaching in the front ranks of all professions. What evidence do we have that this is true?

[8] "McCall's Teacher of the Year," *McCall's*, Vol. 85 (March, 1958), p. 60.

THE PUBLIC IMAGE OF THE TEACHER IS STEADILY GAINING IN PRESTIGE AND IMPORTANCE. The often-inferior caliber of the teacher of the past resulted in an unfortunate stereotype of the teacher which has dogged the profession for years. Even today, in popular periodicals, one may find teaching labeled as the "underdog profession" and teachers pictured as "public drudges" who are "wretchedly overworked, underpaid, and disregarded."[9] The image of the woman teacher has frequently been that of a frustrated, embittered female to whom the joys of normal living are denied. The male teacher, in the past, has been considered vaguely effeminate, and either too incompetent or too lazy to make his way in a nonacademic man's world. In recent years, however, there is some evidence to indicate that this unfavorable stereotype of teaching and teachers is rapidly disappearing. Not a few studies show that the profession is viewed with a steadily increasing regard by the general public.

In 1953, for instance, a Gallup poll survey showed that the professor-teacher ranked below doctor, engineer-builder, clergyman, lawyer, business executive, and dentist as a preferred occupation in the eyes of the public. Nine years later, in 1962, the professor-teacher had moved to third rank, below only doctor and engineer-builder as a preferred profession. Furthermore, in the younger age group (21-29) teaching ranked second only to doctor in preference.[10]

Other studies also show the increasing interest in, and growing prestige of, teaching as a career. For instance, Peckham[11] found that 72 per cent of high school students considered teaching an interesting and challenging career, and almost 50 per cent thought that it was a profession comparable to law and medicine. Of these twelve hundred students, 29 per cent of the girls and 18 per cent of the boys, indicated an interest in teaching. Although Peckham claims that this is a "discouraging" picture, it seems to be encouraging when viewed against the background of earlier studies. In 1952, for instance, a survey of approximately fourteen hundred high school students revealed that only 12.7 per cent chose teaching as a career.[12] Still earlier studies report that the percentage of young people choosing teaching was as low as five[13] and six[14] per cent.

[9] "An Underdog Profession Imperils the Schools," *Life*, Vol. 44 (March 31, 1958), pp. 93-95.

[10] American Institute of Public Opinion Release, August 15, 1962, Princeton, N. J.

[11] Dorothy Reed Peckham and others, "High School Seniors' Opinion of Teaching," *California Journal of Educational Research*, Vol. 13 (January, 1962), pp. 17-30.

[12] Ruth Martinson and Olive L. Thompson, "Attitudes of High School Seniors Toward Teaching," *California Journal of Educational Research*, Vol. 5 (May, 1954), pp. 103-108.

[13] Ward Cramer, "A Vocational Attitudes Survey of Seniors in 28 Ohio High Schools," *School and Society*, Vol. 67 (June 19, 1948), pp. 462-463.

[14] Curtis H. Threlkeld, "Problems in the Recruitment and Adjustment of Teachers," *Bulletin of the National Association of Secondary School Principals*, Vol. 32 (March, 1948), pp. 168-175.

It is interesting to note that occasionally young people have a higher regard for teaching than do teachers themselves. O'Dowd and Beardslee discovered that college students, in general, appeared to have a more favorable image of the teacher than did professors and concluded that, "Of the many images studied in this research program, the school teacher is among the most hopeful. If the economic and social status of the occupation were improved, it would almost certainly demonstrate great drawing power among college men."[15]

In general, then, there seems to be some basis for optimism concerning the increasing prestige of teaching as a career.

THERE ARE CERTAIN SPECIFIC FACTORS THAT ARE ASSOCIATED WITH A FAVORABLE CONCEPT OF TEACHING. Many studies indicate that the favorable factors associated with teaching are both altruistic and practical. In the first category are such motivations as (1) an opportunity to work with children and youth, (2) an opportunity to be of service to society and a benefit to mankind, and (3) an opportunity to impart knowledge. For example, a survey of teachers in service reports that more than one third of them were enthusiastic about, ". . . the love of teaching and the rewarding sense of achievement that comes from work with children and young people and contributing thru their lives to a better future."[16]

This is also true of prospective teachers and such studies as those of Martinson and Thompson,[17] Hardaway,[18] Johnson,[19] Slobetz,[20] and Richey, et al.[21] report that high on the list of factors that motivate young people toward teaching are (1) liking for children and people, (2) service to community and country, (3) satisfaction of watching children grow and learn, and (4) opportunity to improve the world.

In addition, there are certain practical aspects of teaching that are related to its desirability as a career. In general, those mentioned most often include (1) security of job, (2) good hours, (3) long vacation, (4)

[15] Donald D. O'Dowd and David C. Beardslee, "The Student Image of the School Teacher," *Phi Delta Kappan*, Vol. 42 (March, 1961), p. 254.

[16] "The Status of the American Public-School Teacher," *NEA Research Bulletin*, Vol. 35 (February, 1957), p. 40.

[17] Ruth Martinson and Olive L. Thompson, *op. cit.*

[18] Charles Hardaway, "Factors Influencing High School Seniors to Choose or Not to Choose Teaching as a Profession," *Teachers College Journal*, Vol. 27 (May, 1956), pp. 107, 110.

[19] Alfred Harold Johnson, "The Responses of High School Seniors to a Set of Structured Situations Concerning Teaching as a Career," *Journal of Experimental Education*, Vol. 26 (June, 1958), pp. 263-314.

[20] Frank Slobetz, "A Study of Some Attitudes of Prospective Teachers Toward Teaching," *Teachers College Journal*, Vol. 27 (May, 1956), pp. 93-95, 110.

[21] Robert W. Richey, Beeman N. Phillips, and William H. Fox, *Factors that High School Students Associate with Selection of Teaching as a Vocation*, Bulletin of the School of Education, Indiana University, Vol. 28 (March, 1952).

number of employment opportunities, (5) pleasant working conditions, (6) pleasant associates, and (7) interesting work.

THERE ARE ALSO CERTAIN DISADVANTAGES ASSOCIATED WITH TEACHING. Not all attitudes are positive toward teaching, for there are some undesirable features that, according to several studies, deter people from entering the profession or cause them to leave teaching to enter another field. Undoubtedly, the most important of these are summarized as follows: "Foremost among the disadvantages listed by all the students for teaching was low salaries, followed in order of rank by such major factors as: little chance for personal improvement, personal restrictions, too much preparation, dull and monotonous work, too much responsibility, and too much politics."[22]

Many of these so-called disadvantages are examined later in this chapter as well as in other chapters and there is no need for comment here. One, however, is worthy of serious thought because it appears in numerous studies. The evidence appears to be fairly consistent that some young people are reluctant to enter teaching because they consider it to be "dull and monotonous work." Obviously this is a strong indictment of teaching *as they have been exposed to it* for twelve or thirteen years. It would seem, therefore, that one of the best means of placing teaching in a more favorable light, and of recruiting promising young people into the field, is for teachers to demonstrate to their pupils that teaching is exciting and challenging work. If young people think that teaching is dull and uninteresting, it is largely because the teachers they have known have made it dull and uninteresting. On the other hand, if young people think of teaching as an intensely rewarding, satisfying, and stimulating career, it is because their teachers have made it so.

Closely associated with this point is another finding, revealed in some studies, which should be disturbing to any conscientious and dedicated teacher. *An appallingly small number* of students report that they are favorably motivated toward teaching by the example or counsel of any teacher or guidance counselor they have known. Martinson and Thompson report, for instance, that only 2 of the 181 high school students who chose teaching as a career ". . . had been attracted to teaching because of whatever effect their teachers may have had on them."[23] Fox found that 48 per cent of his respondents indicated that in their decisions to become teachers they had been influenced to a significant degree by former teachers, but he states,

One discouraging finding of this study is the relatively small number of respondents who indicated that guidance received from counselors in high school

22 *Ibid.*, p. 43.
23 Ruth Martinson and Olive L. Thompson, *op. cit.*, pp. 104-107.

or college was a significant factor in their decision to become teachers . . . only 9 per cent of the respondents—all of whom are prospective teachers— listed guidance received from a counselor in high school as a significant factor.[24]

There is, therefore, one inescapable fact that must be faced by all teachers. If teaching, as a career, is going to continue to grow in public favor and prestige, teachers and counselors must, through example and counseling, attempt to attract the most capable young people into the field. Thus, a cyclic process is established in which good teachers will continually attract more good teachers who will, in turn, achieve an increasing prestige and status in the eyes of the public.

TEACHING IS RAPIDLY APPROACHING PROFESSIONAL MATURITY. Is teaching a profession? This is a difficult question to answer for it depends, of course, upon the definition of a profession. Many authorities have offered definitions, although none is universally accepted. However, in the numerous lists of criteria suggested by various authorities, the following are among those usually considered as characteristic of a profession.

1. Performs a unique, essential, social service.
2. Emphasizes service above personal gain.
3. Emphasizes a high level of intellectual activity.
4. Requires specific skills, abilities, and a systematic body of knowledge, all of which can be developed only in a long period of specialized preparation.
5. Has high standards of admission.
6. Develops, maintains, and enforces a code of ethics for its members.
7. Maintains a strong professional organization.
8. Emphasizes continual self-growth and professional improvement of its members.
9. Accords a high degree of autonomy to individuals and to the profession as a whole.
10. Emphasizes acceptance of personal responsibility by its members.
11. Is considered a life occupation by its members.

It is readily apparent that teaching has achieved full professional maturity as measured by some of these criteria. There is no doubt, for instance, that it performs an essential social service or that its members place a higher premium upon service than upon personal gain.

As measured by other criteria, teaching is rapidly making progress toward full professional maturity. In recent years, for instance, it has made great strides in developing, emphasizing, and enforcing a code of

[24] Raymond B. Fox, "Factors Influencing the Career Choice of Prospective Teachers," *Journal of Teacher Education*, Vol. 12 (December, 1961), p. 428.

ethics for its members (see Chapter 5). The strength and influence of its professional organizations are, of course, steadily growing. Then too, a large majority of opinion accepts the growing importance of the teacher's continued personal and professional growth (see Chapter 12).

On the other hand, one of the greatest handicaps to the professional maturity of teaching has been the failure of some to recognize the existence of specialized skills, abilities, and knowledges peculiar to teaching. As long as either the general public or teachers themselves think that teaching requires only some "common sense" and a few "tricks of the trade" that can be learned on the job, teaching can never achieve full professional maturity. However, the strenuous efforts of the profession in the past few years to raise the standards of quality performance, to lengthen and strengthen the program of preparation, and to tighten and raise certification requirements (see pp. 23 to 37) have done much to dispel the old craft concept of teaching and consequently to move teaching continuously forward toward its goal of professional maturity.

The eleventh criterion in the preceding list is one that deserves the serious attention of teachers. In the past, teaching was often considered a "steppingstone" to other fields (particularly by men) or as a "stopgap" before marriage and raising a family (by women). This concept has had two unfortunate results. In the first place, it has been an impediment to the full professionalization of teaching. Mason and others, in a study of the career orientation of beginning teachers, state the problem as follows:

Relatively few new teachers intended to stay in teaching until retirement. A large proportion of women expected to leave teaching, at least temporarily, for homemaking responsibilities, indicating that for them their sex role was dominant over their occupational role. On the other hand, many men hoped to move from classroom teaching into administrative and supervisory positions. Both the contingent career commitment of the women and the limited commitment of the men were seen to be impediments to the professionalization of teaching.[25]

The second obvious unfortunate result of the concept of teaching as a contingent career is, of course, a large annual teacher-turnover. This has been a problem for years, although there is some evidence that it is gradually being reduced. One study reports that in 1956 the median teacher service for elementary school teachers was thirteen and a half years which was almost double the median length of service in 1931. The study concludes, "The well-worn jibe that 'teaching isn't a profession, it's a procession' begins to lose its point. Shifts and lack of continuity are still found, but progress toward a stable profession is apparent."[26]

It should be fairly evident that two steps need to be taken to establish the concept of teaching as a life occupation. In regard to the conflict of women between teaching and home-family interests, no person in his right mind would suggest that the former be given preference over the latter. However, some progress can be made by searching for ". . . social inventions which will reduce the conflict between occupational and family responsibilities, and make simultaneous performance in the two roles more feasible."[27]

A more complete solution, however, is to invite professionally minded, career-oriented men and women into teaching by making it as attractive as possible in every respect, particularly in regard to economic status. The progress being made toward this goal is examined in the following section.

ECONOMIC STATUS

From the beginning of time, society has failed to reward its teachers with adequate financial remuneration for their services. Certainly this has been true in our own country, and throughout the years one can find countless statements to the effect that, "the teacher is poorly paid, all will concede"[28] and "the economic status of the teacher has become so pitiable that by far the most popular 'whine' at all the teachers' meetings is 'Teachers are underpaid'."[29]

In short, there can be little quarrel with the following statement.

For a great many years, as far back as we can trace the figures, at least, America has underpaid its school marms, professors, and educational administrators. It has filled the teaching ranks with "dedicated people," men and women who would rather be educators than anything else—who would trade some economic affluence for an academic atmosphere or the way of life that characterizes school teaching, academic research, or similar activities.[30]

There are many reasons why teachers have in the past received low salaries. In general these include: (1) the traditionally low social and professional status as well as the unfavorable stereotype of the teacher, mentioned previously, (2) the fact that public employees have never

---

[26] "The Status of the American Public-School Teacher," *op. cit.*, p. 16.
[27] Ward S. Mason, Robert J. Dressel, and Robert K. Bain, *op. cit.*, p. 383.
[28] "Teachers' Salaries," *Teachers' Institute*, Vol. 22 (April, 1900), p. 322.
[29] Belmont Farley, "From a School Teacher Himself to School Teachers Themselves," *Popular Educator*, Vol. 37 (March, 1920), p. 368.
[30] Sidney G. Tickton, *Teaching Salaries Then and Now—A Second Look* (New York, The Fund for the Advancement of Education, 1961), p. 7.

been paid as well as private employees, (3) the low standards of preparation and education required of teachers, (4) the concept of teaching as a
"part-time" job, (5) the supply of teachers that often exceeded the
demand, and (6) the predominance of women in the profession since
approximately 1850.

IN RECENT YEARS, HOWEVER, THE PICTURE HAS CHANGED CONSIDERABLY.
We have, and will continue to have, a grave shortage of well-qualified
teachers. Standards of preparation and certification are continually being
strengthened (see Section III). Conditions of service are becoming more
attractive (see Section IV). The determination and efforts of the organized profession to achieve higher salaries are finally succeeding. Most
important of all, however, is the new awareness, on the part of the general public, of the importance of teaching. As everyone knows, recent
technological and scientific developments have precipitated an unprecedented amount of criticism of the public schools, most of which has been
entirely unwarranted. However, as Fischer states, out of this criticism has
come a new appreciation of the importance of good schools and good
teachers.[31] The public, perhaps for the first time in our history, is beginning to appreciate the man of thought—the scholar and the teacher. And,
with this new appreciation and recognition, has come a greater willingness
to raise the economic status of teachers.

THE ECONOMIC STATUS OF TEACHERS HAS IMPROVED CONSIDERABLY IN
RECENT YEARS. At the turn of the century, the average annual salary of
teachers was "$270 . . . a standing disgrace to the richest country of the
world."[32] The average monthly salary for teachers in urban areas in
Missouri was $55.30 and for rural areas, $35.75, while blacksmiths received approximately $66.00 per month and carpenters, $56.00 monthly.[33]

In 1919, the minimum annual salary for elementary school teachers was
$1200 in St. Louis, $900 in Buffalo, and $1500 in Detroit.[34]

In 1942-43, ". . . only two states paid all of their teachers $1200 or
more" and several received less than $600 annually.[35]

In 1950-51, the average annual salary of the total instructional staff was
$3126. Twelve years later, in 1961-62, this figure had risen to $5716,
representing an average increase of almost 83 per cent. Furthermore, dur-

---

[31] John H. Fischer, "Why Teach?" *NEA Journal*, Vol. 51 (April, 1962), p. 31.
[32] "The Professional and Financial Side," *Teachers' Institute*, Vol. 27 (September,
1904), p. 69.
[33] "The Professional and Financial Side," *Teachers' Institute*, Vol. 27 (April, 1905),
p. 289.
[34] John W. Withers, "Teachers' Salaries," *Popular Educator*, Vol. 37 (May, 1920),
p. 498.
[35] Helen Fuller, "Teacher Shortages," *Progressive Education*, Vol. 22 (November,
1944), p. 9.

ing this period the average annual salary of elementary school teachers increased almost 90 per cent—from $2806 to $5327. By 1962-63 the average annual salary of elementary teachers had risen to $5,560.[36]

The evidence indicates fairly clearly that teaching salaries have steadily increased with marked acceleration since 1950. However, these figures are not too meaningful unless some comparisons with other occupations are made.

TEACHERS' SALARIES HAVE MADE SOME IMPROVEMENT AS COMPARED WITH THOSE OF WORKERS IN OTHER FIELDS, ALTHOUGH PERHAPS NOT AS MUCH AS THEY SHOULD. Figure 1.1 indicates the estimated average salaries of in-

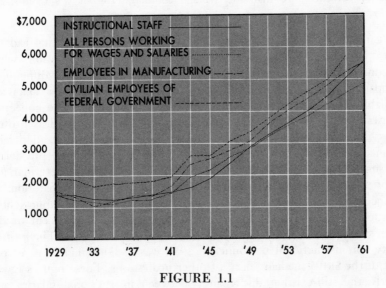

FIGURE 1.1

Trends in earnings of instructional staff compared with earnings of certain other groups. From *Economic Status of Teachers in 1961-62.* Research Report, 1962-R7. (Washington, D. C., National Education Association, Research Division, May, 1962), p. 19.

structural personnel from 1929 to 1961 as compared with the average annual earnings of (1) all persons working for wages and salaries, (2) employees in manufacturing, and (3) civilian employees of the federal government. It can be seen that, since 1952, teachers' salaries have accel-

[36] National Education Association, Research Division, *Economic Status of Teachers in 1961-62*, Research Report 1962-R7 (Washington, D. C., May, 1962), pp. 5-8. The 1962-63 figure is from ———, *Economic Status of Teachers in 1962-63*, Research Report 1963-R9 (Washington, D. C., August, 1963) p. 7.

erated to surpass those of wage and salary workers in general, and to match those of manufacturing employees. The trend is summarized as follows:

Perhaps most significant are the trends from about 1950. This has been in general a time of great prosperity in the United States. It is axiomatic that the salaries of government workers are slow to respond to the business cycle. They fall less rapidly than earnings in private employment during periods of depression, and rise less rapidly than earnings in private employment during periods of prosperity or generally rising wage-and-salary rates . . . The average salary of teachers followed this pattern during the depression and World War II. But since 1953, the average salary of teachers has begun to move away from the average for all workers, so that by 1961, teachers were on the average earning some 14 percent more than the average computed for all wage-and-salary workers.[37]

TEACHERS' SALARIES ARE NOT YET EQUAL WITH THOSE OF OTHER PROFESSIONAL WORKERS. Differences in required periods of preparation, work schedules, duties, and major responsibilities make it extremely difficult to compare teachers' salaries with those of specific professions. Data are available, however, that compare instructional salaries with the collective salaries of seventeen other occupations, commonly designated as professions. These include architects, chemists, clergymen, dentists, dieticians, engineers, foresters and conservationists, lawyers and judges, physicians and surgeons, social and welfare workers, social scientists, and veterinarians, all of which require a minimum of four years of college preparation.

According to recent figures, the *mean* annual salary for public-school instructional personnel in 1958 was $5059. This was 47 per cent of the mean salary of $10,697 made by workers in other professions. The *median* salary for instructional personnel in 1958 was $4831 which was 59 per cent of the $8195 median salary of other professions. These figures reveal clearly the still-existing discrepancy between instructional salaries and those of other professions. Even here, however, there is an encouraging note, for the same source estimates that, upon the basis of available data, by 1960 the *median* income of full-time teachers had risen to ". . . about 63 per cent of the level for the 17 professions."[38]

It should also be remembered that annual salaries are only a part of the picture. When comparing the length and cost of preservice preparation, the actual number of working days per year, and the possible number of years of active service, the average salaries of teachers may compare more favorably with those of other professional fields.

All in all, there seems to be cause for optimism and encouragement concerning teachers' salaries. Most educators would agree that the teacher's

[37] *Ibid.,* p. 12.
[38] *Ibid.,* pp. 12-14, 23.

economic status is not yet what it should be. Indeed, in some areas, it is deplorably low. But, on a national average, there is some cause for hope that the traditionally inadequate salary of the teacher may soon become a thing of the past.

THERE IS A DEFINITE TREND TODAY TOWARD REWARDING TEACHING EXPERI-ENCE AND ADDITIONAL PREPARATION WITH GREATER FINANCIAL GAIN. Of all teachers who have suffered from inadequate salaries in the past, those with several years of experience have usually fared the worst. The beginning teacher is frequently protected by state minimum salary legislation. As of September, 1961, thirty-four states had passed state minimum salary laws. Moreover, to operate in a rising economy, these laws are frequently re-vised. For example, in 1961-62, ten states prescribed a minimum salary of at least $4000 for beginning teachers with bachelor's degrees. This is double the number of states that had this legal minimum in 1959-60.[39]

Furthermore, in order to attract a sufficient quantity and a desirable quality of beginning teachers, many school systems establish minimum salaries far in excess of the state minimum. Minimum salary laws plus the severe teacher shortage have, therefore, in many areas resulted in a fairly respectable salary for the beginning teacher. This is not equally true of the experienced teacher or the teacher with advanced preparation, however, for in many instances the annual increments, the number of steps on the salary scale, and the maximum salaries have not been raised proportion-ately. Thus, the teacher's salary, although fairly adequate at first, may level off after the first few years. The following statement indicates that this shortcoming is gradually being eliminated in the better school districts.

One of the major reasons for lack of interest in teaching as a permanent career is the relatively low reward for experience. As of 1960, a city classroom teacher with 10 years of experience could expect to earn only 49 percent more than a beginning teacher with the same amount of preparation. . . .

Much of the annual loss of teachers (roughly 8.3 percent in 1960-61) can be traced to this factor. Men teachers, especially, resign after a few years to enter more highly paid occupations.

However, school districts are moving toward greater recognition for ad-vanced education and experience. Present salary schedules are usually con-structed to include several classes which recognize different levels of prepara-tion, plus a series of increments in each class based on years of experience. For the past five years, salary schedules generally have shown greater increases at the master's degree level than at the bachelor's degree level. In addition, many districts have a six-year preparation category and some have a seven-year or doctorate class.[40]

[39] *Ibid.*, p. 33.
[40] National Education Association, *Teaching Career Fact Book* (Washington, D. C., 1962), pp. 21-23.

Thus, in evaluating the salary schedule of any system the teacher should pay particular attention to (1) the minimum salary, (2) the maximum salary (should be at least double the minimum), (3) the amount of the annual increment (is usually about 5 per cent of the base, although it may range from 3 per cent to 9 per cent), (4) the recognition of advanced preparation, and (5) the total earnings of life service.

Before leaving this point, we should mention also the present trend toward raising the salaries of top administrative positions. Among the maximum salaries in education today, certain college and university presidents receive from $35,000 to $45,000 annually and the salaries of some outstanding professors range from $24,000 to $35,000.[41] At least two public-school superintendents receive annual salaries of more than $40,000. At the present writing, the current superintendent of Chicago public schools receives a base salary of $48,500 and an additonal compensation of $20,000 for his position as head of the Massachusetts Education Commission. With this annual income of $68,500 he ". . . becomes the nation's highest-paid public official except for [the] President [of U.S.] who gets $100,000."[42]

Admittedly, these high salaries are far removed from that paid to the typical elementary school teacher. The teacher should realize, however, that no longer is there a tight lid on salaries as in the past, for there is a growing trend toward recognizing increased (1) experience, (2) preparation, and (3) responsibility with a properly commensurate salary.

ELEMENTARY SCHOOL TEACHERS HAVE PROFITED GREATLY FROM THE INTRODUCTION OF THE SINGLE SALARY SCALE. For many years, the teacher's salary was determined only by a mutual agreement between the individual and the board of education. To eliminate the gross inequities of individual bargaining, many systems adopted a salary schedule that, simply defined, ". . . is merely a device that automatically determines the salary of a teacher on the basis of certain important factors."[43]

The earliest type of salary schedule was known as the "position-type," in which the amount and range of salary were determined by the position of the teacher. In the typical position-type scale, elementary teachers were ranked lower than secondary school teachers and accordingly received less money. The rationale, of course, was the old idea that elementary teachers needed less skill, less knowledge, and less preparation than high school teachers and should therefore receive less salary.

Gradually, however, such factors as (1) the increased preparation of elementary school teachers, (2) the grave teacher shortage in the ele-

---

[41] Sidney G. Tickton, *op. cit.*, p. 12.

[42] "68,500-a-Year Schoolmaster," *Time*, Vol. 81 (January 25, 1963), p. 55.

[43] Jefferson N. Eastmond, *The Teacher and School Administration* (Boston, Houghton Mifflin Company, 1959), pp. 360-361.

mentary school, (3) the growing competency of the elementary school teacher, (4) the importance of the child study movement and its accent upon early childhood years, (5) the growing emphasis upon professional unity and solidarity, and (6) practically speaking, the sheer number of elementary teachers which constituted a majority in any school system, led to the adoption of a salary schedule based solely upon experience and preparation regardless of the type of teaching position. This is called the "preparation-type" schedule or, more commonly, the single salary schedule.

Since it was introduced in the late nineteen twenties and thirties, the popularity of the single salary schedule has grown phenomenally. The result has been the virtual elimination of inequalities between salaries of elementary and secondary teachers, as indicated in the following statement.

The single-salary schedule now generally in effect throughout the country has abolished inequalities formerly existing between elementary-school and secondary-school teaching salaries. As of 1961, elementary-school teachers received an average salary of $5235, as compared with $5500 for secondary-school teachers. The remaining difference is due primarily to less preparation . . . and fewer years of teaching experience in a single district as a result of the greater mobility of elementary-school teachers.[44]

The typical single-salary schedule contains two to four tracks, each representing a level of preparation. It is organized in a series of steps, representing annual increments, from minimum to maximum levels. The following is an example of a single-salary for the academic year 1964-65, based upon levels of preparation and years of experience. The three levels of training contained in the schedule are defined as follows:

Four Year—To be eligible for the fourth year training level schedule, a staff member must hold a Bachelor's Degree from an accredited college or university and must also present evidence of compliance with the regulations of the New Jersey State Department of Education for a teaching certificate.

Five Year—A staff member is eligible to be placed on the fifth year training level schedule if he holds an earned Master's Degree in his field of specialization granted by an accredited college or university.

Six Year—A staff member is eligible to be placed on the sixth year training level schedule when he offers evidence of satisfactory completion of a program of at least 32 graduate credits beyond the earned Master's Degree. These credits must be approved by the Superintendent of Schools and have been earned at accredited colleges or universities.[45]

[44] *Teaching Career Fact Book*, op. cit., p. 23.
[45] Boards of Education, Princeton Borough, Princeton Township, N. J., *Salary Proposal*, p. 3, mimeographed.

TABLE 1.1
Salary Schedule for the 1964-1965 Academic Year

PRINCETON BOROUGH, NEW JERSEY		PRINCETON TOWNSHIP, NEW JERSEY	
Step/Level	*4 Year*	*5 Year*	*6 Year*
0	$5200	$5500	$5800
1	5450	5750	6050
2	5700	6000	6300
3	6300	6700	7100
4	6600	7000	7400
5	6900	7300	7700
6	7200	7600	8000
7	7500	7900	8300
8	7800	8200	8600
9	8100	8500	8950
10	8400	8800	9300
11	8700	9150	9650
12	9000	9500	10000

Reprinted through the courtesy of Dr. Chester Stroup, Superintendent of Schools, and the Board of Education of Princeton Borough, N. J.

THERE IS CONSIDERABLE DIFFERENCE OF OPINION CONCERNING THE PRACTICE OF RELATING SALARIES TO RATED TEACHER EFFICIENCY. Some feel that the teacher's salary should not be determined solely by preparation and experience (as in the preparation-type schedule) but should be according to demonstrated competency. The practice of paying teachers according to their performance is commonly called *merit rating*. It is far from a new idea but the fact that it has recently been introduced in some systems has created considerable discussion and controversy among educators and laymen alike.

There are many different plans for rewarding merit with salary. Most systems that have instituted the practice, however, use a variation or combination of the following three basic procedures.

1. A planned salary schedule is used but increments are determined by merit instead of, or in addition to, experience and preparation. In other words, advancement to the next salary step is not automatic each year. One teacher may receive two or more increments and consequently jump two or more steps on the salary schedule at one time for outstanding performance. Another may receive one increment for acceptable performance and advance the corresponding single step on the scale. A third may not receive any increment because of inferior work and consequently remains on the same salary step the following year.

2. A planned salary schedule is used with all teachers receiving regular annual increments according to experience and preparation. In addition, however, those teachers who demonstrate superior performance through teaching, research, curriculum construction, etc. may receive an extra compensation or bonus, which usually ranges from 5 per cent to 15 per cent of their salaries. This plan differs from the first one in that the bonus is awarded on an annual basis and does not affect the teacher's placement on the salary schedule. In some systems a teacher may receive such a bonus only once in every so many years. Other systems have no restrictions and a teacher could presumably receive a bonus each year if his work was of high enough quality.

3. A planned salary schedule is used that contains a super-maximum which can be achieved only by teachers who have demonstrated outstanding competency.

There are, of course, many who favor merit rating. Gardner recommended to the President's Commission on National Goals the universal adoption of merit pay with appropriate measures taken to insure its fair implementation.[46]

Typical of the statements supporting merit salary proposals is the following: "This type of salary program rewards superior teachers for outstanding work and tends to attract and retain superior minds in the profession. Another advantage of a merit rating program is that poor teachers may be motivated to improve."[47]

In general, the following advantages are usually cited for merit pay.

1. It stimulates the teacher's professional improvement.
2. It provides reward and recognition for the superior teacher.
3. It improves the quality of the educational program by constantly stimulating teachers to perform at optimum level.
4. It provides superior teachers with salaries comparable to other professions.
5. It helps to attract and retain superior teachers by offering worthwhile salaries.
6. It is used frequently in business and industry, and there is no reason why it cannot be used with equal success in teaching.

The arguments opposing merit rating are many and include refutations of some of the advantages just stated. In general, opposition to the plan is based upon the following.

[46] John W. Gardner, "National Goals in Education," *Goals for Americans* (New York, Columbia University, The American Assembly, 1960), pp. 82-83.
[47] James O. Reiels, "An Approach to Merit Rating," *American School Board Journal*, Vol. 144 (March, 1962), p. 14.

1. There is no reliable, fair, and objective method for appraising and rating teaching competency. (This point is discussed in detail in the following chapter.)

2. Merit rating stimulates competition and rivalry among teachers that may threaten professional morale and unity, as well as the quality of the educational program.

3. Many modern educational responsibilities are assumed by an educational team which makes rating of individual teachers extremely difficult.

4. Many of the teacher's responsibilities and contributions extend beyond the walls of the classroom and are practically impossible to rate.

5. The designation of certain teachers as "superior" creates difficulties in home-school relationships since *all* parents naturally want their children to be taught by a "superior" teacher.

6. It does not necessarily attract better teachers to a school system, for many competent teachers oppose the principle of merit rating and do not wish to join a system where it is in effect.

7. It is not used in business and industry to the degree nor with the success that is usually claimed. As a matter of fact, according to one source,

> Merit rating as a basis of fixing pay is used by considerably less than half of the business and industrial firms.
>
> The firms that use merit ratings are most likely to use them for manual workers; fewer use them for clerical workers; and still fewer for administrative and professional workers.
>
> Studies of the use of merit rating in industry show relatively low measures of reliability and validity.
>
> Problems of merit rating in business and industry closely resemble the problems of merit rating in the public schools.
>
> Many business and industrial firms are now emphasizing merit rating as an instrument for supervision rather than an instrument for determining salary.[48]

The study concludes with the statement,

> Certainly the current practice in business and industry offers no monolithic demonstration of the success either of efficiency ratings themselves, or of the successful use of them in fixing salaries. Experiment, trial and error, success and failure are seen. Fresh ideas are being tried, but the subject continues to be controversial.[49]

8. A higher salary is not necessarily the only, or even the best, method of recognizing superior performance. Certainly everyone would agree that superior service should be recognized and studies of teacher morale reveal

---

[48] "Merit Rating in Business and Industry," *NEA Research Bulletin*, Vol. 39 (February, 1961), p. 16.

[49] *Ibid.*, p. 18.

that "expressions of appreciation and recognition" are closely related to high morale. But financial recognition is only one of these. Redefer says,

> Money increments awarded by a school system are not necessarily the method by which to give personal recognition. There are many ways by which merit can be recognized. For many teachers a pat on the back, a note of appreciation, may be more effective as commendation than a salary increment.[50]

Finally, how do teachers feel about merit rating? The following list of twenty-eight statements is arranged in descending order from those with which teachers most strongly agree to those with which they most strongly disagree.

Teachers tend to *agree* that:

1. It is difficult to identify the results which teachers obtain.
2. Apple polishing would be encouraged by merit rating.
3. Agreement cannot be reached as to how to select persons capable of judging the merits of teachers.
4. Teacher morale would be lowered under merit rating.
5. There is no agreement as to what constitutes superior teaching.
6. Ratings of teachers will reflect the convictions of the raters rather than the excellence of the teacher who was observed.
7. Merit rating would lead teachers to fear supervisors.
8. Feelings of insecurity will be fostered among teachers by merit rating.
9. Merit rating would be unfair because working conditions are not equal for all teachers.
10. Rating is not administratively feasible because all parents will want the merit teachers for their children.
11. Merit rating is statistically unreliable.
12. Teachers will not trust the official who rates them.
13. It is foolish to pay a productive, skillful teacher the same low salary paid the inefficient, uninspired teacher.

Teachers are *uncertain* whether:

14. Merit rating will tend to hold down the nonmerit maximum salary.
15. It is unwise to pay the poor teacher the same high salary paid to the superior teacher.
16. Merit rating provides a way to reward outstanding teachers by means other than promotion.
17. Merit rating will ignore the extracurricular skills and efforts of teachers.

[50] Frederick L. Redefer, "The School Board and Teacher Morale," *American School Board Journal*, Vol. 145 (July, 1962), p. 7.

18. Outstanding teachers would be retained in the classroom under the merit-rating system.

19. Merit rating would be a stimulus to individual development of teachers.

Teachers tend to *disagree* that:

20. Merit rating will help retain outstanding teachers in the profession.

21. Teachers would be motivated by merit rating to do their best teaching.

22. Rating teachers for salary purposes is not distinctively different from rating teachers for promotion.

23. The general public favors merit rating of teachers for salary purposes.

24. The public prestige of the entire profession would be improved under merit rating.

25. The worth of teachers is indicated by the results of testing children's learning.

26. Teachers will trust ratings done by a group of teachers.

27. A healthy competition among teachers would develop under merit rating.

28. Merit rating is psychologically reliable.[51]

How does the organized profession feel about merit rating? The National Education Association has gone on record opposing the practice. Its stand is set forth in the following statement.

The National Education Association believes that it is a major responsibility of the teaching profession, as of other professions, to evaluate the quality of its services. To enable educators to meet this responsibility more effectively, the Association calls for continued research and experimentation to develop means of objective evaluation of the performance of all professional personnel, including identification of (a) factors that determine professional competence; (b) factors that determine the effectiveness of competent professionals; (c) methods of evaluating effective professional service; and (d) methods of recognizing effective professional service through self realization, personal status, and salary.

The Association further believes that use of subjective methods of evaluating professional performance for the purpose of setting salaries has a deleterious effect on the educational process. Plans which require such subjective judgments (commonly known as merit ratings) should be avoided. American education can be better served by continued progress in developing better means of objective evaluation.[52]

[51] Calvin B. Michael, "Equal Pay and Unequal Attitudes," *American School Board Journal*, Vol. 145 (November, 1962), p. 10.

[52] "Policy Statements on Salaries for School Personnel Made by the National Education Association and Some of Its Departments," *NEA Research Memo 1962-30* (Washington, D. C., National Education Association, August, 1962), p. 2.

CERTIFICATION AND EDUCATIONAL PREPARATION

Probably no other aspect of the elementary teacher's position has been the center of more discussion and attention in recent years than his educational preparation and certification. In this section, these two interrelated factors are discussed according to their (1) historical background, (2) purposes and types of certification, and (3) current issues and trends.

Early Beginnings

ALTHOUGH IT WAS NOT STANDARD PRACTICE, LICENSING OF TEACHERS WAS NOT UNKNOWN IN THE EARLY COLONIES. The practice of granting individuals permission to teach dates back to ancient Athens. In our own country, attempts to license some teachers were begun more than a hundred years before the Revolutionary War. In certain colonies, the earliest teachers were licensed by the Bishop of London or by the royal governors. In New England, the Christian magistracy held the authority to decide who should teach. Later, authority for certification was assumed by the local town authorities, or by an appointed school committee which may or may not include the local minister.

In general, attempts at certification were confined to teachers of grammar schools in selected town districts. In the rural schools or in the schools for younger children, such as the dame schools of New England, teacher licensing was not practiced.

Although they were not widespread, it is nevertheless significant that attempts to certify teachers are rooted deep in the history of our country. Elsbree states,

These attempts at licensing schoolmasters in the colonies met with partial success only. The scarcity of qualified candidates, the physical difficulties encountered in supervising all school arrangements, and the religious differences prevalent in many of the colonies seriously complicated the task of licensing. It is significant, however, in the development of the teaching profession in America, that the civil authorities established entrance standards almost from the beginning of our public-school-system and that the church exercised a powerful influence on appointments.[53]

EARLY LICENSING WAS CONCERNED WITH CERTAIN BASIC REQUIREMENTS. Initially, the teacher's license meant only that he was given permission by the proper authorities to teach. To one degree or another, such factors as these were considered in certifying an individual as fit to teach: (1)

[53] Willard S. Elsbree, *The American Teacher* (New York, American Book Company, 1939), p. 51.

religious orthodoxy, (2) moral character, (3) political loyalty, (4) ability to control pupils, and (5) academic knowledge.

There is no doubt that the first of these was of tremendous importance and, "Not to adhere to the prevailing religious tenets of the colony was to disqualify oneself for a profession which was regarded as the half brother of the ministry."[54] The early settlers were God-fearing folk and they took considerable pains to see that their offspring were not contaminated by anyone who was not of their religious beliefs.

A virtuous and moral character was also considered highly important by those granting permission to teach. It is true that early records contain colorful accounts of schoolmasters who were guilty of drunkenness, immorality, profanity, slander, and other misdemeanors. The very fact that these are recorded, however, probably indicates that they were exceptions to the rule, and modern authorities generally agree that the early schoolmaster was not quite the disreputable character that some sources have claimed.

Today, several states require an oath of loyalty or allegiance to our country (see pp. 29-30). It is interesting to note that this practice dates back to colonial times. In many cases, it superseded all other requirements in importance. According to LaBue, the importance attached to the political oaths in many instances ". . . gave it precedence over other requirements for the license."[55] Elsbree states, ". . . considerable emphasis was given in these early days to the loyalty of teachers toward their government. The records do not show that any teachers rebelled against taking oaths of allegiance, nor is there any evidence that as a group they were disloyal."[56]

The ability to maintain order was usually high on the list of requirements. Many of the pupils who attended school (particularly during the winter months) were older and physically larger than the schoolmaster. It is small wonder that school officials were favorably impressed by the applicant whose reputation had established him as a good "licker."

Lastly, academic ability was considered, although to widely varying degrees. As stated in the first section, the grammar schoolmaster, in some communities, was frequently required to be a person of considerable education. In most rural communities, however, the schoolmaster was expected only to have a rudimentary command of reading and writing, and occasionally received an extra stipend if he was also an "arithmeticker." In any case, the teacher's academic shortcomings were frequently overlooked if he possessed the more important qualifications. Then too, according to the following incident, a candidate's persistence often

[54] *Ibid.*, p. 37.
[55] Anthony C. LaBue, "Teacher Certification in the United States: A Brief History," *Journal of Teacher Education*, Vol. 11 (June, 1960), p. 149.
[56] Willard S. Elsbree, *op. cit.*, p. 42.

compensated for his lack of scholarship in securing a certificate to teach, even if the certificate was a somewhat dubious recommendation.

. . . sometimes the examiner ran across a candidate whom even he outranked in mentality and culture. One such, the dumbest of the dumb, pestered an examiner for a certificate, despite the latter's more or less plainly expressed opinion that the would-be instructor of youth didn't know enough to pound sand into a rathole. Finally the examiner, plagued beyond endurance, seized a pen and wrote, "This is to certify that Mr. Amaziah Smith is qualified to teach a common school in Washington Township, and a damned common one at that."[57]

EARLY LICENSES WERE GRANTED UPON THE BASIS OF EXAMINATION. As previously indicated, teaching certification for many years was based entirely upon examination by local authorities. This meant that licenses were valid only in a specific community and only for a single year. Each year the teacher who wanted to renew his license or move to another town, must submit to another examination. Stinnett and Huggett comment upon this haphazard method of certification in the statement, "Teacher licenses were valid only in the school employing the teacher. The results were far from satisfactory. Examination of applicants was haphazard, nepotism was prevalent, standards were disgraceful, teachers rejected or failing in one town could find employment in another."[58]

Although some of the later written examinations were often quite difficult, the early oral ones were usually most perfunctory and blissfully ignored details of academic competency. An account of one such examination follows.

A young man had been engaged to keep his first school, and had already taught two weeks of the term, when he was summoned before the committee for examination, in compliance with the requirement of the law. At the time and place designated, he presented himself. It was on a cold winter evening, at a respectable farmer's house. He went not much fearing a total failure, and yet being without experience in such matters he had vague misgivings as to the result. On arriving, he was soon conducted away from the family, including some of his pupils, gathered around the blazing hearth, to a fireless upper room dimly lighted with a tallow candle. Being seated at a table opposite the chairman of the committee, the interrogatories and answers proceeded as follows:

CHAIRMAN: How old are you?
CANDIDATE: I was eighteen years old the 27th day of last May.

[57] Millard Fillmore Kennedy and Alvin F. Harlow, *Schoolmaster of Yesterday* (New York, McGraw-Hill Book Co., Inc., 1940), p. 76.
[58] T. M. Stinnett and Albert J. Huggett, *Professional Problems of Teachers*, 2nd ed. (New York, The Macmillan Company, 1963), p. 454.

CHAIRMAN: Where did you last attend school?
CANDIDATE: At the Academy at S - - - - -.
CHAIRMAN: Do you think you can make our big youngsters mind?
CANDIDATE: Yes, I think I can.
CHAIRMAN: Well, I am satisfied. I guess you will do for our school. I will
send over the certificate by the children tomorrow.[59]

Purposes and Types

Present day certification has been defined as ". . . the legal authority
for a person to teach in the public schools."[60] It has a trio of broad,
basic, protective functions, all of which have, as their ultimate goal, the
improvement of the quality of education.

CERTIFICATION ATTEMPTS TO PROTECT CHILDREN AND YOUTH FROM INCOM-
PETENT OR UNFIT TEACHERS. Educating the youth of the land is a tre-
mendously responsible and important task. Every precaution must be
taken to guarantee that the task is undertaken only by those who are adequately prepared for it. This is the fundamental rationale for certification.
It should be remembered, however, that the license certifies only that the
candidate has met minimum requirements as specified by existing standards. The certificate is, in no sense, a *guarantee* of teaching competency.

CERTIFICATION ATTEMPTS TO PROTECT SOCIETY AGAINST THE INCOMPETENCY,
MALPRACTICE, OR UNSCRUPULOUSNESS OF UNQUALIFIED PERSONNEL. Certification attempts to guarantee that society is not "cheated" or harmed by
persons performing services for which they are not properly qualified.
It is, of course, essentially for this reason that doctors, lawyers, nurses,
architects, and many other professional workers must be certified. In
some states, even such nonprofessional workers as well-diggers, barbers,
plumbers, beauticians, and dry cleaners need to be certified for exactly
the same reason. Just as certification protects society from any charlatan
who decides to hang out his shingle and practice medicine, so does it
protect society from teachers who do not possess the proper qualifications.

CERTIFICATION ATTEMPTS TO PROTECT TEACHERS FROM UNFAIR COMPETI-
TION. The third basic function of certification is to protect the members
of the profession from competition with unqualified applicants whose
willingness to work under substandard conditions may threaten the security of the teacher as well as the status of the profession.

In addition to these three protective functions, certain secondary purposes of certification are frequently identified. Although there is not
necessarily unanimous agreement on every point, the following are fre-

[59] John D. Philbrick, "Examining and Certificating Teachers," *American Institute
of Instruction Lectures* (Boston, 1870), p. 113.
[60] Anthony C. LaBue, *op. cit.*, p. 147.

quently suggested as subordinate purposes of certification: (1) to insure continuing professional growth, (2) to upgrade the status of the profession, (3) to eliminate or reduce the dangers of incorrect teacher assignment, (4) to call national attention to the improving quality of teacher preparation, (5) to identify publicly persons acceptable to teach children, (6) to recognize professional and personal development, and (7) to develop professional attitudes.[61]

In summary, certification represents an objective, impartial, and standardized attempt to place in public school classrooms those teachers best qualified to be there. It does not pretend to be a badge of teaching effectiveness.

THERE ARE THREE BASIC TYPES OF TEACHING CERTIFICATES. Stinnett[62] points out that the types of certificates presently issued by the various states fall into three categories. The first of these is according to the term or duration of validity. Thus, certificates are classified as life, permanent, limited, continuing, or some short-term designation such as provisional or probationary.

Secondly, certificates are classified according to levels of preparation and include regular, standard, professional, emergency, or substandard.

Thirdly, certificates are classified according to authorization of teaching position or assignment. These include: (1) blanket or general, with no teaching specialization specified; (2) endorsed, which note the specialization for which the candidate is qualified; and (3) special field, which is "either a separate certificate for each special field or one certificate on which separate special fields may be endorsed."[63]

Current Trends and Issues

Certification practices throughout the country have been, and are constantly being modified. This is as it should be, of course, for certification can never be considered in isolation from other education developments. As Von Schlichten says,

. . . it seems evident that certification requirements, once established, can never be considered permanent. As new goals for education are established or old ones dropped, as techniques for identifying and measuring teachers' competencies are developed, as new insights into teacher education are gained, as

[61] J. Fletcher Wellemeyer, "A Summary of Group Discussions," *The Education of Teachers: Certification,* Official Report of the San Diego Conference (Washington, D. C., National Commission on Teacher Education and Professional Standards, National Education Association, 1961), pp. 17-18.

[62] T. M. Stinnett, "Certification Requirements and Procedures Among the States in 1960," *Journal of Teacher Education,* Vol. 11 (June, 1960), p. 178.

[63] *Ibid.*

teaching itself moves increasingly onto the professional level, these developments must inevitably reflect themselves in changes in certification standards.[64]

In some areas of current change, there appears to be almost universal agreement and a definite trend is fairly discernible. In others there is wide disagreement. The current trends and controversial issues which currently occupy considerable attention are discussed in the remainder of this section.

THERE IS A STEADILY INCREASING TREND TOWARD STRENGTHENING THE REQUIREMENTS FOR CERTIFICATION. As we have just pointed out, certification can never be divorced from other educational developments. It is, of course, closely related to teacher preparation and education. Initially, however, this was not true, for certification was based solely upon examination either oral or written. With the establishment of public normal schools in the mid-nineteenth century, the basis for certification changed gradually from an examination to the completion of a specified program of formal preparation. By 1911, only seven states did not issue certificates based upon the completion of courses in normal schools.[65]

Once a period of formal preparation was accepted as the basis for certification, teacher education and certification moved ahead in parallel strides. Cooperative efforts were aimed at steadily strengthening the teacher's preparation. As the program was continually strengthened, it was also gradually lengthened from two to three to four years. Finally, with the evolution of the normal school into a four year college, the Bachelor's Degree became the minimum educational requirement. Today, as shown in Table 1.2, forty-five of the fifty-two states and territories require the Bachelor's Degree for the initial standard elementary school teaching certificate.

Furthermore, there is considerable evidence to indicate that, in order to achieve the type of quality educational program now considered essential, five years of preservice preparation for the elementary teacher will soon become necessary. Such recommendations as the following would seem to presage a trend in this direction.

Length of a program is not an arbitrary figure but is contingent upon what is to be achieved and the kinds of experiences required to realize the desired goals. Assuming a unified, effectively interrelated program and careful selection of students to be admitted to the program:

For most elementary- and secondary-school teachers the preservice program should be five years in length. . .

[64] Erwin W. Von Schlichten, "The Idea and Practice of Teacher Certification in the United States," *Teachers College Record*, Vol. 59 (April, 1958), p. 413.

[65] Harlan Updegraff, *Teachers' Certificates Issued Under General State Laws and Regulations*, Bulletin 1911, No. 18 (Washington, D. C., U. S. Office of Education), p. 182.

TABLE 1.2

General Requirements for Lowest Regular Teaching Certificate for Elementary School Teachers

	Degree or Number of Required Semester Hours	U. S. Citizenship	Allegiance or Loyalty Oath	Must Secure Employment	Recommendation from College or Employing Officer	Minimum Age Required	General Health Certificate Required	Chest X-Ray Required	Special Course Required
Alabama	B	No	No	No	Yes	17	No	Yes	No
Alaska	B	Yes	No	Yes	No	18	No	No	No
Arizona	B	Yes	Yes	No	No	18	No	Yes	Yes
Arkansas	B	No	No	No	Yes	18	Yes	Yes	No
California	B	Yes	Yes	No	No	18	Yes	No	Yes
Colorado	B	No	Yes	No	Yes	none	No	No	No
Connecticut	B	Yes	No	No	Yes	18	Yes	No	Yes
Delaware	B	No	Yes	Yes	Yes	none	Yes	Yes	No
District of Columbia	B	Yes	Yes	No	Yes	none	Yes	Yes	No
Florida	B	Yes	Yes	No	Yes	20	Yes	No	No
Georgia	B	No	No	No	Yes	none	No	No	No
Hawaii	B	Yes	Yes	No	Yes	none	Yes	Yes	No
Idaho	B	Yes	No	No	Yes	18	No	No	No
Illinois	B	Yes	Yes	No	No	19	No	No	Yes
Indiana	B	No	Yes	No	Yes	none	Yes	No	No
Iowa	B	No	No	No	Yes	18	No	No	Yes
Kansas	B	No	Yes	No	Yes	none	No	No	No
Kentucky	B	No	No	No	Yes	18	No	No	No
Louisiana	B	No	No	No	Yes	none	No	No	Yes
Maine	96	No	No	Yes	Yes	17	No	No	No
Maryland	B	Yes	Yes	Yes	Yes	18	No	No	No
Massachusetts	B	Yes	No	No	No	none	Yes	No	No
Michigan	B	Yes	Yes	No	Yes	18	No	No	No
Minnesota	B	No	No	No	Yes	none	Yes	No	No
Mississippi	B	Yes	Yes	No	Yes	18	Yes	No	No
Missouri	B	No	No	No	Yes	none	Yes	No	No
Montana	64	Yes	Yes	No	Yes	18	Yes	Yes	No
Nebraska town	60								
rural	40	Yes	Yes	No	Yes	none	Yes	No	No
Nevada	B	Yes	Yes	No	No	18	Yes	Yes	Yes
New Hampshire	B	No	Yes	Yes	Yes	none	No	No	No
New Jersey	B	Yes	Yes	No	No	18	Yes	No	No
New Mexico	B	Yes	No	No	Yes	18	Yes	Yes	No

TABLE 1.2 (Continued)

	Degree or Number of Required Semester Hours	U. S. Citizenship	Allegiance or Loyalty Oath	Must Secure Employment	Recommendation from College or Employing Officer	Minimum Age Required	General Health Certificate Required	Chest X-Ray Required	Special Course Required
New York	B	Yes	No	No	No	18	No	No	No
North Carolina	B	No	No	Yes	No	18	Yes	Yes	No
North Dakota	64	Yes	Yes	No	Yes	18	No	No	No
Ohio	B	No	No	No	Yes	none	No	No	No
Oklahoma	B	Yes	No	Yes	Yes	none	Yes	No	Yes
Oregon	B	Yes	Yes	No	No	18	No	Yes	No
Pennsylvania	B	Yes	No	No	Yes	18	Yes	No	Yes
Puerto Rico	68	Yes	Yes	Yes	No	18	Yes	Yes	No
Rhode Island	B	Yes	Yes	Yes	Yes	19	Yes	No	Yes
South Carolina	B	Yes	No	No	Yes	18	Yes	Yes	No
South Dakota town	60								
rural	30	Yes	Yes	No	Yes	18	No	No	No
Tennessee	B	No	No	No	Yes	18	No	No	No
Texas	B	Yes	Yes	No	Yes	18	No	No	Yes
Utah	B	No	No	No	Yes	none	No	No	Yes
Vermont	B	No	Yes	Yes	Yes	19	No	No	No
Virginia	B	Yes	No	Yes	Yes	18	No	No	No
Washington	B	Yes	Yes	No	Yes	18	No	Yes	Yes
West Virginia	B	Yes	No	No	Yes	18	No	No	No
Wisconsin	64	No	No	No	Yes	none	No	No	Yes
Wyoming	B	Yes	No	No	Yes	none	No	No	Yes

SOURCE: W. Earl Armstrong and T. M. Stinnett, *A Manual on Certification Requirements for School Personnel in the United States,* 1961 Edition (Washington, D. C., National Commission on Teacher Education and Professional Standards, National Education Association, 1962), pp. 24, 33.

The increased depth of scholarship required to gain the control of knowledge indicated as necessary to begin work as a teaching scholar and to continue to gain in professional stature suggests a five-year unified program as initial preparation for most students. The equivalent of five years would seem to be needed for the preparation of both elementary- and secondary-school teachers, even if content is carefully selected with reference to significance. As colleges move toward this horizon, every effort should be made to improve present four-year programs through focused selection of content and well-designed curricular arrangements. Further, continuous experimentation should take place testing the length of time needed with reference to increasing the efficiency of learning, selecting students of especially high caliber, and modifying the curricular design. Within any five-year program students should be allowed to proceed through the program at differing rates and provision should be made to accommodate the student of advanced ability.[66]

Although no state, at the moment, requires five years of preservice preparation for elementary teachers, some do require the completion of a fifth year of college study within a certain number of years from initial employment. Recent legislation in California, for instance, states, "In California, beginning July 1, 1963, elementary-school teachers will be required to have five years of higher education or its equivalent, with the fifth year to be completed within five years of first employment."[67]

Then too, some of the states which issue permanent or life certificates do so only upon the completion of a fifth year of study, plus a certain number of years of teaching experience. At present, such states as Alaska, Connecticut, Georgia, Indiana, Iowa, Kentucky, Ohio, Rhode Island, and West Virginia require a Master's Degree, or the equivalent of five years of college study, for the life, permanent, or highest certificate.[68]

In line with the raising of legal certification requirements to include the Bachelor's Degree in most states, several professional associations have raised their requirements for membership accordingly. In June, 1961, the Representative Assembly of the National Education Association adopted the following prerequisite for active membership, which should have considerable significance in raising the preparational standards of the profession.

Any person who is actively engaged in the teaching profession or other educational work may become an active member at any time until August 31, 1964. After that time any person who is actively engaged in educational work of a professional nature shall be eligible to become an active member of the Association if he (1) has an earned bachelor's or higher degree and (2) where required holds or is eligible to hold a regular legal certificate of any kind except an emergency substandard certificate or permit . . . Any person who is an active member of the Association for the membership year 1963-64 is entitled to continue as an active member of the Association.[69]

[66] National Commission on Teacher Education and Professional Standards, *New Horizons for the Teaching Profession.* Margaret Lindsey, ed. (Washington, D. C., National Education Association, 1961), p. 75.

[67] "State School Legislation, 1961," *NEA Research Bulletin*, Vol. 39 (December, 1961), pp. 115-116.

[68] W. Earl Armstrong and T. M. Stinnett, *A Manual on Certification Requirements for School Personnel in the United States*, 1961 ed. (Washington, D. C., National Commission on Teacher Education and Professional Standards, National Education Association, 1962), pp. 54-56.

[69] National Education Association, *NEA Handbook, 1961-62* (Washington, D. C., 1961), pp. 29-30.

In addition, several state associations have a similiar prerequisite to active membership. Those requiring the Bachelor's degree of their members by 1961 included Colorado, Connecticut. Florida, Kansas, Maine, Maryland, Michigan, and Washington.[70]

In summary, there are many indications of a current strong trend toward improving the quality of the teacher's preparation and strengthening the requirements of the profession. As Armstrong and Stinnett state, the present trend is in sharp contrast to the agitation of a few years ago suggesting that certification standards particularly for the elementary school teacher be relaxed or lowered.

All in all, there appears to be a new climate of cooperation and concerted effort among college people, both in education and in the liberal arts, public- and private-school personnel, and state directors of teacher education toward achieving higher standards of teacher preparation, certification, and curricula for the lower schools. This developing teamwork is yielding a rapid upgrading all along the line. It is in eloquent contrast to the negative climate of only a few years ago, when criticism and denunciation were the dominating motifs and attempts to bring about reform took on the aspects of a public family brawl.[71]

AUTHORITY FOR CERTIFICATION HAS GENERALLY BEEN TRANSFERRED FROM THE LOCAL TO THE STATE LEVEL. Authority for licensing teachers was originally assumed by town and county officials. During the late nineteenth and early twentieth century, however, as state departments of education grew steadily stronger, certification was gradually centralized within state agencies. By 1911, there was only one state in which all certificates were issued by county authorities. In six states, certificates were issued by both state and local officers; in eight states, by state, county, and local officials; in sixteen states, by state and county officials; and in seventeen states all certification power belonged solely to state agencies.[72] Today, except in rare instances in which certain cities or counties still issue their own certificates, all certification responsibilities are assumed by state agencies.

THE NUMBER OF STATES ISSUING PERMANENT OR LIFE CERTIFICATES HAS STEADILY DECLINED. Today twenty-three states, including the District of Columbia, issue life or permanent certificates. Twenty-eight states, which at one time issued life certificates, have discontinued the practice. Of the states that still issue permanent or life certificates, many require additional study beyond the period of preservice preparation.[73]

[70] W. Earl Armstrong and T. M. Stinnett, *op. cit.*, p. 1.
[71] *Ibid.*, p. 2.
[72] Harlan Updegraff, *op. cit.*, p. 138.
[73] W. Earl Armstrong and T. M. Stinnett, *op. cit.*, pp. 15, 54-56.

Those who oppose the granting of life certificates do so largely on the grounds that it is not conducive to continuing professional improvement (see Chapter 12). They claim that the holder of a life certificate may easily be tempted to relax into a rut of mediocre teaching. Also, such certificates may permit individuals to return to the classroom after an absence of many years, during which elementary school methodology and content may have changed radically, without taking any refresher work. Certainly teaching is more important than driving a car, and if drivers' licenses must be renewed periodically, as in some states, there is little reason why this should not be true of teaching licenses.

There are, of course, many who do not agree with this viewpoint. Allen argues that,

The standard or full license should remain in effect indefinitely, subject to revocation on grounds of incompetence or unprofessional conduct.

Once a person has successfully completed his basic preparation and demonstrated his competence in the eyes of the profession, there is no sound ground for making the meeting of additional requirements of preparation or experience a condition for the continuance of his license. The professional person assumes the obligation to keep abreast of his field and to maintain his competence at the highest possible level. In addition, a responsibility of professional organizations is continually to evaluate the performance of its members and otherwise to stimulate growth in competence.[74]

In spite of some dissension, however, there is little doubt that the practice of issuing life or permanent certificates is steadily declining. "The evidence seems clear . . . that the practice of issuing life certificates to teachers is a declining one. Practically all the states that have revised their certification requirements in recent years have repealed the provisions for life certificates.[75]

THE CONTROVERSY OF GENERAL VS. SPECIAL CERTIFICATES IS CURRENTLY RECEIVING MUCH ATTENTION. The early teacher's license was very general and ". . . carried with it the freedom to practice one's art at any grade level or in any subject from the kindergarten to the university."[76] As education became more complex, however, there was considerable dissatisfaction with this practice and much agitation was directed toward the issuance of specialized certificates, valid only in specific areas. The result was a plethora of certificates (more than sixty different types in a single state) and in recent years the trend in some areas has swung back again in favor of the general or "blanket" certificate. Supporting this

[74] Wendell C. Allen, "Goals of Certification," *Journal of Teacher Education*, Vol. 11 (June, 1960), pp. 272-273.
[75] T. M. Stinnett and Albert J. Huggett, *op. cit.*, p. 473.
[76] Willard S. Elsbree, *op. cit.*, p. 343.

trend are such statements as: "There should be one license based on completion of an accredited program of preparation and demonstration of teaching competence. The license should be accompanied by designation of the teaching responsibilities for which the teacher has been prepared, and recommended by his teacher education institution."[77]

The most serious question relating to the argument for the blanket certificate pertains, of course, to the proper assignment of teachers. If all teachers receive the same general license, what precautions will be taken to insure their assignments to teaching responsibilities for which they are qualified?

Those who argue for the general certificate point out that the proper assignment of teachers should be the responsibility of many. Certainly the teacher-education institution should take the responsibility for recommending the candidate only for the specific fields in which he prepared and demonstrated competency. Certainly the hiring superintendent must be interested enough in the quality of the educational program to place teachers only in assignments for which they are fully qualified. Certainly the accrediting agencies and state departments of education should refuse accreditation and approval to those teacher-education institutions that do not recommend candidates properly, as well as to those schools that do not assign teachers according to such recommendations. Certainly the local professional associations should exert some influence to safeguard the proper assignment of teachers. And most important, the individual teacher should assume the responsibility for accepting an assignment only in an area for which he feels fully qualified. In summary, there *are* ways, other than legal certification, which can be used to safeguard the correct assignment of teachers. The extent to which they can operate successfully depends upon the ethical and professional maturity of those who use them. Bush states,

To insist that a separate state license to teach be granted for each subject in the curriculum would only lead to a multiplicity of licenses, to the tightening of the stranglehold of bureaucracy upon a system already too encumbered by red tape. Effective enforcement of proper assignment and other standards depends upon a disciplined profession of local school administrators, accrediting agencies, local teachers associations, and individual practitioners. None of them should permit a teacher to undertake the teaching of a subject for which he is unprepared. Here is the locale for the enforcement of proper standards of performance. Of ultimate importance, however, is the teacher himself. He is the final source of authority who must be relied upon to judge at the critical time, to enforce standards. He must be fully imbued with what is right and wrong, and he must have the authority to outlaw untenable conditions under which he is working, otherwise his "professional autonomy" becomes a hollow

[77] Wendell C. Allen, *op. cit.*, p. 269.

phrase. The individual practitioner requires support in maintaining standards. He needs to be buttressed by the authority of his organized profession and by the impartial judgment of an accrediting agency. These three—the practitioner, the organized profession, and the accrediting agency—working in concert, can guarantee conditions necessary for optimum professional work and can protect the interest of the public.[78]

THERE IS AN INCREASING INTEREST IN RECIPROCITY AMONG STATES IN MATTERS OF CERTIFICATION. As stated previously, authority for certification has gradually moved from the local to the state level which means that, with few exceptions, teachers' certificates have state-wide validity. This is a big step forward from the days when a teacher had to apply for a new certificate every time he moved to another town. Today, there is considerable interest in extending the validity of certificates across state lines. The mobility of population and the teacher shortage have accented the need; the growing uniformity of requirements has appeared to make the idea feasible and practical. Armstrong points up the general agreement on the idea in the following statement.

Practically everyone concerned with teacher certification favors some form of reciprocity. It just does not make sense to have 50 different bases for the certification of teachers, each different enough from the other to make it difficult for teachers to cross state lines. In general, therefore, school boards favor it; school administrators would like to have it; state departments of education would certainly subscribe to it, at least in principle; colleges and universities that prepare teachers would consider it a great step forward; and the really professional teachers who have no fear of competition from other states would applaud such a move.[79]

There are, of course, several problems that must be solved before widespread reciprocity can be attained. According to Armstrong, major barriers at the moment include: (1) locus of authority for granting certificates, (2) differences among states in the type and scope of certificates offered, and (3) differences among states in specific course and credit-hour requirements for the same certificate.[80]

None of these problems, however, is insurmountable and progress toward interstate reciprocity is being made. One method is regional reciprocity by which several states agree to recognize other's certificates. Typical of this arrangement is the present *Eleven-State Reciprocity Compact* which includes Maine, Vermont, New Hampshire, Massachusetts,

[78] Robert N. Bush, "Responsibility for Professional Performance," *Journal of Teacher Education*, Vol. 11 (June, 1960), p. 264.

[79] W. Earl Armstrong, "A Basis for Reciprocity in Teacher Certification," *Journal of Teacher Education*, Vol. 11 (June, 1960) p. 217.

[80] *Ibid.*, pp. 217-220.

Connecticut, Rhode Island, New York, New Jersey, Delaware, Maryland, and Pennsylvania.

Regional compacts are fine as far as they go but many feel that they are not the real answer. Teachers move freely from one section of the country to another and there is growing interest in a broader framework of reciprocity than that offered by the several regional compacts.

A step in this direction has been taken by those states that recognize the certificates of graduates of institutions, in any state, which have been accredited by the National Council for Accreditation of Teacher Education (NCATE). This council is defined in the following statement.

The National Council for Accreditation of Teacher Education is a nonprofit, autonomous, voluntary accrediting body devoted exclusively to the evaluation and accreditation of teacher education programs. It is recognized by the National Commission on Accrediting as the only national accrediting body for the field of teacher education, which includes the preparation of teachers for all grades and subjects at the elementary and secondary school levels and the preparation of school service personnel for these levels.[81]

At present twenty-nine states have adopted regulations that provide for reciprocity of certification, based upon NCATE accreditation. These are: Alabama, Arizona, Colorado, Delaware, Florida, Georgia, Illinois, Indiana, Iowa, Kentucky, Louisiana, Maine, Maryland, Mississippi, Missouri, Nebraska, North Carolina (September, 1964), North Dakota, Oklahoma (has reciprocity with other states in this group), Oregon, Pennsylvania, Rhode Island, Tennessee, Texas, Utah, Vermont, Washington, West Virginia, and Wyoming.[82]

Typical of the regulations adopted by these states is the resolution adopted in 1962 by the State Board of Education of the State of Delaware: "Graduates of teacher-education programs which have been approved by the National Council for Accreditation of Teacher Education who are fully recommended by their colleges will be certificated automatically for the major teaching area."[83]

THE ISSUANCE OF SUBSTANDARD OR NONSTANDARD CERTIFICATES IS ONE OF THE MOST CRUCIAL PROBLEMS IN CERTIFICATION TODAY. This section has discussed the current concerted trend toward raising certification requirements for elementary teachers. There is no doubt that the last few years have seen most states move in this direction. However, many point out

[81] The National Council for Accreditation of Teacher Education, *A Statement of Purposes, Policies, and Procedures* (Washington, D. C., The Council, October, 1960), p. 1.

[82] The National Council for Accreditation of Teacher Education, *States That Grant Reciprocity to Graduates of NCATE Institutions* (Washington, D. C., The Council, n. d.), mimeographed.

[83] Resolution adopted by the State Board of Education of the State of Delaware, July 19, 1962, reworded as above.

that it may be a trend on paper only, since a large number of teachers presently employed do not meet these requirements.

Over the past ten years, the accelerated birth rate and the competition from business and industry have created a severe shortage of qualified and properly certified teachers for the nation's classrooms. This shortage has not decreased to any significant extent. According to available data, in 1952-53 there were 69,626 emergency teachers employed. In 1962-63 there were 91,556 emergency teachers employed, or 6.1 per cent of the total number of teachers. Of those teachers lacking full certification in 1962-63, 70 per cent were employed in elementary schools.[84]

These figures may not be quite as discouraging as they seem at first glance, however. In the first place, it should be remembered that they include teachers who may have been qualified under previous standards but who have been unable to meet the recently raised requirements. They also include teachers who may have completed an accepted program of preparation in one state but who have not met the specific course requirements of another state. Nevertheless the number of personnel in elementary schools who do not meet minimum professional requirements is a problem of grave concern to all who are interested in improving the quality of education and raising the status of the profession.

What is the solution? Some say that emergency certificates should never have been permitted or that they should be discontinued immediately because of their depressing effect on quality standards. Others argue that the issuance of emergency certificates is the only way to staff classrooms while, at the same time, adhering to, or raising, regular requirements. Some hope that the problem will just eventually disappear. Many state that it will be with us until teaching is made attractive enough to recruit and retain the numbers of capable, fully qualified teachers we need.

As with most issues, the problem cannot be considered in isolation. It is a part of the entire, widespread concern with the complex problems of recruiting, selecting, educating, and retaining quality teachers and will be solved only in proportion to the progress achieved in these interrelated fields.

CONDITIONS OF SERVICE

Tenure

Simply defined, *tenure* means the legal protection of the teacher against unjust dismissal. The purposes of tenure are outlined clearly in the following statement.

[84] National Education Association, Research Division, *Estimates of School Statistics, 1962-63*, Research Report 1962-R13 (Washington, D. C., December, 1962), pp. 12-13.

Public schools exist to provide the best possible education for the children and adults in the community. It is essential, therefore, that school systems be competent and efficient. A key figure in these schools is the competent teacher, freed from the fear of insecurity and the danger of unfair dismissal.

Competent school boards exercise the utmost vigilance in maintaining and improving the professional status of the teacher. They seek potential candidates for teaching who will exemplify high ideals. To retain this professional personnel, they provide adequate tenure measures in an effort to keep their schools effective.

For the teacher, tenure provides

> reasonable security in employment
> effectiveness in position resulting from a sense of well-being
> freedom to teach without unreasonable restraint or censorship
> opportunity to become an established participating citizen in the community
> warning, if services are unsatisfactory.

For the students, tenure provides

> teachers freed from uneasiness, able to devote their full energies to their classwork
> better school conditions because teachers are free to speak up for improvements
> opportunity to develop critical thinking under teachers with courage, initiative, and independence.

For the board of education, tenure provides

> a stable faculty of competent personnel
> an evaluation of teacher services
> an orderly procedure for dismissing unsatisfactory personnel
> an assurance against charges of unjust dismissal.

For the community, tenure provides

> an efficient school system
> teachers sincerely interested in their pupils and the school system
> teacher-citizens with pride in the community.

Tenure prevents

> the dismissal of a teacher because
> he failed "to vote right"
> he expressed an honest opinion
> he became "too popular"
> he disturbed the status quo
> a school board member had a friend he wanted to employ
> someone thought it would be "for the good of the schools" regardless of the teacher's competence
> the dismissal of a teacher in a capricious or unethical manner
> the dismissal of a teacher without proof of reasonable cause.[85]

[85] Committee on Tenure and Academic Freedom, *Tenure—What and Why* (Washington, D. C., National Education Association, n. d.) pp. 2-3.

It should be clearly understood that tenure laws (1) protect the teacher against unfair dismissal and (2) guarantee orderly dismissal procedures, *only*. They do not guarantee to the teacher a specific position in a school system. (Some teachers labor under the illusion that they cannot be transferred to another school or to another grade "because they are under tenure." This is completely false.) Nor do tenure laws guarantee absolutely permanent employment for the tenured teacher. If, for instance, school enrollments drop to the point where the size of the staff must be reduced, a tenured teacher may be dismissed. In such a case, seniority should prevail and the teachers with the most years of service are retained longest.

THERE ARE TWO BASIC TYPES OF TENURE LEGISLATION. A tenure law

(*a*) provides for continuing employment of teachers who, under its terms, have acquired permanent, tenure, or continuing contract status; and (*b*) requires boards to comply with prescribed procedural provisions of notice, statement of charges, and right to a hearing before a tenure teacher can be dismissed, or before nonrenewal of the teacher's contract of employment can be effective.[86]

The second type is the "continuing contract law" which,

lacks the essential provisions of notice, statement of charges, and right of hearing before a teacher's employment can be terminated; it requires only that the teacher be given advance notice of nonrenewal of his employment contract, and ordinarily no reasons need be furnished. Under statutory provisions of this kind, the teaching contract is automatically renewed for the ensuing school year unless notice to the contrary is received by a specified date.[87]

TENURE LEGISLATION IS A FAIRLY RECENT DEVELOPMENT. In 1930, no more than a half-dozen states had any type of statewide tenure provisions. In 1960-61, thirty-seven states and the District of Columbia had tenure legislation on a state-wide basis or in certain designated areas. The remaining thirteen states had either continuing contract laws of the spring notification type, or annual or long-term contract provisions.[88]

THERE ARE CERTAIN GENERAL CHARACTERISTICS OF MOST TENURE LEGISLATION. These are:

1. *Stipulation of a probationary period*. The large majority of tenure laws specify a probationary period prior to granting tenure. This may

[86] "Teacher Tenure Laws," *NEA Research Bulletin*, Vol. 38 (October, 1960), p. 81.
[87] *Ibid.*, p. 82.
[88] *Ibid.*

vary from a few months to five years, with three years as the most common. At the end of the probationary period, most states require the superintendent to recommend the candidate for tenure, although in some cases tenure becomes automatic with the signing of the fourth year contract, or where no notice is given of dismissal at the close of the probationary period.

In many states, tenure applies only to a specific school district and the teacher breaks his tenure by moving to another system. In Connecticut, Ohio, and Kentucky, however, the probationary period is shortened for teachers who held tenure status in another district and in Pennsylvania, tenured teachers of one district need not serve another probationary period when moving to another district within the state.[89]

2. *Procedures for orderly dismissal.* Causes for dismissal may or may not be specified by law. If specified, they usually include immorality, inefficiency, incompetency, insubordination, or negligence. If not specified, the law usually states for "good" or "just" or "reasonable" cause.

Procedures for dismissal usually include: (1) a written notice of dismissal, delivered personally or by registered mail to the teacher a certain number of days in advance, (2) a hearing before the employing school board, and (3) provision for appeal to higher educational authorities, either the county superintendent of schools or board of education or both, or the state board of education or the chief state school officer or both.

TENURE LEGISLATION REPRESENTS A LARGE STEP FORWARD IN PERSONNEL PRACTICES. Tenure laws have developed rapidly in the last few decades, although not without some opposition. In general, opposition to tenure is based upon the fact that it tends to protect the mediocre teacher as well as to promote professional stagnation. It is true, of course, that there are isolated instances in which this is true. However, the general value of tenure in promoting teacher security and morale greatly outweighs any individual cases where it has been misused or abused. Certainly there are better ways to rid the profession of mediocrity than to eliminate a very important contribution to teacher welfare. There can be little argument with Eastmond's conclusion that "Although there are many shortcomings . . . it is generally recognized that the good achieved by the tenure laws in safeguarding the interests of children, in raising professional standards, and in protecting the competent against arbitrary dismissal, has, in the long run, far outweighed the disadvantages.[90]

[89] *Ibid.,* p. 83.
[90] Jefferson N. Eastmond, *op. cit.,* p. 421.

Leaves of Absence

The most common leaves of absence, for which local or state provision or both is made include the following:

1. *Sick leave.* Provisions for absence for personal illness without loss of salary are fairly common in most schools. The purposes of such a provision are (1) to protect the health and welfare of pupils by not exposing them to a teacher too ill to be in the classroom, (2) to protect the physical health of the teacher, and (3) to provide security and freedom from worry about the expenses of personal illness.

The most common practice is to permit ten days of fully paid sick leave per year. In addition, some systems grant an extra number of days with partial salary or with full salary from which a substitute's pay has been deducted.

The typical sick leave regulation makes some provision for the accumulation of unused days, up to a specified total amount. In the state of Washington, the teacher may accumulate as many as 180 days of fully paid sick leave, the equivalent of one full school year. In other states, the number of days permitted to accumulate is not specified. In still others, (Kentucky, Vermont, and West Virginia) teachers are allowed to accumulate only twenty days of leave, and in at least one state, there is no provision for accumulation.[91]

2. *Miscellaneous leaves.* Most systems permit, without loss of salary, a few days absence each year for (1) illness or death in the immediate family, (2) professional visitation, and (3) attendance at professional conferences, workshops, and institutes.

3. *Professional improvement leaves.* Some systems have provisions for granting extended leaves of absence, with full or partial salary, for purposes of professional improvement. Such leaves may be granted for purposes of travel, graduate study, research, professional writing, or similar activities. The following provisions for professional leaves of absence adopted by Princeton Township, New Jersey are fairly typical of the regulations governing this type of leave.

A. Requests for one year's sabbatical leave of absence to be spent in study or travel or both may be made to the Superintendent of Schools.

1. Requests may be made by teachers and administrators who have completed seven years' service in the Princeton Township Schools.

[91] National Education Association, Research Division, *School Law Summaries: Leaves of Absence* (Washington, D. C., June, 1961).

   2. Requests shall be made on the proper form and shall delineate the plan of study or travel.

B. An approved sabbatical leave of absence shall carry a grant of one-half salary.

C. Personnel granted a sabbatical year's leave of absence will receive experience credit on the salary guide.

D. Sabbatical leaves of absence are subject to the following provisions:

   1. Personnel who accept a sabbatical leave of absence agree to return to the Princeton Township Schools and to remain on the staff of the Princeton Township Schools for three years. Requests to be released from this obligation must include an offer to reimburse the Princeton Township Board of Education according to this formula: A person who requests a release for the entire three years shall agree to repay the entire amount received from the Board of Education during the sabbatical leave. A person who completes one year of service after the sabbatical leave before requesting a release shall agree to repay two-thirds of the total received during the sabbatical leave. A person who serves two years after returning from a sabbatical leave before requesting a release shall agree to repay one-third of the amount received during the sabbatical leave.

   2. Requests for sabbatical leave must be made before March 1 of the year in which the leave is to take place.

   3. Sabbatical leaves of absence shall begin September 1 and terminate June 30.

   4. The total number of teachers and administrators granted sabbatical leave during one academic year may not exceed two.

   5. During the period of the sabbatical leave of absence personnel may not engage in any remunerative employment without written permission from the Superintendent of Schools.

   6. During the sabbatical leave of absence personnel will report to the Superintendent of Schools fully, in writing, (October 31, January 31, March 31, June 30, and at other times on request) concerning their progress in those activities for which leave was granted, and will report specifically any information or ideas gained during the leave which may be of value to the Princeton Township Schools. The final report will include a summary of all the experiences and the conclusions drawn which have any bearing on the future performance of their duties and which suggest possible improvements for the Princeton Township Schools.[92]

4. *Exchange teaching.* Opportunities for exchange teaching are discussed in Chapter 12. Regulations governing the release of personnel for

[92] Princeton Township Board of Education, "Leaves of Absence Policy" (Princeton Township, N. J.), pp. 3-4, mimeographed.

teaching abroad vary according to the school system and the type of exchange program. Those adopted by one school system are stated below.

Requests for leave of absence for one school year to permit teachers and administrators to participate in the International Educational Exchange Program or similar government sponsored educational programs carried on by the Department of State will be considered. The maximum number of teachers and administrators granted leave to participate under this provision may not exceed three in any one year. Requests will be considered in the order in which they are made.

The matter of leave with pay or leave without pay will be stated as one of the provisions of the request since conditions of the International Educational Exchange Program vary.

Permission to participate in the International Educational Exchange Program will be granted not more than once in seven years.

Requests will be limited to teachers and administrators on tenure.

Personnel participating in the International Educational Exchange Program will receive experience credit on the salary guide.[93]

Retirement

It was stated previously that one of the attractions of teaching as a career is the security it offers. One aspect of this security is a retirement and pension plan, now operative in almost every state in the nation.

In general, retirement plans are of two types: The first is the pension plan to which the teacher makes no financial contribution. The second and much more prevalent type is the joint-contributory plan in which the teacher is a joint contributor with the state or local system. In most cases, enrollment is compulsory and a certain percentage, usually from 2 per cent to 6 per cent, is automatically deducted from the teacher's salary.

Retirement plans usually specify minimum and maximum retirement ages. The most common age for normal retirement is sixty, although some systems specify a certain number of years of service, with twenty years as a common minimum.

A recent survey of sixty-four retirement systems reveals that the median annual allowance paid to retired teachers in 1961 was $1748 and the range was from $439 to $3918. The survey notes, however, that these averages may be misleading although they still do not approximate the now-accepted goal that retirement allowances should be at least half of the average final salary.

Averages, however, can be misleading, for included in them are benefits paid to teachers who were *not* career teachers—teachers who retired early and

[93] *Ibid.*, p. 3.

with few years of service. Also, the benefits reported were from the retirement systems only. Many of these teachers also receive social security benefits which are not reflected in the benefits reported.

These factors must be considered when averages are discussed. The fact still remains, however, that the goal of 50 percent of average final salary— which most who work in retirement think should be the benefit paid to career teachers upon retirement—has not been met by all the systems to which teachers belong.[94]

SUMMARY

This chapter has examined some of the distinctive features characteristic of the position of the elementary school teacher.

The first section was devoted to a discussion of the social and professional status of teaching. It was pointed out that the traditionally low prestige of the teacher is gradually disappearing for there is evidence to indicate that teaching is steadily achieving the status of a highly respected profession. One of the factors that influences a profession's status is its attractiveness in the eyes of the public. In general, those factors that enhance the desirability of teaching are both altruistic and practical. They include: (1) opportunity to work with children and youth, (2) opportunity to be of service, (3) opportunity to impart knowledge, (4) security of position, (5) good hours, (6) long vacations, (7) number of employment opportunities, (8) pleasant working conditions, (9) pleasant associates, and (10) interesting work.

The major disadvantage associated with teaching has long been its low economic status. This factor was examined in the second section of the chapter. Recent surveys reveal that the economic status of teachers has unquestionably risen in recent years, although it is not yet equal to certain other professions. One of the major steps forward in raising teachers' salaries has been the introduction of a standard salary schedule. Various types of schedules were discussed and the controversial issue of relating salary to rated teacher effectiveness was examined in some detail.

The history and current status of certification and educational preparation were discussed in the third section. Certification was considered to have a triple protective function, (1) to protect children and youth from unqualified teachers, (2) to protect society from unfit practitioners, and (3) to protect teachers from unfair competition. Among the trends or issues in this area that are currently receiving emphasis are: (1) steady strengthening of certification requirements, (2) transfer of certification authority from local to state level, (3) gradually decreasing number of permanent or life certificates issued, (4) controversy concerning general

[94] "Retirement Systems: 1961 Statistics," *NEA Research Bulletin*, Vol. 39 (December, 1961), p. 126.

versus special certificates, (5) increasing attempts at interstate reciprocity, and (6) the prevalence of substandard or nonstandard certificates.

The last section dealt briefly with three conditions of service in teaching, namely: (1) tenure, (2) leaves of absence, and (3) retirement.

ADDITIONAL LEARNING EXPERIENCES

Topics for Thought and Discussion

1. What were your major motivations for choosing teaching as a career? Were they primarily altruistic or practical or a combination of both?

2. If your state adopted a "blanket" teaching certificate, would you accept a position for which you did not feel qualified?

3. If you worked in a system using merit rating, would your relationships with fellow teachers be more competitive than if merit rating were not used?

4. Do you think you would work harder under a merit rating plan than under another plan?

5. Do you think we will eventually have national reciprocity in teacher certification?

6. Are you in favor of life and permanent certificates?

7. What is your greatest single satisfaction in teaching?

8. Is teaching a career profession for you?

9. Do you think that the great deal of publicity given recently to the need for raising teachers' salaries has helped or hurt the prestige of the profession in the eyes of the public?

10. What do you think of *moonlighting* (working at additional jobs after school hours) by teachers?

11. Have you ever felt the stigma of the traditional unfavorable stereotype associated with teaching? Have you ever been slightly apologetic about being "just a teacher?"

Projects and Activities

1. Interview at least ten members of a profession in your community. Make a composite list of what they consider to be the distinctive criteria of a profession. How does your list compare with the one contained in this chapter?

2. Some secondary teachers resent the single salary schedule and in one city some high school teachers recently went on strike opposing it. Write an article for your local teachers' publication, defending the single salary schedule from the elementary teachers' point of view.

3. Write to your state department of education. How many teaching certificates are currently issued in your state? How does your state compare

with others? Is there any activity or interest in your state toward decreasing (or increasing) the number of different types of certificates?

4. Several studies show that young people frequently cite low salary as a major reason for not entering teaching, although, in many instances, those questioned were unable to estimate the actual salary paid to a typical teacher in their community. Try to get permission to interview a class of high school students. Ask them such questions as: (1) What is the starting salary of an elementary school teacher in your town? (2) What is maximum salary? (3) How much does an average teacher earn during a lifetime? (4) How does this compare with other fields? Do their answers reveal that these young people have an accurate or inaccurate concept of teaching salaries today?

5. Prepare a twenty-minute talk on teaching for a high school Career Night. Be sure that you present an honest and fair picture of teaching, including what you consider to be its major advantages and drawbacks.

6. Some people argue that teacher certification should be extended to the college and university level. Others strongly disagree. Explain your viewpoint on this subject in a well-written statement.

7. Write a brief skit to be presented to a PTA or local community agency on the general theme, "The Teacher—Today and Yesterday." Try to show the changes that have evolved in the position over the past.

8. The fact that many laymen consider teaching to be a "part-time" job has been a deterrent to raising salaries in some systems. Interview ten elementary school teachers. Would they be willing to work on a twelve-month basis (one month's vacation) if their salaries were raised accordingly? What are the advantages and disadvantages of an all-year school from the teacher's point of view?

9. Write a description of a female literary character who has been portrayed as an unfavorable stereotype of the teacher. A male literary character.

10. The month of April each year is designated as "Teaching Career Month." Prepare an exhibit that could be displayed in a nearby high school in observance of this month.

Selected Bibliography

Armstrong, W. Earl, and Stinnett, T. M., *A Manual on Certification Requirements for School Personnel in the United States,* 1961 ed. National Commission on Teacher Education and Professional Standards of the National Education Association, Washington, D. C., 1962.

Chandler, Bobby J., *Education and the Teacher.* New York, Dodd, Mead & Co., 1961.

Elsbree, Willard S., *The American Teacher.* New York, American Book Company, 1939.

Kennedy, Millard Fillmore, and Harlow, Alvin F., *Schoolmaster of Yesterday.* New York, McGraw-Hill Book Co., Inc., 1940.

KERSHAW, Joseph A., and McKEAN, Roland N., *Teacher Shortages and Salary Schedules.* New York, McGraw-Hill Book Co., Inc., 1962.

LIEBERMAN, Myron, *Education as a Profession.* Englewood Cliffs, N. J., Prentice-Hall, Inc., 1956.

National Education Association, *Teaching Career Fact Book.* Washington, D. C., 1962.

NEA Research Division, *Economic Status of Teachers in 1961-62.* NEA Research Report 1962-R7. Washington, D. C., National Education Association, May, 1962.

———, *Economic Status of Teachers in 1962-63.* NEA Research Report 1963-R9. Washington, D. C., National Education Association, August, 1963.

New Horizons for the Teaching Profession, Margaret Lindsey, ed. National Commission on Teacher Education and Professional Standards of the National Education Association. Washington, D. C., 1961.

RICHEY, Robert W., PHILLIPS, Beeman N., and Fox, William H., *Factors That High School Students Associate with Selection of Teaching as a Vocation.* Bloomington, Ind., Indiana University, Division of Research and Field Service, 1952.

RUML, Beardsley, and TICKTON, Sidney G., *Teaching Salaries Then and Now.* New York, The Fund for the Advancement of Education, 1955.

SMILEY, Marjorie B., and DIEKHOFF, John S., *Prologue to Teaching.* New York, Oxford University Press, 1959.

STINNETT, Timothy M., *The Profession of Teaching.* Washington, D. C., The Center for Applied Research in Education, Inc., 1962.

———, T. M., and HUGGETT, Albert J., *Professional Problems of Teachers,* 2nd ed. New York, The Macmillan Company, 1963.

"The Education of Teachers: Certification." *Journal of Teacher Education,* Vol. 11 (June, 1960).

The San Diego Conference, *The Education of Teachers: Certification,* Official Report. National Commission on Teacher Education and Professional Standards of the National Education Association. Washington, D. C., 1961.

The Status of the American Public-School Teacher. NEA Research Bulletin, Vol. 35 (February, 1957).

The Teacher's Role in American Society, Lindley J. Stiles, ed. New York, Harper & Row, Publishers, Inc., 1962.

TICKTON, Sidney G., *Teaching Salaries Then and Now—A Second Look.* New York, The Fund for the Advancement of Education, 1961.

WOELLNER, Elizabeth H., and WOOD, M. Aurilla, *Requirements for Certification.* 27th ed., 1962-63. Chicago, University of Chicago Press, 1962.

CHAPTER 2

Qualities and Competencies of Effective Teachers

"WHAT MAKES A GOOD TEACHER?" is a question that almost everyone past the age of six feels well-qualified to answer. The housewife, the business executive, the taxi driver, the pulp magazine writer, the department store clerk, the editor of the local newspaper—in short, the butcher, the baker, and candlestick maker do not hesitate to offer their opinions concerning the requirements of good teaching, particularly in the elementary school. Such opinions, however, are usually based on little more than personal experience and convictions and are extremely contradictory. One individual may claim that, "A good teacher is tough with the kids and doesn't let them get away with murder." Another may state that, "A good teacher has the patience of a saint in order to work with thirty children every day." A third may answer that, "A good teacher stresses the three *R*'s," while a fourth may feel strongly that, "A good teacher is one who knows how to have a little fun with the kids." And so it goes on and on.

Among educators who know their business there is, of course, considerably more agreement on the procedures and behavioral patterns that constitute good teaching. Some schools have been able to develop lists of teaching procedures that find fairly general agreement among teachers and administrators as being those factors which, if done correctly, almost certainly produce learning. Developing an agreed-upon list of criteria of teaching effectiveness is not, however, the same as identifying a scientific, objective, research-based, inclusive definition of teaching competency. For years numerous studies have been made in an attempt to define scientifically the distinguishing characteristics of the "good" teacher. In recent years, much progress has been made but the final answer has not yet been found.

THE IMPORTANCE AND DIFFICULTY OF DEFINING TEACHER EFFECTIVENESS

THE IMPORTANCE OF IDENTIFYING COMPETENT TEACHERS IS GENERALLY RECOGNIZED. It should be fairly obvious that this is an important problem. Certainly if we are going to improve our schools, we must know what good teaching is. We must know its components and the proportion in which they should be combined. We must be able to distinguish objectively and surely between the good teacher and the poor teacher. We can then find ways of encouraging the first and helping the latter. The vital importance of this problem is so universally recognized that almost every educator would agree with Ryans who states that, "The identification of qualified and able teaching personnel . . . constitutes one of the most important of all educational concerns."[1] Specifically, this problem is so important because its answer would help us in the following important tasks.

1. *The improvement of instruction.* Certainly we could take giant strides in improving the quality of instruction in our elementary schools if we knew what qualities and competencies constitute effective teaching and what conditions or factors help or hinder its development. Good education depends on good teachers. Must we not, therefore, know what a good teacher is?

2. *Determining personnel policies within a school system.* Such decisions as employing or dismissing teachers, granting tenure, determining salary increases (in some cases), and making promotions depend upon the concept of teaching effectiveness. The more valid that concept, the more objective will be these important decisions.

3. *Refining recruitment and selection procedures.* A scientific concept of teaching effectiveness would greatly assist high schools and schools of education to recruit and select those candidates who have the greatest potential for success in the field.

4. *Improving teacher education programs.* If, and when, the exact ingredients of teaching excellence are known, the teacher education institutions will be in a better position to offer their students the knowledges and experiences that will best equip them for superior performance in the classroom.

There seems to be little doubt or disagreement, therefore, that the definition of teaching competency merits the intensive study and research directed toward it for the past several decades. Unfortunately, however,

---

[1] David G. Ryans, *Characteristics of Teachers* (Washington, D. C., American Council on Education, 1960), p. 1.

research has not made as much progress in this area as in some others, mainly because it has been confronted with the following problems.

TEACHING IS A COMPLEX PROCESS. As Barr points out, "The first set of difficulties arises in defining teaching. Teaching is not one thing but many things."[2] Undoubtedly, the fact that teaching is a multidimensional rather than a unidimensional process presents the chief stumbling block in arriving at a clear-cut definition. True, one may formulate a general definition such as Ryans' statement that, ". . . teaching is effective to the extent that the teacher acts in ways that are favorable to the development of basic skills, understanding, work habits, desirable attitudes, value judgments, and adequate personal adjustment of the pupil"[3] but, as he readily admits, this is an abstract statement and is not easily translatable to specific teacher dimensions. On the other hand, the number of dimensions, including personal and behaviorable characteristics, is almost inexhaustible. An early study by Charters and Waples, for instance, lists 1001 activities and eighty-three personality traits thought to be related to effective teaching.[4] To combine all of these into a composite labeled "teaching effectiveness" is obviously almost an impossible task. For this reason, some suggest that the term itself is completely misleading and that teaching can be described only in terms of *effectivenesses* rather than a composite effectiveness.[5]

Adding to the complexity of the problem is the fact that many of the traits commonly mentioned are intangible and are, therefore, exceedingly difficult to appraise. Personality traits such as sense of humor, integrity, and buoyancy are almost universally *thought* to be related to successful teaching but their *exact* importance is difficult to determine.

Another contributor to the complexity of the problem is the interrelatedness of the factors. The various qualities, for instance, of the teacher's personality are interrelated with each other and with his behavior in a variety of situations and it is not easy to isolate or study them to any exacting degree.

TEACHING COMPETENCE DEPENDS TO SOME EXTENT ON THE INDIVIDUAL SITUATION. All of us have known some teachers who, regardless of the situation, appeared to do a consistently superior job in the classroom. Miss H, for example, was considered by everyone to be an excellent second grade teacher—but she was equally successful when she was transferred to a sixth grade. Another was Mr. B who, after two years of out-

[2] Arvil S. Barr, "Problems Associated with the Measurement and Prediction of Teacher Success," *Journal of Educational Research*, Vol. 51 (May, 1958), p. 695.

[3] David G. Ryans, *op. cit.*, p. 2.

[4] Werrett W. Charters and Douglas Waples, *The Commonwealth Teacher-Training Study* (Chicago, Ill., University of Chicago Press, 1929).

[5] H. H. Remmers and others, "Second Report of the Committee on Criteria of Teacher Effectiveness," *Journal of Educational Research*, Vol. 46 (May, 1953), p. 652.

standing success in fifth grade, accepted an assignment to teach a special class for the mentally retarded—where he was equally competent. But perhaps these are the unusual teachers, for, in many cases, the teacher's competency, *at least to some extent*, is influenced by the individual situation. The superior first grade teacher, for instance, may possess different qualities or qualities in different proportions from the sixth grade teacher. The successful teacher of socially deprived children may differ in many respects from his colleague who does outstanding work with privileged children. Or the teacher who has done only average work with her third grade class one year may do a superior job with another third grade the following year. Generally speaking, therefore, the grade level, the intellectual level of the pupils, the size of the class, the socio-economic level of the community, and numerous other factors appear to influence the quality of teaching. All of these, of course, add to the difficulty of defining teacher effectiveness.

THE CONCEPT OF THE "GOOD" TEACHER IS A CONSTANTLY CHANGING ONE. The definition of the competent teacher is not only very complex but it is constantly being modified and revised. As Getzels and Jackson[6] point out, the general concept of teaching, along with that of other professions, has changed steadily with the times. These writers state, for instance, that the concept of the competent physician has slowly changed from that of the kindly, fatherly, general practitioner to that of the highly skilled specialist. So, also, has the concept of the successful teacher changed with the changing philosophy of the twentieth century. Not too many years ago, for example, the concept of the successful teacher closely resembled the drillmaster whose efforts resulted in extensive memorization, accumulation of factual knowledge, unquestioning obedience, and deathlike quiet among his pupils. Then, as the philosophy and goals of education changed, the concept of what constituted good teaching changed accordingly and the emphasis was placed upon teaching which would implement a democratic philosophy of education, which would guide pupils toward emotional adjustment and sound value judgments, and which would motivate learning through problem-solving procedures and the awakening of intellectual curiosities and interests. Thus, as our philosophy of education is modified by research in child development and the learning process, as well as by socio-political ideologies, so does the concept of effective teaching change accordingly.

IT IS VERY DIFFICULT TO ESTABLISH FIRM CRITERIA OF TEACHER COMPETENCY. In colonial days the "good" teacher was usually one who could maintain order in the classroom. Today, the problem of determining a valid cri-

[6] J. W. Getzels and P. W. Jackson, "Research on the Variable Teacher: Some Comments," *School Review*, Vol. 68 (Winter, 1960), pp. 450-462.

terion of teaching effectiveness is one of the most difficult ones facing students in the field. A thorough examination of the advantages and disadvantages of criteria used most frequently today is contained in pages 72 to 74.

The discussion thus far has emphasized the difficulty and impracticality of presenting an absolute image of the competent elementary school teacher at the present time. As has been stated, research findings are inconclusive and contradictory as to the *exact* components of teaching success. On the other hand, it is possible to arrive at some generalizations concerning the major qualities or competencies upon which there appears to be most agreement at present. These are examined in the following section.

PERSONAL AND BEHAVIORAL CHARACTERISTICS USUALLY ASSOCIATED WITH EFFECTIVE ELEMENTARY SCHOOL TEACHING

NUMEROUS APPROACHES HAVE BEEN USED TO DISTINGUISH BETWEEN "GOOD" AND "POOR" TEACHING. As was stated previously, there has been extensive investigation of the problem of teaching competence for more than half a century. The thousands of studies in this field range from comprehensive research designs to superficial surveys and use varied techniques in collecting data. Of the various approaches used, the following seem to be most common.

1. *Survey of opinions of experts.* According to Tomlinson, "The first recorded efforts to determine the factors of teaching efficiency were based upon collections of opinions about teachers, usually those of eminent educators."[7] These early studies usually depended upon interviews or questionnaires to gather the opinions of principals, superintendents, or professors of education which were then classified and tabulated in order of importance. For several years this technique enjoyed wide popularity, although recently its limitations and unreliability have been generally realized and the number of such studies has decreased substantially.

2. *Survey of opinions of pupils.* Another popular approach is to ask pupils their opinions of good and poor teachers. This is far from a new approach, for in 1896 Kratz[8] surveyed 2411 children in grades two through eight and found that among the characteristics of good teachers mentioned most frequently were, "helped me in my work," "helped me to be good," "good and/or kind," "patient," "polite," and "neat in work and

[7] Loren R. Tomlinson, "Pioneer Studies in the Evaluation of Teaching," *Educational Research Bulletin*, Vol. 34 (March 9, 1955), p. 63.

[8] H. E. Kratz, "Characteristics of the Best Teacher as Recognized by Children," *Pedagogical Seminary*, Vol. 3 (June, 1896), pp. 413-418.

appearance." On the whole, most studies of this type are fairly consistent, as revealed by the following findings of a very similar study done exactly sixty years later.

The ability to maintain good discipline was mentioned twice as often as any other quality . . . wanted teachers to look neat and nice . . . sense of humor . . . friendly in and out of class . . . assignments justifiable and amount reasonable . . . patience and even temper held in high regard . . . understand children . . . fairness frequently mentioned . . . voice often mentioned.[9]

It is interesting to note that, not only are children's comments relatively consistent, but they are also fairly penetrating and revealing and are worthy of study by all teachers. As an example, the following comments are quoted verbatim from 563 children in the fifth and sixth grades of five schools in a city school system who were asked by the author to write a short composition entitled, "My Idea of a Good Teacher." The traits mentioned most frequently (and their similarity to those previously mentioned is very evident) were classified into three general categories, namely: (1) personal qualities, (2) relationships with pupils, and (3) teaching procedures or techniques. The traits most often mentioned in each classification are listed below in order of frequency, with some of the typical comments offered by the children.

A. TEACHER'S PERSONAL QUALITIES

Pleasant, kind, nice personality

A teacher should be kind and thoughtful and happy . . .
Should have fun with the kids . . .
Should come to school in a good mood every morning . . .
Should be nice to the children and they will be nice to her . . .
A good teacher is a kind person that we love . . .
Is agreeable . . .
Generous . . .
A kind teacher is a wonderful thing to have . . .
I like a friendly teacher who has a nice smile . . .
Should not always have a mean look on her face . . .
Considerate . . .

Well-Informed

Should know all about maps and globes and birds . . .
Should know what he or she is teaching . . .
Should know how to spell and write clearly . . .
A good teacher is a good thinker . . .
Should have a college education . . .

[9] C. F. A. Powell, "The Ideal Teacher," *NEA Journal*, Vol. 45 (January, 1956), p. 31.

I like a teacher who knows what's going on in the world . . .
First of all, a teacher should know how to spell . . .
One who knows about countries, continents, and cities . . .
Should know how to write on the blackboard . . .
Should keep the children up-to-date about the news around us . . .
Should know a lot of things . . .
Good teachers should be very smart so they know the answers to everything . . .
Should be sure of herself when she tells a kid something . . .
A good teacher is an intelligent teacher . . .

Courteous

Talks politely to us . . .
When a teacher is wrong he should apologize . . .
I would like a teacher to be polite to me as I would be to her . . .
Doesn't interrupt me when I am talking and I don't interrupt her when she is
    talking . . .
Teachers and pupils should be polite to each other . . .

Even-Tempered

Should not get upset . . .
Should be calm when something happens . . .
Not too cranky . . .
Shouldn't lose their tempers all the time . . .
Doesn't get mad over little things . . .
Have self-control . . .

Patient

Have a lot of patience . . .
Most teachers do not have enough patience . . .
Patience is the most important thing in the world . . .

Pleasant Voice

Soft and pleasant voice . . .
I like a teacher who talks in a nice low voice . . .
Doesn't holler at us . . .
I like my teacher because she is nice and talks softly . . .
I don't like a teacher who yells all day . . .

Appearance

Should be neat and clean at all times . . .
A teacher that can dress pretty . . .
Well, I like a pretty good-looking teacher . . .
Should come to school properly dressed . . .
I do like a pretty teacher . . .

Honest

Must not tell a lie . . .
Be truthful at all times . . .
Should mean what he says . . .

B. RELATIONSHIPS WITH CHILDREN

Helpful

Should help you when you need help . . .

Is willing to spell some words for you . . .

Should not be too busy to help children with their work . . .

Should help a child if he doesn't know how to do the work instead of letting him find out on his own . . .

Willing and able to help every child . . .

If someone needs help she should go to his desk and help him . . .

A reliable teacher that you could go to when a little help is needed . . .

When you are sick the teacher will help you catch up when you come back . . .

Will help you when you're in trouble . . .

Should listen to our problems and help us in every way . . .

Helps kids when they are stuck in their work. . .

Should be a friend and helper . . .

Understands and Enjoys Children

Should know his or her students . . .

Should know how to handle children . . .

I like a teacher that understands me . . .

I think a good teacher is a person who not only has the ability to teach a class of children but actually likes children and tries to understand them. I think that if teachers were like this it would bring up a better relationship between teachers and kids.

Is Fair in Relationships with Children

Not think one person is better than another . . .

Give every child a chance to prove himself . . .

Should not show too much likeness for one child . . .

Does not show partiality . . .

Should punish children only when they deserve it . . .

Gives you a chance to explain . . .

A good teacher treats children as she would like to be treated herself . . .

Should treat all children equally . . .

Likes all children the same . . .

Is Firm in Relationships with Children

Should be very strict with children who are bad . . .

A teacher should not be too softhearted . . .

He should be stern about rules . . .

Is a little on the strict side . . .

Is strict but nice . . .

Should be stern but not too stern . . .

Should be strict about things children know they are doing wrong . . .

Is Not Too Firm in Relationships with Children

Shouldn't be too rough on children . . .

Shouldn't be too strict . . .

Should be a little strict but not a lot . . .

Should not hurt children . . .

I would like a teacher who is not too strict but yet serious . . .

I would like to have a teacher who is not too harsh or strict. I know this seems
simple but I just feel that this is the right way to go about things . . .

Respects Children

A good teacher respects me and I respect her . . .

I want respect and cooperation from my teacher . . .

I would like my teacher to be reasonable and respect me at all times . . .

I think she respects us the way we respect her . . .

She treats us right and we treat her right . . .

C. TEACHING PROCEDURES AND TECHNIQUES

Provides Challenging Material

I like a teacher who teaches me a lot . . .

One that gives a lot of hard work . . .

Gives you extra work . . .

I like a teacher that makes you do the work . . .

I like a teacher who gives a lot of arithmetic and science work . . .

Gives hard work sometimes and easy work sometimes but mostly hard work . . .

Paces the Amount and Type of Work Correctly

Doesn't give too much work at one time . . .

Gives you a chance to finish your work . . .

Should not give the words too fast or too slow in spelling . . .

Would give you time to finish your assignments . . .

I like a teacher who gives the right amount of work . . .

Should make sure children understand before going on to new work . . .

If you give them some division problems and the class doesn't understand
them, don't just skip to fractions but work with them awhile until they do
understand . . .

Explains Things Clearly and Thoroughly

I like a teacher who takes time to explain things to you . . .

You can tell if a teacher is good by the way she explains things to you . . .

Almost all the time a good teacher explains things clearly . . .

Should be willing to explain things over and over to children who don't understand at first . . .

My idea of a good teacher is to make children understand the work before
giving it because some teachers think that you know it . . .

Try to explain good when kids are puzzled . . .

Makes Work Interesting

It would be nice if we could have a few more projects such as making pictures
of different cities . . .

A good teacher brings lots of interesting things to school . . .

Gets many materials for her children to work with . . .

Should try to get things that will interest the class in their work . . .

Should make maps and charts for arithmetic, spelling, reading, and social studies . . .

Takes us on trips . . .

Organizes Well

Knows what she is doing and has the day planned . . .

Keeps to the schedule . . .

Should make a good schedule so there isn't too much rushing through lessons . . .

Dismisses you on time . . .

Teaches Social and Safety Habits

Must teach children how to get along with each other . . .

Must teach difference between right and wrong . . .

Should teach you good manners . . .

Should teach children to be good . . .

A good teacher teaches us to be unselfish . . .

Maintains an Interesting and Attractive Classroom

She keeps the room in order . . .

Has flowers in the room . . .

Puts interesting things on the bulletin board . . .

Puts things the children make around the room . . .

Lets us have a library corner . . .

In summary, it may be said that pupils' opinions of good teachers and good teaching are revealing, interesting, and consistent. That they are held in high regard by some educators is revealed in the following statement: "The only persons in the school system who were found to be professionally competent to judge the worth of teachers were their sixth-grade pupils . . . and the teachers themselves."[10]

3. *Comprehensive research designs.* By far the most ambitious, sophisticated, and worthwhile type of investigation into the problem of teacher competency is the comprehensive research design that seeks an answer through the use and development of several criteria, techniques, and instruments. Such studies as the *Teacher Characteristics Study* of the American Council on Education, the *Harvard Teacher Education Research Project*, and the work of the Division of Teacher Education of the New York City Board of Higher Education are typical of the studies recently done in this field. The *Teacher Characteristics Study* extended over approximately a ten year period during which approximately one hundred separate research projects were developed involving more than six thou-

[10] William A. McCall and Gertrude R. Krause, "Measurement of Teacher Merit for Salary Purposes," *Journal of Educational Research*, Vol. 53 (October, 1959), p. 73.

sand teachers in seventeen hundred schools and 450 school systems. As one outcome of the study, the following generalizations emerged which appear to be characteristics of outstanding teachers.

Superior intellectual abilities, above-average school achievement, good emotional adjustment, attitudes favorable to pupils, enjoyment of pupil relationships, generosity in the appraisal of the behavior and motives of other persons, strong interests in reading and literary matters, interest in music and painting, participation in social and community affairs, early experiences in caring for children and teaching (such as reading to children and taking a class for the teacher), history of teaching in family, family support of teaching as a vocation, strong social service interests . . . appear to apply very generally to teachers judged by various kinds and sets of criteria to be outstanding.[11]

Another interesting study is that reported by Heil and others which attempted to discover what characteristics of teacher behavior and competency affected pupil growth. Fifty-five teachers of grades four, five, and six were classified into three personality types designated as Type A (turbulent personality), Type B (self-controlling personality), and Type C (fearful personality). It was discovered that the greatest gains in pupil growth were achieved by the Type-B teacher who was described as:

. . . focuses on structure, order and planning. This focus is also accompanied by high work-orientation. There is likely to be a sensitivity to children's feelings and a warmth toward children, which is an integral part of this personality-type's character and which is not, therefore, predicated upon a need for her to feed upon the children's offering her affection. This teacher is also likely to emphasize interpersonal relationships in the classroom.[12]

FROM THE LITERATURE NOW AVAILABLE, CERTAIN GENERALIZATIONS MAY BE MADE CONCERNING THE EFFECTIVE ELEMENTARY SCHOOL TEACHER. From the studies mentioned previously and many others, there emerge certain basic essentials that may be said to have a definite relationship with teaching competence. The most important of these are discussed in the remainder of this section. It should be kept in mind that they are not listed in any order of importance and that no one of them is the absolute determinant of the quality of teaching. On the other hand, *all of them are vitally important and all good teachers possess most of them to a high degree.*

1. *High intellectual ability and academic background.* It should be said immediately that this does *not* mean that all persons of high intellec-

---

[11] David G. Ryans, *op. cit.,* p. 366.

[12] Louis M. Heil, Marion Powell, and Irwin Feifer, *Characteristics of Teacher Behavior and Competency Related to the Achievement of Different Kinds of Children in Several Elementary Grades* (New York, Brooklyn College, 1960), p. 70.

tual capacity would be good elementary teachers. This, of course, is absurd and everyone knows many extremely intelligent and capable students who are obviously ill-suited to teaching. On the other hand, most of the research and evidence now available indicates that the superior teacher *is* a person of high intelligence and good scholastic preparation. It will be noticed, for instance, that Ryans' generalized description of the outstanding teacher which was quoted on page 58 includes "superior intellectual abilities." Numerous other studies support this statement, one of which investigated characteristics of "employable" and "nonemployable" teachers. The authors state that among the eighteen outstanding teachers who comprised the "highly employable" group, there was "ample evidence of great intellectual capacity" and, further, that, when contrasting the two groups, "Intellectual capacity would seem decisive."[13]

It is obvious that such statements are directly contradictory to the old-fashioned idea that the successful teacher did not have to "know very much" to teach young children. Furthermore, the fact that some people still have this idea is one of the greatest deterrents to improving the elementary school program that exists today. Witness, for instance, the parents, and even some high school guidance counselors, who attempt to discourage the more able young people from entering elementary education because of its lack of "intellectual challenge." Fortunately, the stereotype of the elementary teacher as nothing more than a certified baby sitter is disappearing very rapidly, for most people realize that good teaching, *on any level*, demands an alert and inquiring mind as well as an extensive backlog of good, solid knowledge. Let us examine the reasons behind this statement.

John Steinbeck, winner of the Nobel prize in literature, in describing one of the best teachers he had ever known, said, "She breathed curiosity into us so that we brought in facts or truths shielded in our hands like captured fireflies."[14] Most educators would agree with this famous author that the stimulation of children's intellectual curiosities and interests is a primary function of good teaching. It should be obvious, moreover, that only a teacher who possesses an active intellectual curiosity can "breathe curiosity" into his pupils so that they become problem-solving, seeking, questioning, thirsting, exploring, and discovering individuals. As Chandler says,

The relationship between desire to know on the part of the teacher and ability to motivate students to learn has long been recognized. The individual who is himself curious, who finds in intellectual activities stimulation and excitement,

[13] Ben Bohnhorst and others, "Good and Bad Teachers," *Overview*, Vol. 2 (March, 1961), p. 55.

[14] John Steinbeck, ". . . like captured fireflies," *CTA Journal*, Vol. 51 (November, 1955), p. 7.

**The stimulation of children's intellectual curiosities
and interests is a primary function of good teaching.**

who demonstrates genuine respect for knowledge, whose habits of scholarship
are well established, will kindle the enthusiasm of his pupils along similar lines.
This realization supports the pedagogical slogan: "What we hope for our
youth, we must demand of our teachers."[15]

Another reason for the emphasis upon the intelligent teacher is the
changed concept of his duties and responsibilities. In the days when a
teacher was a hearer of lessons and his sole function was to transmit the
subject matter of the textbook to the head of the pupil, perhaps there
was no real need for more than a very ordinary intelligence level. But
today teaching is considered to be much more than this. The modern
teacher must diagnose the intellectual, social-emotional, and physical needs
of *each* of his pupils; must observe and interpret behavior; must appraise
growth in relationship to specific directional goals; and must measure and
evaluate all types of learning outcomes. Teaching is a matter of getting
inside a child—of discovering why he is what he is—and of deciding
upon the very best method for helping him along every inch of the way.
That this requires a keen, alert, intelligent, and perceptive mind should be
readily apparent.

[15] B. J. Chandler, "The Teacher as a Scholar," *School and Society*, Vol. 89 (April
22, 1961), p. 198.

Then, too, it should be remembered that knowledge—the teacher's basic commodity—is an ever-changing, ever-growing property. Today, as never before in our history, we are pushing back the boundaries of knowledge *in every field*. This modern, much-publicized explosion of knowledge has great significance for the classroom teacher, who must continually strive to keep up with developments in almost every academic sphere. How will he do this unless he possesses a hunger for understanding characteristic of the intelligent individual?

Lastly, it is almost impossible to overestimate the wide range of interests, backgrounds, experiences, and abilities that exist among a class of elementary school children. Youngsters today are infinitely more experienced and more knowledgeable than were those of a few years ago, and even primary grade children talk, with some degree of understanding, about astronauts, space travel, and the changing world scene. Furthermore, the questions they ask would keep a genius on his toes! Recently, for instance, an English professor accompanied his eight-year-old grandson on the boy's first plane trip. While in flight, the captain announced the plane's altitude and mentioned that the temperature was twenty degrees below zero. The boy turned to his grandfather and asked, "Why is it so much colder up here than it is on the ground when we're nearer the sun?" The professor, a learned man, confessed that he did not know the answer, and furthermore, had never even had the question occur to him! Imagine the task of the elementary teacher who must not only "keep up with" his students but should be ahead of them. Nothing but sheer brain power will enable him to do it! (Note: No case is made here that the teacher should be a walking encyclopedia—only that he should be the possessor of a keen, active mind!)

Let us now consider briefly the *spheres* of knowledge which should be at the command of the elementary teacher. The typical teacher of the self-contained classroom is responsible for teaching most, if not all, of the subjects and should therefore possess a cultural and academic background of considerable breadth. For this reason, most teacher education institutions today require elementary education majors to take a generous portion of their college work in general education. Such a background should include study in the following areas:

(1) Languages—his own and one other: reading, writing, speaking, listening—in all, communication.
(2) Literature, the fine arts, and music.
(3) Philosophy.
(4) Mathematics.
(5) The social and behavioral sciences—history, anthropology, political science, economics, geography, sociology, psychology.

(6) The physical sciences.

(7) The life sciences.[16]

In all these fields, the elementary teacher should have some strength for not only must he be a well-educated person himself (like all other teachers) but he will actually teach content from most of these disciplines to his pupils. Furthermore, although all areas are important, a particular emphasis today is placed upon the teacher's *communication skills*. (Notice the pupils' comments on page 56 concerning the teacher's ability to explain clearly.) Ability to express oneself clearly and fluently in speech and writing, to listen intelligently and intensively, and to read critically are some of the basic assets of the superior elementary teacher.

Many authorities recommend today that the elementary teacher not only have a *breadth* of academic preparation but a *depth* as well. For this reason, some schools of education are encouraging, or requiring, prospective elementary teachers to major or minor in an academic area. At this time it is impossible to predict a trend in this direction, although it does seem that at least one academic specialization, *if not developed at the cost of other important areas*, may have two major advantages. In the first place, it contributes to the elementary teacher's own scholastic command and stature. Secondly, it enables him to give specialized services to his school over and above his classroom teaching. Such services might consist of serving on specialized curriculum committees (for which he is well prepared) or acting in an advisory capacity for the rest of the staff in purchasing textbooks, references, audio-visual aids, and other materials within his area of specialization.

Equally as important as general education is the elementary teacher's command of professional knowledge. This includes, among other things, (1) a basic understanding of the historical, psychological, philosophical, and sociological foundations of education, (2) a firm knowledge of child growth and development, (3) a command of the fundamental principles governing a desirable teaching-learning situation, and (4) an understanding of the basic procedures and methods involved in teaching each of the elementary subjects. Robinson stresses the importance of the teacher's being well-versed in this area in the following statement:

The superior teacher, intelligent, flexible, well educated in the subject he is to teach, eager to learn and eager to teach, and in tune with his community, should have in addition the advantages of knowing all that is known about

[16] Roy Harvey Pearce and L. O. Andrews, "Toward the End of the Beginning," *Curriculum Programs*, Official Report of the Kansas Conference, National Commission on Teacher Education and Professional Standards (Washington, D. C., National Education Association, 1959), p. 19.

teaching. . . . Because we care about providing the best possible learning for all children, we cannot accept the notion that knowledge of the subject alone is enough to make a good teacher, or even almost enough.[17]

Last, but not least, the elementary teacher needs a firm knowledge of the sociological factors that have a bearing upon his particular school situation. A clear understanding of the environmental factors operative in his particular situation will enable the teacher to gain a deeper insight into the needs and problems of his pupils as well as help him to work effectively with their parents and other members of the community (see Chapter 4).

The foregoing discussion might be summarized by repeating that the competent elementary teacher has a firm command of: (1) subject matter,. (2) children and their needs, (3) the teaching-learning process, and (4) the immediate school situation. It should be repeated that *all* of these are essential to the academic background of the successful teacher. There seems to be little point in arguing here over which takes precedence over the others. Without the first, the elementary teacher, *at his best*, becomes only a competent baby sitter; without the second, only an earnest pedant; without the third, only a hearer of lessons; and without the fourth, only an ivory-towered pedagogue. *All* are important and should be recognized as such by all those interested in the future of elementary education.

2. *Physical and mental health.* As any experienced elementary teacher knows, teaching is a physically demanding profession. Daily association with twenty-five or thirty active, healthy, and lively youngsters demands that the teacher have considerable physical stamina. Moreover, nothing is more detrimental to pupils' learning than a high rate of faculty absentee-ism. The author remembers clearly, for instance, one first grade class who had a succession of substitute teachers throughout the year due to the illnesses of their regular teacher. This was, of course, no one's "fault" but the fact remains that the children did suffer immensely. It seemed to the author, as she watched them progress through the six grades, that they never fully recovered the learning loss they experienced in first grade from not having the consistent, everyday instruction of a physically healthy teacher.

The total concept of fitness today includes not only physical health, but mental and emotional health as well. This latter factor is of extreme concern to all those responsible for recruiting and selecting teachers. Some systems go so far as to require a psychiatric examination of all can-didates for employment or promotion. VanderWerf makes the following

---

[17] Donald W. Robinson, "Who is a Good Teacher?" *The Clearing House*, Vol. 35 (February, 1961), p. 325.

**Daily association with lively active youngsters
requires the teacher to have physical health
and vigor.**

suggestions to insure the employment and retention of only physically
and emotionally fit teachers.

(1) School boards should expect from institutions which prepare teachers a
    fairly adequate appraisal of the graduate's health, physical and mental . . .

(2) During interviews references should be made to items in the candidate's
    health history and an informal evaluation made by some expert in psycho-
    logical services . . .

(3) A fairly complete health record should be kept on each staff member with
    periodic examinations required to keep the records up to date . . .

(4) At strategic points in the teacher's career in the school system, election to
    tenure, or promotion to administrative or supervisory positions complete
    psychiatric examinations should be required.

(5) Regardless of position it seems desirable for teachers to have complete and
    thorough health examinations every few years as a matter of routine . . .

(6) School boards should set policies governing matters of health as part of
    minutes of their meetings and publish them. Such matters as health re-
    quirements, sequence of examinations, and sick leave should be included.

(7) Since teachers are subject to the same frustrations and tensions as other people, school systems should seriously consider making available to their staffs adequate consulting services.[18]

Although not all educators would agree with all of these suggestions, the fact remains that school systems throughout the country are devoting more attention to the teacher's physical and mental health than has ever been true in the past. However, the responsibility rests not completely upon school administrators and boards of education but upon teachers as well, who should do everything in their power to *maintain* a clean bill of health. Proper attention to fundamental health habits such as proper rest, diet, and exercise, is so obviously important that it need not be dwelt upon here. As far as mental health is concerned, however, there are two considerations worthy of our attention.

In the first place, it is important to bear in mind that teachers are subject to the same frustrations and tensions as all other adults. Worries about finances, personal or family illnesses, interpersonal relationships, and other problems are part of adult living and should be met with equilibrium and maturity if the teacher is a mentally healthy person.

Secondly, there are certain conditions *inherent in the nature of elementary teaching* which may be causes of poor mental health unless teachers make a deliberate attempt to counterbalance them. As every experienced teacher knows, elementary teaching can be a lonely and confining job. Being the only adult in a room of children day after day is an intensely challenging and satisfying experience—but it can also be a lonely and confining one. The elementary teacher, therefore, *must* make a deliberate attempt to cultivate adult friendships and enjoy a wide variety of adult interests and hobbies during out-of-school hours in order to maintain a sound mental balance. In connection with this point, also, the importance of recreation should be stressed and the teacher owes it to his own sound mental health to provide some time in his workday and work week for recreational activities.

In the past, the elementary teacher has been subject to certain social restrictions not normally imposed on those in other professions. Depending upon the community, the teacher was often restricted as to her dress, choice of friends, recreational activities, church affiliation, political participation and numerous other things. As a matter of fact, it was only recently that one school board repealed a ruling on its books forbidding teachers from wearing nail polish!! Fortunately, some of the more rigid restrictions have disappeared in most communities, although the teacher's personal life is, and to a large extent should be, a matter of public concern.

[18] Lester S. VanderWerf, *How to Evaluate Teachers and Teaching* (New York, Holt, Rinehart and Winston, Inc., 1958), p. 3.

However, the closer the teacher can come to living as any other respectable, decent, law-abiding, contributing community member lives, the less he will feel socially restricted and isolated, and the greater may be his chance for positive mental-emotional health.

Kaplan's investigation discovered that most annoying to more than two-thirds of the teachers studied were the items concerned with child behavior that challenged the standards and role of the teacher. He suggests that the mental health of the teacher would be greatly improved if he would "accept and tolerate the normal behavior patterns of children[19] . . ." instead of attempting to force them to conform to adult standards. Any teacher who lacks an understanding of children and places unrealistic demands upon them will certainly encounter frustrations and tensions which may eventually affect his mental health.

It should be repeated, therefore, that the teacher's total fitness is a matter of supreme importance. It is the responsibility of many people including those responsible for recruiting and selecting applicants to a teacher education program; those responsible for selecting, employing, and supervising in-service teachers; and, lastly, the teachers themselves. As Stoops aptly states, "The world at its worst needs teachers at their best."[20]

3. *Interest in, and satisfaction from, working with children.* It is almost too obvious to state that the successful teacher must like children. However, most normal adults like children. What is demanded of the elementary teacher is not only an affection for children, but a dedicated interest in working with them and a deep concern for their all-around growth. The good teacher is intensely interested in the progress of *each* individual pupil and is unreservedly committed to encouraging that progress to the very best of his ability. This is the quality to which Alexander refers when he characterizes the superior teachers he has known with the statement, "Each of these teachers showed great concern for the quality of their students' work."[21]

Because of their deep interest in and concern for pupil growth, superior teachers usually realize their greatest work satisfactions from observing and stimulating this growth. Gowan, for instance, found that superior teachers, when questioned concerning the satisfactions they received from their work, gave such answers as, ". . . being with children . . . watching change, growth . . . changing attitudes . . . dealing with leaders

[19] Louis Kaplan, "The Annoyances of Elementary School Teachers," *Journal of Educational Research*, Vol. 45 (May, 1952), p. 665.

[20] Emery Stoops, "Schoolmarm Neurosis and the Golden Mean," *Understanding the Child*, Vol. 21 (April, 1952), p. 45.

[21] William M. Alexander, *Are You a Good Teacher?* (New York, Holt, Rinehart and Winston, Inc., 1959), p. 21.

**A good teacher is intensely interested in the progress
of each individual.**

of tomorrow . . . encouraging progress of children . . . and stimulating
pupil reactions."[22] It seems to be fairly evident, therefore, that a dedication to the task of helping young people to develop to their optimum
potential is a trait that distinguishes the competent teacher from his less
effective colleagues.

4. *Personal magnetism.* Although there is no standard pattern, superior
teachers have consistently been found to possess, for want of a more
specific term, a pleasing personality. These are the teachers who are
usually described by children as "good," "kind," "pleasant," or "friendly"
teachers (see page 53). Actually, traits mentioned most frequently in this
category include enthusiasm, warmth, buoyancy, sense of humor, pleasing voice, kindness, thoughtfulness, unselfishness, integrity, generosity,
creativity, inventiveness, and resourcefulness. All of these are very important but perhaps a very special case can be made for the last three
mentioned. Many years of working with all types of elementary teachers

[22] John C. Gowan, "A Summary of the Intensive Study of Twenty Highly Selected
Elementary Women Teachers," *Journal of Experimental Education,* Vol. 26 (December, 1957), p. 118.

have led to the conviction in the author that nothing is more important than a *spirit of creativeness*. The ability to approach ordinary situations with a fresh outlook, to inject originality and spontaneity into the routine task is a quality that has strong appeal for young children. The teacher with a million ideas, the one who can always think of new ways and new ideas to occupy the attention, stimulate the interest, and capture the imagination of a class of young children, is a mighty valuable person to have on an elementary school faculty!

5. *Acceptance of one's self and others*. This quality could probably be included in the previous personality category but it seems to be important enough to merit special mention. It has been the subject of interest to several investigators who state that the "self-accepting" person is likely to be well-adjusted, emotionally mature, and nonthreatened. Such a personality feels little need, therefore, to be either aggressive or defensive in his relationships with others. That this trait is related to effective teaching is proposed by Reed in the following statement: "A relationship far beyond chance expectancy was found to exist between the teacher's effectiveness in the classroom as evaluated by the students and that aspect of the teacher's personality organization, or attitude, which permits him to be an accepting person."[23]

Not only is the effective teacher accepting of himself but also of others. Thus, the hypercritical, overly demanding, withdrawn, insecure, and emotionally immature individual would appear to have definite personality traits that would hinder his ability as a teacher.

The present-day agreement upon the important relationship between the attitude of acceptance and competent teaching is summarized thus: "The teacher's attitude of acceptance has been found to be closely related to his effectiveness as perceived by his pupils. The teacher who accepts himself and his environment as well as his pupils is likely to be effective in his work.[24]

6. *Ego-involvement in teaching*. There is some interesting evidence that indicates that ego-involvement is an important factor in teaching success. In defining this quality, Jersild states,

Where there is meaning, there is involvement. When something has meaning, one is committed to it. Where there is meaning, there is conviction. Such commitment and conviction is something different from conformity, or merely playing a part, or living as a cog in a machine, or losing one's indi-

[23] Harold J. Reed, "An Investigation of the Relationship Between Teaching Effectiveness and the Teacher's Attitude of Acceptance," *Journal of Experimental Education*, Vol. 21 (June, 1953), p. 324.
[24] K. M. Evans, "The Teacher-Pupil Relationship," *Educational Research*, Vol. 2 (November, 1959), p. 4.

viduality in what Kierkegaard has called the 'featureless crowd.' Where meaning is lacking in one's work as a teacher, the self is uninvolved. The substance is lacking, and teaching is just an empty formality.[25]

This author goes on to report that meaninglessness was a problem of many of the teachers studied, and that, ". . . some said they saw little or no meaning in many of the things they had to learn or teach."[26] These are the teachers who merely go through the motions of teaching; who blindly "follow" a textbook, workbook, or course of study; who never really see their pupils as individuals; and who never enjoy the satisfaction that results from the achievement of clearly formulated goals.

In direct contrast, most superior teachers appear to have a high work-libido and ego-involvement. These teachers not only have a deep interest in teaching but they also have a high regard for it. They feel that it is a vitally important profession and they are proud to be a part of it. Often they come from a home in which teaching is greatly respected and many of them are motivated early in their lives toward teaching as a career. They derive intense personal satisfaction from their work. Frequently they identify themselves with one or two school systems instead of constantly changing locations; and they have a high degree of permanency in teaching. Concerning this last point. Leiderman and others include in their summary of teacher behavior studies the statement that, ". . . ego-involvement is the best predictor of permanency in teaching.[27]

7. *Administrative and organizational leadership.* Ordinarily one thinks of these qualities as important requirements for the principal, superintendent, or supervisor—for almost everyone, in fact, *but* the classroom teacher. Actually, the classroom teacher is, in every sense of the word, an administrator. Think for a moment of some of his duties and responsibilities to realize the truth of this statement! He must plan, organize, schedule, and conduct a wide variety of activities designed to meet individual pupil needs; he must take care of innumerable details which range from collecting milk money to tracking down lost mittens; he must budget time wisely in order to accomplish specified goals; he must establish and adhere to a regular, but flexible, schedule; he must supervise the activities of numerous individuals and several groups, all working simultaneously; he must make daily judgments of far-reaching consequence to many individuals; and he must make immediate and arbitrary decisions in times of emergency or crisis. These and countless other tasks require that the

[25] Arthur T. Jersild, *When Teachers Face Themselves* (New York, Bureau of Publications, Teachers College, Columbia University, 1955), pp. 78-79.
[26] *Ibid.*
[27] Gloria F. Leiderman, Thomas L. Hilton, and Harry Levin, "Studies of Teachers' Behavior: A Summary Report," *Journal of Teacher Education*, Vol. 8 (December, 1957), p. 437.

effective elementary teacher be a methodical, well-organized, and efficient administrator who is capable of planning and implementing his plans down to the finest detail.

It is important to note here that this quality also has a strong appeal for children. Children *do not like* a disorganized, haphazard, chaotic kind of teacher or classroom. To the contrary, they do like the security of a well-planned, well-organized, purposeful, and somewhat structured situation. A fourth grade class, as an example, had the misfortune of having a teacher who was extremely disorganized. She was simply incapable of administering to the details involved in working with thirty children every day and finally resigned her position. She was followed by a succession of substitutes and things went from bad to worse until pure chaos reigned. The classroom was dirty and ill-kept; materials were lost or broken; and children were noisy, impudent and inattentive. Nothing was accomplished and, in desperation, the principal prevailed upon an outstanding teacher who had retired the year previously to substitute in the class for the remainder of the year. On her first day, ten minutes after school had opened, Mrs. R had everything running like clockwork. Children's assignments were placed on the chalkboard and all were busily working; attendance had been taken; materials were distributed with no noise or confusion; and all other routine matters were dispensed with quietly and efficiently. Peace and serenity reigned. After about fifteen minutes of such bliss, one youngster leaned his head back, rolled his eyes heavenward, and murmured, "Hey, somebody pinch me! I must've died and gone to heaven!!"

The discussion thus far has examined seven general and basic essentials that are most related to effective teaching in the modern elementary school. The remainder of this section is concerned with those dimensions that apparently have little relationship to the quality of teaching performance.

CERTAIN QUALITIES APPEAR TO BE ONLY SLIGHTLY, OR NOT AT ALL, RELATED TO TEACHING EFFECTIVENESS. Again, evidence is inconclusive and contradictory but the following factors do not appear to have any significant relationship to teaching success.

1. *Age and experience.* One would ordinarily think that the longer a person taught, the more competent he would become. Interestingly enough, research does not substantiate this assumption. Concerning the importance of age and experience, Gowan's study of twenty outstanding teachers revealed that, "Evidently there is little relationship between experience and effectiveness. The range was from thirty-six to two years, with the median at ten years. There were six teachers of more than twenty

years' experience and six with less than five years.[28] McCall and Krause report similar findings to the effect that, "Years of service . . . showed a zero . . . correlation with merit."[29] A summary of research studies states, "Age of the teacher and amount of teaching experience seem to manifest an over-all negative relationship with teaching effectiveness, although there is evidence of curvilinearity, increase in effectiveness being positively correlated with experience during the early years of teaching careers."[30] Still another summary concludes that,

There is considerable conflict in the research literature as to whether age and experience are related to teaching competence. A few studies have indicated no relationship. Others have found that teaching ability improves very rapidly at first, but the rate of improvement quickly slows and eventually begins a slow decline. One researcher found evidence that the improvement continues for only one or two years; others have found that the rise is rapid for about five years, slower for another five years, and unchanged for a fairly long period. Since this finding is consistent with learning patterns in a number of other areas, it seems reasonable to believe that it may be accurate for development of teaching ability. Studies of the over-all relationship between age and experience and development of competence generally show a low but positive relationship.[31]

It can only be concluded, therefore, from these and other statements that the relationship of age and experience to teaching effectiveness is a question to which no one, at present, has a final answer.

2. *Sex.* Some studies report a higher degree of effectiveness among women than men teachers, although these pertain more to the secondary school than to the elementary school. In general, it appears to be true that, "Sex differences in teacher effectiveness do not appear to be pronounced among elementary teachers. . . ."[32]

3. *Marital status.* Again, the evidence is far from conclusive although there appears to be a very slight margin in favor of married teachers, as evidenced from the following statements: ". . . within the elementary school the evidence somewhat favors married teachers . . ."[33] "In general married women have been more favorably reported than have single though the differences are neither great nor uniform."[34]

[28] John C. Gowan, *op. cit.*, p. 118.
[29] William A. McCall and Gertrude R. Krause, *op. cit.*, p. 73.
[30] David G. Ryans, "Prediction of Teacher Effectiveness," *Encyclopedia of Educational Research*, 3rd ed., Chester W. Harris, ed. (New York, The Macmillan Company, 1960), p. 1490.
[31] Robert B. Howsam, "*Who's a Good Teacher?*" (Burlingame, Calif., California Teachers Association, 1960), p. 25.
[32] David G. Ryans, *op. cit.*, p. 1490.
[33] *Ibid.*
[34] Robert B. Howsam, *op. cit.*, p. 25.

4. *Cultural background.* The following statement meets with general agreement: "There appears to be no substantial evidence that race or color, socio-economic status, or similar factors are significantly related to success in teaching."[35]

In summary, from the vast amount of research done on teacher competency, one may conclude that certain general constellations of factors are definitely related to teaching effectiveness. Other narrower, single factors are not.

THE MEASUREMENT AND PREDICTION OF TEACHER COMPETENCY

The attempt to define teacher competency is paralled by an attempt to measure and predict it. Although it has been greatly accelerated in the twentieth century, interest in measuring teacher efficiency is probably as old as teaching itself. In general, attempts in this direction have been slowed down by all of the problems mentioned on pages 50 to 52 namely, that good teaching is a multidimensional, complex, individualized, and ever-changing concept that does not lend itself easily to either accurate definition or measurement. In addition, the major problem of suitable criteria is a formidable one and needs to be examined in detail.

IT IS DIFFICULT TO ESTABLISH A VALID CRITERION FOR THE MEASUREMENT OF TEACHER COMPETENCY. Against what yardstick should the teacher's performance be measured? What criteria can one use to say that Mr. X is a good teacher but Mrs. Y is not? Generally speaking, there are two main ways by which a teacher can be measured, namely: (1) pupil growth and (2) a study of the teacher's behavior or his personality characteristics or both.

1. *Pupil growth.* Pupil growth is sometimes called a "product criterion" or an "ultimate criterion" since it is concerned with the *final product of teaching*. It has been used extensively to measure the teacher's worth and, on the face of it, would appear to be a valid criterion. After all, the teacher is supposed to teach! The better he teaches, the better his pupils will learn! It would seem to follow, therefore, that the pupils of the best teacher will learn the most. Measure the extent of their learning and you have also measured the level of their teacher's ability. Simply put, this is the rationale behind the use of this criterion and there are many who favor it, as evidenced from the following statement: ". . . most educational researchers now agree that pupil gains in learning are the most valid

[35] *Ibid.,* p. 24.

criteria of a teacher's competence."[36] There is little doubt that pupil gain in learning is one criterion of teaching effectiveness. However, reliance upon it entirely, or without qualification, presents some serious problems, among which are the following.

In the first place, even if pupil growth is interpreted in *its narrowest sense* as meaning only academic growth, it is still very hard to measure it accurately. Pupil achievement tests can measure the possession of certain knowledges and skills, but they are much less successful in measuring problem-solving skills; ability to organize, locate, and evaluate information; and other learning outcomes upon which there is so much emphasis today. The question simply put, therefore, is Do pupil achievement tests really measure academic achievement or *only certain aspects of academic achievement?* If it is the latter, is it fair to judge a teacher's competence by them?

Secondly, pupil growth should certainly *not* be interpreted to mean only academic growth, for today the good teacher is concerned about social acceptance, emotional adjustments, positive value judgments, and other equally important learnings. These are, of course, extremely difficult, if not impossible, to measure accurately. As Tyler says,

There are many suitable instruments for detecting improvement in school achievement, but techniques for the evaluation of non-cognitive functions (changes in social behavior; in mental health; in attitudes, values, and beliefs; in life adjustment) are much less satisfactory. Indeed, evidence about growth in affective behavior is difficult to come by.[37]

Thirdly, it is difficult to exclude the other factors that affect pupil growth, for no one can say that the teacher alone is responsible for the learning or nonlearning of his pupils. Many factors inherent in the students themselves such as their intellectual capacities, motivations, physical well-being, interests, and many others certainly affect the extent of their learning. External factors also play an important part, such as home backgrounds, size of class, availability of teaching aids, and classroom environment. All of these help or hinder pupil growth to a considerable degree. One can hardly, therefore, afford to discount them and relate pupil growth only to the teacher's effectiveness.

Lastly, in considering pupil gain it is necessary to distinguish between immediate and long-range gain. Is the best teacher one whose pupils learn

---

[36] Horace B. Reed, "Teacher Variables of Warmth, Demand and Utilization of Intrinsic Motivation Related to Pupils' Science Interests: A Study Illustrating Several Potentials of Variance-Covariance," *Journal of Experimental Education*, Vol. 29 (March, 1961), p. 205.

[37] Fred T. Tyler, "Teachers' Personalities and Teaching Competencies," *School Review*, Vol. 68 (Winter, 1960), p. 431.

the most—or one whose pupils retain the most over the longest period of time? Is the best teacher one who has the most direct influence on children —or one whose influence is felt and remembered years later?

These and other problems must be taken into consideration by those who would use pupil gain as the criterion of teacher effectiveness. It is true that some of the more recent studies have made statistical allowances for all such factors, but the fact remains that there are fewer studies using pupil growth criteria than those using the second criterion, discussed below.

2. *Studies of teacher behavior or characteristics or both*. This criterion has been called the "process" or "proximate" criterion because it attempts to measure the process used to achieve the final goal. It includes the use of numerous types of ratings and observational devices as well as standardized tests, all of which present some advantages and disadvantages. The remainder of the chapter is devoted to a brief discussion of the major issues involved in the use of these instruments.

NUMEROUS OBSERVATIONAL DEVICES HAVE BEEN USED TO EVALUATE TEACHER EFFECTIVENESS. Rating of teachers through the technique of classroom visitation and observation is not new. On the contrary, this device has occupied the attention of educators for years, and many attempts have been made to devise instruments of various forms upon which the teacher is rated according to the judgment of the observer, usually the principal or supervisor. As in the case of pupil growth, this criterion poses many problems.

In the first place, many teachers object strenuously to such ratings because of their widely publicized subjectivity and invalidity. It is difficult to compose a rating instrument that eliminates the element of subjectivity and early attempts often produced crude instruments which were biased, incomplete, and superficial. In recent years, however, more sophisticated research has produced more refined methods and instruments which are more objective and reliable for assessing teaching effectiveness. An example of such a scale is the *Classroom Observation Scale* described briefly on pages 75 to 76.

Secondly, observers differ in their evaluations and in the relative importance they attach to certain aspects of the teacher's behavior or personality. There have been many studies that show that one observer may rate a teacher "average" while another will rate the same teacher as "outstanding," even though both observers have witnessed the same lesson and both are persons of equal experience and training.

Thirdly, in observing the classroom situation, it is very difficult to discount the effect of the observer's presence. In order to offset this factor as much as possible, frequent visitations over a long period of time are often recommended. Even this procedure, however, does not entirely negate the factor. A more promising possibility may be the use, as proposed by Howsam,[38] of kinescopic recordings to analyze, and perhaps evaluate teacher performance, although it is obvious that this too will present many complications.

Fourthly, observers, when checking specific items on a rating scale, tend to mark most or all items almost the same. This produces only a generalized estimate, usually termed the halo effect, which reduces considerably the value of the rating.

Lastly, it is well known that most observers do not tend to be genuinely critical or analytical in their evaluation of teaching performance. As a matter of fact, there is usually a tendency to be overly lenient. Bass states, "The bias of leniency is an error commonly found in merit ratings. Most ratees are assigned very complimentary evaluations; few or none are assigned unfavorable scores."[39]

The above problems do not suggest that the evaluation and analysis of teacher behavior-personality be eliminated as a criterion of competence. To the contrary, they point toward the need for continual refinement and improvement of these procedures. In general, there appear to be three hopeful signs in this direction, namely: (1) the continued refinement of adequate rating instruments, (2) the training of competent raters, and (3) the trend toward greater emphasis on self-evaluation and cooperative evaluation.

RECENT INSTRUMENTS FOR ASSESSING TEACHING EFFECTIVENESS ARE GREATLY IMPROVED OVER EARLIER ATTEMPTS. There seems to be some indication that progress is being made in devising evaluative instruments relatively free from the limitations previously noted. The *Classroom Observation Scale* used in the Teacher Characteristics Study, for instance, is "an extension and refinement" of earlier instruments and has the following unique features:

(1) it provides for judgment of teacher behavior as based (*a*) on the immediate observation of the teacher's performance in the classroom and (*b*) on inferences regarding teacher behavior derived from pupil behavior; (2) it assumes that many teacher traits or qualities constitute dimensions of behavior, the opposite poles of which may be described with precise and meaningful terms referring to specific behaviors of the teacher; (3) it demands that the judge avoid the "central tendency error" by *forcing* the rating in the direction of one or the other of the poles; (4) it makes use of a detailed "Glossary"

[38] Robert B. Howsam, *New Designs . . . For Research in Teacher Competence* (Burlingame, Calif., California Teachers Association, 1960).

[39] Bernard M. Bass, "Reducing Leniency in Merit Ratings," *Personnel Psychology,* Vol. 9 (Autumn, 1956), p. 359.

which provides supplementary descriptions of the teacher behaviors under consideration, and, of course, demands thorough acquaintance with the instrument.[40]

OBSERVERS SHOULD BE THOROUGHLY TRAINED IN ORDER TO MAKE THE RATING AS VALID AS POSSIBLE. This is a fairly obvious need and requires little explanation here. The more expert and trained the raters are, the more valid the rating will be. Ryans goes so far as to propose that ratings should be done not by principals or supervisors but by "highly selected and trained teams of judges . . . employed in a school system for that sole purpose."[41] There are, of course, many, many, people who would be opposed to this practice for various reasons. Few, however, would deny the vital importance of the careful training of the observer, whoever he may be.

THERE IS CONSIDERABLE INTEREST TODAY IN PROMOTING SELF-EVALUATION AMONG TEACHERS. Since the primary goal of teacher evaluation should be the improvement of instruction, it follows that helping teachers to evaluate themselves objectively is a major step in this direction. If self-evaluation procedures are used, however, they should be used *solely for this purpose* and never to serve as the basis for administrative decisions concerning the teacher's reemployment, promotion, or salary increase. Many systems today are using some sort of self-evaluation, either alone, or in combination with the evaluation of the principal or supervisor. In the latter case, the teacher evaluates himself, the principal, the supervisor or both evaluate him (often on the same instrument), and the results are compared and discussed in a conference among all individuals involved. Systems using self-evaluation or cooperative evaluation frequently use a scale such as the *Almy-Sorenson Self Rating Scale*. Other systems prefer to construct their own instruments which, of course, can be tailored to the individual needs and goals of the particular situation. The following is an example of a self-rating scale presently in use in Portland, Oregon.[42]

TEACHER'S SELF EVALUATION GUIDE

TEACHER_____ DATE_____

GRADE OR SUBJECT_____ SCHOOL_____

BEGAN TEACHING IN PORTLAND_____ 19_____

A. *Personal Attributes:*

    1. Emotional stability:
       a. Is well-balanced emotionally.

[40] David G. Ryans, "Notes on the Rating of Teacher Performance," *Journal of Educational Research*, Vol. 47 (May, 1954), p. 698.
[41] *Ibid.*, p. 702.
[42] Teacher's Self-Evaluation Guide, Portland, Oregon.

      b. Shows mature self-control.

      c. Is adaptable, open minded.

2. Health and vitality:

      a. Has adequate energy to meet full demands of position.

      b. Is seldom absent due to ill health.

3. Personality:

      a. Is well groomed.

      b. Dresses appropriately.

      c. Has a pleasing voice, well modulated.

      d. Has a sense of humor.

      e. Is considerate of the feelings of others.

      f. Wears well.

B. *Teaching Skills:*

1. Classroom techniques and procedures:

      a. Lessons are well planned.

      b. Pupil-teacher planning is evident.

      c. Purposeful activities are evident in classroom.

      d. Work is well planned and organized.

      e. Develops attitudes, habits, and skills in terms of pupil capacities.

2. Success in group control:

      a. Pupils are well adjusted in classroom.

      b. Controls through pupils' interest in work.

      c. Avoids autocratic domination when possible.

      d. Is firm but fair in handling pupils.

      e. Democratic principles are practiced in classes.

      f. Room is neat, orderly, and attractive.

3. Results in terms of pupil growth:

      a. Pupils work up to capacity.

      b. Pupils have learned good work habits.

      c. There is evidence of good citizenship being practiced.

      d. Provisions are made for individual differences.

4. Professional equipment:

      a. Seeks continuous growth through observation, professional study, and reading.

      b. Vitalizes teaching through preparation and study.

C. *Relations with Others:*

1. Teacher-pupil relationships:

      a. Pupils admire and respect teacher.

      b. Uses subject matter as a vehicle of child development.

      c. Pupils consult with him about their personal problems.

      d. Teacher is available for help outside the classroom.

      e. Respects pupil's personality, a guide rather than a taskmaster.

2. Teacher-co-workers relationships:
   a. Relations with teachers are cordial.
   b. Is respected by fellow teachers.
   c. Is willing to help other teachers with extra duties.
   d. Is friendly at all times.

3. Teacher-principal relationships:
   a. Is loyal to school program and policies.
   b. Is a good team worker.
   c. Takes suggestions for his own improvement.

4. Public relations:
   a. Meets parents easily, deals frankly but sympathetically with different adjustment problems.
   b. Makes friends for the school system.

5. Professional relations:
   a. Manifests pride in the teaching profession.
   b. Is frank and honest in his criticisms.
   c. Creates good will among individuals or groups.
   d. Supports PTA and teacher organizations.

NUMEROUS PAPER-AND-PENCIL TESTS HAVE BEEN DEVELOPED TO PREDICT TEACHER COMPETENCY. Although written tests are occasionally used to measure the competency of in-service teachers, for the most part they are used by colleges and some school systems to ascertain the potential of future teachers. There are a wide variety of them, designed to test the individual's intelligence, academic background, professional knowledge, motivations for teaching, attitude toward teaching and children, personality traits, and numerous other factors. It should be fairly obvious that, if the *definition* and *measurement* of teaching competency are difficult tasks, the *prediction* of it is even more so. Consequently, there are very few people who are willing to rely heavily upon *any* single test as a predictor of teaching success. Some school systems, however, and several teacher education institutions use a battery of them to screen the most desirable candidates for college admission or teacher recruitment. A few of the more common tests now in use for these purposes are mentioned below.

1. *Tests of scholastic aptitude and achievement.* Tests in this classification which may be required by schools of education and some school boards include the *Graduate Record Examinations*,[43] the *Miller Analogies Test*,[44] and others of a similar type.

---

[43] *The Graduate Record Examinations* (Princeton, N. J., Educational Testing Service).
[44] W. S. Miller, *Miller Analogies Test* (New York, Psychological Corporation).

2. *Tests of professional knowledge.* Slightly different are the tests that test for professional as well as general knowledge such as the well-known *National Teacher Examination* (NTE)[45] and a newer form, the *Teacher Education Examination Program* (TEEP).[46]

3. *Tests of personality and attitudes.* These may be of a clinical nature such as the *Minnesota Multiphasic Personality Inventory* (MMPI)[47] although, as Gowan points out,[48] there are many problems associated with using clinical screening devices on normal populations. Much more promising would seem to be tests designed to test specific traits and attitudes toward teaching. Of these, a widely studied one has been the *Minnesota Teacher Attitude Inventory* (MTAI)[49] which purports to measure ". . . those attitudes of a teacher which predict how well he will get along with pupils in interpersonal relations, and indirectly how well satisfied he will be with teaching as a vocation."[50] However, some people feel that the MTAI goes beyond this sphere and can be used as a general predictor of teaching effectiveness. Popham and Trimble state that, ". . . the MTAI may be utilized not only as an index of the type of social atmosphere a teacher will maintain in the classroom, but also as an indication of a teacher's general competence."[51] Barr and Jones summarize the studies made of this instrument as follows: "It would appear from these and other investigations reported earlier that the MTAI is well on the way toward being established as a useful instrument for the measurement and prediction of teacher efficiency."[52]

Not all people agree with these assertions, however, for some report a failure of the MTAI to predict teacher-pupil rapport[53] while others claim that it is subject to faking, and still others claim that it ". . . certainly

[45] *The National Teacher Examination* (Princeton, N. J., Educational Testing Service).

[46] *Teacher Education Examination Program* (Princeton, N. J., Educational Testing Service).

[47] Starke R. Hathaway and J. Charnley McKinley, *Minnesota Multiphasic Personality Inventory* (New York, Psychological Corporation).

[48] John C. Gowan, "Self-report Tests in the Prediction of Teaching Effectiveness," *School Review*, Vol. 68 (Winter, 1960), p. 411.

[49] Walter W. Cook, Carroll H. Leeds, and Robert Calis, *Minnesota Teacher Attitude Inventory* (New York, Psychological Corporation).

[50] *Ibid.*

[51] W. James Popham and Robert R. Trimble, "The Minnesota Teacher Attitude Inventory as an Index of General Teaching Competence," *Educational and Psychological Measurement*, Vol. 20 (Autumn, 1960), p. 512.

[52] Arvil S. Barr and Robert E. Jones, "The Measurement and Prediction of Teacher Efficiency," *Review of Educational Research*, Vol. 28 (June, 1958), p. 260.

[53] William Rabinowitz and Ira Rosenbaum, "A Failure in the Prediction of Pupil-Teacher Rapport," *Journal of Educational Psychology*, Vol. 49 (April, 1958), pp. 93-98.

cannot be expected to reveal the totality of a teacher's effectiveness or ineffectiveness."[54]

Lack of space prohibits mention of numerous other tests in the three categories mentioned and other additional ones. It is sufficient only to state that much time and study have gone into the preparation of instruments concerned with the prediction of teaching success. It appears that certain of these are generally successful in predicting certain aspects of teaching effectiveness. Whether or not they can be used to predict a composite effectiveness is still an unanswered question.

SUMMARY

The present chapter has been concerned with one of the most crucial tasks facing elementary education today, namely, the definition, measurement, and prediction of teaching competency. The difficulties involved in attempting to answer the question, "Who is a good teacher?" are many, for teaching is a complex, multidimensional, individualized, ever-changing process that does not lend itself easily to exact definition or measurement. In spite of the difficulties, however, it does seem possible, at present, to reach some degree of agreement on the general essentials most frequently related to quality teaching. Those proposed in this chapter included: (1) high level of intellectual ability and academic background; (2) physical and mental health; (3) interest in, and satisfaction from, working with children; (4) personal magnetism; (5) acceptance of one's self and others; (6) ego-involvement in teaching; and (7) administrative and organizational leadership. Such isolated single factors as age and experience, sex, marital status, and cultural background have been found to have very little, if any, relationship to effective teaching.

The last part of the chapter was devoted to a discussion of the measurement and prediction of teaching success. The problem of establishing a valid criterion was examined. The advantages and disadvantages of using pupil growth (the product criterion) were compared to those using the analysis of teacher behavior-personality (the process criterion). It was stated that research is moving ahead in both areas, and that hopeful trends involving the latter appear to be (1) the development and refinement of more adequate instruments, (2) the recognition of the need to train teacher-raters carefully, and (3) the present interest in self-evaluation and cooperative evaluation.

Instruments presently being used to predict teaching competency were discussed briefly according to the classifications of (1) tests of scholastic

[54] Harry P. Day, "A Study of Predictive Validity of the Minnesota Teacher Attitude Inventory," *Journal of Educational Research*, Vol. 53 (September, 1959), p. 37.

aptitude, (2) tests of professional knowledge, and (3) tests of personality and attitudes.

In conclusion, it should be reiterated that educators and researchers recognize full well the importance of clarifying and evaluating scientifically the concept of the "good" teacher. Much progress has been made, but much more needs to be realized, before this objective is attained.

ADDITIONAL LEARNING EXPERIENCES

Topics for Thought and Discussion

1. What is your greatest single teaching asset? Your limitations?

2. What do people usually mean who refer to someone as "a born teacher"?

3. Do you think you are more effective with a certain type of child or on a certain grade level than another? Why?

4. Should elementary majors be permitted to concentrate all their student teaching experience on one grade level or should they be required to have experience in several grades prior to graduation?

5. How would you evaluate your "ego-involvement" in teaching?

6. Are you in favor of the present policy of some boards of education to require a psychiatric examination of teachers prior to employment?

7. To what degree would you say that you are a "self-accepting person"? Do you think this has any relationship to your teaching effectiveness?

8. Many studies show that teachers find it very difficult to evaluate themselves objectively. "Good" teachers tend to underrate themselves. "Poor" teachers tend to overrate themselves. Do you think you can objectively evaluate your own teaching performance?

9. It has been said that the hallmark of teaching excellence is ". . . the capacity to draw from the routine tasks of the day, a spark that lifts the teaching act out of the ordinary." To what degree do you feel you have this "spark"?[60]

10. Many teachers object to being rated by supervisors on the basis that such ratings are often subjective and biased. Yet these same teachers assume constantly, and often confidently, the task of rating children. Since teachers are frequently called upon to rate others, should they, in turn, be willing to be rated by others?

11. Do you think that the public concept of a good elementary teacher has changed at all in the last twenty years? In what respect?

[60] Howard B. Holt, "Artist and Artisan in the Teaching Profession," *Educational Forum*, Vol. 25 (January, 1961), p. 234.

Projects and Activities

1. Your state professional association is awarding a prize for the best essay entitled, "My Most Unforgettable Teacher." Submit your entry in five hundred words or less.

2. Ask a fifth or sixth grade class of pupils to write an essay entitled, "My Idea of a Good Teacher." Classify the traits mentioned into categories of (1) teacher's personal qualities, (2) relationships with children, and (3) teaching procedures and techniques. Compare the results of your survey with those mentioned in this chapter. What degree of consistency do you find?

3. Talk with several high school guidance counselors or teachers. What qualities do they consider important when advising high school students who are considering a career in elementary school teaching?

4. Observe for at least one hour each in the classrooms of four primary (K-1-2) grade teachers and four upper grade (5-6) teachers. Write a brief personality sketch of each teacher. Do you notice any consistent differences in personality between the two groups?

5. Write a rebuttal to the old cliche that, "Those who can, do; those who can't, teach."

6. Interview a superintendent of schools. What qualities does he say he looks for most in interviewing prospective elementary school teachers? Compare your data with the findings of Item 3.

7. Talk with several elementary teachers. Do they feel that teaching offers a genuine intellectual challenge. In what respect?

8. Evaluate yourself according to the *Self-Evaluation Scale* contained on pp. 76-78.

Selected Bibliography

ALEXANDER, William M., *Are You a Good Teacher?* New York, Holt, Rinehart, and Winston, Inc., 1959.

BARR, Arvil S., and JONES, Robert E., "The Measurement and Prediction of Teacher Efficiency." *Review of Educational Research*, Vol. 28 (June, 1958).

———, and others, *Wisconsin Studies of the Measurement and Prediction of Teacher Effectiveness.* Madison, Wis., Dembar Publications, Inc., 1961.

CHARTERS, Werrett W., and WAPLES, Douglas, *The Commonwealth Teacher-Training Study.* Chicago, University of Chicago Press, 1929.

HATCH, Winslow R., and BENNET, Ann, *Effectiveness in Teaching.* Washington, D. C., U. S. Department of Health, Education, and Welfare, 1960.

HEIL, Louis M., POWELL, Marion, and FEIFER, Irwin, *Characteristics of Teacher Behavior and Competency Related to the Achievement of Different Kinds of Children in Several Elementary Schools.* New York, Brooklyn College, 1960.

Howsam, Robert B., *Who's a Good Teacher?* Joint Committee on Personnel Procedures of the California School Boards Association and the California Teachers Association. Burlingame, Calif., California Teachers Association, 1960.

——, *New Designs . . . For Research in Teacher Competence.* Joint Committee on Personnel Procedures of the California School Boards Association and the California Teachers Association. Burlingame, Calif., California Teachers Association, 1960.

Jenkins, David H., and Lippitt, Ronald, *Interpersonal Perceptions of Teachers, Students, and Parents.* Washington, D. C., National Education Association, Division of Adult Education Service, 1951.

Jersild, Arthur T., *When Teachers Face Themselves.* New York, Bureau of Publications, Teachers College, Columbia University, 1955.

Leiderman, Gloria F., Hilton, Thomas L., and Levin, Harry, "Studies of Teachers' Behavior: A Summary Report." *Journal of Teacher Education,* Vol. 8 (December, 1957).

Medley, Donald M., and Klein, Alix A., *Studies of Teacher Behavior: Inferring Classroom Behavior from Pupil Responses.* Research Series 30. Board of Higher Education of the City of New York, Division of Teacher Education, Office of Research and Evaluation. New York, February, 1956, mimeographed.

——, and Mitzel, Harold E., *Studies of Teacher Behavior: The Refinement of Two Techniques for Observing Teachers' Classroom Behaviors.* Research Series 28. Board of Higher Education of the City of New York, Division of Teacher Education, Office of Research and Evaluation, New York, October, 1955, mimeographed.

Mitzel, Harold E., and Gross, Cecily F., *A Critical Review of the Development of Pupil Growth Criteria in Studies of Teacher Effectiveness.* Research Series 31. Board of Higher Education of the City of New York, Division of Teacher Education, Office of Research and Evaluation, New York, April, 1956, mimeographed.

New York State School Boards Association, *Identifying Superior Teachers.* A Report of a Study by a Committee of Central School Teachers and Lawrence M. Knolle. New York, Institute of Administrative Research, 1959.

Ryans, David G., *Characteristics of Teachers: Their Description, Comparison, and Appraisal, A Research Study.* Washington, D. C., American Council on Education, 1960.

Tomlinson, Loren R., "Pioneer Studies in the Evaluation of Teaching." *Educational Research Bulletin,* Vol. 34 (March 9, 1955).

VanderWerf, Lester S., *How to Evaluate Teachers and Teaching.* New York, Holt, Rinehart and Winston, Inc., 1958.

Who's a Good Teacher? William J. Ellena, Margaret Stevenson, and Harold V. Webb, eds. American Association of School Administrators, Department of Classroom Teachers of NEA, National School Boards Association. Washington, D. C., 1961.

PART **II**

WORKING WITH OTHERS

CHAPTER **3**

Working With Children

"WHAT IN THE WORLD am I going to do with Mickey? He can't seem to stay out of trouble for five minutes. I've tried everything I know but now I'm at my wit's end. . . ."

"I met Mrs. Hartley, Tommy's mother, on the bus yesterday. She invited me to dinner Monday night. . . ."

"Mrs. DeMazzio stopped in yesterday to talk about Gloria. She told me some things about their home situation that threw some light on Gloria's crying spell the other day. I feel that I understand the child much better now. . . ."

"I certainly appreciated Mr. MacKenzie's stopping in to see our science exhibit. No matter how busy he is, he always has time to give every teacher some help and encouragement. I think he's the best principal in the city.. . ."

"Wouldn't you think Miss Keldnar would keep her class on its own side of the playground? If her children interrupt our game once more, I'm going to complain. . . ."

A school is primarily the interaction of people. Teaching is, to a considerable extent, a problem in varied and complex interpersonal relationships. Relationships between teacher-pupil, pupil-pupil, parent-teacher, teacher-group, principal-teacher, pupil-group, teacher-teacher and numerous others are like the threads of a tapestry. Individually they may be invisible but together they comprise the strength and quality and beauty of the total product. At the center of many of these relationships is the teacher—and the extent to which he can work harmoniously and constructively with all individuals contributes inestimably to his total effectiveness.

OF ALL THE RELATIONSHIPS IN WHICH THE TEACHER IS INVOLVED, NONE IS MORE IMPORTANT THAN THOSE HE HAS WITH HIS PUPILS. Today, even the most die-hard traditionalist admits that the establishment of healthy pupil-teacher relationships is a major responsibility of every teacher. Some, of course, admit the importance of such relationships only because of the now-accepted fact that they affect learning. Therefore, these individuals reason, if children are to learn and teachers are to teach, the relationships between them must be taken into account. A second school of thought recognizes the importance of interpersonal relationships as a primary factor in maintaining peace and order in the classroom. Children will behave better if they are on good terms with their teacher, hence the human relationship is important in preventing classroom chaos. Although a third point of view recognizes the worth of both these ideas, it goes considerably further in stressing the importance of human relationships *as a factor in the total personality development of the child.* In other words, human relations in education are important, not only because they affect learning and classroom control, but because the school is vitally concerned with the complete, integrative personality growth of every individual boy and girl. This concern for all factors and phases of child personality and behavior has frequently been called the "mental hygiene emphasis" in teaching. It is one of the basic concepts of our modern educational philosophy, and its importance is reiterated frequently in this chapter and others.

THE TEACHER HAS A DOUBLE-EDGED RELATIONSHIP WITH HIS PUPILS. More than ever before, educational emphasis today is upon *the individual child.* In general, three major forces have contributed to the emergence of the individual as the focus of the educative process. In the first place, the child study movement of the early twentieth century made teachers fully aware of the existence and importance of individual differences. Today's teachers recognize and understand that each child is different from all others in an untold number of dimensions and that they must react to him accordingly. Secondly, the scientific movement and research into the learning process has emphasized individual motivations, satisfactions, goals, capacities, and aptitudes. Lockstep learning is no more. Thirdly, the fact that we live in a democratic rather than a totalitarian state leads us to respect and value the dignity, worth, and unique contribution of each individual. As Sheviakov and Redl state, "A democracy is distinguished . . . by its solicitude for every individual. Differences are not only accepted, but are valued for the contribution which they can make to the welfare and progress of all."[1]

Thus, our educational and social principles adhere strongly to the

[1] George V. Sheviakov and Fritz Redl, new rev. by Sybil K. Richardson, *Discipline for Today's Children and Youth* (Washington, D. C., Association for Supervision and Curriculum Development, NEA, 1956), p. 7.

A good teacher must always be concerned with both the individual and the total group.

belief in the importance of the individual. The warm, personal, one-to-one relationship between teacher and pupil, therefore, may be regarded as the very heart and core of the entire school experience.

In view of the great importance placed upon the individual, it is paradoxical that the teacher seldom meets him except as he is part of a group. By far the greatest portion of the teacher's time is spent in working and dealing with children *as a group*. Consequently, the teacher-group relationship is of extreme importance. This means that the teacher must not only have an understanding of individual behavior but also a knowledge of group dynamics as well. He must be, not only a guide to individuals, but also an expert in group engineering!

From this double-edged relationship with the individual and with the group, comes one of the major problems of the teacher, namely, "How can I balance both relationships without sacrificing one for the other? If I concern myself primarily with giving Rocco the attention I know that he needs—my class will literally fall apart. On the other hand, I know I'm being unfair to Rocco if I force him to conform to the standards of the group." This dilemma of the teacher is referred to by Redl as "the law of marginal antisepsis" which he interprets in the following statement:

. . . everything you do to impress the group and get them organized has to be at least harmless in its effect on the individual; and everything you do to the individual has to be at least harmless in its effect on the total group. If you do something right for Johnny and that makes the group a mess the following morning, that's the wrong treatment. If you do something which gets the group badly organized, or the other children scared, that's wrong, too. And that is where the tremendous problem of the classroom teacher on the job comes in. There is no magic bagful of tricks with which to solve it.[2]

Recognizing the importance of this problem, the following suggestions for working successfully with children are based upon two important considerations, namely, the concern for the personality development of the individual and the concern for the cohesiveness and harmony of the group.

GUIDEPOSTS TO WORKING SUCCESSFULLY WITH CHILDREN

THE MOST IMPORTANT SINGLE STEP TOWARD WORKING SUCCESSFULLY WITH CHILDREN IS TO UNDERSTAND THEM. For many years, educators and psychologists have stressed the importance of the teacher's understanding his pupils. Schools of education have introduced child psychology courses into their curricula, in-service programs have stressed child study techniques, and state certification requirements have been strengthened to insure the teacher's having a foundational knowledge of child growth and development. All of these are the result of the steadily growing evidence that the teacher must know and understand children in order to be effective in the classroom. Bush, for instance, reports the result of an investigation which indicated that, "In general, the teachers who know most about their pupils and are aware of and sympathize with their individual needs and interests have effective relationships with a larger number than do the teachers whose major concern is knowledge of subject matter.[3]

Since it is accepted today that the teacher must understand children in order to guide their development and establish desirable relationships with them, two questions come to mind, (1) What knowledge should the teacher have about his pupils? and (2) How can he obtain this information?

---

[2] Fritz Redl, "Discipline in the Classroom," *Child Study*, Vol. 21 (Summer, 1944), p. 104.

[3] Robert Nelson Bush, *The Teacher-Pupil Relationship* (Englewood Cliffs, N. J., Prentice-Hall, Inc., 1954), p. 189.

1. What knowledge should the teacher have about his pupils?

   a. *Latitudinal knowledge of child growth and development.* It is a well-known fact that each child develops according to his own unique growth pattern. It is equally well-known that there are "average" or "typical" growth patterns for each age level. It would seem that, *as the barest minimum,* the teacher should have full knowledge of his pupils' typical growth pattern *at their particular stage of development.* The third-grade teacher, for instance, should know that the "average" eight-year-old is,

   . . . less brooding . . . more centrifugal . . . more perceptive in the responses of others. He may be characterized by speediness, expansiveness, and evaluativeness. He is in general healthier and less fatigable. . . The eight-year-old listens closely when adults talk among themselves. He watches their facial expressions; he keeps looking and listening for cues and indicators in the social environment. . . He is naively docile and compliant. . . He is a little sensitive about being told too directly what to do. He prefers a cue or hint. He expects and asks for praise. . . His sense of self is becoming a sense of status.[4]

   Similarly, the fifth-grade teacher should be aware that,

   The ten-year-old is peculiarly receptive to social information, to broadening ideas, and to prejudice, good and bad. It is relatively easy to appeal to his reason. He is ready to participate in elementary discussions of social problems. . .[5]

   If the teacher withstands the temptation to categorize *all* of his pupils according to such chronological age slots, the latitudinal knowledge of child growth and development is of inestimable value in helping him to understand the pupils in his class. In addition, of course, he needs the following specific knowledge of each individual.

   b. *Health knowledge.* The physical and mental health of the child is a primary factor in his behavior. Consequently, the teacher should have accurate knowledge of his health history including (1) his general state of physical health, (2) the presence of any chronic diseases or infirmities, (3) his physiological state of development, and (4) the presence or treatment of any mental or emotional disorders.

   c. *Knowledge of academic aptitudes and special interests.* Data concerning the pupil's intelligence level and scholastic achievement are readily available to most teachers today. In addition, teachers should

---

[4] Arnold Gesell and Frances L. Ilg, *The Child from Five to Ten* (New York, Harper & Row, Publishers, Inc., 1946), pp. 160-161.
[5] *Ibid.,* pp. 213-214.

have as much knowledge as possible concerning individual aptitudes and interests. Many a relationship has been strengthened and many a child has been helped over a behavior problem because the teacher just happened to know that he played the trombone, collected Indian arrowheads, raised prize pigs, or pitched a no-hit Little League game.

    d. *Home environment.* Knowledge of the home that will help the teacher to better understand the child includes (1) any special strains or stresses such as the chronic illness or disability of any family member, (2) the cohesiveness of the family unit, (3) the influence of the broken home or excessive parental absence, and (4) the economic-cultural level of the home. This last item is becoming increasingly important. Sociologists stress that, because the large majority of American teachers come from middle-class socio-economic homes, they fail to understand the social patterns and codes of the lower-class socio-economic child. Poor teacher-pupil relationships and unacceptable pupil behavior are the inevitable result. This problem is examined in detail in Chapter 6.

    e. *Group relationships.* In view of the double-edged relationship stressed earlier in the chapter, the teacher must not only have a knowledge of the *individual* but must also have an understanding of his group. Knowledge of the group structure, group roles, and social climate is of vital importance to the teacher as he builds strong teacher-pupil relationships (see Chapter 6).

2. How may the teacher obtain information about his pupils?

    a. *Records.* Cumulative records should be consulted by teachers who wish to learn as well as teach children. Most schools have a central records system. Regardless of the elaborateness and detail of the records, the real test of their value is the extent to which teachers use them to obtain enlightening and constructive information about their pupils.

    b. *Observation.* Any teacher may learn a great deal by merely observing his pupils carefully. Is David always on the fringe of the group? How many days in succession has Alice complained of feeling ill just before physical education period? Are Dick and Tom vying for leadership roles in the group? Why have Beth and Linda, usually the best of friends, suddenly stopped speaking to each other? Light can be thrown on these and countless other questions that teachers have about their pupils by careful and critical observation of pupils in the classroom, at the lunch table, on the school bus, in the gymnasium, on the class trip, and other such situations.

c. *Anecdotal records.* Teachers often record their observations of pupil behavior in thumbnail sketches which are helpful in revealing a *pattern of behavior* that may appear or develop over a period of time. Usually such records contain, in three parallel columns, the (1) incident of behavior observed, (2) teacher's comment, and (3) action suggested (see sample anecdotal record on pages 478 to 480.

d. *Art and writing experiences.* Children's art work may often be indicative of their feelings or problems and many perceptive teachers have found help from this source in understanding their pupils. In addition, various creative writing experiences such as autobiographies, diaries, logs, etc., are often used in the upper grades. Suggested titles for compositions such as "A Happy Day," "My Most Exciting Experience," "If I Could Have Three Wishes," "What I Remember Most About Last Summer," may be helpful in yielding enlightening information.

e. *Standardized tests and rating scales.* Many of these are now available and are helpful in yielding objective data concerning the child's progress (see Chapter 11).

f. *Conference and visitations.* Probably the most valuable of these is the individual pupil-teacher counseling conference. The success of these conferences depends upon certain basic principles:

The teacher must be an effective listener.

A feeling of rapport must exist between teacher and pupil.

Pupils should be given an opportunity to express negative feelings in a permissive and objective atmosphere.

After rapport has been established and negative feelings expressed, the teacher must help the child evaluate these negative feelings and develop more positive ones.

Children must be given an opportunity to arrive at, and to try out, tentative solutions to their problems.

Summaries and evaluations of the counseling sessions should be developed by the child, not by the teacher.[6]

Other conferences that will yield helpful information are those the teacher has with such specialized personnel as the principal, school nurse, school psychologist, and guidance worker. Conferences with the child's former teachers may be of great value provided they are on a professional and constructive level and never deteriorate to idle gossip. Home visitations, another valuable source of information, are discussed in the following chapter.

[6] Dorothy G. Petersen and Velma D. Hayden, *Teaching and Learning in the Elementary School* (New York, Appleton-Century-Crofts, 1961), pp. 440-442.

IN ORDER TO WORK SUCCESSFULLY WITH CHILDREN, RAPPORT MUST EXIST BETWEEN TEACHER AND PUPILS. The same ingredients are necessary for teacher-pupil rapport as for any other type of harmonious human relationship. The teacher who consistently treats his pupils with courtesy, tact, consideration, respect, warmth, and friendliness is building a strong bond of rapport that will inevitably affect the social relationships and behavior in his classroom.

CONSIDERATION MUST BE GIVEN TO THE PUPILS' BASIC NEEDS. There are certain basic needs which, if deprived or thwarted, will result in severe social misbehavior and personality maladjustment. Those that are most pertinent to this discussion are examined below.

1. *Physiological needs.* Of the physical needs demanded by the human body, rest and activity are two that concern the classroom teacher greatly. The wise teacher will recognize the existence of these needs in all growing children and will make adequate provision for them in the daily program. Occasionally a brief period of rest or relaxation, or a few minutes of bodily exercise or movement, are all that are needed to forestall an undesirable social incident.

Another technique some teachers use most effectively is to legitimize the behavior of certain individuals who have an excessive need for exercise and activity. For example, Jake is constantly out of his seat, walking around the room, making excuses to sharpen his pencil a dozen times, making endless trips to the wastebasket, all of which can be disturbing to other childen. Instead of trying to force Jake to be inactive, the teacher may provide certain positive opportunities to satisfy his need for physical movement. Asking him to distribute or collect supplies, run necessary errands, or assume other classroom duties will help Jake to get the activity his body demands in a socially accepted manner.

2. *Social needs.* Every child is a social human being who needs contact and interaction with others. Youngsters are intensely interested in others and have a strong need for social communication and group belongingness. As Redl says, ". . . no normal growing youngster can keep his mind and thoughts and eyes off other human beings."[7] To attempt to force each child to mind his own business and to refrain from normal social contact or communication during the school day is to invite disaster.

3. *Emotional needs.* The emotional needs of greatest concern to classroom teachers may be thought of as *The Three A's:*

Affection. Every child feels the need of love. It is also true, as someone has said, that, "The least lovable is in most need of love." This has great

[7] Fritz Redl, *op. cit.*, p. 105.

**A good teacher makes adequate provision for the
physiological needs of children.**

significance for the teacher. It is, for instance, easy enough for any teacher
to like pretty, sweet, clean, neat, charming little Susan, or intelligent,
popular, dependable, courteous Billy. Who wouldn't like such charming
children? The ironic thing is, of course, that these children are probably
receiving most of the affection and attention they need from their devoted
parents, doting relatives, and numerous friends. They may not need the
attention of the teacher nearly as much as some others. What about
Katherine, for instance? Unkempt, sullen, from a broken home, uninter-
ested in school, disagreeable to other children—can the teacher give her
the affection she is not receiving from anyone else?

While on this point, it may be well to clarify the meaning of "affection" as used in this sense. It does *not* mean a cloying, sentimentalized,
gushing show of emotion toward a child. Overemotionalized behavior has
no place in the classroom. It *does* mean, however, that the teacher should,
in a hundred subtle ways, show that he generally likes and thinks about
the individual child. For instance, to show any overt signs of affection
for hard-to-handle, twelve-year-old Ed would be simply disastrous. He
would be resentful and suspicious, making the teacher-pupil relationship
worse instead of better. However, to stop briefly by his desk one morning

**Every child feels the need for love and
affection.**

to say casually, "Ed, I know you're interested in sailing. I thought you
might like to look over this book I happened to see in the library," might
be a highly acceptable way of showing your regard for the child. Redl
and Wattenberg emphasize that *helping the child to learn* is the best way
the teacher can show his affection toward him. "When any youngster needs
affection, the simplest way for teachers to administer it is not by honeyed
words or sympathetic smiles, but by friendly assistance in learning."[8]

Acceptance. It has been said that rejection is the chief cause of insecurity. A basic need of children is to be accepted by their peers, their
teachers, and others. There is an untold number of ways a teacher may
help a child to be part of the group and to feel accepted by it. These
involve everything from praising his art work in front of the class to

[8] Fritz Redl and William W. Wattenberg, *Mental Hygiene in Teaching*, 2nd ed.
(New York, Harcourt, Brace & World, Inc., 1959), p. 206.

recommending him for a post on the school patrol. All good teachers recognize the existence in all of us of the basic need to be accepted, and devise hundreds of subtle ways to meet this need among their pupils.

Achievement. Every child needs to experience the thrill of achievement. Every child needs to feel adequate to the tasks that confront him. Every child needs to feel occasionally the inner satisfaction that comes from having done a job well. When he is continually deprived of this feeling, personality maladjustment is inevitable. As D'Evelyn says,

Schools unwittingly foster mental illness and maladjustment when they fail in this important function, that of helping the young child to gain a feeling of *accomplishment*. It is through this feeling that self-confidence is born, and self-confidence is one of the roots of good mental health. In most maladjustments and mental ills, the lack of self-confidence and its concomitant feeling of worthlessness are present.[9]

This author goes on to state, however, that the emphasis upon achievement or accomplishment does not necessarily mean that children should never experience failure. On the contrary,

Small children can learn from failure if certain conditions are present. They must have the interest, the motivation, the skill, the intellectual and emotional readiness for a certain task. If these conditions are present, they can and do learn from failure.[10]

Burton examines the place of failure in the school program at length and summarizes the desirable and undesirable results of two types of failure in the following statement.

First, failure imposed arbitrarily upon individuals and by circumstances beyond the control of those individuals is definitely destructive of personality values and of mental hygiene and conducive to the most undesirable attitudes and practices. Second, failure resulting from the individual's own immature judgment, hasty or ill-considered reactions, or emotional interferences, and definitely recognized as such, is definitely educative.[11]

We may conclude, therefore, that under certain conditions, elementary school children do and should experience failure and that this experience may have educative value. On the other hand, to expose a child to a never-ending succession of failure day after day is vicious and cruel. On the whole, success in achievement is a much stronger motivating force than

[9] Katherine E. D'Evelyn, *Meeting Children's Emotional Needs* (Englewood Cliffs, N. J., Prentice-Hall, Inc., 1957), p. 9.
[10] *Ibid.*
[11] William H. Burton, *The Guidance of Learning Activities*, 3rd ed. (New York, Appleton-Century-Crofts, 1962), p. 494.

failure and there is abundant evidence to support the old statement that, "Nothing succeeds like success."

STANDARDS OF BEHAVIOR SHOULD BE DEVELOPED COOPERATIVELY. Our knowledge of learning tells us that children learn best when the experience involves purposing, planning, and problem solving. Our belief in democracy means that, "We believe in the right of people to have a voice in plans and policies which directly affect them."[12] Obviously, therefore, standards governing desirable relationships and behavior can best be fostered by permitting children to participate in their development. Frequent group sessions throughout the entire year, *in every grade*, should be devoted to helping children understand their own and others' behavior, as well as formulating guidelines for future action. Children should be helped in these sessions to probe into their own actions—"Why did we spend so much time quarreling and arguing that we didn't have any time left to play the game?" or "What is the *real* reason why we wasted so much time today?" Similarly, they should be helped to arrive at solutions for misbehavior—"How can we remember not to disturb Miss Schwartz's class when we go through the hall today?" or "What rules should we make about working in committees, today?" Through such techniques, children are given an elementary insight into the causal factors behind human behavior as well as an opportunity to define standards of acceptable conduct. Concerning this technique, Ojemann says,

If the child is provided with opportunity for understanding both the behavior of people about him and his own behavior, he will be able to make more effective adjustments . . . pupils can be taught some of the elementary principles regarding the causes and effects of behavior, and this understanding appears to have some influence on the adjustment of the child toward his associates and toward himself.[13]

There are, of course, certain times when children will not be given the opportunity to develop their own behavioral standards. A directive may come from the principal's office saying that, "No hard baseballs may be used on the playground," or that, "All children living on Evergreen Road must cross at the intersection of Evergreen and Broad." The effective teacher will not merely relay these directions to his pupils but will stress the *rationale* behind them. "Why do you think Mr. Watson made this rule about hard baseballs on the playground? Do you think it's a good idea? What do you think might happen if one child forgets or disobeys

[12] George V. Sheviakov and Fritz Redl, *op. cit.*, p. 13.
[13] Ralph H. Ojemann, *Personality Adjustment of Individual Children*, What Research Says to the Teacher, No. 5, Department of Classroom Teachers and American Educational Research Association (Washington, D. C., National Education Association, 1954), pp. 17-18.

Standards of behavior should be developed cooperatively.

this rule? What can we do to help us remember it?" Discussions of this type stress the fact that there is a *reason* for all sensible rules governing social conduct. If the reason is understood, there is much more likelihood that the ruling will be accepted.

Persistency AND *consistency* ARE KEY WORDS IN WORKING EFFECTIVELY WITH CHILDREN. Children do not learn desirable social behavior in one day or through one incident. On the contrary, they learn only through the persistent efforts of a patient teacher. The teacher, for instance, who is trying to develop more cohesiveness in his group, or who is trying to alter Andy's habit of constantly interrupting during a discussion, must recognize that these are long-range goals. Only by moving toward them slowly, steadily, patiently, and persistently will they be attained.

Most teachers recognize the importance of consistency in working with children. Children place much emphasis upon the "fair" teacher and reject the teacher who shows partiality or favoritism (see Chapter 2). Educators and psychologists also stress this quality, for many studies have shown that inconsistent behavior toward a child is more devastating than either strict control or overpermissiveness. It is important to realize, however, that consistency should *not* be confused with rigidity! There are no absolutes when dealing with human behavior, and the teacher who applies one set of standards to all children and all occasions is on psychologically unsafe ground. For instance, it would be extremely unrealistic to establish the same rules of conduct to apply to the physical education period, the social studies discussion, the auditorium concert, and the lunch hour. Each of these situations determines its own type of acceptable behavior. Just as adults know that acceptable behavior at a picnic is not acceptable at a formal dinner, so children should be taught that behavior standards are flexible and are determined by the individual situation.

Thus far in this chapter, considerable emphasis has been placed upon understanding *each individual child*. It is easily apparent that an over-emphasis on unrealistic consistency is directly contradictory to this viewpoint. The wise teacher, therefore, *within a certain framework*, will react in different ways to different behavior incidents. He may be a little more demanding in one, a little more permissive in another, a little quicker to act arbitrarily in one, a little more inclined to let the matter rest awhile with another. Such actions stem, not from inconsistency, but from an insight into the complex problem of human behavior. Again, this does not mean that the teacher's relationship with pupil or class should be ephemeral, ambiguous, or vacillating. It does mean that consistency is a desirable virtue while rigidity is not. As Sheviakov and Redl state,

We cannot stress too often that consistency does not lie in a set repertory of standard penalties. Because individuals differ so widely in what they have experienced in the past and what they need in the future this is indeed the height of psychological inconsistency. . . Consistency for the teacher-leader results through an analytic study of causes and through the clarity of purpose toward which action is directed in any given incident.[14]

To conclude, we should reiterate that consistency *is* important, it is desirable, and it *does* play an important role in establishing desirable social relationships and behavior. The effective teacher will use it wisely and well, always keeping in the back of his mind Emerson's admonition that, "A foolish consistency is the hobgoblin of little minds!"

One cannot go far in a discussion of pupil relationships and behavior without considering the important problem of discipline. The following section examines the modern concept of this word.

THE MODERN CONCEPT OF DISCIPLINE

THERE ARE MANY INTERPRETATIONS OF THE WORD *discipline*. Current literature and conversation is filled with varying interpretations and definitions of this frequently used word. For example, one well-known

[14] George V. Sheviakov and Fritz Redl, *op. cit.*, p. 58.

source lists six definitions of the general term and follows with eleven definitions of specific types of discipline including constructive discipline, military discipline, preventive discipline, therapeutic discipline, and others.[15] In the context of the classroom, however, the term is usually used as a noun, verb, or adjective. The first of these refers to discipline as the state of order or harmony existing in the classroom or school. Thus, one says that Mr. Purcell has "good" discipline meaning that his classroom is relatively free of confusion, disorder, and antisocial behavior. Secondly, the term is used as a verb, for instance, Mr. Purcell disciplines children very effectively. Thirdly, the term is frequently used as an adjective in describing certain children as discipline problems. This latter connotation is, of course, a direct contradiction of the first two for here the term is used to mean a problem of disorder and lack of control. To be consistent, we probably should refer to such problems as lack-of-discipline problems or nondiscipline problems, rather than discipline problems!

For purposes of our discussion here, the term can be interpreted to mean the *constructive guidance of children toward the development of healthful social relationships and desirable social behavior as well as the extent of social harmony resulting from such guidance.* In order to clarify this definition, it is necessary to examine some of the basic misconceptions concerning discipline today.

THERE ARE MANY MISCONCEPTIONS CONCERNING THE MEANING AND USE OF *discipline*. The following statements are an attempt to clear up some of the most common misunderstandings concerning modern discipline.

1. *Discipline is not synonymous with control.* It will be noticed that the above definition stresses the guidance rather than mere control of the child's behavior. In this context, discipline is considered to be a directing, guiding, channeling influence upon the personality of the child. It is not considered to be the mere imposition of adult authority or standards. Its primary aim is not the *repression* of behavior as much as the *changing* of behavior.

2. *Discipline is not synonymous with punishment.* Unfortunately, many teachers still consider discipline to be synonymous with punishment. Miss Bennett, for instance, defends her frequent use of punishment on the grounds that she believes in being a "firm disciplinarian." It is apparent that to her, discipline still "refers to 'woodshed' tactics more than to guidance, supervision, directing the child's choices, and other meanings which are both practical and in keeping with good mental hygiene."[16]

---

[15] *Dictionary of Education*, 2nd ed., Carter V. Good, ed. (New York, McGraw-Hill Book Co., Inc., 1959), pp. 176-177.

[16] E. Lakin Phillips, Daniel N. Wiener, and Norris G. Haring, *Discipline, Achievement, and Mental Health* (Englewood Cliffs, N. J., Prentice-Hall, Inc., 1960), p. 13.

It should be made clear that punishment may, or may not, be a necessary technique of discipline, see pages 115 to 119, but it can *never* be considered as the sum total of the concept.

3. *Discipline does not imply a constant state of war between teacher and pupils.* Some of the most persistent battles in history have been fought in the classrooms. In these rooms, the flag of truce never goes up for a minute. Teacher and children are endlessly engaged in squabbling, bullying, bickering, arguing, hurting, scolding, annoying, punishing, insulting, and retaliating. The whole dreary process is usually referred to as "disciplining" which is a travesty of the word as it has been previously defined.

4. *The modern concept of discipline does not encourage extreme permissiveness.* Because the modern concept deemphasizes control, repression, and punishment, some people go to the other extreme and intrepret it to be synonymous with no discipline. A careful examination of our definition will reveal that this viewpoint is certainly not justified. Discipline means, essentially, guidance. It does not mean license. It does not mean ultra-permissiveness. It does not mean complete freedom. It does not mean disorder, chaos, and confusion. It does not mean that the child has the right to do anything he pleases. On the other hand, it *does* mean that the child is taught the difference between acceptable and nonacceptable behavior. It does mean that he is taught to channel his behavior toward a consideration of the rights and property of others. It does mean that he is taught to handle the delicate balance between conformity and freedom. It does mean that he learns the democratic meaning of the motto, which appears in some classrooms, that, "Obedience to law is liberty."

5. *Discipline is a necessary and desirable part of the educative experience.* Again, some teachers misinterpret discipline in feeling that it is somehow unhealthy, undesirable, and has no place in the modern classroom. Nothing could be further from the truth! There are three main arguments that should dispel any doubts teachers have concerning the necessity of discipline.

In the first place, discipline is a need of society. It is fairly obvious that any society, whether it be a classroom or nation, cannot exist long without some degree of order, law, and harmony. As Hymes says, "The world needs discipline. Our country needs discipline. Children need discipline. You cannot have a decent family or a decent business or a decent school or a decent town without discipline."[17] Havighurst also agrees with this need for discipline. "Discipline can be successful or it can be unsuccessful, but it is essential . . . It can be a power for good in the child's life,

[17] James L. Hymes, Jr., *Behavior and Misbehavior* (Englewood Cliffs, N. J., Prentice-Hall, Inc., 1955), p. 2.

or a power for evil, but it is essential to the relation of child to the older person or persons who take responsibility for rearing the child."[18]

Discipline, therefore, is a requirement of every orderly society and, as such, is a definite responsibility of every classroom teacher.

Secondly, discipline can be considered, not only as a need of society, but as a developmental need of the child. Geisel states that children have, within themselves, a definite need for discipline. He summarizes this viewpoint as follows:

. . . the child has a need within himself to live according to certain standards, to live a well-disciplined life, because: (1) He gets a feeling of security if he knows where his limits are and then lives according to these limits. (2) As he lives according to his limits and freedoms, he has less cause to feel guilty for having broken them, or for having been confused about them. (3) As he lives according to the rules and regulations, he gives parents many opportunities for praise, which in turn stimulate him to continue his orderly behavior. (4) It is ego-bolstering for the child to accomplish what is required of him. Furthermore, pressure exerted by a loving adult over a long period of time becomes a pattern for the internalized voice of the conscience, guiding the child in making choices along the progress of his activity.[19]

Thirdly, teachers who are apprehensive about discipline because it may not be compatible with principles of mental hygiene need have no fear, for this is not so. Discipline, as defined previously, is definitely compatible with all we know about mental hygiene and is accepted as such by the leaders in this field. Redl and Wattenberg support this viewpoint in the following statement:

A chaotic, disorganized classroom in which children can do no learning because there is so much noise that they cannot think, will find no defenders among mental hygienists. For a child, to spend all day in a room where he cannot carry through any activity because other children interfere with him is a frustrating experience. It creates emotional disturbances. Bad discipline of this type is also bad for mental hygiene . . .

. . . the mental hygienist has no quarrel with good discipline, but would emphasize that the type of order the teacher is trying to establish and the means being used to support it should not be injurious to the sound emotional development of children.[20]

Thus, on several grounds we can defend the necessity of desirable discipline in the classroom and no teacher should be under the delusion

[18] Robert J. Havighurst, "The Functions of Successful Discipline," *Understanding the Child*, Vol. 21 (April, 1952), p. 35.

[19] John B. Geisel, "Discipline Viewed as a Developmental Need of the Child," *Nervous Child*, Vol. 9 (March, 1951), p. 118.

[20] Fritz Redl and William W. Wattenberg, *op. cit.*, pp. 383-384.

that discipline is a fact of life that exists but which is just not talked about in polite society.

6. *Concern over discipline should not receive an exaggerated emphasis.* It is extremely unfortunate that present day publicity about juvenile delinquency and blackboard jungles has caused many teachers to exaggerate the problems of classroom discipline. It is an area that frequently causes prospective teachers to approach their first teaching positions with fear and trembling. One study indicates, for instance, that of 3000 prospective teachers, 2481 reported discipline as their major worry when planning for their first teaching assignments.[21]

It is true, of course, that discipline is frequently reported by teachers as one of the major factors that handicap teaching effectiveness (see Chapter 13). But it is entirely possible that much of the difficulty lies in the attitude of the teacher himself. If teachers, regardless of the number of years of experience, *expect* discipline to be a major problem, it will be. If teachers *expect* children to misbehave, they will.

Ordinary children do not come to school for the purpose of making the teacher's life miserable. They do not continually try to misbehave. They receive little satisfaction from teacher-pupil friction and antagonism, nor do they enjoy doing wrong or being punished. On the contrary, most of them are more than anxious to please. Most are eager to learn and want to like the teacher, and be liked by him.

Realizing the importance of good discipline is one thing; allowing it to become an obsession that threatens self-security and wholesome attitudes toward children and teaching is quite another.

THE ULTIMATE GOAL OF ALL DISCIPLINE IS SELF-DISCIPLINE. One of the most important characteristics of the modern concept of discipline is its emphasis upon self-discipline, which involves self-direction, self-reliance, and self-control. This is the purpose of all externally-imposed discipline upon the child, and the ultimate success of such discipline can be measured only to the extent it achieves this purpose. Consequently, the teacher has a relatively simple yardstick with which to measure the effectiveness of any disciplinary device or technique, namely, Will this contribute, in some measure, to the pupils' growth toward self-discipline? If the answer is yes, the device is good and constructive and should be used. Making allowances for rare and emergency cases when stop-gap measures are demanded, if the answer is no, the technique should be reexamined and abandoned for another that will build toward this long-range goal of self-discipline.

[21] Lawrence E. Vredevoe, "Practices in School Discipline," *American School Board Journal*, Vol. 139 (July, 1959), p. 20.

It is important to state here that self-discipline must be taught and learned! No child comes into the world automatically equipped with self-disciplinary devices. On the contrary, these must be learned slowly and gradually. As in other areas, learning is acquired best through direct experience. Thus, from the day he enters kindergarten, the pupil should be given numerous opportunities to learn self-direction and self-control such as being increasingly responsible for his own behavior, participating in group planning and abiding by group decisions, analyzing and discussing his own as well as others' behavior, and many more. Above all else, *timing is important!* Too much, too soon, too little, and too late are all to be avoided. Children learn self-discipline much as they learn to swim. They do not learn by being forbidden to go near the water. Neither do they learn by suddenly being tossed into the pool. On the contrary, they learn by exploring, experiencing, and achieving alternating degrees of dependence and independence.

It is unfortunate that some teachers still do not recognize the concept of self-discipline as the ultimate goal of all discipline. An example of such a teacher is Mrs. F who recently was called from her classroom on an emergency matter. As she left the room, she heard the noise and confusion start up, as on a given signal. However, as soon as the pupils heard her footsteps returning to the room, complete silence fell upon the group and every child was busily working when she reached the doorway. Mrs. F related this incident to illustrate her effectiveness as a disciplinarian because, in her words, she "really made children toe the mark!" Actually, of course, the incident is a striking example, not only of her ineffectuality as a disciplinarian, but of her complete lack of understanding of the concept and goals of good classroom discipline. Fortunately, teachers of this type are comparatively rare today because now most recognize and evaluate the success of their discipline according to the extent to which it moves in the direction of self-discipline.

DISCIPLINE IS AN INTEGRAL PART OF TEACHING. Occasionally, one meets a teacher who feels that discipline is something *apart* from teaching. Such an individual may complain that, "I have to spend so much time disciplining, I don't have time to teach," or state that, "I don't have any trouble with teaching—my only trouble is discipline." This concept of discipline and teaching as two separate, unrelated entities is incompatible with the modern concept, which states that, "Good discipline in the classroom is a partner of good teaching and good learning."[22] In other words, disciplining is a kind of teaching, a teaching that concentrates on social

[22] Alice V. Keliher, "Talks with Teachers," *Grade Teacher*, Vol. 78 (April, 1961). p. 153.

learnings just as other aspects of teaching focus on academic learnings. Consequently, good disciplining uses the same techniques as does good teaching: explaining, discussing, interpreting, clarifying, illustrating, repeating, and many others. Furthermore, the pupil acquires social learnings in much the same way he acquires academic learnings. He does not learn that $9 + 8 = 17$ by having this fact explained to him once, nor does he learn it by being punished for forgetting it. On the contrary, he learns through exploring, discovering, and experiencing. Furthermore, *even after he learns it,* he may occasionally forget. This means that he simply needs more reteaching and restrengthening of the original concept. Exactly the same theory applies to social learnings. Most misbehavior of ordinary boys and girls is due to the fact that they have not yet learned to subordinate their own immediate desires and goals to a consideration of others and an adherence to standards of acceptable conduct. This is a difficult and complex concept to learn and it takes time, patience, and skillful teaching of all teachers. Hymes emphasizes this concept of discipline in the following statement.

Youngsters do not get the hang of good behavior right off. No more than they get the knack of reading or spelling or dancing or typing immediately. No more than they can practice driving a car once and then have it. No more than they can pick up sewing in a jiffy, or baseball or swimming or working with tools. Children want to be good, but the ways of behavior—the right things to do, the appropriate actions—are hard to master.

You have to explain. You have to talk over things. You have to find out what part was not clear. You have to emphasize certain points again. You have to make the generalizations clearer. You have to give the underlying reasons again. You have to give some more examples. You have to talk through with the youngsters what could happen and what might happen and why the right way is the best. *You have to teach.*[23]

Teachers often ask, "What is the best way to discipline my class?" From our discussion here, the answer is fairly obvious. Teach them! Teach them exactly as you teach them anything else you want them to learn! (It should be noted here, that we are now talking only about the normal, everyday misbehavior of ordinary boys and girls. Misbehavior of another sort is discussed in the last section of this chapter.)

The discussion thus far has emphasized the establishment of positive pupil-teacher relationships and the concept of preventive discipline. As long as we have schools and children, however, we will probably have occasional problems of poor discipline. The basic causes of these problems are examined in the following section.

[23] James L. Hymes, Jr., *op. cit.,* pp. 18-19.

UNDERLYING CAUSES OF POOR DISCIPLINE

Poor discipline, or ordinary poor group behavior, is usually a symptom of a basic weakness in the educational program. It was stressed earlier that teaching and discipline are integral parts of the same experience. This is true. Therefore, good teaching is usually, if not always, accompanied by good discipline. A good teacher is a good disciplinarian. A poor disciplinarian is a poor teacher, again making allowances for extremely rare cases.

Since poor discipline is a symptom, rather than an entity in itself, it can only be improved by finding the source of the problem. Some people draw an analogy between poor discipline and the elevated temperature of a physically sick person. To the physician, for instance, the 103° temperature of a patient indicates that something is basically wrong. He will, therefore, devote most of his attention to *finding the cause and treating it*. He will not be satisfied with merely treating the symptom. The same procedure holds true for the classroom. Consistently poor discipline is the 103° temperature of a group of children, and the wise teacher will look for the cause instead of treating the symptom.

In attempting to diagnose the cause, the teacher is warned against being misled by false or superficial clues. For instance, some teachers comfort themselves by the thought that their poor discipline may be attributed to its being Friday afternoon, or just before lunch, its having rained every day for a week, its being just before Halloween or just after a long vacation, and so forth. A little logic will reveal that these are superficial and not underlying causes of poor school discipline. If they were, every class in every school in the country would be misbehaving most of the time. Obviously this is ridiculous. The teacher is urged to go far beyond these superficial reasons in search of the cause of his poor discipline.

It seems almost too obvious to state that search for causal factors should be the long-range concern of the teacher, if not always the immediate one. To go back to the physician analogy, occasionally his *immediate* concern is to lower the elevated temperature, but he does not stop there. Or, to use one more analogy, the teacher may be compared to the fireman, whose first concern is to put the fire out. He then turns his attention to finding the cause. Similarly, when confronted by an emergency problem of poor discipline, which may involve physical as well as other dangers, the teacher is concerned primarily with handling the immediate incident. Once this is done, however, he should start his search for the cause, unless he wants to spend his entire professional life putting out one fire after another! Let us now examine some of the most common and basic causes of poor group discipline.

1. *Uninteresting teaching-learning situation.* The dull, boring lesson, the sterile, uninteresting, dreary classroom, the same monotonous routine day after day, are the primary causes of ordinary group misbehavior. If mediocre teachers are guilty of one crime more than all others, it is the crime of boring children to death. From this boredom may arise numerous types of poor conduct and attitudes, including aggressiveness, overt disturbances, listlessness, hostility, apathy, or antipathy toward learning. Of one thing the teacher may be certain. No healthy child will submit to the prospect of complete boredom week after week, year after year, without putting up a strenuous fight. As Redl says, "Every normal child will kick if you bore or tire him more than is legally permissible. Only idiots don't care. Normal children will become indifferent and wander off in fantasy, or become obstreperous, or play with each other, or kick each other—in other words, create a behavior problem.[24]

All of the knowledge about teaching the creative and resourceful teacher has at his command can be brought to bear on the problem of boredom and resultant undesirable behavior. Careful planning of lessons, securing many and varied learning materials and aids, utilizing unusual approaches to a problem, recognizing and attending to individual needs, establishing a stimulating learning environment, and all of the other techniques discussed in Part III of this book are, in effect, antidotes for poor discipline. Numerous studies of classroom situations reveal a positive correlation between such practices and good discipline. For example, conclusions from one study state,

The practice of using all available equipment and visual aids to embellish and enrich a lesson so as to interest and promote the learning growth of pupils is closely associated with effective discipline. . . .

The practice of presenting the subject matter in a vital and enthusiastic manner, of making the subject matter appealing to the point that the interest and the enthusiasm catches on enough so that the subject matter itself acts as a check or control to incipient misbehavior is also closely associated with effective discipline.[25]

It seems unnecessary to belabor this point. We can summarize, therefore, by saying that any practice or device that increases the effectiveness of teaching will, at the same time, decrease the possibility of poor discipline.

2. *Unwise academic pacing.* Poor discipline frequently results from the teacher's failure to gauge correctly the academic abilities of his stu-

[24] Fritz Redl, *op. cit.*, p. 105.
[25] Sidney L. Celler, "Practices Associated with Effective Discipline: A Descriptive Statistical Study of Discipline," *Journal of Experimental Education,* Vol. 19 (June, 1951), p. 357.

An interesting lesson is the best guarantee of good classroom discipline.

dents. Assignments that are too long, too difficult, or for which the directions are not clear will frequently cause resentment and frustration. On the other hand, assignments and content lacking challenge are quickly dispensed with, leaving children much time on their hands to do nothing. Often, also, content woefully below the level of children's capacities and interests constitutes a real insult to their intelligence. One of the poorest examples of classroom discipline ever witnessed by the author occurred in a second grade. For some unexplainable reason, the teacher had chosen to teach the class how to tell time. Throughout the entire lesson, the youngsters giggled, conversed with each other, insulted or ignored the teacher, and created every kind of disturbance they could think of. They were both resentful and amused that the teacher should teach them this particular concept, for practically every child in that particular class had known how to tell time for a year or more. Such an abysmal lack of knowledge concerning her youngsters' abilities obviously created serious disciplinary problems for this teacher. This is, of course, an extreme case but any teacher experiencing disciplinary trouble is advised to consider seriously the question of whether he is gauging content and assignments to the precise academic level of his pupils. A final word of advice—any teacher who follows religiously a rigid course of study, or whose pupils proceed page by page through the prescribed text and workbook, may want to ponder long and hard as to whether this has any relationship to the poor discipline that seems to be giving him trouble.

3. *Unhealthy classroom environment.* The physical, intellectual, social, and emotional climates of the classroom undoubtedly play a part in determining children's behavior. Because this topic is discussed fully in Chapter 6, it will only be mentioned here. Poor ventilation, poor lighting, poor acoustics, poor housekeeping, overcrowding, uninviting decor, and lack of space and equipment are physical factors that have a relationship to discipline. Equally important causal factors are a nonchallenging intellectual climate and certain types of unhealthy social and emotional climates discussed on pages 228 to 256.

4. *Lack of organization.* It cannot be stressed too often that organizational ability is an asset for effective teaching. A classroom that is *not* organized according to some fundamental routines and regulations will quickly become disintegrated and chaotic. All children have the right to the security of knowing what is expected of them. Thus, the daily schedule should be posted on the bulletin board or chalk board. Assignments should be written on the board so that all may see and understand. Supplies and equipment should be stored in certain definite places. Agreed-upon standards of conduct may be written on charts to serve as reminders for recalcitrant offenders. These and other organizational guidelines will help to prevent needless confusion and misbehavior.

Although good organization is vitally important, the teacher is warned against an overemphasis on routinization. Routines to cover every single aspect of the school day may produce overconformity on the part of the youngsters. Although it is hard to generalize, it would seem that fixed routines should be necessary primarily to cover the following activities.

a. Entering the room in the morning and leaving in the afternoon.

b. Distributing and collecting supplies.

c. Leaving the room, either singly or in a group.

d. Emergency measures such as air raid or fire drills.

e. Use of free time.

In addition to these, routines and standards should be cooperatively developed to govern such activities as group work, playground activities, and field trips, although, as has been previously stated, these will be determined by each individual situation.

5. *Weak teaching personality.* Personal traits probably most related to securing good discipline in the classroom are:

a. *Forcefulness and conviction.* Some teachers, and parents, state their expectations to children in a calm, pleasant manner which seldom motivates resentment or disobedience. Others may raise their voices, wave hands in the air, or pound the table, and children pay absolutely no attention. The difference appears to lie in the inner force and conviction of the first type of person which, as children sense, is lacking in the second.

b. *Security.* The teacher who is secure in his knowledge of children as well as all aspects of his job can afford to relax and enjoy teaching. It is usually insecurity and fear which turns a teacher into a strict militaristic diciplinarian, thereby worsening his relationships with pupils. As Symonds states, "An insecure teacher does not dare to relax control for fear that his authority will be irrevocably undermined."[26]

c. *Self-control.* Emotionalism has little place in the classroom and the effective disciplinarian keeps his anger or indignation under tight rein, realizing always that his primary concern with children is *guidance* not *retaliation.* Also, if the teacher can control any nervous gestures or mannerisms the children find amusing, distracting, or irritating, he will find this an aid to developing a strong teaching personality.

d. *Self-respect.* We have placed considerable emphasis upon treating children with respect and courtesy. The teacher also has a right to expect such treatment from his pupils, within the limits of their understanding. No teacher should consider it part of his job to accept continually insulting and impudent behavior from heedless and thoughtless pupils. The teacher who allows children to walk all over him does not have the self-respect needed for a strong teaching personality.

In summary, the teacher is reminded that superficial group misbehavior is usually rooted in some fundamental underlying weaknesses in the educational program. Only when these causes are removed, will the behavior improve.

TECHNIQUES FOR INFLUENCING AND GUIDING PUPIL BEHAVIOR

It is impossible to propose a specific set of blueprints the teacher can follow in establishing good discipline in his classroom. The entire process depends almost entirely upon the individual situation and persons involved. What is a *right* procedure one day—is a *wrong* one the next. An approach which works for one teacher is ineffective when used by another. For example, Joe's voice becomes noisy and disturbing during a committee work period. Mr. Brown merely catches his eye, shakes his head in disapproval, and Joe immediately lowers his voice and the incident is closed. Across the hall, an identical incident takes place when

[26] Percival M. Symonds, "Classroom Discipline," *Teachers College Record*, Vol. 51 (December, 1949), p. 154.

Ronald's voice becomes disturbing to the group. Mr. Harper uses the exact signal that solved the problem for Mr. Brown. Ronald, however, reacts in an entirely different manner from Joe. He slams his book on the desk, slumps down in his seat, and complains loudly that, "I don't want to work on any old committee, anyway!" Obviously these two different reactions were influenced by a multiplicity of factors, all of which emphasize that the development of desirable social behavior and attitudes is a highly individualized process. It should be understood, therefore, that the following techniques are suggested because (1) they are compatible with the philosophy of discipline thus far discussed and (2) they have been found to be effective by many teachers. They are not necessarily guarantees of desirable pupil behavior in every classroom and for every individual teacher.

1. *Wise and sparing use of the voice.* The teacher's voice can play a major role in influencing the behavior of pupils. Often, when the class gets noisy, the teacher will, consciously or unconsciously, raise his voice louder and higher to be heard over the confusion. Obviously, he is simply adding to the noise. On the contrary, deliberately *lowering* his voice, sometimes almost to a whisper, has a quieting effect upon the situation. This simple procedure is one of the most reliable tricks of good discipline available. It is unfortunate that it is not used by more teachers.

Carrying the above suggestion still further, many teachers find it effective not to use their voices at all to gain the attention of pupils. Such teachers may often merely wait for quiet to descend on the group, or go to the chalkboard without saying a word and write directions or a note asking for immediate attention. Often, also, a pleasant signal will help such as a chord on the piano or a few notes on the autoharp. (Note that such signals do *not* include clapping hands, snapping fingers, banging rulers on desks, etc.)

Signals may also be used to control the behavior of an individual child. Interrupting the lesson a dozen times with, "John, put that book away," "John, turn around," or "John, please pay attention," is not only nagging poor John, but it is also slowing down the pace of the lesson to the point where other children become disinterested. It is far more desirable to control John's behavior through such signals as shaking the head, putting fingers to the lips, or frowning. Concerning the use of signals, Redl and Wattenberg state that they are "usually most effective in the early stages of misconduct or when an ordinarily normal and well-controlled child has literally forgotten himself."[27]

Similar to the use of signals is the technique which these authors refer to as "proximity control."[28] Every good teacher, especially in the primary

[27] Fritz Redl and William W. Wattenberg, *op. cit.*, p. 349.
[28] *Ibid.*

grades, knows the beneficial effect of simply standing by an individual's desk momentarily or asking, "Alma, come sit next to me for awhile."

2. *Probationary isolation.* At certain times, it is necessary and desirable to remove a child from the group. This procedure is most effective if the teacher can make clear to the child and the class that the isolation is not a rejection or punishment but is done only ". . . to help the young person and the group to regain self-control."[29] The child who is disturbing the reading group, for instance, may be sent back to his desk with the admonition, "You may come back to the group as soon as you are ready to help us." In isolating children, the teacher must be extremely careful that she does not remove him from her sight. Sending a child into the hall or into an empty classroom may magnify the original incident if he decides to run away, go home, wander down the hall and annoy other classes, roam around the school, or do damage upon himself. (Several cases are on record in which children have hurt themselves or committed suicide when banished to an empty room for a long period of time.)

Another type of isolation is voluntary on the part of the child. As Anderson says, "Among the needs of some children is the need to be alone. Some primary rooms have a corner where a child may go when he no longer feels that he can conform, participate, or listen."[30] An interesting example of this need was displayed by first-grader Milton who entered the principal's office one day to ask permission to sit in the nurse's room (presently unoccupied) for a while. The principal, with natural concern, asked him if he felt ill, if he were upset by anything that happened in the classroom, or if he had hurt himself. The answer was always, "No."

Finally, the principal asked, "But why do you want to sit in the nurse's room all by yourself?"

Milton replied, "I just feel like being lonely!"

Many other children are like Milton and occasionally feel the need "to be lonely." Providing a spot not far from the watchful eye of the teacher or principal for the child to be alone with his thoughts once in a while has a decided therapeutic value and may be helpful in lessening the strains of continual group living which weigh heavily upon some children.

3. *Knowledgeable ignorance.* Deliberately ignoring certain types of behavior can be extremely effective in the right situation. Occasionally, for instance, a child will deliberately seek attention through some form of misbehavior. Children in a particularly rebellious or defiant mood may deliberately challenge the authority of the teacher. At such times, the

[29] *Ibid.,* p. 356.
[30] Paul S. Anderson, "Discipline in the Classroom Today," *Phi Delta Kappan,* Vol. 41 (December, 1959), p. 115.

wisest and best course of action may be not to appear to see the incident at all. Miss Cunningham, for instance, left the school building late one afternoon with a fellow teacher. Out of the corner of her eye, she saw Rudy, one of her sixth graders who had been in a particularly ugly mood all day, deliberately light a cigarette thereby breaking a very strict school rule. Miss Cunningham kept her eyes straight ahead and said to her friend, "I'm sorry to disappoint Rudy, but I'm *not* going to see him smoke that cigarette!"

Miss Cunningham's reaction did not mean that she was not seriously concerned about Rudy's breaking a school law or about his developing poor health habits at an early age. These she would work on at the proper time. At the moment her keen understanding of Rudy told her not to aggravate his emotional state which would, in all probability, only lead to more serious resistance and defiance. Sometimes the best course of action is no action!

Less serious incidents happen frequently in even the most ideal classroom, and the wise teacher knows that knowledgeable ignorance is often the best technique to use in dealing with them. As Symonds says, "A good teacher refuses to be drawn into a contest of wills. I have seen some excellent teachers permit a child to spend a whole hour with head on desk or reading some book not connected with the lesson rather than to reach a deadlock with a child who is in a highly resistant mood.[31]

Obviously, it is impossible to make a blanket statement concerning the use of this technique for although it can be extremely effective at times, it can be equally dangerous at others. It is sufficient to state, therefore, that any good teacher knows there is a time to see and a time not to see!

4. *Positive versus negative approach.* Several years ago a popular song was titled, "Accentuate the Positive," which is about the best advice that can be given to an elementary school teacher. Unfortunately, some teachers allow themselves to fall into the trap of continually nagging, scolding, criticizing, and faultfinding, thus relying solely upon negative approaches to behavior problems. Everything accomplished by these techniques can be accomplished infinitely better through a positive approach. For instance, instead of saying, "Not one person is ready to go home," the teacher may say, "I think James is almost ready to go home." In actuality, she is saying the same thing, but the effect is much different.

Many people advocate "divertive discipline" as one of the most effective positive techniques, especially with younger children. In other words, instead of telling the youngster not to do something, it is much more helpful if you suggest that he do something else, for example, not "Marjorie, don't go near that mud puddle," but "Marjorie, come play on

[31] Percival M. Symonds, *op. cit.,* p. 155.

this side of the playground." Similarly, it is comparatively ineffective to tell a child who is wasting time by aimlessly wandering about the room to stop it. Rather, the teacher may suggest that he either choose a library book or work in the art corner until it is time for his reading group.

The positive statement of desired behavior, the use of praise and encouragement instead of criticism and fault finding, and constructive suggestions to children as to what they *should* do rather than commands only to stop what they are doing are some of the positive disciplinary techniques that will pay worthwhile dividends in the elementary classroom.

5. *Cognizance of the ripple effect.* Teachers know, and some studies support, the fact that there is a *ripple effect* in discipline. In other words, disciplining an individual affects not only him but many other members of the group as well. The wise teacher will recognize and use this ripple effect to advantage in many ways. For instance, "John is holding his reading book correctly," will not only reward John but will also have an effect on the other children, many of whom will immediately emulate John's behavior. Kounin and Gump studied the relationship of three dimensions of control—clarity, firmness, and roughness—with the ripple effect among kindergarten children. They found that clarity and reasonable firmness sometimes produced increased conformance among the observant children but that roughness did not.[32] Thus, the teacher should always be aware that his treatment of one child will not only affect that individual but will produce either positive or negative attitudes and behavior among the observing children.

6. *Wise and infrequent use of punishment.* Even the most superior elementary teacher is forced to resort to punishing children now and then. Infrequent and effective punishment can be used under certain conditions with desirable results. On the other hand, excessive or wrong punishments can be damaging to the personality of the child, to the teacher's relationships with his pupils, and to the general improvement of children's behavior. It is fairly safe to state that most punishments do more harm than good, most punishments create more problems than they solve, most punishments create more undesirable than desirable aftereffects, and most punishments destroy rather than develop positive attitudes within the offender. Punishment is like dynamite; it can be used to advantage in certain situations, but it can wreak untold damage when handled injudiciously. The following guidelines concerning its use should be examined carefully by every elementary teacher interested in a mental hygiene approach to teaching.

[32] Jacob S. Kounin and Paul V. Gump, "The Ripple Effect in Discipline," *Elementary School Journal,* Vol. 59 (December, 1958), pp. 158-162.

a. *Punishment should always be considered a last resort.* When all else fails, when every other technique and approach have been tried and re-tried, the teacher may feel the need to resort to punishment. Because of its damaging emotional effects, however, it *must* be used just as little as possible. It is with this possibility of emotional damage in mind, that Redl and Wattenberg state, "In view of the high risk of undesirable results, punishment should be employed rarely, and then only with the greatest caution."[33] Also, the classroom teacher should be aware of a very practical fact, the more punishment is used, the less effective it becomes. Thus a vicious circle is created in which the punishment must get stricter and stricter in order to be effective and where that will end no one knows. Punishment is a tool in the teacher's disciplinary kit but, like many other tools, the less it is used, the sharper it remains.

b. *Punishment should not constitute retaliation or rejection.* Punishment should be aimed at improving the child's behavior; it should not be simply a way of getting back at him. Furthermore, the child should understand clearly that the punishment does *not* constitute rejection of him *as a person.* Some people advise, on this point, that the teacher keep in mind that *he is punishing the deed, not the child.* Geisel states, for instance, that punishment should always convey the attitude that, "I like you just the same, Johnny; it's only what you did that I don't like."[34]

Because punishment should not be associated with rejection, the teacher must be sure to let bygones be bygones once the incident is closed. To punish a child and then to continue to ignore him, reject him, or continually remind him of the original offense is contradictory to everything we know today about good mental health.

c. *The punishment should be related to the offense.* The most effective punishment is not superimposed by an authority figure but is the natural result of the offense. For instance, during an art lesson on making paper masks for the Halloween party, Ray and Don waste time, misbehave, and consequently do not finish their masks. The natural, and best, punishment for this offense is that the boys do not have masks to wear to the party when all the other children do. Such punishment is much more effective, and much less damaging, than an unrelated act such as depriving the boys of recess period, keeping them after school, or forbidding them to attend the party. Concerning this principle of effective punishment, Phillips, Wiener, and Haring state, "Let the deed carry its own consequences, and we need not punish the doer. In place of punishment, think of the natural or logical consequences that would follow an action—or

[33] Fritz Redl and William W. Wattenberg, *op. cit.,* p. 374.
[34] John B. Geisel, *op. cit.,* p. 121.

that you would want to follow any action—and see that these consequences do follow, as night follows day."[35]

d. *Aspects of the school and school program should never be used as punishment.* The stereotype of the whining schoolboy creeping like a snail unwillingly to school is perpetuated in the feature stories and cartoons of newspapers and magazines. Such a stereotype is more fiction than fact, however, because under normal circumstances children like and enjoy school. Many factors contribute to a positive attitude toward school, not the least of which is the fact that it is never used as a threat or form of punishment. Detention, therefore, is *not* a recommended form of punishment because of the unpleasant connotation placed upon the school. In addition, keeping a child after school is unwise because (1) it is usually ineffective (simply sitting in the classroom for an extra fifteen or thirty minutes usually means little to a child); and (2) it involves numerous other factors such as school bus schedules, children crossing streets while unprotected by school policemen or patrol members, and older children who may be expected to run errands or do odd jobs after school hours. For many reasons, therefore, detaining a child after school is usually considered to be a poor type of punishment. This does *not*, of course, refer to the practice of detaining a child after others have left in order to have a private conference with him.

Assigning extra school work as punishment is also unwise because it may produce undesirable attitudes toward academic learning as well as toward the school itself.

e. *Punishment should not produce the same effect as the offense.* This is an important principle and one frequently overlooked by teachers. For instance, George misbehaves in such a manner that it is pretty evident he is seeking peer attention and approval. To punish him, therefore, by seating him in such a spot that he is the center of attraction is, obviously, unwise. Or, to punish George unreasonably so that he gains peer sympathy is equally unwise. As Cutts and Moseley state, "Punishment is most ineffective when it serves the same end as the behavior that occasioned it."[36]

f. *Mass punishment is undesirable.* Punishing the entire class for an individual infraction is, obviously, a poor type of punishment. Usually, its only result is the straining of the teacher-group relationship.

g. *The use of peer control or punishment should be avoided.* We have stated repeatedly that effective punishment depends upon a deep under-

[35] E. Lakin Phillips, Daniel N. Wiener, and Norris G. Haring, *op. cit.*, p. 24.
[36] Norma E. Cutts and Nicholas Moseley, *Teaching the Disorderly Pupil in Elementary and Secondary School* (New York, Longmans, Green & Co., Inc., 1957), p. 27.

standing of individual behavior and that it is a *means*, never an *end* in itself. It is apparent, therefore, that children should not be permitted to impose penalties or punishment on each other. Some teachers use this device in the belief that it is "teaching democracy." It is not. Young children do not have the wisdom, the objectivity, or the insight needed to impose penalties on another individual. Stendler cites the danger of using peer judgment when she states that, ". . . when children are put in the position of being able to pass judgment on other children they may use this opportunity to give vent to underlying hostilities."[37] Hymes also warns the teacher against this procedure in the following statement: "Only one part of the whole process do you not turn over to youngsters: how the individual "law-breaker" will be dealt with. This is your special, trained, professional adult job."[38]

For this reason, class or school councils, whose chief purpose is to act as law-enforcing agencies, are not recommended for the elementary school. This is in no way contradictory to the philosophy expressed on page 98 to the effect that standards of behavior should be developed cooperatively. Group planning, group discussion, group evaluation of behavior is educationally and psychologically sound; group penalization of an individual is not.

h. *The use of punishment should reflect the teacher's understanding of human behavior.* The necessity of understanding children and their behavior was stressed earlier in the chapter. It is an interesting paradox that, although teachers do seem to understand the causes of human behavior, their use of punishment is not guided by this knowledge. Smitter found, for instance, that teachers understood, or at least verbalized an understanding of behavior, yet the punishments they invoked were ". . . age-old, superficial, sometimes cruel, and frequently ineffective."[39] It would seem, therefore, that classroom teachers need to close the gap between their professed knowledge of child behavior and their application of this knowledge to their classroom situation. Apparently, also, teacher-education institutions and in-service programs should assume greater responsibility for emphasizing the practical application of knowledge concerning human behavior.

i. *Punishment should be reasonable.* After all that has been said so far, it seems unnecessary to state that cruel, prolonged punishment which ridicules, hurts, embarrasses, or humiliates the child is completely unacceptable in the modern elementary school. It is particularly unfortunate

---

[37] Celia B. Stendler, "Group Ways in Discipline," *Childhood Education,* Vol. 31 (February, 1955), p. 271.

[38] James L. Hymes, Jr., *op. cit.,* p. 27.

[39] Faith W. Smitter, "A Study of Teachers' Beliefs Regarding Control of Child Behavior," *California Journal of Elementary Education,* Vol. 27 (August, 1958), p. 13.

that occasional publicity is given to the efforts of certain groups to defend the use of corporal punishment in the school. At present, New Jersey is the only state that prohibits corporal punishment, although certain cities and individual school systems forbid its use. The New Jersey law reads as follows:

No person employed or engaged in a school or educational institution, whether public or private, shall inflict or cause to be inflicted corporal punishment upon a pupil attending such school or institution. Every resolution, by-law, rule, ordinance, or other act or authority permitting or authorizing corporal punishment to be inflicted upon a pupil attending a school or educational institution shall be void.[40]

It is difficult to understand how *any* teacher can defend its use on sound educational ground, and it is hoped that all teachers agree with the statement that, "Corporal punishment is a denial of everything an educator should stand for."[41]

Thus far, our discussion has been concerned solely with the relationships and behavior of healthy, active, "normal" boys and girls. The following section is devoted to a far different problem that occasionally confronts the elementary teacher.

TEACHING THE TROUBLED CHILD

Because of the difficulties of definition, it is difficult to estimate the number of socially and emotionally maladjusted pupils who are now enrolled in our elementary schools. D'Evelyn, however, states that about 10 per cent of children ". . . show behavior deviant enough to cause real concern to the teacher."[42] Regardless of the exact number, the fact remains that the classroom teacher does have an occasional member of his group who is seriously emotionally disturbed. With such an individual, the teacher has a twofold concern, (1) to help the child as much as is humanly possible and (2) to prevent the child from being a disturbing element in the group. The following suggestions are given to achieve these goals.

TEACHERS MUST LEARN TO RECOGNIZE SYMPTOMS OF MALADJUSTMENT. This does not mean that teachers should attempt to be amateur psychiatrists or to pin a psychological label on every child. It does mean that the teacher's knowledge of personality and behavior should be such that he recognizes the child in his class who needs specialized help. Fortunately, there is some evidence to show that teachers are more skillful in this

40 New Jersey Statutes Annotated, Title 18, Chapter 19, Article 1.
41 Fritz Redl and William W. Wattenberg, *op. cit.*, p. 375.
42 Katherine E. D'Evelyn, *op. cit.*, pp. 39-40.

respect than they were in the past. Wickman's famous study of 1925-26 revealed a wide difference of opinion between teachers and mental hygienists concerning the seriousness of certain types of pupil behavior. At that time, teachers stressed the importance of such antisocial behavior as sex problems, dishonesty, disobedience, disorderliness, and failure to learn. They accorded little significance to problems indicating withdrawing, recessive behavior. The mental hygienists, on the other hand, considered "these unsocial forms of behavior most serious," and discounted "the stress which teachers lay on anti-social conduct."[43] Since this original study, many others have been done and the results compared with those of Wickman. Findings vary but the consensus of opinion seems to be that, although teachers still are most concerned about aggressive behavior, they do attach more significance to withdrawn behavior than they did almost thirty years ago. The following statements support his conclusion.

The attitudes of 1951 teachers toward the behavior problems of children were much more in agreement with the criterion attitudes established by clinicians than was true for 1927 teachers . . . Disagreements between attitudes of teachers and the criterion attitude established by clinicians, though not as pronounced as in 1927, still exist, and these disagreements are of the same nature as those pointed out by Wickman.[44]

In analyzing the lists of problems it would seem that the behavior problem child in school is still, as he was twenty-five years ago, identified chiefly by annoying, disorderly, irresponsible, aggressive, untruthful, disobedient behavior. Teachers of today, however, were not as oblivious to behavior indicative of social and emotional maladjustment as those reported by Wickman in his inquiry.[45]

It would seem, therefore, that teachers today have gained some insight, and look at pupil behavior more from the mental hygienist's point of view than they did several years ago. There is, however, still room for improvement, although it seems to be unrealistic to expect teachers to agree absolutely with the clinician's viewpoint. Teachers will naturally always be more concerned with the child who disrupts their group than will the clinician who is interested only in individual therapy. But the fact that teachers are beginning to recognize the seriousness of withdrawal behavior as much as aggressive behavior may reduce the number of criminal in-

[43] E. K. Wickman, *Children's Behavior and Teachers' Attitudes* (New York, The Commonwealth Fund, 1928), p. 129.

[44] Manfred H. Schrupp and Clayton M. Gjerde, "Teacher Growth in Attitudes Toward Behavior Problems of Children," *Journal of Educational Psychology*, Vol. 44 (April, 1953), p. 214.

[45] George A. W. Stouffer, Jr. and Jennie Owens, "Behavior Problems of Children as Identified by Today's Teachers and Compared with Those Reported by E. K. Wickman," *Journal of Educational Research*, Vol. 48 (January, 1955), p. 331.

cidents about which one reads in the newspapers and which contain such statements as, "Teacher says he was a model pupil," or, "I don't remember much about him—except that he was always very quiet and never caused any trouble!"

There are many sources available to teachers who are interested in studying the symptoms of severe personality maladjustment. In general, symptoms most frequently met in the classroom include: "resistance to learning, extreme dependence on the teacher or classmates, resistance to classroom routine or group living, tantrums, quarreling, fighting, stealing, lying, bragging, bullying, crying, teasing, destructiveness, withdrawal, fear of physical injury, truancy, school phobia, stuttering, and tics."[46]

MULTIPLICITY OF CAUSATION IS IMPORTANT TO UNDERSTANDING PERSONALITY MALADJUSTMENT. One of the most important factors to the teacher who works with the troubled child is the understanding that his personality maladjustment can be traced to *no single cause*. Causes of emotional disturbance are many, complex, interrelated, and deep-seated. This fact has contradictory significance for the teacher. On the one hand, it limits his effectiveness because he cannot, obviously, control *all* the causes. At the same time, as Wattenberg points out, it gives teachers a wide range within which to work, meaning, ". . . if there is any one item which we can control, then through it we may be able to alter the pattern sufficiently to be effective."[47] Thus, teachers are not justified in simply attributing the sole cause of the child's trouble to his home or out-of-school environment, thereby justifying a defeatist attitude that they can do nothing for him. On the contrary, the teacher should realize that the problem is unbelievably complex and, if he can relieve any one tiny cause or contributing factor, he is helping to solve the problem.

THE TEACHER SHOULD NOT HESITATE TO ASK FOR SPECIALIZED ASSISTANCE. It is unfair and unrealistic to expect the teacher to help the troubled youngster without assistance from specialized personnel. If the teacher is convinced, after sufficient study, that the child is disturbed enough to need expert help, he should not hesitate to seek that help from every available source. The school psychiatrist, psychologist, guidance worker, physician, nurse, principal, and other functionaries should be consulted, as well as any available child guidance clinic. It should be stressed strongly that no teacher should consider it a sign of defeat to ask for help from these sources. It is exactly the opposite. Many a child has been helped immeasurably by a wise classroom teacher who recognized signs of his maladjustment and referred him to the specialized help he needed.

[46] Katherine E. D'Evelyn, *op. cit.*, p. 40.
[47] William W. Wattenberg, "Causes of Child Behavior," *Understanding the Child*, Vol. 25 (June, 1956), p. 82.

TEACHERS SHOULD REALIZE THAT THE EMOTIONALLY DISTURBED CHILD IS A HANDICAPPED CHILD. He is not a bad child. He is not a nasty child. He is not a mean child. He is not a coward or a weakling. He is a handicapped individual who needs essentially the same understanding and treatment as other handicapped children. How does the teacher treat the physically handicapped child? He tries to understand the extent of his handicap, he is careful neither to minimize nor magnify it, he does not overtax him nor pamper him, he expects as high a level of performance as he is capable of giving, and he works on building positive relationships and attitudes between the individual and the group. Essentially the same treatment may be applied to the emotionally disturbed child. The teacher attempts to understand thoroughly the nature of his handicap; he is careful to permit and encourage him to express his thoughts, emotions, and fears (knowing that expression is infinitely more desirable than repression); he does not reject nor punish him for his handicap; and he attempts to relate him positively to the group.

Building positive relationships between the handicapped child and the group is not nearly as difficult as some teachers imagine. Children can be taught rather easily to accept the fact that Jane has problems and they will not necessarily expect her to be held to the same standards of conduct that apply to themselves. Nor will they necessarily try to imitate her behavior. To the contrary, they can be taught to regard Jane's temper tantrums or crying spells with the same understanding they show toward Martin's epileptic attacks or Marianne's hearing handicap. When, occasionally, the disturbed child must be temporarily removed from the group, for his own and others' benefit, children can understand and accept the wisdom of this move with no damage to their own emotional equilibrium. In attempting to develop these attitudes, the teacher should do so by setting an example more than by much direct teaching. It is usually inadvisable, except in extreme cases, to give children lengthy explanations such as "Jane is sick," or, "We must all try to help Jane." The teacher's own behavior and attitude are much more important than verbal explanations. If the teacher regards Jane with hostility, disapproval, punishment, indignation, or retaliation, the children may follow suit. On the other hand, if he consistently shows a sympathetic understanding and warmth toward Jane, the children will react accordingly.

In summary, the classroom teacher should remember that his own attitude toward the emotionally disturbed child is the most important factor. He should understand the basic principle of working with the handicapped, namely, that they have essentially the same needs (affection, security, acceptance, etc.) as all individuals, but that they may have them in different proportion or degree.

SUMMARY

Today, a major focus of teaching is centered upon the problem of human relationships. Of these, none are more important than the relationships between the teacher and his pupils. This chapter has discussed the responsibilities of the teacher in building desirable teacher-pupil relationships and in developing desirable social behavior in his children.

The first section of the chapter presented five basic guideposts for working successfully with children. It was stressed that the teacher's knowledge of his pupils was a foundation for building a strong relationship with them. Two aspects of this area were considered. (1) What knowledge should the teacher have about his pupils, and (2) How may the teacher obtain information about his pupils?

One of the major concerns of the elementary school teacher is discipline. There are, however, many definitions as well as misconceptions concerning this problem. The modern concept of the word was defined and examined in detail in the second section. It was stressed that poor group discipline is usually a symptom of a basic weakness in the educational program and that, therefore, the only way to eliminate it is to locate its cause. The underlying causes of "normal" group misbehavior were considered to be: (1) uninteresting teaching-learning situation, (2) unwise academic pacing, (3) unhealthy classroom environment, (4) lack of organization, and (5) weak teaching personality.

Specific techniques for influencing and controlling child behavior were examined in the next section. It was emphasized that suggestions were based upon techniques found to be effective by many teachers. Because discipline is such a highly personalized problem, no guarantee can be made that a technique will work in every individual situation. Suggested techniques included: (1) wise and sparing use of the voice, (2) probationary isolation, (3) knowledgeable ignorance, (4) positive versus negative approach, (5) cognizance of the ripple effect, and (6) wise and infrequent use of punishment.

The last section examined briefly the problem of the emotionally maladjusted child in the classroom. It was stressed that this individual is a handicapped child, and that the teacher's understanding and attitude are important in (1) helping him and (2) helping other children to make a positive adjustment to the situation.

ADDITIONAL LEARNING EXPERIENCES

Topics for Thought and Discussion

1. What do you think is probably the most common misconception of discipline held by most teachers?

2. Do you think discipline is a greater problem in the schools today than it was twenty-five years ago? One hundred years ago? Why?

3. One study states that teachers who were rated superior in discipline generally possessed traits of (1) constructive leadership, (2) understanding of young people, and (3) forcefulness.[48] To what degree do you feel that you possess these traits?

4. Do you think that corporal punishment by the teacher can ever be justified?

5. Do you think that the elementary school teacher should send a child who misbehaves to the principal? Defend your answer.

6. Are you familiar with your state's statutes concerning the use of corporal punishment in the schools?

7. What types of punishment do you remember teachers using when you were in the elementary school? Do you think the situation has changed in most schools since then?

8. A boy in your classroom is continually tardy. You have spoken to him several times about being more prompt, but no improvement has been shown. What would you do?

9. In some communities, serious acts of vandalism are committed by children on Halloween night or the preceding night. Does the school have any responsibility in this matter?

10. What is your concept of discipline? Has it changed at all in recent years?

11. There is general agreement on the fact that a good teacher is a good disciplinarian. Is it possible for a good disciplinarian to be a poor teacher? Be careful to define your concept of a good disciplinarian as you answer this question.

Projects and Activities

1. Interview approximately fifteen or twenty parents in your town on the questions, How successful do you feel most elementary schools are today in the general area of discipline? and Upon what sources of information do you base your opinion? What conclusions can you draw from your findings?

2. Ask a sample group of lay people in the community the question, Do you favor the use of corporal punishment in the elementary school? Compare their answers with those of a similar sample of elementary school teachers. With school administrators and supervisors.

3. Write an analytical report of the literature concerning school discipline which has appeared in popular magazines during the past several years.

[48] Jesse A. Bond, "Analysis of Observed Traits of Teachers Who Were Rated Superior in School Discipline," *Journal of Educational Research*, Vol. 45 (March, 1952), p. 513.

4. Prepare an illustrated lecture (using slides, filmstrips, charts, or opaque projector) on "Acceptable Techniques for Securing and Maintaining Desirable Classroom Discipline."

5. You are the principal of an elementary school. The school bus driver complains to you about the behavior of children on the bus, such as throwing articles out of the window, indulging in horseplay, shouting at each other, and refusing to stay seated. Outline the specific steps you would take to correct this situation.

6. Describe in detail an example of poor classroom discipline that you remember from your own elementary school days or that you have recently observed. Analyze the underlying causes. The proximate cause. To what extent did the action or attitude of the teacher contribute to the incident? What would have been a preferred course of action?

7. You have noticed, from time to time over the past several months, that a few cents have been missing from the small box for milk money you keep in your desk. One day you see Mary Beth, a pleasant and intelligent child from a well-to-do home, take the money. Outline your course of action.

8. Prepare a series of cartoons to illustrate a set of behavior standards that could be developed cooperatively by an elementary teacher and his pupils.

9. Prepare a concise practical list of "Do's and Don'ts of Classroom Discipline" which would be of help to a student teacher or beginning teacher.

Selected Bibliography

Association for Childhood Education International, *Discipline*. Washington, D. C., 1957.

BARUCH, Dorothy Walter, *New Ways in Discipline*. New York, McGraw-Hill Book Co., Inc., 1949.

BERNARD, Harold W., *Mental Hygiene for Classroom Teachers*, 2nd ed. New York, McGraw-Hill Book Co., Inc., 1961.

BUHLER, Charlotte, SMITTER, Faith, and RICHARDSON, Sybil, *Childhood Problems and the Teacher*. New York, Holt, Rinehart and Winston, Inc., 1952.

BUSH, Robert Nelson, *The Teacher-Pupil Relationship*. Englewood Cliffs, N. J., Prentice-Hall, Inc., 1954 .

CASSEL, Russell N., *The Psychology of Child Discipline*. Cincinnati, C. A. Gregory Company, 1955.

CUTTS, Norma E., and MOSELEY, Nicholas, *Teaching the Disorderly Pupil in Elementary and Secondary School*. New York, Longmans, Green and Company, 1957.

Discipline, NEA Journal, Vol. 52, September, 1963, pp. 9-22.

D'EVELYN, Katherine E., *Meeting Children's Emotional Needs*. Englewood Cliffs, N. J., Prentice-Hall, Inc., 1957.

HYMES, James L., Jr., *Behavior and Misbehavior: A Teacher's Guide to Action*. Englewood Cliffs, N .J., Prentice-Hall, Inc., 1955.

KAPLAN, Louis, *Mental Health and Human Relations in Education.* New York, Harper & Row, Publishers, Inc., 1959.

KRUG, Othilda, and BECK, Helen L., *A Guide to Better Discipline.* Chicago, Science Research Associates, Inc., 1954.

LANE, Howard A., and BEAUCHAMP, Mary, *Human Relations in Teaching.* Englewood Cliffs, N. J., Prentice-Hall, Inc., 1955.

LONG, Nicholas J., and NEWMAN, Ruth G., *The Teacher's Handling of Children in Conflict.* Bulletin of the School of Education, Indiana University, Vol. 37 (July, 1961).

MACKIE, Romaine P., and others, *Teachers of Children Who Are Socially and Emotionally Maladjusted.* Bulletin 1957, No. 11, U. S. Department of Health, Education, and Welfare, Office of Education, Washington, D. C., 1957.

MOUSTAKAS, Clark E., *The Teacher and the Child.* New York, McGraw-Hill Book Co., Inc., 1956.

MUUSS, Rolf E., *First-aid for Classroom Discipline Problems.* New York, Holt, Rinehart and Winston, Inc., 1962.

OJEMANN, Ralph H., *Personality Adjustment of Individual Children.* What Research Says to the Teacher, No. 5. Department of Classroom Teachers, American Educational Research Association. Washington, D. C., National Education Association, 1954.

PHILLIPS, E. Lakin, WIENER, Daniel N., and HARING, Norris G., *Discipline, Achievement, and Mental Health.* Englewood Cliffs, N. J., Prentice-Hall, Inc., 1960.

REDL, Fritz, *Understanding Children's Behavior.* New York, Bureau of Publications, Teachers College, Columbia University, 1949.

———, and WATTENBERG, William W., *Mental Hygiene in Teaching,* 2nd ed. New York, Harcourt, Brace and World, Inc., 1959.

———, and WINEMAN, David, *Children Who Hate.* Glencoe, Ill., The Free Press of Glencoe, 1951.

———, and ———, *Controls from Within.* Glencoe, Ill., The Free Press of Glencoe, 1952.

SHEVIAKOV, George V., and REDL, Fritz, *Discipline for Today's Children and Youth,* rev. by Sybil K. Richardson. Association for Supervision and Curriculum Development. Washington, D. C., National Education Association, 1956.

"Teacher Opinion on Pupil Behavior, 1955-56." *NEA Research Bulletin,* Vol. 34 (April, 1956).

CHAPTER 4

Working With the Home and Community

THE YEAR WAS 1800. The day was an eventful one for people of the tiny New England village. It was near the close of the term, and the annual school exhibit, for which the schoolmaster and his pupils had been preparing for months, was in full progress. Everyone in town, from the youngest to the oldest, was there in his Sunday best clothes. They listened attentively to the recitations and dialogues spoken by the pupils and to the speeches of the community's leading citizens. They admired the examples of spelling, handwriting, and other schoolwork displayed prominently on the walls. When the lengthy program was over, the day's social festivities began. The lunch or outdoor picnic of fried chicken, cheese, baked beans, milk, bread and marmalade, applesauce, and candied fruits and nuts was a highlight of the occasion and was followed by an afternoon of varied recreation and relaxation. Finally, tired but pleased with the success of the day, the group voted to ask the schoolmaster to return for another term, and the occasion closed on a note of well-being and satisfaction.

During the early years of American public education, the schoolmaster and schoolhouse were integral parts of the community. The schoolmaster boarded around at the homes of his pupils and thus came to know the child and his home background to an extent today's most conscientious teacher would envy. The schoolhouse was the educational and social center of the town, from which all community activities radiated. To separate the school from the community was unheard of and practically impossible.

As urbanization increased, however, and as the educational program became more specialized and complex, the school and community grew further and further apart. Apathy, disinterest, and in some cases, resentment and opposition of each group toward the other became so prevalent that, in the early years of the twentieth century, alert school administrators realized that something needed to be done. Unfortunately, these schoolmen took their cue from the fields of public relations and advertising, which were growing rapidly then; and so began an era in which educators were primarily concerned with "selling the schools" to the public in order to secure its "acceptance, acquiescence, and financial support when needed."[1] The basic fallacies and limitations of this one-way street emphasis gradually became apparent, however, and today the development of an interactive, positive home-school-community relationship is considered by most people to be one of the most crucial challenges facing modern American education. Mutual cooperation and understanding between home and school will not, like Topsy, just grow. On the contrary, there exist today some sources of tension and misunderstanding that militate against home-school cooperation unless they are overcome by a well-planned, consistent, and purposeful program of action.

POSSIBLE SOURCES OF TENSION BETWEEN HOME AND SCHOOL

Tensions and misunderstandings that may arise between home and school can usually be traced to one or more of the following sources.

1. *Role confusion.* In the past, the school assumed the responsibility for the academic development of the child and the home took care of all other phases of his growth. The lines of responsibility were clearly drawn and left little room for confusion. In more recent years, however, the school has assumed increased responsibility for the total growth of the child, physically, socially, emotionally, and mentally. Some of this responsibility is assumed by the school voluntarily because of a changing philosophy of education. Some, however, is thrust upon the school by a changing social scene and the abdication of responsibility on the part of the home and sometimes other agencies. But at the same time the parent still has the ultimate responsibility for the total growth of the child and this leads to some confusion as to just whose job it is to do what. For instance, should the school be concerned as to whether or not the child has an adequate breakfast? Most teachers will say, "Yes," but many parents may feel that this is none of the school's business. On the other hand, is it the parent's prerogative to help his first-grade son with reading during the evening? Most parents will say, "Yes," but some teachers may disagree.

[1] William A. Yeager, *School-Community Relations* (New York, Holt, Rinehart and Winston, Inc., 1951), p. 108.

This confusion of roles often leads to resentment, suspicion, and antagonism between home and school as well as a tendency of each to shift responsibility and blame to the other. According to McNassor, this "search for mutually exclusive roles" is a major obstacle to be overcome before a program of genuine home-school interaction is realized.

As we no longer feel guilty about the change in roles that has come about, the great confusion will have ended, and talk about who does which part of the job in influencing children's development will begin to disappear. When this happens, both parents and teachers will be much more self-confident in what each is doing for the child. *The search for mutually exclusive roles will have ended.*[2]

2. *Changing theories of education.* Probably one of the greatest sources of confusion and tension between the public and the school lies in the fact that most people tend to interpret and evaluate the educational program in terms of the one they knew when they were pupils twenty or thirty years ago. As any teacher knows, educational goals, procedures, materials, and methods have changed considerably since then. Furthermore, they will and must continue to change in a changing world. But some parents do not understand this, and lack of understanding is only one step away from criticism and resentment. A similar situation may arise, also, when parents who have more than one child see the program change in a very few years. For instance, MaryAnn Smith, now in fourth grade, is studying something in social studies entirely different from what her older brother did a few years ago when he was in the same fourth grade in the same school. Naturally Mr. and Mrs. Smith are somewhat puzzled and occasionally haunted by the nagging doubt, "Does the school really know what it's doing? If so, why does it keep changing every few years?" Obviously, the solution to this problem is a program of steady communication and close cooperation, as is discussed later in the chapter. It is sufficient here simply to remind all teachers, as McNassor does, that, "contact between school people and lay citizens in appraising schools in light of changes in society and science must be facilitated . . . parents of children need to feel welcome in proposing and evaluating changed school practices."[3]

3. *Differences among schools and school systems.* Compounding the problem stated above, is the fact that educational philosophy and practice not only change over the years, but they also vary widely from school to school. The situation in which a family moves to another town only to find the new school curriculum and program completely different is,

[2] Donald McNassor, "Barriers and Gateways in School-Community Relationships," *Journal of Educational Sociology*, Vol. 28 (September, 1954), p. 9.
[3] *Ibid.*, p. 10.

of course, not unusual. There can be little doubt that this is a source of misunderstanding between home and school of which the alert teacher and administrator should be well aware. It should be kept in mind, however, that the solution lies, *not in standardizing the schools*, but rather in *each* school's consistent emphasis upon interpreting *its* program to *its* community.

4. *Prevalence of stereotypes.* As in many other human relationships, misunderstanding and distrust between teacher and parent may be caused by the stereotyped image each has of the other. The parent, for instance, may view the teacher as a bookish person who "has a few queer traits, is not quite as earthy as other folk, has an easy job with a long vacation, and is inclined to feel that he has 'congressional immunity' when it comes to educating children."[4] This stereotype, although it is gradually disappearing, is still perpetuated to some extent by the frequent, unflattering portrayals of teachers in films, television, and other mass media. There can be little doubt that it works to the detriment of the profession as well as to a sound community-school relationship, for as long as parents consider teachers to be unapproachable, misunderstanding is inevitable.

Equally important, also, is the image of the parent frequently held by the teacher. Many insecure teachers tend to view the parent as an intruder who threatens their authority and status. (See the statements of beginning teachers in Chapter 13.) As Langdon and Stout state, "It probably would surprise parents to know how often a teacher is fearful of them, fearful that they will criticize or interfere or ask questions that might be hard to answer."[5]

Thus, the stereotypes of the teacher as a stand-offish individual not quite like other people and the parent as a faultfinder and status-threat may contribute to a mutual distrust and lack of cooperation which must be replaced by a dynamic home-school-community program.

5. *Failure to Recognize the Importance of the Problem.* In many systems, home-school cooperation does not exist simply because neither group recognizes its importance and the advantage it offers. Some teachers, for instance, may still be blind to the fact that much of their success and effectiveness depends upon enlisting the understanding and support of the parents. Or, they may simply not realize how much their every action either strengthens or weakens the home relationship. Second grade teacher Mrs. Jones, for instance, hurriedly dashed off a last-minute note to Karen's mother the other day, explaining how Karen had spilled paint on her dress. Karen's mother appreciated the thoughtful gesture but she did not

[4] *Ibid.*, p. 5.
[5] Grace Langdon and Irving W. Stout, *Teacher-Parent Interviews* (Englewood Cliffs, N. J., Prentice-Hall, Inc., 1954), p. 53.

appreciate the fact that the note was written in careless penmanship and contained two misspelled words. Obviously this incident, well-intentioned though it was, did not help to strengthen the parent's confidence in the teacher or school.

Some parents, also, frequently fail to recognize the importance of mutual cooperation and interest. Their coolness toward teachers who visit their homes, their refusal to attend any school events, and their general disinterest in the entire school program indicates that they have little recognition of today's vital need for a unified home-school-community program.

6. *Concerted attacks on public education.* Criticism of public education is not new. Nor is it entirely bad. Much of it is of a positive nature and, over the years, has helped American education to move ahead. Today, however, some of the criticism of the public schools is of an entirely different nature. In many cases, this type of criticism represents a well-organized, concentrated attempt to undermine deliberately the confidence of the public in its system of public education. Now, it is not our purpose here to explore the roots of such criticism, nor to expose its misrepresentation of truth, nor even to rise to the defense of the schools.[6] The point is made only that an increasing criticism by certain groups has not helped to bring home and school closer together. On the contrary, it has led many well-meaning and interested parents to view the school with a certain amount of distrust and alarm. At the same time it has caused teachers to become resentful and discouraged because their efforts appear to be seldom appreciated. Heffernan says,

Teachers are no more thin-skinned than other people, but they cannot do effective work for children to the continuous accompaniment of an anvil chorus of criticism. Unfortunately, the people who value what the schools are doing for children rarely express their positive approval. This leaves a field day for crackpots who are loudly vocal in behalf of educational methods that violate what is known about how children learn.

Educators know a great deal about how children learn and about the obstacles which militate against children's learning. Vigorous moral support of the schools from socially-minded citizens is long overdue. The destructive game of creating confusion and distrust will continue until the American sense of fair play reasserts itself and schools are protected in their right to render the professional service for which they were established.[7]

[6] Students who desire to explore this topic further will find such books as *Public Education Under Criticism* edited by Scott and Hill (Prentice-Hall, Inc., 1954), *Public Education and Its Critics* by V. T. Thayer (The Macmillan Company, 1954), and *American Education, Facts, Fancies, and Folklore* by Raymond P. Harris (Random House, Inc., 1961) interesting reading.

[7] Reprinted by permission of the Association for Childhood Education International, 3615 Wisconsin Avenue, N.W., Washington 16, D. C. "What Obstructs Learning?" by Helen Heffernan. From *Childhood Education*, October, 1962. Vol. 39, No. 2, p. 70.

Thus far we have examined the major sources of confusion and tension, which should convince every teacher of the need for a well-defined, carefully-planned, forward-looking program of home-school-community relationships. The major goals of such a program are discussed in the following section.

GOALS OF HOME-SCHOOL-COMMUNITY COOPERATION

1. To ENABLE THE SCHOOL TO ACCOMPLISH BETTER ITS MAJOR TASK OF EDUCATING CHILDREN. All knowledge of human development and behavior points to one inescapable conclusion: the person is the sum total of *all* his experiences. No child lives a mere five hours a day. Every child lives a full twenty-four hours and each brings with him to the classroom each morning the knowledges, experiences, and impressions of his total environment. The phrase *the whole child* is not a fragment of meaningless educational jargon. On the contrary, it is an actuality that faces every teacher every day. The more the teacher knows and understands the wholeness of his pupils and their lives, the better job he will do in the classroom, a fact substantiated by research (see Chapter 3) and vast personal experience. (The author remembers, for instance, one teacher who told how his entire attitude toward a pupil changed overnight after he visited the home and found a family of seven living in a one-room squalid shack without electricity, plumbing, or any other modern convenience.) No school nor teacher can perform his function adequately unless he is thoroughly familiar with his pupils, with their home backgrounds, family situations, peer relationships, hobbies, interests, out-of-school activities, and innumerable other influences bearing upon their total development. Recognition by the school of its need to have thorough knowledge of the pupils' total life experiences has been translated into a major goal of home-school-community cooperation and many of the aids suggested in the last section of this chapter are directly aimed at its realization.

2. To HELP THE PARENT IN HIS TASK OF REARING THE CHILD. In no other nation in the world are children more highly regarded than in our own country. American parents work and plan and sacrifice all of their lives to give their children the advantages and benefits which they themselves were not able to enjoy. Mothers read Dr. Spock, serve as den mothers, and spend hours chauffering their offspring to piano lessons, ballet lessons, dental appointments, Scout meetings, and basketball practice. Fathers coach Little Leagues, build game rooms in their basements, help with homework problems, and open bank accounts for the child's college education the day he is born. "Nothing is too good for my child," has become the motto of a large portion of our American population. In short, most American parents *are* interested in their children, *are* trying

to rear them to the best of their knowledge and ability, and *are* appreciative of any help they are offered. The school, as the expert in child growth and behavior, has an obligation to offer this help and to share its specialized knowledge with parents through a consistent program of home-school cooperation. Gabbard emphasizes the importance of this goal in the following statement: "The job of the school is only partially done when it has educated the children of the Nation . . . helping the parent to feel more adequate for his task is fully as important from the point of view of public education and the welfare of society as is the education of children themselves."[8]

3. TO DEVELOP A PROGRAM OF CONSISTENT EDUCATION AND GUIDANCE OF THE CHILD. Many studies show that inconsistency among adults can be most harmful to the healthful development of a child. In a home, for instance, where one parent tends to be overly permissive while the other is relatively strict, the child becomes confused and insecure. The same principle applies to home and school guidance. When these are inconsistent toward their mutual interest, the child, or, even worse, when they are in opposition to each other, the effect upon the child can only be harmful. Antagonism, open criticism, resentment, and sharp differences of opinion between home and school inevitably work to the disadvantage of both but, more important, they constitute a seriously demoralizing influence upon the child's development. As McNassor states, "Children have enough of a load on their hands in growing up without the added burden of taking on the problem of adult anxiety and inconsistency as to how to educate them."[9]

4. TO HELP THE PARENT UNDERSTAND MODERN THEORIES OF CHILD GROWTH AND LEARNING. Like everything else, educational theory and practice change over the years. Added knowledge, continuing research, new facilities, and the problems, needs, and demands of today's world require a far different educational program than that of thirty, or even five, years ago. As pointed out earlier, this causes parents to become confused, distrustful, and critical of the school. Hymes comments upon this situation as follows:

Schools cannot simply plunge into new programs. They can be sure that parents want the best for their children, but not all parents are as eager for change in education as they are for new cooking stoves. The first step for schools is to know realistically that many parents are already out of touch with school practices, they feel left behind, and they are suspicious.[10]

[8] Hazel F. Gabbard, *Working with Parents* (Washington, D. C., U. S. Department of Health, Education, and Welfare, Office of Education, 1949), p. 1.
[9] Donald McNassor, *op. cit.,* p. 10.
[10] James L. Hymes, *Effective Home-School Relations* (Englewood Cliffs, N. J., Prentice-Hall, Inc., 1953), p. 50.

It should be fairly obvious that the school has a real opportunity as well as an obligation to keep parents informed of the constantly changing developments in education. Such a program of parent education should, for instance, not only tell parents that the school is teaching a new method of long division in fourth grade but should also explain *why* the new method was adopted and in what respects it is believed to be superior to the one learned by the parent when he was an elementary school pupil. Through such an approach, the school will not only help the parent to become a more enlightened citizen but will also strengthen the bonds of mutual cooperation.

5. To ENLIST THE SUPPORT OF THE HOME AND COMMUNITY. Many years ago, Horace Mann said, "The people will sustain no better schools and have no better education than they personally see the need of." At no time was this statement more true than it is today. The one inescapable fact teachers must face is that *the people will have the type of schools they want.* They elect legislators who appropriate money and determine educational policy, they elect school board members, they vote on school budgets, they elect (to some degree) educational officers and, in numerous other ways, they make their voices heard on educational concerns. The public does have the final word on the education of the children of the state. Any teacher or school which thinks that it can determine its educational program in an academic ivory tower is in for a rude awakening. The relationship of public support to the quality of education is clearly stated in the following:

Good schools must have good public relations. One doesn't have to look far to see the proof. In a community where the people understand the school program and have faith in the staff the quality of education is usually high. There the classroom teachers have essential instructional materials, salaries and working conditions reach professional levels, and the educational opportunities of pupils are outstanding. Where schools are *not* good the cause may often be found in the indifference, misinformation, and distrust among the people. Public education is not likely to be better than the public's understanding of the schools.[11]

6. To IMPROVE THE STANDARD OF LIVING IN A COMMUNITY. Several years ago the concept of the *community school* was introduced into American public education. The broad purpose of the true community school is, simply ". . . better persons in a better community."[12] To achieve this

[11] National School Public Relations Association, *It Starts in the Classroom* (Washington, D. C., National Education Association, 1951), p. 6.
[12] Ruth Strang, "Community Schools and the People Working Together," *The Community School*, Nelson B. Henry, ed. Fifty-second Yearbook, National Society for the Study of Education, Part II (Washington, D. C., 1953), p. 157.

goal, school and community work together to study and improve the problems of the community. Projects such as (1) improving the dietary or other health habits of the community, (2) beautifying the landscaping of parks, playgrounds, and similar public places, (3) reducing racial, religious, or other intergroup tensions, (4) educating youth for marriage and family life, (5) providing healthful recreational activities and facilities, and (6) making the wisest use of community resources provide the bases for the community school's educational program. Although the extent of the school's identification with the problems of the community varies widely according to the individual situation, each is, to some degree, a community school. Thus, the goal of developing better citizens for a better community is inherent in a public relations program.

CHARACTERISTICS OF A POSITIVE PROGRAM OF HOME-SCHOOL-COMMUNITY COOPERATION

The achievement of the goals stated above depends upon a dynamic, positive program of home-school-community relationships. In general, such a program is distinguished by the following characteristics:

1. A POSITIVE PROGRAM EMPHASIZES *two-way* COMMUNICATION AND INTERACTION. It was stated previously that an earlier concept of public relations was selling the schools to the public. Such a concept implied a one-way communication system with the schools on the giving end, the parents on the receiving end. Schools recognized their responsibility to *inform* and *appraise* parents of new developments in order to insure public support. Rarely, however, did the schools welcome information, assistance, and advice from parents. Today, of course, this has changed. Parents and teachers are mutually dependent on each other. They are involved in a two-way program of communication and cooperation involving numerous activities and experiences. Cooperative planning sessions, group evaluation projects, attacks upon common problems, and the establishment of mutual goals are the benchmarks characterizing the modern school's relations with its community.

2. IT INCLUDES PARENTS IN ALL TYPES AND LEVELS OF ACTIVITIES. Unfortunately, in some cases, a school's so-called public relations program is nothing more than an exploitation of parents' interest and willingness to help. In other words, schools may call upon parents to help in the cafeteria or assist with field trips, but they *do not* include them in such activities as curriculum planning sessions, lay advisory committees, or others of a similar educational level. Restricting parental participation to only routine tasks is, of course, reducing the public relations program to a farce. The ideal program being discussed here includes parents in a wide

variety of activities and aims at genuine cooperation and assistance rather than mere exploitation.

3. IT IS CONSISTENT IN ITS EMPHASIS. A major strength of a desirable program is its consistent emphasis upon harmonious relationships. In this respect, it differs greatly from a superficial program which limps along in low-gear until a crisis arises. Then, all of a sudden, parents are deluged with letters, newspaper articles, and various other propaganda devices urging their support and assistance. That such a program is ultimately ineffectual is obvious. Only a program of steady day-in, day-out, year-in, and year-out emphasis will yield the type of home-school unity necessary to a sound educational program.

4. THE INDIVIDUAL TEACHER IS THE MOST IMPORTANT FIGURE IN A DESIRABLE PUBLIC RELATIONS PROGRAM. The school's relationship with the community is of such concern today that many systems have employed full-time public relations directors to establish and supervise a coordinated, well-planned program. Regardless of the specialized personnel available, however, *the classroom teacher remains the most crucial person in the entire program*. The unanimous agreement upon this statement is revealed in the following statement: "As workers in school public relations have explored the processes involved, they have repeatedly held the role of the classroom teacher to be the most fundamental link in the entire process."[13] Specifically, the teacher may contribute to a positive home-school relationship through the following channels.

His participation in community life. Some authorities feel that, "In order to understand the culture of its people and learn about their needs and interest, it is essential that the teacher live in a full sense in the community, including week-ends."[14] Although the author would not disagree strongly with this statement, it does represent the ideal rather than the practical viewpoint. For economic, social, family, or cultural reasons, the classroom teacher often cannot make his home in the community in which he teaches. However, regardless of where he lives, the teacher should make a conscientious effort to participate as fully as practically possible in the affairs of the community. Membership in service clubs, home-school organizations, and civic associations as well as patronage of local businesses will help the teacher to really understand the community of his pupils as well as enlist the interest and support of local leaders in the

[13] "Teachers View Public Relations," *NEA Research Bulletin*, Vol. 37 (April, 1959), p. 35.

[14] Marie A. Mehl, Hubert H. Mills, and Harl R. Douglass, *Teaching in Elementary School*, 2nd ed. (New York, The Ronald Press Company, 1958), p. 12.

school's program. The participation of teachers in community activities, according to one survey, is as follows:[15]

	Percent of Teachers Who Regularly Participate
General church activities	73.6
Social or recreational clubs	37.9
Church related clubs	29.2
Fraternal or lodge activities	26.3
Service clubs	24.3
Civic and welfare organizations	25.0
Teach in church school	17.8
Political clubs	4.9

His personal and professional life. Simply by being himself, the classroom teacher helps or hinders good public relations. The public's attitude toward the individual teacher inevitably becomes its attitude toward the entire school. Thus, the teacher whose personal life is above reproach and whose professional life reflects his sincere interest in his work gains the respect of the community and helps to strengthen the school's public relations.

His pride in the profession. In recent years, considerable publicity has been given to such negative aspects of teaching as low salaries, inadequate facilities, and overcrowded classrooms. There can be little doubt that this type of publicity was necessary or that it has not accomplished a great deal in helping to raise the level of the profession. In some places, however, the situation has gotten out of hand and the public is weary of teachers complaining about their hard lot in life. There is a vast difference between working to raise the status of the profession and merely complaining in order to attract public sympathy and attention. In other words, while the teacher is striving constantly to further the welfare of the profession, he can also, in hundreds of different ways, tell the public that teaching is a wonderful profession and that he is proud to be a member of it. Justifiable pride in his chosen work is an absolute *must* if the teacher expects to (1) attract capable young people into the profession, (2) raise the professional level of teaching, and (3) win the respect and support of the public for education.

The following statement supports the crucial importance to good public relations of the teacher's pride in his profession. "PRIDE IN THE PROFESSION, then, is the first requisite to a teacher's effectiveness in public

[15] National Education Association, Research Division, *The Classroom Teacher and Public Relations*, Research Monograph 1959-M2 (Washington, D. C., National Education Association, July, 1959), p. 37.

relations. Without it he can build no goodwill for the profession. With it he can build goodwill for his colleagues and the schools. A community that appreciates its teachers takes pride in its schools."[16]

His classroom performance. Just as the teacher is the most important person in the public relations program, so is his classroom performance the most important single factor. The teacher who makes pupils happy, makes parents happy. The teacher who wins the respect and admiration of his pupils, wins the respect and admiration of their parents. As someone has said, the school's best public relations device walks on two legs back and forth from home to school every day. If each morning the child leaves his home happily anticipating another interesting day in school, and each afternoon returns home bursting with enthusiasm about the things he has done in school, this contributes, as nothing else possibly can, toward an enduring program of home-school cooperation and harmony.

His awareness of the importance of good public relations. Over and above a superior classroom performance, the teacher can contribute even more to good home-school relations through inserting in his teaching some effective public relations techniques. Consider the following situation. George (age seven) is asked at the dinner table the routine question, "What did you learn in school today?"

His answer is just as routine—"Nothing!"

The next day the question is made more specific, "What did you do in arithmetic today?"

The answer may be, "Nothing much—we just played some games."

Now, as any teacher knows, "Nothing," was merely a youngster's way of avoiding an involved answer and the "games" were probably some intensive drill devices designed to strengthen certain mathematical understandings carefully developed in previous lessons. But parents don't know this! Small wonder, then, that after a while they begin to wonder exactly what the school is accomplishing. Good teachers, of course, prevent things from getting to this point through using a variety of public relations techniques. One Robinson includes among the ten best is asking pupils at the close of a lesson, "What will you tell your parents that you learned in this class today?"[17] Such a question is an excellent way to summarize and clinch the main points of the lesson as well as to create a good impression in the home. A variation with the same values is the question asked by some teachers at the close of the day, What do you know as you leave our classroom tonight that you didn't know when you entered it this

[16] National School Public Relations Association, *op. cit.*, p. 8.
[17] Thomas E. Robinson, "Ten Best Public Relations Devices," *School Executive,* Vol. 68 (August, 1949), p. 37.

morning? Equally valuable, also, is the technique some teachers use of always closing the school day on a note of anticipation. To remind children that, "Tomorrow, I'll have some brand new books on the library table when you arrive," or, "Try to think of a science experiment we can do tomorrow to help us answer our science questions," may encourage children to talk more about their classroom activities at home and also make them eager to return to school the following day.

Another way the classroom teacher can combine good education with good public relations is to teach his pupils, according to their level of understanding, content related to the American public school system. This can be done on many grade levels. For instance, when studying a faraway land (perhaps in fourth grade) the teacher may include not only subject matter on such things as the food, the homes, the customs of the land but also on its schools. A comparison with our own country might then reveal our emphasis upon free educational opportunity for *all* children and the fact that this is not true in many other parts of the world. Or, when studying colonial life, the teacher may include content about the colonial schools and how they differed in philosophy and curriculum from our modern schools. As Eastmond points out, "From the public relations viewpoint, the parents of tomorrow are the pupils of today," and we cannot begin to build too early "a solid background of understanding and support"[18] for our educational system.

A third excellent technique for good education and good public relations is the frequent use of informal phone calls and notes to the home. Most teachers, for instance, are well aware of the world of good a little individual encouragement and attention can do for the child. What some do not realize, however, is that this can be extended with an added advantage to the home. Take, for instance, the teacher who comments to John, "I am certainly proud of how much you have improved in spelling this week." This is fine. It may be, however, even finer if she took a minute to write a short note saying the same thing to John's parents. Or perhaps a short telephone call might be equally effective. It is difficult for teachers, busy with thirty pupils, to realize fully how very important even a small gesture is to the parent of the individual child. The following anecdote is revealing.

A teacher sent a note to a boy's home praising the work he had done in school that term and the next day she asked the child what his mother had said when she received the note. "Nothing," the boy replied, "She cried."[19]

All kinds of informal notes, telephone cards, birthday cards, get-well-

[18] Jefferson N. Eastmond, *The Teacher and School Administration* (Boston, Houghton Mifflin Company, 1959), pp. 258-259.
[19] National School Public Relations Association, *op. cit.*, p. 58.

wishes are used by capable teachers as they work with parents for the welfare and happiness of the child.

Two other very important public relations devices used by all classroom teachers are (1) methods of reporting pupil progress to parents including parent-teacher conferences and (2) homework. For a discussion of these the reader is referred to Chapters 11 and 9 respectively.

Suggestions offered here, of course, pertain to only a few of the ways in which effective teachers combine good teaching with good public relations. They have been included only to emphasize the important contribution of the *individual teacher* to home-school cooperation. Others, of which *all* school personnel should be aware, are discussed in the following section.

AIDS TO HOME-SCHOOL-COMMUNITY COOPERATION

A well-coordinated consistent program of home-school-community cooperation is successful only if it is designed to fit the needs of a particular school and a particular community. Thus, it is impossible to suggest devices that will be equally successful in all situations. In general, however, schools that have achieved a genuine interaction with their community find the following aids to be of value.

THE SCHOOL MUST PROVIDE NUMEROUS OPPORTUNITIES FOR PARENTS AND OTHER INTERESTED PERSONS IN THE COMMUNITY TO OBSERVE THE SCHOOL PROGRAM. It has been stated repeatedly that parents are and should be interested in the school's program. In order to capitalize upon this interest and acquaint parents with the work of the classroom, most schools provide the following observational opportunities.

All-School Parents Night. That this is very common practice is revealed by a recent survey of urban systems which states that more than nine in ten teachers indicated the existence of an open-house or parents' night in their schools.[20] Such an event may take several forms although it usually includes some sort of a general program in the auditorium or gymnasium. In addition, some opportunity is given for parents to visit individual classrooms and chat briefly with various teachers. In some schools, the parents move through an abbreviated facsimile of their child's daily schedule although this is more common on the secondary level than in the elementary school. Although the nature of the event varies widely, the goal is essentially the same, to furnish an opportunity for parents and others "to inspect the school, to talk with the teachers about the work and about individual children, and to become informed concerning general school policies and philosophy."[21]

[20] "Teachers View Public Relations," *op. cit.*, p. 37.
[21] *Ibid.*

American Education Week. For more than thirty years, American Education Week has been an important feature of the schools' public relations programs. Held traditionally during the week of November 11, it is sponsored jointly by the National Education Association, the National Congress of Parents and Teachers, the American Legion, and the United States Office of Education. Most schools make an earnest effort to encourage parental visitation throughout the entire week. In addition, many write letters, prepare newspaper releases, arrange for special programs in the school or on radio and television, and utilize numerous other devices to publicize the school's activities in the community. Helpful materials and suggestions for making the week most profitable may be secured from the National Education Association. These include, among others, such recent pamphlets as *How Can I Help My Child with Arithmetic*, *How Schools Test Your Child's Potential*, *What Every Parent Should Know About Homework*, and *Your Child Can't Sit and Stay Fit*.

Classroom visitation. Although both of the all-school events discussed above have many advantages, generally they cannot provide opportunity for extended observation in a single classroom. To meet this need, many teachers arrange for classroom teas or programs for the parents of their pupils. Such an event is usually held during the school day although some prefer the evening or Saturday afternoon when both parents are usually able to atttend. Such classroom events have several advantages. In the first place, they permit parents to observe and talk with teachers in a more intimate setting than the all-school affair. Secondly, if a program is presented, it is usually centered around a unit of work so that the event has real educational value for pupils and is not merely putting on a show for parents. On the whole, there can be little doubt that classroom get-togethers involving parents, teachers, and pupils are valuable educational and public relations devices. Most schools require or strongly urge their teachers to take advantage of the values they offer at least once or twice a year.

Another type of classroom visitation, designed for a slightly different purpose, is the program of informal and individual observation extending over the entire year. Some schools encourage parents to visit by publicizing the fact that on a certain day each week or month (the third Monday, for instance) they will be very welcome to visit any classroom they choose for as long as they like. In other schools, teachers write to groups of about six to eight parents at regular intervals naming a day on which they would be very welcome. The advantage of this type of informal visitation is, of course, that it permits the parent to observe *the regular daily work of the classroom*. However, in order to capitalize upon this advantage, the teacher is urged to close the visitation day with a short discussion period after the pupils have left the room. He can then explain the purpose of some of the activities the parents witnessed as well as answer questions. Such a discussion period greatly adds to the value of the observation since it helps to prevent parents from "seeing with eyes unseeing."

It is interesting to note that classroom visitation and teacher-parent discussion may not only help to strengthen home-school relations but may also help to improve pupils' performances in the classroom. Conner reports a study in which parents of a control group of pupils participated in the regular public relations devices while those of pupils in an experimental group spent two hours (one for observation and one for discussion) each week in the classroom. At the close of the experiment, it was found that, "In all of the regular subjects of the curriculum that could be tested by means of standardized achievement tests, the children in the experimental group exceeded the achievements of their matched partners in the control schools by differences that were statistically significant."[22]

THE SCHOOL SHOULD ENCOURAGE PARENTS TO PARTICIPATE IN NUMEROUS TYPES OF SCHOOL ACTIVITIES. Popular techniques for encouraging parental participation in school affairs include the following:

1. *Participation at the planning and policy-making level.* One method of community participation is through the *unmet-needs conference.* In general, this type of conference is an open meeting to which all interested persons are invited. After a general session including an orientation address, the large group is divided into several small sections of approximately ten to twelve persons to identify needs and to specify community and individual problems that are not adequately met by the schools. The success of this technique obviously depends upon the careful balance of professional and lay personnel involved, as well as upon the skill of trained discussion leaders. There is little doubt that this type of conference has the advantages of the grass roots approach to professional problems and, if handled well, can be immensely successful.

Another type of community participation is through *lay advisory committees.* Many schools use these groups to assist in planning and determining policy concerning curriculum, methods of evaluating and reporting pupil progress, appraising building needs, and others.

In summary, parent participation at the planning and policy-making level offers obvious advantages. The reader is also reminded, however, that it presents certain problems. Difficulties of scheduling meetings equally convenient for professional and lay personnel, unfamiliarity of laymen with professional language and educational research, differences of educational backgrounds, and many others demand extremely careful

[22] Jay Davis Conner, "Parent Participation Pays Dividends," *California Journal of Elementary Education,* Vol. 19 (February, 1951), p. 140.

planning in order to realize the advantages of lay-professional cooperation at this level. The following example illustrates the method and advantage of this technique.

A model of citizen participation in curriculum building developed out of a single classroom incident. In a western state where cotton raising has become a major industry, a fourth-grade teacher was instructing her class in how cotton is grown.

"But Miss Carver, that's not the way we do it," one boy piped up. The teacher's instructional material, it developed, was produced in South Carolina, where farmers' methods did not correspond with western dry farming.

This teacher began to do some investigating and studying herself. Much of the fourth-grade curriculum in that state is built around community living. She discovered other areas where instruction was poorly adapted to life in her community. Under her leadership, the problem was attacked countywide.

Top leaders in each major industry—cotton, petroleum, merchandising, irrigation, livestock raising, and dairying—were called together. Need for localized instructional materials and guidance was explained. Each industry was asked to prepare a complete story—history of the industry locally, technics used, local and national significance—and provide about 10 glossy pictures to illustrate every phase.

Industry committees then delegated responsibilities, did research, and compiled the full story. County-school employees and teacher committees rewrote the material in fourth-grade vocabulary and in a form suitable for instructional use. Industrial committees reviewed the rewrite job for accuracy in every detail. Copies of the completed unit were mimeographed for use by pilot teachers whose suggestions were incorporated in final printed units.

Scores of community agricultural and industrial leaders thus had a direct part in planning these instructional units for their schools. Many of them said that they had learned more about their own industry in the process than they had ever known before.

All are staunch advocates of schools and teachers because they've experienced what is involved in modern school programs to develop good citizens. They saw how instruction in reading, arithmetic, writing, art, and geography were injected into activities for the unit they helped prepare.[23]

2. *Assisting with school activities.* Opportunities for parents to assist with school activities and tasks are almost too numerous to mention. For instance, in one school that has a fairly good library but no librarian a group of mothers organized and operate a Library Service Corps. They rotate hours on duty and, through their combined efforts, the school enjoys full librarian service every day of the week.

In a rural elementary school, volunteer parents assist with lunchroom and playground supervisory duties, much to the gratitude of teachers

[23] National School Public Relations Association, *op. cit.*, pp. 18-19.

who, for the first time in years, now have a brief noon respite before beginning afternoon classes.

Still another system has achieved success in using parents as volunteer *classroom aides* to assist the teacher with such noninstructional duties as collecting monies, taking attendance, distributing supplies, and others. In this system also certain parents act as *lay readers* to read and mark examinations and written compositions although this is much more prevalent in the secondary schools than on the elementary level.

Another school is fortunate enough to have a group of parents who have formed a stenographic pool. Typing, duplicating, and other clerical duties for principal and teachers are performed by these parents, each of whom contributes a few hours per week of her time.

Mrs. Y, a skilled pianist, has earned the lasting gratitude of the teachers in another elementary school. Each week she spends several hours in the school playing the piano for school assemblies, rhythmic and dance lessons, and special programs. She offers assistance occasionally with the school orchestra and glee club and in every way evidences her strong interest and support of the school program.

These illustrations are, of course, only a few of the ways in which parents may make a valuable contribution to the activities of the school. It should be repeated that most parents are interested in the school and many who have the time are happy to offer their assistance. That such interest and willingness should not be merely exploited by the school in order to capitalize upon some free labor should be, of course, fairly obvious. Exploiting parents merely for the selfish benefit of the school and teachers is certainly contradictory to the teacher-parent cooperation we are discussing here and must obviously be avoided at all costs.

3. *Resource personnel.* Many parents possess unusual talents, backgrounds, or hobbies that should be utilized by the school as a source of enrichment for its program. As Hymes says, "Sitting at home in every community are photographers, cabinet makers, tennis players, trumpeters and cellists, square-dancing enthusiasts, story-telling experts."[24] All these and many, many others comprise a rich resource for the classroom. Parents are usually more than happy to show to the sixth grade a film of their trip to Africa, to display their skill as a puppeteer for the first grade, or to tell the third grade about their job at the city filtration plant. The values of such parental contributions are several: (1) they provide a wonderful enrichment resource for the school curriculum, (2) they cement home-school cooperation, and (3) they may be a means of building a pupil's much-needed peer status. An example of this occurred recently in one school with Jimmy S, a timid, insecure fourth-grader who yearned

[24] James L. Hymes, *op. cit.,* p. 171.

for group status and approval but without much success. His father happened to be a fairly well-known artist. Jimmy's teacher asked his father if he would care to exhibit six or eight of his paintings in the main hall of the school for a week or two. The exhibit attracted wide attention from all classes, the pupils enjoyed a rich art experience, Jimmy's father was flattered and pleased by the school's invitation, and Jimmy's ego was bolstered every time he heard, "Say! Your father's a pretty good artist!"

However, in order to realize all of the advantages of this practice there are a few cautions the teacher should observe. It is important to make sure that the parent's contribution is suited to the interest and comprehension of young children and that the parent understand a child audience, its sphere of interest, level of comprehension, and span of attention. As any teacher knows, not everyone is adept at working with young children and the invited resource person, regardless of how gifted he is, will be unsuccessful unless he is well acquainted with an immature audience.

The point was made earlier that parents should not be exploited when helping with school activities. This same caution should be observed when they are asked to serve as resource personnel. It is assumed that most parents are happy to contribute but, after all, there is a limit! If Mrs. Jones is asked to speak to the fourth grade one week, the sixth the next week, and still another class two weeks later it is fairly easy to predict the ultimate outcome. In order to avoid this situation, many schools keep a resource file in the central office. Such a file lists available resource materials, facilities, and people in the community and notes when and how they have contributed to the school. It obviously has the double advantage of informing all teachers of available resources and avoiding the overuse of any of them. The following account describes how teachers and parents cooperatively developed and maintained a functional resource file for the school's use and the benefits it yielded.

During the opening weeks of the school year in a new elementary building, teachers and principal were impressed with the wide range of occupations, interests, and special skills represented by the parents of the children in the school. At the organization meeting of the parents' group early in the fall, plans were set in motion to find out just what talents and hobbies were available for use in the classrooms of the school. A committee, consisting of two parents, a teacher, and the principal, was organized to look into the possibilities . . .

The school-community coordinator summarized the information and set up a filing system under four large headings: collections, hobbies, occupations, and talents. Under "collections" were such items as foreign travels, rocks, stamps, plants, tropical fish, model airplanes, coins, records, and Indian relics. Hobbies which were listed included woodworking, photography, ceramics, weaving, leather and metalcraft, magic, puppet-making, radio, and Indian lore. A variety of special talents was represented—painting, dramatics, travel talks, playing musical instruments, speaking foreign languages. Among the parents in the school were geologists, ministers, teachers, lawyers, doctors, psychologists, and many more.

The resource file was placed in the office for use by teachers and others who had need of it. Original questionnaires were filed alphabetically in a central place for use by teachers and other school personnel. Records are kept up to date by the secretary. Newcomers to the school and community constantly add to the file.

As a result of the activity, many people have had and continue to have the experience of participation in a school-community project. Parents enjoy coming to the school to share their particular resources with children. Boys and girls profit greatly from their visits. Teachers, in turn, learn to know the community better and have a deeper understanding of the youngsters they teach and the homes from which they come. Parents seem to feel the school belongs to them, and an increasing number of civic groups are using the school auditorium. As a result of the participation of so many individuals in the program, parents are eager to have teachers use the vast resources at hand to provide a richer learning experience for children.[25]

4. *Parent-teacher organizations.* Probably the most common channel of parent participation is membership in an organization for teachers and parents. Although there are various types of these associations today, the largest and best known is the National Congress of Parents and Teachers, commonly known as the PTA.

The National Congress of Mothers was formed in 1897 through the efforts of Mrs. Alice Birney and Mrs. Phoebe Hearst. The first meeting, held on February 17 in Washington, D. C., was an overwhelming success. The more than two thousand who "swept into Washington like a tidal wave—filling and overflowing the ballroom of the Arlington Hotel, sitting on window ledges, blocking the doors" and the hundreds who were turned away well exceeded Mrs. Birney's modest hope, "I shall be satisfied . . . even if only twenty-five are there."[26] From its inception, the members of the congress were occupied with a dual concern, (1) "to learn how to be good parents and teachers of their children" and (2) "to take the institutions of their common life in hand and make them help rather than hinder the growth of children."[27] This concern included, of course, the education of the child and over the next few years the need for home-school cooperation received such emphasis that in 1908 the name was

[25] Gertrude H. Fitzwater, "Cooperation Helps Individual Classrooms," *Citizen Cooperation for Better Public Schools,* Nelson B. Henry, ed., Fifty-third Yearbook, National Society for the Study of Education, Part I (Washington, D. C., 1954), pp. 87-88.

[26] National Conference of Parents and Teachers, *Golden Jubilee History* (Chicago, 1947), p .18.

[27] Harry and Bonaro Overstreet, *Where Children Come First* (Chicago, National Congress of Parents and Teachers, 1949), p. 5.

changed to the National Congress of Mothers and Parent-Teacher Associations which was streamlined in 1924 to its present title, the National Congress of Parents and Teachers.

During the sixty-seven years of its existence, the PTA has grown steadily. As of April 15, 1963 its total membership was 12,131,318.[28] This figure includes more than 47,000 local units, fifty state congresses, and a state branch for overseas dependent schools which is known as the European Congress of American Parents and Teachers. There are also chapters in other parts of the world.

The objectives that guide the association have remained fairly standard and are:

To promote the welfare of children in home, school, church, and community.

To raise the standards of home life.

To secure adequate laws for the care and protection of children and youth.

To bring into closer relation the home and the school, that parents and teachers may cooperate intelligently in the training of the child.

To develop between educators and the general public such united efforts as will secure for every child the highest advantages in physical, mental, social, and spiritual education.

5. *Room mothers and room councils.* A very common practice in many schools is the designation of certain parents to assist the teacher in organizing certain activities and to act as a liaison between the school and other parents in the classroom. Most of the time a room mother acts in this capacity although in some schools a married couple is appointed to serve as room parents. In still others, a small group acts as a room council. Assisting with field trips, organizing special programs and projects, and contacting or enlisting the aid of other parents for various events are usually the chief channels through which these parents assist and participate in the school program.

THE SCHOOL MUST EXERT EVERY EFFORT TO INTERPRET ITS GOALS AND PROGRAM TO THE COMMUNITY. It was stated earlier that one of the fundamental goals of good public relations is a consistent program of information and interpretation of the school program. The techniques through which this can be achieved are numerous. Some found to be most successful are the following:

1. *School publications.* The school newspaper or magazine is an excellent public relations device, since it usually contains accounts of special events as well as a full coverage of classroom activities. In addition, many schools send out newsletters to parents at regular intervals to keep them

[28] Letter to the author.

informed of important happenings. Other brochures and booklets on special subjects such as *How Children Learn to Read, The Kindergarten Program,* or *Your Child's First Year in School* are extremely valuable in helping parents to understand the important facets of the educational program. Of a slightly different nature but equally valuable and appreciated are the helpful bulletins some schools send to parents on such topics as *Suggestions for Your Child's Summertime Reading, Rainy Day Activities for Lively Youngsters,* and *Safety Hints for Vacation Fun.*

2. *Intelligent use of mass media.* There is no more important device for taking the school into the home than the daily newspaper. Most schools designate one teacher as a school reporter whose job it is to see that accounts of all interesting and important events appear in the local newspaper. A distinguished visitor to the school, an unusual classroom visit, a special program, a special distinction awarded to the school or to an individual pupil or teacher all receive proper publicity in the community press. Human relations stories make good news, for example, the story of second-grader Mary who brought her baby lamb to school one day. Some schools also prepare weekly columns introducing their staff to the community; the subject of "Meet Mr. X" may be a story of the principal, a teacher, the custodian, the policeman who assists with the school patrol, the school doctor, a cafeteria worker, or the dairyman who delivers the daily milk to the school.

In recent years, radio and television programs have been used to advantage in publicizing the school program. Programs involving teachers, pupils, or both, such as plays, reading, quiz shows, panel discussions and debates are exceedingly helpful in acquainting the public with the achievements of the school.

Equally valuable are displays and exhibits in such places as community centers and store windows which some schools have used with success. To acquaint the general public with modern methods of education one teacher, for instance, "transformed a large store window into a classroom and conducted a full-day's instruction, with crowds outside watching avidly as loud speakers brought them every teacher question or direction and pupil response."[29]

There is little doubt that mass media are powerful forces in our modern culture and the wise teacher will take advantage of them to further the community's understanding of his responsibilities and achievements.

3. *Devices for reporting pupil progress.* Many schools consider report cards and parent-teacher conferences to be excellent opportunities for interpreting their goals to parents. For further discussion of these techniques, the reader is referred to Chapter 11.

[29] National School Public Relations Association, *op. cit.,* p. 16.

THE SCHOOL MUST MAKE A CONSISTENT EFFORT TO LEARN AND TO UNDER-
STAND THE COMMUNITY. It has been stated repeatedly in this chapter and
others, that no teacher can function to optimum effectiveness unless he is
familiar with the home and community environments of his pupils. The
following devices are among the most common used to achieve this goal.

1. *Home visits.* Visiting the pupil's home is, undoubtedly, one of the
most valuable ways of (1) learning about the child, and (2) establishing
friendly relationships with the parents. It is unfortunate that, today, most
teachers realize fully the value of the home visit and yet evidence indicates that comparatively few make such visits. According to a recent
survey, "Teachers regard visits to pupils' homes as constructive public
relations techniques, but relatively few teachers make such visits a part of
their program. Less than 10 percent of the schools have an organized program to encourage home visits."[30]

This discrepancy between belief and practice is probably caused by
two factors. In the first place, a consistent program of home visits involves
such practical problems as time and transportation. The only solution
to this is, obviously, that the teacher must have a cooperative administration that will do everything possible to encourage and facilitate home
visitation. Secondly, some teachers may be hesitant because they have had,
or have heard of others who have had, an unpleasant experience while
visiting a pupil's home. Adherence to a few practical do's and don'ts, however, is usually all that is needed to make the visit successful.

a. *Do* make the visit at your own volition. The school administration
should encourage but not absolutely insist that teachers visit their pupils'
homes. There are some systems that require *every* teacher to visit the
home of each of his pupils once, twice, or even more times a year. This
seems to be defeating the purpose of the visit. Unless the teacher visits
voluntarily, because he sees the value of the experience, the visit may
become an empty formality with no genuine educational value.

b. *Don't* assume that home visitation is the responsibility of personnel
other than the classroom teacher. In some systems, the school nurse, *visiting teacher*, or social worker acts as the liaison between the home and
the classroom teacher. This is all to the good, but it does not relieve the
teacher from the responsibility of becoming acquainted with the home.
No knowledge, learned secondhand from another school official, will
substitute for the direct experience of being a guest in a pupil's home,
becoming acquainted with his parents, and thus seeing the child in the
total context of his environment.

c. *Do* make proper arrangements for a visit. It seems almost unnecessary
to remind teachers that they should not merely drop in on parents. Im-

[30] "Teachers View Public Relations," *op. cit.*, p. 35.

promptu visiting is usually reserved only for very close friends and may cause embarrassment or inconvenience if done by a socially insensitive teacher. A short note or telephone call asking if a certain day or time would be convenient will greatly help to insure the success of the visit.

d. *Do* consult with your principal before visiting a pupil's home. In a few communities, particularly in certain cosmopolitan areas, the neighborhood is such that any home visitation may be unwise and probably should be discouraged. In others, visits to certain homes known to be strongly antischool may have embarrassing results. It is strongly suggested, therefore, that the teacher, particularly if he is new to the community, check first with the principal or social worker concerning the attitude of a home he wishes to visit.

e. *Do* apply the same rules of social etiquette to home visitations as to any other informal visit. It seems a little insulting to the teacher's social intelligence to spell out the rules of conduct governing a home visit. Obviously the visit should not be too lengthy, obviously the teacher is a guest in another's home, obviously he should not give any indication of inspecting the home, and obviously the conversation should be of mutual interest. One of the primary goals of the visit is to build a bond of friendship between home and school and the teacher's conduct should be guided accordingly. As Hymes says, "Nothing in making a home visit differs in any way from the countless other visits you have made in all the years of your past: visits to new neighbors, to church members, to fellow alumni of your college, to new colleagues."[31]

f. *Don't* make the home visit an occasion for discussing a pupil's faults or shortcomings. In the past, many parents have been apprehensive about the teacher's visits because they were only precipitated by the child's difficulty or misbehavior in school. Today, if a pupil's behavior demands a conference with the parent most schools insist that it be held *in the school* and *not in the home*. There are several reasons for this: (1) If home visits are to be successful they should be removed entirely from a negative concept, (2) the atmosphere of the classroom or school office is more conducive to a business conference than that of the living room, (3) there is less likelihood of distraction in the school than in the home, (4) the teacher has available in school the pupil's complete record, and (5) the teacher may determine the tone and context of the conference more than in the home. This last point was brought home very forcefully to Miss G one day when she decided to call upon Frank's parents to discuss Frank's antisocial behavior on the playground. Unfortunately, she found Frank's parents extremely defensive and resentful of her criticism of their son. In Frank's presence (if the conference had been held in her classroom or in the school office, the teacher could easily have asked the child to wait

[31] James L. Hymes, *op. cit.,* p. 133.

in another room) they defended his actions and berated Miss G at length for "picking on him." Needless to say, the unhappy Miss G left as soon as possible, thoroughly discomforted, but with a well-learned lesson. In a conference that may become unpleasant or disagreeable the teacher is at an advantage if it is held on his home base, the school.

2. *Business education day.* In recent years, many schools and communities have participated in a Business-Education-Industry Day sponsored by the United States Chamber of Commerce. The usual procedure is to close school for the day to permit all teachers and school administrators to tour one or more of the local business or industrial plants. The goal is obviously to orient educators to their community and to acquaint them with the community resources available to them for expanding their classroom program. In general, the day appears to be well received by both school and community and represents another step toward mutual understanding and support.

3. *Community study or orientation programs.* Some school systems sponsor rather detailed community studies, done by a corps of teachers, which are then placed on file for use by new teachers. Such studies contain valuable information concerning population growth and distribution, socio-economic status, commercial interests, housing trends, socio-ethnic groups, and other items of interest.

Somewhat similar are the community orientation programs of certain systems. Usually designed for new teachers, these programs may encompass a week or more of intensive community study prior to the opening of school in September. Beginning staff members are conducted on intensive tours of various parts of the community, are helped to find suitable housing, are introduced to local business men, are invited to attend meetings of church, civic, and service organizations and, in general, are thoroughly oriented to the community in which they are going to work.

THE SCHOOL MAY SPONSOR MANY WORTHWHILE PUPIL ACTIVITIES THAT CONTRIBUTE TO SCHOOL-COMMUNITY UNDERSTANDING. It cannot be stressed too strongly, that certain pupil activities can provide a strong link in the public relations program. An individual or group of pupils, operating in the community, demonstrates more forcefully than any other single factor the school's goals and achievements. The teacher should be constantly alert to the public relations value of such desirable educational activities as the following:

1. *Field trips and excursions.* In addition to what children receive from a field trip, they also give something. They give an impression—to the storekeeper, factory manager, or police captain they visit and interview as well as to the public at large. Their conduct speaks louder than any words of the discipline and social knowledge they have learned at school.

Their questions and comments indicate the background, interest, and knowledge they have of the subject they are studying. A noisy, disobedient group of children whose irrelevant and superficial questions convey little grasp of the problem they are trying to solve or the goal they are trying to reach can be a real stumbling block to a positive public-relations program. Good teachers are well aware of the educational values of field trips; they are equally aware of their importance as a public-relations device when handled correctly.

2. *Participation in community affairs.* Cooperating with community agencies by having pupils participate in certain events is another important step toward mutual support. The school orchestra or Glee Club can give a short performance, for instance, one night a week in a local store during the busy pre-Christmas shopping season. Or a sixth grade class may present a program consisting of a social studies quiz at a meeting of the local Kiwanis or Rotary club. Or an exhibit of children's art work may be displayed in a store window or community center. The now popular Science Fair, often sponsored by the local newspaper or group of merchants, is another example of how school activities can penetrate the life of the community. Certain assignments, also, can be used to weld school and community into a unified educational organization, for example:

Sending representative pupils to interview aged citizens or prominent leaders.

Polling neighbors to discover opinions on current school or civic problems.

Writing the history of the community.

Writing biographical sketches of former mayors.

Preparing materials on personages for whom local streets are named.

Getting reactions of older citizens regarding "the best teacher I ever had."

Ringing doorbells on the night preceding election to remind citizens of their voting privilege.

Making reports on local industries and customs.

Digging up the facts of local history.[32]

Another type of community project is that which approaches the community school concept, in other words that which is aimed at the improvement of the community through the solution of a definite problem. Such service projects, for instance, as (1) improving the dietary habits of the community, (2) studying and making recommendations concerning the elimination of certain traffic hazards, (3) beautifying a public park, and (4) assuming a leadership role in removing racial or ethnic tensions have been undertaken by schools with considerable success both from the

[32] National School Public Relations Association, *op. cit.*, p. 34.

educational and public relations points of view. More frequently than not, these are, of course, one and the same.

SUMMARY

The relationship of the American public school to its community has passed through several distinct stages since the early years of our country. During the colonial era, the schoolmaster and school house were central features from which all educational and many social and civic activities radiated. As the community pattern became more complex and as education became more specialized, the two tended to drift apart, occasionally to the point of complete disinterest or overt antagonism. The emphasis of the early nineteen hundreds on selling the schools to the public was an attempt to correct this situation which, however, met with limited success. Today, in order to realize the school's maximum effectiveness, teachers recognize that the development of a dynamic, two-way program of mutual understanding and cooperation between home, school, and community is one of the most vital challenges on the educational horizon.

The first section of this chapter examined the major sources of tension and misunderstanding between parents and teachers, emphasizing the need for a positive public relations program. The chief sources considered were (1) confusion of roles among teachers and parents, (2) changing theories of education, (3) differences in educational philosophy and practice among the individual schools and school systems, (4) the stereotyped image parent and teacher may have of each other, (5) failure of all concerned to recognize the importance of the problem, and (6) today's increasing attempts on the part of certain groups to undermine the public's faith in its educational system.

The second section considered the goals of a worthwhile program to be (1) to enable the school to accomplish better its task of educating children, (2) to help the parent with his responsibility for rearing his children, (3) to develop a program of consistent guidance for the child, (4) to help the parent understand modern educational theories, (5) to enable the school to enlist the support and interest of the community, and (6) to improve the standard of living in the community. In order to achieve these goals it was recognized that a certain type of program was required. Characteristics of a worthwhile program examined in the next section were (1) the program must emphasize two-way communication and interaction, (2) it should include parents in all types and levels of activities, (3) it should be consistent rather than sporadic, and, most important, (4) it recognizes that the classroom teacher is the most important single factor, upon whom rests the ultimate success or failure of the program.

The last section discussed some of the most successful aids to home-school-community cooperation now used by capable teachers. Aids were examined which (1) provide opportunity for parents to observe the school in action, (2) provide functional opportunities for parents to participate in and contribute to the educational program, (3) enable the school to interpret its program to the public, (4) help the school to become more familiar with its community, and, finally, (5) improve the standard of living and the quality of education for all children and adults.

ADDITIONAL LEARNING EXPERIENCES

Topics for Thought and Discussion

1. What (or who) do you think is behind the scenes of some of the sharp criticism directed toward the public schools in recent years?

2. Do you think that a book such as *Why Johnny Can't Read* or *What Ivan Knows that Johnny Doesn't* ultimately works more to the advantage or disadvantage of the school? To what extent does this answer depend upon the actions of the school and teachers?

3. Some teachers say they prefer *not* to live in the community in which they teach because they do not want to become too familiar with parents and pupils. What is your reaction to this statement? Would you prefer to live in the community in which you teach?

4. What do you think of the policy of some school boards which *requires* teachers to live in the community?

5. Should teachers take an active voice in the political affairs of the community, such as campaigning, running for office, etc.?

6. Should schools reciprocate Business Education Day and invite personnel from business and industry to take a thorough tour of the schools at least one day each year?

7. Recently a principal forbade his staff from shopping in the local stores during their free noon hour on the basis that "it didn't make a good public impression for teachers to be seen shopping during the middle of the day." What is your reaction to this viewpoint?

8. Should teachers' salaries be published in the local newspapers?

9. Some teachers complain because parents frequently call them at their homes in the evening to discuss their child's progress. Are these teachers justified?

10. Do you think that teachers should be required to join the PTA? To attend meetings? To hold office or serve on committees?

11. Do you occasionally view as intruders parents who ask frequently about their child's progress?

12. Do you sometimes see parents as a threat to your authority or security?

Projects and Activities

1. Secure permission from a local merchant to display in his store window an exhibit that will acquaint the community with the philosophy and goals of the modern elementary school.

2. Interview several members of your community. How do they feel about home visits by teachers? What suggestions do they offer? Do they think such visits help to bring about closer understanding and cooperation between home and school? Compare their answers with those of a similar sampling of teachers.

3. Prepare an illustrated booklet which could be sent home to parents explaining a certain facet of the school program such as (1) reading readiness, (2) the new mathematics, (3) the transition from manuscript to cursive writing, (4) the kindergarten program, or (5) the guidance program.

4. Prepare an analytical survey of research on the criticism which has been directed toward public education in popular lay magazines in recent years.

5. Examine a social studies elementary school curriculum guide. Does it reveal a public relations awareness by including a study of schools or education in any unit of work? What possibilities could you suggest to extend this awareness through other units.

6. Prepare a field trip file of twenty-five educationally valuable community resources in or near your community. Describe each resource as to (1) location, (2) necessary arrangements and preparations for visiting, (3) personnel to be contacted, (4) cost, (5) special cautions to be observed, (6) special areas of interest, and (7) particular educational values to be derived.

7. Write an article for your state Parent-Teacher Magazine entitled, "Problem Children or Problem Parents?"

8. List some practical suggestions which can help to eliminate the role confusion which now exists between some teachers and parents.

9. Prepare a radio or television program, a feature article for the newspaper, or an assembly program for American Education Week to acquaint parents with the work of the schools.

10. Describe an existing problem in your community which would motivate a worthwhile and functional school study.

11. Keep a scrapbook of clippings from one or more local newspapers over a several week period. How much space has been devoted to news of the schools? What type of news has been emphasized? What implications do your findings have for the local school system?

12. Distribute a questionnaire to a group of elementary school teachers to determine their participation in certain specific community activities. In what types of activities are these teachers most active? Least active? What conclusions can you draw?

Selected Bibliography

American Association of School Administrators, *Public Relations for America's Schools*. Twenty-eighth Yearbook. Washington, D. C., 1950.

BORTNER, Doyle M., *Public Relations for Teachers*. New York, Simmons-Boardman Books, 1959.

CAMPBELL, Roald, and RAMSEYER, John A., *The Dynamics of School-Community Relationships*. Boston, Allyn and Bacon, Inc., 1955.

Citizen Co-operation for Better Public Schools, Nelson B. Henry, ed. Fifty-third Yearbook, National Society for the Study of Education, Part I. Chicago, 1954.

FINE, Benjamin, *Educational Publicity*, rev. ed. New York, Harper & Row, Publishers, Inc., 1951.

GABBARD, Hazel F., *Working with Parents*. Washington, D. C., U. S. Department of Health, Education, and Welfare, Office of Education, 1949.

HYMES, James L., Jr., *Effective Home-School Relations*. New York, Prentice-Hall, Inc., 1953.

JENSON, Theodore J., and STAUB, W. Frederick, "School-Community Relations." *Review of Educational Research*, Vol. 31 (October, 1961).

KINDRED, Leslie W., *How to Tell the School Story*. Englewood Cliffs, N. J., Prentice-Hall, Inc., 1960.

———, *School Public Relations*. Englewood Cliffs, N. J., Prentice-Hall, Inc., 1957.

LANGDON, Grace, and STOUT, Irving W., *Helping Parents Understand Their Child's School*. Englewood Cliffs, N. J., Prentice-Hall, Inc., 1957.

———, and ———, *Teacher-Parent Interviews*. Englewood Cliffs, N. J., Prentice-Hall, Inc., 1954.

MENGE, J. Wilmer, and FAUNCE, Roland C., *Working Together for Better Schools*. New York, American Book Company, 1953.

MOEHLMAN, Arthur B., and VAN ZWOLL, James A., *School Public Relations*. New York, Appleton-Century-Crofts, 1957.

National Congress of Parents and Teachers, *Golden Jubilee History*. Chicago, 1947.

National School Public Relations Association, *It Starts in the Classroom*. Washington, D. C., National Education Association, 1951.

NEA Research Division, *The Classroom Teacher and Public Relations*. NEA Research Monograph 1959-M2. Washington, D. C., National Education Association, July, 1959.

OSBORNE, Ernest, *The Parent-Teacher Partnership*. New York, Teachers College, Columbia University, 1959.

OVERSTREET, Harry, and Bonaro, *Where Children Come First*. Chicago, National Congress of Parents and Teachers, 1949.

"Teachers View Public Relations." *NEA Research Bulletin*, Vol. 37 (April, 1959).

The Community School, Nelson B. Henry, ed. Fifty-second Yearbook, National Society for the Study of Education, Part II. Chicago, 1953.

The Modern Community School, Edward G. Olsen, ed. New York, Appleton-Century-Crofts, 1953.

The National Elementary Principal, *Parents and the Schools*. Thirty-sixth Yearbook, Department of Elementary School Principals. Washington, D. C., National Education Association, 1957.

The School and Community Reader: Education in Perspective. Edward G. Olsen, ed. New York, The Macmillan Company, 1963.

YEAGER, William A., *School-Community Relations*. New York, Holt, Rinehart, and Winston, Inc., 1951.

CHAPTER 5

Working With Professional Colleagues

MRS. REED IS A CONSCIENTIOUS, capable, and highly regarded third grade teacher. This afternoon, after she dismisses her pupils, she will attend a meeting of a city-wide social studies curriculum committee of which she is a member. This committee has been charged with the responsibility of evaluating and revising the social studies curriculum guide for the entire system. Mrs. Reed realizes fully the importance of this task and has spent, and will spend, many hours on the study, investigation, consultation, and discussion needed for successful results. Tomorrow evening, she will attend a joint meeting of her local professional association and the Board of Education at which the teachers' proposal for a revised salary scale will be reviewed. Later this month, she will travel to the state capital with several friends for the state association's convention, at which she will serve on a panel in a sectional meeting devoted to the topic, "Creative Teaching in the Elementary School."

Does Mrs. Reed consider herself to be an overburdened, imposed-upon individual? Does she consider the above-mentioned responsibilities to be extras or additions to her regular job of teaching? Not at all. On the contrary, Mrs. Reed is fully aware that her role as a teacher is considerably expanded over that of her predecessors many years ago. There was a time, of course, when the teacher's responsibilities and interests, for the most part, were confined within the four walls of his classroom. His relatively low level of scholarliness, status, and professional awareness did not equip him to view teaching as anything more than that activity that took place in the schoolroom. Today, of course, this picture is radically changed. The competent teacher is a well prepared, knowledgeable, and professionally oriented worker. His educational horizons extend far beyond his immediate classroom. He is informed about, and participates in, a variety of professional activities, all of which are directed toward the ultimate improvement of education for every boy and girl in the land. This broadening awareness of multiple dimensions of teacher competence includes two specific roles which are examined in this chapter, namely: (1) a member of the school organization and (2) a member of the organized teaching profession. Consider the first of these for a moment.

The fact that the elementary teacher in the typical self-contained classroom works for several hours each day virtually isolated from his colleagues may lead him occasionally to view himself as a solitary or autonomous figure. This is, of course, a fallacy. The teacher, far from being an isolate, really plays a central role in a complex and highly organized educational system. The successful fulfillment of this role makes several demands upon the teacher, the first of which is that he be thoroughly informed and knowledgeable concerning the organization and administration of our present educational system. The following section is devoted to a brief discussion of this subject.

ORGANIZATION AND ADMINISTRATION OF THE EDUCATIONAL SYSTEM

In order to be an alert and functioning member of a school system, the elementary teacher should be informed about the administration and organization of education on the national, state, and local levels.

THE TEACHER SHOULD BE FAMILIAR WITH THE FEDERAL GOVERNMENT'S RESPONSIBILITY TOWARD EDUCATION. No mention of education is made in the United States Constitution. The Tenth Amendment leaves, by implication, the responsibility, organization, and control of education to the individual states. Because of this decentralized pattern, some assume that the national government is almost completely detached from educational concerns; this is not the case. On the contrary, the federal government, over the years, has manifested its interest in education through the following activities.[1]

1. Providing funds and resources for establishing and conducting numerous educational programs. Of these, a familiar one to all elementary teachers is the subsidized school lunch program for which several hundred million dollars worth of commodities and federal funds have been allocated.

2. Establishing and administering such educational programs as those for armed forces personnel and their dependents.

3. Providing funds and resources for the education of special groups, for instance, the GI educational provisions for veterans.

[1] John K. Norton, "Federal Relations to Education," *Encyclopedia of Educational Research*, 3rd ed., Chester W. Harris, ed. (New York, The Macmillan Company, 1960), pp. 522-541.

4. Establishing advisory, consulting, and research services, most of which are conducted by the United States Office of Education, mentioned below.

The United States Office of Education was created by an act of Congress in 1867. Two years later, the office ceased to become a separate unit and was attached to the Department of the Interior. In 1939, the Office of Education became one of the constituent units of the Federal Security Agency which was replaced in 1953 by the Department of Health, Education, and Welfare. The Office of Education consequently became one of the units of this new department and retains that status at the present time.

The three major functions of the Office are (1) to conduct and make available research findings, studies, and surveys, (2) to provide educational services through conference participation, speaking, writing, consultation, and field work, and (3) to administer grant funds as stipulated by Congress.[2]

The United States Commissioner of Education is the chief federal officer of education and is appointed directly by the President. His major functions are "To determine policy and program objectives; to provide executive leadership for the operations; to render consultive service to educational agencies; to coordinate Office work with related programs within the Department of Health, Education, and Welfare; to conduct liaison with the Executive, Legislative, and Judicial Branches of the Government; and to advise with National, State, and local officials on educational problems."[3]

Those who have held this office since its inception are:

Henry Barnard
John Eaton
N. H. R. Dawson
William T. Harris
Elmer E. Brown
Philander P. Claxton
John James Tigert
William John Cooper
George F. Zook
John W. Studebaker
Earl James McGrath
Lee M. Thurston
Samuel Miller Brownell
Lawrence G. Derthick
Sterling M. McMurrin
Francis Keppel

[2] Office of Education, *Handbook* (Washington, D. C., U. S. Department of Health, Education, and Welfare, 1957), pp. 4-5.
[3] *Ibid.*, p. 7.

In summary, then, the teacher should be aware of the fact that, in spite of our decentralized educational pattern, the national government does play an important role in many educational concerns and interests.

THE CLASSROOM TEACHER IS PART OF A STATE EDUCATIONAL SYSTEM. As was stated previously, each state has autonomy in its administration and organization of education. Among the many state agencies concerned with education, the following are the most important and are those with which the teacher should be thoroughly familiar.

1. *The State Legislature.* Except for restrictions placed upon it by the state or federal constitutions, the state legislature has plenary power over all school districts. The relationship of the state legislature to education is stated in the following basic legal principles.

(1) State legislatures have absolute power to control public schools unless limited by constitutional provisions. (State constitutions generally turn the subject over to the legislatures.)

(2) The control of education is in no way inherent in the local self-government except as the legislatures have chosen to make it so.

(3) Public education may be a separate field distinct from local government.

(4) The legislature having tried one method of school administration and maintenance is not precluded from trying another.

(5) Education is a State function even though the legislature provides no State central control or State agency for its administration.[4]

2. *The Governor.* The governor, as the chief executive officer of the state, possesses considerable responsibility for, and control over, the educational program. His powers involving education are generally located in one or more of the following areas:

(1) appointment of policy-making and administrative personnel of State educational agencies, (2) membership on, or chairmanship of, commissions and boards which make State educational policy, (3) authority over budget and other central administrative services of State education agencies, and (4) influence over proposed new educational legislation.[5]

3. *The State Board of Education.* This term, as used here, refers to general state boards of education, and not to those that perform specialized functions such as state boards for vocational education. At present all states but Illinois and Wisconsin have such general boards. The number of members on the board varies from three in Mississippi and Oregon

---

[4] Ward W. Keesecker, *State Boards of Education and Chief State School Officers* (Washington, D. C., Federal Security Agency, Office of Education, 1950), p. 6.
[5] Fred F. Beach and Robert F. Will, *The State and Education* (Washington, D. C., U. S. Department of Health, Education, and Welfare, Office of Education, 1955), p. 5.

to twenty-three in Ohio. The method of selecting members varies according to states and includes the following: (1) ex officio membership (consisting of state officials such as the state treasurer, secretary, and attorney general, (2) election by popular vote, (3) election by school board conventions, (4) election by the state legislature, and (5) appointment by the governor.

The state board's degree of responsibility for public education varies also according to states. In some states it has the sole or major responsibility; in others it shares responsibility with one or more other state agencies.

4. *The Chief State School Officer.* Every state has a chief administrative officer of its public educational system, who may be known as the Superintendent of Public Instruction, Commissioner of Education, Superintendent of Education, or by a similar title.

There are three methods used to select the chief state school officer. In five states (New Jersey, Pennsylvania, Tennessee, Virginia, and Alaska) he is appointed by the Governor. In twenty-two states he is elected by popular vote, five of which are on a nonpartisan ballot. In twenty-three states he is appointed by the state board of education.[6] All three methods have their advantages and disadvantages, and arguments supporting or rejecting each are readily available. In general, however, students of educational administration appear to favor appointment by the state board and, over the years, this method has grown in popularity.

The qualifications, responsibilities, powers, duties, length of term, and salary of the chief state school officer vary widely according to states. In general, however, it may be said that an outstanding trend of recent years has been the steadily increasing stature of the office. The following statement summarizes the nature of this trend.

The chief state school officer is far more important in the administration of education than he was a decade ago. Even then he was adding many professional responsibilities to the predominantly statistical and clerical duties that had long characterized his office, but recently his duties have multiplied. He has gained in professional stature. His older functions of inspection and approval have given way to professional leadership and stimulation of educational programs in local school districts throughout the state. The theme of his principal work tends increasingly toward professional leadership and away from routine official functions.[7]

5. *The State Department of Education.* As with its chief officer, the status of the entire department of education is generally rising. During

[6] National Education Association, *Selection of Chief State School Officers and State Boards of Education* (Washington, D. C., May, 1962), mimeographed.

[7] Edgar Fuller, "State School Systems," *Encyclopedia of Educational Research,* 3rd ed., Chester W. Harris, ed. (New York, The Macmillan Company, 1960), p. 1387.

the past decade, it has greatly increased its number of personnel and has assumed added responsibilities and services. As a consequence, most state departments today are vital forces, contributing greatly to the improvement of education within the state. As a general rule, their services may be classified into three categories:

a. *The administration of federal programs of education.* For the most part, federal programs (such as the National Defense Education Act) are administered through the state department of education and *not* directly from the national level to the local system.

b. *Consulting and leadership services.* The personnel of the state departments are active in providing services designed to strengthen and coordinate instructional and curriculum programs throughout the state. Indicative of the extent of these services is a survey by Savage of eight midwestern states, which reports that the state departments "provided consultative service to the local school systems in a wider range of school activities and problems than did any other source" and that they are "the most powerful outside influence in the improvement of local programs of education."[8]

c. *Conducting research and investigation.* Each state department maintains a staff whose major responsibility is the continual survey and evaluation of educational programs and facilities. For example, in 1954 the New Jersey State Department of Education conducted a survey of the number of mentally retarded children in the state. This survey resulted in legislation that required each school system to provide special classes and facilities for the mentally retarded.

It has been possible in these few pages to present only a skeletal description of the state educational system. It should be repeated, however, that each classroom teacher has a definite responsibility to be thoroughly informed concerning the organization and services of his state department of education if he is to function at his maximum professional level.

THE CLASSROOM TEACHER SHOULD BE THOROUGHLY INFORMED CONCERNING HIS LOCAL ADMINISTRATIVE UNIT. There are, at present, more than 50,000 local administrative units, ranging in size from one teacher and a few pupils to very large, complex organizations. In general, the local system has a high degree of autonomy concerning its educational regulations and requirements. It is usually administered by a board of education and a professional staff of administrators and teachers. A very common organizational pattern is the *line-and-staff* system described briefly below.

THE LINE-AND-STAFF DESIGNATION OF AUTHORITY IS THE OLDEST AND MOST COMMON ORGANIZATIONAL PATTERN. It is the hierarchical pattern used tradi-

[8] William W. Savage, "Local School Systems and Their Consultants," *Administrator's Notebook*, Vol. 4 (October, 1955), n. p.

tionally by industry and the military forces and was adopted by education when the growing size of the local unit demanded a clear-cut delegation of authority. The *line* of authority is clearly designated and runs vertically down from the board of education to the superintendent to his assistant, district, or deputy superintendents to the building principal to the classroom teacher. The authority of each line personnel is clearly defined and each is subordinate to the position just above him.

Staff personnel are usually those persons who serve in an advisory capacity. In most systems, they report directly to the superintendent or his assistants. They work closely with teachers and principals although, if they are strictly staff personnel, they have no authority over either. Staff officers employed by many local systems include the following:

General Supervisor. Since his primary concern is the improvement of instruction, the general supervisor usually works very closely with the classroom teacher. His duties usually consist of (1) observing the work of the teacher and offering constructive guidance, assistance, and advice for his improvement, (2) acquainting teachers with worthwhile instructional aids and materials, (3) teaching occasional demonstration lessons for individuals or small groups, and (4) offering leadership and consultant service to committees, institutes, and workshops directly related to the improvement of instruction or curriculum.

The scope of the general supervisor's responsibility usually depends upon the size of the school system. In some systems, he is responsible for all grades in the elementary school. In others, he may work only on certain grade levels, for instance, kindergarten through third grades, or perhaps only a single grade. In still other systems, he may be assigned to work only with first-year teachers or those not under tenure.

Personnel who serve in this capacity are known by a variety of titles although supervisor or helping teacher may be the most common. Regardless of the title, however, these persons are concerned almost solely with the improvement of instruction and, consequently, work closely and directly with the classroom teacher.

Special Area Personnel. Many systems employ specialized personnel in such areas as reading, art, science, music, foreign languages, or physical education. Such individuals usually assume overall responsibility for the quality of instruction in their particular areas. Depending upon their titles and specific assignments, specialized personnel usually function in one of two classifications:

1. *As a special teacher.* Some specialized personnel have the title and duties of special teachers which means they work directly with pupils in the classrooms. Depending upon the size and philosophy of the system, the special teacher either assumes full responsibility for instruction in his area or works

cooperatively with the classroom teacher. In any case, he works directly with pupils, usually on a fairly fixed schedule, a:.d thus differs from the consultant who works primarily with teachers.

2. *As a consultant.* The newer trend with specialized personnel is to use them as consultants. This means that they work most closely with teachers and principals and only indirectly with pupils in the classroom. The consultant's duties consist of (1) apprising teachers of new materials and promising curriculum developments in his field, (2) organizing and chairing committees for curriculum revision and improvement, (3) teaching demonstration lessons, (4) arranging teachers' institutes and workshops, (5) developing and maintaining a curriculum laboratory of materials and teaching aids which he makes available to teachers, (6) routing to teachers the best professional books and periodicals in his field, and (7) being on call to visit classrooms by request to offer assistance and advice.

Using specialized personnel as consultants appears to have several advantages over using them as special teachers. In the first place, they can offer a much wider variety of services to the educational program. Secondly, their more flexible schedule permits them to give concentrated help to teachers when and where it is needed as compared to the special teacher who works on a fixed schedule, dividing his time evenly among all classes for which he is responsible. Lastly, the use of these individuals on a consultant basis appears to keep intact all the advantages of the self-contained classroom, while, at the same time, it offers to the classroom teacher specialized assistance in those areas in which he is most deficient.

It should be remembered that this discussion is necessarily very general, for the *exact* duties, responsibilities, and relationships of the specialized functionaries are, of course, determined by each individual system's need and facilities.

Child Guidance Personnel. With the increasing emphasis upon child guidance and mental health, many school systems have added specialized staff personnel in this area. The school psychologist, psychiatrist, guidance counselor, nurse, physician, dentist, and others are usually classified as staff personnel. These individuals work almost entirely with individual children and serve in a liaison capacity between the school and the home, clinic, or any other agency affecting the physical and mental health of the child.

In summary, the line-and-staff pattern is the oldest and probably the most common type of administrative organization used by school systems today. Figure 5.1 on page 166 illustrates a typical administrative system organized according to the line-and-staff theory.

IN SOME SYSTEMS, A PATTERN OF DEMOCRATIC ADMINISTRATION HAS REPLACED OR MODIFIED THE OLDER LINE-AND-STAFF ORGANIZATION. The line-and-staff pattern has long been under fire from students of educational

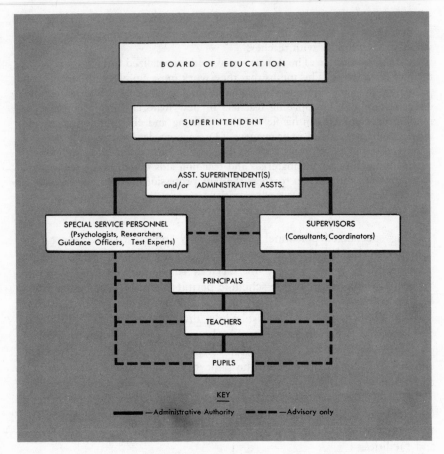

FIGURE 5.1

Conventional line and staff organization of schools. From Jefferson N.
Eastmond, *The Teacher and School Administration,* (Boston, Houghton
Mifflin Company, 1959), p. 164.

administration. It has been criticized on many bases, chief of which are
its authoritarianism, lack of flexibility, and failure to recognize and encourage the full potential of the classroom teacher. As a consequence,
many systems are moving today toward a more democratic administrative
pattern which encourages widespread teacher participation. In general,
there are two main channels for this teacher participation. There is the
faculty advisory council consisting of teachers elected or appointed to
serve in an advisory capacity to the superintendent or, in the case of individual schools, to the principal. Such councils came into being during the
early years of the twentieth century, and are today fairly common

throughout the country. Where they are successful, they ". . . work in harmony with teachers on the one hand, and the administration and board of education on the other for the solution of common problems."[9] The other major channel of teacher participation in democratic administration is through numerous committees, formed to attack a wide variety of problems. A more extensive discussion of teacher participation in administrative matters, usually through these two major media, is contained in the following section.

TEACHER-ADMINISTRATIVE RELATIONSHIPS

On page 159 it was stated that the teacher's role as a member of a school system makes several demands upon him, the first one of which was that he be *informed* concerning the organization and administration of education in this country as discussed in the previous section. The second demand is that he be *able and willing to participate* in certain administrative responsibilities. Before proceeding on this point further, however, it seems wise to caution the teacher in two respects. First, his assuming an active role and interest in administrative concerns *does not mean* that he should usurp the responsibility of the administrator. Many duties and decisions are, and should be, solely the concern of the superintendent or principal and need not involve the classroom teacher. Secondly, the teacher's interest and participation in administrative matters should not be so demanding of his time that he neglects his classroom responsibilities. With these two cautions in mind, let us examine the teacher's role in certain administrative concerns.

THE CLASSROOM TEACHER'S PARTICIPATION IN ADMINISTRATION IS A FORWARD STEP IN EDUCATION. The expanding role of the teacher has resulted in a far different teacher-administrative relationship from that of a few years ago. Far from being only a passive recipient, today's teacher is actively interested and engaged in certain policy-making areas. Eastmond emphasizes this changed relationship in the following statement.

Undoubtedly the greatest change in a teacher's role and responsibilities during the most recent decades is related to the actual administration of schools. No longer can the good teacher confine his efforts solely to classroom instruction and leave administration to someone else. The time is gone when governing and conducting a school system were legitimately the concern of only a handful of administrators. In those days the teachers remained suspicious and uninformed about such matters and were content to form their passive opinions about administration on the basis of newspaper stories or information via the

---

[9] William A. Yeager, *Administration and the Teacher* (New York, Harper & Row, Publishers, 1954), p. 416.

grapevine. Today the teacher must keep interested and active in administration. He is expected to work with others in actually assuming some administrative duties and exercising whatever leadership he may be capable of rendering.[10]

THE CLASSROOM TEACHER'S PARTICIPATION IN ADMINISTRATION CAN BE DEFENDED ON SEVERAL BASES. There are several sound reasons why the teacher should be encouraged to take an active part in administration:

1. In earlier days, the teacher's meagre professional preparation and scholarly background did not equip him to meet the broader challenges of educational administration. Today, this is not true. The classroom teacher is well prepared, professionally alert, and well able to assume a leadership role along with his administrative colleagues.

2. The idea that several heads are better than one is trite but true. Administrative policy based upon the experiences, suggestions, and contributions of several individuals is usually superior to that stemming from a single authoritative source.

3. Research shows a direct relationship between the teacher's opportunity to participate in policy making and his satisfaction with teaching. Participation is, therefore, a decided positive morale factor. Supporting this viewpoint is a study which concludes that,

> Teachers who report opportunity to participate regularly and actively in making policies are much more likely to be enthusiastic about their school systems than those who report limited opportunity to participate.
>
> ...many teachers today feel that they have a right to participate in the determination of policies related to the curriculum and instruction, to salaries and working conditions, and to many other aspects of educational planning. They are likely to become resentful and unhappy if such opportunities are denied.[11]

4. Most important of all, the teacher's participation in democratic administration implements our generally accepted modern philosophy of education. Today, considerable emphasis is placed upon the development of self-direction, self-discipline, initiative, and creative thinking in the classroom. No teacher can be expected to understand or implement this democratic objective in his classroom if he himself is operating within a strictly rigid and authoritarian system. If teachers are expected to develop abilities of democratic leadership and creativity among their pupils, it seems fairly obvious that they must function in an environment conducive to the development of these qualities in themselves.

We may conclude, therefore, that the teacher's participation in administration is a wholesome, forward-looking, and thoroughly sound edu-

[10] Jefferson N. Eastmond, *The Teacher and School Administration* (Boston, Houghton Mifflin Company, 1959), p. 161.
[11] "The Teacher and Policy Making," *Administrator's Notebook*, Vol. 1 (May, 1952), n. p.

cational development, contributing directly to the improvement of the profession and the quality of education.

THERE ARE SEVERAL TYPES AND DEGREES OF TEACHER PARTICIPATION IN PLANNING AND POLICY MAKING. The kind and amount of teacher participation in determining policy range from nearly none in some communities to a great deal in others. In general, the following activities are usually mentioned as those in which teachers most often participate.

1. *Curriculum development.* Except for certain restrictions or prescriptions imposed by the legislature or the state department of education, each local system has autonomy in determining its curriculum content and pattern. Usually this is done by committees composed jointly of classroom teachers and supervisory personnel. On the whole, there appears to be general agreement that teachers should, and do, participate strongly in this activity. One study, for instance, reports that the majority of the 568 teachers questioned believed that teachers should be solely or jointly responsible for the determination of instructional objectives and curriculum content.[12] That this is often supported by actual practice, is indicated in another survey in which 62 per cent of elementary principals replied that "classroom teachers, principals, and supervisors develop the curriculum cooperatively for the school system with adaptation to individual schools up to the principal and teachers."[13]

2. *Selecting and requesting the purchase of instructional materials.* This is another area in which theory and practice support teacher participation. It is reported by 59 per cent of elementary principals that "the faculty, working together, makes requests for materials in terms of the school program."[14] Opinions of teachers as to who should be responsible for specific duties in this area are summarized as follows:

Establishment of criteria for the selection of instructional materials—groups of teachers and principal.

Selection of materials for a subject or class—individual teachers.

Determination of amount of money to be set aside in school's budget for instructional materials—superintendent.

Determination of amount of money to be given to each department and teacher for instructional materials—superintendent and principal.[15]

The importance teachers attach to this responsibility was also discovered in a study of job expectations of experienced teachers. August

[12] "Who Should Make What Decisions?" *Administrator's Notebook*, Vol. 3 (April, 1955), n. p.

[13] "Elementary School Principals," *NEA Research Bulletin*, Vol. 36 (December, 1958), pp. 105-106.

[14] *Ibid.*, p. 106.

[15] "Who Should Make What Decisions?" *op. cit.*

reports that experienced teachers, seeking new positions, attach major importance to provision for participating in the selection of school supplies.[16]

3. *Determining policies affecting teacher welfare.* Today's teacher is keenly interested and actively participates in decision making affecting teacher welfare and status. In most communities, representatives of the local educational association are actively involved in decisions concerning such matters as salary, sick leave, and promotional policies.

4. *Developing the system of pupil accounting.* Teachers are frequently asked to assume partial responsibility for developing or revising record forms, report cards, evaluation procedures, testing programs and other matters related to pupil accounting.

5. *Determining the grade placement of pupils.* In the previously mentioned survey, 76 per cent of the elementary principals reported that, ". . . within the framework of general school system policies, the teacher works with parents, child, and principal on placing each child."[17]

6. *Recruiting, selecting, and recommending teachers for employment.* There appears to be a conflict between theory and practice on this point. Many students of educational administration strongly recommend that teachers be involved in the selection of new personnel on the theory that they may have a clearer concept of the competencies needed for a specific teaching assignment than either the principal or superintendent. Illustrative of this position is the following statement.

Teachers whose assignments are similar to those inherent in the vacancies to be filled often have insights and knowledge regarding the qualifications needed which administrators and supervisors do not possess. Experience indicates that one of the most important sources of information about qualified applicants is the classroom teacher. Therefore, teachers should be encouraged to suggest names and their recommendations should be given full consideration.[18]

Although this appears to be a defensible theory, it is apparently not implemented to a great extent in actual practice. On the contrary, there appears to be some evidence that principals *and* teachers disagree strongly with the idea, teachers more so than principals, probably because they are still reluctant to assume responsibilities that traditionally and legally have

[16] Stephen August, "Comparison of Connecticut Superintendents' Beliefs Concerning Job Expectations of Experienced Teachers with Reported Expectations of the Same Teachers" (unpublished Doctoral thesis, University of Connecticut, 1958).

[17] "Elementary School Principals," *op. cit.*, p. 106.

[18] American Association of School Administrators, *Staff Relations in School Administration*, Thirty-third Yearbook (Washington, D. C., National Education Association, 1955), p. 35.

been exclusively those of the administrator.[19] Another study reports that teachers feel that the exact responsibilities in this area should be delegated to the following persons.

Determination of policies relating to the selection, promotion, retention, or dismissal of teachers—superintendent and board of education.

Recommendation of a particular candidate for employment—superintendent.

Promotion, dismissal or rehiring of teachers—superintendent and principal.[20]

7. *Planning and conducting faculty meetings.* This is another area on which there is disagreement. In general, authorities strongly advocate the involvement of teachers in this responsibility and administrators tend to agree. On the other hand, teachers apparently do not support the principle as strongly, probably again because they have long viewed their role as *receivers* rather than participants in such activities.[21]

THE CLASSROOM TEACHER SHOULD RECOGNIZE AND MEET HIS OBLIGATIONS TOWARD THE ADMINISTRATION. Harmonious teacher-administrative relationships depend greatly upon the extent to which each group fulfills the expectations of the other. What are the competencies and attitudes every school administration may justifiably expect of its teachers?

First, the administration has a right to expect each teacher to perform to the best of his ability. This is such an obvious truth that it needs no elaboration. The teacher who cheats children by doing a second or third rate job of teaching is obviously unfair and dishonest to his pupils, his profession, and to the school system paying his salary.

Secondly, the administration is entitled to *loyalty* and *support* from its teachers. No school administration can function successfully unless it has allegiance and cooperation from the teaching staff. Teachers, as professional persons, *must* refrain from openly criticizing their administration and from creating unrest or disharmony among its employees. This does *not* mean, however, that the teacher must become a complete conformist deprived of any voice or action that conflicts with the philosophy or policies of the system. On the contrary, if the teacher finds himself in disagreement with the administration, the following alternatives are open to him.

It is entirely possible that a teacher joins a school system only to discover that its educational philosophy or administrative organization are completely incompatible with his own ideas. If this is the case, the teacher owes it to himself and his pupils to leave the system at the termination of

[19] Harry J. Merigis, "Attitudinal Differences between Principals and Teachers," *National Elementary Principal*, Vol. 40 (April, 1961), p. 36.
[20] "Who Should Make What Decisions?", *op. cit.*
[21] Harry J. Merigis, *op. cit.*, p. 37.

his contract. To do otherwise will create inner frustrations and tensions which will inevitably affect, not only his personal happiness, but the effectiveness of his teaching as well.

In cases where the disagreement is not serious enough to warrant leaving the system, the teacher should keep in mind that he is free to voice his ideas, grievances, suggestions, and complaints through *regularly established channels*. He may call the matter to the attention of his immediate administrative officer (usually the principal in the elementary school) and, if satisfaction is not received, he can continue up the line of administrative authority. Or he can take his problem to certain other groups such as (1) the grievance committee (which exists in some systems), (2) the faculty advisory council, or (3) the local or state professional association. Each of these groups, if it performs as it should, will examine the teacher's problem or grievance and take action on it if the facts so warrant.

To summarize this point, every teacher owes his administration his loyalty, cooperation, and support. This does not mean, however, that the teacher is not free to act as a self-directing individual. He is *always* free to voice his grievances or disagreements through proper and professional channels. He is *not* free to criticize the administration indiscriminately to either fellowteachers or community members; he is *not* free to create dissatisfaction and tension among the various employees; and he is *not* free to indulge in endless griping and petty complaining, the chief purpose of which is always destructive and never constructive!

Thirdly, the administration has a right to expect teachers to comply with the established policies and routines upon which an efficient organization depends. Certain rules and regulations are needed to administer any complex organization and, for the sake of efficiency, even the most individualistic must comply. Reporting attendance, requisitioning supplies, completing statistical reports, and collecting lunch money are typical of the routine and clerical tasks which demand promptness and accuracy from every teacher in the system. Mr. Jones may be a creative teacher in the classroom but he is a thorn in the side of his principal if his attendance report is never submitted on time, or his supply inventory is invariably inaccurate.

Fourthly, the classroom teacher should recognize his obligation to keep the principal informed concerning events happening in his classroom or to his pupils. Pupil accidents, parental complaints, or serious infractions of school rules should, unless otherwise stated, be reported to the principal so that he will not be completely in the dark if he hears about them from other sources. Also, inviting the principal frequently to the classroom, notifying him of certain pupils' progress, or informing him of classroom events of interest are sincerely appreciated by the administrator who is interested in all aspects of the school program.

Fifthly, the administration has a right to expect every teacher to recognize existing channels of authority. The teacher, in all matters, works closely with his immediate administrative superior, usually the building principal. He does *not* go over the principal's head and confer with other administrative personnel unless he notifies the principal that he intends to do so. If, as was stated earlier, the teacher has a grievance, he has an unqualified right to take this to the highest administrative officer in the system. He must, however, proceed through the proper avenues of authority and advise each officer that, if necessary, he intends to take his problem to the next highest level. Furthermore, this procedure is not only followed in grievance cases but in ordinary daily contacts as well. For instance, if the teacher wants to invite the superintendent to an assembly program for which his class is responsible, professional courtesy dictates that he consult first with the principal concerning the wisdom of this action or, at the very least, notify him of his intent.

There are, of course, many other obligations the teacher has toward his administrative officers, depending upon the individual system. As a rule, personal consideration and respect, professional courtesy, and observance of the policies of the system are all the teacher needs to guide his relationships toward his administration.

THE ADMINISTRATION SHOULD RECOGNIZE AND MEET ITS OBLIGATION TOWARD THE CLASSROOM TEACHER. What may a classroom teacher expect from a democratic administration?

First, the teacher expects that his individuality and unique talents will be respected and encouraged. Teaching is a creative process and no two good teachers have exactly the same personal traits or teaching competencies. The able administrator recognizes, encourages, and capitalizes upon diversity in his staff rather than striving for conformity. The importance of this viewpoint in creating harmonious staff relationships is emphasized by Tyler who says,

Effective working relationships require us to recognize the potential variety of abilities, interests, and points of view among the staff members and to seek to capitalize on this variety. Instead of trying to mold others to be like us, we shall profit more by trying to identify the individual's unique potential, by encouraging him to develop it, and by giving him opportunities to use it constructively in the service of education. This releases great energy and increases the zest and morale of the staff.[22]

22 Ralph W. Tyler, "Recent Research Sheds Light on School Staff Relationships," *Elementary School Journal*, Vol. 56 (May, 1956), pp. 395-396.

It is encouraging to note that this principle is almost unanimously accepted by educators today, according to the previously mentioned survey that reports that 100 per cent of the principals and 97 per cent of the teachers agreed that, "The principal should, when exploring educational problems, strive for individuality rather than uniformity on the part of his staff."[23]

Second, the classroom teacher is entitled to a *relative* or *reasonable* amount of freedom within his own classroom. This is a point upon which teachers feel very strongly, according to a study of teacher satisfactions with their jobs which states that, "Freedom to plan one's own work is given the highest possible rating by more than three-fourths of all respondents, and achieves a considerably higher average rating than any other factor."[24]

There is, in the author's opinion, much justification for this strong feeling among teachers. It has been stated repeatedly in this chapter that the classroom teacher is steadily becoming a more highly educated, prepared, and competent individual. As such, he is well equipped to plan his program and organize his classroom according to the needs of his individual situation. There seems to be little point in refining our recruitment techniques and strengthening our preservice and inservice programs to secure superior teachers, if all they are expected to do is to adhere to a program prescribed by another. Any competent teacher will, and should, chafe under a system which demands that he adhere to an inflexible time schedule, follow blindly a prescribed course of study, or use in his classroom only the single textbook advocated by a certain administrative officer.

On the other hand, no teacher should be unrealistic enough to expect *absolute* freedom or autonomy. This is ridiculous for several reasons. In the first place, the teacher *is* part of a system and *is* expected to conform to certain policies and procedures. Many systems today expect a teacher to adhere to a planned, but flexible, curriculum guide. Many expect him to conform generally with certain large weekly blocks of time for certain subjects. But these should serve primarily as *guides* permitting *relative freedom* but not complete autonomy. A second limitation upon the teacher's freedom in the classroom stems from the community. Yauch states that,

Teachers who unrealistically assume that it is their business to determine how the classroom work should be carried on, and stubbornly ignore the deep biases of the community, will discover that the outcomes are not only disastrous for good school-community relations, but their plans will eventuate in poor results.

[23] Harry J. Merigis, *op. cit.*, p. 37.
[24] Francis S. Chase, "Factors for Satisfaction in Teaching," *Phi Delta Kappan,* Vol. 33 (November, 1951), p. 129.

Successful teachers have long since concluded that their freedom to teach is and must be modified by community expectations.[25]

Any person who is at all familiar with teaching recognizes the truth of this statement and there is little need to discuss it further. It can only be reiterated that the teacher should expect a considerable degree of freedom in planning his classroom program, but if he expects absolute autonomy he is bound for a rude awakening.

Third, teachers have a right to expect favorable working conditions. Again it is unnecessary to add—within reason. Oversized classes, substandard classrooms, inadequate facilities and equipment, no release time even during the noon hour, and numerous extraclassroom duties are among frequently mentioned deterrents to high teacher morale. They lead to frustration and prevent the competent teacher from doing the kind of job he can and wants to do. He certainly should expect the administration to make a concerted effort to eliminate or minimize them as much as is humanly possible.

Fourth, teachers obviously expect the administration to be concerned about teacher welfare. Provisions for tenure, sick leave, salary schedules, retirement, professional recognition, promotion, and others are directly related to teachers' morale and the quality of teacher-administrative relationships.

Fifth, the teacher is vitally concerned about the problem of communication. In the first place, he expects to be *informed* of school factors, events, or policies that affect him. Ideally, of course, the teacher, or his elected representative, should participate in formulating policy or making decisions that affect him. Many decisions, however, are and should be made at the administrative level. When such is the case, provision should be made for promptly conveying this information to the teacher. Administrative bulletins, teacher handbooks, and daily announcements, are usually the devices employed by efficient administrators to circulate information to all staff members.

There is also another aspect to be considered in discussing channels of information from administration to teacher. Just as it was stated in Chapter 3 that pupils are more apt to obey a regulation if they know the *why* behind it, so are teachers more inclined to support a decision if they are aware of its rationale.

Distilling information, no matter how efficient, is not, of course, synonymous with communication. Communication implies a *two-way* exchange of ideas. The teacher, therefore, is not only concerned with *receiving* information but also with the opportunity to offer reactions, ideas, and

[25] Wilbur A. Yauch, *Helping Teachers Understand Principals* (New York, Appleton-Century-Crofts, 1957), p. 16.

suggestions. Again, the administrator recognizes this and provides ample opportunity for it through democratic faculty meetings, group enterprises, administrator-teacher conferences and many others. Adequate communication has always been a necessary part of good human relationships. Culbertson recognizes its importance in the following statement.

Certainly the quantity and quality of administrator-staff communication are basic determinants of organizational effectiveness. At the same time the quality of this communication either contributes to the satisfaction and professional growth of personnel or, on the other hand, adds to their frustrations and leaves unexplored the avenues which could increase their personal and professional excellence.[26]

Last, but far from least, the teacher is vitally concerned about the quality of professional leadership among administrative personnel and many surveys report the relationship of this factor to teacher morale. In general, teachers have two categories of expectancies concerning their administrators. They want a human, sympathetic, and understanding person who is concerned about their problems and upon whom they can always call for support and reassurance. In addition, they expect their principal to be knowledgeable and competent in his professional responsibilities. Yauch describes the professional competencies of the principal who deserves the respect of his teachers as follows:

The outstanding principal

has a profound knowledge of the basic design of American society and its value system . . .

has an intimate knowledge of the community the school attempts to serve . . .

has a command of modern educational theory and of the newer developments in the psychology of learning . . .

is a student of curricular design and construction . . .

is skilled in the organization and administration of the school as a whole . . .

is a leader of people in the school and outside . . .

is able to translate ideals into practical realities . . .

is capable of and skillful in making practical concessions . . .[27]

TEACHER-TEACHER RELATIONSHIPS

Positive intrafaculty relationships are important. Almost nothing affects the teacher's job satisfaction and quality of performance more than the type of relationships he enjoys with his fellow teachers. In

[26] Jack Culbertson, "Recognizing Roadblocks in Communication Channels," *Administrator's Notebook*, Vol. 7 (March, 1959), n. p.
[27] Wilbur A. Yauch, *op. cit.*, pp. 85-91.

general, of course, good relationships in this area depend upon courtesy, respect, integrity, honesty, consideration, and other characteristics necessary for any desirable adult relationship. Specifically, the major contributors to harmonious relationships among teachers have usually been found to be the following:

1. *Mutual respect.* It was stated above that each teacher's unique talents and contributions should be recognized and respected by the administration. This is probably even more important in teacher-teacher relationships. It is evidenced by teachers who willingly seek help from, and give help to each other, thus recognizing the strengths of each other; as it is by teachers who are as proud of a colleague's success as they would be of their own and who don't hesitate to let him know this. It is evidenced by teachers who derive intense satisfaction from working with other competent teachers, and by teachers who feel they are part of a team of professionals, all well equipped and all moving toward the attainment of common goals.

2. *Absence of cliques.* Many faculties are divided into small groups, each vying for favor and competing with others. In such a faculty, petty gossip, competition, and rivalry are rampant. It is obvious that good human relations are not operative at all in such a climate and that tensions, frustrations, and dissatisfactions are the inevitable results.

3. *Observance of professional ethics.* The teacher's relationship with his colleagues is based, not only on personal considerations, but upon professionally ethical standards as well. This topic is examined more fully in the last section of this chapter.

4. *Lack of interference with another's sphere of authority.* Good staff relations demand that the teacher not interfere with matters relating to another teacher's relationships with his pupils. Sympathizing with pupils reprimanded by another teacher, or disciplining pupils in another class (except in cases of the teacher's absence) are procedures that tend to create conflict among the various staff members, and are avoided by the teacher sensitive to his relationships with others.

5. *Lack of criticism.* Openly criticizing fellow teachers has long been regarded as unethical by teachers; most of them refrain from this practice. There is, however, a type of subtle criticism some teachers use against their colleagues. Each September, you will hear some teachers complain about the poor work habits, behavior, or academic preparation of their pupils. Such complaints are, of course, a direct reflection upon the pupils' previous teacher. Sometimes this is deliberate. Probably more often, it is used as a defense mechanism. Consider the teacher, for instance, who tells a complaining parent, "John is really making excellent progress considering that he was reading far below grade level when he came to

me this year." Isn't this individual defending himself by casting doubt upon the competency of John's former teachers? This is an insidious kind of criticism to which even the most professional teacher may succumb unless he makes a conscious effort to avoid it.

There are, of course, many other factors upon which harmonious teacher-teacher relationships depend but most of them are apparent to the intelligent individual who has personal integrity, social sensitivity, and awareness of professional ethics.

TEACHER RELATIONSHIPS WITH OTHER SCHOOL PERSONNEL

The custodian, school secretary, cafeteria worker, traffic policeman and others are important members of the school group. The teacher's relationships with these personnel can make or break the overall effectiveness of the program. Each teacher should be sensitive to the role expectations and needs of these workers and do his utmost to establish with them relationships based upon mutual consideration, understanding, and respect.

The second role of the teacher considered in this chapter is as a member of an organized profession. The remainder of the chapter deals with two important aspects of this role.

PROFESSIONAL ASSOCIATIONS

Organizations concerned with the advancement of public education were formed in this country early in the eighteenth century although their membership usually included more lay persons than educators. Early in the nineteenth century, however, various local associations of public or semipublic school teachers appeared in New York, Boston, and other cities. By 1850 such local or county teacher organizations were fairly common and paved the way for the formation of the National Teachers Association (later to become the National Education Association) in 1857. The professional association movement has grown rapidly in the last century and today various estimates place the number of such groups between 7500 and 10,000. Although they differ widely in specific aims and interests, in general, most of the associations have two underlying aims: (1) improvement of instruction and (2) concern for teacher welfare.

Usually the classroom teacher, faced with many other concerns, has two predominant questions concerning professional associations. First, he wants to know what benefits he will receive from membership in a professional group. Secondly, he wants to know which of the many organizations he will join. Let us consider the first of these.

THE CLASSROOM TEACHER DERIVES MANY BENEFITS AND ADVANTAGES FROM MEMBERSHIP IN PROFESSIONAL ASSOCIATIONS. The familiar refrain of many teachers is, "What am I going to get out of it?" This is a good question and a fairly easy one to answer. He will get a great deal out of it. The following are only some of the benefits derived from membership in a professional group.

1. *Opportunity to broaden one's professional horizons and contacts.* There is no better opportunity for the teacher to become aware of broad educational concerns, or to enjoy numerous contacts with persons of similar professional interests than to join an association of his choice.

2. *Professional growth.* Closely related to the above advantage, is the opportunity for professional growth offered by such associations. Most of them hold district and national conventions devoted to the examination of important educational questions. Group discussions, exhibits of new professional materials and books, and addresses by national authorities usually characterize these meetings. There is little doubt that the teacher can gain much from attending.

Another avenue of growth is the excellent literature published by many associations. Monthly periodicals, yearbooks, pamphlets, bulletins, and other publications are invaluable in informing the teacher about research, theory, and desirable practices in his particular field of interest.

3. *Opportunity to improve the quality of education.* Many, many improvements in education over the years have resulted directly from the work of professional organizations. Affiliation with these groups gives the teacher opportunity to work in the front line on many needed educational improvements.

4. *Opportunity to promote teacher welfare.* There is little doubt that professional associations can take most of the credit for the steady improvement of teacher welfare and status over the years. Again, membership in various groups gives the teacher an opportunity to work directly in this important area of professional concern.

5. *Social contacts.* Membership with any group will inevitably provide a widened circle of social participation and contacts.

With the hope that these brief statements have convinced the teacher of the benefits he will derive from joining certain professional groups, let us now turn to the question of which of the many currently functioning groups will probably be of the most interest to the elementary teacher.

THE ELEMENTARY TEACHER SHOULD BE ACQUAINTED WITH CERTAIN NATIONAL ORGANIZATIONS. The most prominent national associations of a general nature include the following.

1. *The National Education Association.* This is the largest educational association in the world with enrollment figures, as of June, 1963 at 859,505.[28] It was formed in 1857 in Philadelphia as the National Teachers Association and in 1927 changed its name to its present one, popularly known as the NEA. Its original charter stated its purpose as "to elevate the character and advance the interests of the profession of teaching and to promote the cause of education in the United States." This purpose has remained constant to the present day. To implement this overall purpose, the platform of the NEA lists the following goals.

(1) Educational opportunity for every individual to develop his full potential for responsible and useful citizenship and for intellectual and spiritual growth . . .

(2) Balanced educational programs to provide for the varied needs and talents of individual students and for the strength and progress of the nation . . .

(3) The services of a professionally prepared and competent educator in every professional position . . .

(4) School plant, equipment, and instructional materials appropriate to the educational needs of all learners . . .

(5) Effective organization, control, administration, and financial support of public education in every state . . .

(6) A local-state-federal partnership in the financial support of public education with control of education residing in the states . . .

(7) Public understanding and appreciation of the vital role of education in our American democracy . . .

(8) Understanding and support of the teacher's right to participate fully in public affairs . . .

(9) Fair standards of professional welfare for teachers . . .

(10) Professional associations that evolve the active participation of all educators in working toward the highest goals for education . . .[29]

The NEA has offered, and is offering, valuable service to all phases of the profession. It is impossible to mention all such services, only a few of which include its continual concern with teacher welfare; its concerted efforts to elevate the status of the profession; its sponsorship of research; and its publication of research findings and articles of interest in the *NEA Journal, Research Bulletin,* and numerous others.

The organization of the NEA includes thirty-three departments, twenty-six commissions and committees, and fourteen headquarters divisions, structured according to Figure 5.2 on page 181.

[28] *NEA Handbook 1963-1964,* p. 343.
[29] "The Platform of the National Education Association," *NEA Handbook, 1961-1962* (Washington, D. C., National Education Association, 1961).

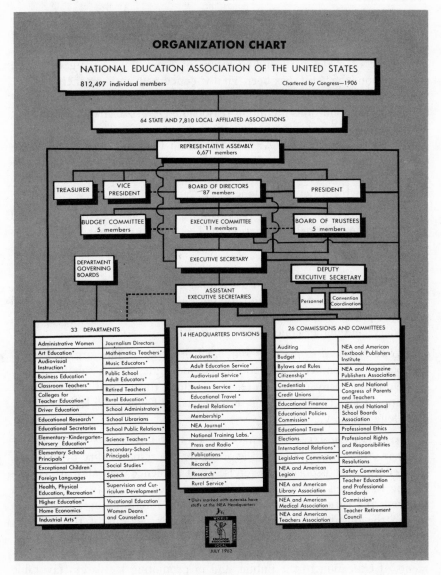

FIGURE 5.2

Organization chart of the National Education Association of the United States.

2. *The American Federation of Teachers*. Commonly referred to as the AFT, this organization is the second largest educational association in the country. Enrollment figures as of May, 1963, were 81,798 distributed among five hundred local units.

Although there existed some teachers' unions during the early years of the twentieth century (such as the Chicago Teachers Federation, organized in 1897), it was in 1916 that the American Federation of Teachers, an affiliate of the American Federation of Labor, was organized. Since its inception, the AFT has been vitally concerned with teacher welfare. It has worked for higher salaries, tenure rights, academic freedom, favorable working conditions including reasonable class size, adequate facilities, and others.

The membership of the AFT differs from that of many other educational groups in that it is restricted only to classroom teachers. Administrative officers may, however, form their own local chapter although instances in which they have done so are rare.

3. *The American Teachers Association.* This organization was formed in 1902 as the National Association of Teachers in Colored Schools. It is an organization of Negro teachers of fourteen southern and Middle Atlantic States.

4. *The National Catholic Educational Association.* Formed in 1904, membership in this organization includes all levels of Catholic parochial education, including classroom teachers and administrators in elementary, secondary, and higher education.

5. *The National Council of Independent Schools.* This organization is composed of membership of educators from independent schools.

In addition, many classroom teachers belong to such national honorary educational societies as Phi Delta Kappa, Kappa Delta Pi, Pi Lamba Theta, and Delta Kappa Gamma.

STATE EDUCATIONAL ASSOCIATIONS ARE VITALLY IMPORTANT TO THE CLASSROOM TEACHER. Since education is primarily the responsibility of the state, state educational associations exercise great influence over all matters pertaining to schools and teachers. They have been particularly effective in unifying the various agencies within the state interested in education, in raising the quality of education in the poorer sections of the state, in awakening and stimulating the professional outlook of teachers, in developing codes of ethics for teachers, in interpreting the goals and achievements of education to the public, and in promoting legislation favorable to all phases of education. Summarizing the outstanding achievements of state associations, Stinnett says,

State education associations have been chiefly responsible for almost every gain in public education which has resulted from legal enactments . . . State education associations have led in efforts to secure adequate financial support, to bring about larger administrative school units, to institute equalization of educational opportunity, and to obtain teacher welfare provisions. They have served as effective instruments of professional growth of their members. State education associations speak for the organized profession before the state legislature, state departments of education, and meetings of lay organizations; they defend their members against unjust dismissals or unfair treatment; and they present viewpoints of the profession to the people.[30]

There is little doubt that the state associations are loyally supported by most teachers today. One evidence of this is their membership records. In 1955, for example, of all public school teachers, *91 per cent* belonged to their respective state associations.[31] Another evidence of support is the ever-increasing number of staff members attached to the state organizations. These personnel may operate from the association's headquarters or serve as field representatives on specialized assignments in various parts of the state. They are responsible to the Executive Secretary of the Association, second only to the Chief State School Officer in influence in many states. Another evidence of support from teachers is the provision for housing of the state association. Today, almost all groups have their own building headquarters. Many of them are spacious and impressive enough to permit an efficient functioning of staff as well as to serve as a symbol of the growth and importance of the profession.

THERE ARE MANY AND VARIED TYPES OF LOCAL ASSOCIATIONS. The number and variety of local education associations is so great that it is impossible to discuss them here with any clarity. They range from the all-inclusive type consisting of all teachers in a school system to a system, county, or regional group of teachers with specialized interests. The local group may be affiliated with a national or state organization or it may be completely independent. In general, local associations enjoy a relatively high percentage of membership. They provide opportunities for professional leadership to large numbers of teachers and are the chief medium ". . . thru which the voice of every teacher can be heard and translated . . . into educational policy."[32]

SPECIAL INTEREST GROUPS ATTRACT MANY TEACHERS. There are many specialized organizations (some independent and some affiliated with the NEA) whose membership is composed largely of classroom teachers. Such groups are primarily concerned with the improvement of instruction in their particular area. To this end, they conduct conferences and conventions, provide consulting services, sponsor and conduct research, and publish yearbooks, bulletins, and regular periodicals. Such magazines as *The Arithmetic Teacher, The Reading Teacher, Social Studies, Elementary English,* and many others are official organs of specialized in-

[30] T. M. Stinnett, *The Teacher and Professional Organizations*, 3rd ed. (Washington, D. C., National Education Association, 1956), p. 93.

[31] *Ibid.*, p. 94.

[32] *Ibid.*, p. 87.

terest associations. They perform invaluable service in bringing directly to the classroom teacher the best and most recent theory and research available in their particular field.

Obviously, the present discussion has made no attempt to acquaint the teacher with all the professional associations now functioning. It is important only to restate that the large majority of such groups perform valuable professional services and have been responsible for many of the educational gains realized during recent years. As such, they deserve the support of all professionally minded teachers.

PROFESSIONAL ETHICS

Chapters 3, 4, and 5 have repeatedly stressed the ever-increasing importance educators place upon human relationships in teaching. As was frequently stated, many of these relationships are governed by the same rules of conduct that operate in any type of personal interaction. In addition, however, there are certain types of acceptable teacher behavior and relationships that are firmly based upon a code of professional ethics. This is an important area of professional development and should be a major concern of every classroom teacher.

THERE IS AN EVER-INCREASING AWARENESS OF THE IMPORTANCE OF PROFESSIONAL ETHICS AMONG EDUCATORS. Education has lagged noticeably behind other professions in establishing national standards of ethical conduct. Although there were several local and state codes in existence during the early years of the century (the first one was adopted by the Georgia Education Association in 1896), it was not until 1929 that the need for a national code was met by the National Education Association. This was twenty-one years after the American Bar Association adopted its Canons of Professional Ethics and twenty-six years later than the American Medical Association adopted the Principles of Medical Ethics (although it had had for centuries the Hippocratic Oath). The reason for the relatively late interest of education in a code of ethics, however, was not mere laxness on its part. As Perry points out, education *is* different from other professions in at least two major respects, both of which have implications for formulating ethical standards. In the first place, teachers practice in a governmental, tax-supported enterprise (unlike other professions). Secondly, teachers are unique in that they have ". . . direct and varying ethical obligations to a multiple clientele," including pupils, parents, the schoolboard, and community.[33] Although, therefore, the development of a code of ethics for education has been slower than in other fields, the

[33] Cyrus C. Perry, "A Code of Ethics for Public School Teachers," *Annals of The American Academy of Political and Social Science*, Vol. 297 (January, 1955), p. 76.

reasons are understandable and our recent acceleration of interest more than compensates for our slow start. Evidence of this lies in the fact that today, *all* states have operating codes. Many have adopted a national code, some have their own codes, and some adhere to both the national code and their own. In addition, there are numerous local codes in effect.

The multiplicity of codes is a concern to some educators who argue that uniformly high standards of ethical conduct will be achieved only through adherence to a single code. On the other hand, there are those who argue that a single code would have to be so general to cover all situations, that it would be very ineffectual. Probably the best solution is a clear, direct, and forceful national code with general application, with supplementary statements in operation where the need is felt. Such appears to be the condition the profession is rapidly approaching.

IN ORDER THAT CODES MAY BE EFFECTIVE, IT IS NECESSARY FOR TEACHERS TO BE KNOWLEDGEABLE OF THEM. Although recent years have seen increased interest in establishing ethical standards for teachers, numerous surveys still show that an amazing number of teachers are unfamiliar with any code of ethics. This appalling situation is partly the result of various groups tending to shift the blame to each other. Schools of education claim that informing the teacher concerning the code of ethics is primarily the responsibility of the state and local professional associations and school systems. On the other hand, these groups insist that the teacher education institutions are lax in not including a unit of study on professional ethics in their curricula. This is a pointless argument which does no one any good. It seems obvious that acquainting the teacher with the ethics governing his actions is the joint responsibility of both preservice and inservice programs and must be assumed by both if the profession is going to continue to move forward.

SOME PROVISION FOR THE ENFORCEMENT OF CODES OF ETHICS MUST BE MADE. This is another area in which there is disagreement. Some argue that no code will ever become operative until adequate provision is made for enforcement. Others claim that most teachers are conscientious and well-intentioned persons whose ethical misconduct, if and when it occurs, is due more to lack of knowledge than willful disregard of the existing codes. Such persons argue that developing inner controls among teachers is more important than initiating disciplinary procedures. Obviously there is something to be said for both points of view. Thoroughly acquainting teachers with existing codes and continuously emphasizing their principles will do much to encourage professional conduct. On the other hand, as one source states, ". . . some way must be found to make it clear to the small minority that certain ethical principles are to be observed by all."[34] Today, several steps have been taken in this direction, among which the most interesting are the following.

In the first place, every state (and some local units) now has operating an Ethics Committee, sometimes called a Personnel Standards Commission. Such a group reviews cases of unethical conduct referred to it. Its recommendations depend upon the seriousness of the violation, and range from merely explaining the correct procedure to the offender to recommending to his local system that he be discharged or recommending to the state department of education that his certificate be revoked.

Another promising step forward is the body of opinions handed down by the Professional Ethics Committee of the National Education Association. This committee reviews all questions submitted to it by individuals or groups concerning a possible infraction of the national code of ethics. The opinions of this committee are published over the years in the NEA Journal and in various volumes published from time to time. Although such opinions are not really disciplinary actions, they do strengthen the national code by interpreting it and thus broadening its sphere of influence.

It is apparent, therefore, that the profession is making progress in developing ethical behavior and relationships by moving ahead on three major fronts: (1) formulating and developing a uniform code of ethics for the education profession, (2) educating teachers concerning ethical codes, and (3) making provision for enforcement of the codes when necessary.

As has been stated, the early national codes were developed by the National Education Association and were generally referred to as the NEA codes of ethics. These have been recently replaced by a code of ethics for the education profession which has been agreed upon by many groups within the profession, under the leadership of the NEA Ethics Committee through which it has been made available.

THE CODE OF ETHICS OF THE EDUCATION PROFESSION

PREAMBLE

We, professional educators of the United States of America, affirm our belief in the worth and dignity of man. We recognize the supreme importance of the pursuit of truth, the encouragement of scholarship, and the promotion of democratic citizenship. We regard as essential to these goals the protection of freedom to learn and to teach and the guarantee of equal educational opportunity for all. We affirm and accept our responsibility to practice our profession according to the highest ethical standards.

[34] Department of Classroom Teachers and Research Division, *Ethics for Teachers* (Washington, D. C., National Education Association, 1958), p. 15.

We acknowledge the magnitude of the profession we have chosen, and engage ourselves, individually and collectively, to judge our colleagues and to be judged by them in accordance with the applicable provisions of this code.

PRINCIPLE I

Commitment to the Student

We measure success by the progress of each student toward achievement of his maximum potential. We therefore work to stimulate the spirit of inquiry, the acquisition of knowledge and understanding, and the thoughtful formulation of worthy goals. We recognize the importance of cooperative relationships with other community institutions, especially the home.

In fulfilling our obligations to the student, we—

1. Deal justly and considerately with each student.

2. Encourage the student to study varying points of view and respect his right to form his own judgment.

3. Withhold confidential information about a student or his home unless we deem that its release serves professional purposes, benefits the student, or is required by law.

4. Make discreet use of available information about the student.

5. Conduct conferences with or concerning students in an appropriate place and manner.

6. Refrain from commenting unprofessionally about a student or his home.

7. Avoid exploiting our professional relationship with any student.

8. Tutor only in accordance with officially approved policies.

9. Inform appropriate individuals and agencies of the student's educational needs and assist in providing an understanding of his educational experiences.

10. Seek constantly to improve learning facilities and opportunities.

PRINCIPLE II

Commitment to the Community

We believe that patriotism in its highest form requires dedication to the principles of our democratic heritage. We share with all other citizens the responsibility for the development of sound public policy. As educators, we are particularly accountable for participating in the development of educational programs and policies and for interpreting them to the public.

In fulfilling our obligations to the community, we—

1. Share the responsibility for improving the educational opportunities for all.

2. Recognize that each educational institution may have a person authorized to interpret its official policies.

3. Acknowledge the right and responsibility of the public to participate in the formulation of educational policy.

4. Evaluate through appropriate professional procedures conditions within a district or institution of learning, make known serious deficiencies, and take any action deemed necessary and proper.

5. Use educational facilities for intended purposes consistent with applicable policy, law, and regulation.

6. Assume full political and citizenship responsibilities, but refrain from exploiting the institutional privileges of our professional positions to promote political candidates or partisan activities.

7. Protect the educational program against undesirable infringement.

Principle III

Commitment to the Profession

We believe that the quality of the services of the education profession directly influences the future of the nation and its citizens. We therefore exert every effort to raise educational standards, to improve our service, to promote a climate in which the exercise of professional judgment is encouraged, and to achieve conditions which attract persons worthy of the trust to careers in education. Aware of the value of united effort, we contribute actively to the support, planning, and programs of our professional organizations.

In fulfilling our obligations to the profession, we—

1. Recognize that a profession must accept responsibility for the conduct of its members and understand that our own conduct may be regarded as representative.

2. Participate and conduct ourselves in a responsible manner in the development and implementation of policies affecting education.

3. Cooperate in the selective recruitment of prospective teachers and in the orientation of student teachers, interns, and those colleagues new to their positions.

4. Accord just and equitable treatment to all members of the profession in the exercise of their professional rights and responsibilities, and support them when unjustly accused or mistreated.

5. Refrain from assigning professional duties to non-professional personnel when such assignment is not in the best interest of the student.

6. Provide, upon request, a statement of specific reason for administrative recommendations that lead to the denial of increments, significant changes in employment, or termination of employment.

7. Refrain from exerting undue influence based on the authority of our positions in the determination of professional decisions by colleagues.

8. Keep the trust under which confidential information is exchanged.

9. Make appropriate use of time granted for professional purposes.

10. Interpret and use the writings of others and the findings of educational research with intellectual honesty.

11. Maintain our integrity when dissenting by basing our public criticism of education on valid assumptions as established by careful evaluation of facts or hypotheses.

12. Represent honestly our professional qualifications and identify ourselves only with reputable educational institutions.

13. Respond accurately to requests for evaluations of colleagues seeking professional positions.

14. Provide applicants seeking information about a position with an honest description of the assignment, the conditions of work, and related matters.

PRINCIPLE IV

Commitment to Professional Employment Practices

We regard the employment agreement as a solemn pledge to be executed both in spirit and in fact in a manner consistent with the highest ideals of professional service. Sound professional personnel relationships with governing boards are built upon personal integrity, dignity, and mutual respect.

In fulfilling our obligations to professional employment practices, we—

1. Apply for or offer a position on the basis of professional and legal qualifications.

2. Apply for a specific position only when it is known to be vacant and refrain from such practices as underbidding or commenting adversely about other candidates.

3. Fill no vacancy except where the terms, conditions, policies, and practices permit the exercise of our professional judgment and skill, and where a climate conducive to professional service exists.

4. Adhere to the conditions of a contract or to the terms of an appointment until either has been terminated legally or by mutual consent.

5. Give prompt notice of any change in availability of service, in status of applications, or in change in position.

6. Conduct professional business through the recognized educational and professional channels.

7. Accept no gratuities or gifts of significance that might influence our judgment in the exercise of our professional duties.

8. Engage in no outside employment that will impair the effectiveness of our professional service and permit no commercial exploitation of our professional position.

SUMMARY

The present chapter has been concerned with the multiple relationships the classroom teacher enjoys with his professional colleagues. The roles of the teacher as (1) a member of a school organization and (2) a member of an organized profession were examined. Concerning the first of these, certain major emphases were made. It was stressed that the teacher should be informed concerning the organization of the system of education in this country. To this end, the national, state, and local systems were examined according to their organization, major functions, and personnel. The question of the teacher's *participation* in certain administrative matters, as a member of a school organization, was also stressed. Lastly, reciprocal relationships between the teacher and administration, teacher and fellow teachers, and teacher and other personnel were examined.

The role of the teacher as a member of an organized profession was also examined. The benefits accruing to the teacher through membership in professional organizations were enumerated. The discussion in this chapter also included an examination of the major types of organizations in which the classroom teacher is most interested: national, state, local, and special interest associations.

To conclude the discussions of Chapters 3, 4, and 5 concerning the teacher's relationships with others, the last section of the present chapter dealt with the important subject of professional ethics. It was stated that certain of the teacher's relationships were governed by the same personal characteristics operative in any desirable type of social contact, but that certain others were determined only by adherence to a definite code of ethics. The teacher's knowledge of ethical conduct, therefore, is most important and is the joint responsibility of all preservice and inservice programs.

The chapter concluded on a note of optimism, that the profession is moving steadily forward in its task of developing, interpreting, and enforcing a vital and functional code of ethics for all its members.

ADDITIONAL LEARNING EXPERIENCES

Topics for Thought and Discussion

1. Some people today advocate that the position of U.S. Commissioner of Education be elevated to cabinet rank instead of being part of the Department of Health, Education, and Welfare. How do you feel about this proposal? Would there be advantages? Disadvantages?

2. Who is the present U. S. Commissioner of Education? What are his qualifications for the position?

3. Does your state have its own code of ethics? How does its code compare with the national Code of Ethics of the Education Profession?

4. Do you think there is need for greater enforcement of ethical behavior among teachers? What suggestions do you have for accomplishing this?

5. Do you know of any system that has a faculty advisory council? How does it operate?

6. Do you think teachers should participate in recruiting, selecting, and recommending teachers for employment? Is it true that a third-grade teacher may have a clearer concept of the needs of that position than a principal or superintendent may have?

7. What should be the attitude of the beginning teacher toward the few chronic complainers who are on almost every school staff?

8. What would you do if a fellow-teacher complained to you constantly about another member of the staff?

9. Should a new teacher adopt the philosophy and procedures of his experienced colleagues, or should he be encouraged to experiment with his own philosophy and techniques he considers educationally sound?

10. Many people recommend that a person should have some elementary school teaching experience (usually two to five years) before qualifying as an elementary school principal. Do you think this is a good idea?

11. While a student-teacher was teaching a class, the teacher next door left her room for a few minutes. The noise from her class became so disturbing that the student teacher left his own class to scold the other class. Was this action justified?

12. To what professional associations do you belong, or will you belong when you begin to teach?

13. Who is the executive secretary of your state professional association? The president? The other officers? What is the official organ of the association?

14. Suppose your principal asked for your opinion of the competency of a fellow teacher? What would you do?

15. Does the staff position of *consultant* require different competencies from that of *special teacher?*

Projects and Activities

1. Prepare or secure an organizational chart of your state department of education, listing names and positions with which every elementary teacher in your state should be familiar.

2. Henry Barnard, first U. S. Commissioner of Education, is considered one of the outstanding leaders in American education. Prepare a paper on Barnard, mentioning the many contributions he made to public education in this country.

3. Compare the 1952 NEA Code of Ethics with the 1963 Code of Ethics of the Education Profession. What major changes have been made in the new statement? What are the implications of these changes?

4. Secure information, through correspondence and reading, on your state ethics committee. What is the function and influence of this agency?

5. See if you can discover any local school system that has its own ethics committee. If so, explain its origin and function.

6. Compare the Code of Ethics of the Education Profession with the Canons of Professional Ethics of the American Bar Association and the Principles of Medical Ethics of the American Medical Association. What major similarities and differences do you note?

7. Interview an officer or staff member of your state education association. What per cent of your state's teachers belong to the association? What gains in teacher welfare legislation has the association strongly supported in recent years?

8. Prepare a research paper on "The Changing Role of the Chief State School Officer."

9. Compare the platforms of the National Education Association and the American Federation of Teachers.

10. Organize a debate on the subject, "Should Teachers Unionize?"

11. Study your state constitution. What specific references to education does it contain?

12. Find out the name of your chief state school officer. How is he appointed? What are his qualifications for office? His length of term? His salary?

13. Find out if your state has a general board of education. How many members are on it? Who is president? How are members appointed?

14. Write a "Hippocratic Oath" for teachers

Selected Bibliography

American Association of School Administrators, *Staff Relations in School Administration*. Thirty-third Yearbook. Washington, D. C., National Education Association, 1955.

BEACH, Fred F., *The Functions of State Departments of Education*. Washington, D. C., Federal Security Agency, Office of Education, 1950.

———, and GIBBS, Andrew H., *The Personnel of State Departments of Education*. Washington, D. C., Federal Security Agency, Office of Education, 1952.

———, and ———, *The Structure of State Departments of Education*. Washington, D. C., Federal Security Agency, Office of Education, 1949.

———, and WILL, Robert F., *The State and Education*. Washington, D. C., U. S. Department of Health, Education, and Welfare, Office of Education, 1955.

BURRUP, Percy E., *The Teacher and the Public School System*. New York, Harper & Row, Publishers, Inc., 1960.

CHAMBERLAIN, Leo M., and KINDRED, Leslie W., *The Teacher and School Organization*, 3rd ed. Englewood Cliffs, N. J., Prentice-Hall, Inc., 1958.

Committee on Professional Ethics, *Opinions of the Committee on Professional Ethics*, 3rd ed. Washington, D. C., National Education Association, 1960.

Council of Chief State School Officers, *Responsibilities of State Departments of Education for Instruction.* Washington, D. C., 1958.

Department of Classroom Teachers and Research Division, *Ethics for Teachers,* 3rd ed. Washington, D. C., National Education Association, 1958.

EASTMOND, Jefferson N., *The Teacher and School Administration.* Boston, Houghton Mifflin Company, 1959.

GRIFFITHS, Daniel E., *Human Relations in School Administration.* New York, Appleton-Century-Crofts, 1956.

KEESECKER, Ward W., *State Boards of Education and Chief State School Officers.* Bulletin 1950, No. 12, Federal Security Agency, Office of Education, Washington, D. C., 1950.

"Local Education Associations at Work." *NEA Research Bulletin,* Vol. 26 (October, 1948).

MARTIN, Theodore Day, *Building a Teaching Profession.* Middletown, N. Y., The Whitlock Press, Inc., 1957.

National Education Association and American Association of School Administrators, Educational Policies Commission, *Professional Organizations in American Education.* Washington, D. C., National Education Association, 1957.

NEA Handbook. Washington, D. C., National Education Association, Annual.

NORTON, John K., "Federal Relations to Education," in Chester W. Harris, ed., *Encyclopedia of Educational Research,* New York, The Macmillan Company, 1960.

PERRY, Cyrus C., "Code of Ethics for Public School Teachers." *Annals of the American Academy of Political and Social Science,* Vol. 297 (January, 1955), pp. 76-82.

STINNETT, T. M., *The Teacher and Professional Organizations,* 3rd ed. Washington, D. C., National Education Association, 1956.

———, and HUGGETT, Albert J., Professional Problems of Teachers, 2nd ed. New York, The Macmillan Company, 1963.

THURSTON, Lee M., and ROE, William H., *State School Administration,* New York, Harper & Row, Publishers, Inc., 1957.

WESLEY, Edgar B., *NEA: The First Hundred Years.* New York, Harper & Row, Publishers, Inc., 1957.

YAUCH, Wilbur A., *Helping Teachers Understand Principals.* New York, Appleton-Century-Crofts, 1957.

YEAGER, William A., *Administration and the Teacher.* New York, Harper & Row, Publishers, Inc., 1954.

PART **III**

GUIDING THE LEARNING PROCESS

CHAPTER 6

Creating a Desirable
Learning Environment

PSYCHOLOGISTS LONG AGO convinced most of us, beyond any reasonable doubt, of the tremendous influence an individual's environment has on his total development and behavior. This is such an accepted truth that there is little need for examining it in any detail here. Add to this fact the realization that the typical elementary school child spends almost half his waking hours in school, and the crucial importance of the classroom environment becomes crystal clear. In its broadest sense, the term *environment* embraces all of the tangible and intangible elements, forces, and factors that surround the child day after day in the school situation. It includes all elements of the physical plant such as the lighting, heating, and equipment which comprise the physical environment. It includes the materials, devices, and resources that can be used to stimulate and satisfy intellectual curiosities and which together comprise the intellectual environment. It includes the subtle and intangible patterns of group relationships, group structure, and group temperament which characterize the social-emotional environment. In examining each type of environment the present chapter is directed toward two basic questions: (1) What are the distinguishing characteristics of a desirable environment? and (2) What are the responsibilities of the classroom teacher in creating and maintaining a desirable environment? With these two questions in mind, let us turn to a closer examination of the physical environment.

THE PHYSICAL ENVIRONMENT

The physical environment includes every detail of construction and every piece of equipment of the school plant. It is, of course, of primary importance to the physical growth, well-being, safety, and comfort of pupils and teachers. The difference between good and poor lighting, between proper and improper furniture, or between adequate and inadequate ventilation is the difference between healthy, happy, comfortable pupils and restless, unhappy, and inattentive pupils.

In addition to its importance to the comfort, health, and safety of pupils, the physical environment affects each of the other types of environment. For instance, a room with inadequate lighting or ventilation is hardly conducive to the intellectual development of pupils. Neither is a room with rigid and immovable seating arrangements conducive to the development of an informal, friendly, social environment. By the same reasoning, a cramped, crowded, or overheated classroom will not contribute to the development of a healthful emotional climate. Thus, the physical environment is important, not only for its own sake, but also because of its influence on all other environmental conditions.

When considering the importance of the physical environment, it is necessary to keep in mind that many individuals assume a greater responsibility for it than the classroom teacher. Indeed, there are many teachers who are well aware of the limitations of their classrooms' physical facilities but who are helpless to do anything to improve them. The school architect, illuminating engineer, landscape designer, acoustical expert, member of the board of education, school principal, and custodian are among those who are ultimately more responsible for the physical facilities than the classroom teacher. Moreover, this field is so technical and so specialized that it is unreasonable to expect classroom teachers to become experts in it. This does not mean, however, that the classroom teacher has no responsibility for the physical environment. Within reasonable limits there are many things the teacher can do to make the classroom a healthful, comfortable, and safe place for children. Specifically, the teacher's responsibilities may be considered to be:

1. He should be acutely aware of the importance of every aspect of the physical environment upon the comfort and safety of his pupils as well as on their intellectual, social, and emotional development.

2. He should have knowledge of the basic principles underlying good school design.

3. He should be aware of the modern trends and innovations in this area and their relationship to overall advances in education.

4. He should be able to appraise critically his classroom's physical environment and make recommendations for improvement to the proper authorities.

5. He should be able to use whatever facilities and controls are available to obtain optimum living conditions for his pupils and himself.

With these responsibilities in mind, most of the following discussion is concentrated upon an adequate environment for the typical elementary school self-contained classroom. Before concentrating directly upon the classroom, however, let us look at the most recent and important trends affecting total school design.

THERE ARE MANY INTERESTING TRENDS AND INNOVATIONS IN THE FIELD OF SCHOOL DESIGN. In recent years there has been no more dramatic change in education than the revolution in school design. Some say this movement began in approximately 1950 and will continue for some years to come. One has only to compare a school built in 1930 with one recently completed to be fully aware of the changes that have taken place. The forbidding multistoried building with its rectangular classrooms running down long dark corridors, high ceilings, stationary rows of desks and chairs, poorly ventilated cloakrooms or long rows of metal lockers, gang toilets, and extravagant use of basement storage space is disappearing gradually from the American landscape. In its place has come the school of the present and future, radically different in design, construction, materials, and equipment. Many influences have contributed to this revolution but none is more important than the now-accepted philosophy that the physical plant must be determined by the type of program it is to house. *Today, school design begins with a consideration of the educational program.* It begins with a study of the needs, interests, and characteristics of the learners to be housed in the new building, with a study of the varied experiences and activities through which learning will take place, and with a study of the materials and facilities needed to make learning an active and dynamic process. All of these, and many other aspects of the total educational program are determined by teachers and administrators *before* the architect is called into the picture. This single step is one of the most hopeful developments in the entire field of school construction. It means that the school program determines the school plant which is vastly different from a few years ago when the physical plant dictated to teachers the type of educational program they would have.

THE PATTERN OF PROGRAM-TO-PLANT PLANNING IS REFLECTED IN THE MODERN TRENDS IN SCHOOL DESIGN AND CONSTRUCTION. The following trends are worthy of examination by all teachers and administrators.

1. *Experimental overall design.* The train-type building with classrooms located symetrically on either side of a long corridor is being replaced by buildings of more experimental design. *Cluster* schools (schools within schools), *finger-type* buildings, *campus* schools, and *schools-in-the-round* are among those which represent a sharp break with the traditional concept of an elementary school.

2. *More functional use of space.* Space has become an important consideration in many communities and much thought is given to the most functional and economical use of it. In many systems, auditoriums, gym-

THERE HAS BEEN A DRAMATIC CHANGE IN SCHOOL DESIGN IN RECENT YEARS.

ABRAHAM LINCOLN ELEMENTARY SCHOOL
Glen Ellyn, Illinois
Orput-Orput and Associates, Inc., Architects

JONAS E. SALK SCHOOL
Lawndale, California
Carmichael-Kemp, Architects

CACTUS ELEMENTARY SCHOOL
Dumas, Texas
Brasher and Goyette, Architects

L. F. JOY ELEMENTARY SCHOOL
Fairbanks, Alaska
Alaska Architectural and Engineering Co., Architects

nasiums, and large storage areas with limited uses have been replaced with *multipurpose* rooms, work centers, skills laboratories, and curriculum workrooms which may be used for a variety of purposes.

In the interests of conserving space, the wide corridors of yesteryear are also missing from the new schools. In some cases they have simply become narrower; in others, they have disappeared or have become outside walkways depending upon the overall design; and in others they have been built with alcoves or surfaced with tackboard to provide additional display and exhibit space. In one elementary school known to the author, the corridors are used for a continual art exhibit either of pieces on loan from another source or done by the pupils themselves. Small benches have been placed at intervals along the corridors and it is a common occurrence to see children sitting singly or in small groups studying those pieces that interest them. Thus, thought is given to making every square inch of space contribute to the educational goals of the school.

3. *Greater flexibility.* No other trend in school building is accented today more than the emphasis on flexibility. The increasing use of all types of learning aids (including television and auto-instructional devices) as well as experimentation with various organizational patterns has highlighted the need for flexibility in the schools of the future. It may, for instance, be desirable to teach children in groups of ten at one time and to combine them into groups of ninety or more at another time. Thus, some schools are built with movable walls which will permit considerable flexibility to accommodate a variety of purposes.

Furthermore, flexibility includes also the element of *convertibility* which means that teaching areas may be used for different purposes in different years. Many architects and administrators consider this to be a more important factor than day-to-day flexibility. A room, for instance, with movable furniture, adjustable cabinet and shelf space, and chalkboards and tackboards that may be moved, raised, or lowered can easily be used to accommodate a third grade one year and a sixth grade the next year, or it may be used as a self-contained classroom one year and a skills laboratory the following year. One has only to recall the vast amount of time, effort, and money needed to convert a traditional classroom from one grade level to another to realize it is a tremendous step forward to provide for convertibility.

Emphasis upon flexibility also permits a wide range of activities within the classroom. Movable shelves, which serve as room dividers, furniture that can be grouped according to the activity, and chalkboards or tackboards that can be moved at will enable the teacher to make adequate physical provision for the numerous individual and group activities that take place in the self-contained classroom. Further discussion of possibilities in this area are discussed later in this section.

4. *Increased use of the physical plant.* There is little doubt that school buildings will be used a greater proportion of the day and year by a greater number of people than has been true in the past. For this reason, many new schools are being built as community centers designed to house a variety of community activities such as educational programs, social gatherings, and basketball games. This increased use of school buildings is highlighted in the following prediction: "School facilities will be more extensively used for both school and community activities. Trends toward a longer school year, a longer school day, more adult education programs —all these will increase the use of school facilities . . . Groups in many communities will use school facilities more and more for such purposes as recreation, meetings, and projects."[1]

5. *Greater attention to the physical comfort and well-being of pupils and teacher.* There is no doubt that a well-designed modern building is more attractive, more comfortable, safer, and more healthful than an antiquated structure. Advances in lighting, air conditioning, acoustics, and use of newer materials, have resulted in optimum physical conditions for learning in the modern elementary school classroom.

CERTAIN ESSENTIAL FEATURES COMPRISE THE PHYSICAL ENVIRONMENT OF THE CLASSROOM. Features that should be considered in appraising the physical environment of the classroom include the following:

Size. The trend in elementary classroom size over the past one hundred years is related closely to the change in educational program and philosophy. During the latter part of the nineteenth century, classrooms ranged in size from approximately 1200 to 1400 square feet to accommodate classes of fifty to eighty pupils. The trend toward smaller classes, however, was accompanied by smaller classrooms. Between the two World Wars the standard classroom of 660 square feet (22 feet wide by 30 feet long) designed to accommodate thirty-five pupils in five straight rows was the common pattern. Today, of course, this classroom is considered woefully inadequate to house an educational program that places emphasis upon learning as an active rather than passive process. The numerous and varied experiences and activities of the modern elementary program demand, above all else, adequate space and there are many who agree with Hayward who says, "To give children room to learn is neither wasteful nor extravagant. To force them into patterns of conflict, regimentation, and limitation because of classrooms which are too small is worse than wasteful."[2]

[1] "Educational Administration in the Decade Ahead," *School Life,* Vol. 43 (January, 1961), p. 9.
[2] W. George Hayward, "School Buildings and the Learning Program," *National Elementary Principal,* Vol. 39 (September, 1959), p. 22.

It is, of course, difficult to say exactly how much space is adequate because obviously this depends on many factors. In general, however, the minimum today seems to be about 30 to 50 square feet per child with most authorities recommending an overall size of 1000 to 1200 square feet for a class of twenty-five children. Kindergarten rooms should be larger.

What can the classroom teacher do to provide adequate space in a classroom that does not meet these requirements? Obviously, he cannot push out the walls of the classroom or remodel the school plant. A very simple solution, however, which lies within the power of every teacher is the careful selection and arrangement of furniture, thereby avoiding an extravagant waste of space (see pages 211 to 212).

Shape. What is the most desirable shape for an elementary classroom? In the rural one-room schools most of the classrooms were square. As schools increased in size, most of them contained rectangular classrooms placed on either side of a central corridor. Today, architects are exploring the possibilities of new shapes, among which are the circular, octagonal, hexagonal, and triangular classrooms. Such experimentation is to be commended provided, of course, that it is not done simply in an attempt to be different but rather in a sincere attempt to fit the physical environment to the needs of the learning situation.

Lighting. No single feature of the physical environment is of greater importance than proper lighting. Research has demonstrated rather conclusively that a satisfactory visual environment increases learning efficiency and reduces bodily fatigue and nervous tension among teachers and pupils. In addition, of course, it plays a major role in reducing safety hazards in the classroom, on stairways, in corridors, and in other parts of the school plant. Because of its prime importance, the subject of proper lighting has been the target of intensive research and study for several years. The literature on the topic is abundant but much of it is of a highly technical nature and of relatively little significance to the classroom teacher. There are, however, three key concepts of proper lighting with which *every* classroom teacher should be thoroughly familiar: quantity of light, quality of light, and balance of light.

The most fundamental requirement of good lighting is enough light. This depends on *the intensity of the source* and *the distance of the areas in question from the source.* These two factors combined result in illumination, which is measured in foot-candles. A foot-candle is the amount of illumination produced by a standard candle on a surface one foot away from it. The number of foot-candles required varies according to the task to be performed. Most authorities state that 30 foot-candles is the minimum illumination level for classroom activities for individuals of normal vision, and Seagers recommends that ". . . the general level of illumination at pupils' desks should be about seventy foot-candles."[3] The amount of illumination can be measured by a foot-candle meter which is a relatively inexpensive and small piece of equipment. There is little excuse for any school to be without a light meter or for any teacher to be unfamiliar with its use.

The quantitative approach to proper lighting is important but it, alone, is no longer recognized as a true indication of an adequate visual environment, for it is possible to have an abundance of light and still have unsatisfactory visual conditions. Much more important is the *quality* of light which is usually referred to as *brightness*. Brightness depends not only upon the intensity of light but also upon the amount reflected by any surface. Most surfaces reflect some light but there is wide variation depending upon color and texture. A dark surface, for instance, may reflect less than 10 per cent of the light falling upon it while a white surface may reflect approximately 85 to 90 per cent. It becomes apparent, therefore, that the reflectance factors of various surfaces of the classroom are important contributions to the overall quality of light secured. The following recommendations concerning the proper finish for the common surfaces of the classroom meet with wide agreement.

For ceilings, a reflectance factor of 80 to 85% may be achieved by use of white or off-white finish. Ceiling color should extend 18 to 20 inches down the side wall, unless the ceiling is extremely low. Average wall reflectance factors should be 50 to 60 or 70%, obtainable by light pastel colors. It is important to give the window wall a little higher reflectance (as high as 75-80% around the windows) than other walls, as daylight enters here and there are contrasts with the windows of high brightness. For floors, reflectance factors are 15 to 30%. Light colored linoleum, asphalt, and vinyl tile, as well as cork, help produce a desirable effect and are also easier to clean than dark tiles. Colors of desks and tables should be light or natural with non-gloss finish.[4]

Figure 6.1 illustrates desirable reflectance factors of the common surfaces of the classroom.

Brightness, thus, represents the *product* of the illumination (in foot-candles) and the reflection value of the surface. It is measured in terms of foot-lamberts. (Foot-candles x reflectance value = foot lamberts.) Thus, if fifty foot-candles of light fall upon a surface with a reflectance factor of 50%, the brightness can be figured as 50 x 50 or 25 foot-lamberts. If the illumination is known, it becomes very simple to figure the brightness

[3] Paul W. Seagers, "Lighting the Classroom," *NEA Journal*, Vol. 51 (October, 1962), p. 30.
[4] U. S. Department of Health, Education, and Welfare, *Environmental Engineering for the School* (Washington, D. C., 1961), p. 18.

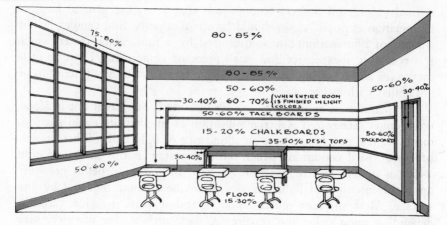

FIGURE 6.1

Recommended classroom reflectable values. From *Environmental Engineering for the School* (Washington, D. C., U. S. Department of Health, Education, and Welfare, 1961), p. 11.

since today almost all paint manufacturers state the reflectance value of their product on the label.

It has been stated that concern with proper lighting has progressed from an emphasis on *quantity* to one on *quality* or *brightness*. We have not stopped there, however, for today's concept of an adequate visual environment goes one step further and stresses brightness-balance. This simply means that the brightness of all surfaces, within the visual range, should be in proper balance. To achieve a correct balance, the following simplified standards are recommended.

1. The contrast *within* the *task* (the child's book or piece of paper) should be high, i. e. dark lead or ink on light paper.

2. No part of the *immediate* visual surroundings (the desk top, for instance) should be more than 3 times the brightness of the "task". (A high glossy finish on a desk top would violate this standard.)

3. No part of the child's *remote* visual environment (the classroom) should be more than 10 times (some say less) the brightness of the task. (An unshielded light bulb would violate this standard.)

4. No part of the child's *remote* visual environment should be less than ⅓ the brightness of the task. (A very dark chalkboard, floor, or tackboard would violate this standard.)

The above may be considered very lenient by some who advocate a closer balance among the various visual elements in the classroom. However, it is safe to say that if the above standards were followed in every elementary classroom, the visual environment would be considerably improved over what it has been in the past.

In considering the brightness-balance of the classroom, considerable attention should be given to the problem of *glare*. Glare may be defined as "the effect of brightness or brightness differences within the visual field sufficiently high to cause annoyance, discomfort, or loss in visual performance."[5] One may have either *direct glare*, due to bright sources of light in the field of vision (strong sunlight through an unshielded window, or a direct lighting fixture) or *reflected glare*, caused by light falling upon shiny surfaces. Let us consider each of these briefly.

To eliminate the problem of direct glare from wide window expanse, architects and designers are experimenting with various shades, blinds (horizontal and vertical), draperies, baffles, and louvers. Some of these are designed to be controlled by the classroom teacher; others operate automatically. Another solution may be to decrease the amount of window space per classroom, and several school architects have voiced the opinion that we may have reached the peak in the amount of glass we are using in schools. In some situations, of course, this reverse trend has gone so far as to result in the *windowless classroom*. McDonald summarizes the advantages of this innovation as:

1. High comfort level—no glare, no heavy shadows, no drafts, no overheating, no excess noise, no dust or grit.

2. Easily controlled conditions—light for study or darkness for films in seconds, silence for film narration or lecturing, no distractions from outside.

3. More space and time for learning—four full walls for displays, chalkboards, bulletin boards, pictures; no time wasted pulling shades, opening and closing windows, waiting for that truck to go by outside.

4. It can be more economical.[6]

There are, of course, many, many educators and architects who are not in favor of this type classroom for several reasons. The idea of living all day in a windowless cell seems to be highly objectionable to many of us and, in addition, depriving children of the valuable learning opportunities gained from observing the out-of-doors appears to be highly questionable. This viewpoint is expressed in the following statement by F. Lee Cochran, quoted by Burts.

I suspect there are many unanswered questions relative to the ultimate desirability, for the human organism, of living in an environment which is con-

[5] "Lighting Glossary," *Nation's Schools*, Vol. 66 (September, 1960), p. 78.
[6] Eva G. McDonald and Eleanor Burts, "Opinions Differ on Windowless Classrooms," *NEA Journal*, Vol. 50 (October, 1961), p. 14.

trolled by artificial means within very narrow limits, both thermally and visually. I suspect that the change of light intensity due to clouds passing over the sky, the changing quality of daylight from dawn to dusk, and the changing seasons with varied quality of light and air, which are made a part of an interior environment by the use of classroom windows, form a sort of human heritage that we will banish at our peril.[7]

The second source of direct glare, incorrect lighting fixtures, has been greatly eliminated by the widespread use of indirect and diffuse lighting. Several methods and kinds of equipment are now in use which are generally satisfactory. Probably the luminous ceiling through which soft light is diffused over the entire surface is one of the most forward-looking steps in controlling direct glare.

Reflected glare can be eliminated by removing shiny surfaces from the classroom. The use of varnish or high-gloss paints should be avoided. Glass surfaces such as those in cupboard doors and in framed pictures should either be removed or covered, and in every other possible way, the harmful effects of glare should be eliminated from the classroom.

Color. One of the most dramatic changes in the physical environment in recent years has been the wide use of color. Schools, like hospitals and factories, have discovered that color affects human morale and temperament to a high degree. Consequently, the dull schoolhouse browns and grays of the past have been replaced by soft, pleasing pastels with a higher reflectance value. In general, the warmer pastels, such as soft rose or pale yellow are used for rooms with northern exposure while the cooler blues, violets, and greens are used for southern exposures. In addition to these soft basic colors, many elementary classrooms are also painted with some of the bold, bright colors many children love so dearly. Bright red, blue, green, orange, or yellow can be used very effectively in wall murals or as decorative accents and can help to make the classroom a gay and inviting place for children.

It is interesting to note that there has been some research that indicates that color not only affects vision and mood, but may also affect the academic performance of children. An interesting experiment conducted several years ago in three Baltimore, Maryland schools compared the performance of children in (1) a school repainted according to the principles of color dynamics; (2) a school repainted with the traditional light buff walls and white ceilings; and (3) a school which was not repainted. Among the findings were "that color had the greatest beneficial results on behavior and scholastic performance traits among kindergarten children; that greater improvement as a result of planned color was in scho-

[7] *Ibid.,* p. 14.

lastic achievement rather than behavior traits; and that boys show greater color response than girls."[8]

In summarizing the research on the use of color in schools, Rice states that, "Color in the environment of a child affects his moods, his scholastic achievements, and his physical well-being."[9] In view of this statement, the importance of making wise and knowledgeable decisions regarding the selection and use of color should be apparent to every classroom teacher and administrator.

Acoustics. Equal in importance to the visual environment are the acoustical features of the classroom. Recent years have seen much improvement in this field and today, beginning first with the all-important decision of site selection, much thought is given to the proper control of sound. In general, acoustical engineers and architects are faced with two problems in this area. The first of these is the problem of *comfort*, or how to eliminate or reduce undesirable noise in the classroom. The second is the problem of *communication*, or how to transmit desired sound and create conditions for adequate hearing and listening. Perkins summarizes the progress made in solving these problems in the following statement.

Today, there is really no excuse for an acoustical problem. Available to the architect is a storehouse of knowledge and materials to solve any situation. Acoustical plasters, ceiling tiles (both decorative and practical), and other materials, used properly, can make any room quiet, while at the same time permitting the proper sound levels in all areas of the room. Even without standard acoustical treatment, a classroom can be relatively quiet by employing architectural features such as slanting ceilings and exposed beams to cup up the sound patterns.[10]

As with the visual environment, most of the responsibility for providing proper acoustical conditions in the classroom lies with specialized personnel rather than the classroom teacher. Concern, however, for the comfort and learning efficiency of his pupils should alert the teacher constantly to the importance of (1) being aware of, and reporting to the proper authorities, sources of internal or external noises that can be controlled such as noisy ventilators, (2) proper use of his own voice as a model for children to emulate, (3) careful attention to the needs of individual children, particularly those suffering from a hearing loss, and (4) carefully arranging the daily schedule to minimize distractions from ex-

[8] Condensed Report of the Johns Hopkins University Experiment collaborating with the Baltimore City Schools and the Pittsburgh Plate Glass Company, p. 1, mimeographed.

[9] Arthur H. Rice, "What Research Knows About Color in the Classroom," *Nation's Schools*, Vol. 52 (November, 1953), portfolio insert.

[10] Lawrence B. Perkins, "The Physical Environment," *National Elementary Principal*, Vol. 39 (September, 1959), p. 121.

ternal noises such as other children playing on the playground, heavy out-of-doors traffic, or band rehearsals in the school auditorium.

Air conditioning. Today's inclusive concept of air conditioning embraces heating, cooling, humidity control, and ventilation. The importance of this feature of the physical environment is so obvious that it needs little elaboration here. In most schools, except in the warmest parts of our country, it is necessary to use some type of heating system for a certain part of the year. Authorities generally agree that the temperature of the room for usual classroom activities should be between 68 and 72 degrees and controlled by an individual classroom thermostat. The teacher's responsibility for heating the classroom properly is summarized by Anderson as follows:

Whatever the heating system in use, the teacher needs to understand its operation. If a custodian or building engineer has responsibility for the regulation of the system, the teacher may merely need to know the channels through which he reports any questions relating to room heating. But if the teacher is responsible for regulating the heat within the classroom, he should ask the principal how he can obtain expert instruction.[11]

Air cooling is, of course, a relatively new feature in schools although certainly the time is close at hand when it will be considered as necessary as a heating system. The trend toward the longer school year and increasing use of the school plant mentioned earlier will most certainly highlight the need for supplying these buildings with air cooling systems.

The problem of proper ventilation has received considerable study in recent years for its relationship to bodily comfort and hence learning efficiency is apparent. The early belief that there was something "unhealthful, if not poisonous, about air in a room occupied by a number of people . . . was reflected in state ventilating codes requiring 30 cubic feet of fresh air per occupant per minute."[12] Today, the need for such a large intake of fresh air has been generally discredited, although, of course, no one will deny the importance of adequate ventilation. What is meant by "adequate," however is debatable although ". . . 10 to 15 cubic feet of air per minute per person, or two to three air changes per hour, are commonly recommended."[13] This may be accomplished through window ventilation or through a mechanical system. Anderson compares the two types, and the teacher's responsibility for controlling them in the following statement.

[11] C. L. Anderson, "Heating and Ventilating," *NEA Journal,* Vol. 51 (October, 1962), p. 29.

[12] John H. Herrick and others, *From School Program to School Plant* (New York, Holt, Rinehart, and Winston, Inc., 1956), p. 449.

[13] *Ibid.*, p. 450.

The most common type of classroom ventilation is the window-gravity method: An open window with a glass or other composition deflecting board at the bottom of the window causes the outdoor air to rise upward as it enters the room. Because this cool air from outdoors is heavier than the warm air in the room, it soon begins to settle toward the floor. As the air warms, it rises and is drawn from the room through an exhaust flue on the wall opposite the windows.

If the room is not equipped with an exhaust flue, the teacher should see that the window is open from the top, as well as the bottom, to allow the warm, moist air to escape outdoors. An open door on the side of the room opposite the windows also can substitute for an exhaust flue. In addition, the teacher may be able to experiment by varying the angle of the baffle board and the height of the window opening, to assure a comfortable flow of air.

Mechanical ventilation is another method of circulating air through a room: Fresh air enters the building, usually in the basement, and is forced through various flues or ducts into the classroom by fans or blowers. The blowers or fans operate at a set rate and there is little a teacher can do to vary conditions.

If the teacher finds that the ventilation is not removing enough heat and moisture from the room, he should report this condition to the school office. An exhaust duct could be blocked or a fan stopped. These conditions can be corrected if they are called to the attention of the proper person.

Window-gravity ventilation usually is preferable to mechanical ventilation, but is unsatisfactory in excessively crowded classrooms.[14]

Furniture. The main item of classroom furniture is pupil seating and work facilities. In most classrooms, the pattern of furnishing each pupil with an individual desk and chair is still standard practice. Some schools, however, are furnishing classrooms with tables to seat two to six or eight children instead of individual desks, or they are combining a few larger tables with perhaps ten or twelve desks per classroom. Such a seating arrangement is obviously more economical of space than individual chairs and desks and also lends itself more easily to accommodating a variety of individual and group activities.

Where individual desks and chairs are used, they are of a light-weight movable type designed for maximum eye and body comfort. In general, there are two types, (1) the *tubular unit* in which desk and chair are connected by a metal tubing and (2) the separate chair and desk. Advantages of each are claimed by authorities although the desk and chair type probably lends itself more easily to a wide variety of purposes. Desks and chairs should be purchased and assigned to the classroom with full consideration of the wide range of physical differences existing among children in any one class. Some authorities recommend that every classroom should be equipped with at least three different sizes of chairs in an attempt to provide proper seating for all children. In judging whether or

[14] C. L. Anderson, *op. cit.*, p. 29.

not the equipment is comfortable and correct for a child, the teacher should ask himself the following questions:

Are the chairs and desks the right height for the children? Can each child place his feet flat on the floor while sitting with the base of his spine against the back of the seat? . . . When a child is at his desk or table, does he appear comfortable? Is the table a convenient height or must he hunch his shoulders or reach to rest his arms on the table? Are his toes touching the floor under his chair, are his feet dangling, or is he able to place his feet flat on the floor? . . . If the child is left-handed, is his table built so he can use his left hand comfortably or must he twist himself around so he can write or draw?[15]

It has been suggested earlier that, of all types of furniture arrangements, the most space consuming, the most rigid, and the least satisfactory from a modern educational point of view is the arrangement of straight rows of individual desks and chairs. In addition to the space needed for each desk to be a little island unto itself, this arrangement is least conducive to developing desirable communication skills, and an informal and wholesome social climate. Decidedly more preferable is the informal arrangement some teachers use of combining individual desks to form larger tables or to arrange desks in an informal semicircle, circle, or open-square pattern. Regardless of which of these is used, it should be kept in mind that no arrangement should become absolutely fixed, for desks and chairs should be moved at will to accommodate the purposes and activities of the moment.

Concerning the finish of the desk or table top, it is generally agreed that the best materials for working surfaces "appear to be hard melamine plastics with a dull finish and a light color with a reflectance factor of 40 to 50 per cent."[16] These are very satisfactory from the visual standpoint and are also extremely durable and easy to clean. It is interesting to note that soon we may hope to improve these still further by having desks with "soft" surfaces, "comparable in writing ease to a pad of paper and yet rugged enough to withstand classroom wear and stains."[17]

Another important furniture item in the classroom is the teacher's desk. Fortunately, the teacher's desk on a raised platform in the front of the room can be found today only in Hollywood film sets, for most teachers have relegated it to a relatively obscure section of the room where they can use it as a teacher-pupil work or conference center. Russell and Hood comment upon the trend toward considering the teacher's desk, not just as a desk and chair, but as a small suite including (1) a large

[15] Evelyn A. Davies, *The Elementary School Child and His Posture Patterns* (New York, Appleton-Century Crofts, 1958), pp. 46-47.

[16] Russell E. Wilson and James R. Hood, "Equipment for the Elementary School," *National Elementary Principal*, Vol. 39 (September, 1959), p. 142.

[17] *Ibid.*

flat-top work area on a table or desk, (2) conference area as part of the table or desk, (3) at least one two-drawer file on casters to accompany the table, (4) a book truck, (5) a television and visual aids unit.[18]

It has already been mentioned that supplementary chairs and tables are necessary pieces of furniture in the modern classroom. The latter may be provided in varying sizes, heights, and newer shapes such as round, half-round, S-shaped, and trapezoidal.

Chalkboards. Many innovations have been made in this standard piece of equipment since the days of the dark slate boards. Although some teachers still prefer slate boards, most of the newer schools contain chalkboards of higher reflectance value and greater aesthetic appeal. These boards are made of a wide variety of materials and colors. For some time green was the most widely used color, although today gray seems to be gaining in popularity with various shades of blue, brown, tan, coral, and blue-green also available. White or ivory boards have also been installed in some classrooms and are used primarily for art work.

In general, the footage devoted to chalkboards has steadily decreased over the years and few modern classrooms have boards extending the full length of two walls as was true thirty years ago. Some think that this trend has gone too far, however, for some teachers in modern schools complain about too little chalkboard space. A sensible compromise between adequate chalkboard footage and sufficient wall space for other purposes appears to be the trend toward making chalkboards in sliding, movable, reversible, or portable sections. Also, the fact that these boards can now be raised or lowered to suit the height of children is an important improvement over the older stationary type.

Tackboards. Part of the trend toward decreasing space for chalkboards is increasing space for tackboards. Today, educators recognize bulletin boards to be a valuable feature of the intellectual environment (see following section) and consequently the newer classrooms contain more than twice as much wall space devoted to cork and composition boards than the classrooms of the past. Indeed, in some schools, entire walls of classrooms are surfaced to permit them to be used for display purposes. In others, increased tackboard space is gained through using reversible chalkboard-tackboard units or by installing portable boards, sliding boards, boards mounted on folding panels, or free-standing boards that can double as space dividers. Pegboards which accommodate many types and sizes of hangers and clips are also popular items in some of the newer classrooms. In general, display boards may be purchased in a variety of attractive colors similar to those mentioned for chalkboards. The modern colors are aesthetically pleasing and, of course, have a sufficiently high reflectance

[18] *Ibid.*

value for a balanced visual environment. In older schools, the advantages of the newer boards can be gained by covering the dark-brown surface with several coats of light paint or with a pastel wallpaper.

Storage equipment. To the intense relief of the classroom teacher, more and more thought is given today to designing classrooms with adequate storage space. The trend is toward *more* storage space as well as functional storage equipment designed to serve a variety of purposes. The stationary wall cabinets and the waste-consuming cloakrooms are rapidly disappearing. In their place are substituted cabinets of various sizes and shapes which can be used to house audio-visual aids, books, children's clothing and belongings, and various school supplies and pieces of equipment. Some of these are closed cabinets but many are open to permit easy access and proper ventilation. Cabinets, book-cases, and shelving units are now made so that they can be moved easily and can double as book trucks, room-dividers, or work counters. In general, the advantages of this new concept of storage space are (1) it provides more space for storing the increasing number and variety of materials used in a modern program, (2) it permits greater flexibility of room arrangement and pupil activities, (3) it permits a higher degree of convertibility from year to year, and (4) it is more economical, easier to clean, and offers greater convenience to teacher and pupils.

As part of the physical environment, we have considered only the permanent features and equipment of the classroom. Supplementary materials designed for specific curriculum areas are discussed in the following section.

THE INTELLECTUAL ENVIRONMENT

This section is discussed according to three basic considerations: (1) What is meant by the term *intellectual environment?* (2) What are the functions of the intellectual environment? and (3) What elements are necessary to a positive intellectual environment?

WHAT IS MEANT BY THE TERM *intellectual environment?* Perhaps the simplest way to answer this question is to visit two elementary classrooms. As you open the door to the first, you notice that the room is neat, clean, quiet, and orderly. Most of the floor space is consumed by the straight rows of children's desks. As a matter of fact, the teacher's desk and a single bookcase are the only other items of furniture in the room. The lone bulletin board exhibits the week's perfect spelling papers and the assignments on the chalkboard indicate the workbook pages, arithmetic examples, and questions to be completed that day. All in all, the classroom conveys an orderly and not unpleasant impression but it is impossible to see how its barrenness and sterility could be conducive to any keen intellectual activity—by either teacher or pupils.

The first thing you notice as you visit the second classroom is the hum of purposeful activity that greets you. The children are engaged in a wide variety of tasks as the teacher circulates around the room, helping individuals and groups with their work. Some children are working at their desks. Three boys are sprawled on the floor carefully tracing an outline map on a huge sheet of brown paper. Two others are engrossed in the atlas on the library table. One child is busy at the easel while another energetic individual is industriously cleaning the aquarium. You notice, also, the abundance of materials in this room which apparently includes everything from a television set to an old black umbrella presently serving as a miniature planetarium. As you watch the teacher and children working together, you begin to sense a dynamic feeling of excitement and you discover that these pupils are actually excited about learning! They are eagerly seeking answers, finding new sources of knowledge, uncovering strange and puzzling problems, testing hunches, and discovering satisfying solutions. The zest, vitality, and enthusiasm they have for intellectual adventuring have been carefully nurtured in a classroom climate far different from that of the first classroom you visited. Specifically, this type of climate has been structured to serve the basic functions discussed below.

WHAT ARE THE MAJOR FUNCTIONS OF THE INTELLECTUAL ENVIRONMENT? First and foremost, the environment of the classroom should stimulate the pupils' intellectual curiosities. Every normal, healthy youngster has within him a driving need to know and every phase of the environment should be arranged and manipulated to whet this desire to razor sharpness. For instance, a bulletin board containing pictures of various types of erosion with the caption, "Do You Know What These Pictures Illustrate?" will help to arouse some children's curiosities. Or an empty tank with the sign near it, "Can you submit a good plan for a balanced aquarium in this tank?" will present a not-to-be ignored challenge to other pupils. Or perhaps a writing assignment to "Describe the preparations you will make for your first trip to Mars," will encourage some original and creative thinking. Through these, and untold other ways, the classroom environment can be contrived to confront children continuously with problems or questions that stimulate intellectual curiosity and develop creative, independent thought.

Of equal importance with intellectual curiosity is intellectual initiative. In other words, when children have been confronted with a problem, they must be encouraged to exert the initiative and effort needed to find its solution. In order to accomplish this, they must have ready access to numerous references, materials, and resources. If these are not available, interest and curiosity will quickly change to disinterest and frustration. Strickland emphasizes this point in the following statement.

The material for solving the problems, finding answers to the questions and carrying on the suggested exploration must be available without too much frustrating search and labor or the child will put forth some effort and then give up the matter and be almost worse off for his experience. Intellectual curiosity and interest are valuable and rewarding only as the child learns to satisfy them. Curiosity without initiative in finding answers produces no real growth.[19]

Another area of intellectual growth that should be fostered by the classroom environment is intellectual resourcefulness which Lewis defines as the "wise use of knowledge and skills."[20] In other words, the classroom environment should provide plentiful opportunities for children to use their knowledges and skills. For instance, a classroom shell collection, to be worthwhile, demands that each shell be accompanied by a card identifying and describing it. What better functional reading and writing experiences can be offered to children? An empty picture frame cries for an attractive painting from a pupil. A small section of a bulletin board devoted to a review of "The Book of the Week" invites children to post illustrated reviews of their favorite books. A setting hen demands a house and the house demands some measuring, computing, estimating, designing, and constructing skills. In these, and in thousands of other ways, the classroom environment can be manipulated to provide opportunities for each pupil to further his intellectual resourcefulness.

Lastly, a favorable academic climate will provide for the wide range of intellectual abilities and interests that exists among thirty children. In a classroom rich with learning materials and varied opportunities, no child needs to feel held back because his neighbor does not parallel him in intellectual growth, nor pressured to keep pace with his more advanced neighbors. Books on all levels of difficulty, periodicals ranging from *Scientific American* to *Jack and Jill;* materials from the simplest to the relatively complex; and opportunities for individual study that differ in frequency and length will help to stimulate and satisfy unique intellectual appetites. As Fox states,

In a classroom deliberately and skillfully set up for gearing children's choice toward learning the skills, every child in the group is provided for. No child will ever reach the ceiling, as it were, will ever exhaust the challenges in his classroom because the teacher, planning with him in mind, will set out materials

[19] Ruth G. Strickland, "Creating a Challenging Classroom Environment," *The Reading Teacher,* Vol. 15 (December, 1961), p. 194.
[20] Gertrude M. Lewis, *Educating Children in Grades Four, Five and Six,* Bulletin 1958, No. 3 (Washington, D. C., U. S. Office of Education, 1958), p. 70.

and set up situations accordingly. Similarly, a child who is restless and seems not to latch on will not be blamed but rather will lead the teacher to seek and try out other materials or ideas to challenge him. Thus every child in the group is challenged to select and reach out—to find his own kind of "giftedness", resources and growing skills—within a framework of good social living.[21]

WHAT ELEMENTS CONSTITUTE A FAVORABLE INTELLECTUAL ENVIRONMENT? In our discussion thus far, certain elements have been mentioned that determine a favorable intellectual climate in the classroom. Obviously, the most important of these is the teacher. What the teacher is, says, and does are reflected in a classroom atmosphere that either nourishes or inhibits intellectual growth. In order to create a positive academic climate, the teacher must himself be an intellectually alert individual, a point strongly emphasized in Chapter 2. Secondly, the teacher must be sensitive to the varying abilities and interests that exist among his pupils and structure the environment to accommodate them. Thirdly, and very important, the teacher must be able to recognize, and capitalize upon, the spontaneous opportunities for learning that arise daily in every classroom. For instance, David, aged eight, one winter morning described to his classmates the very large icicle he had seen hanging from a branch of a tree, as he walked to school. A fairly ordinary incident? Certainly. But it was turned into a valuable learning experience by a creative teacher who followed up with such questions as:

"How is it possible for David to see an icicle when we haven't had snow or rain in a long time?"

"Are all icicles made of water? Could there be anything special about this one?"

"Could David have seen this icicle on any tree or only on a certain kind of tree?"

"Does anyone know the name of the tree David is talking about? How could we find out?"

"Does anyone remember the story we read about sugaring in New England? Does this give you a hint about this icicle? Do we have sugar maples around here? What kind of maple trees do we have?"

The second element necessary for a desirable intellectual environment is *time*. Children and teacher must have time to wonder, time to peruse individual problems, time to browse among books, time to observe living phenomena, and time to think. This means that the daily schedule should be carefully planned (see Chapter 7) but should not be so highly organ-

[21] Reprinted by permission of the Association for Childhood Education International, 3615 Wisconsin Avenue, N.W., Washington 16, D. C. "Building on Children's Eagerness to Read," by Lorene K. Fox. From *Childhood Education*, January, 1962, Vol. 38, No. 5, p. 219.

ized or so rigid that children have no time for their special intellectual pursuits. Classrooms in which children are rushed from one lesson or assignment to the next according to the inflexible hands of the clock remind one of the classic remark of the elderly Quaker gentleman. To his friend, who had explained how he organized his day so that every minute was accounted for, the old gentleman replied, "But when dost thee do thy thinking?" In a positive intellectual environment, children must be given some time occasionally to do their thinking.

The third element which has been mentioned repeatedly in our discussion of an intellectual environment is that of adequate materials, tools, and resources for learning. The remainder of this section is devoted to those most often considered as part of the classroom environment with additional instructional aids examined in Chapter 10.

Bulletin boards. It was stated in the previous section that one of the most noticeable trends in schoolroom construction is the increasing amount of wall space devoted to tackboards or bulletin boards. This area today is recognized as one of the most important features of the intellectual environment. Gone are the days when the bulletin board was used solely to exhibit pictures of holiday or seasonal interest, the week's crop of perfect arithmetic papers, or mimeographed announcements from the central office. Today, the bulletin board is considered one of the most valuable and most functional instructional devices available to the teacher, *if it is used correctly*. It can, for instance, be profitably used to motivate interest in a future unit of work. Or it can be used to expand and enrich a unit already underway. Occasionally it may be devoted to an exhibit prepared by an individual or small group on a special or unique interest. It is an extremely valuable aid to a study of current news events and a *News Board* of well-chosen clippings is a must in every intermediate or upper grade. It can, of course, be used as a display area for children's paintings or such three-dimensional art forms as paper sculpture or collages. It may be decorative; it may be utilitarian; but, above all else, it *must* have educational value. DeBernardis suggests the following guidelines for making the bulletin board an effective instructional tool.

1. Collect suitable illustrations and other materials which will cover topics and units being taught.
2. Classify and file the materials so they can be easily located.
3. Select illustrations pertaining to the specific subject or area under consideration.
4. Arrange the materials in an interesting, eye-catching manner.
5. Use the principles of good composition and display.
6. Prepare a title and brief captions.

7. Integrate the display with the instructional unit.
8. Encourage students to observe and evaluate the bulletin board.[22]

Centers of interest. In discussing materials and displays that should be integral features of the classroom environment, the question is usually asked, "Can a classroom contain so many materials that the environment is distracting rather than stimulating?" Admittedly some classrooms are overcrowded and cluttered but the cause is usually one of poor house-keeping or disorganization rather than an overabundance of learning resources. In order to avoid this possibility, many teachers organize their classroom space and materials into *centers of interest*. Resourceful utilization of space, careful grouping of movable storage and display areas, wise arrangement of movable furniture, and improvisation of temporary shelves and tables permit various sections of the room to be devoted to particular interests or curriculum areas. Such centers, corners, or clusters are used primarily to (1) encourage individual and small group participation, (2) display projects and activities of pupils, (3) provide numerous suggestions for independent study, (4) motivate interest in a future area of study, (5) expand and continue an academic interest produced during a class discussion, and (6) store, whenever feasible, materials usually kept permanently in the classroom.

The following are generally the most popular centers found in the modern elementary classroom. It should be kept in mind, however, that few of them (except the classroom library) should be considered as absolutely permanent features of the classroom. To the contrary, they should be formed, dismantled, expanded, or reduced according to the on-going activities and interests of the children.

Classroom library. No other factor is more important for stimulating children's interest in reading than an adequate supply of the fascinating and wonderful books written for children today. Consequently, one of the most important spots in the elementary classroom is the library nook. It is important to remember, however, that the classroom collection should supplement, *but never supplant*, the school library. A small reading table; some comfortable chairs; and skillfully arranged bookcases, shelves, and room dividers are the basic pieces of equipment of the library center. Here is kept the classroom collection of books and periodicals, some of which may belong permanently to the classroom as well as others that have been borrowed from the school library, the traveling county library, the public library, or from the teacher's and pupils' personal collections. (Note: This last source should not be overlooked by teachers for very often a sizable collection of books can be accumulated in the classroom

[22] Amo DeBernardis, *The Use of Instructional Materials* (New York, Appleton-Century-Crofts, 1960), p. 28.

merely by suggesting that pupils share their own books temporarily with their classmates.)

The library center also contains the room's collection of reference and research materials. Reference books, at least one set of encyclopedia, dictionaries of varying levels of difficulty, maps, globes, atlases, newspapers, periodicals, and other tools may be kept permanently in the library center. A bulletin board may be used to display illustrations or attractive book jackets made by children of their favorite books. A small display area or an accumulative class booklet can provide children with the means of sharing their written book reviews with each other. A bulletin board or scrapbook of pictures of well-known authors will interest many pupils. Original stories and poems by children can also be displayed or collected in a scrapbook for the library corner. Then too, the library center may be used to teach certain habits and attitudes toward books and reading. A chart of acceptable standards of conduct in a library may be displayed prominently on a wall or nearby chart rack. Perhaps another chart reminding children how to care for a book properly may be needed occasionally. There is literally no end to the type and number of learning experiences to be gained from a classroom library corner and it is difficult to see how any teacher, on any grade level, could create a favorable intellectual environment without it.

Art center. Another very popular area in the elementary classroom is the art center designed to provide children with a variety of creative experiences. A large, flat-surfaced table and from two to four easels are usually musts in this section although many teachers improvise painting surfaces by covering chalkboard or tackboard surfaces with protective wrapping paper or newspaper. Very often these surfaces contain a printed invitation such as "Do you want to paint a picture today?" and some teachers provide a convenient space where children may sign up for the use of an easel. In addition, the art center should contain a drying rack for children's painting, storage space for art materials kept permanently in the classroom, and storage space for children's work such as an oversized filing cabinet which can be purchased or made from a large sturdy cardboard carton.

If running water is available, the art center should be located next to the sink. Some of the newer classrooms have adjoining alcoves or workrooms which contain the sink, storage facilities, and space needed for a functional art center. Storage space is at a premium in the art center and the ingenious teacher organizes and utilizes every inch possible in order to accommodate the numerous materials needed for a rich art program. Tools and supplies basic to the elementary school program and kept permanently in the classroom or borrowed from the central art room include the following:

1. brushes   painting, flat, hog bristle, one inch to one-quarter inch wide

                       painting, pointed sable, large (size 6 or 7)

                       paste

2. chalk   soft, 10 or 12 colors, black, white

3. crayons   wax, soft, 10 or 12 colors, black, white

4. drawing boards about 18″ x 24″, soft plywood at least "B C" grade (i. e., clear of knots on at least one side)

5. erasers   Artgum type

6. inks   ordinary blue-black fountain pen

                       black India, 2-oz. bottles

7. paint   poster, liquid in pints or powder in pounds (white, black, yellow, blue, brown, green, red, as basic; magenta, purple, turquoise as luxuries; probably twice the quantity of black, white, and yellow as of other colors chosen)

                       water colors in boxes of 8 colors (sometimes useful but not entirely necessary . . .)

8. paper   roll of kraft (i. e., brown wrapping), about 36″ wide, or "project roll", 36″ wide manila, 18″ x 24″, cream and gray colored construction, 12″ x 18″ (red, yellow, blue, light green, dark green, black, gray, and perhaps some in-between colors like blue-green, red-orange; some 40 colors are obtainable)

                       newsprint, natural, 18″ x 24″

9. paint tins   muffin tins, with at least 6 depressions

10. paste   school, in quarts

11. pencils   black, drawing, soft, about 5B

12. work boards plywood (3-ply) 18″ x 24″ (old drawing boards are suitable)[23]

In addition to the above basic list, many classroom art centers contain such materials as plasticene (in various colors); clay (dry or ready-to-use); bits of colored glass, tile, seeds, or cereals for making mosaics; string and wool for making collages or weaving; paper of all kinds including cellophane, aluminum foil and gift wrappings; pieces of cloth, leather, metal, and felt for three-dimensional forms; bits of sponge or wooden dowels for making block prints; linoleum block printing equipment (in the upper grades); and others too numerous to mention.

In addition to providing creative experiences, the art center should be structured to develop children's appreciation of fine art. Art masterpieces

[23] Charles D. Gaitskell, *Children and Their Art* (New York, Harcourt, Brace & World, Inc., 1958), pp. 108-109.

(classic and modern) that appeal to children can be attractively displayed in this section of the room. Realistic or abstract pieces of sculpture will also add an interesting and artistic note to the environment. In summary, the art center should provide the opportunity, the inspiration, and the materials to develop the varied artistic talents of all pupils. It should be, without question, one of the most dynamic and vibrant features of the classroom environment.

Industrial arts center. Another important center is the industrial arts center which is becoming increasingly important in the elementary school program. Many of the newer schools have a central workshop used by all grades. Others have self-contained classrooms constructed to provide a work corner or small adjoining shop. In classrooms without these built-in facilities, the resourceful teacher may requisition materials and allot space in order to provide his pupils with firsthand experiences in using a variety of tools and materials.

In most self-contained classrooms, all that is needed to provide a fairly adequate industrial arts center are a few simple tools and a place to work. A sturdy general-purpose workbench equipped with two woodworking vises will provide adequate work space for the average classroom. The bench height will vary from 24 inches for kindergarten and grade one to 28 inches for grades five and six. The bench should be of the enclosed type in order to provide a storage area for tools and projects. A small vibrating type jig saw is a safe power tool suitable for all grade levels. Hand tools that should be basic to the elementary classroom industrial arts center include the following, all of which can be purchased for an approximate total cost of seventy-five dollars.

2 — 10 point crosscut saws
1 — backsaw
2 — coping saws
1 — hand drill (¼" capacity)
2 — sets, assorted twist drills ⅟₁₆" to ¼"
1 — brace, 10" swing
1 — each, auger bits—¼", ⅜", ½", ¾", and 1"
1 — try square
1 — combination pliers
1 — side-cutting pliers
1 — straight tin snips
2 — C clamps
2 — claw hammers, 7 oz.
1 — claw hammer, 16 oz.
2 — half round cabinet file with handle
1 — block plane
2 — screwdrivers—4" and 6"
2 — bench rules, 24"

**The industrial arts corner is a vital center of interest
in the modern elementary classroom.**

A word of caution concerning the above suggested list: The elementary teacher, when requisitioning or purchasing tools for his classroom, should be guided by two basic principles: (1) The appropriate size and weight of all tools should be determined by the physical capacities of the pupils as well as the purposes for which the tools are intended, and (2) All tools should be of high quality. It is a false and even dangerous economy to buy cheap tools for children, a lesson which many teachers have learned from bitter experience. Finally, since safety is always a factor to be considered in this area, charts containing directions and reminders as to the proper use, care, cleaning, and storage of tools and materials should be prominently displayed in the industrial arts center.

Science center. One can scarcely imagine a modern elementary classroom that does not have a section of it devoted to the science activities and interests of children. Here can be displayed to advantage the various collections that interest children such as rocks, shells, fossils, leaves, and insects. A worktable or cabinet top surfaced with plastic, linoleum, or oilcloth may be provided on which children may conduct individual experiments during their free time. If the table is on casters, it may be rolled to the center or front of the room to serve as an experiment table during science lessons. Scientific books and magazines are, of course, valuable additions to this area. Then too, all types of living things may be kept from time to time in the science center. The goldfish or tropical fish aquarium, terrarium, and formicarium are usually spots of interest. Hamsters, turtles, chickens, frogs, toads, snakes, tadpoles, rabbits, guinea pigs, and others offer wonderful opportunities for learning. Experiments in progress, table displays, bulletin board exhibits, charts and notebooks of accumulated data, many varieties of plants, and other items too numerous to mention are frequently found in the science center. Basic materials which, if kept in the classroom, should be stored in or as near the science center as possible include the following:

Chemicals (To be collected or purchased)

    Ammonia—household
    Iodine
    Lime—for limewater (drugstore)
    Limewater—to test for carbon dioxide
    Litmus paper—to test acids, bases, and salts
    Paraffin
    Red ink
    Baking soda
    Soil tester
    Starch
    Sugar
    Table salt

Glassware (To be purchased)

    Battery jars, small and large
    Beakers, Pyrex, assorted sizes
    Flask, boiling, flat-bottom, Pyrex, 1-pint size
    Funnel, 7-inch top diameter (for filtration experiments)
    Glass tubing, 6-mm. outside diameter (5 lb.)
    Graduate
    Lamp chimneys
    Petri dishes (for growth of bacteria)
    Window glass, assorted shapes and sizes

Other Apparatus (To be purchased)

    Asbestos mats
    Clamp for ring stand
    Corks, assorted sizes, Nos. 12-25 and Nos. 0-11
    Forceps, for handling heated objects
    Iron ring stand, large size
    Iron ring, with clamp, for fastening on ring stand

Iron tripod

Magnifying glass, 4-inch diameter or larger

Rubber stoppers, solid, and 1- and 2-hole, assorted sizes, Nos. 2-6

Rubber tubing to fit glass tubing, 3/16-inch inside diameter

Test tubes, 6" x 3/4"

Test-tube brushes

Test-tube clamp (holder)

Test-tube rack (to hold 12 tubes)

Thistle tube

Triangular file (to cut glass tubing)

Wire gauze with asbestos center for placing over ring or tripod

Miscellaneous (To be collected)

Bags, paper, and cellophane

Boxes, wooden and cardboard, assorted sizes, for storage and other uses

Candles

Cellophane, clear and colored

Construction materials: ball of string, colored chalk, crayons, glue and cement, needles, nails, paring knife, pins, rubber bands, scissors, spools of thread, thumbtacks, and similar equipment

Dowels, assorted diameters

Flowerpots, assorted sizes

Fruit jars, milk bottles, glass tumblers, for storage and other uses

Globes and maps of the world

Labels, gummed, assorted

Lumber, assorted sizes, scraps

Medicine dropper

Paints, oil, water color, show card

Pans, various shapes and sizes

Plates, assorted sizes

Pot holder

Pots and pans, large and small

Razor blades, single-edge

Rubber balloons and balls

Ruler, foot

Sandpaper, assorted

Saucers and sauce dishes

Scraps of different kinds of cloth (silk, wool, cotton, etc.)

Spoons for handling heated materials and other purposes

Tin cans, assorted sizes, tops cut out carefully

Tools . . .

Wire, steel and copper

Sources of Heat (To be purchased)

Alcohol burner

Alcohol for burner

Bunsen burner (Usable only with gas. Four feet of ¼-inch inside diameter rubber tubing for use with Bunsen burner)
Canned heat
Hot plate[24]

Arithmetic center. The increasing use of concrete and semiconcrete materials to teach the mathematical and social significances of numbers has resulted in the creation of an arithmetic center in many classrooms. The exact type of materials in each classroom will, of course, depend upon the maturity and mathematical experiences of the pupils. In order to enrich and give meaning to the arithmetic curriculum, Brueckner suggests the following basic list of materials, all of which may, at one time or another, find their way into the arithmetic center where they can be used freely and extensively by the children.

MATERIALS USEFUL IN MAKING NUMBERS AND NUMBER OPERATIONS MEANINGFUL

1. Tickets or sticks to show groupings and regroupings of ones, tens, and hundreds.
2. Hundreds' board to visualize meanings and groupings.
3. Disks and fact finders to find number facts.
4. Place-value charts to show the meaning of place-value in whole numbers and decimals and to visualize operations with numbers.
5. Abacus to demonstrate place-value and operations.
6. Practice cards for learning number facts.
7. Fraction chart to compare values of fractions and to find answers of examples.
8. Cut-outs of fractional parts to demonstrate meanings and solutions, involving especially halves, fourths, and eighths.
9. Diagrams to visualize the meaning and relative value of decimal fractions.
10. Diagrams to show actual sizes of units of square measure, such as square inch, square foot, and square yard.

MATERIALS FOR TEACHING ABOUT SYSTEMS AND INSTRUMENTS OF MEASUREMENT

1. Quantity: abacus, adding machine, number charts, dial telephone, tallying devices, automobile license plates, street numbers, fact finders, counting block.

[24] Glenn O. Blough and Marjorie H. Campbell, *Making and Using Classroom Science Materials in the Elementary School* (New York, Holt, Rinehart and Winston, Inc., 1954), pp. 35-38.

2. Lengths: ruler, yardstick, tape measure, meter stick, standards for measuring height, micrometer, pedometer, speedometer.

3. Time: calendar, clock, watch, stop-watch, sun dial, shadow stick, candle clock, hourglass, time table, metronome, school clock system, standard time chart.

4. Value: coins, bills, checks, wampum, tax tokens, stamps, tickets, bonds, price lists, tokens, price tags, cash register.

5. Weight: postal scales, balances, spring scales, nurses' scales, grocer scales, druggist scales, pressure gauges, height-weight charts, pictures of scales for weighing large amounts, labels showing weights of things.

6. Area: square-inch cards, square-foot cards, sizes of rugs and rooms, house plans, garden plans, maps.

7. Volume: pint, quart, gallon measures; cup, teaspoon, tablespoon; cooking measures; cans by sizes; peck and bushel measures; boxes, cases, bottles; water meter, gas meter, rainfall gauge; cubic inch blocks.

8. Temperature: thermometer, clinical thermometer, cooking thermometer, thermostat, automobile temperature gauge, furnace gauge.[25]

In addition to the above materials, teachers using one of the modern mathematics programs include in the arithmetic center those manipulative materials specially designed for the program.

Music center. The music center should be designed to provide children with worthwhile creative and appreciational activities as well as to house the various materials and instruments. A record collection, a record-player (preferably with earphones), and a tape-recorder will provide valuable listening experiences. If a small bulletin board is part of this area, it can be used to display pictures of musical instruments, pictures of famous composers, or original songs composed by children. A group scrapbook kept on the table or nearby shelf may serve the same purpose. In addition, storage cabinets with movable shelves may be grouped or arranged to hold the various song books; simple instruments such as musical glasses, inexpensive flutes, and auto-harp; and the numerous commercial or pupil-made rhythm instruments. Last, but not least, of course, is the piano which should be a permanent feature of all primary and most upper elementary grade classrooms.

Writing center. A desk or table and one or two chairs grouped into a cozy corner and relatively isolated from the main stream of activity are all that is necessary to provide a quiet place for children to express themselves creatively in writing. Lewis describes a classroom that contains one corner designated as "Our Writers' Corner" where, according

[25] Leo J. Brueckner, *Improving the Arithmetic Program* (New York, Appleton-Century-Crofts, 1957), pp. 95-100.

to classroom policy, "writers are *not* to be disturbed by anyone but the teacher, and she, only if necessary."[26] This is only one example of how an ingenious teacher may structure the classroom environment to stimulate creative expression from his pupils.

Hobby center. In many intermediate and upper grades, the hobby center is one of the most popular spots in the room. Here children are encouraged to display and share their hobbies with each other which, incidentally, utilizes a variety of functional oral and writing experiences. Collections are, of course, very popular and, from time to time, the hobby center may display collections of dolls, stamps, dried flowers, baseball heroes, coins, match covers, and numerous others which have a never-ending fascination for children. Other hobbies such as model building, weaving, sewing, or writing to overseas "pen pals" are equally welcome in the hobby center and can be used to stimulate a variety of interests, develop numerous types of skills, and, very important, teach the wise use of leisure time.

The present section has suggested only some of the numerous possibilities open to the resourceful teacher who wishes to surround his pupils with a rich, exciting, and dynamic academic climate. It should be kept in mind that no single factor will accomplish this goal. On the contrary, the quality of the intellectual environment is the result of the interaction of numerous tangible and intangible factors, a point well summarized by Strickland: "A challenging environment is in part physical and material, to be sure, but it is mainly psychological and inspirational; it is the social, emotional, and intellectual challenge that counts and everything in the environment is built to that end."[27]

THE SOCIAL-EMOTIONAL ENVIRONMENT

Any discussion of a desirable learning environment would be woefully inadequate without a consideration of the social-emotional aspects of the classroom. Most elementary school children live, work, and play together in a single school group, day in and day out, for the better part of the year. Some of these groups are formed with extreme care by the school personnel. Others are determined with a minimum of thought or concern by those responsible. Some groups contain fifty or more members; others less than half as many. Some may be fairly homogeneous in the culture they represent. Others may be aggregates of individuals from widely divergent ethnic groups and socio-economic strata. Regardless of the size or type of group, however, the degree to which each individual re-

[26] Gertrude M. Lewis, *op. cit.,* p. 175.
[27] Ruth G. Strickland, *op. cit.,* p. 201.

lates to all other members greatly influences his mental health, academic achievement, and all other phases of his total personality.

For several years now, the elementary school has recognized that one of its greatest tasks is the development of social intelligence. Five-year-olds enter the kindergarten from a predominantly self-centered "me and my world." As they transfer from a world that revolved largely around them to one in which they are only a small part, many learnings and adjustments must be accomplished. As they progress through the grades, the elementary school tries consistently to teach these youngsters to respect the dignity and worth of each member of the group, to participate in and abide by group decisions, to contribute to group projects and activities, to act effectively in a variety of social situations, and to develop the numerous other skills and attitudes that characterize the socially competent democratic citizen.

As teacher and pupils work toward the refinement of these skills, a kind of atmosphere or climate is generated which we will refer to as the social-emotional environment. This environment, in one classroom, may be one of harmony, security, respect, and well-being. In another it may be one of hostility, tension, rivalry, and discord. When comparing these two environments, it is important to remember that appearances are often deceiving. In other words, a classroom and group may present an outward picture of friendship and accord and yet have deep-rooted antagonisms and frustrations of which only a very perceptive teacher can be aware. What are some of the questions a sensitive teacher asks himself as he appraises the social-emotional environment of his classroom? The following are a few suggestions.

Are the children happy? Do they look happy? Do they smile often? Do they laugh frequently? Does their laughter stem from healthy, wholesome humor? Or is it the nervous giggle or hysterical laughter that indicates underlying tensions and deep-seated frustrations? Is it the laughter of friendship? Or of ridicule and derision? Do children laugh *with* each other or *at* each other?

Are the children busily engaged in a satisfying, productive enterprise? Are they doing the busy work created by the teacher solely for that purpose? Or are they busy at jobs and problems they have identified and uncovered? Purposeful, self-directed activity was mentioned in a previous section as a sign of a desirable intellectual climate. It is an equally important indication of a healthy social environment. It is important to remember that normal, healthy children are busy and active people; they are not, by nature, lazy, disinterested, or apathetic. One hears a teacher complain occasionally, "My children never want to do anything," or "My class just isn't interested in anything." Such apathy may be a serious sign of a poor social-emotional climate. Lane and Beauchamp emphasize this point in the following statement.

A good people are a busy people. One senses among them an active living of life rather than the dull routines through which one must go because someone says we must. When we were little children in school, teachers liked to hear pins drop and clocks tick. Today they welcome the hum of industry as a sign that this is a healthy group. They have challenging things to do.[28]

Do the children operate efficiently and productively? In some classrooms, nothing ever seems to get done. Work is never completed; plans are never accomplished; goals are never reached. Children and teacher appear to flounder endlessly in a quagmire of futility and confusion. Such a condition may, of course, have numerous causes but one of them may very definitely be a disintegrated group structure and correspondingly negative social atmosphere.

Do the children appear to be concerned about each other? Do they show by their questions and actions that they miss a member who is absent? Do they want to help when someone loses his lunch money or doesn't understand the assignment? There are innumerable small ways in which members of a group show respect and concern for each other, all of which indicate, in some measure, the quality of interpersonal relationships and interactions.

Lastly, is the classroom relatively free from widespread epidemics of anti-social behavior? Behavior problems of "normal" children as well as the emotionally disturbed child were examined in Chapter 3. There are, however, certain types of classroom behavior that do not stem from the normal mischievousness of children, nor from their lack of social skills, nor even from a severely disturbed mental state. Such behaviors as fighting, cheating, stealing, vandalism, and scapegoating, *when they occur in epidemic proportions*, may be serious symptoms of an unhealthy social-emotional group atmosphere.

It should be fairly obvious that the number of factors that are related to the quality of the classroom social climate is infinite. In the remainder of this section, however, the discussion is limited to three major ones that should be of significance to every classroom teacher.

Intergroup Conflicts and Tensions

MANY ELEMENTARY SCHOOL CHILDREN DEVELOP INTERGROUP AWARENESSES AT A RELATIVELY EARLY AGE. In recent years, several interesting studies have been made of the social prejudices and attitudes of children. In general, research indicates rather conclusively that certain social aware-

[28] Howard Lane and Mary Beauchamp, *Human Relations in Teaching* (Englewood Cliffs, N. J., Prentice-Hall, Inc., 1955), p. 147.

nesses and prejudices may be present in some children at a very early age. Early studies, for instance, by Lasker[29] and Minard[30] indicate that elementary school children were aware of racial differences. Several years later, the well-known Philadelphia Early Childhood Project which studied the social prejudices of kindergarten, first, and second grade children concluded that, "It is evident from the data that at an early age children learn about and adopt attitudes toward different racial and religious groups.[31]

In agreement with these studies are the findings of Goodman who studied the racial awarenesses of approximately one hundred four-year-olds.

The high degree of race awareness we have seen in many of these children is startling, and not only because it does not fit our adult expectations. The fact is that mere intellectual awareness of the physical signs of race is not all of the story. There is another part which is not merely startling but quite shocking for liberal-humanitarian sensibilities. It is shocking to find that four-year-olds, particularly white ones, show unmistakable signs of the onset of racial bigotry.[32]

A recent summary of available research on this point states that, ". . . studies of the attitudes of children and young people clearly show that children *do* recognize differences and that these "anti" feelings are related to the attitudes and feelings of adults. A school interested in promoting better group relations must recognize the nature and the sources of such negative feelings.[33]

Although the studies are not entirely consistent, there is also some evidence that elementary school children may be aware of socio-economic differences as well as racial and religious differences. Hollingshead, for instance, found that first-grade children knew the difference between rich and poor people.[34] Neugarten studied the peer status and reputations of children in fifth and sixth grades and found that social class dinstinctions were clearly marked. Concerning peer status, she concluded that,

The child from a family of upper status occupies an enviable position—many of his classmates consider him their friend or would choose him for a friend

[29] Bruno Lasker, *Race Attitudes in Children* (New York, Holt, Rinehart and Winston, Inc., 1929).

[30] Ralph D. Minard, *Race Attitudes of Iowa Children* (University of Iowa, Studies in Character, Vol. 4, No. 2, 1931).

[31] Helen G. Trager and Marian Radke Yarrow, *They Learn What They Live* (New York, Harper & Row, Publishers, 1952), p. 345.

[32] Mary Ellen Goodman, *Race Awareness in Young Children* (Reading, Mass., Addison-Wesley Publishing Co., Inc., 1952), pp. 217-218.

[33] Jean D. Grambs, *Understanding Intergroup Relations* (Washington, D. C., Department of Classroom Teachers, American Educational Research Association, National Education Association, 1960), p. 17.

[34] August B. Hollingshead, *Elmtown's Youth* (New York, John Wiley and Sons, Inc., 1949).

or mention him as their parents' choice. Very few of his classmates mention him as a person they would not want for a friend.

The child from a family of lower status faces the opposite situation. He is seldom mentioned as a friend (and then only by children of the same social position as his own), but he is often mentioned as a person his classmates do not like and whom parents do not want their children to play with.[35]

Concerning the reputations children held of each other, Neugarten states,

The lower-class child . . . has the reputation of being poorly dressed, not good looking, unpopular, aggressive; of not liking school; of being dirty and bad mannered; of never having a good time; and of not playing fair. These opinions of him are shared even by members of his own class group. The child of a family of upper status, on the other hand, enjoys a reputation almost exactly opposite—he is considered well-dressed, good looking, popular, a leader; as liking school; as being clean and well-mannered; as always having a good time; and as playing fair.[36]

TEACHERS SHOULD BE AWARE OF THE FACT THAT SOCIAL AWARENESSES AND PREJUDICES MAY BE PRESENT IN THE CLASSROOM. In the past, most adults either have not known or have refused to admit that young children may have social prejudices. Teachers and school administrators have been particularly guilty of taking an ostrich-like attitude toward this problem. The author remembers, for instance, a principal of a large elementary school in an urban neighborhood who commented proudly one day, "These children get along fine together. They never even think of who is Negro and who is white." Not a week later in that same school a playground riot erupted between Negro and white children which was halted only by the arrival of the police. Trager and Yarrow comment on the traditional tendency of teachers to ignore the possibility of prejudice in children in the following statement.

At the beginning of the Project many teachers were not conscious of the fact that young children have attitudes about racial and religious differences. They rejected the implication that prejudice might begin in early childhood. They offered as "proof" of children's natural friendliness toward everyone that they all play together, especially in the public school. Those who acknowledged the existence of a problem saw it primarily in the form of "name-calling," and they wanted to know what to do about it. Few, if any, regarded the name-calling as a symptom or manifestation of a deeper problem. Some dismissed it as "just parroting of adults."[37]

[35] Bernice L. Neugarten, "Social Class and Friendship Among School Children," *American Journal of Sociology*, Vol. 51 (January, 1946), p. 309.
[36] *Ibid.*, p. 310.
[37] Helen G. Trager and Marian Radke Yarrow, *op. cit.*, p. 349.

IT IS IMPORTANT TO REMEMBER THAT SOCIAL ATTITUDES ARE LEARNED PERCEPTIONS. To assume that social prejudices are innate or that they exist in all children to the same degree is just as fallacious as to assume that they do not exist at all. Obviously children are not born with these awarenesses. On the contrary, they learn them as they learn everything else, from what they see, hear, and experience within the context of their total culture. This means, of course, that the extent and type of awarenesses vary considerably among the members of the group. Children who, from their earliest years, have been exposed repeatedly to such remarks as, "You play with your own kind," or, "I want you to stay away from those dirty kids down the street," naturally mirror such attitudes. Other children may be *aware* of group differences (just as they are aware of sex differences) but, at the same time, be relatively free from ethnocentrism or the feeling that their group is the *in* group and all others are *out* groups. The fact that most social attitudes are *learned* during childhood, of course, places a very heavy responsibility upon the elementary school teacher. *No adult other than the elementary teacher works with a single group of children each day over an extended period of time.* What he does or does not do with that group will greatly influence the social attitudes children will learn, relearn or unlearn. These will, in turn, lay the groundwork for all future interpersonal contacts and relationships. What courses of action are open to the teacher?

IN ORDER TO PROMOTE A POSITIVE SOCIAL-EMOTIONAL ENVIRONMENT, TEACHERS MUST EXAMINE CAREFULLY THEIR OWN PREJUDICES. We have stated repeatedly in this chapter that the teacher is the most crucial factor in a desirable learning environment. Hopefully, no teacher consciously favors some children more than others. But teachers are human. They are, themselves, products of their cultures and may unknowingly hold certain attitudes or stereotypes that may seriously affect the total classroom climate. Grambs, for instance, raises the question of "whether teachers who are strongly against minority-group persons in out-of-school contacts can genuinely accept such children when they appear in their classrooms."[38] This is an important question and calls for continual soul-searching on the part of each teacher as he examines his relationships with, and attitudes toward, his pupils. If, in this process, the teacher finds that he does hold certain prejudices, there is no better weapon with which to combat them than his own intelligence. Exploring the reasons for his ethnocentric feelings, as well as recognizing that they are not substantiated by a scrap of scientific evidence or reliable research will help the conscientious and intelligent teacher to deal with all pupils, regardless of their cultural backgrounds, with fairness and objectivity.

[38] Jean D. Grambs, *op. cit.,* p. 14.

THE GROUP STATUS OF THE LOWER SOCIO-ECONOMIC CHILD SHOULD BE EX-
AMINED CAREFULLY. Many writers have stated that the public school is a
middle-class institution and that, with some exceptions, the cards are generally stacked against the child of the lower socio-economic class. Let us
examine this statement somewhat in detail.

In the first place, the youngster from a low socio-economic bracket
often does not enjoy the social acceptance in the classroom which is
afforded to the more economically privileged child. Neugarten, Davis,
Havighurst, and others have emphasized the fact that social class distinction may be more common in the elementary classroom than most teachers
imagine, even though the youngsters are not necessarily concerned with
class structure as such.

Secondly, there is considerable evidence to support the theory that
teachers, themselves, are unconsciously prejudiced against the lower class
child. In a study, for instance, of pupil-teacher contacts, Hoehn found
that the lower-class child received as *much* attention from the teacher
as the higher-status pupil but that the "quality of teacher contacts experienced by high status pupils tends to be better from the mental hygiene
standpoint than that of contacts experienced by low status pupils."[39]

The rationale behind the teacher's unconscious prejudice against the
lower class child is, of course, fairly obvious. People tend to favor the
familiar. Since the large majority of our teachers (Davis estimates it at
ninety-five percent[40]) are themselves from the middle class, they are
familiar with its values, standards, motivations, and customs and are correspondingly unfamiliar with those of the lower socio-economic level. As
Kaplan states,

Teachers try to be democratic and fair in their relationships with children,
but they cannot escape their middleclass indoctrination. They have difficulty
understanding and relating themselves to children from the lower classes and
reflect this in their attitudes toward these children, their disciplinary approaches,
and their teaching techniques.[41]

Thus, the lower-class child, slum child, culturally deprived child, or
disadvantaged child (as he is variously called) is pretty much of an unknown quantity to the classroom teacher. The average teacher doesn't
understand this child's dietary habits or table manners, his standards of

[39] Arthur J. Hoehn, "A Study of Social Status Differentiation in the Classroom
Behavior of Nineteen Third Grade Teachers," *Journal of Social Psychology*, Vol. 39
(May, 1954), p. 291.

[40] Allison Davis, "Socio-Economic Influences on Learning," *Phi Delta Kappan*,
Vol. 32 (January, 1951), p. 253.

[41] Louis Kaplan, *Mental Health and Human Relations in Education* (New York,
Harper & Row, Publishers, Inc., 1959), p. 216.

dress and cleanliness, his family relationships, his code of behavior, his frequent lack of motivation toward a formal education, or his more direct and less inhibited acts of physical aggression and sexual interest. But, most of all, the teacher often fails to understand the conflict he sets up within the child as he tries to teach him to conform to middle-class standards. If the child obeys, he finds himself in conflict with his home and is often punished accordingly. If he does not, he is punished or rejected by the teacher and school. Rich states,

Many teachers, failing to recognize the characteristics and social patterns of the lower class child, find that the lower class child is a disciplinary problem, lacks motivation, and does not demonstrate the manners and morals becoming to youth . . .

Many teachers, unintentionally and without realization of the far-reaching consequences, try to get lower class children to adopt a code of behavior that is, on the one hand, quite foreign and unnatural to them and, on the other hand, a code whose adoption goes not only unrewarded in the home environment, but may, in fact, draw censure and rebuke. Many teachers discipline in terms of etiquette and manners sanctioned by the middle class and, as a result of this inculcation, many teachers are dismayed to find their efforts unproductive in converting lower class children to their way of behaving.[42]

This is a harsh dilemma which is compounded even further when the child is of foreign-born parentage. The following example illustrates the point.

One day early in November, a third grade class was discussing preparations for Thanksgiving. The discussion centered upon the Thanksgiving turkey and progressed to the fact that the turkey belongs to the bird family. Miss F., a young, conscientious teacher, asked, "What other birds do we eat?" One child answered, "Chickens," which was, of course, accepted. Another said, "Pheasants and quail," and Miss F nodded approvingly. Tony then added, "Robins and starlings." The class laughed. Miss F frowned slightly and patiently explained that, "Robins and starlings *are* birds but we don't eat them. We eat only game birds." Of course, she had no way of knowing that Tony's father continued to trap robins and starlings as he had done as a boy in Europe and that they often appeared as delicacies on the family's dinner table. Nor did she ever know of the confusion that her kindly meant, but completely incorrect answer, created in Tony's mind as he wondered, "Is my father doing something wrong? Is the teacher right or wrong? Can they both be right?" A pretty difficult situation for an eight-year-old to puzzle out!

[42] John M. Rich, "How Social Class Values Affect Teacher-Pupil Relations," *Journal of Educational Sociology*, Vol. 33 (May, 1960), p. 357.

Grambs summarizes the situation of Tony and others like him in the following statement.

The child of foreign-born parents, particularly if English is not the primary language at home, is affected by other group pressures and differences. He may be torn between two conflicting expectations. From his parents he learns manners, food habits, family role relationships, attitudes towards education and the future, and these may differ in many respects from those of the American school and of the American culture as conveyed through the mass media. To what shall the child be loyal? If he rejects his parents' attitudes and values, he feels highly insecure and uncertain and is inevitably involved in conflict and trouble at home. If he does not accept the school's version of what is "American," he is apt to be left out of school activities, to receive poor grades, and in many crude or subtle ways to be made to feel unworthy. He may avoid conflict by adopting the school's image of an American child and be rewarded by the school, but then, more likely than not, he will be punished by his parents. This is, indeed, a cruel dilemma.[43]

Another reason for the possible discrimination against the lower-class child is the fact that he is often a low academic achiever. This is *not* necessarily because of low intelligence but rather because of such factors as (1) poor social adjustment and low peer status with resultant feelings of inferiority, (2) lack of teacher-pupil rapport, (3) culture bias of many standardized tests, (4) lack of motivation toward education usually evidenced by a "what's the use" attitude, (5) language barrier, in the case of the foreign-born child, (6) possible physical fatigue from working after school, inadequate rest, and irregular eating habits, (7) possible emotional unrest from crowded conditions and lack of privacy in the home, and (8) generally inferior environmental conditions and experiences. These, and others, contribute to the low scholastic achievement of the disadvantaged child which, in turn, may foster a poor teacher-pupil relationship, for teachers are only human and they are very prone to look with favor on pupils with whom their efforts are rewarded and with disfavor on pupils who do not make them feel successful. As Becker states, "In short, the differences between groups make it possible for the teacher to feel successful at her job only with the top group; with the other groups she feels, in greater or lesser measure, that she has failed."[44]

Warner, Havighurst, and Loeb make the point as follows:

...there is no doubt that ability is frequently rewarded regardless of class. It is true though that the lower-class child must show greater ability to be recog-

---

[43] Jean D. Grambs, *op. cit.*, pp. 21-22.
[44] Howard S. Becker, "Social-Class Variations in the Teacher-Pupil Relationship," *Journal of Educational Sociology*, Vol. 25 (April, 1952), p. 455.

nized than does the higher-class child . . . whenever a lower-class child shows in his behavior that he or she is quick to learn the middle-class standards of acting, the teacher is more likely to reward that child. Or if the child shows any exceptional talent, the teacher will act encouragingly. What appears to happen is that the teacher, like a speculator, puts her efforts and rewards where she thinks they will bring in the biggest gain. She knows that those who are most likely to succeed, here placed in their order of probability, are those from better-class families, those who have exceptional ability, and those who seem to have the stuff to learn the ways of living which make them comparable to children of the better-class families.[45]

Redl and Wattenberg emphasize the same point in the following statement.

The child who cannot be helped quickly, whose stubborn difficulties prevent the teacher from reaching a goal of professional triumph, may seem to be willfully ungrateful. At the very least, he is an obstacle in the path, and, as such, arouses aggressive feelings. At worst, he seems to be an enemy who is deliberately refusing to learn and his actions, obviously conceived in malice, deserve punishment.[46]

Our discussion thus far of the lower socio-economic class child has examined the possible prejudice against him of (1) his peers, and (2) his teacher. A third possibility is worth considering.

Several writers have pointed out the fact that most school curricula and textbooks reflect a middle-class bias. Many curricula, for instance, are oriented largely toward verbal learnings and experiences at which the culturally deprived child obviously does not excel. Textbooks and other reading materials, in the past, have been largely concerned with middle-class values and experiences, although some interesting new materials now coming off the press are attempting to correct this limitation. Kaplan presents a strong indictment against the bias of many textbooks in the following statement.

From the time the lower-class child is first handed a book, the pattern of life presented to him in the classroom is the typical middle-class culture. In his primer he will read about the Joneses who have two children, a boy and a girl. They live in a pleasant little suburban house in a well-cared-for neighborhood. Each child has a private room with closets, dressers, and play space. The bathroom is clean and sparkling with separate towel racks for each individual and a place for each person to keep his toothbrush. Father is pictured as coming home from work nattily dressed and carrying a brief case. Everyone is clean, happy, emotionally secure, and well adjusted.

[45] W. Lloyd Warner, Robert J. Havighurst, and Martin B. Loeb, *Who Shall Be Educated?* (New York, Harper & Row, Publishers, Inc., 1944), pp. 81-82.
[46] Fritz Redl and William W. Wattenberg, *Mental Hygiene in Teaching*, 2nd ed. (New York, Harcourt, Brace & World, Inc., 1959), p. 234.

All of this is the prototype of the middle-class, white, liberal Protestant, Anglo-Saxon, politically and religiously apathetic, middle-of-the-road pattern of life. At least one-fourth of the children who read about this "typical" American family will find no resemblance to their own home life in the congested slum areas of the city or the shanty dwellings on farms and in rural areas. They are familiar with crowded quarters where they sleep two and three in a bed, share a bathroom with other families, if they have a bathroom, hang their clothes on nails or hooks fastened to the wall, and do most of their washing in the kitchen. Their father comes home dirty and tired. Family life is congested, noisy, and not at all like the idyllic storybook conception of what home life ought to be. Lower-class children are often hurt by this contrast and confused by the unreal picture it presents.[47]

Bettelheim agrees, and emphasizes the frustrations that may result from the child's comparing his own experiences with the unrealistic content of many of his textbooks.

... while parents play a large role in our readers, the stories never describe occasions when even the slightest differences arise between parents. What does this tell the child about his own parents? Either that these stories are not true, and that reading is therefore not worthwhile, or else that something is wrong with his parents because they argue on occasion. Actually, what children need to learn is that people can have differences of opinion, can even argue, and still live successfully together, and that this is better, though much more difficult, than to deny that any difference of opinion exists.

In these reader stories about families, the mother is always ready to go out for walks or to play, is never preoccupied with housework, is never a working mother, though the mothers of many of these children are. The father is never tired or in need of rest when he comes home from work. The conclusion is that the child's own parents are not good parents because they do not behave like the mother and father in the stories. Instead his parents act like human beings who are sometimes tired, preoccupied, or even irritated as they go about their chores, which is very different from how characters are described in the child's reader.

True, some progress toward reality has been made, at least in some readers. No longer are all good children blond and of fair complexion; no longer are the dark-haired, dark-skinned children the bad ones. But even this is only a partial accomplishment, and only in the last few years. In many ways the images we create of what are usual or desirable homes and forms of behavior still contradict the child's everyday experiences. The result is that either these images set the child against his own life experiences or they suggest to him that little truth can be derived from reading.[48]

[47] Louis Kaplan, *op. cit.*, pp. 207-208.
[48] Bruno Bettelheim, "The Decision to Fail," *School Review*, Vol. 69 (Winter, 1961), pp. 386-387.

MANY SUBGROUPS OPERATE WITHIN THE TOTAL CLASS GROUP. No elementary school teacher should be under the impression that his class is one big, happy family or that he can make it so. The elementary class is an artificial, adult-created, *in name only* children's group, and subgroups are bound to develop. Thus far, we have examined the possibility of subgroups forming according to ethnic or socio-economic differences and their resulting influence upon the social-emotional climate of the classroom. There are, however, many other types of subgroups that may have as great or greater influence upon the social climate. Subgroups may evolve according to which children do or do not buy their lunches at the school cafeteria, do or do not ride the school bus, live in the township or the borough, or live above or below a certain city block. Actually, the problem, as stated by Redl and Wattenberg, is not the mere existence of subgroups but the basis for their formation and the feelings they have toward each other. "The formation of subgroups in any aggregation as large as the average class is inevitable. The questions are, How many will form? On what basis? How will they feel toward each other?"[49]

There are many aids available to help the teacher answer these questions concerning his class. Some of the most widely used are discussed below.

SOCIOMETRIC TECHNIQUES WILL HELP THE TEACHER TO UNDERSTAND THE GROUP STRUCTURE OF HIS CLASS. The sociometric test was originated by Jacob L. Moreno, popularly known as the Father of Sociometry. It is a simple, convenient, practical, and easily constructed instrument which may help the teacher to determine the internal social structure of a group.

On a typical sociometric test (written in the intermediate and upper grades; oral informal interviews in the primary grades) children are asked to name the classmates with whom they would like to associate in a specific activity. Example: "We have decided that, for our next social studies unit, we will work in committees. On this piece of paper, will you please write the names of the classmates with whom you would like to work on this unit?" A reverse question that would indicate rejections would be, "Please list the names of the classmates with whom you do not want to work in a committee." Many authorities recommend, however, that the negative choice test be reserved for clinical or extreme cases rather than for ordinary classroom usage.

The questions which indicate pupil choices are usually called the *sociometric criteria* and sometimes they alone comprise the sociometric test. At other times they are hidden among five or ten other questions designed also to determine pupil preference such as, "I am going to order some films for us to watch during rainy noon hours. Please write the kinds of

[49] Fritz Redl and William W. Wattenberg, *op. cit.*, p. 267.

films you like best and that you would like me to order." The purpose of inserting the sociometric criteria among other questions is, of course, to make the technique attract less attention from pupils or parents. Obviously, the type of sociometric test will depend upon many factors in the total situation.

After the desired information has been secured on a sociometric test, it is usually transferred to a chart or table from which a sociogram or friendship chart is prepared. There are numerous types of individual, partial, and total group sociograms although the *mutual choice group sociogram* is probably the most practical and valuable for classroom use. In this type of sociogram, a symbol for each child (usually different for boys and girls) is placed on a chart and connected by lines to mutual choices (children who chose and were chosen by each other). Through this relatively simple technique, the teacher may observe the internal structure of the group and note the appearance of the stars (those who have a high number of mutual choices), of isolates (those who have none), of neglectees (those who have few), of cliques (the very small groups whose members choose each other and rarely anyone else), of cleavages between certain subgroups, and others. The mutual choice sociogram in Figure 6.2 reveals the structure of a combined fifth and sixth grade. It was constructed from children's responses to a question concerning with whom they would like to work on an art project the following week. It is evident at a glance that this is a fairly cohesive group. There were no isolates. No child was chosen by less than two classmates whom he also chose. The star of the girls and the star of the boys each received seven mutual choices, although several other children received four or five choices. It is true, of course, that there is a sharp division according to sex, although this is to be expected with this age group. Other than sex, the most noticeable cleavage is along age-grade lines. Age-grade differences appear to be particularly noticeable among the boys, as indicated by the fact that the three sixth-graders remained almost entirely aloof from the other boys. This may be, of course, because they constituted such a small minority, because they had little of common interest with the younger boys, or because of a variety of other reasons. Age-grade differences are also noticeable among the girls but not to such a marked extent. Each of the three sixth grade girls chose the other two, but one was also mutually attracted to three fifth grade girls.

In summary, the sociogram reveals that this is a fairly cohesive, homogeneous group. The children appear to accept each other to a high degree. The classroom teacher's main task would appear to be an attempt to minimize a tendency toward forming a clique on the part of the small group of sixth graders.

Newer modifications of the sociogram include the *target sociogram*

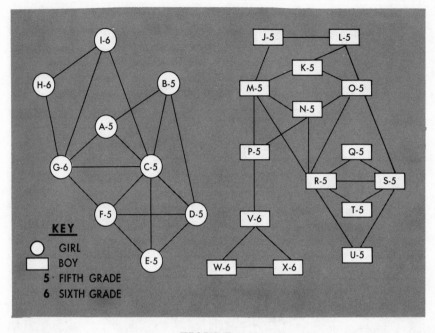

FIGURE 6.2

Mutual choice sociogram of a combined fifth and sixth grade class.
Constructed by Maryminta Konrad, teacher in the Monroe Township
Elementary School, No. 2, Cranbury, N. J.

which involves charting the sociogram upon a series of concentric circles.
In this type, pupils receiving the most number of mutual choices are
placed in the center circle with each circle showing a decreasing number
of mutual choices. The sociogram in Figure 6.3, together with explanations and interpretations, is from Gronlund's very readable and practical
book on the subject.[50]

Stars. The two stars (numbers 6 and 12) appear in the center of the sociogram. The girl (number 12) has five mutual choices with other girls, which
provides a chain of relationships with all but two of the girls. The boy (number 6) has only two mutual choices with other boys, but these choices attach
him indirectly to six of the boys. His two mutual choices with girls provides
him with a chain of contact with eight of the girls. Is he the real leader in the
class? Is he vying with number 12 for the leadership of the girls as well as the
boys (note that he rejects number 12)? What factors account for the leader-

[50] Pp. 72-76 from *Sociometry in the Classroom* by Norman E. Gronlund. Copyright © 1959 by Norman E. Gronlund. Reprinted with permission of Harper & Row,
Publishers, Inc.

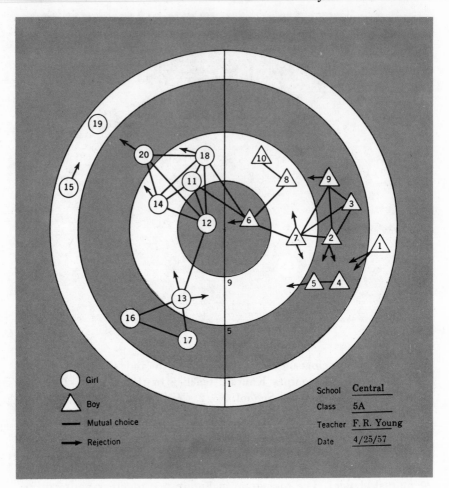

FIGURE 6.3

Sociogram of choices and rejections of work companions. From *Socio-metry in the Classroom* by Norman E. Gronlund. Copyright © 1959 by Norman E. Gronlund. Reprinted with permission of Harper & Row, Publishers, Inc.

ship positions of number 6 and number 12? Do their leadership positions pro-vide a constructive influence on the classroom as a whole? Are they exercising actual leadership in classroom activities? . . .

Isolates and Neglectee. Girls number 15 and 19 received no choices on the sociometric test, and boy number 1 received one choice. All are in the outer ring of the sociogram. Why are these three pupils isolated or neglected by the group? Do they have any characteristics in common which account for their fringe positions? Is there anything in the teaching procedure or classroom arrangement that is contributing to their isolation and neglect? What can the teacher do to help them become accepted by the group? . . .

Rejectee. Girl number 19, who received no positive choices from her classmates, was rejected by four of the girls. What accounts for these rejections? Does she need help with her social skills or personal grooming? Is she emotionally disturbed? Is she of a different race or nationality than the other pupils? How are her parents accepted in the community? Are they also rejected? . . .

Mutual Choices. There are numerous mutual choices depicted in the sociogram. What factors might account for these various pairs of pupils choosing each other? Do they choose each other in actual work situations? How do these mutual friendships affect the classroom process? Which ones contribute to classroom harmony and which ones result in classroom disturbances?

Pupils number 4 and 5 form a separate *pair.* Although they have mutually chosen each other, they are below average in acceptance and are rejected by pupils number 1, 2, and 7. Why did they choose each other? Why are they rejected by several students? How do they differ from the other boys in class? What do they have in common? . . .

Pupils number 13, 16, and 17 form a *triangle* of mutual choices. How do they work with the other pupils in class? Do they exclude others from their little group? What do they have in common? Would it be desirable to integrate them into the larger group? Can the mutual choice between number 13 and number 12 be used to bring about a more integrated social structure?

Pupils number 10, 8, and 6 form a *chain* of mutual choices. What caused this structure to form? How do pupils number 10 and 6 get along in their personal relations? Does pupil number 8 have to divide his time between pupil number 10 and pupil number 6? If pupils number 10 and 6 are not compatible, how does number 8's in-between position affect his social relations and his personal adjustment? . . .

Cliques. There are two relatively large subgroups, or cliques, observable in the sociogram. Boys number 2, 3, 7, and 9 form one, and girls number 11, 12, 14, 18, and 20 form the other. What seems to account for the formation of these cliques? What characteristics do the members of each clique have in common? How do these cliques affect the harmony of the classroom and the attainment of classroom goals? What procedures will most effectively weaken these cliques and provide for a more general distribution of mutual choices? Cliques are not necessarily harmful, but they can lead to a disintegrated social structure which interferes with harmonious and purposeful relations in the classroom.

Cleavages. Although minor cleavages are apparent between small subgroups, the most obvious cleavage is between boys and girls. There are only two mutual choices between the sexes and both of these are with the same boy. This is a fairly common phenomenon in sociometric testing at the fifth-grade level. However, sociometric results from different schools show considerable variation in the amount of cleavage between the sexes. What factors might account for this rather extreme cleavage? Do the school procedures . . . contribute to this cleavage? To what extent can this cleavage be diminished? What classroom procedures will contribute to more harmonious boy-girl relations?

As has been stated, the sociometric test and sociogram offer a fairly simple and practical means of determining the internal structure of a group. A teacher who is interested in applying it to his classroom, however, should be thoroughly familiar with its purposes, values, limitations, and cautions. Obviously, our discussion here is too limited to examine these factors in detail and the reader is strongly urged to consult the many excellent references now available on the subject, some of which are included in the bibliography at the close of the chapter. The following list of *do's* includes only some major suggestions and does not pretend to cover all of the points with which the teacher should be familiar.

1. *Do* make the sociometric criterion specific rather than general. Most authorities advocate that a specific question such as, "On our field trip next week, what persons would you like to sit next to on the bus?" be used in preference to a more general type such as, "Which people in our class do you like best?"

2. *Do* make it clear to children that their choices will be kept strictly confidential.

3. *Do* follow through with the information received on the sociometric test. If, for instance, children have been asked with whom they would like to work on a committee, the teacher should certainly take these choices into consideration when actually organizing the groups. Incidentally, this also applies to the questions on the sociometric test among which the sociometric criteria may be hidden. Children's answers to the question concerning noontime movies mentioned previously, for instance, should certainly be considered by the teacher as he orders these films.

4. *Do* keep in mind the limitations of the sociometric test. Remember that it reveals the group structure *at one given time according to one stated criterion*. If another criterion were applied, the results may be different. Also, because group structure is often shifting rather than static, a test at another time may yield different results. For this reason, a series of tests, administered at intervals throughout the year, is usually recommended.

Remember also that the test merely indicates group structure. It does not reveal the reasons for the structure nor does it give any hints as to how it may be improved.

5. *Do* be careful about interpreting the results of the test or jumping to hasty conclusions. John, for instance, may be revealed as an isolate.

This *may* be because he is a member of a minority group or it *may* be that he entered the class only a few days ago and is a relative stranger to the group. Any sociometric device may be subject to various interpretations, and the teacher must combine its results with his total knowledge of the pupils gained from many sources before he may draw valid conclusions.

In addition to the sociometric test and sociogram, there are other techniques that may help the teacher to understand the relationships underlying the group structure. Such instruments as the *Guess-Who Test* (in which children are asked to name a classmate who best fits a certain description) and the *Classroom Social Distance Scale* have been used by teachers with worthwhile results.

Another technique advocated by many is role playing or the sociodrama. In this activity children are encouraged to play through or act out spontaneously a representative situation involving a social relationship or problem. As the group selects the theme, acts out the situation, analyzes and discusses the presentation, and reenacts the situation with different children assuming the roles according to suggestions offered during the group discussion, the teacher and pupils may gain insights that will provide a springboard to the improvement of the social structure and climate of the group.

THERE ARE MANY AVENUES OF ACTION OPEN TO THE TEACHER WHO WISHES TO IMPROVE PUPILS' SOCIAL RELATIONSHIPS. The perceptive and capable teacher will discover innumerable techniques he can use to improve the interpersonal relationships of his pupils. Those which most teachers find to be valuable include the following.

1. Creating numerous opportunities for children to work in different groups. The elementary school program and classroom should be so organized as to provide numerous opportunities for each individual pupil to work intimately and become acquainted with all other members. As a pupil becomes a member of a reading group, a social studies committee, a baseball team, a stage-lighting crew, a school patrol, a playground clean-up detail, a stamp club, or a refreshment serving committee, he experiences a wide variety of social contacts that should help him to develop new friendships and deeper social understandings.

2. Providing numerous opportunities for *each child* to contribute to the total group living. As Ambrose and Hilliard say,

Teachers know that healthy group living provides responsibilities and opportunities for each child to contribute to the good living of all—to care for paints, crayons, toys, puzzles, books and records which are used; to carry messages, greet guests, take turns in making lunch time pleasant and comfortable; to help care for window plants, garden plots, bulletin boards or other

Cooperative projects promote social understandings and cohesiveness.

commonly shared spaces and facilities. Good group living provides opportunities to do some jobs alone, others with a chosen friend or friends, still others because the job needs to be done and it is one's time to do it.[51]

3. Eliminating traditional school practices that inhibit social interaction. Certain practices left over from the past such as (1) formal and rigid seating arrangements, (2) assigning classroom, lunchroom, or auditorium seating according to alphabetical or other teacher-determined order, (3) forbidding any normal conversational interchange during class hours, (4) insisting that children raise their hands or stand before they are permitted to speak, and (5) passing through the halls in straight lines, are socially artificial situations that serve only to inhibit the social growth and development of children.

[51] Reprinted by permission of Childhood Education International, 3615 Wisconsin Avenue, N.W., Washington, D. C. "A Setting for Effective Social Learnings" by Edna Ambrose and Pauline Hilliard. From *Childhood Education*, January, 1962, Vol. 38, No. 5, pp. 221-222.

**A good teacher provides numerous opportunities for
each child to contribute to the total group.**

4. Adapting the curriculum to the needs of the group. It was stated earlier that many curricula emphasize reading and verbal activities at which the culturally disadvantaged child does not excel. On the other hand, this child may excel in artistic, musical, athletic, or constructional activities. A rich curriculum, adapted to the varied needs of all pupils, will help to improve pupils' attitudes toward the school, toward themselves, and toward other members of the group.

5. Integrating intergroup education into the school curriculum. Many teachers have initiated and developed successful units of study designed to improve intergroup relations. During the past year, for instance, Mrs. B noticed considerable group hostility directed against three Puerto Rican children in her fourth grade class. She consequently developed a short unit on Puerto Rico, and its people, emphasizing personalities prominent in the fields of athletics, music, government, and literature. According to sociometric tests, administered before and after the unit, the project was highly successful in improving the intergroup attitudes within the classroom.

6. Bringing to light the hidden or latent talents of each individual. Someone has said that the thrill of research is "looking at something everyone else has looked at and seeing something that no one else has seen." This, in essence, is the thrill of teaching, to look at a child everyone else has looked at and to see within him something that no one else has seen. As Hoppock says, "All children have gifts,"[52] and the teacher who can bring these gifts to light so that they may be respected by, and shared with, other members of the group improves the social and emotional health of the individual and group to a degree impossible to measure.

The following section is concerned with a second major factor that may relate to the quality of the social-emotional environment.

Over-emphasis Upon Competition

There is little doubt that we live in a competitive *and* cooperative world. Mr. Jones tries desperately each day to show a better sales record than his colleagues, thereby hoping to win a generous Christmas bonus and perhaps the district sales manager's job. But at the same time, he gladly volunteers his service during week-ends to help build a badly-needed addition on his church. Mrs. Jones is elated when her chocolate cake wins first prize at the county fair. But she is also happy to be a member of a car-pool that transports the children of the neighborhood back and forth to day camp each summer. Young Dick Jones competes fiercely against football rivals. But he knows that only teamwork will win the game for his college.

The same thing is true in the classroom. Each day, in hundreds of different ways, children cooperate with, and compete against, each other. Contrary to the opinion of some, it is not necessary to eliminate all competition from the classroom in order to achieve a healthful social-emotional climate. It is, however, essential that the classroom teacher examine the issue of competition versus cooperation according to valid research and educational theory. What are the facts concerning the use of competition in the elementary classroom?

COMPETITION MAY BE DETRIMENTAL TO THE SOCIAL COHESIVENESS OF THE GROUP. Research is not conclusive on this point. However, the fact that several studies have revealed that cooperation, more than competition, increased the social cohesiveness of the group should give the classroom teacher much food for thought. Phillips and D'Amico, experimenting with fourth graders, reported ". . . groups which worked under co-

[52] Anne S. Hoppock, *All Children Have Gifts* (Washington, D. C., Association for Childhood Education International, 1958).

operative conditions during the experiment increased in cohesiveness . . . This means that individuals who worked together under cooperative conditions liked each other better at the end of the experiment than they did at the beginning of the experiment."[53]

Stendler and others report similar results from an experiment with seven-year-olds to the effect that "results showed that positive interactions do not equal or exceed negative interactions under individual reward conditions."[54]

Comparing the results of competition and cooperation upon college students, Deutsch states,

To the extent that the results have any generality, greater group or organizational productivity may be expected when the members or sub-units are cooperative rather than competitive in their interrelationships. The communication of ideas, coordination of efforts, friendliness, and pride in one's group which are basic to group harmony and effectiveness appear to be disrupted when members see themselves to be competing for mutually exclusive goals. Further, there is some indication that competition produces greater personal insecurity through expectations of hostility from others than does cooperation. Implications for committees, conferences, and small groups in general appear to be fairly obvious.[55]

The significance of these studies is clear, and the possible detrimental effects of competition upon group cohesiveness should be considered carefully by a teacher interested in building a healthful social-emotional climate in his classroom.

COMPETITION MAY BE DETRIMENTAL TO AN INDIVIDUAL'S MENTAL HEALTH. On this point, there is virtually unanimous agreement, and most psychologists warn repeatedly against the possible harmful effects of competition upon the individual's mental health. A psychiatrist points out that most suicides are "the fruits of failures in competition" and adds,

The commonest source of anxiety today is repressed hostility or aggression . . . And these hostilities develop out of competition. Whether he is an advertising executive, a school teacher or a pupil, he cannot remain long in a bath of

53 Beeman N. Phillips and Louis A. D'Amico, "Effects of Cooperation and Competition on the Cohesiveness of Small Face-to-Face Groups," *Journal of Educational Psychology*, Vol. 47 (February, 1956), p. 68.

54 Celia Stendler, Dora Damrin, and Aleyne Clayton Haines, "Studies in Cooperation and Competition: The Effects of Working for Group and Individual Rewards on the Social Climate of Children's Groups," *Journal of Genetic Psychology*, Vol. 79 (December, 1951), p. 196.

55 Morton Deutsch, "The Effects of Cooperation and Competition upon Group Process," *Group Dynamics*, Dorwin Cartwright and Alvin Zander, eds. (New York, Harper & Row, Publishers, Inc., 1953), p. 352.

competition without developing hostility to his rivals, and then some anxiety and guilt because of the hostility.[56]

Danger to the individual's mental health is, of course, greatly increased when the competition is unfair. Competition, of short duration, and between evenly matched individuals or groups, need not be accompanied by feelings of failure and frustration. But most competition in the classroom is not of this type. It is, instead, competition that is grossly unfair because it pits against each other individuals of widely varying abilities. No teacher would dream of forcing seven-year-olds, ten-year-olds, and thirteen-year-olds to race against each other on the playground every day. Yet this is exactly what happens in the classroom when children with mental ages of seven, ten, and thirteen are forced to compete against each other daily. The harmful results of this incessant, unfair competition upon the mental health of children cannot be overemphasized. It has been stressed in numerous statements similar to the following.

Whenever children of unequal ability, backgrounds, and interests are placed under pressure to meet rigid and graded standards of subject matter mastery, the pupils with below average ability will experience monotonous failure day after day and eventually develop feelings of inadequacy. In the same situation, the bright pupils may be rewarded for a mediocre performance and develop unhealthy attitudes toward true scholarship, and, too, they may fail to develop feelings of success or adequacy. The traditional curriculum of the typical American school with its reliance on the cheap and easy technique of competition and of a comparative marking system condemns too many children to daily frustrations and feelings of inadequacy which leave a mark on mental health. Given years of this type of crippling influence in the life of the typical American child, the school becomes a powerfully contributing factor to adult feelings of hostility or futility.[57]

Competition without rules is inconceivable, and one of the rules of true competition is that the competitors shall be evenly matched. Much of our school competition has been far from evenly matched. For the child who has little chance to win, such competition becomes a real threat. He is doomed to fail (or believes he is) and will probably either openly resist or merely go through the motions.[58]

COMPETITION DOES NOT NECESSARILY STIMULATE GREATER EFFORT. Undoubtedly, most teachers employ competitive techniques to stimulate pupils to greater effort. Comparative grades, gold stars, rewards, and such

[56] Henry A. Davidson, "Competition, The Cradle of Anxiety," *Education*, Vol. 76 (November, 1955), pp. 165-166. Reprinted from the November, 1955, issue of *Education*, by special permission of The Bobbs-Merrill Company, Inc., Indianapolis, Indiana.
[57] W. Ray Rucker, *Curriculum Development in the Elementary School* (New York, Harper & Row, Publishers, Inc., 1960), pp. 54-55.
[58] Robert M. Isenberg, "Competition and Cooperation in Our Society," *National Elementary Principal*, Vol. 36 (May, 1957), pp. 23-24.

daily remarks as, "If you work hard, you may be able to move up to the first reading group," or, "All those who had perfect papers stand up so that we may take a good look at you," or, "Look at Ellen's paper. Don't you wish you could do as well?" are used constantly by teachers in the naive hope that they will stimulate children to greater effort. But there is little evidence to support this hope. Some claim that the effort produced may be greater but very temporary. Others claim that competition and rivalry are incentives *only* to the few who have a chance of winning; they have little effect on the others. Combs says,

Psychologists, sociologists and educators who have been doing research on competition for several decades tell us that the people who work for prizes—who enter into competition with other people—are only those who feel they have a chance of winning. Competition is of limited value as a means of motivation since it motivates few. We do not work for things we feel we cannot achieve . . . We are motivated by competition only *when we feel we have a chance of winning.*[59]

Every teacher, if he really thinks about it, can support this statement from his own experience. Who are the children who like the chart with the gold stars? Usually those with an impressive array of stars beside their names. Who are the pupils who enjoy spelling bees? Usually those who can outspell the others. Who are the parents who favor a competitive grading system? Usually those whose children will get the A's and B's. Competition can be a motivating force to some, but not necessarily to all.

COMPETITION MAY NOT NECESSARILY PRODUCE BETTER RESULTS. As Davidson says, "Competition brings us better cosmetics, cars, and cabbages, but no one has yet proved that it brings us better education.[60]

This is true. There is no conclusive research that supports the assumption of some teachers that children will consistently learn better through competition and rivalry. True, in some areas of learning, competition may produce this desired result. But there is no evidence that, as a general rule, children learn faster or more thoroughly when motivated only by a desire to excel over others. Otto states that his data show that overall scholastic achievement is not increased by use of a competitive grading system.

My file includes unpublished data from three school systems in which the comprehensive type of achievement test was given each year for one or more years before an A-B-C-D-F marking system was abandoned and then given each year for four to six years after the marking system was discontinued.

[59] Reprinted by permission of the Association for Childhood Education International, 3615 Wisconsin Avenue, N.W., Washington 16, D. C. "The Myth of Competition" by Arthur W. Combs. From *Childhood Education*, February, 1957, Vol. 33, No. 6, p. 266.

[60] Henry A. Davison, *op. cit.*, p. 162.

A comparison of children's achievement before and after the elimination of a competitive marking system shows that there not only was no drop in the median achievement scores by grades, but in most grades there was actually a slight increase. Undoubtedly the nature of these findings is due to the fact that teachers substituted more effective motivations in lieu of the threat of low marks or rewards for good marks.[61]

THE CLASSROOM TEACHER SHOULD NOT BE MISLED BY THE POPULAR MYTH THAT COMPETITION IS NECESSARY TO PREPARE CHILDREN FOR "LIFE." In spite of the fact that research points to certain possible harmful effects from an overemphasis upon competition, many teachers continue to use it in the belief that since competition is part of our way of life, children should be exposed to it in school. This argument is fallacious for several reasons.

1. Life is both cooperative and competitive. As we said earlier, both elements are part of our modern society. But it is a fact that we are living in a more cooperative, more interdependent society, than the world has ever known. The old idea of fierce competition as the rule of life is disappearing rapidly, and, as Combs says, "Whether we like it or not, we are thoroughly and completely dependent upon the goodwill and cooperation of others at every moment of our lives."[62]

Burton emphasizes the importance of cooperation in our modern way of life in the following statement.

Cooperation, mutual assistance, and ethical restraint are not only as "natural" as competition but are necessary if the fanatical type of individualism is not to destroy civilization. The benefits of competition, properly operated, are apparent to everyone. The benefits and absolute necessity of cooperation must be realized and quickly if we are to avoid serious evil. The proponents of the ruggedly individualistic competitive life make a serious error in harping constantly on the achievements and benefits of this system while neglecting the serious evils which also attend it. This is more than a matter of application to the classroom or to community affairs; it is a cosmic matter and might involve survival.[63]

2. The modern emphasis upon competition and getting ahead usually places an exaggerated emphasis upon material gains and false values while, at the same time, it downgrades the more important social, moral, and spiritual values. Is this what we want to teach our children?

3. The greatest gains to mankind have been achieved through the cooperative efforts of many rather than through the singlehanded endeavors of any one individual. By the same token, the greatest humanitarians, artists, scientists, and leaders have been motivated by inner curiosities, creative urges, *or* desires to benefit their fellowmen. It is doubtful whether

[61] Henry J. Otto, "What Price Competition?" *Texas Outlook*, Vol. 38 (February, 1954), pp. 8-9.

[62] Arthur W. Combs, *op. cit.*, p. 265.

[63] William H. Burton, *The Guidance of Learning Activities*, 3rd ed. (New York, Appleton-Century-Crofts, 1962), p. 61.

any human being has ever achieved greatness in any field who has been motivated solely by a selfish desire to get ahead of others.

4. Where competition does occur in life, the individual usually has an opportunity to choose his field of competition. Thus, the competition is fair in that people compete against others of similar abilities, interests, and talents. If, for instance, the adult finds that he is a "failure" as a salesman, he usually leaves that field and enters another where he may realize some degree of success. He is not compelled by law (as the elementary school child is) to return to the same arena day after day and to compete against others of widely varying abilities and interests. Bernard expresses this point as follows:

The grading system would be more lifelike if every citizen were employed to do the same task at the same salary, if everyone were expected to produce the same results from his efforts. But this is not what happens in life. Employees are selected to do different jobs at different rates of pay . . . all workers do not do the same thing. They tend to do the things for which they have the interest, talent, and background. They might do them even better and work more cheerfully if they did not have school backgrounds which had implanted feelings of inferiority and the anticipation of failure.[64]

5. Lastly, and most importantly, to make an analogy between a business or industrial concern and the elementary school is ridiculous. They are different institutions designed for different purposes. The elementary school is not a factory. It is not a business. It is not a battleground nor a racetrack. It is an institution designed for only one purpose, to help children to learn. It is not concerned with earning greater profits; it is not concerned with increasing production. It is concerned only with helping children to learn the many skills, attitudes, and knowledges they need to know in order to function effectively. And, as far as we now know, this function is achieved to a higher degree in an atmosphere of security, mutual respect, and cooperation than in an environment characterized by competition and rivalry.

In summary, we may conclude that both cooperation and competition operate in an elementary classroom. Competition of short duration, in some fields, and between evenly matched opponents may not necessarily produce harmful results. Competition that continues day after day, between unfairly matched adversaries, should be carefully avoided by the teacher interested in the good mental and social health of his pupils. This does *not* mean, however, that we do not hold children to high standards nor that they never experience failure (see Chapter 3). Nor does it mean that we should try to delude children into thinking that they are all equally competent in all fields. This is not only ridiculous but impossible. Children, even at a very young age, recognize readily that Mary is a

[64] Harold W. Bernard, *Mental Hygiene for Classroom Teachers*, 2nd ed. (New York, McGraw-Hill Book Co., Inc., 1961), pp. 264-265.

good reader, Annette a fine artist, and Mickey a fast runner. The point is that we try to teach them to recognize the talents and capabilities of others with respect and admiration, *not* with rancor and bitterness because they may not possess them all to an equal or greater degree.

Undemocratic Leadership

A third, and very important, hazard to the development of a healthful social-emotional environment is the type of leadership exerted by the teacher. Many studies have shown that the influence of the teacher's personality and behavior is a crucial factor in determining the quality of the social climate. In 1938, the well-known studies of Lewin, Lippitt, and White were conducted to determine the effects of adult leadership and personality upon children's groups. These experiments were designed to detect the effects of (1) authoritarian, (2) democratic, and (3) laissez-faire leadership upon informal club groups of eleven-year-old children. The three leadership roles were defined as follows:[65]

Autocratic (or Authoritarian)	Democratic	Laissez-Faire
1. All determination of policy by the leader.	1. All policies a matter of group discussion and decision, encouraged and assisted by the leader.	1. Complete freedom for group or individual decision, with a minimum of leader participation.
2. Techniques and activity steps dictated by the authority, one at a time, so that future steps are always uncertain to a large degree.	2. Activity perspective gained during discussion period. General steps to group goal sketched, and where technical advice is needed the leader suggests two or more alternative procedures from which choice can be made.	2. Various materials supplied by the leader, who makes it clear that he will supply information when asked. He takes no other part in work discussion.
3. The leader usually dictates the particular work task and work companion of each member.	3. The members are free to work with whomever they choose, and the division of tasks is left up to the group.	3. Complete nonparticipation of the leader in determining tasks and companions.
4. The leader tends to be "personal" in his praise and criticism of the work of each member, but remains aloof from active group participation except when demonstrating.	4. The leader is "objective" or "factminded" in his praise and criticism, and tries to be a regular group member in spirit without doing too much of the work.	4. Infrequent spontaneous comments on member activities unless questioned, and no attempt to appraise or regulate the course of events.

[65] Table, pages 26-27 from *Autocracy and Democracy* by Ralph K. White and Ronald Lippitt. Copyright © 1960 by Ralph K. White and Ronald Lippitt. Reprinted with permission of Harper & Row, Publishers, Inc.

The findings of these studies indicated that democratic leadership produced more originality, higher work-motivation, and a higher degree of
friendliness and group-mindedness than either of the other two types.

In general, the laissez-faire, passive, or do-nothing leadership produced
confusion of roles, discontent, more play, less work, and poorer work.
These behaviors are often duplicated in the elementary classroom situation in which the teacher abdicates leadership. Children become confused
and disorganized and the quality of the social climate deteriorates greatly.

In contrast to the other two types, the authoritarian leader-figure produced considerably more hostility and aggression in the group. It is
interesting to note, however, that this hostility was not always directed
toward the autocrat but rather toward other members of the group, and
frequently toward an individual or subgroup. This phenomenon is called
scapegoating and was mentioned earlier in the section as a common
symptom of an undesirable social environment. Redl and Wattenberg say,

When a group is under pressure or is meeting many frustrations, it is likely
to displace its feelings of hostility upon an unpopular individual or sub-group
. . . From the mental hygiene point of view, scapegoating of this kind is not
only a symptom of poor emotional health conditions within a group, but is
especially serious in its effects upon the victims.[66]

Nedelsky makes a similar comment to the effect that children become
tense and irritable in a situation where adult control places unrealistic
demands upon them and that,

These tensions and resentments are often expressed against each other. Children may pick on the "teacher's pet", or they may "gang up" on some child
who is particularly vulnerable. The groups that do spring up are likely to be
closely knit, with strong loyalties within each group and little movement
from group to group.[67]

Many other studies have revealed that the leader's personality and behavior are reflected within the group. Anderson, Brewer, and Reed,[68] for
instance, in studies of elementary teachers and pupil groups, found that
pupil behavior appeared to be generally consistent with teacher behavior.
The teacher's tendency to dominate the group was reflected by the pupils'

[66] Fritz Redl and William W. Wattenberg, *op. cit.*, p. 284.

[67] Ruth Nedelsky, "The Teacher's Role in the Peer Group During Middle Childhood," *Elementary School Journal*, Vol. 52 (February, 1952), p. 331.

[68] Harold H. Anderson and Joseph E. Brewer, *Studies of Teachers' Classroom
Personalities, II.* Effects of Teachers' Dominative and Integrative Contacts on Chil-
dren's Classroom Behavior (Stanford University Press, 1946). Harold H. Anderson,
Joseph E. Brewer, and Mary Frances Reed, *Studies of Teachers' Classroom Personali-
ties, III.* Follow-up Studies of the Effects of Dominative and Integrative Contacts on
Children's Behavior (Stanford University Press, 1946).

tendencies to dominate each other. Children with an integrative teacher, on the other hand, tended to show socially integrative behavior and greater spontaneity and initiative.

Many other situations could be cited to illustrate the extent to which authoritarianism breeds hostilities and resentments among the group. A friend of the author once commented upon this phenomenon as he experienced it while a prisoner of war. He said that one of the most difficult and depressing things about his year in a prison camp was not the strict punishment, starvation diet, or constant fear of death but rather the friction and hostility among the prisoners themselves. In other words, instead of becoming united through a common bond of sympathy and resentment of authoritarian rule, the members of this particular group became hostile and aggressive toward each other.

Intragroup and intergroup frictions and aggressions are not the only undesirable behaviors produced by an authoritarian rule. When the aggression is directed toward the leader, it may take such undesirable forms as stealing or vandalism. Children who are fearful of rebelling openly against a dictatorial teacher may retaliate by stealing or destroying property they associate with the teacher or school.

According to the consistent evidence now available, therefore, we may conclude that the personality and behavior of the teacher exert a tremendous influence upon the relationships and structure of the group. Our present knowledges of, and beliefs in, democracy and education leave little room for doubt that the truly democratic teacher will motivate a more desirable and healthful social-emotional environment than will either the authoritarian or the passive type of teacher.

SUMMARY

Today we know, without reservation, that the individual's environment exerts a tremendous effect upon his total growth and development. This chapter was concerned with the teacher's responsibility for creating a desirable classroom learning climate, which was considered to be the composite of the physical environment, the intellectual environment, and the social-emotional environment.

The physical environment was discussed both from the standpoint of its own importance and of its influence upon all types of environment. Certain modern trends and innovations such as (1) experimental overall design, (2) more functional use of space, (3) greater flexibility and convertibility, (4) increased use of the physical plant, and (5) greater attention to the physical comfort and well-being of pupils were examined. The remainder of this section examined the teacher's responsibility for being knowledgeable concerning the desirable qualities of such classroom features as (1) size, (2) shape, (3) lighting, (4) color, (5) acoustics, (6) air conditioning, (7) furniture, (8) chalkboards, (9) tackboards, and (10) storage equipment.

The discussion of the intellectual environment was guided by three considerations: (1) What is meant by the term *intellectual environment?* (2) What are the functions of the intellectual environment? and (3) What elements are necessary for a desirable intellectual environment?

The third section dealt with the importance and influence upon learning of a positive social-emotional environment. Three major factors that bear a relationship to the quality of this environment were examined. Concerning the first, intergroup conflicts and tensions, it was stated that elementary school children may be aware of certain ethnic and socioeconomic differences and that these awarenesses may be hazardous to a healthful social classroom climate. The classroom status of the lower socioeconomic class child (or the culturally deprived or disadvantaged child, as he is sometimes called) was examined somewhat in detail. Certain techniques for ascertaining the group structure and existing relationships were discussed and several suggestions for improving these were offered.

The second major factor related to the social-emotional environment which was examined was the undue stress placed by some teachers on competition and rivalry. It was pointed out that some competition, of short duration, and between evenly matched adversaries may not necessarily be detrimental to mental and social health. But incessant competition, between individuals of widely varying abilities, should be carefully avoided by the conscientious classroom teacher.

Lastly, the leadership role of the teacher and its relationship to the social-emotional climate was examined. Research studies, as well as our own modern beliefs in education and democracy, support the statement that democratic leadership is a vital factor in the fostering of desirable social relationships and a positive social-emotional environment in the elementary classroom.

ADDITIONAL LEARNING EXPERIENCES

Topics for Thought and Discussion

1. Do you think the windowless classroom will become more popular in future years? Why?
2. Are you generally sensitive to the use of color in your physical environment? Can you analyze how various colors affect you?
3. Should pupils be responsible for controlling any aspects of the physical environment? How?
4. Do you consider yourself to be an intellectually curious person?
5. Do you have racial, religious, or socio-ethnic biases? How did you acquire

them? Have they increased or decreased since you were a child? To what extent do you think they will influence your attitude toward pupils in your classroom?

6. Do middle-class teachers have as much difficulty understanding the pupil from the upper socio-economic classes as they do in understanding the pupil from the lower socio-economic classes?

7. As a child, were you ever torn between the teachings of the school and the teachings of your home? How did you resolve the conflict?

8. During a spelling test you notice sixth-grader John copying his words from a list he has hidden in his desk. What would you do?

9. What do you think of the honor system used in some colleges and universities?

10. Would you establish an honor system in your sixth grade classroom?

Projects and Activities

1. Construct a model, or make a scale drawing, of a "classroom of tomorrow." Describe the type of furniture, storage space, equipment, chalkboard, and tackboard areas you have provided.

2. Evaluate the lighting of an elementary school or your college classroom. If it is not satisfactory, give specific suggestions for improvement.

3. Examine three recent basal reading series. Are the current criticisms concerning textbook socio-economic bias applicable to these series? Write to the publishers. Ask them for their reaction to the current criticism and their plans, if any, for further revision of their texts.

4. Talk with a school nurse. What is her role in establishing a correct classroom physical environment? How does she work with the classroom teacher, principal, and custodian on this phase of the school health program?

5. Write a description of a person you know, or have known, who possesses a high degree of intellectual curiosity. Can you analyze or speculate on what factors contributed to the development of this trait in this particular person?

6. Arrange a sample elementary classroom exhibit for Book Week.

7. Make a place value chart for an upper grade arithmetic classroom center which could be used to visualize operations with whole numbers and decimals.

8. Visit an elementary classroom. What tentative conclusions can you make concerning the social-emotional environment? Upon what specific evidence do you base your conclusions?

9. Observe a class of elementary school children on the playground or in the playroom for several consecutive days. Do you notice any consciousness of race, religion, or socioeconomic bias?

10. Compile an annotated bibliography of children's books that may help to develop healthy and positive intergroup attitudes and relationships.

11. Prepare a research project on "The Culturally Deprived Child." Be sure to include recommendations for the elementary school through which it can meet the needs of this child.

12. Write a description of a teacher who, in your opinion, represents an authoritarian personality. A democratic personality. A laissez-faire personality.
13. If possible, administer a sociometric test to an elementary class. Construct a mutual choice sociogram from the results. How does your sociogram compare with the observation and judgment of the pupils' teacher?
14. Talk with several primary grade teachers. Do they think racial and religious biases exist among their pupils? Upon what do they base their opinions? Are they familiar with some of the research done in this field? What are their reactions to the findings of this research?

Selected Bibliography

ADORNO, T. W., and others, *The Authoritarian Personality*. New York, Harper & Row, Publishers, Inc., 1950.

Aluminum Company of America, *Schoolhouse*, Eggers and Higgins, architects, Walter McQuade ed. New York, Simon and Schuster, Inc., 1958.

American Association of School Administrators, *Planning America's School Buildings*. Washington, D. C., 1960.

Association for Supervision and Curriculum Development, *Creating a Good Environment for Learning*. 1954 Yearbook. Washington, D. C., National Education Association, 1954.

BERNARD, Harold W., *Mental Hygiene for Classroom Teachers*, 2nd ed. New York, McGraw-Hill Book Co., Inc., 1961.

CALDWELL, Edson, *Creating Better Social Climate in the Classroom through Sociometric Techniques*. San Francisco, Fearon Publishers, Inc., 1959.

CUNNINGHAM, Ruth, and associates, *Understanding Group Behavior of Boys and Girls*. New York, Bureau of Publications, Teachers College, Columbia University, 1951.

DAVIES, Evelyn A., *The Elementary School Child and His Posture Patterns*. New York, Appleton-Century-Crofts, 1958.

DAVIS, Allison, *Social-Class Influences upon Learning*. Cambridge, Mass., Harvard University Press, 1948.

DEBERNARDIS, Amo, *The Use of Instructional Materials*. New York, Appleton-Century-Crofts, 1960.

Educational Policies Commission, *Education and the Disadvantaged American*. Washington, D. C., National Education Association, 1962.

"Elementary School Buildings . . . Design for Learning." *The National Elementary Principal*, Vol. 39 (September, 1959).

GOODMAN, Mary Ellen, *Race Awareness in Young Children*. Reading, Mass., Addison-Wesley Publishing Co., 1952.

GRAMBS, Jean D., *Understanding Intergroup Relations*. Department of Classroom Teachers, American Educational Research Association of the National Education Association. Washington, D. C., 1960.

GRONLUND, Norman E., *Sociometry in the Classroom*. New York, Harper & Row, Publishers, Inc., 1959.

HERRICK, John H., and others, *From School Program to School Plant*. New York, Holt, Rinehart and Winston, Inc., 1956.

HOLLINGSHEAD, August B., *Elmtown's Youth*. New York, John Wiley and Sons, Inc., 1949.

KAPLAN, Louis, *Mental Health and Human Relations in Education*. New York, Harper & Row, Publishers, Inc., 1959.

LANE, Howard A., and BEAUCHAMP, Mary, *Human Relations in Teaching*. Englewood Cliffs, N. J., Prentice-Hall, Inc., 1955.

MORENO, Jacob L., *Who Shall Survive?* Beacon, N. Y., Beacon House, Inc., 1953.

National Council on Schoolhouse Construction, *Elementary School Plant Planning*. Nashville, Tenn., Peabody College, 1958.

REDL, Fritz, and WATTENBERG, William W., *Mental Hygiene in Teaching*, 2nd ed. New York, Harcourt, Brace & World, Inc., 1959.

RIESSMAN, Frank, *The Culturally Deprived Child*. New York, Harper and Row, Publishers, Inc., 1962.

"School Plant and Equipment." *Review of Educational Research*, Vol. 21 (February, 1951).

Space, Arrangement, Beauty in School. Washington, D. C., Association for Childhood Education International, Bulletin 102, 1958.

STENDLER, Celia B., *Children of Brasstown*. Urbana, Ill., University of Illinois Press, 1949.

TAYLOR, James L., GORE, Lillian L., and GABBARD, Hazel F., *Functional Schools for Young Children*. Washington, D. C., U. S. Department of Health, Education, and Welfare, Office of Education, 1961.

The Dynamics of Instructional Groups, Nelson B. Henry, ed. Fifty-ninth Yearbook, National Society for the Study of Education. Chicago, University of Chicago Press, 1960.

TRAGER, Helen G., and YARROW, Marian Radke, *They Learn What They Live*. New York, Harper & Row, Publishers, Inc., 1952.

U. S. Department of Health, Education, and Welfare, Office of Education, *Environmental Engineering for the School*. Washington, D. C., 1961.

WARNER, W. Lloyd, HAVIGHURST, Robert J., and LOEB, Martin B., *Who Shall Be Educated?* New York, Harper & Row, Publishers, Inc., 1944.

WHITE, Ralph K., and LIPPITT, Ronald, *Autocracy and Democracy*. New York, Harper & Row, Publishers, Inc., 1960.

CHAPTER 7

Planning and Organizing
For Learning

The right decision at the right moment is the essence of good teaching. Right decisions are those that time learning perfectly for the individual student. A series of such decisions moves the student forward at an optimum pace. Obviously, such timing and pacing are no more accidental than is a perfect catch by the professional outfielder. They are the result of careful planning and organizing on the part of the teacher.[1]

PLANNING IS AN INESCAPABLE PART of living. One plans what he will eat for breakfast, how he will finance the payments on his car, where he will go on his vacation, and how he will propose marriage to his true love. Some plans are immediate; some are long range; but all are a necessary part of responsible human action. This is particularly true in teaching. The teacher has more freedom (and more responsibility) for planning than do workers in many other fields. He must establish goals, organize activities and procedures for attaining them, select appropriate content, secure necessary instructional materials, and budget the available time with efficiency and economy. Furthermore, as Goodlad says, all of this must be done at exactly the opportune moment if learning is to take place. The following basic principles of effective classroom planning should help the teacher in this all-important task.

PRINCIPLES OF EFFECTIVE PLANNING

THE TEACHER'S PLANNING BEGINS WITH AN UNDERSTANDING AND ACCEPTANCE OF THE BASIC GOALS OF MODERN ELEMENTARY EDUCATION. Many comprehensive statements of the fundamental aims of the elementary school

[1] John I. Goodlad, "The Teacher Selects, Plans, Organizes," 1959 Yearbook, *Learning and the Teacher* (Washington, D. C., Association for Supervision and Curriculum Development, NEA, 1959), p. 39.

have been formulated in recent years. Obvious limitations of time and space prevent our examining these in detail here. It should be sufficient to remind the teacher that the elementary school, as the broad base of the entire educational system, is purposed to promote the total integrative growth of *each* individual so that he may be a constructive participating member of our society, according to his unique and optimum potential. To realize this goal, classroom activities must be planned and organized to develop understandings, skills, competencies, attitudes, and interests in the broad areas of (1) Physical Development, Health, and Body Care, (2) Individual Social and Emotional Development, (3) Ethical Behavior, Standards, Values, (4) Social Relations, (5) The Social World, (6) The Physical World (The Natural Environment), (7) Esthetic Development, (8) Communication, and (9) Quantitative Relationships.[2]

THE TEACHER'S PLANNING SHOULD BE GUIDED BY THE NEEDS AND ABILITIES OF A PARTICULAR GROUP OF INDIVIDUALS. This is a basic premise of effective planning and would seem to be almost too obvious to merit mention here. Unfortunately, this is not the case for there are still some teachers who either do not know or do not heed this tenet. Mr. B, for instance, teaches in a school in which he is required to write weekly plans in a plan book supplied by the system. Recently, he complained bitterly to a fellow teacher that his principal would not allow him to reuse the same plans he used the previous year. According to Mr. B, "After all, I teach the same grade and same subjects I taught last year. What's the sense in writing all new plans?" Apparently Mr. B had not the foggiest notion of what planning is all about, or what teaching is all about for that matter!

This illustration does not mean that last year's plans cannot be of some value to the teacher. On the contrary, the exact opposite is true. The efficient teacher will frequently make brief notations and evaluations on his daily or long-range plans as he develops them: this particular procedure was very effective; these references were helpful only to the more able children; this activity was very popular with all pupils, and so forth. Former plans, with carefully noted evaluations and revisions may serve as valuable guides in planning for the following year. But this is far different from Mr. B's short-sighted "same grade—same plans" idea.

As the year progresses and the teacher becomes increasingly familiar with his pupils, it becomes easier to put this principle into practice. However, at the beginning of the year, the inexperienced teacher may wonder how he is going to plan according to the needs and abilities of

[2] Nolan C. Kearney, *Elementary School Objectives* (New York, Russell Sage Foundation, 1953), pp. 52-120. For a more detailed discussion of elementary school objectives see also Chapter 2 in Petersen and Hayden, *Teaching and Learning in the Elementary School* (Appleton-Century-Crofts, 1961).

children whom he has never seen. A careful examination of children's records, and if possible, conferences with their previous teachers will help him to overcome this limitation. If he can get some idea from these sources as to children's previous learning experiences, dominant interests, and approximate abilities he may be able to avoid the first-day-of-teaching-catastrophe experienced by the author. Armed with what she thought were adequate plans for a day's activities for childen about whom she knew nothing, by ten-thirty in the morning she had completed all of them and faced the rest of the day in a "What shall I do now?" panic. One needs only one such experience in a lifetime of teaching to be thoroughly convinced of the importance of planning adequately and carefully with the specific needs, abilities, and interests of a particular class in mind.

THE TEACHER'S PLANNING OF CLASSROOM ACTIVITIES MUST RECOGNIZE CERTAIN EXISTING BOUNDARIES. It has been previously stated that the typical teacher has considerable freedom in, and responsibility for, planning the learning activities that take place in the classroom. No teacher, however, has complete autonomy in this area. Most teachers work in situations that are generally permissive and self-directed but are also bounded by some broad, flexible restrictions. These boundaries may be imposed by state law; state, local, or individual school policy; or simply by the mores of the community. In general, restrictions of varying type and degree which must be recognized by the teacher in planning his work exist in the following areas.

1. *Scope of content.* There is no doubt that the trend in curriculum development is toward a planned but flexible program and away from the planless or free program found in some school systems a few years ago. This means the individual teacher in most systems is limited and guided by some type of curriculum guide in the content he teaches. It may be a state-wide guide or it may be a guide developed by the local school system or, in some cases, by an individual school. In any case, it is usually a broad, flexible document organized according to major educational goals for each age or grade level with accompanying suggestions as to desirable content, procedures, and materials for their achievement. Rarely is it the rigid and detailed type popular during the early decades of the century.

Even in systems that have no curriculum guides, the teacher is not one hundred per cent free to determine the content he will teach. All states have some legislation that makes the teaching of certain content mandatory. Although varying widely from state to state, legislation of the elementary school curriculum usually pertains to such broad areas as (a) nationalism (i.e., devotion to the interests of state and nation), (b) health and prohibition, (c) conservation of life and property, (d) practical and cultural subjects, (e) humaneness, (f) fundamental subjects, (g) religious and ethical subjects, and (h) miscellaneous subjects (i. e., science, social studies, etc.).[3]

Curriculum legislation is, of course, much more liberal for the elementary school than the secondary school. But the fact remains that all states have such legislative prescriptions and the elementary teacher should be aware of this fact. For instance, Nebraska requires that American history be taught for three periods a week in at least two of the three years from fifth to eighth grade, while Massachusetts requires the Declaration of Independence and the Bill of Rights to be taught in the elementary school. Louisiana also specifies that the Declaration of Independence be made a required topic of study in all elementary schools, and Wisconsin includes instruction in conservation and the wise use of natural resources as a required part of the elementary school program. Among examples of recently enacted statutes are California's requirement that, starting July 1, 1965, foreign language instruction is required not later than sixth grade, and New York's requirement that science be included in the required courses of study for the first eight years of school.

According to Moreland, the social studies areas most frequently prescribed by state statutes for the elementary school are: Federal Constitution (26 states), American History (22 states), Civics (13 states), State and Local History (9 states), State Constitution (18 states), and Geography (3 states).[4] In addition,

Almost all states prescribe certain holidays which should be commemorated in the school program. Thanksgiving, Flag Day, Memorial Day and the birthdays of Washington and Lincoln are the most common, although many states have local patriots to whom special attention is given. Likewise, there are many statutes involving the teaching of "harmful effects of alcohol and narcotics" which are a required part of the school program.[5]

2. *Time allotment.* The most formidable bugbear of the elementary teacher is TIME. "Where am I going to get the time?" is the despairing lament of all conscientious teachers. It is true, of course, that limitations of time must be considered carefully in planning the classroom program. The most obvious limitation is the length of the school day and school year. The average length of the elementary school day, according to a recent survey of urban districts, is five and a half hours, exclusive of noon and recess periods. It is interesting to note that increasing pressures may result in a longer school day in the future for, according to this survey, ". . . almost one-quarter of the urban places predicted an increase in the

---

[3] John R. Plischke, *Legislative Control of the Elementary Curriculum from 1941 to 1950* (unpublished Doctoral Dissertation, University of Pittsburgh, 1953).

[4] W. D. Moreland, "State Statutes Affecting the Social Studies Curriculum," *The Social Studies*, Vol. 53 (April, 1962), p. 131.

[5] *Ibid.,* p. 133.

number of hours an elementary school child will attend school each day in the future."[6]

The school year ranges from 168 days to 194 days although ". . . over two-thirds of the urban places of the United States maintained public elementary school programs of between 175 and 180 school days during the school year 1957-1958"[7] with 180 days mentioned most frequently. Here, again, it is interesting to note that there may be a trend toward increasing the time the elementary school youngster spends in school for ". . . 42.7 per cent of the respondents indicated the likelihood of adding days to the elementary school year within the next 5 years."

Within the broad confines of the school day and year, the majority of systems require, suggest, or recommend that the elementary teacher allocate certain amounts of time to certain areas of instruction. A survey of New England school systems revealed that three systems *required* teachers to adhere to a prescribed time budget while forty-eight reported that they provided a *recommended* schedule.[8] These findings are consistent with those of the previously mentioned survey of urban systems which reports that, "In summarizing . . . instructional time allocation, it is found that the most common policy for the first six grades of the public elementary school is the 'suggested time' approach . . ."[9]

In general, there are two major trends in time allocation among those systems that provide a guide. First, allocations are suggested according to broad integrated curricular areas such as communication arts, social studies, and creative arts rather than according to narrow, discrete subjects. In addition, most guides remind the teacher that a recommended time proportionment is not intended to prohibit in any way the functional integration of various curriculum areas. Secondly, allocations are usually stated in terms of suggested minimums and maximums per *week* rather than per day which was characteristic of earlier practice. Thus, an attempt is made to avoid compartmentalizing or segmenting the curriculum by the imposition of arbitrary time limits.

Table 7.1 on pages 266-267 is an example of a suggested time allotment recommended by one school system.

3. *Use of instructional materials.* Except for limited availability of materials, by far the most common restriction placed upon the teacher in this area concerns the use of the textbook. A very few states still have a single-textbook-adoption policy that restricts the teacher's choice of a

[6] Stuart E. Dean, *Elementary School Administration and Organization* (Washington, D. C., U. S. Department of Health, Education, and Welfare, Office of Education, 1960), p. 38.

[7] *Ibid.,* pp. 39-40.

[8] New England School Development Council, *Time Allocation in the Elementary School* (Cambridge, Mass., New England School Development Council, 1959).

[9] Stuart E. Dean, *op. cit.,* p. 56.

TABLE 7.1
Weekly Time Allotment—Grade 1

		Approximate Time in Minutes	Approximate Time in Percentage
LANGUAGE ARTS		770	47
Opening Exercises	75		
Reading and Library	570		
Literature	50		
Handwriting and Spelling*	75		
SOCIAL LIVING		140	8
Social Studies			
Science			
Health			
Safety			
ARITHMETIC		150	9
ART		80	5
MUSIC		60	4
PHYSICAL EDUCATION		150	9
LUNCH AND FREE PLAY		300	18
		1650	100

* . . . will not be taught until children are ready to begin this work. Prior to this, the teacher will distribute the allotted time to other areas.

Weekly Time Allotment—Grades 2 and 3

		Approximate Time in Minutes	Approximate Time in Percentage
LANGUAGE ARTS		900	46
Opening Exercises	75		
Reading and Library	570		
Literature	45		
Handwriting and Spelling	155		
Language	55		
SOCIAL LIVING		200	10
Social Studies			
Science			
Health			
Safety			
ARITHMETIC		225	12
ART		80	4
MUSIC		70	4
PHYSICAL EDUCATION		150	7
LUNCH AND FREE PLAY		325	17
		1950	100

Weekly Time Allotment—Grades 4, 5 and 6

		Approximate Time in Minutes	*Approximate Time in Percentage*
LANGUAGE ARTS		775	40
Opening Exercises	75		
Reading and Library	280		
Handwriting and Spelling	165		
Literature	45		
Language	210		
SOCIAL LIVING		300	15
Social Studies			
Science			
Health			
Safety			
ARITHMETIC		225	12
ART		85	4
MUSIC		90	5
PHYSICAL EDUCATION		150	7
LUNCH AND FREE PLAY		325	17
		1950	100

SOURCE: Board of Education of Baltimore County, *A Handbook for Elementary School Teachers* (Towson, Maryland, 1956), pp. 18-20.

basal text in certain curricular areas, but most states that had a single adoption in the past have recently moved toward a more liberalized policy. Florida, for instance, recently changed to a multiple-adoption policy that "provides for multiple adoption of not more than three textbooks in each grade and subject field, except for reading in the elementary school where the limit is five."[10] However, even within those states that have no statutes governing the use of textbooks, many individual systems require the teacher to use prescribed basal texts. Obviously, the teacher when planning his program must investigate the availability of textbooks as well as the system's regulation concerning their use. Equally important, he must investigate resources for securing additional materials and supplementary references because, although many situations prescribe the basal text to be used, *no* system prohibits enriching the program through the use of numerous and varied learning aids.

In addition to the textbook, the use of certain other aids such as field trips and films is occasionally determined by system-wide policies that must, of course, be considered in the teacher's planning.

[10] National Education Association, Research Division, *High Spots in State School Legislation, January 1—August 1, 1959*, Research Report 1959-R-22 (Washington, D.C., National Education Association, November 1959), p. 43.

THE TEACHER'S PLANNING SHOULD REFLECT HIS KNOWLEDGE OF THE LEARN-
ING PROCESS. Bigge and Hunt distinguish between three broad levels of
learning. Concerning the first, or memory-level learning, they say,

The capacity to memorize and retain material probably bears no relationship
to the capacity for intelligent behavior . . . Memory-level teaching may, of
course, contribute indirectly to intelligent behavior. If memorized facts become pertinent on an occasion when a problem requires solving, they contribute to usable background and hence to the effectiveness of the problem
solving. However, memorized facts usually contribute little. One reason is
that, as already suggested, they tend to be forgotten quickly. Another reason
is that a large proportion of the facts memorized in school are irrelevant to
future thought needs.
     It is no longer a matter for speculation that not much in the way of durable
or useful results can be expected from memory-level instruction. Its contribution to intelligent behavior is too unpredictable and undependable for
us to set much store by it as a favored instructional procedure.[11]

For years, many teachers were content to aim their teaching toward
this level of learning and rote memorization is still prevalent in some
classrooms. Most teachers, however, have recognized the shortcomings
of this learning level and have consequently tried to raise their teaching
to the next plateau or the understanding-level. On this level, the teacher
is concerned that the pupil understand rules, generalizations, and meanings according to his level of maturation. That it is decidedly preferable
to the first level is evident in the following statement.

A contrast may be drawn between understanding-level and memory-level
teaching as follows: if understanding-level teaching is successful, students will
know, in addition to facts, the principles by which the facts are related;
memory-level teaching tends to ignore principles, or at best handles them on
such a superficial level that they have no meaning . . .
     Understanding-level teaching gives students a tool for more intelligent be-
havior. It equips them with generalized insights which can be applied in
problematic situations inside and outside of school. It provides them with a
mental kit of rules. If the rules learned are the best which are known at the
time—by people in a position to have expert knowledge—then students have
at least gained something from their education.[12]

Today, the competent teacher is interested in a still higher plateau of
teaching aimed at the development of a type of learning usually called
creative learning, critical learning, inferential thinking, problem-solving
behavior, or reflection-level learning. This may be defined as follows:

[11] Morris L. Bigge and Maurice P. Hunt, *Psychological Foundations of Education*
(New York, Harper and Row, Publishers, Inc., 1962), pp. 429-430.
     [12] *Ibid.*, p. 432.

Reflection-level learning leads to understanding, but with reflection the search for understanding is pursued in different fashion from that described in the preceding section. Instead of being given a collection of facts and generalizations by a teacher, students are confronted with something which is unclear or puzzling. Reflective learning may begin with what a student brings with him to school—his own attitudes, beliefs, values, and knowledge. If he can be convinced that there is something seriously inadequate about his present mental furniture, he may be led to reflect. Or reflective learning may begin with some observed inadequacy in the subject matter: inconsistency, incompleteness, irrelevance, etc. In any case, a problematic situation appears about which a student centers his thinking and research. In the process, he examines facts and generalizations, and . . . he tries to seek out new ones.

There are these crucial differences between understanding- and reflection-level teaching: the latter requires more active participation of students, more criticism by them of conventional thinking, and more imagination and creativeness.[13]

Thus, although memory and understanding may contribute to the learner's growth, it is the third or reflection-level learning that becomes synonymous with intelligent behavior. This concept of learning rests upon certain foundational cornerstones. Those that probably have the greatest implications upon the teacher's planning and organizing classroom activities are examined briefly here.

1. *Readiness.* The term *teachable moment* refers to the commonly recognized fact that there is a "best" time to introduce a new learning experience to children. When this time occurs, of course, depends upon the maturity of the learners. Furthermore, "maturity" as used here refers not necessarily to chronological maturity but rather to physiological and psychological maturation, both of which must be carefully considered by the teacher in planning. It is important, however, to remember that the teacher constantly asks himself when planning an activity, not, "Are these children ready?" but rather, "How can I help these children to become ready?" and "What degree of readiness now exists that I can extend further through wisely chosen sequential experiences?" To illustrate: A misuse of the concept of readiness is for the teacher to ask himself, "Are these children 'ready' to develop this unit through large-scale group work?" and to conclude that, since they do not possess certain social skills, "No, they are not ready for group work." With this kind of reasoning, how will children ever get ready? After all, one does not "get ready" for swimming if one never goes near the water. A much more intelligent approach is for the teacher to ask himself, "How can I begin group work with these children? What types of group work would be most successful at their stage of development? Which individuals would

13 *Ibid.*, pp. 432-433.

benefit most from this type of work? and To what extent should I balance group work with more familiar procedures in developing this unit?" Readiness, therefore, is not considered as a static state but rather as a series of carefully graded steps toward a predetermined goal. The wise teacher will carefully appraise the level of each pupil for each specific activity and consider how and when he can take him to the next step. Thus, the principle of readiness becomes an inherent factor in guiding the teacher's planning.

2. *Motivation.* Motivation is generally considered to be of two types, extrinsic and intrinsic. Extrinsic classroom motivation refers to the external factors teachers bring to bear upon the learning process such as marks, rewards, punishments, prizes, and social approval. As the child progresses through school, many short-sighted and ineffectual teachers resort more and more to this type of motivation. Thus, the high school or college student interested only in a mark and who couldn't care less about what he is learning in the course is not an uncommon phenomenon. He is, however, a sharp contrast to the first-grade youngster who is so eager to read, so interested to learn, and so ready to ask questions and seek answers. This youngster is motivated by *intrinsic* motivation which, simply defined, is an inner search for meaning. Furthermore, this type of motivation is not peculiar to primary grade children nor does it automatically disappear as individuals mature. On the contrary, it can be stimulated in most individuals on any age level by a creative and perceptive teacher.

Intrinsic motivation is initiated through an active, learner-centric, self-recognized goal. The individual is confronted with a problem, with a situation he doesn't understand, or with a condition that upsets his mental complacency. As he consciously organizes his resources to meet this situation, a purpose emerges that guides his actions until satisfaction is realized.

The implications of this type of motivation upon the teacher's planning are twofold. First, if the teacher has considerable freedom in determining the content of his program, he may simply capitalize upon the genuine, spontaneously voiced interests and questions of the pupils. A class, for instance, may become so interested, so concerned, so excited, and so voluble about last week's tornado scare that they may raise in class such questions as, "What is a tornado?" "What causes tornadoes?" "What does wind velocity mean?" "Why are tornados more frequently found in some parts of our country than in others?" A clever teacher may then use these questions as a guide to a very worthwhile learning experience for the class. This type of intrinsic motivation, when used in the classroom, is usually referred to as *natural* motivation. It can motivate, when used correctly, a very desirable learning experience.

But there are also many dangers in the teacher's relying solely upon children's spontaneous interests, or natural motivation in planning his program. Blough summarizes the limitations of this approach in the following statement.

Several points should be considered before building a learning experience entirely around children's questions.

First, children cannot ask questions about something with which they have had little or no experience.

Second, children should continually grow to see the difference between a trivial question and a thought-provoking problem.

Third, the question asked by the child who always waves his hand hardest and is recognized by the teacher may not necessarily represent the interest of the group.

Fourth, the process of assembling questions needs direction from the teacher if anything worth studying is to result. There is nothing wrong with the teacher's frequently saying, "Have you ever wondered about this?" and writing her problem with the others.

Fifth, important questions arise from the puzzlement and curiosity that develops when children observe and explore on their own.

Sixth, it makes a difference what subject matter is studied. The method of discovery is important, but while using this method children should be studying something that will make them better informed and more capable of identifying and solving problems . . .

Children's interests are important, but they can easily be overemphasized and underdeveloped. With the elementary curriculum as crowded as it is, there is no time for nonsense. In our zeal to build on pupil interests, let us not forget that they are often transitory and need broadening and that their pursuit needs direction by the teacher.[14]

Someone has said that the happiest classroom situations occur when pupils voluntarily desire to learn what the teacher has already decided they should learn. This is essentially the case with another type of intrinsic motivation, frequently referred to as contrived motivation. This type of motivation occurs when the teacher contrives a situation out of which a pupil-felt problem will emerge. If, for instance, the teacher has planned in advance that his pupils will study a unit on Africa, he may (1) show several films or filmstrips on the topic, (2) arrange an attractive bulletin board and table display, (3) provide opportunities for class discussion of current news happenings related to the topic, or (4) introduce stories, poems, songs that will arouse children's interests and stimulate them to voice problems or questions that can then be used as a basis for study.

[14] Glenn O. Blough, "Using Children's Questions," *NEA Journal*, Vol. 51 (October, 1962), pp. 23-24.

Whether contrived or natural, there is little doubt that intrinsic motivation which leads to pupil-felt and pupil-expressed problems produces a more desirable learning experience than does extrinsic motivation. Provision for intrinsic motivation should be, therefore, a major consideration of the teacher in planning his total program.

3. *Unity*. Rigid boundaries between academic disciplines exist only within the walls of the classroom. They do not exist in a real-life situation. It is literally impossible for one to delve very deeply in any area without involving many other fields. One cannot, for instance, study nor understand very much of the history of a people before he needs to learn something about geography, language, anthropology, sociology, political science, art, music, science, and arithmetic. By the same token, the deeper one goes into physics the more he delves into other fields, including foreign languages. As a matter of fact, as the frontiers of science advance today in every field, scientists are discovering a higher degree of inter-relationship among specializations than was heretofore realized, and the *unity of science concept* is increasingly accepted. A high level of classroom teaching recognizes this fact and provides for functional, purposeful unity of learning experiences rather than compartmentalized and discrete packages of subject matter neatly labeled history, reading, composition, or spelling. The newer curricular patterns (see Chapter 8), the pronounced trend toward unit teaching, and the emphasis upon scheduling the day according to large blocks of time are examples of how the concept of unity is applied to classroom practice.

4. *Continuity and sequence.* Just as learning is a unified experience, so is it a continuous and sequential one, and considerable thought should be given to these basic principles when planning or organizing a classroom program. It is important to note that continuity and sequence may be attained through a logical, psychological, or sociological organization of content or, ideally, through a combination of all three. Some areas, for instance, are preferably taught and learned according to the logical organization of the subject. One cannot, for instance, multiply very efficiently by a two-digit multiplier unless he has previously learned to add. On the other hand, many subjects taught in logical or chronological order may have continuity and sequence for the teacher but certainly not for the learner. In many areas, individuals do not learn according to a logical or chronological sequence but rather according to a psychological pattern that begins with their most immediate needs and interests and radiates outward toward more distant spheres. Of course, as learning takes place, the learner takes each newly acquired knowledge and relates it to his previously acquired background. Thus, the logical organization of the learner's knowledge is a *result* not a *pattern* of learning. The following

example of a natural learning experience on an adult level illustrates this point.

A friend of the author recently inherited her first piece of antique furniture, a rare and expensive Chippendale table. Eager to learn about her prized possession, she immediately began to study about Thomas Chippendale—when and where he lived, the characteristics of his style, and so forth. Now a person thoroughly familiar with English antique furniture would instantly protest, "But you can't start there! You simply can't understand nor appreciate the Chippendale period without first understanding the influences of the earlier periods." But this learner didn't learn (and wasn't interested in learning) in this neat, chronological order. She learned according to her immediate interest and, as that interest grew, it led her "backward" to explore earlier periods and styles and "forward" to become thoroughly acquainted with later periods. Thus, she learned in a pattern that completely defied chronology but definitely had psychological sequence and continuity *for her as a learner.*

The implications for planning are obvious. Many teachers, when developing a study of Great Britain, will insist that the children study first the location, then the size, then the climate, and so on in what seems to them to be a correct logical organization. But it is very possible that children may be most interested in newspaper and television discussions of an item of current interest relating to Great Britain. If so, the study may be initiated on this note and then proceed to such other topics as location, industry, etc. of this land. Thus, the study would be organized in a psychological if not logical or chronological sequence.

Another organizational pattern is the sociological organization that begins with the study of the child's immediate environment and proceeds methodically to environments that become increasingly remote in time and space. The principle of widening horizons upon which many elementary school social studies programs are based is a well-known example of this type of organization. In a typical program organized in this fashion, the child begins his study with his most immediate environment, the home and school, and proceeds year by year to widen his horizons through sequential studies of the local community, state, region, nation, and finally the world. Although it is true that this curricular pattern is currently criticized by many, the concept of a sociological organization is a sound and important factor to be considered by the teacher in planning his program.

5. *Relatedness.* Learning takes place most effectively when pupils are able to relate the topic to their own experiences. A study of ancient Greece in the sixth grade, for instance, may produce very little genuine learning because children fail to see any relationship between it and their

own lives. After all, ancient Greece is several thousand miles and several thousand years removed, and what can it possibly mean to children who find it difficult to believe that people actually existed without telephones, automobiles, and transistor radios. But if the teacher makes a consistent effort to show that a relationship does exist through a study of such things as language (root words, derivations, etc.), architecture, literature, and sculpture, he may help to bridge the gap of years and miles and thus strengthen the pupils' awareness of the dependence of the present upon the past.

PUPIL INVOLVEMENT IN ALL TYPES OF PLANNING IS IMPORTANT. The principles of learning just discussed emphasized continually the involvement of the learner. Although widely accepted today by most teachers, the theory that pupils should be involved in planning their learning activities is a relatively recent educational innovation. In approximately 1920-1930 the idea of teacher-pupil planning or pupil-teacher planning was introduced. It represented a sharp contrast to the practice of ". . . one person's making all the plans for 30 or more other persons, who are then expected wholeheartedly and enthusiastically to implement those plans which they have had no part in contriving."[15]

Today, the term, *teacher-pupil* planning has generally been replaced by the broader term, *cooperative planning* or *cooperative procedures*. The original concept, also, has been expanded to mean that pupils should not only be involved in the planning of activities but, equally important, in all phases of the implementation and evaluation of these plans. The following definitions are indicative of this broader concept of cooperative planning.

. . . cooperative planning among pupils and teacher is regarded as a method by which a problem-oriented, experimental-minded group can determine its goals and direct its efforts toward the achievement of those goals.[16]

[Teacher-pupil planning] . . . provides for the teacher and students to share in the identification of purposes, the planning of learning experiences, the collection of materials and information, and the evaluation of group results and individual accomplishment.[17]

[15] Louise Parrish and Yvonne Waskin, "Curriculum Planning Through Teacher-Pupil Planning," *The Self-Contained Classroom*, Edith Roach Snyder, ed. (Washington, D. C., Association for Supervision and Curriculum Development, National Education Association, 1960), p. 23.

[16] Kenneth J. Rehage, "A Comparison of Pupil-Teacher Planning and Teacher-Directed Procedures in Eighth Grade Social Studies Classes," *Journal of Educational Research*, Vol. 45 (October, 1951), p. 111.

[17] G. Max Wingo, "Methods of Teaching," *Encyclopedia of Educational Research*, 3rd ed., Chester W. Harris, ed. (New York, The Macmillan Company, 1960), p. 853.

Pupil involvement in daily planning is important.

The values of teacher and pupils working together to purpose, to plan, to seek, to select, to develop, to implement, and to evaluate have been set forth in numerous statements similar to the following.

. . . violence is done to children whenever they are denied some share in decisions, plans, procedures and evaluation of enterprises they are expected to engage in. The more one engages in such activities, the greater is the investment and the greater is the learner's responsibility for the success of the enterprise. If we desire to insure better continuity within a learner, we will not repudiate the importance of affording ample opportunities for him to be in on the planning and executing of the enterprise to the fullest degree possible.[18]

. . . when learners are involved in the process of planning their own learning experiences, problems with which they are genuinely concerned are more likely to be considered. There is no better way for teachers to gain insight into the concepts children have developed than during the process of planning learning activities. The questions children ask, their grasp of the ramifications of a problem, and the ways they propose for studying problems are indicative of the growth and understanding they have achieved. For these reasons, coop-

[18] Reprinted by permission of the Association for Childhood Education International, 3615 Wisconsin Avenue, N.W., Washington, D. C. "Meeting the Challenge to Continuous Learning," by Beatrice Davis Hurley. From *Childhood Education*, October, 1962, Vol. 39, No. 2, pp. 55-56.

erative planning at all levels is one of the best means of promoting continuous learning.[19]

Skillful planning with pupils is the very core of teaching for efficient learning. Without pupil-teacher planning, motivation may be superficial and class time may be a waste of the teacher's energy and the pupils' opportunities.[20]

Successful learning occurs in teaching-learning situations in which the child is actively involved. His learning is effective to the extent that he comes to appreciate the relationships that exist between his goals and the activities in which he participates to attain these goals.[21]

According to our present knowledge of the learning process, therefore, there seems to be little room to question the superiority of cooperative planning over teacher-directed methods. Unfortunately, however, the idea of involving pupils in planning and evaluating learning activities has been woefully misunderstood and distorted by some teachers. Classroom practices that masquerade as cooperative planning but are simply indications of ineffective and incorrect teaching include the following.

1. *Puppeteering.* Some teachers delude themselves into thinking that they are planning cooperatively when they merely permit children to verbalize established routines and procedures. In such situations children are little more than puppets reciting what they know they are expected to say. A common example is the morning "planning" period during which children merely verbalize the day's routine. "What shall we do first?" brings forth the dutiful answer, "Put our News Story on the board." "What shall we do next?" elicits the rote response, "Have our reading groups." "What shall we do while another group is reading?" prompts such replies as, "Copy our News Story," "Read at the library table," and, "Work on our pictures." The whole repetitious process is dreary, boring, time-consuming, and dishonest. Children are not really planning the day. They are merely verbalizing what they know the teacher has previously planned.

The group planning session must not deteriorate to this type of activity. Nor does it have to be held the first thing in the morning each day. The group should sit down and plan together when a need arises. As a matter of fact, many teachers prefer combining evaluation and planning periods into one session at the close of the day. This has the advantages of ending the day on an anticipatory note; of permitting children to enter the fol-

[19] Association for Supervision and Curriculum Development, *A Look at Continuity in the School Program,* 1958 Yearbook (Washington, D. C., Association for Supervision and Curriculum Development, NEA, 1958), p. 139.

[20] Kimball Wiles, *Teaching for Better Schools* (Englewood Cliffs, N. J., Prentice-Hall, Inc., 1952), p. 159.

[21] Walter Murray and Lester D. Crow, "Teaching Science in the Elementary School," *Education,* Vol. 80 (March, 1960), p. 416.

lowing day and start right to work on individual tasks without waiting for a daily planning session; and of being of inestimable value to any substitute teacher.

2. *Fishing.* This is really a wholesale guessing game in which children try desperately to give the teacher what he wants. The following is an example.

TEACHER: How can we ask Miss M, our principal, if we may visit the firehouse?

PUPIL: I could go to the office and ask her.

TEACHER: Well . . . er . . . I don't know whether or not she's in the office now. What other way could we use?

PUPIL: You could ask her when you go to the office for your mail.

TEACHER: Well . . . er . . . I may not see her. Who has another idea?

PUPIL: I live right next door to her and see her every afternoon after school. Do you want me to ask her?

TEACHER: Well . . . er . . . I don't think you should bother her when she is at home. (*Desperately*) Doesn't anyone have another idea?

PUPIL: We could write her a letter.

TEACHER: (*Intense relief*) That's a splendid idea. Let's do that. Let's write Miss M a letter!

3. *Letting children do as they please.* Most educators are pretty weary of the cartoons and jokes about the teacher who addresses a class in the morning with the question, "What do you want to do today?" A competent teacher does not, and never did, believe that cooperative planning was synonymous with complete pupil freedom. As Burton forcefully says, "No competent and responsible educational leader has ever said anywhere at any time that the pupil is to do what he wants to do."[22]

We have mentioned briefly three of the most common distortions of cooperative planning. Many writers have written at length on how to avoid these pitfalls. Actually, two major suggestions, if carefully observed, should help to guarantee the success of pupil-involved planning.

First, advance planning, preplanning, or anticipatory planning, as it is variously called, is vitally important to the success of cooperative planning. Cooperative planning does not preclude the necessity of teacher planning. On the contrary, it often demands more extensive and skillful planning by the teacher. The teacher must determine the educational outcomes that should emerge from a particular activity in terms of pupil needs and abilities; he must set up broad outlines within which children may be permitted to operate; he must select a wide range of resources and materials suited to varying pupil abilities; he must plan how he will stimulate and sustain pupil interest over an approximate period of time; and he must weigh carefully the various procedures and activities which children may choose to attain their goals. In planning immediate or long-range learning experiences, advance planning by the teacher is an absolute necessity for the success of the cooperative planning that will follow.

Second, and extremely important, cooperative planning is successful only to the extent that the teacher is completely honest with pupils. This involves several factors, primarily, acquainting children with the limits within which they may operate. If teacher and pupils are operating within a rigid curriculum framework, it is futile and dishonest of the teacher to attempt to hide this fact from children. In such a situation, an honest approach that may be used occasionally is simply to say to children, "Boys and girls, our curriculum guide suggests that we study the Pacific States next. Shall we talk a little now to see what information we already have about this section of the country? Perhaps we can discover some important things we don't know, or we may also find that we don't all agree on our facts. This may help us to plan and organize our study of this new region." An entirely honest approach such as this will acquaint children with the broad limits within which they must operate but will also, as the study progresses, permit numerous opportunities for cooperative planning as pupils set up subproblems, organize the procedures they will use to attack their problems, select suitable references, and continually evaluate their progress. Concerning the importance of setting limits, Miel says,

It is the function of the status leader to help the group define the limits of its authority. This setting of limits should be open and above board and, if possible, done in advance to avoid the necessity of a veto. In other words, as a group starts to make a plan, members should be able to feel confident that plans made by the group will be followed if they stay within recognized limits.[23]

Being honest with children also means accepting pupil suggestions within any limits that have been defined. In the previous illustration, all suggestions offered to the question, "How can we ask Miss M if we may visit the firehouse?" were equally sensible and practical. Yet the teacher accepted only the one that suited her purposes. It would have been far better (1) to accept the suggestion which met with general group approval, and (2) to motivate a genuine need for a functional letter-writing experience through such an approach as, "We have listed several questions we want answered on our trip to the firehouse. Do you think the

[23] Alice Miel, *Cooperative Procedures in Learning* (New York, Bureau of Publications, Teachers College, Columbia University, 1952), p. 17.

firemen should know what things we are interested in before we actually arrive? Why? What is the best way to let them know?"

Not only should pupil suggestions be accepted, but honesty demands that the teacher, as a member of the group, be permitted to offer suggestions when the need arises. As was stated in the previous chapter, democratic leadership should not be confused with no leadership. The teacher is a respected and vital member of the group and should never hesitate to exert leadership and guidance through suggestions, recommendations, and cautions to be observed. As Miel says, "If the teacher has an idea he should contribute it to the group as simply and directly as any other group member would, with the special qualification that in general he will bend backward to give the children plenty of opportunities to express their ideas first."[24]

This section has discussed the major principles underlying the effective planning and organizing of classroom activities. Let us now examine how these principles may be applied to the three major areas of planning for which the elementary teacher is responsible.

PLANNING AND DEVELOPING THE UNIT

Long-range planning is the most crucial guarantee of a worthwhile and sequential yearly program. Most teachers begin such planning with an overview of curriculum guides, available instructional resources, and existing school records. From this point they begin to sketch in lightly the work of a semester or quarter, and then proceed to plan the major units of work around which many of the daily and weekly activities will be organized.

For at least three decades, the unit has been accepted as the most desirable method of organizing and developing classroom learning experiences. In spite of this, many teachers still admit that they do not fully understand how to plan and develop a unit of work. This section will attempt to shed some light on the situation by (1) defining and examining the distinguishing features of a unit, and (2) analyzing each part of the unit as it is organized and put into practice.

What is a Unit?

Many competent authorities have proposed clear and specific definitions of a unit. The following reveal the high degree of consistency that exists among educators today concerning the concept of a unit.

A unit is any combination of subject-matter content and outcomes and thought processes into learning experiences suited to the maturity and needs (personal

[24] *Ibid.*, p. 318.

and social) of the learners, all combined into a whole with internal integrity determined by immediate and ultimate goals.[25]

A unit, or a unit of work, can be defined as a purposeful learning experience focused upon some socially significant understanding that will modify the behavior of the learner and enable him to adjust to a life situation more effectively.[26]

Units of work represent an effort on the part of the school to relate subject matter and the development of skills in the organization of children's learning about important interests, topics, or problems.[27]

Our own definition is: A classroom unit is a cohesive sequence of learning experiences generated by a pupil-centric interest or problem, the solution of which satisfies both the immediate needs of the learners and the long-range goals of the school.

A UNIT HAS SEVERAL DISTINGUISHING FEATURES. Regardless of type or level, the unit is characterized by certain features that distinguish it from other general types of organizations. In general, they are the following:

1. *The ultimate goal of the unit is integration within the learner of his needs, organized subject matter, and processes of study and thought.* In the past some authors have distinguished between subject matter units, experience units, and process units. Such distinctions, however, may be artificial for, as Burton points out, "All units will deal with subject matter and materials, with processes of study and thought, combined in educative experiences best suited to ultimate and immediate goals."[28] The difference among units, therefore, becomes one of *emphasis* rather than of type. For instance, with young children, the unit will be primarily determined by their immediate problems, interests, and needs. An example of such a unit might be, "Why Does the Doctor Vaccinate Us?" As children progress through the grades, the emphasis of the unit may be placed more on organized subject matter, although it should still be related to the learners' needs and interests. An example of such a unit may be "Early Settlers of Our Town." Still other units, such as "Do Newspapers Always Tell the Truth?" may emphasize critical skills of reading and thinking although, here again, organized knowledge and the satisfaction of learners' needs are definite outcomes as well.

[25] William H. Burton, *op. cit.*, p. 329.

[26] Lavone A. Hanna, Gladys L. Potter, and Neva Hagaman, *Unit Teaching in the Elementary School*, rev. ed. (New York, Holt, Rinehart and Winston, Inc., 1963) p. 117.

[27] Ruth G. Strickland, *How to Build a Unit of Work* (Washington, D. C., U. S. Office of Education, 1946), p. 1.

[28] William H. Burton, *op. cit.*, p. 328.

2. *It is a long-range, comprehensive learning experience.* A primary unit such as "Kinds of Christmas Greens" may easily be completed in one or two weeks. Most elementary school units, however, are somewhat more comprehensive in scope and extend generally over a four to eight week period.

3. *It transcends artificially created boundaries of subject matter.* As was stated previously, the hard and fast compartmentalization of subject matter is a thoroughly artificial situation. The unit adheres to a natural learning experience in that it uses whatever disciplines are needed to solve the problem. One cannot, for instance, gain much of an understanding of the kinds of evergreens used at Christmas time unless one crosses over artificial subject limits into the fields of science, geography, history, art, reading, and probably others.

It should be stressed here, however, that the utilization of content from many fields is far different from the older idea of *correlation* in which each school subject had to be related to a central topic. (See following chapter.) Arithmetic learnings become part of the unit when they are needed to solve a problem or accomplish a purpose. This does not mean that, if the Christmas greens unit is in progress, all arithmetic problems should be of the "If I had 20 spruce trees and sold them for $3.75 each, how much money would I have?" type. Thank goodness this type of artificial teaching is fast disappearing from most of our classrooms.

The question is frequently asked, "Is it possible to have two units in progress simultaneously in a classroom?" The answer should be fairly obvious from this discussion. One may easily develop a social studies and, perhaps, a science unit at the same time. Several units progressing simultaneously will, however, tend to disintegrate rather than integrate pupils' progress toward a comprehensive goal.

4. *It provides for a wide range of activities adapted to individual needs and interests.* The comprehensiveness of a unit makes it an ideal vehicle for recognizing and providing for individual differences. As children engage in research, group work, creative activities, problem-solving procedures, communication skills, and others the teacher may capitalize upon numerous opportunities to develop the unique talents and skills of each pupil.

5. *It utilizes the accepted principles of learning.* Unit planning and teaching consistently recognize the elementary principles of learning mentioned in the first section of this chapter.

THE PLAN AND ORGANIZATION OF A UNIT ADHERE CLOSELY TO THE SEQUENCE OF A NATURAL EDUCATIVE EXPERIENCE. Some naive teachers appear to think that the plan and organization of a unit have been arbitrarily

TABLE 7.2

Sequential Steps in Learning

1	2	3	4	5	6
Motivation within the learner makes him receptive to stimulation.	A goal becomes related to the motivation. A. The goal is not at once attainable. B. A barrier exists.	Tension arises. A. Energy is released within the learner; he is ready to act. B. The barrier prevents an appropriate discharge of the energy and creates tension.	Learner seeks an appropriate line of action to reach goal. A. In every situation there are a number of possible ways of acting. B. The selection of one of those ways of acting will involve elements of chance and/or analysis. C. When the selection is made action toward the goal is attempted. D. If the selected line of action is inappropriate steps A, B, and C will be repeated until an appropriate action occurs. E. When an appropriate action occurs it will involve: 1. Some degree of success in terms of the goal. 2. A sense of satisfaction and a reduction of tension to the extent that the motive is satisfied.	Learner fixes the appropriate line of action. A. Skills are acquired by drill or practice. B. Concepts are developed by becoming familiar with the referent. C. Memorization is accomplished through meaningful repetition. D. Tastes and preferences are established by the satisfyingness or annoyingness of the experience. E. Ability to solve problems is a product of A and B above. Speed of Learning Varies A. May be relatively sudden. B. May be very slow. C. Depends on: 1. Nature of the problem. 2. Degree of motivation. 3. Capacity of the learner.	Inappropriate behaviors are dropped. A. Yielding no satisfaction, they lose attractiveness.

SOURCE: Asahel B. Woodruff, *The Psychology of Teaching*, 3rd ed. (New York, Longmans, Green and Company, Inc., 1951), p. 241. Courtesy of David McKay Company, Inc.

decided by a professor of education or a curriculum coordinator sitting somewhere in a comfortable office with nothing else to do. Not true! The sequence of a unit is based squarely upon what we now know about the natural learning process. As Woodruff says, "When all theories and schools of thought are peeled aside, and the bare facts about learning are exposed, it becomes clear that regardless of theoretical points of view the learning process contains certain common sequential steps."[29]

The sequence of these steps is illustrated by Woodruff in Table 7.2 on page 282.

Very similar is Hanna's *Flow Chart of a Complete Educational Experience*,[30] outlined in the left-hand column below. The right-hand column lists the steps in the normal development of a unit. The relationship between the two is clearly evident.

A Flow Chart of a Complete Educational Experience

Individual with past experience

faces a new situation, novel to him, resulting in

a disturbance, disequilibrium

out of which emerges a *purpose*

To Do Something,

i.e., share a thought or feeling, acquire object or information, express a mood, etc.

The Organization of a Classroom Unit of Work

Anticipatory Planning

a. Examination of Available Resource Units

b. Formulation of Teacher's Objectives

c. Examination of Broad Outlines and Limitations of Future Cooperative Planning

d. Preliminary Overview of Available Resources and Materials

Initiatory Activities

e. Motivating Activities and

f. Exploratory Discussions and/or Activities

g. Formulation of Major Problems and/or Subproblems

h. Cooperative Planning of Necessary Procedures and Activities

[29] Asahel D. Woodruff, *The Psychology of Teaching*, 3rd ed. (New York, Longmans, Green and Company, Inc., 1951), p. 239.

[30] Paul R. Hanna, *A Flow Chart of a Complete Educational Experience* (Palo Alto, California, Stanford University).

A Flow Chart of a Complete Educational Experience		*The Organization of a Classroom Unit of Work*
Each type of behavior suggested has its own medium or expression		i. Exploration of Subtopics According to Planned Procedures and Activities
constructing, dramatizing, reading, asking questions, writing, speaking, figuring, drawing, etc.	Development	j. Utilization of Numerous Learning Materials and Resources
and each medium has its own appropriate skills, techniques, facts, attitudes, appreciations, etc.		
which have to be acquired in the normal process of achieving the purpose set,		k. Frequent Intermediate Planning and Evaluation Sessions
and when these skills, facts, attitudes are thus built into the learner in normal goal-seeking	Culmination	l. Summary and Evaluation
They give satisfaction in restoring the equilibrium of the personality and leave him ready to face the next novel situation with increased power to live and learn.		m. Possible Emergence of Related Problems for Future Study (Assignment and/or Forward Look)

The following is a brief examination of each step of the unit according to the order in which it appeared above.

Anticipatory Planning

a. *Examination of Available Resource Units.* Source units or resource units are comprehensive and valuable references that should be consulted by the teacher when preparing a classroom unit. These teacher-aids are usually prepared by curriculum committees and contain numerous suggestions as to the possible content, procedures, activities, resources, and materials the individual teacher may use in developing a unit for his particular group of pupils. Many source units are deliberately made comprehensive enough to be adapted to several grade levels. A resource unit, for instance, on "The Meaning of Democracy" may be a worthwhile reference for either a third or sixth grade teacher who wishes to organize a unit around this central theme. According to Wagner,

The better resource units are characterized by: (1) coverage of a relatively broad area dealing with a central theme; (2) ideas and activities emerging from many subject-matter fields as they relate naturally to the basic problem;

(3) a suggested variety of methods for achieving the same objectives; (4) provision for experiences of varying difficulties in order to challenge individual tasks and group projects; (5) a listing of valuable sources of information; and (6) emphasis upon materials available in the local environment.[31]

b. *Formulation of teacher's objectives.* Basic to the entire success of the unit is the teacher's ability to formulate clearly the goals or educational outcomes he wishes his pupils to realize from this learning experience. If the teacher does not know precisely what his objectives are, the whole unit simply becomes a case of the halt leading the blind. In formulating his objectives, the teacher should keep the following cautions in mind.

Objectives should be specific and reasonably attainable. Too many teachers fall into a trap of formulating broad, sweeping objectives that are valid goals for the entire school program but cannot, by any stretch of the imagination, be attained in a single unit. "To develop artistic appreciation" or "To develop scientific attitudes" are general aims of all teachers and are of little help in evaluating the success of any single unit.

Objectives should distinguish between the goal and the procedure. The teacher's objectives represent what he hopes children will *learn*, not what they will *do* in the process of learning. This sounds very simple and yet many, many, many teachers fail to make a distinction between the two. "To build a grocery store," "To visit the planetarium," "To study the industries of New England," and "To work in committees" appear over and over again in teachers' unit plans as objectives. They are not objectives. They are activities and procedures. They are not an end. They are a means to an end. Most of the mechanical, imitative and low-gear teaching characterizing some of our modern classrooms may be traced directly to this point. To illustrate:

As part of a unit on "Transportation" in her third grade, Miss Q listed as one of her objectives, "To have the children make a mural illustrating the various methods of early travel." This is not an objective. This is an activity. When Miss Q's supervisor asked the *purpose* of the activity, Miss Q replied that she thought the children would enjoy it, that it would provide work for some pupils while others were in reading groups, that an attractive mural would brighten the classroom, and finally that she had learned at college that making a mural was a desirable activity for children. The sad truth was, of course, that Miss Q had no objectives in mind when planning this activity. She had planned simply in terms of deciding upon the experience without giving any thought to the educational outcomes toward which it should contribute. She had decided upon

[31] Guy Wagner, *"What Schools Are Doing: Unit Teaching," Education,* Vol. 80, p. 508. Reprinted from the April, 1960, issue of *Education.* Copyright, 1960, by The Bobbs-Merrill Company, Inc., Indianapolis, Indiana.

having her pupils paint a mural simply because she thought it was a good thing to do.

Now, the point is that this is, or can be, a good experience, provided it is designed to accomplish certain specific desirable educational outcomes. It can provide an excellent opportunity to teach certain basic art principles such as balance and color harmony. It can be an excellent vehicle for developing certain skills of group work. It can introduce children to new art media. It can be a means of encouraging art appreciation. It can test children's understanding of certain basic concepts developed as the unit progressed. It can help to develop group planning and evaluation skills. It can help to develop group approval and appreciation of the abilities of certain members of the class. It can provide purposeful motivation for extended reading and research. In short, it can serve a variety of educationally valid purposes, provided the teacher has planned the activity with these specific purposes in mind.

Objectives should not be confused with pupils' objectives. On this point, Burton states,

The teacher's objectives and the pupil's objectives in any learning situation are not similar in form, but they are intimately related. The teacher's objectives are the desirable educational outcomes . . . which he hopes the pupil will achieve. The pupil's objectives are the immediate results which he sees and desires and which will result from his activity in solving the question in which he is interested. The teacher hopes so to guide the learning experience that desirable educational results (the teacher's objectives) will be achieved while the pupil is achieving his objectives. Failure to realize the difference and relation between teacher's and learner's objectives has caused not only much ineffective and useless teaching but has developed detrimental attitudes and practices and much pupil antagonism toward education. In many schools the pupil does not know or care what the teacher's objectives are. Worse, the teacher too often does not know or care what the pupil's objectives are. Because of this, teachers often cover the ground, go through the motions, and think that they have achieved their objectives when, in fact, they have achieved no educative results. The pupil has realized neither objectives of his own, nor those of the teacher.[32]

c. *Examination of broad outlines and limitations of future cooperative planning* and d. *Preliminary overview of available resource materials.* Both of these steps have been examined in the preceding discussion on cooperative planning.

Initiatory Activities

e. *Motivating activities* and f. *Exploratory discussions and/or activities.* If natural motivation is used, these phases of the unit will be devoted

[32] William H. Burton, *op. cit.*, p. 130.

to a pulling together of the spontaneously expressed interests and problems of pupils. Example: "Yesterday, most of us spent our play period watching the bulldozer work across the street. You asked many questions about the bulldozer and what the men were doing. Do you remember what they were? If we write these questions on the board, so that we may remember them, maybe we can find the answers someplace."

If contrived motivation is used, the teacher will set the stage for the unit several days in advance by such devices as:

1. Arranging attractive bulletin board and table displays.
2. Showing films, filmstrips, or other appropriate audio-visual aids.
3. Collecting and exhibiting pertinent books and periodicals.
4. Emphasizing current news events of related interest.
5. Utilizing the services of an available resource person in the school or community.

When sufficient interest has been aroused, the teacher may then introduce preliminary discussions from which pupils' problems will emerge.

g. *Formulation of major problems and/or subproblems.* These are the pupils' goals and, if properly motivated, represent the genuine, learner-involved, learner-stated problems for which pupils desire solutions.

h. *Cooperative planning of necessary procedures and activities.* The initial planning session may be completed in a single lesson or may extend over several days. Teacher and pupils may plan (1) the scope and sequence of the study, (2) the materials and resources needed, (3) the appropriate activities involved, and (4) the division of responsibilities among individuals, groups, or both. Very often the planned layout may be put on a chart to which children may regularly refer. This does not mean, however, that the initial plan should be so rigid as to prohibit changes and modifications as the unit progresses.

Development

i. *Exploration of subtopics according to planned procedures and activities;* j. *Utilization of numerous learning materials and resources;* and k. *Frequent intermediate planning and evaluation sessions.* All of these are self-explanatory and are the means by which the study is guided toward its predetermined goals.

Culmination

1. *Summary and evaluation.* When all data have been collected, when all problems have been solved, children and teacher may evaluate together their success. "Did we answer all of our questions? Did we choose the best methods and materials for doing the job? How could we have im-

proved? What did we learn, not only about our problem, but about other things as well? Which of these are worth remembering? How can we help ourselves to remember them?" These and other techniques will help children to evaluate and appraise the satisfaction they have received from their efforts.

m. *Possible emergence of related problems for future study.* It was said previously that few learning experiences are isolated and discrete. Units are merely links in a year-long educative experience. As one unit nears completion, the teacher will begin to motivate the next unit so that there is a natural and easy transfer from one to the next. In most classrooms, the older idea of an elaborate unit culmination has been replaced by an emphasis upon the smooth and natural flow from one unit to the next.

THERE ARE MANY ACCEPTABLE FORMS FOR WRITTEN UNIT PLANS. In this section we have examined the plan and organization of the unit as it develops in the classroom. In what form and in what detail the teacher places this plan on paper depends upon many factors. The following is an outline of a fifth grade unit that was motivated naturally by children's interest and concern in the previous week's serious power failure in their community, as the result of a sleet storm.

UNIT PLAN

TOPIC: *ELECTRICITY AND MAGNETISM*
GRADE: Five
TIME: Approximately 6-8 weeks

LEARNERS' CONCERNS AND INTERESTS

Major Topic

Why Electricity is Important to Us

Sub-problems

Where does electricity come from?
How does electricity get to my house?
What makes a battery work?
What are conductors and insulators?
What is an electric current?
What makes a person get an electric shock?
What is static electricity?
What makes static on the radio and television set?
How does an electric light work?
Why doesn't the electricity in my flashlight need wires like a lamp?
How does an electric doorbell work?
How does electricity work in a radio?

How does electricity heat homes?

How can electricity make a stove hot and a refrigerator cold?

What is magnetism?

How does electricity make magnetism?

What can a magnet do?

Are there different kinds of magnets?

How has electricity changed man's way of life?

TEACHER'S OBJECTIVES

Knowledges and Understandings

To develop an understanding that electricity is a form of energy.

To develop certain concepts basic to understanding electricity, namely:

    a. Scientists believe electricity is a flow of electrons.

    b. Man can control electricity and make it serve him.

    c. An electric current needs a complete circuit.

    d. There are two kinds of electrical charges, negative and positive.

    e. Some materials allow electricity to flow easier than others.

    f. Magnetism is one of the results of the motion of electric current.

To develop an understanding of the extent of man's dependence today on electricity.

To develop an understanding of the extent to which science has benefited mankind.

Attitudes and Appreciations

To develop the realization that man has only begun to capitalize upon the potential contributions and benefits of electricity.

To develop an interest in the natural phenomena of our immediate environment.

To develop an appreciation of the limitations and dangers of electricity as well as its benefits.

To strengthen a spirit of inquiry and intellectual curiosity.

To strengthen the ability to appraise data objectively.

To emphasize the dangers of formulating hasty conclusions upon the evidence of limited data.

To develop an appreciation of the role science plays in our modern society.

Habits and Skills

To develop the skills of locating information with particular emphasis on:

    a. The use of the index

    b. The use of the table of contents

    c. The use of tables and illustrations

    d. The use of the card catalogue

To develop the habit of utilizing many resources and methods for securing information.

To develop skill in communicating information through giving oral reports and demonstrations to the class.

To develop judgmental skills with particular emphasis on:

    a. The ability to evaluate sources of data

    b. The ability to differentiate between important ideas and irrevelant facts

To develop the habit of challenging explanations made by others and accepting challenges from others.

To strengthen the intellectual resourcefulness of pupils with particular emphasis on substituting available materials for an experiment in place of those suggested but nonavailable.

To strengthen pupils' abilities to utilize scientific methods in solving problems.

To develop the habit of exercising all necessary cautions when working with electrical equipment.

AREA OF INVESTIGATION	TENTATIVE PROCEDURES AND ACTIVITIES	CHILDREN'S REFERENCES
Initiatory Activities	Science Table Exhibit	
	Bulletin Board Displays of News Clippings of Last Week's Power Failure	
	Work Bench Display	
	Library Corner	
	Collection of Electrical Toys	

Cooperative Planning Sessions	Discuss how to solve problems
	  a. Reading
	  b. Experimentation
	  c. Observation
	  d. Field Trips
	  e. Resource people
	  f. Films, etc.	

	Organize methods of procedures
	  a. Individual research
	  b. Special projects
	  c. Class activities
	  d. Committee work
	  e. Responsibilities for reports
	  f. Plan tentative sequence of topics
	  g. Block out an approximate schedule	

AREA OF INVESTIGATION	TENTATIVE PROCEDURES AND ACTIVITIES	CHILDREN'S REFERENCES
Electricity as Energy Light Heat Power	Experiments and Demonstrations Film—*The Story of Edison* Filmstrip—*How Water Power Produces Electricity* Discussion Group work Examine inside of light bulb Start individual booklets Start vocabulary chart Film—*Introduction to Electricity*	*The Storybook of Science* *The First Electrical Book for Boys* *The Story of Power* *Junior Science Book of Electricity*
Origin and History of Electricity	Special Report—John L. Discussion of early theories Group project and report by first reading group Film—*Lightning and Thunder*	*Lightning and Thunder* *Exploring Electricity* *Men of Science and Invention* *The Boy Scientist* *The Bright Design* *Lightning*
Static Electricity	Experiments and Demonstrations "Magic Show" for Second Grade Film—*Static Electricity*	*Adventuring in Science* *All About Electricity*
Magnetism	Film—*Magnetism* Film—*Electromagnets* Discussion—Basic Principles Make a compass Make diagrams and charts Individual experiments—share with class later Special report—Group II	*The Golden Book of Science* *Magnets and How To Use Them* *The Storybook of Science*

AREA OF INVESTIGATION	TENTATIVE PROCEDURES AND ACTIVITIES	CHILDREN'S REFERENCES
Current Electricity	Experiments and Demonstrations	*The First Book of Electricity*
What is current electricity?	Work at Science Table— conductors and insulators	*All About Electricity*
electrons conductors and insulators	Film—*Learning About Electric Current*	*Rusty Rings a Bell*
circuit series parallel	Film—*Making Electricity* Field Trip—Power Plant	*Discovering with Science*
		The Storybook of Science
How is it produced?	Filmstrip—*Electricity*	*Science in Our World*
battery generator	Complete individual notebooks	
How is it controlled? switches wires		
The Safe Use of Electricity	Prepare a list of safety rules	*Discovering with Science*
electric appliances electric wires switches grounds	Prepare displays and talks for other classes concerning dangers of overloading wiring during coming Christmas season	
Terminal Activities	Wire up an intercom system between classroom and office (tentative)	*Experiments with Electricity* *Electrical Things Boys Like to Make*
	Wire kindergarten's doll house as Christmas surprise	

COOPERATIVE EVALUATION

Intermediate and terminal evaluative sessions directed toward following:
1. Have we answered our questions?
2. What are we learning about the possible ways of solving problems?
3. What *do's* and *don'ts* have we discovered for working experiments and giving demonstrations?
4. How have we enlarged our vocabularies through this study?
5. Was our committee work successful? What did we learn about being a leader or member of a work group?

6. How have we improved in giving and listening to reports?
7. What new sources of information have we discovered?
8. Did we try to help each other in this unit?
9. What did we learn about the scientist's method of drawing conclusions and evaluating data?
10. Have we learned anything new about magic and superstition?
11. Have our study skills improved?
12. Can we locate information more efficiently than we used to?
13. Are we learning to use time economically?
14. How will we put our knowledge into practice and use outside of the classroom?
15. Has this unit helped us to live more intelligent and safer lives?

CHILDREN'S SUPPLEMENTARY REFERENCES

1. American Heritage, *Men of Science and Invention* (New York, American Heritage Publishing Company, 1960).
2. Beeler, Nelson F. and Branley, Franklyn M. *Experiments with Electricity* (New York, Thomas Y. Crowell Company, 1949).
3. Branley, Franklyn M. and Vaughan, Eleanor K. *Rusty Rings a Bell* (New York, Thomas Y. Crowell Company, 1953).
4. Cook, Sherman B. *Electrical Things Boys Like to Make* (Milwaukee, Bruce Publishing Company, 1954).
5. Craig, Gerald S. and Hill, Katherine E. *Adventuring in Science* (New York, Ginn and Company, 1954).
6. Craig, Gerald S. and Hurley, Beatrice D. *Discovering with Science* (New York, Ginn and Company, 1954).
7. Epstein, Samuel and Beryl W. *The First Book of Electricity* (New York, Franklin Watts, Inc., 1953).
8. Freeman, Ira, *All About Electricity* (New York, Random House, 1957).
9. Notkin, Jerome J. and Gulkin, Sidney, *The How and Why Wonder Book of Science* (New York, Grosset and Dunlap, Inc., 1960).
10. Feravolo, Rocco V. *Junior Science Book of Electricity* (New York, Grosset and Dunlap, Inc., 1962).
11. Keelor, Katharine L. *Working with Electricity* (New York, The Macmillan Company, 1931).
12. Lewellen, John, *The Boy Scientist* (New York, Simon and Schuster, 1955).
13. Morgan, Alfred, *Things a Boy Can Do with Electricity* (New York, Charles Scribner's Sons, 1938).
14. Morgan, Alfred, *A First Electrical Book for Boys*, Revised edition (New York, Charles Scribner's Sons, 1951).
15. Pine, Tillie S. and Levine, Joseph, *Magnets and How to Use Them* (New York, McGraw-Hill Book Company, Inc., 1958).
16. Shippen, Katherine, *The Bright Design* (New York, The Viking Press, 1949).
17. Skilling, Hugh H. *Exploring Electricity* (New York, The Ronald Press, 1948).

18. Stoddard, Edward, *The Story of Power* (New York, Doubleday and Company, 1956).
19. Zim, Herbert S. *Lightning and Thunder* (New York, William Morrow and Company, 1952).

LESSON PLANNING

Planning individual lessons requires the same careful thought as does unit planning and much of what has been said previously about the importance of organization, direction, pupil involvement, cohesiveness, and sequence applies equally well to this important type of planning. Furthermore, the sequence of a lesson, although it is telescoped into a time interval of one or a few days, parallels the steps of a unit outlined in the previous section. Careful anticipatory planning (including formulation of teacher's objectives), recognition of the learner's purpose, the methodical progress toward stated objectives, the employment of varied activities and resources, the closing evaluation, and the assignment or forward look are the important steps in a well-organized lesson. Because there is such a wide variety among the types of lessons employed in the elementary school, however, it is usually possible to make individual plans in terms of certain basic essentials only.

AN EFFECTIVE LESSON PLAN CONTAINS CERTAIN BASIC ESSENTIALS. Most educators readily concede that there is no *one* best type of written lesson plan for several reasons. First, today's emphasis upon creative teaching encourages teachers to develop and use the type of plan that best serves their specific needs at a specific time. Second, the plan should depend upon the *type* of lesson and it is fairly obvious that a plan for a creative rhythms lesson may differ from that of a lesson designed to teach children the use of an index and table of contents. Third, the demands placed upon teachers in this area vary widely from system to system. Some schools require the teacher to use a commercially prepared plan book, others print and distribute their own forms to teachers. Still others allow the teacher freedom to keep his own type of plans. Some principals request that weekly plans be submitted to the central office for approval; most do not. As a matter of fact, about the only pertinent generalization that should be stated concerning the writing of individual lesson plans is that *all adequate lesson plans contain certain basic essentials*. Simply stated, the written plan for each lesson, regardless of detail, type of lesson, grade, or subject, should contain the following information.

1. *What we expect to accomplish through this experience.*
   (Teacher's and pupils' objectives)
2. *How we expect to accomplish it.*
   (Content, procedures, materials, activities, and resources)

3. *How we can evaluate the results.*
   (Summary and evaluation)
4. *What is our next step?*
   (Assignment and/or forward look)

Many inexperienced teachers appreciate the security of fairly detailed lesson planning. During their initial teaching experience, many teachers find they need the direction and security that result from preparing detailed lesson plans. This is very commendable, provided the plan does not become a strait-jacket. No advance planning by the teacher should be rigid to the point where it stifles the spontaneous contributions and cooperative planning of the pupils. Incidentally, much of the fishing mentioned earlier is caused by teachers who do not make their plans flexible enough to permit the lesson to go in one of several directions and can, therefore, accept from children only the exact responses they have anticipated in their previous planning. It should be noted, however, that *detail* and *organization* are not necessarily synonymous with *rigidity*. The following is an example of a plan prepared by an inexperienced teacher which strikes a desirable balance between thoughtful organization and desirable flexibility.

LESSON PLAN

GRADE: Four

TIME: Approximately three days

TEACHER'S OBJECTIVES

To further children's interest in their local natural environment.

To teach the names and properties of the more common local rock specimens.

To emphasize the importance of carefully checking tentative conclusions with authoritative sources.

To familiarize children with common procedures for identifying rock specimens.

To strengthen skills of locating, summarizing, and organizing information.

To strengthen skills of written communication with particular emphasis upon
   a. legible handwriting
   b. proper spelling
   c. capitalization of proper nouns

LEARNERS' PURPOSE

To set up in the hall for the benefit of other classes a table display of rocks including those collected on yesterday's trip to the quarry.

MATERIALS

Rocks collected by children, including those found yesterday on trip to the quarry.

Geologist's hammer, knife, diluted hydrochloric acid.

References and text books.

PROCEDURES

1. Discussion of criteria for worthwhile display (List on board)
   a. Attractive (neat, clean, well-organized, etc.)
   b. Informative (accurate labels and interesting descriptions for all items)
2. Discussion of information needed for each specimen included in the display (List on board)
   a. Name
   b. Where and when found
   c. Description
   d. Use
   e. Miscellaneous interesting information
3. Discussion of procedures for identifying rock samples
   a. Consult available references for possible identification
   b. Check tentative identification by
      (1) General appearance
      (2) Scratch test
      (3) Acid test
   c. Draw conclusions
   d. Check conclusions with references
4. Examination by class of one or two sample specimens to illustrate the procedures for tentative identification, choose from the following.
   a. Mica Schist
   b. Quartz
   c. Limestone
   d. Shale
   e. Sandstone
5. Individual and/or small group research until identification is completed
6. Discussion of division of responsibilities for display
   a. Writing labels and descriptions—emphasize particularly the importance of
      (1) Legible handwriting (labels will be read by many people)
      (2) Correct spelling (scientists must be accurate!)
      (3) Use of capital letters for proper nouns
      (4) Good organization of subject matter
   b. Setting up display in hall
   c. Writing notices and invitations to see the exhibit
   d. Dismantling the exhibit when it has served its purpose

EVALUATION AND ASSIGNMENT

What did we, and other classes in the school, learn from our rock display? On what things do we need further work or study?

MOST EXPERIENCED TEACHERS PREFER TO WRITE WEEKLY OR SEMI-MONTHLY PLANS. Writing detailed plans for each day is very time-consuming and the experienced teacher usually finds that he can more profitably devote his time to other aspects of his job. Another disadvantage of maintaining plans day by day is that it tends to segment rather than unify the natural flow of learning experiences. Most experienced teachers, therefore, prefer to plan in terms of weekly or biweekly periods. This does not mean, however, that these plans should be so condensed that they omit the basic essentials of adequate planning previously mentioned. Many teachers who maintain a weekly plan book do not, in fact, write any plans but merely outline a weekly layout of subject matter. Mrs. T, for instance, for a February day's social studies lesson in second grade recorded in her plan book just two words, "George Washington." Sure enough, she started the lesson by showing a picture of the noble gentleman and from there the discussion went to why the school would be closed Friday, to what the pupils would do on their holiday, to how they spent their previous vacations, to why they wished the spring vacation would soon arrive, to why they liked to go to baseball games, to what record would be set for home runs during the coming season, and they never did manage to get back to the neglected Father of Our Country. This is an actual illustration of the kind of disorganized and ineffectual teaching that results from the woefully false idea that two words constitute an adequate plan for any teaching-learning experience.

Table 7.3 on pages 298 to 299 is a plan written by an experienced first grade teacher for the development of certain arithmetic skills. It will be noticed that, although much unnecessary writing has been omitted, the plan contains the basic essentials that will guarantee an organized and purposeful educational experience for pupils, even if a substitute teacher is in the room.

DAILY PROGRAMMING

The last major area of planning with which we are concerned is the teacher's responsibility for planning his daily program. Here again, although operating within the broad boundaries previously mentioned, most teachers have considerable freedom to organize the daily program to meet the needs of their particular pupils. From the research, study, and literature that have been devoted to this area over past years, it is possible to identify certain broad trends in schedule making. In general, these may be summarized as follows:

THE DAILY TIME SCHEDULE SHOULD BE FLEXIBLE. One of the great joys of teaching in the elementary school self-contained classroom is that one does not have to turn a lesson off or on like a faucet at precisely 10:32

TABLE 7.3

TEACHER Mary Robbins   SUBJECT Arithmetic
GRADE First (John's Group)   DATE Week of October 15

	MONDAY	TUESDAY	WEDNESDAY	THURSDAY	FRIDAY
Teacher's Objectives	To reinforce the skill of rational counting by 1's and 2's from 1 to 40. To strengthen the ability to read and write numbers from 1 to 40. To develop an understanding of place value in numbers from 1 to 40.				To develop concept of day, week, month
Learner's Purpose	How many children are present today? How many are absent? (Capitalize upon other functional counting opportunities as they arise.)				What holiday is coming soon?
Procedures	Review counting to 40 by 1's and 2's. (1) People (2) Money (3) Pegs, etc. Write sequence of 1 to 40 on chalkboard. Take turns. Read and discuss.	Review counting by 1's and 2's. Write 14 on chalkboard. What number is this? Form group of 14 Regroup — 1 dime and 4 cents Repeat—pegs, disks, flannel board cutouts, etc.	Read sequence 1–29 on chalkboard. Review — Show us the tens numbers. What did we learn about this number (14) yesterday? Redemonstrate with money, pegs, disks, etc. Further review—13, 15, 17, etc. as necessary.	Discuss follow-up of yesterday — functional use of numbers in every day life. Develop concept of numbers from 31 to 39 according to procedures of Tuesday and Wednesday.	Examine calendar. How many days in October? Count them? How many days in a week? Name them? How many weeks in October? How many days in October have passed? Count.

Procedures	Game—which number comes after 14 when counting by 1's? By 2's? Which number comes before 22 when counting by 1's? by 2's? etc. . . . Vary with oral and written answers. Demonstrate groupings from 1 to 9.	Look at 14 — What does the 1 stand for? The 4? Continue procedure for 13, 18, 16, 12, 11, etc.	Look at this number—23. What does it mean? Demonstrate. Repeat. *How do we know which numeral means tens and which means ones?*	*Independent work* pp. 32-34 in workbook. Special Help with concrete groupings for those who need it.	How many weeks in October have passed? How many days until Halloween? How many weeks until Halloween? Discussion—other special days in October (Columbus Day, birthdays, etc.).
Summary and Evaluation	What two ways can we count to 40? Which is faster? Why?	Show us the tens numbers on the chalkboard. Why are they called tens numbers? What did we learn about them today?	In this number (22) point to the 2 which tells how many tens. To the 2 which tells how many ones. State rule.	Check written work with independent group.	
Assignment-Forward Look	*Ditto Sheets* Fill in missing numbers in sequence.	Flannel Board Stories 14 is ___ tens and ___ ones, 16 is ___ tens and ___ ones, etc.	See if you can find where any of the numbers we have been talking about are used in your home or outside of school.		What do we need to do to get ready for Halloween?

A.M. or 2:04 P.M. It is true, as mentioned previously, that most systems recommend certain time apportionments to certain curricular areas, but these are very elastic and there are few elementary teachers who are obliged to regulate their day's program strictly by the clock. Flexibility of program is desirable for several reasons. It will permit the teacher to prolong or terminate activities according to children's interests which is of vital importance when working with the limited concentration spans and ephemeral interests of young children. It will allow time for the development of planning, evaluating, and the all-important social skills. It will permit teachers to capitalize upon the spontaneous learning opportunities that continually arise in a class of thirty youngsters. And, last but not least, it will permit spending some time on such crises as a lost overshoe or a wounded pigeon on the window sill without driving the teacher into a nervous breakdown because he feels pressed for time. Timetable precision is fine for railroads, but not for elementary classrooms. To summarize, a carefully planned and budgeted daily time schedule is necessary to the efficiency of every classroom, provided it contains a suitable amount of flexibility and elasticity.

THE DAILY PROGRAM SHOULD PROVIDE FOR A DESIRABLE BALANCE OF LEARNING ACTIVITIES. The shortsighted but, in some cases, extremely vocal emphasis on tightening up the elementary school program, has led some teachers to tip the scale each day in favor of certain curricular areas. This is unfortunate. Teachers who have been panicked into neglecting certain important areas of the child's development should be reminded of the broad basic goal of elementary education stated previously in this chapter. Only through providing rich and varied experiences in *all* curricular areas can this goal be achieved.

A balanced program means not only a balance of curricular areas but of types of learning experiences as well. Unfortunately, research indicates that many elementary youngsters engage in the single activity of listening during more than half their school day.[33] The remainder of the time is frequently spent in reading and study activities. In order to provide children with a variety of learning experiences, it is necessary to establish a desirable balance between such types of learning activities as the following.

Group activities *versus* individual activities.

Verbal *versus* nonverbal activities.

Pen-and-pencil tasks *versus* large muscular activity.

[33] Miriam E. Wilt, "A Study of Teacher Awareness of Listening as a Factor in Elementary Education," *Journal of Educational Research*, Vol. 43 (April, 1950), pp. 626-636.

Activities aimed at developmental concepts *versus* activities aimed at skill reinforcement.

Study and research activities *versus* creative and/or expressional activities.

Expressionistic communicative activities (speaking and writing) *versus* impressionistic communicative activities (listening and reading).

Indoor learning experiences *versus* outdoor learning experiences.

Direct learning experiences *versus* vicarious learning experiences.

ACCORDING TO RESEARCH, THERE IS NO SINGLE PATTERN THAT DETERMINES THE ORDER OF THE DAY'S ACTIVITIES. For years elementary school teachers have planned their daily programs upon the false assumption that children are mentally more alert early in the morning and that, therefore, the "hard" subjects should be scheduled first in the day. Many teachers still continue to base their daily programs on this idea even though it has been thoroughly disproved by research. Thirty years ago, Gates wrote, "One thing is quite certain: the ordinary work of the school day is not so severe as to reduce efficiency perceptibly. In fact, achievement is higher at nearly every other hour than it is at the beginning of the day although the differences are small.[34]

Recent research at the University of Chicago also indicates that there is no standard curve of efficiency but rather that it varies widely among individuals and may be related to the rise and fall of the body temperature. According to these studies,

Our temperature regularly goes up and down each day on a fairly smooth, wave-like curve, with a peak or plateau in the middle of the waking period and a minimum at night during sleep . . . Our body temperature is about the same just before we go to bed at night as when we rise in the morning, which explains why there is no difference in efficiency of performance.[35]

In other words, according to this research, the daily curve of mental and physical efficiency parallels the fluctuation of the body temperature which is highest at approximately the midpoint of our waking period and lowest at the middle of our sleeping period.

Now, what does this mean to the classroom teacher? It means simply that the teacher has much more freedom to schedule activities at various times of the day than he frequently realizes. The "hard" subjects do not have to, and should not necessarily, be scheduled always during the morning. On the contrary, they can be scheduled at any time. This is assuming, of course, that the ordinary schedule of events is not so taxing that children become abnormally fatigued as the day wears on. With this

[34] Arthur I. Gates, *Psychology for Students of Education*, rev. ed. (New York, The Macmillan Company, 1933), p. 472.
[35] Nathaniel Kleitman, "Sleep," *Scientific American*, Vol. 187 (November, 1952), p. 37.

greater latitude in scheduling, the classroom teacher may (1) take into consideration various environmental factors (band rehearsals across the hall, classes playing beneath the windows, traffic noises, etc.) that influence learning efficiency and schedule his classroom activities accordingly and (2) experiment with the daily schedule from time to time to determine the best possible sequence of activities.

THE MODERN DAILY PROGRAM IS PLANNED ACCORDING TO LARGE BLOCKS OF TIME. Today's emphasis upon an integrated and unified educational program makes it neither possible nor desirable to dole out the entire day according to fifteen minutes for spelling or ten minutes for handwriting. The more functional schedules today, in all grades, are planned in terms of large, uninterrupted blocks of time. Sometimes, these blocks are reserved for activities within a certain curricular area and consequently one finds teachers scheduling communication arts for one hour, followed perhaps by social studies for the remainder of the session. Other teachers, working in a more integrated program, schedule the time according to *type* of activity rather than the curricular area. Thus, there will be allotted time for a skills period, work period, or simply independent activities. Again, it should be stressed that the daily schedule should meet the needs of the particular situation while at the same time reflecting a positive philosophy of education and a knowledge of children and how they learn.

PUPILS SHOULD BE ENCOURAGED TO PARTICIPATE IN PROGRAM MAKING. There are many opportunities for the teacher to involve children in planning for their use of the school day. These do not resemble in the slightest the puppeteering example mentioned earlier in the chapter. Children may culminate the day's activities by planning what they are going to do the following day. They may cooperate in some long-range planning to determine how much time will be needed to rehearse for their assembly program or finish making drapes for the windows. Many times teachers in the upper grades will briefly overview the required work of the semester with pupils and secure from them suggestions as to how the time may be used to the best advantage. Most authorities agree that pupil planning of the wise use of time is without question a desirable educational opportunity and there are many ways to provide children with this opportunity other than having them dutifully recite the firmly established roster of the day's events.

SUMMARY

Basic to the success of the entire educational program is the teacher's ability to plan and organize an effective sequence of learning experiences. The first section of this chapter discussed the fundamental principles or guideposts of effective planning. It was stated that the teacher's planning begins with an understanding and acceptance of the fundamental goals of modern elementary education. From this point, the teacher's plans will be successful to the extent that: (1) they are guided by the needs and abilities of a particular class of children, (2) they recognize certain existing boundaries imposed upon all teachers, although to widely varying degrees, (3) they reflect a knowledge of the learning process, and (4) they employ a high degree of pupil involvement. Techniques for securing pupil involvement were discussed together with some distortions under which cooperative planning may masquerade in some situations.

The second section was devoted to the steadily increasing trend toward planning and organizing the elementary school program according to units of work. The term *unit* was defined and examined according to the fundamental features that distinguish it from other types and methods of organizing content and classroom activities. The similarity between the plan and organization of a classroom unit and the sequence of a natural educative experience was examined. Included in this section was a sample written plan of a unit, although it was stressed that the unit plan would vary considerably according to the individual situation.

Equally as important as the long-range and unit plans of the teacher are the plans he makes for specific lessons. These plans vary widely according to the type of lesson, skill of the teacher, and demands of the specific situation. All plans, however, contain four basic essentials: (1) What is expected to be accomplished, (2) How it will be accomplished, (3) How the results will be evaluated, and (4) What is the next step.

The last major area of planning for which the classroom teacher is responsible is daily programming. The most desirable daily programs are characterized by (1) flexibility and elasticity, (2) balance among curricular areas as well as types of learning activities, (3) freedom and latitude which permit experimentation concerning the scheduling of activities at certain hours of the day, and (4) numerous opportunities for pupils to engage in planning the use of their school time.

ADDITIONAL LEARNING EXPERIENCES

Topics for Thought and Discussion

1. What factors do you think have influenced the modern trend toward the planned program and away from the planless program?
2. Are you in favor of the present trend toward increasing the length of the elementary school day and year?
3. Would you work just as hard in all your college courses if you received no grades? In which courses would you work just as hard as you do now? In which courses would you work less? Why?

4. If extrinsic motivation has questionable educational value, why do so many teachers use it?

5. At what time of the day do you think you are at your peak of mental efficiency? At your lowest?

6. In spite of the fact that educational theory has recognized the superiority of the unit method for years, many teachers still do not use it. Why not?

7. In one school system recently, a teacher flatly refused to comply with school policy requiring every teacher to submit his written plans to the principal one week in advance. He gave as his reason the fact that such required detailed advanced planning prohibited teacher-pupil planning and forced him to adhere to a rigid program. The principal countered with the argument that detailed advance planning was necessary to insure continuity of instruction in case of a teacher's unexpected absence. Which person was justified? What would you decide if you were a member of the school board to whom the case was referred?

Projects and Activities

1. Investigate the legislative prescriptions in your state concerning the elementary school curriculum. Has this type of legislation increased or decreased in recent years?

2. Observe for a full day in an elementary classroom. Make a list of the spontaneous questions, comments, or experiences of the children that could be capitalized upon by the teacher to motivate an educationally valid unit of work. Which of these units are suggested for this grade in the school's curriculum guide? What are the implications of your findings?

4. Observe for a full day in an elementary classroom. What thought has the teacher given to the balance of learning activities throughout the day? If you are teaching, answer this question for a typical day in your own classroom.

5. Write an outline of a unit for a grade of your choice according to the suggested outline in this chapter.

6. List the specific experiences you would provide for sixth-grade pupils in a study of ancient Rome to develop their understanding of the relationship of an ancient culture to their own society.

7. Prepare a series of cartoons that could be used in a faculty meeting or professional conference to illustrate the *do's* and *don'ts* of successful cooperative planning.

8. The following are samples of teachers' stated objectives as they have appeared on daily lesson plans. Examine them carefully. Which are valid objectives? Which are not? Why not?

    (1) To give practice in oral reading.
    (2) To teach children to read with comprehension.
    (3) To teach the proper use of the comma in a series.

(4) To develop an understanding of the vowel rule that determines the pronunciation of a one syllable word which ends in a silent *e*.

(5) To talk about how people prepare for winter.

(6) To reinforce the skill of carrying in two-column addition.

(7) To review the correct form for writing a business letter.

(8) To have children express themselves creatively.

(9) To develop an understanding and appreciation of the hardships faced by the early New England settlers.

(10) To read the story orally for enjoyment.

(11) To have children decorate place mats and paper plates for the Valentine party on Friday.

Selected Bibliography

Association for Supervision and Curriculum Development, *Learning and the Teacher*. 1959 Yearbook. Washington, D. C., National Education Association, 1959.

Bigge, Morris L., and Hunt, Maurice P., *Psychological Foundations of Education*. New York, Harper & Row, Publishers, Inc., 1962.

Bruner, Jerome S., *The Process of Education*. Cambridge, Mass., Harvard University Press, 1962.

Burton, William H., The Guidance of Learning Activities, 3rd ed. New York, Appleton-Century-Crofts, 1962.

———, Kimball, Roland B., and Wing, Richard L., *Education for Effective Thinking*. New York, Appleton-Century-Crofts, 1960.

Cantor, Nathaniel, *The Teaching-Learning Process*. New York, Holt, Rinehart and Winston, Inc., 1953.

Crow, Lester D., and Alice, *Readings in Human Learning*. New York, David McKay Co., Inc., 1963.

Frandsen, Arden N., *How Children Learn*. New York, McGraw-Hill Book Co., 1957.

Hanna, Lavone A., Potter, Gladys L., and Hagaman, Neva, *Unit Teaching in the Elementary School*, rev. ed. New York, Holt, Rinehart and Winston, 1963.

Hilgard, Ernest R., *Theories of Learning*, 2nd ed. New York, Appleton-Century-Crofts, 1956.

"Invitation to Learning." *Childhood Education*, Vol. 39 (October, 1962).

Klee, Loretta E., *How to Do Cooperative Planning*. Washington, D. C., National Council for the Social Studies, 1951.

Learning and Instruction, Nelson B. Henry, ed. Forty-ninth Yearbook, National Society for the Study of Education, Part I. Chicago, University of Chicago Press, 1950.

Miel, Alice, and others, *Cooperative Procedures in Learning*. New York, Bureau of Publications, Teachers College, Columbia University, 1952.

Parrish, Louise, and Waskin, Yvonne, *Teacher-Pupil Planning*. New York, Harper & Row, Publishers, Inc., 1958.

RUSSELL, David H., *Children's Thinking*. New York, Ginn and Company, 1956.

SEAGOE, May V., *A Teacher's Guide to the Learning Process*, 2nd ed. Dubuque, Iowa, William C. Brown Company, Publishers, 1961.

STRICKLAND, Ruth G., *How to Build a Unit of Work*. Washington, D. C., U. S. Office of Education, 1946.

TROW, William Clark, *The Learning Process*. What Research Says to the Teacher, No. 6. Department of Classroom Teachers, American Educational Research Association of the National Education Association. Washington, D. C., 1954.

WILES, Kimball, *Teaching for Better Schools*. Englewood Cliffs, N. J., Prentice-Hall, Inc., 1952.

WINGO, G. Max, "Methods of Teaching," in Chester W. Harris, ed., *Encyclopedia of Educational Research*, 3rd ed. New York, The Macmillan Company, 1960.

CHAPTER 8

Improving the Curriculum

"WELL, I'M REALLY TRYING something different this year!"

"What are you doing?"

"You know in our sixth grade we usually do a unit on transportation. For several years I started this unit with a study of early means of transportation—children always seemed interested in that approach. This year I thought we'd start there again or maybe at the other extreme for I thought perhaps these sixth graders might be fascinated with space travel. But when we started to talk about transportation, I couldn't get them off the subject of automobiles!"

"Why are they so interested in cars?"

"I don't know and I never knew they were until now. Three or four have parents who are antique car hobbyists and they were telling the others about the early models. Danny said his brother belonged to a hot rod club and then they started discussing drag races and what not—I didn't even know what they were talking about! They know the new compacts and foreign cars—which ones take the least gas, which are cooled by air instead of water, and much more. So—I'm wondering if it might be a good idea this year to devote a large part of our transportation unit to the automobile.

"What would that include?"

"Well, as I begin to think about it, there are a few big areas I'd like to stress. As we get into it, I'd like to emphasize the social changes the automobile has brought with it, and try to give children some understanding of the great influence technology has on all phases of modern living. Then I thought it would be a good opportunity to develop some truly functional concepts concerning highway safety including cars, bicycles, and pedestrians. My children need this, I know—and they'll certainly need it in a few years when many of them will be driving cars. But where will

I get material on this? After all, how much is there in our sixth grade books on the place of the automobile in modern society?"

"Why not have children write to the National Safety Council and also to the National Safety Commission of the NEA? I'd try the U. S. Bureau of Public Roads, too, if I were you. And probably you could get some help from the car manufacturers themselves. And I'm sure there are lots of things in magazines which would help. Put your class to work looking through their old magazines at home!"

"Thanks, that's a good idea. I don't know how this will turn out, but wish me luck!"

Whenever teachers share ideas, experiment with new procedures, develop new understandings of their pupils, discover new ways to attain educational goals, the result may be curriculum improvement. Whenever teachers improve units or find better ways to use new materials, the result may be curriculum improvement. Pritzkau states that curriculum improvement happens

. . . whenever a teacher is concerned about how a child learns. Curriculum improvement takes place whenever a teacher discusses with other teachers or with the principal the appropriate uses of certain types of materials. The curriculum is improved when there is a consideration of better ways of communicating to parents about the progress of children in school. Curriculum change occurs when teachers request more shelving for the placing of books and other materials to use with learning experiences. The improvement of lighting conditions in a classroom is an important step to curriculum development. Any set of conditions which is provided by teachers, children, principal, and citizens to improve learning experiences for children can be classified as curriculum development.[1]

In a certain sense, therefore, we have discussed curriculum improvement throughout this entire volume. We have discussed it very directly in the preceding chapter as we examined the ways in which the teacher plans and organizes his classroom program. Although everything that the teacher does to improve his classroom program is, in a sense, curriculum improvement, this chapter is concerned with the teacher's understanding of and participation in the structured process of curriculum development and improvement. For it is not enough for the teacher to improve his own skills in his own classroom. In addition, he must assume an active and responsible role for developing the overall design of the curriculum, whether it be on a large-scale basis or for his individual school. In order to fulfill this role, the teacher needs, first of all, a basic understanding of the present status of the elementary school curriculum.

[1] Philo T. Pritzkau, *Dynamics of Curriculum Improvement* (Englewood Cliffs, N. J., Prentice-Hall, Inc., 1959), p. 4.

PRESENT STATUS OF THE ELEMENTARY SCHOOL CURRICULUM

This section is concerned with the current definition, scope, and most common organizational patterns of the modern elementary school curriculum.

THERE IS NO UNANIMOUS AGREEMENT ON THE DEFINITION OF THE TERM *curriculum*. Although it probably appears in educational literature and discussion more frequently than any other word, there is no single, unanimously accepted definition of the term *curriculum*. Concepts of the curriculum range all the way from the very broad idea that it includes everything the children learn to the narrow idea that it is a body of subject matter organized and presented by the teacher to the pupils. For the purposes of our discussion here, we will accept the definition that comes closest to meeting with general agreement, namely, that the curriculum is ". . . all the learning experiences which children and youth have under the direction of the school."[2]

A second viewpoint defines the curriculum as a planned, written document that represents ". . . the design of a social group for the educational experiences of their children in school."[3] This definition is not as common as the first since to many people it refers to the written statement of the curriculum which is usually called the curriculum guide, curriculum outline, or course of study.

A third definition which appears in current literature states that the curriculum is ". . . the sum of the experiences—the learnings, skills, habits, and attitudes—that the child has made a part of himself, and that govern his behavior, as a result of the environment provided by the school.[4] It would seem that this psychological definition of the curriculum as the changed behavior of the learner is really synonymous with learning or education. In any case, the first definition appears to be most accurate, least confusing, and most widely accepted. It is the one that will guide our use of the term throughout the entire chapter.

THE SCOPE OF THE ELEMENTARY SCHOOL CURRICULUM HAS EXPANDED CONTINUALLY OVER THE YEARS. The earliest colonial schools concentrated exclusively on two R's—religion and reading, with the second introduced

---

[2] Edward A. Krug, *Curriculum Planning* (New York, Harper & Row, Publishers, Inc., 1950), p. 4.

[3] George A. Beauchamp, *Planning the Elementary School Curriculum* (Boston, Allyn and Bacon, Inc., 1956), p. 41.

[4] Harold G. Shane and E. T. McSwain, *Evaluation and the Elementary Curriculum*, rev. ed. (New York, Holt, Rinehart and Winston, Inc., 1958), p. 170.

Curriculum of 1775[5]	*Curriculum of 1900*[5]	*Curriculum of 1960's*
MAJOR IMPORTANCE	MAJOR IMPORTANCE	LANGUAGE ARTS
Reading	Reading	—including
Bible	Literature	Listening
	Arithmetic	Reading
MEDIUM IMPORTANCE	Oral Language	Spelling
Catechism	Text Geography	Handwriting
	Text History	Speech
MINOR IMPORTANCE		Composition
Spelling	MEDIUM IMPORTANCE	Foreign Languages
Writing	Nature Study	
Arithmetic	Spelling	SOCIAL STUDIES
	Writing	—including
	Grammar	History
	Home Geography	Geography
	History Stories	Civics
	Music	Anthropology
		Economics
	MINOR IMPORTANCE	Ethics
	Play	Jurisprudence
	Physical Training	Political science
	Sewing	Social psychology
	Cooking	Sociology
	Manual Training	
	Drawing	ARITHMETIC
	Elementary Science	
		SCIENCE
		Biological Sciences
		Physical Sciences
		Earth Sciences
		HEALTHFUL LIVING
		Health
		Safety
		Physical Education
		CREATIVE ARTS
		Art
		Music
		Dance
		Drama
		Industrial Arts

primarily to facilitate the learning of the first. Later, when it became clear that education had a utilitarian value, writing and arithmetic were included in the curriculum of the lower schools. Independence from Eng-

[5] Elwood P. Cubberley, *Public Education in the United States*, rev. ed. (Boston, Houghton-Mifflin Company, 1934), p. 473.

land brought with it a flush of nationalism and patriotism which resulted in geography being introduced into the schools, along with the first American-authored textbooks. It was not until approximately the middle of the nineteenth century that history became a common study in the schools, and still later came the arts and sciences. Today, the expansion still continues with foreign languages as the most recent addition in many schools.

The ever-widening scope of the content of the elementary school curriculum is illustrated on page 310.

Equally important is the expansion of types of learning experiences included in the elementary school curriculum. At the beginning of the century, most learning experiences were verbal in nature although, as seen on page 310, there was some provision made for drawing, music, play, physical training, manual training, and homemaking training. Changed concepts of learning, increased knowledge of child growth and development, and technological advances in communication have resulted in an expanded range of learning experiences which includes an infinite number and variety of activities and utilizes countless resources such as field trips, motion pictures, television, teaching machines, and others too numerous to mention. As Tyler says, these new developments have removed the restrictions placed upon the curriculum by the physical limitations of the classroom's four walls and now permit the school to offer ". . . a range of learning experiences as wide as those of life outside."[6]

Thus, from its earliest beginnings, the development of the elementary school curriculum has been additive in nature. New content has been introduced; new experiences have been incorporated. The problem of the bulging curriculum was recognized more than sixty years ago, according to the following statement: "One of the difficulties which all teachers must encounter in present day school is the multiplication of subjects in the curriculum. Every programme is overcrowded, and most teachers are bewildered by the demands which are made upon their times."[7]

The problem has become more acute with every passing year. No absolute solution has been found, although a helpful and partial answer has been the change in organizational pattern which has evolved gradually over the years.

THERE ARE A FEW BASIC ORGANIZATIONAL PATTERNS OF TODAY'S ELEMENTARY CURRICULUM. In spite of the fact that such terms as *experience curriculum, subject-matter curriculum, problems-of-living curriculum,*

[6] Ralph W. Tyler, "The Curriculum—Then and Now," *Elementary School Journal,* Vol. 57 (April, 1957), p. 370.
[7] Sarah Louise Arnold, "The Morning Talk," *American Primary Teacher,* Vol. 23 (December, 1899), p. 126.

core curriculum, and *developmental curriculum* appear continually in the literature, there are essentially two basic schools of thought concerning the organization of the curriculum. At one pole is the philosophy that places primary emphasis upon the content to be taught. Thus, considerable attention is directed toward the most efficient and most logical selection and organization of content. At the other extreme is the *learner-centric philosophy* which places primary emphasis upon the needs of the learner. The curriculum consequently is selected and organized to meet these needs.

There are very few, if any, schools that operate today at either of these extremes. Most patterns range along a continuum between the two poles, and may be discussed according to the following major classifications.

Separate-subjects curriculum. Nearest to the subject-matter-oriented pole is the traditional organizational pattern usually referred to as the separate-subjects curriculum. In this pattern, each subject is organized and taught with little or no attempt to relate it to other areas. Thus, the separate-subjects curriculum really consists of compartmentalized and unrelated bodies of subject matter that have been carefully selected and organized by adults for mastery by the pupils. Figure 8.1 illustrates the lack of unity and the tendency to treat every subject as an entity, totally divorced from all others. (The diagram illustrates only this lack of unity; it does not include all the subjects that actually comprise the curriculum.) It should be obvious from this very brief description that this

FIGURE 8.1

Separate-subjects curriculum.

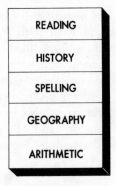

FIGURE 8.2

Correlated curriculum.

curricular pattern has been under fire for several decades. Smith, Stanley, and Shores discuss the following common indictments leveled against it.

1. Its compartmentalized and fragmentary approach is not conducive to the total development of the learner.
2. It ignores the interests and activities of the learner.
3. Its logical arrangement of subject matter ignores the psychological sequence or the "personal organization of functional knowledge."
4. It is frequently divorced from current and persistent social problems. '
5. It fails to develop habits of effective thinking.[8]

Correlated curriculum. Dissatisfaction with the separate-subjects approach led to the development of the correlated curriculum. As shown in Figure 8.2, a step toward unity was taken by hinging the subjects together through relating the content of each to the other. Thus, if pupils studied the Louisiana Purchase in history class, they studied the geography of that section of the country in geography class. Both areas, however, retained their hard-and-fast subject matter boundaries. There are many inherent weaknesses of this pattern. Since it demands no essential reorganization of content nor new approach to learning, it represents only a minor improvement over the traditional separate-subjects curriculum and most of the indictments leveled at the earlier pattern are applicable here also. Then, too, when inept teachers tried to relate all subjects, an artificial learning situation was the inevitable result. In general, it is safe to say that the correlated curriculum is worthy of note chiefly because it paved the way for the more promising patterns that followed.

[8] B. Othanel Smith, William O. Stanley, and J. Harlan Shores, *Fundamentals of Curriculum Development* (New York, Harcourt, Brace and World, Inc., 1950), pp. 392-399.

Broad-fields curriculum. The broad-fields curriculum is often called the fusion pattern and represents an attempt to fuse or weld several related subjects into one large curriculum block. In this pattern, reading, spelling, handwriting, composition, speech, and grammar cease to be separate entities and merge into a broad area labeled either Language Arts or Communication Arts. Similarly, history, geography, civics, and various elements from other social sciences are welded together into a Social Studies area. Music, art, creative dramatics and others frequently become the Creative Arts section of the curriculum. Figure 8.3 illustrates a portion

LANGUAGE ARTS

SOCIAL STUDIES

CREATIVE ARTS

FIGURE 8.3

Broad-fields curriculum.

of the broad-fields curriculum as it is organized into broad fields of learning rather than discrete subjects. The major advantages of this pattern over the others discussed previously are (1) it dissolves certain artificial boundaries of subject mater, (2) it permits greater flexibility of program, (3) it allows for a wide variety of activities and experiences, (4) it permits expansion of content by delving into fields hitherto excluded from the elementary school program, and (5) its flexibility encourages creativity, originality, and inventiveness of both teacher and pupils.

Unified curriculum. Close to the learner-centric pole is the unified curriculum which is frequently called the developmental-activity pattern or the integrated curriculum. In this type of organization, the emphasis is upon the problems and needs of the learner and content is selected and organized accordingly. It should be noted, moreover, that the boundaries between the curricular areas may become blurred and frequently disappear. Attention is directed toward the problem and whatever knowledges and activities are needed for its solution with little concern as to whether they can be classified as social studies, communication, or any other area. When children compose and present a playlet, for instance, about the hardships faced by the Jamestown colonists, does this belong under the category of communication arts? On the other hand, it demands considerable knowledge of history and geography, so maybe it's social studies. But, then again, isn't it in the area of the creative arts? The point is obvious. The unified curriculum is organized in terms of broad learner-oriented problems, and content is selected and organized on that basis.

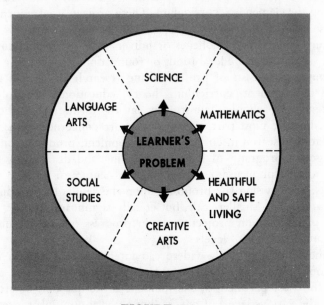

FIGURE 8.4
Unified curriculum.

It should be repeated here that very few schools today adhere strictly to any single type of organizational pattern. Most schools combine and modify the features of all four basic patterns, with the more traditional schools clustered toward the subject-centered pole and the more forward-looking programs moving toward the learner-centric pole.

BASIC PRINCIPLES OF CURRICULUM IMPROVEMENT

Never before in the history of American education has there been more interest and more activity directed toward the improvement of the curriculum than there is at the present time. Numerous attempts to strengthen, revise, reshape, and upgrade the curriculum are presently in progress and include large-scale national projects as well as local school action. Such projects as the University of California Elementary School Science Project and the Science Curriculum Improvement Study, University of Illinois Elementary School Science Project, School Mathematics Study Group (SMSG) Project on elementary school mathematics, Syracuse-Webster Elementary Mathematics Project, Greater Cleveland Mathematics Program, and the Joint Project of the National Council for the Social Studies and the American Council of Learned Societies are only a few of the large-scale projects recently or currently directed toward improving the elementary curriculum. These projects are frequently sponsored by national organizations, state professional associations, regional curriculum councils, and colleges or universities. Often, but not always, they are supported by federal funds or foundation grants. Their membership commonly consists of professors and research scholars in the fields of child development, curriculum theory, educational psychology, and the content field; school administrators; lay representatives; and classroom teachers. For the most part, these projects are concerned with analyzing and initiating research in curriculum development, proposing one or several suggested programs of study; developing and distributing materials for teacher and pupil use; establishing pilot centers to try out suggested proposals; and revising the proposals upon the results of experimentation and research. On a smaller scale, but equally significant, are the countless number of curriculum projects now in progress on the regional, state, system, and local school levels.

It is inevitable that such widespread interest in curriculum improvement would be accompanied by numerous controversies and problems. One of the most pertinent at the moment is the question of articulation between the various levels of curriculum activity now in progress. There are those, of course, who argue for the creation of a National Curriculum Commission which would be responsible for providing ". . . leadership in formulating educational objectives and in recommending ways of improving the curriculum and of keeping it abreast of the swift material progress of the nation and the world."[9] At the other extreme are many who argue that the individual school must always be the primary focus of curriculum development. A major problem at the moment, therefore, is how to reconcile the advantages of both these viewpoints. Certainly widespread attempts to improve the curriculum (not necessarily a single curriculum commission) may utilize resources and make contributions not possible on a single-school level. On the other hand, it is necessary that the curriculum, if it is truly functional, be developed in accordance with the needs of a particular situation. In any case, the problem of how to articulate and utilize the many levels of curricular activity now in

[9] Paul R. Hanna, "A National Curriculum Commission?" *NEA Journal*, Vol. 49 (January, 1960), p. 25.

progress is one that is increasingly demanding the attention of all those interested in curriculum improvement.

The present spurt of curricular activity has been characterized, not only by some controversies, but more frequently by widespread agreement on certain basic principles, among which the following are most important.

CURRICULUM IMPROVEMENT IS A CONTINUOUS, ON-GOING PROCESS. Two things are certain. First, we are living in an era of unbelievably rapid and bewildering change which, according to present predictions, will accelerate at a faster pace with each passing year. As Mead says, "No one will live all his life in the world into which he was born, and no one will die in the world in which he worked in his maturity."[10]

Secondly, the curriculum of the American school has traditionally lagged far behind cultural changes. Almost forty years ago Rugg wrote, "Not once in a century and a half of national history has the curriculum of the school caught up with the dynamic content of American life."[11] Twenty years later Miel revealed the same concern: "In spite of all the attention and energy that has been directed toward solution of curriculum problems during the last two decades, it is rather generally agreed that there has been relatively little fundamental change in the curriculum of American schools in the years when rapid advances in technology have been making drastic changes in the whole culture surrounding the schools."[12]

In order to close this gap between society and the school, it is necessary to view curriculum improvement as a fluid, dynamic, and never-ending process. This means that there is no longer a detailed and voluminous course of study (called the "bible" by the more irreverent) rigidly dictating the program from its exalted perch in the principal's office, until the next revision fifteen years later. Today, curriculum improvement and revision must occur continually, not at fifteen or twenty year intervals.

There are many techniques to facilitate the mechanical operation of this philosophy. Several school systems have standing curriculum councils which assume the task each year of evaluating the present curriculum and attacking the most apparent weaknesses or limitations. In other schools, the staff each September identifies a major curricular area for concentrated scrutiny and evaluation. Some schools insure against curriculum ossification by issuing a series of curriculum bulletins in prefer-

[10] Margaret Mead, "A Redefinition of Education," *NEA Journal,* Vol. 48 (October, 1959), p. 16.

[11] Harold Rugg, "The School Curriculum and the Drama of American Life," *Curriculum Making: Past and Present.* Twenty-sixth Yearbook, National Society for the Study of Education, Part I, Guy Montrose Whipple, ed. (Bloomington, Illinois, Public School Publishing Company, 1926), p. 3.

[12] Alice Miel, *Changing the Curriculum* (New York, Appleton-Century-Crofts, 1946), p. 11.

ence to a single bound volume. Others prepare the curriculum guide in looseleaf notebook form, which makes revision, addition, or deletion relatively painless.

It should not be interpreted from these remarks that curriculum revision is a willy-nilly process that keeps the classroom teacher in a state of perpetual confusion and insecurity. Change does not have to be haphazard and disorganized. It can, and should, be done with forethought, deliberation, and direction. Curriculum improvement is a methodical, continual, and on-going process. It is not mounting a tired horse to ride off in all directions.

MANY ASPECTS OF MODERN LIVING DEMAND THE RECONSIDERATION AND IMPROVEMENT OF THE PRESENT ELEMENTARY CURRICULUM. Modern forces that call for widesweeping changes in the present program can be grouped into three classifications. First, there are the innumerable social forces, among which are (1) the expansion and mobility of the population in recent years, (2) racial and intercultural needs, (3) rapid expansion of knowledge in all fields and particularly in the sciences, (4) changes in family life including teen-age marriages and employed mothers, (5) increasing concern with such symptoms of mental and social ill health as delinquency, crime, alcoholism, and marital unhappiness, (6) increasing availability of leisure time, (7) changing moral and spiritual values, and (8) international tensions and developments.

Secondly, such technological developments as auto-instruction, more and better instructional aids, and newly developed media of communication make the traditional curriculum as outdated as the Model T Ford. Thirdly, changing educational ideology and increasing research with emphases on (1) the nature of learning, (2) the growth of the learner, (3) provision for individual differences, (4) importance of group dynamics, and (5) improved administrative organizations contribute in large measure to the need for a dynamic and adequate curriculum.

THE CLASSROOM TEACHER IS A KEY FIGURE IN A PROGRAM OF CURRICULUM IMPROVEMENT. The scope of involvement in curriculum planning has continually enlarged in recent years. At one time, most of the responsibility was assumed by subject matter specialists, administrators, and curriculum directors. This resulted in some very beautiful courses of study but, strangely enough, very little change in classroom practice. Gradually the idea grew that curriculum improvement was really teacher improvement and that any worthwhile curriculum planning must involve the active and interested participation of the teacher. Today, the importance of the teacher is universally recognized in such statements as the following.

The teacher is the most important of the "curriculum makers." In the final analysis, he is the one who determines what the experiences of pupils will be . . . Whether or not the classroom will be a continuous source of adventure and exploration in learning or a monotonous repetition is a choice that rests mainly with the teacher.[13]

. . . the classroom teacher, since he works directly with the learner, is a key person in curriculum planning and action . . .[14]

Teachers are the key persons in curriculum planning . . . of necessity teachers have and always will have very important responsibilities for actually determining the nature of the educational experiences that are developed in the school.[15]

. . . we can't get along without teachers in planning the curriculum—not if we want to plan it in terms of children's growth and development, and have it tailor-made for the needs of individuals.[16]

Of particular importance is the fact that teacher participation in curriculum planning is on the increase . . .[17]

In order for teacher participation in curriculum improvement to become more than well-intentioned theory several things are necessary. In the first place, the participation must be voluntary rather than through an edict handed down from administration. This implies that the teacher must view curriculum planning *as a part of teaching*. As emphasized in Chapter 5, today's teacher does not consider that his sole responsibility is classroom instruction and that everything else is something extra. Assuming a leadership role in determining curriculum through serving on committees, engaging in action research, and experimenting with new procedures is a definite responsibility of the teacher. It must be so considered if curriculum improvement is to become anything more than a futile and idle gesture. As Pritzkau says,

In some school systems, the staff has already equated the task of curriculum development to teaching. Teachers have recognized and accepted the responsibility of curriculum improvement as an essential and integral part of professional services. It is hoped that the leadership in teacher education institutions and school systems develop the conditions which will encourage all teachers to facilitate this unity of tasks in the teaching profession.[18]

[13] Vernon E. Anderson, *Principles and Procedures of Curriculum Improvement*, pp. 13-14. Copyright © 1956, The Ronald Press Company.

[14] Association for Supervision and Curriculum Development, "Platform of Beliefs," *Educational Leadership*, Vol. 14 (January, 1957), p. 233.

[15] J. Galen Saylor and William M. Alexander, *Curriculum Planning for Better Teaching and Learning* (New York, Holt, Rinehart and Winston, Inc., 1954), p. 63.

[16] Robert S. Gilchrist, "Promising Practices in Education, II," *Phi Delta Kappan*, Vol. 41 (March, 1960), p. 272.

[17] George A. Beauchamp, "Some Issues and Trends in Curriculum Planning," *Elementary School Journal*, Vol. 56 (April, 1956), p. 343.

[18] Philo T. Pritzkau, *op. cit.*, p. 4.

Voluntary participation also demands that the teacher consider himself *capable* of engaging in responsible and large-scale curriculum improvement. It is hoped that the day is not far off when teachers will cease to view themselves as "just classroom teachers" or low men on the totem pole. Today's competent teacher is a well-prepared, professionally-minded person fully capable of making significant contributions to education on every front. He must be so considered in his own and others' eyes if he is to fulfill his role as a key figure in curriculum development.

Secondly, curriculum improvement can be facilitated if the special interests of teachers are recognized and encouraged. More than 75 per cent (see Chapter 9) of elementary school teachers today teach in self-contained classrooms and are responsible for most or all areas of the curriculum. This does not mean, however, that they are equally competent and equally interested in all areas, and even the most ardent advocate of the self-contained classroom never claimed that they were. Many have specialized competencies in certain areas. Some recent college graduates have specialized in a content area in addition to their major concentration in elementary education, and there is evidence that this trend may grow in the future. Older teachers have, over the years, discovered that they do a better job in some areas than others and have tried to build steadily on their talents in these fields. Such individuals should be encouraged to develop their specialized abilities. This is not an argument for departmentalization (see the following chapter for a discussion of this point). It is simply a recognition of the fact that some teachers possess special competencies and knowledges that enable them to make high-level contributions to curriculum improvement, over and above their performance in the self-contained classroom. In a sense, these persons may be regarded as teacher-consultants. Their contributions to curriculum improvement may consist of such activities as (1) assuming a leadership role on local, state, or national curriculum committees, (2) acting as staff advisers in the purchase of materials and equipment, (3) acquainting other teachers with the recent literature and research findings in their special fields of interest, (4) teaching occasional demonstration lessons for other staff members, and (5) implementing a dynamic program of action research in their classrooms.

It should be repeated that capitalizing upon a teacher's special strength does not imply departmentalizing the program. It does suggest, however, an efficient method for utilizing the contributions of the classroom teacher to an optimum degree. Such concentrated utilization of talent would appear to be superior to naively expecting Mrs. J to make an outstanding contribution to a social studies committee one year, a science project the next, and an arithmetic study the next. Mrs. J is not superhuman, and she knows it. She can, and does, do a superior job in the self-contained classroom. Over and above that, she can make a significant contribution to structured curriculum development provided her talents are concentrated in her fields of interest rather than directed indiscriminately toward any and every curriculum area. Pritzkau agrees with this viewpoint in the following statement.

Although there is no intention to advocate departmentalism, it is, nevertheless, reasonable to assume that individual teachers are often more effective in working with one subject than another. It is proposed that every classroom become some kind of center or laboratory for ideas. It is extremely important, also, that there be unity in ideas as between one subject area and others. It is perfectly logical and conducive to resourcefulness, however, to encourage individual staff members to expand the laboratory of ideas in terms of the special strengths and capabilities . . . Each teacher, in connection with the responsibility for a self-contained classroom, would have all areas represented even though a particular area is emphasized.[19]

Lastly, the teacher's participation in curriculum planning can be facilitated through careful attention to the mechanical details of scheduling meetings, providing a budget for necessary expenses, and making available a wide variety of consultant and material resources. In many situations, curriculum committee meetings are scheduled during after-school hours when there are only a few hours available and the teacher's energy is at low ebb. Much more desirable is the practice of many progressive systems of employing teachers on a voluntary basis to work on curriculum revision during the summer months. This gives the group a long, uninterrupted period to devote to the problem, provides summer employment for those who desire it, stimulates the in-service growth of teachers, and raises the career level of teaching to where it is considered a full-time profession rather than a 180 day occupation.

Other systems attempt to meet the problem by hiring substitute teachers and freeing the regular teacher for an occasional uninterrupted day for curriculum work. Still others provide expenses for dinner and travel so that committee meetings may continue from the late afternoon through the early evenings. Although these are steps in the right direction, they are not as desirable as the summer curriculum workshops and institutes of the better school systems. It is hoped that an increasing number of administrators, boards of education, and teachers will recognize in the future the advantages of the summer projects in raising the level of education as well as of the profession itself.

LAY PARTICIPATION IN CERTAIN AREAS OF CURRICULUM IMPROVEMENT IS IMPORTANT. The expanding scope of involvement in curriculum development includes not only teachers, but laymen as well. In a sense, of

[19] *Ibid.*, pp. 31-32.

course, laymen have always been involved in curriculum planning since the board of education is the legally constituted lay body that has final responsibility for the entire educational program. However, in recent years, the idea has grown that lay participation should be extended to include community representatives in numerous aspects of curriculum improvement. There is virtually no disagreement on this point. All able schoolmen deplore, from every angle, the idea of professional personnel taking a solo flight into curriculum improvement with the community left standing on the ground. Among the many statements supporting the professional-lay partnership concept is the following.

Lay citizens have the right to determine the role of our public elementary schools just as they have the obligation to support them; furthermore, the political philosophy upon which our democracy is based demands such participation. Lay participation in curriculum matters is inevitable to some degree, and professional personnel must make use of the important aid in organized curriculum planning.[20]

Among the numerous values gained from including the community in this activity, Caswell suggests the following:

1. Laymen may bring to the project a knowledge of the community and of pupils which supplements that of the teaching staff.
2. Lay participation in curriculum planning may result in the development of a better informed public that supports desirable curriculum change.
3. Useful resources are almost always available among laymen in a community and these may be brought to bear on the educational program.[21]

Although there is general agreement on the desirability and value of lay participation in curriculum planning, there is also recognition of some problems that must be met. In general, these problems revolve around two central questions.

1. In what areas or types of curriculum planning can lay participation make the greatest contributions?
2. How can lay participation be best coordinated with professional participation and responsibility?

In the first place, it is generally agreed that lay participation makes the greatest contribution when it is *advisory* in nature. Secondly, it should be recognized that decisions of a professional or technical nature should

[20] George A. Beauchamp, *Planning the Elementary School Curriculum* (Boston, Allyn and Bacon, Inc., 1956), pp. 11-12.
[21] Hollis L. Caswell and Associates, *Curriculum Improvement in Public School Systems* (New York, Bureau of Publications, Teachers College, Columbia University, 1950), pp. 94-95.

be delegated to the professional staff by virtue of its specialized training and knowledge. Saylor and Alexander identify the four major tasks of curriculum development as follows.

. . . (1) a definition of the kinds of outcomes desired from school experience, (2) the selection of the learning experiences and the subject matter content as part of such experiences which will contribute maximally to the attainment of these desired outcomes, (3) the guidance and development of such learning experiences in the school effectively and skillfully so that the desired learning may be achieved, and (4) the evaluation of behavior in terms of the desired outcomes, so that subsequent experiences may be planned more efficiently.[22]

These authors suggest that, of the four listed above, the first and last are those in which lay participation may make its greatest contribution. The third and fourth they would reserve for professional personnel. They defend this division of responsibility in the following statement.

It is our own belief that parents and citizens can make significant contributions to the process of curriculum making in the first and fourth aspects of planning and guiding learning . . . and that curriculum workers should utilize them directly and fully in these phases of the process. Would not parents and citizens be highly competent to advise with members of the school staff on the kinds of behavior that is considered by the social group to be desirable and essential for effective citizenship in our modern democratic society? This is simply another way of saying that parents and citizens should help define the objectives of education or the desired outcomes of the educational program. Furthermore, who could make more effective evaluations of the attainment of these desired goals by pupils than their own parents or citizens generally in the community? They are the ones who see the pupils in action in many more ways than the teacher does.

We believe that little is to be gained by asking parents to help teachers select learning experiences for the attainment of our desired outcomes or to advise the teacher on how to develop these experiences with pupils. That does seem to be a highly professional job, and one for which the educator is trained.[23]

There are innumerable ways schools have used to coordinate the responsibilities of both groups. Some include community representatives on all standing curriculum committees and councils. Others maintain separate Professional Councils and Parents' Councils but provide for close interaction and communication between the two bodies.[24] Many, of course, rely heavily upon the Parent-Teacher Association and its study

---

[22] J. Galen Saylor and William M. Alexander, *op. cit.*, p. 61.
[23] *Ibid.*
[24] Maurice R. Ahrens, "Parents and Staff Cooperate in System-Wide Improvement," *Educational Leadership*, Vol. 11 (March, 1954), pp. 337-342.

groups. In any case, the question of lay participation in curriculum making is no longer a debatable issue. The only question is how each individual situation can best organize and delegate responsibilities to capitalize upon its recognized values.

THE EXPANDING SCOPE OF INVOLVEMENT IN CURRICULUM PLANNING INCLUDES MANY OTHERS. In addition to teachers, administrators, curriculum directors, and community representatives, many others are included in curriculum planning. In most situations, these include consultants from colleges and universities, representatives from business and industrial concerns, representatives from community agencies, representatives from professional organizations, and members of the state department of education.

THERE IS AN INCREASING TREND TOWARD THE LONGITUDINAL APPROACH TO CURRICULUM DEVELOPMENT. One of the most serious handicaps to curriculum improvement in the past has been the lack of articulation between educational levels. Elementary school groups have embarked upon intensive curricular study with a total disregard of the high school. Secondary teachers have attacked their problems without knowing anything about their pupils' previous experiences. Even within these units there was often stratification. Witness, for example, the typical elementary curriculum project in which committees were formed solely on a grade level basis. Each group decided what was needed at its level. As a final step, their recommendations were put together in jig-saw puzzle fashion with the duplicate pieces discarded and additional pieces hastily contrived to plug existing holes.

Modern attempts at curriculum improvement are making serious efforts to develop a smoothly coordinated, comprehensive, sequential program from the kindergarten through the twelfth grade. Such programs are built upon a ". . . set of threads or organizing elements, of both behavior and content, running vertically through the curriculum, around which learning activities can be organized."[25] Many of the nation-wide curriculum projects now in process are interested in developing this type of fluid, dynamic program. There are two obvious advantages to the comprehensive longitudinal approach to curriculum planning. First, it provides for sequence and continuity through the spiral-like expansion of concepts in difficulty and complexity. Secondly, it permits schools to break away from the rigid, grade-by-grade organizational concept that has dominated the scene for over a hundred years. There is little doubt that the concept of the curriculum as a fluid, flexible, and longitudinal

[25] Ole Sand and others, "Components of the Curriculum," *Review of Educational Research*, Vol. 30 (June, 1960), p. 231.

sequence instead of as a succession of separate steps, one built upon the other, is an educational improvement that will receive increasing emphasis in the days to come.

SEQUENTIAL PROCEDURES FOR CURRICULUM IMPROVEMENT

Whether on the local, state, or national level, certain basic sequential procedures are usually employed for structured curriculum improvement. In general, these include the following.

Awareness of need and identification of problem. Action for curriculum improvement is obviously generated by a recognition of the inadequacy of the existing program. On the local level, this may arise from the action research of an individual teacher and gradually move in a centrifugal direction to include other classrooms or other schools. Or it may arise through community pressures to reexamine present offerings. It may arise in the central office with the superintendent or curriculum director who perceives in the system a weakness in a certain area. Today, many professional associations are assuming leadership roles in curriculum planning. The National Council of Teachers of English, the National Council for the Social Studies, and the National Council for Teachers of Mathematics are only a few of the groups actively engaged in curriculum improvement for the elementary school at the present time. In any case, structured curriculum improvement begins with a felt need and a determination to do something about it.

Organization for study. The organizational plan varies so widely, depending upon the purpose and size of the project, that it is almost impossible to generalize about it. Committee work is, of course, the most popular instrument for curriculum revision. In a single school project, the most common approach is to consider the entire staff as a curriculum committee. In a system project, a coordinating council, central committee, or steering committee usually assumes the major responsibility and is assisted by numerous substudy groups. As mentioned previously, these various committees are composed of administrators, specialists and consultants, teachers, and lay representatives.

Examination of literature and appraisal of current practice. This is one of the most important and, unfortunately, one of the most neglected steps in the entire process. Many groups, particularly on a local level, embark upon the serious responsibility of completely overhauling their present curriculums without a careful study of available literature and research. In recent years, there has been an almost unbelievable amount of study conducted on every facet of the curriculum. To overlook this vast wealth is to allow curriculum planning to deteriorate into a mere pooling of ignorance. Good intentions and honest effort are not adequate substitutes for sound knowledge. Time and energy devoted initially to the study of existing research will pay rich dividends as the project progresses. It is an important step and cannot be stressed too strongly.

In addition to studying research, many committees undertake to appraise current practice and opinions. Questionnaires sent to systems with similar populations and problems are helpful in this respect. Surveys of teachers' needs and opinions may also help to guide the direction of the study. Opinions of authorities concerning certain practices are also frequently helpful to committees at this stage.

As valuable as this step is, as with all other good things, it can be over-done in the hands of incompetent groups. Care must be taken to avoid getting bogged down in this phase of the process. In other words, the examination of current literature and practice in other systems is a valuable step in curriculum improvement provided it doesn't result in squandering valuable time in discussing minutiae or groping through a philosophical fog.

Preparation of curriculum guide. Most attempts at structured curriculum improvement eventuate in some kind of a written curriculum guide or proposed program. Such documents usually contain the following.

1. *Statement of objectives.* The importance of formulating clear, specific, attainable, and educationally valid goals was emphasized strongly in the previous chapter and there is little need for repetition here. Of course, objectives that appear in a curriculum guide will be more comprehensive than those formulated by a classroom teacher for a specific lesson or unit, but they will still be clearly stated. They will be objectives, not procedures or activities. They will be definite. And, most important, they will be stated in such a way that the teacher is able to evaluate his progress toward their achievement.

2. *Selection and organization of content.* As Miel says, "With the whole wide world to choose from, where to dip in with a group of learners is a continuing problem for educators.[26]

There are three primary sources of content from which curriculum experiences are derived. First, the school derives its curriculum content from the needs of society. Obviously, the school must prepare the child for responsible democratic and social living. To do this, it must know what the needs of society are and develop a curriculum according to those needs. There are innumerable examples of content derived from social needs in present-day curriculums. The attempt to base a social studies

[26] Alice Miel, "A View of Curriculum Content," *Educational Leadership*, Vol. 13 (March, 1956), p. 339.

curriculum upon problems of living is one. The accent upon languages as a tool of communication is another. An emphasis upon the social significance of arithmetic is another. The plan of basing the spelling program upon words taken from children's writing experiences is another. One could go on and on. The selection of content according to the needs of society is an absolute necessity if the curriculum is to have functional value for pupils.

Secondly, the selection of content is derived from the needs of the learners. The school looks to the longitudinal and latitudinal studies of child psychology for help in determining appropriate content for children. The developmental tasks theory[27] has served as a guide to the types of learning experiences that should be provided at various levels in the school program. Studies of the emotional, physical, social, and mental maturation of childen have contributed a great deal. Investigations of children's interests in reading, science, and other fields have helped to determine content. Studies of children's fears, anxieties, and attitudes have thrown some light on the subject. Attempts to ascertain children's abilities to comprehend abstract concepts have great significance for curriculum workers. The work of Gesell, Havighurst, Piaget, and scores of others has helped the school to determine the learners' needs and to develop a curriculum accordingly.

The needs of society and the needs of the learner have traditionally been the major sources of content for the twentieth-century elementary school curriculum. Today, a third source is receiving increasing attention. Many advocate that the patterns, nature, and structure of an academic discipline itself be considered as a major source of curriculum content. This is, of course, a major emphasis in the new mathematics programs. It also underlies the current interest in the science of linguistics and its implications upon the elementary school curriculum. It has resulted in many of the changes now being felt in the science program. In short, there appears to be a growing interest in helping children to explore and discover the patterns and structure of knowledge, whether that knowledge be in the area of mathematics, language, science, or any other subject. Bruner explains the need to study the structure of the subject in the following statement.

. . . the curriculum of a subject should be determined by the most fundamental understanding that can be achieved of the underlying principles that give structure to that subject. Teaching specific topics or skills without making clear their context in the broader fundamental structure of a field of knowledge is uneconomical in several deep senses. In the first place, such teaching

---

[27] Robert Havighurst, *Human Development and Education* (New York, Longmans, Green and Company, Inc., 1953).

makes it exceedingly difficult for the student to generalize from what he has learned to what he will encounter later. In the second place, learning that has fallen short of a grasp of general principles has little reward in terms of intellectual excitement. The best way to create interest in a subject is to render it worth knowing, which means to make the knowledge gained usable in one's thinking beyond the situation in which the learning has occurred. Third, knowledge one has acquired without sufficient structure to tie it together is knowledge that is likely to be forgotten. An unconnected set of facts has a pitiably short half-life in memory. Organizing facts in terms of principles and ideas from which they may be inferred is the only known way of reducing the quick rate of loss of human memory.[28]

At this point, it appears that all three sources of content hold promise for an improved curriculum. It seems almost unnecessary to add that the main problem is one of balance and proportion. Many of us have lived through unfortunate experiences in which there was a curriculum imbalance between the first two. We do not want to repeat them. On the other hand, there are already some faint indications that overemphasis upon the third source may lead to the neglect of important psychological considerations and social needs of the learner. There is little doubt that proper balance of content is one of the greatest problems facing the curriculum worker of the present and future. A further discussion of this point is contained in the last section of this chapter.

The previous chapter discussed the problem of determining sequence of content according to a (1) logical, (2) psychological, or (3) sociological pattern. As with the individual teacher in the classroom, the curriculum worker will be guided in his determination of content sequence according to the nature of the subject as well as the needs and maturity of the learners.

3. *Statement of suggested experiences, activities, and resources.* Most curriculum guides accompany the statement of suggested content with a list of appropriate experiences, activities, and resources the teacher may use or adapt in his classroom.

4. *Preparation of materials.* Many current curriculum projects, particularly those on a large-scale basis, prepare teaching and learning materials to accompany the suggested program. Textbooks, workbooks, teachers' manuals, and various instructional aids are developed to acquaint the teacher with the new program and to facilitate its implementation in classroom practice.

Selection of pilot centers. After the curriculum guide and accompanying materials have been prepared, they are usually tried out in selected pilot schools or experimental centers. Such trial balloons are

[28] Jerome S. Bruner, *The Process of Education* (Cambridge, Mass., Harvard University Press, 1962), pp. 31-32.

extremely helpful in determining the limitations and strengths of the proposed plan before it is finally put into action. Even on the local level, the plan may be in a tentative state for a year or more while it is tried out in various classrooms. After a sufficient trial period has elapsed, the weaknesses revealed through observation or from teachers' and pupils' opinions are brought before the proper committees for diagnosis and further study, and the program is revised along the lines indicated.

Translation into classroom practice. Obviously, this is the most important step in the entire process. Whether it is relatively simple or difficult depends largely on what has gone before. It is not difficult if participation in the earlier stages has been widespread, involving many teachers and parents. It is not difficult if channels of communication between the curriculum study groups and teachers (and parents) have been kept open through frequent discussions, newsletters, and bulletins. It is not difficult if teachers' opinions have been sought and respected. It is not difficult if teachers are helped to understand the new program through a series of workshops, meetings, demonstration lessons, or other in-service projects. It is not difficult if helpful materials and aids are made available through a centralized curriculum center. It *is* difficult, and probably impossible, if any of these are neglected.

Evaluation. As McNally and Passow[29] point out, evaluation of curriculum improvement involves evaluation of both the product and the process. The *product* of all curriculum work should be, of course, a curriculum that improves the quality of pupils' learning experiences. Saylor and Alexander list seven major criteria of such a program.

1. A good curriculum develops social understandings.
2. A good curriculum promotes maximum personal development.
3. A good curriculum promotes continuity of experience.
4. A good curriculum provides for all educational goals.
5. A good curriculum maintains balance among all goals.
6. A good curriculum emerges in learning situations.
7. A good curriculum uses effective learning experiences and needed resources.[30]

Equally important is the *process* used in curriculum improvement. It should contribute to improved teacher behaviors and attitudes, better human relationships, and better school-community relationships. The

[29] Harold J. McNally, A. Harry Passow, and Associates, *Improving the Quality of Public School Programs* (New York, Bureau of Publications, Teachers College, Columbia University, 1960), p. 106.

[30] J. Galen Saylor and William M. Alexander, *op. cit.*, pp. 14-15.

following are some of the criteria suggested by Caswell for evaluating the process of curriculum improvement.

Lay Participation

Is provision made for the assistance of laymen in relation to general curriculum problems and for direct participation as opportunity affords at the classroom level?

Is the advisory role of laymen clearly recognized?

Procedures

Is teacher growth considered the primary avenue of curriculum improvement?

Are means employed to stimulate leadership in curriculum work on a wide basis?

Is a variety of activities provided in order that each member of the instructional staff may participate in the program in a way recognized by him as being of value?

Is provision made for those who have to carry out plans to participate in making them?

Is provision made for work on both individual school and system-wide problems?

Is provision made for the practical testing on a limited basis of ideas for curriculum improvement and for the dissemination of good results?

Committees

Are the assignments for committees clearly stated and the committees discharged when their work is completed?

Do committees function in such a way that their responsibility to the larger instructional staff is clearly recognized?

Is time provided for committees to do their work?

Curriculum Materials

Are written materials used as a means of aiding teachers to do better work with pupils rather than as a direct goal?

Are written materials of a flexible, tentative nature which encourages continued improvement rather than adoption of a fixed pattern?[31]

In order for the teacher to fulfill his role in developing and improving the curriculum, it is necessary for him to have knowledge of the current edge of curriculum thought and experimentation now in progress. The following section examines the major curriculum emphases currently receiving considerable attention and study.

[31] Hollis L. Caswell and Associates, *op. cit.*, pp. 100-101.

PROMISING CURRICULUM TRENDS

Elementary education is in a transitory state. There is exciting experimentation being carried on in every curriculum area. Dynamic new developments and challenges with far-reaching implications are emerging daily from research. This section is concerned with three basic current trends that appear to hold promise for improved educational experiences for children in most or all of the curriculum areas.

At the outset, it should be understood that by "promising trends" are meant those developments that appear to be gaining widespread acceptance among educators because they seem to offer hope of an improved school program. Such trends are the results of careful study, experimentation, research, and deliberation. They are initiated and supported by educators who weigh their values and consequences carefully. They are not change for the sake of change nor crash programs born of panic and misinformed community pressures. They are not shiny new bandwagons on which all the young and eager are anxious to climb aboard. They are not necessarily the most dramatic of innovations. Neither are they promoted by individuals who hold a wet thumb aloft before deciding which way to jump. Promising trends include those changes made by able and courageous educators vitally interested in improving teaching and learning. Caswell suggests the following criteria for evaluating proposed curricular changes.

1. The proposed change is consistent with democratic values.
2. The proposed change is a reasonable area of activity for schools.
3. The proposed change either has the support or will gain the support of public-spirited leaders in the community.
4. The proposed change relates to the lives of pupils in such a way that meaningful and useful experiences will be afforded them.
5. To meet the demand would not require displacing other curriculum areas of greater potential value.[32]

A careful study of the above criteria is suggested for those who think that the Montessori method is a new panacea for all educational ills, or who advocate returning to McGuffey's readers, modeling Johnny's textbook after Ivan's, eliminating "fads and frills," abandoning certification requirements for teachers, or any other proposal of a similar caliber.

THERE ARE SEVERAL RECOGNIZED GENERAL CURRICULUM TRENDS IN ELEMENTARY EDUCATION. Among the general curriculum trends that have

[32] *Ibid.*, pp. 38-40.

gained increasing acceptance in recent years are the following, all of which have been emphasized in one or more chapters of this text:

Large groupings of subject matter, and large blocks of time.

Unit organization of whole program; breakdown of subject boundaries.

More attention to the needs, aptitudes and interests of individuals and adaptation of materials and activities to meet those needs.

More cooperative planning; teacher-pupil planning.

Modifying the curriculum to serve the physical, social, emotional and intellectual needs of children.

Building the curriculum around the needs and resources of the community.

Emphasis on democratic living and democratic relationships in the school.

Greater freedom for teacher to make adaptations in the curriculum.

Increased consideration of readiness.

Greater variety of curriculum materials.

Provision of school camping experiences.[33]

In addition to the above, there are three recent developments that merit the attention of all elementary school teachers.

THERE IS A VERY PRONOUNCED EMPHASIS UPON CREATIVITY. There are many who agree with Carpenter who says, "The weakest single phase of America's educational effort is the matter of developing the creative abilities of children."[34]

At no other time has there been greater concern over this weakness than at the present time. We are just beginning to realize that the typical school's accent upon conformity, docility, and intelligence as measured by standardized tests has led to a neglect of those creative individuals whose talents cannot be measured by our present tests. These are the individuals who are inventive, resourceful, curious, and experimental-minded. These are the individuals who may comprise our greatest intellectual reservoir if we can learn how to identify and develop their talents. Promising research is just beginning in this area but much has already been learned. Some of the basic generalizations about creativity that are very significant for every teacher are the following.

1. Creativity is not restricted to a select few. It is generally agreed that *all* individuals have an element of creativity within them, although obviously not in equal proportions. Mallinson says, "Without doubt, as is

---

[33] Jesse A. Bond and John A. Hockett, *Curriculum Trends and Teacher Education,* 1953 Yearbook (Lock Haven, Pa., Association for Student Teaching, 1953), p. 29.

[34] Regan Carpenter, "Creativity: Its Nature and Nurture," *Education,* Vol. 82 (March, 1962), p. 391.

true with all attributes, every person possesses creativity to some degree."[35] Scofield agrees, "Recent experiments and researches have demonstrated that all students, even mental retardates, can be creative."[36]

2. Creativity is not restricted to certain curriculum areas. The old idea that creativity could be developed only in the arts and music has been completely abandoned. Today, we are interested in the creative aspects of language, mathematics, science, and, in fact, all curriculum areas.

3. Creativity demands much self-discipline and hard work. Here again, many teachers are misled by the popular stereotype of the creative person as a Bohemian nonconformist who derives his creative powers solely from flashes of inspiration. Anyone familiar with the creative mind will recognize the fallacy of this concept. As Keiler points out, "We know that self-discipline and concentrated effort as well as imagination and experience are particulars which are constituents of creativity."[37]

4. Creativity can be developed in children of all ages. The author has discovered that many teachers unconsciously feel that developing creativity is a job for the primary grade teacher. Upper grade teachers appear to feel that the pupil either "has it or doesn't have it" by the time he reaches them. This is, of course, absurd. There are many creative teachers on the secondary and college levels who have discovered and stimulated creative abilities the individual himself never knew he possessed.

In summary, we can say that the present experimentation in the realm of creativity is one of the more promising trends on the educational horizon. It may result in more widespread changes in our educational program than many of us can possibly conceive of at the present time.

THE IMPORTANCE OF DISCOVERY, EXPLORATION, AND UNDERSTANDING IS STRESSED IN ALL CURRICULUM FIELDS. Closely related to the emphasis on creative thinking is the emphasis upon discovery, exploration, and understanding. This is not, of course, a new trend. Rather, it is a continuation and extension of the reaction against rote learning which began with the progressive education movement of forty years ago. Never, however, has it been stressed in all curricular fields to the extent that it is today. It means that no longer is arithmetic considered as a set of skills to be mastered through drill exercises and rote memorization. No longer, for instance, is the pupil taught to divide fractions by inverting the divisor and multiplying, without the slightest understanding of what he is doing. Arithmetic is taught as a science of numbers and pupils are led to dis-

[35] George G. Mallinson, "Creativity in Science and Mathematics," *Educational Leadership*, Vol. 18 (October, 1960), p. 25.

[36] Robert W. Scofield, "A Creative Climate," *Educational Leadership*, Vol. 18 (October, 1960), p. 5.

[37] Manfred L. Keiler, "Creativity: Core of Art Education," *Educational Leadership*, Vol. 18 (October, 1960), p. 32.

THERE IS A PRONOUNCED EMPHASIS UPON CREATIVITY IN THE MODERN EDUCATIONAL PROGRAM.

Art.

Creative writing: dictation.

Instrumental music.

cover the basic patterns and formulate the fundamental generalizations that govern the science. They are urged to think creatively, to find new ways of solving problems. Such statements as the following attest to the importance of discovery and exploration in the new mathematics program.

Inherent in the new programs in mathematics is a method of teaching which encourages student discovery, creativity, and proof . . . Textbooks which provide a poorly worded rule in a red box, followed by an example and 25 exercises requiring only that the reader follow directions, are not compatible with the new look in mathematics.[38]

Real learning in mathematics is done through discovery, and discoverers must know how to observe, select, make generalizations and act. At all stages of learning arithmetic these activities are demanded.[39]

The following is an example of how arithmetic is taught through an emphasis upon pupil discovery.

A fifth grader who answered $7 + ? = 5$ with "two in the hole," and symbolized it with ②, had invented a wealth of possibilities. Most fifth graders, and many teachers, would have replied, "There is no number which can be added to 7, giving 5." This boy created something new, and he was excited about it. He wanted to add these new "in-the-hole numbers." After that, he wanted to subtract them. Recalling that $10 - 8$ is another name for the number

[38] Vern D. Hiebert, "Preparing Elementary Teachers in Mathematics," *Educational Leadership*, Vol. 19 (March, 1962), p. 383.

[39] Howard F. Fehr, "Trends in the Teaching of Arithmetic," *Frontiers of Elementary Education, VII*, Vincent J. Glennon, ed. (Syracuse, N. Y., Syracuse University Press, 1961), p. 36.

2 because $8 + 2 = 10$, he concluded that $10 - ⑧$ must be another name for the number 18, because $⑧ + 18 = 10$.[40]

The emphasis upon discovery as a method of learning is also felt strongly in science. Science today is not taught as an accumulation of facts. Experiments are not done according to steps outlined in cookbook fashion by either the teacher or the textbook. Instead children are urged to devise their own experiments, to find out what a flame needs to burn or to find out how to transfer water from one container to another without pouring it. As Blough says, "Science is a method of discovery—it is a creative intellectual activity—it is learning how to find the answers—it is an attitude—and it is the body of organized subject matter that is the result of this intellectual activity."[41]

The same emphasis is felt in the fresh new approach some teachers are taking toward the social studies. In the past, many children learned these subjects almost solely through the memorization of long lists of facts, dates, places, events, and persons. This is no longer true. Foshay illustrates how a discovery approach to history can be developed through such questions as:

What kinds of events after Lincoln would be most worth knowing? . . . How can we discover what these events were? What do historians say they were? . . . What are the principal ways the period has been interpreted by the historians? Do you, as a student, think of other ways? What information do you think the historians might include that they appear to have omitted? Why do you suppose they omitted this information? Because they couldn't find it? Because it didn't fit with their interpretation?[42]

A similar approach can be taken to the study of geography as illustrated by the following:

A sixth-grade class, having been through a conventional unit on the social and economic geography of the Southeastern states, was introduced to the North Central region by being asked to locate the major cities of the area on a map containing physical features and natural resources, but no place names. The resulting class discussion very rapidly produced a variety of plausible theories concerning the requirements of a city—a water transportation theory that placed Chicago at the junction of the three lakes, a mineral resources theory that placed it near the Mesabi range, a food-supply theory that put a great city on the rich soil of Iowa, and so on. The level of interest as well as the level of conceptual sophistication was far above that of control classes. Most

[40] Vern D. Hiebert, *op. cit.*, p. 383.
[41] Glenn O. Blough, "Improving the Science Program," *Educational Leadership*, Vol. 19 (January, 1962), p. 221.
[42] Arthur W. Foshay, "A Modest Proposal," *Educational Leadership*, Vol. 18 (May, 1961), p. 512.

striking, however, was the attitude of children to whom, for the first time, the location of a city appeared as a problem, and one to which an answer could be discovered by taking thought. Not only was there pleasure and excitement in the pursuit of a question, but in the end the discovery was worth making, at least for urban children for whom the phenomenon of the city was something that had before been taken for granted.[43]

One could go on and on with similar illustrations. The point, however, should be clear. A promising current trend that will almost certainly have far-reaching implications upon curriculum method and content is the unprecedented emphasis upon learning through discovery and understanding.

Somewhat related to this trend is the increasing regard with which curriculum builders are viewing the importance of intuitive thinking in various curriculum areas. In the past, the school has stressed the importance of analytic thinking. For example, there was a time when many teachers taught children to solve problems through a single series of formal steps. Today this is no longer true. Children are encouraged to think intuitively, to sense relationships and solutions in problem-oriented situations. The emphasis upon intuitive thought by some present-day curriculum builders is evident in the following statement.

The complementary nature of intuitive and analytic thinking should, we think, be recognized. Through intuitive thinking the individual may often arrive at solutions to problems which he would not achieve at all, or at best more slowly, through analytic thinking. Once achieved by intuitive methods, they should if possible be checked by analytic methods, while at the same time being respected as worthy hypotheses for such checking. Indeed, the intuitive thinker may even invent or discover problems that the analyst would not. But it may be the analyst who gives these problems the proper formalism. Unfortunately, the formalism of school learning has somehow devalued intuition. It is the very strong conviction of men who have been designing curricula, in mathematics and the sciences particularly, over the last several years that much more work is needed to discover how we may develop the intuitive gifts of our students from the earliest grades onwards. For, as we have seen, it may be of the first importance to establish an intuitive understanding of materials before we expose our students to more traditional and formal methods of deduction and proof.[44]

NEW CONTENT IS BEING INTRODUCED INTO THE ELEMENTARY SCHOOL CURRICULUM. We are living in an age of rapidly expanding knowledge in all fields. There is a strong emphasis upon the development of intellectual vigor in the schools. Many studies of children reveal that they are capable

[43] Jerome S. Bruner, *op. cit.*, pp. 21-22.
[44] *Ibid.*, pp. 58-59.

of assimilating more difficult concepts than was previously believed. The combination of these factors has resulted in the introduction of much new content into the elementary school curriculum. Some, of course, is new to the elementary school only in that it has been extended downward from the secondary level. Other areas are genuinely new.

This trend is noticeable in all fields. In the language areas, the emphasis upon linguistics may result in new curriculum content. According to the linguists, it is not true that language is primarily a means of communication with no content of its own. As a consequence, some predict that, ". . . the notion that elementary teachers should plan some 'English units,' in addition to 'social studies units' or 'science units' is a concept which will be explored rather fully in the years immediately ahead."[45]

An example of such a language unit was a unit on words the author recently saw developed in a sixth grade. As part of their study, the pupils explored such topics as (1) What is a word? (2) the origin of words, (3) the derivation of words, (4) the multiple meaning of words, (5) the similarity of sound and/or meaning of some words, (6) the jobs of words, (7) the importance of "silent words" such as gestures and signals, (8) the history of words, and (9) the same word as it appears in various languages. There is little doubt that the study was meaningful for these pupils and it is possible that other units of a similar nature might profitably be incorporated into the elementary curriculum.

In no other field is the introduction of new content more noticeable than in arithmetic. The new or modern mathematics has not discarded all of the content of the traditional program. But it undoubtedly has added to it. Content related to sets and sentences, the structure and development of the number system, approximation and estimation, geometry, algebra, mathematical language and symbolism, statistics and probability, and many other areas of content are included in the new elementary school mathematics programs.

The content of the social studies is also receiving much attention today. A recent source[46] lists the following important emphases in social studies content, many of which represent innovations in the traditional program that has long dominated the elementary school.

1. *World understandings.* New advances in transportation and communication continue to make our world grow steadily smaller. International tensions continue to mount. Never was there a greater need for peoples of the world to understand each other. It is imperative that a beginning be made in this direction in the elementary school. Beginning

[45] James R. Squire, "Tension on the Rope: English in 1962," *Educational Leadership*, Vol. 19 (February, 1962), p. 283.

[46] "Social Studies in the Elementary Schools," *Education Briefs* (Washington, D. C., Office of Education, September, 1960), p. 5.

Social Studies are becoming world-centered.

a study of current events as early as the primary grades; participating in numerous activities including the exchange of letters, gifts, and CARE boxes; developing units on such international organizations as the UN, UNESCO, and UNICEF; and supplying children with a wealth of books that contain interesting and accurate information about children in other lands are some of the activities that can help develop international understandings in elementary school children.

It should be mentioned here, that this emphasis must be world-centered rather than only Europe-centered as has been true in the past. The emerging importance of the countries of Asia, Africa, and South America has tremendous implications for the social studies curriculum of the future.

2. *Geographic education.* The vital need for world understanding highlights the importance of geography in the elementary curriculum. Man's interaction with his environment and the cultural, economic, political, and social interdependence of all nations are basic understandings that should receive attention in the elementary program.

3. *Citizenship education.* This is not a new but rather a continuing emphasis of the social studies. Knowledge of the privileges, duties, and responsibilities of a democratic citizen has been, and will continue to be, an important emphasis on all levels.

4. *Conservation education.* There is much interest in science and social studies directed toward the conservation of natural and social resources.

In some states, the need for adequate understandings and positive attitudes has prompted legislation requiring the subject to be taught in all schools. There is little doubt that it will receive increasing attention in future years.

5. *Community study*. The previously-mentioned emphasis upon world understanding does not imply a neglect of community study. On the contrary, modern curriculum planners are striving for a functional balance and integration of both areas.

There has also been an expansion of content in elementary school science. In the past, content was derived almost solely from the biological sciences for two major reasons. In the first place, this was a natural continuation of the nature study emphasis of the early nineteen hundreds. Secondly, most educators believed that the biological sciences were more easily understood by children and more closely related to their interests than other sciences. Recent research, however, has indicated that this is not the case, and today the comprehensive science program consists of elements from the physical sciences and the earth sciences, as well as the biological sciences.

Part of the trend toward the inclusion of new content has been the introduction of new subjects into the curriculum. A conspicuous example is listening. According to Duker, "An increase in interest in the nature of the listening process and in the best procedures for teaching efficient use of this process has marked the past three years . . . There has been an amazing increase in space allotted to listening in textbooks on speech and language arts as well as in recent curriculum bulletins."[47]

As recently as ten years ago, the teaching of listening was generally omitted from the elementary curriculum because teachers (1) did not realize its importance and (2) assumed that children automatically developed listening skills as they matured. Recent research has demonstrated that listening is one of man's major activities and that it can and must be taught. As a consequence, it has gained a firm foothold in the curricula of the forward-looking elementary schools. In general, listening is taught through many informal games and activities, as well as through direct instructional procedures designed to develop and evaluate the growth of specific listening skills. Such skills include listening to determine the major idea of a selection, listening for specific details, listening to determine the sequence of events, listening to determine the relationships of ideas, and many others.

It is not entirely accurate to call modern languages a new addition to the elementary curriculum because they appeared in some schools as early as the turn of the century. It is only within the last decade, how-

[47] Sam Duker, "Listening," *Review of Educational Research*, Vol. 31 (April, 1961), p. 145.

ever, that there has been a pronounced interest in this field. There is little doubt that the number of programs has grown steadily in recent years and today, according to one source, ". . . languages are being studied by more children in the elementary schools than by students in our colleges and universities."[48] Gilchrist comments upon this growth with the statement, "Perhaps the most dramatic revolution that is taking place [in the school program] is in foreign language instruction."[49]

In spite of this rapid growth there is still, however, some disagreement among educators concerning the value of foreign language in the elementary school. The movement has its ardent advocates and its severe critics. Advantages and disadvantages are claimed with equal vigor. Such differences of opinion indicate that there is still need for considerable study of the subject. The following questions were formulated by a study group interested in ". . . defining the purposes of and establishing criteria for, program development in the elementary school." They are indicative of the general questions that must be answered by continued research before it is possible to predict the place of foreign languages in the future elementary curriculum.

1. *Purpose.* . . .

    What purposes are proposed?

    How realistic are these purposes?

    How do they relate to the general purposes of the elementary-school program?

    May there be differences in purpose proposed by specialists and general teachers that will have to be reconciled?

    For whom are the various purposes most appropriate?

    Which purposes do we believe to be most defensible in our situations?

    What difference will selection of purpose make in our program planning?

2. *Content.* . . .

    Are there choices to be made in the vocabulary presented to children? If so, what differences might be tested in what they are to learn?

    To what extent do we need to plan to make sure that basic language patterns are learned in our program?

    Do children's interests enter into the teaching of modern language in the elementary school? What may children themselves suggest?

    Can modern-language teaching be related to other parts of the program?

[48] Edward D. Allen, "Foreign Language in the Elementary School," *Educational Research Bulletin*, Vol.-40 (April 12, 1961), p. 87.

[49] Robert S. Gilchrist, "Promising Practices in Education," *Phi Delta Kappan*, Vol. 41 (February, 1960), p. 209.

3. *Method.* . . .

How much proficiency in oral language should be required of elementary-school language teachers? How can they be helped to obtain it?

In the development of ability to speak and understand, how much attention should be given to hearing other speakers besides the teacher?

To what extent is printed material of value in the elementary-school program?

What kinds of guides will help teachers improve their methods?

To what extent can individual needs and interests be provided for in a program geared largely to skill development and group instruction?

4. *Materials.* . . .

Are there other kinds of materials that teachers might find useful?

What materials are now available? How useful are these?

Do tapes have a place in the elementary-school program?

Can television make a unique contribution?

What kinds of help do teachers of modern language in the elementary school think they need?

Is there a place for the language laboratory in the elementary school?

5. *Teachers.* . . .

What kinds of teachers are we presently using in the modern-language program of the elementary school?

What problems do we encounter in using teachers who are not adequately prepared in elementary education or perhaps have not received any professional education?

What kinds of help do such teachers need?

Can we teach general teachers enough modern language so that some of them can either follow up or actually teach the language?

How do regular teachers feel about the modern-language program? What kinds of contributions can they make to its success?

6. *Grade Placement.* . . .

How will objectives differ according to the level at which the program is begun?

Is it possible to recommend a grade level at which instruction might best begin?

Are there problems of confusion when children begin the study of another language during their first year at school. What influences may affect the rest of the program in later grades?

How much value is there in beginning a language later in the elementary school; that is, how much learning may be expected?

7. *Pupil Selection.* . . .

What happens when the program is voluntary?

What happens when the program is offered only to superior students?

What kinds of problems have to be faced when all children are involved?

Is there a point at which a program that begins with all children might be expected to become more selective?

Is there such a thing as language aptitude? If so, should it be considered at this level?

To what extent is cross-grade grouping a possibility?

8. *Selection of Language.* . . .

What criteria would seem best for use in selecting the language or languages to be taught?

Does it matter which language is selected?

Should criteria differ from one community or situation to another?

9. *Time and Scheduling.* . . .

Is there a minimum amount of time that should be devoted to language study?

Is it better to have more short periods than fewer long periods?

Is there a preferred time of day for language instruction?

What about after-school or Saturday scheduling?

Should the amount of time involved be closely related to age?

Is flexibility of time important?

10. *Continuity.* . . .

Can we plan so that content is really cumulative?

How are we to provide for new pupils who may not have had prior language study?

Can we help prepare for continuity by working with our junior-high school colleagues in getting ready to receive our pupils?

How can we help in planning a multitrack program?

11. *Evaluation.* . . .

How can we provide for continuous evaluation of the success of the program?

Should we specify what is to be learned by grade levels so that growth can be measured in vocabulary, sentence patterns, and so on; or should we avoid setting standards by grades, especially in early years?

Can we measure ability to speak and understand the language?

How important is evaluation in this program?

Can we keep track of attitudes and the like?

Who should be involved in over-all evaluation?[50]

There are, of course, many cautions to be heeded in adding new content to the elementary curriculum. The problem of the bulging curriculum has previously been mentioned. Subjects and areas are added steadily. Few, if any, are deleted. Then too, there is the problem of balance. As content is added steadily to some areas, there is danger of minimizing the importance of other areas such as art, music, and physical education. As Foshay says, "In pursuing high intellectual goals, it is not necessary for a moment that we overlook the fact that man, in addition to being an intellectual creature, is also an emotional, a social, an aesthetic, a biological, a creative, and a spiritual creature."[51]

Lastly, there is the problem mentioned earlier of maintaining a proper balance between the three sources of content. Much of the new content, in most fields, comes from a study of the nature and structure of the discipline itself. This is fine and there is no doubt that it can be challenging and stimulating to pupil intellect. But we must also balance this with content that has social value and that is derived from the felt needs of the learners. In the new mathematics programs, for instance, there are already some faint indications that children may become very skilled at discovering patterns and understanding relationships, but less than adequately prepared in computational skills needed for responsible living. Some mathematicians have sounded a note of warning in this regard similar to the following.

Another note of caution is to be found in the desires of some mathematicians to make mathematicians out of all children who can become mathematicians, and as far as the rest are concerned, that is a problem for those interested in the less capable. I happen to believe that arithmetic as a social instrument and as an applied science is far more valuable to most of the human population than arithmetic as a pure game. I also happen to believe that learning arithmetic out of the world so that it can be applied to the world is a greater and more important aim of elementary school arithmetic instruction than creating future mathematicians. I also believe that learning arithmetic as a game will turn as many children away from learning and liking arithmetic as the meaningless rote teaching that is still being widely practiced.[52]

[50] Alexander Frazier and others, "Modern Language in the Elementary School: A Study of Purposes and Programs," *Educational Research Bulletin*, Vol. 40 (May 10, 1961), pp. 122-125.

[51] Arthur W. Foshay, *op. cit.*, pp. 516-528.

[52] Howard F. Fehr, *op. cit.*, p. 34.

The same thing is true of the third source of content, that derived from the study of children's needs. Some recent studies have indicated that children can learn more difficult and different content than was previously believed. This is probably true. But the fact that children can learn certain subject matter does not necessarily mean that they should learn it. Close attention to children's needs, abilities, and interests is as important now as it ever was. It would indeed be a serious error if teachers, in their enthusiasm for some of the new content, ignored the fact that it may be far removed from the interests and experiences of children.

In summary, the major concern of curriculum builders today is one of proper balance. As Foshay points out, ". . . sometimes, despite the best efforts of wise men, the result [of curriculum change] has been only to substitute one distortion for another."[53] This is the danger against which all teachers must be constantly on guard.

SUMMARY

This chapter has discussed the role of the teacher in structured curriculum development and improvement. It was stated that every teacher, as he seeks daily to refine his classroom procedures, is improving the curriculum. But over and beyond that, the teacher has a definite responsibility to participate in developing a structured curriculum design for the elementary school.

Three definitions of the curriculum were examined with the most commonly accepted one usually considered to be ". . . all the learning experiences which children and youth have under the direction of the school." The expanding scope and patterns of organization of the elementary school curriculum were also examined in the first section. The two basic philosophies of curriculum organization, the subject matter approach and the learner-centric approach, were placed at both ends of a continuum. Along this continuum were placed four common organizational patterns. These were (1) the separate subjects curriculum, (2) the correlated curriculum, (3) the broad fields curriculum, and (4) the unified curriculum.

The second section was concerned with the basic principles of curriculum improvement. It was stressed that functional curriculum improvement is an on-going, continuous responsibility of many individuals including teachers, parents, subject matter specialists, educators, psychologists, and many others.

[53] Arthur W. Foshay, "From the Association," *Balance in the Curriculum*, Yearbook, 1961 (Washington, D. C., The Association for Supervision and Curriculum Development, 1961), p. iii.

Whether on a state, national, or local level, there are certain common sequential procedures for developing or revising the curriculum. These begin with an awareness of the need, and end, if the project is successful, in being incorporated into the daily work of the classroom.

Since all teachers are curriculum builders, it is necessary that they be familiar with the current edge of curriculum experimentation and research. Three basic trends that today permeate practically all curriculum areas were examined in the last section of the chapter. All three appear to hold promise for an improved curriculum, provided teachers are constantly aware of the need for maintaining a proper balance among the areas and types of content that can be translated into functional and valuable learning experiences for children.

ADDITIONAL LEARNING EXPERIENCES

Topics for Thought and Discussion

1. Does your state have a state-wide curriculum guide? Who developed it? How flexible is it? How is provision for continuous revision and improvement made?

2. What is your reaction toward the proposal of a National Curriculum Commission?

3. Are you in favor of the requirement of some states that an elementary teacher must have an academic major in addition to his specialization in elementary education? Why?

4. There is some concern today that curriculum making may be taken out of the hands of teachers and educators and delegated primarily to subject-matter specialists. Is this concern justified? What would be the result of such a move? If curriculum making is a cooperative responsibility, what specializations should be represented? How can a proper balance be maintained?

5. What is your concept of a creative person? How is he different from other people?

6. Does a creative artist have essentially the same qualities and attributes as a creative scientist? Check your answer to this question with findings from research and with current writing on the subject.

7. Do you think a foreign language should be a required part of the pre-service education of every elementary teacher? How many years should be required? Why?

8. Which of the four curriculum patterns discussed in this chapter do you think is the most common? In what direction is the trend moving?

9. To some, a magic word today is *specialist*. Are elementary teachers specialists? Or generalists? Or both?

10. If an elementary education teacher has specialized in one academic area and teaches in a self-contained classroom, will he naturally tend to emphasize his area of specialization and neglect or minimize other curriculum areas? What controls could be established to prevent this from happening?

Projects and Activities

1. Conduct an informal poll of several elementary teachers. Do they feel that they have special strengths in certain curricular areas? Are these strengths recognized and capitalized upon by their administration? Are such strengths utilized in structured curriculum revision or development?

2. Observe in an elementary classroom. List any evidence you see of pupils learning through discovery and exploration. Compare each of these with the way the same concept would be taught in a traditional manner.

3. There is currently in progress much research and experimentation in the area of creativity. Study the writings of Torrance, Guilford, Getzels and Jackson, and others in this field. What implications do their findings have on the elementary school curriculum? On other aspects of the school program?

4. Examine several recent social studies curriculum guides. To what extent do they reflect an awareness of the five current emphases in this area mentioned on pp. 338 to 340. Is content in these areas confined to certain grade levels or is it developed in a cyclic manner throughout all grades?

5. Try to determine, through a questionnaire, the opinions of a sampling of elementary teachers in your state as to the advisability of including modern languages in the elementary school curriculum. What are the advantages? The problems or limitations?

6. Prepare a research report on the influence of the science of linguistics upon the changing content of the elementary school curriculum.

7. You are the principal of a school. Several parents have questioned you as to your opinion of parental participation in curriculum improvement. Prepare a fifteen minute talk to give at the next PTA meeting on this topic. Outline carefully the areas in which your school would, or would not, welcome parental participation. Defend your statements with concrete illustrations as well as supporting statements from authorities in the field.

8. You have just been appointed to the newly-created position of curriculum coordinator in your school. List the steps you will take to involve teachers in curriculum improvement.

9. From visitations, observations, reading, and interviews with people in the field, give several specific examples of content that has recently been moved down from the secondary school to the elementary school. Are your examples in one or two curriculum areas or in most areas?

10. Prepare a panel discussion on the pros and cons of a national curriculum for the elementary school.

Selected Bibliography

ALCORN, Marvin D., and LINLEY, James M., *Issues in Curriculum Development*. New York, Harcourt, Brace & World, Inc., 1959.

ANDERSON, Vernon E., *Principles and Procedures of Curriculum Improvement*. New York, The Ronald Press Company, 1956.

Association for Supervision and Curriculum Development, *Balance in the Curriculum*. 1961 Yearbook. Washington, D. C., National Education Association, 1961.

Association for Supervision and Curriculum Development. *Research for Curriculum Improvement*. 1957 Yearbook. Washington, D. C., National Education Association, 1957.

BEAUCHAMP, George A., *Planning the Elementary School Curriculum*. Boston, Allyn and Bacon, Inc., 1956.

BECK, Robert H., COOK, Walter W., and KEARNEY, Nolan C., *Curriculum in the Modern Elementary School*, 2nd ed. Englewood Cliffs, N. J., Prentice-Hall, Inc., 1960.

BRUNER, Jerome S., *The Process of Education*. Cambridge, Mass., Harvard University Press, 1962.

CASWELL, Hollis L., and associates, *Curriculum Improvement in Public School Systems*. New York, Bureau of Publications, Teachers College, Columbia University, 1950.

————, and FOSHAY, Arthur W., *Education in the Elementary School*, 3rd ed. New York, American Book Company, 1957.

Curriculum Crossroads, A. Harry Passow, ed. New York, Bureau of Publications, Teachers College, Columbia University, 1962.

"Curriculum and Survival." *Educational Leadership*, Vol. 16 (October, 1958).

"Curriculum Planning and Development." *Review of Educational Research*, Vol. 27 (June, 1957).

"Curriculum Planning and Development." *Review of Educational Research*, Vol. 30 (June, 1960).

DOLL, Ronald C., and others, *Organizing for Curriculum Improvement*. New York, Bureau of Publications, Teachers College, Columbia University, 1953.

DUTTON, Wilbur H., and HOCKETT, John A., *The Modern Elementary School Curriculum and Methods*. New York, Holt, Rinehart, and Winston, Inc., 1959.

FLEMING, Robert S., *Curriculum for Today's Boys and Girls*. Columbus, Ohio, Charles E. Merrill Books, Inc., 1963.

GETZELS, Jacob W., and JACKSON, Philip W., *Creativity and Intelligence*. New York, John Wiley & Sons, Inc., 1962.

GWYNN, J. Minor, *Curriculum Principles and Social Trends*, 3rd ed. New York, The Macmillan Company, 1960.

HAAN, Aubrey, *Elementary School Curriculum: Theory and Research*. Boston, Allyn and Bacon, Inc., 1961.

HURLEY, Beatrice D., *Curriculum for Elementary School Children*. New York, The Ronald Press Company, 1957.

JAMESON, Marshall C., and HICKS, William V., *Elementary School Curriculum from Theory to Practice*. New York, American Book Company, 1960.

KRUG, Edward A., *Curriculum Planning*. New York, Harper & Row, Publishers, Inc., 1950.

"Lay Participation in Curriculum Development Reexamined." *Educational Leadership*, Vol. 15 (April, 1958).

LEE, J. Murray, and Dorris May, *The Child and His Curriculum*, 3rd ed. New York, Appleton-Century-Crofts, 1960.

McNALLY, Harold J., PASSOW, A. Harry, and associates, *Improving the Quality of Public School Programs*. New York, Bureau of Publications, Teachers College, Columbia University, 1960.

PARKER, J. Cecil, EDWARDS, T. Bentley, and STEGEMAN, William H., *Curriculum in America*. New York, Thomas Y. Crowell Company, 1962.

PETERSEN, Dorothy G., and HAYDEN, Velma D., *Teaching and Learning in the Elementary School*. New York, Appleton-Century-Crofts, 1961.

PRITZKAU, Philo T., *Dynamics of Curriculum Improvement*. Englewood Cliffs, N. J., Prentice-Hall, Inc., 1959.

RAGAN, William B., *Modern Elementary Curriculum*, rev. ed. New York, Holt, Rinehart and Winston, Inc., 1960.

RUCKER, W. Ray, *Curriculum Development in the Elementary School*. New York, Harper & Row, Publishers, Inc., 1960.

SAYLOR, J. Galen, and ALEXANDER, William M., *Curriculum Planning for Better Teaching and Learning*. New York, Holt, Rinehart, and Winston, Inc., 1954.

SHANE, Harold G., and McSWAIN, Eldridge T., *Evaluation and the Elementary Curriculum*, rev. ed. New York, Holt, Rinehart, and Winston, Inc., 1958.

SHARP, George, *Curriculum Development as Re-education of the Teacher*. New York, Bureau of Publications, Teachers College, Columbia University, 1951.

SMITH, B. Othanel, STANLEY, William O., and SHORES, J. Harlan, *Fundamentals of Curriculum Development*. New York, Harcourt, Brace & World, Inc., 1950.

SPEARS, Harold, *Curriculum Planning through In-Service Programs*. Englewood Cliffs, N. J., Prentice-Hall, Inc., 1957.

———, *The Teacher and Curriculum Planning*. Englewood Cliffs, N. J., Prentice-Hall, Inc., 1951.

"Staff Participation in Curriculum Development—A Searching Look." *Educational Leadership*, Vol. 15 (March, 1958).

STRATEMEYER, Florence, and others, *Developing a Curriculum for Modern Living*, 2nd ed. New York, Bureau of Publications, Teachers College, Columbia University, 1957.

TABA, Hilda, *Curriculum Development: Theory and Practice*, New York, Harcourt, Brace & World, Inc., 1962.

"The Curriculum: Learning and Teaching." *Review of Educational Research*, Vol. 21 (June, 1951).

"The Curriculum: Organization and Development." *Review of Educational Research*, Vol. 24 (June, 1954).

TORRANCE, Ellis P., *Guiding Creative Talent*. Englewood Cliffs, N. J., Prentice-Hall, Inc., 1962.

"Who Should Plan the Curriculum?" *Educational Leadership*, Vol. 19 (October, 1961).

WILT, Miriam, *Creativity in the Elementary School*. New York, Appleton-Century-Crofts, 1959.

CHAPTER **9**

Providing for
Individual Differences

WHAT DO I DO WITH A FOURTH-GRADER who can't read a preprimer? How do I help a stutterer? How can I keep a child from constantly interrupting when another is speaking? What can I do with a pupil who always finishes his work before the others? What is the trouble with a child who just can't tell the truth? How can I tactfully help a sixth-grade girl with problems of personal cleanliness and grooming? What is the best way to treat a third-grader whose parents still consider him a baby? Why didn't any instructor in college tell me how to handle an epileptic child in the classroom? How did I fail one of my boys who has just been assigned to a correctional institution? What is wrong with a youngster who has an I. Q. of 135 but can't spell?

These and similar questions are asked daily by conscientious teachers. They reveal their recognition of, and concern with, the many differences existing among their pupils. The sum of these differences is incalculable. Some are of relatively little significance to the teacher. Jean's fair skin and Joe's swarthy complexion are an interesting contrast, but no more than that. Mary and Sally go to different churches, but this is of little concern to the teacher. Other differences, however, do concern the teacher greatly in that they affect all of his instructional procedures and pupil relationships. In general, such differences may be classified in the following categories:

Physical differences. These are, of course, the most apparent and, therefore, the most easily observed. Differences in height, weight, and general appearance are readily recognized and may or may not be of significance to the teacher. Physical handicaps, such as obesity, hearing

351

Physical differences are most apparent and easily observed.

loss, poor sight, speech difficulties, and various types of orthopedic impairments may influence the total personality of the child and are, therefore, of enormous concern to the teacher. Other physical differences, in strength, coordination, dexterity, and energy, are less detectable but may be equally significant.

Sex differences. Three general categories of variability between the sexes should be of interest to the teacher. In the first place, there is a general difference in academic achievement. Girls generally appear to excel in this area, particularly according to teachers' grades. The difference is less marked on standardized achievement tests, on which girls generally excel in language skills and boys in scientific and mathematical areas. Many educators today, however, suggest that such differences are learned rather than innate and that they are fast disappearing in our changing social world. Burton says,

The sexes do differ greatly in certain interests and special abilities, but these are usually the result of training or social pressure. Certain attitudes have developed toward women which in turn determine many of the interests and occupations open to women. Furthermore, the part to be played by each in the world has further accentuated the differences in interests, tastes, and skills. Girls are not given mechanical toys and are not expected to study the physical and mechanical sciences, whereas boys are directed to these fields. Girls are more often guided to esthetic fields and to those connected with homemaking. However, the wars of this century have broken down many of the barriers which have kept girls and women out of certain occupations.[1]

There is, at the moment, no evidence to indicate a difference between the sexes as far as general intelligence is concerned. As Tyler says, ". . . at the present stage of mental measurement it is not possible to give an unequivocal answer to the question, 'Which sex is superior in intelligence?' "[2]

The second category of difference is noted in the interests and personality traits of the sexes. Such differences as the following emerge from the various studies.

. . . boys are more variable than girls in their play life. Boys more often engage in the following types of activity: active, vigorous plays and games; those involving muscular dexterity and skill; those involving competition; and the more highly organized plays and games. Girls, on the other hand, are more conservative in their play life; they participate more often in sedentary activities and in activities involving a restricted range of action. . . .

. . . marked sex differences in reading preferences are evident as early as the primary school grades and persist to adult years . . . girls read more than boys, and . . . their choices run to milder stories of home and school as contrasted with the active or violent adventure preferred by the boys. . . .

Studies of radio listening habits show a trend toward high popularity and not much differentiation. . . .

In movie interests we find patterns of sex difference similar to those for reading.[3]

The third category of difference is the rate of over-all physical maturation with girls exceeding boys by about one to two years.

Social-emotional differences. Wide differences in social intelligence and emotional maturity exist among pupils in every elementary classroom. The perceptive teacher recognizes and adjusts his program to the varying degrees existing among his pupils in such traits as gregariousness, sensitivity, timidity, aggressiveness, optimism, poise, shyness, tenacity, confidence, introspection, cheerfulness, and innumerable others.

[1] William H. Burton, *The Guidance of Learning Activities,* 3rd ed. (New York, Appleton-Century-Crofts, 1962), p. 234.
[2] Fred T. Tyler, "Individual and Sex Differences," *Encyclopedia of Educational Research,* 3rd ed., Chester W. Harris, ed. (New York, The Macmillan Company, 1960), p. 685.
[3] Lewis M. Terman and Leona E. Tyler, "Psychological Sex Differences," *Manual of Child Psychology,* 2nd ed., Leonard Carmichael, ed. (New York, John Wiley and Sons, Inc., 1954), pp. 1077-1080.

Environmental and experiential differences. Differences in home backgrounds and their significance to the teacher were discussed in Chapter 6. Such differences influence greatly pupils' academic achievements, motivations, value judgments, and attitudes toward the school. Some children are strongly motivated toward a formal education as a status symbol or steppingstone to a higher social position. Others regard school success as a threat to their peer relationships and gang status. Some children accept the luxuries of life as a matter of course. Others have never been free from hunger. Some youngsters have traveled the globe before they reach the kindergarten door. Others have never left their backyards. The range and significance of experiential and environmental differences cannot be too important to the teacher who is genuinely concerned about each individual in the classroom.

Mental and academic differences. Least observable, least understood, and least accepted by teachers are the differences in mental ability that exist in the classroom. As a matter of fact, the traditional school either refused to admit, or chose to ignore, the existence of these differences. The graded school came into existence approximately one hundred years ago, largely upon the naive assumption that children of approximately the same chronological age possessed approximately the same mental abilities. Thus, academic standards were assigned to grade levels and the child who did not meet them was either lazy or contrary. His punishment was, of course, to repeat the grade. The fact that some children were retained in one grade for as long as nine years only showed that they were uncommonly successful in resisting the efforts of the teacher!

It was not until the child study and scientific measurement movements of the twentieth century that educators realized the full significance of the differences in mental ability that exist among individuals. Today teachers know that, on the average, there is a four-year range of mental ages among children entering the first grade. Some six-year-olds enter first grade with a mental age of 4.0, others with 8.0, and a very small per cent are even more widely distributed from the norm. The range continues to expand on each succeeding grade level until it about doubles in the sixth grade. Consequently, the typical sixth grade teacher may expect an eight-year mental age range, from approximately 8.0 to 16.0 in his classroom. Furthermore, it should be recognized that this pertains only to *general mental maturity as measured by existing tests*. The wide ranges existing among the more than fifty individual aspects of intelligence are, at present, nonmeasurable and can be recognized only by the extremely competent and observant teacher.

To compound the problem, the now generally recognized complex nature of intelligence means that wide ranges of ability exist in each individual. Thus, the intra-individual as well as the inter-individual differences in mental capacities among children have great significance in planning an educational program.

In summary, the fact of individual differences is indisputable and inescapable. For many years conscientious and competent educators have faced the problem. Numerous attempts have been made to devise an educational program that would be efficient, economical, and practical enough to serve all youth, while simultaneously recognizing the unique potential of each individual. In general, these attempts involve changes, modifications, and innovations in the (1) administrative organization of the school or (2) the instructional procedures of the classroom. The first of these is discussed in the following section.

ADMINISTRATIVE PROVISIONS FOR INDIVIDUAL DIFFERENCES

The increasing population, the trend toward urbanization, the growing emphasis upon efficiency in business and industry, and the interest of some educators in European educational systems were some of the factors that led to the establishment of the graded school in the mid-nineteenth century. Many claimed that the increased efficiency of the graded school provided more adequately for individual differences than the one-room schoolhouse. Actually, it probably did just the opposite. The weaknesses of the early graded school are evident in the following statement.

The school officials endeavored to create an organization through which an elementary school education could be provided as economically as possible for the increasing school population. The trend in American cities was toward elaborate mechanical organization. The desired goal appeared to be the installation of smoothly operating machinery with which a large student body could be handled with ease, order and efficiency. The outcome, as might be expected, was an elementary school that was rigid in its administrative, supervisory and instructional practices. Consideration of the individual pupil was ignored by a rigid curriculum, lock-step methods of teaching and inelastic methods of marking, grading and promoting. The efficiency of classroom instruction was measured primarily by the process used, rather than by progress made by pupils. The mechanical phases of teaching were overemphasized; red tape and routine were rampant. Smaller school systems imitated large ones, with their printed forms, regulations, rules and records. In general, the rural school was the only type in which the teaching of individuals survived.[4]

[4] James Henry Dougherty, Frank Hermon Gorman, and Claude Anderson Phillips, *Elementary School Organization and Management*, rev. ed. (New York, The Macmillan Company, 1950), p. 18.

These weaknesses became apparent to some educators before the turn of the century, and attempts to eliminate them have been made from approximately 1875 to the present day. Early plans which have since been discarded or radically modified include the following.

Flexible promotions. Superintendent William T. Harris instituted in the 1860's a plan in St. Louis which permitted semiannual, quarterly, and eventually semiquarterly promotions. Two advantages claimed were: (1) Children were better able to progress at their own rates of speed, and (2) Frequent reclassifications of pupils reduced the range of differences in each group.

Multiple-track programs. In 1888, a three-track program (later known as the Pueblo Plan) was introduced in Pueblo, Colorado. This plan permitted the group on the fast track to complete the eight grades of the elementary school in seven years. The slow group took nine years, and the average, eight.

Acceleration and retardation. The earliest form of acceleration consisted simply of grade-skipping and was probably first used in Elizabeth, New Jersey. Today, the term is used to define "progress through an educational program at rates faster or ages younger than conventional."[5] Probably the most common forms of acceleration in use today are (1) some types of ungraded organizational plans and (2) early admission to school for those youngsters of superior mental ability. Advantages and disadvantages of acceleration have been well summarized by Passow. The major arguments for acceleration are:

1. Since the gifted child learns more rapidly than do other students, he needs to be provided with opportunities commensurate with his ability to progress. These opportunities help to place him in the grade which corresponds to his maturity level rather than his chronological age.

2. Students should not be forced to spend traditional blocks of time simply to facilitate academic bookkeeping. They should take the least time needed for desired educational attainment. Research studies indicate that there is little correlation between achievement in a given subject and the length of time devoted to its study. A gifted student should be encouraged to master a particular area at his own rate of speed.

3. Evidence indicates that "the years of maximum health, physical strength and endurance, intellectual alertness and productivity, vigorous interest and enthusiasm, all come near the beginning of adult life.". . . Acceleration capitalizes on this biological peak by putting an earlier end to full-time educational preparation and enables earlier entry into productive careers.

[5] Sidney L. Pressey, *Educational Acceleration: Appraisals and Basic Problems* (Columbus, Ohio, Ohio State University, 1949), p. 2.

4. Children kept in classes in which they are not challenged develop attitudes and habits which may result in emotional maladjustments. The temporary difficulties which can result from being with students older and more mature may, in the long run, be less damaging than achieving below one's potential ability. Classmates who are chronological peers may or may not be intellectual or social peers.

5. Acceleration invites varied educational opportunities and more of them, either in a major interest or talent area or in fields unfamiliar to the student. Thus acceleration is actually a form of enrichment.

6. The period of full-time schooling has been lengthened to the point where intellectual, social, and economic "adolescence" is prolonged unduly. A year or two saved in early schooling can mean the completion of graduate study without delaying the age for marriage and self-support unduly.

7. Fewer school years mean lower costs and substantial savings for students, their parents, schools, and communities. Any saving of a year or more for as few as 1 per cent of the students in elementary and secondary school would mean the equivalent of thousands of additional man-years of productivity.

The major arguments against acceleration are:

1. Education does not consist of neatly compartmentalized, logically organized units of learning in preordained sequences. While some skills may be developed in sequence, rich learning experiences do not necessarily come from a fixed pattern of subject matter. While it is possible to decrease time spent on particular activities, certain learnings arise only from studies in depth and breadth.

2. The boredom that breeds on lack of challenge can be eliminated in other and better ways than reducing time spent in a class.

3. Younger students may be intellectually mature, but socially and emotionally disadvantaged among older students. Opportunities for leadership in some areas may be denied students because of physical or social immaturity with older groups.

4. Acceleration deprives gifted children of opportunities for full living and learning. Bright students cannot compensate for the learnings which come from time and opportunity to think, reflect, explore, and appreciate. Creativity may be curbed by lack of leisure and by pressures to maintain rapid progress in all areas.

5. Comparability of mental age does not necessarily mean similar intellectual functioning or maturity. A six-year-old with a mental age of nine years and the nine-year-old with a mental age of nine perform qualitatively quite differently. Acceleration into an advanced grade may provide more difficult work but, in terms of the child's total educational development, may not result in more appropriate experiences.

6. Because of different maturation rates, the child's development may be quite uneven. While he might profit from accelerated experiences in one area, he may not be ready for rapid progress in others. Pressures to achieve and maintain standards of equal attainment in all areas may affect his motivation as well as his over-all educational development.

7. Acceleration tends to emphasize differences in ability and to set the gifted apart from his age peers. Undesirable social and emotional behavior patterns may result from this separation.

8. When skipping occurs, serious gaps may result in the student's learning, affecting the quality of later performance. This is especially true in skill areas where there are sequential developments.[6]

Retardation refers to the policy of retaining a pupil in a grade until he meets the standards of the next higher level. Numerous surveys over the years have revealed the steady decline of this practice, largely because research strongly supports the following conclusions.

1. Nonpromotion (retardation) does not result in greater academic gain by the retainees.

2. Nonpromotion produces a greater, not lesser, range of academic performance on any given level.

3. Nonpromotion is threatening to the social adjustment and personal development of children.

Individualized instruction. The history of our country has always reflected a deep regard for the individual. Whenever his rights have been threatened, many have become concerned. This was true late in the nineteenth century when certain educators protested against the harmful effects of mass education upon the individual. Some advocated the abolition of group teaching and proposed a "school of individualism"[7] in which each child worked alone, under the direction of the teacher. In spite of considerable opposition, the idea of individualized instruction grew and finally culminated in the Winnetka, Dalton, and other plans of the 1920's. These plans utilized individualized assignments and permitted the pupil to proceed at his own rate through a series of "job sheets" or contracts. Some plans attempted to eliminate the disadvantages of complete individualized instruction by making some provision for group and social activity. In general, however, their popularity dropped sharply in the thirties and forties, although certain modified types are still used in some school systems today.

[6] A. Harry Passow, "Enrichment of Education for the Gifted," *Education for the Gifted*, Nelson B. Henry, ed., Fifty-seventh Yearbook, National Society for the Study of Education (Chicago, University of Chicago Press, 1958), pp. 212-214.

[7] Preston W. Search, "Individualism in Mass Education," *Journal of the Proceedings and Addresses of the National Education Association* (St. Paul, Minn., Pioneer Press Company, 1895), pp. 398-406.

Specialized educational facilities and programs are now found in most elementary schools.

Specialized Facilities

Over the years, public education, in the form of special classes and schools, has been extended in some degree to the (1) physically handicapped, (2) mentally retarded, (3) socially and emotionally handicapped, and (4) academically talented.

Physically handicapped. A few residential schools for the blind and deaf were established in this country fairly early in the nineteenth century. It was not until a century later that the needs of the speech and orthopedically handicapped were met with specialized facilities. Today, many public school systems provide sight-saving classes, special speech and hearing classes, and special classes for children suffering from cerebral palsy, cardiac disorders, and orthopedic impairments. In the larger cities, special schools may serve the needs of the physically handicapped.

Mentally handicapped. The first public school classes for backward children were established in Providence, Rhode Island in 1896. Since that time much progress has been made, particularly since the mid-forties, in securing compulsory or permissive legislation to meet the needs of this group through public education. Broadly speaking, two classifications of mentally handicapped are served through public school programs. The mentally retarded (I. Q. approximately 50 to 70) are educated in one type of program and the mentally deficient (I. Q. approximately 25 to 50) are grouped into training classes. It should be understood, of course, that the I. Q. is only one narrow criterion and that many additional criteria are used as a basis of classification and instruction of these children.

Socially handicapped. Less common are special public educational facilities for the socially and emotionally maladjusted. However, many large cities, such as Chicago, Detroit, and New York, have attempted to meet the needs of delinquent and maladjusted children through specialized classes or schools.

Academically talented. More controversial than any other type of specialized education is that provided for the intellectually gifted. In the past, provision for these children was made through acceleration or various types of groupings. These gradually, however, were replaced by a strong emphasis on enrichment within the regular classroom and special provisions for the gifted, with a few exceptions such as Cleveland's Major Work Classes, became almost nonexistent.

Today there is a decided renewal of interest in an adequate educational program for these children. A few states have enacted legislation to provide especially for this group, although most states include provision for them in legislation designed to serve the needs of all atypical children.

The vast amount of current literature concerning gifted children reveals far from unanimous agreement among educators on the best means of providing for these youngsters. Many argue for enrichment within the regular class program on such grounds as (1) educational desirability, (2) administrative feasibility (in smaller systems where the number of such pupils may be very small), (3) undemocratic implications of specialized facilities for a favored few, (4) increased costs of special provisions, (5) problems of identification and classification, and (6) failure of research to demonstrate the increased academic gain resulting from segregated classes. Equally vocal are arguments for specialized provisions such as (1) failure of the typical classroom to challenge the gifted pupil, (2) the national need to develop the optimum intellectual potential of future leaders, (3) the dangers of developing a "cult of mediocrity," and (4) the rationale that special provisions represent, not *segregation*, but only lifelike *congregation*. Concerning the last point, Freehill states,

Both pitch and volume increase when discussions turn to the question of separating the gifted. The common use of the word *segregation* accentuates the conflict. The semantic problem is partly avoided by using the term *ability grouping* and more vigorously avoided by using the term *congregation*. Advocates of the latter maintain that boys congregate to play baseball, that children congregate to put on a play or to pursue other common interests, so why not have them congregate in the pursuit of intellectual interests and academic learning?[8]

A modified type of segregation (or congregation) used by some schools is the *enrichment* or *opportunity* class. Such a class may function for a single school, or pupils from several schools may be transported to it. It may meet every day or several times a week. Usually in the charge of a special teacher, the enrichment class offers gifted children literary, artistic, mathematical, or scientific experiences not normally included in the regular school program.

Another administrative device for providing for these children is to group them together for only part of the school day. In such a plan, the abler may be placed with children of various levels of ability for a half-day and be grouped into special classes for the other half of the day.

Still another device currently in use is *cluster grouping*. In this plan, a cluster of academically talented children may be placed in a class whose members range from average to above average in academic achievement. Proponents of the plan claim that it places the gifted child among others of similar talent while, at the same time, he enjoys daily contact and relationships with children of varying abilities.

One of the oldest and most prevalent means of providing for the gifted is through the use of ability grouping, discussed below.

Ability Grouping

This discussion of ability grouping refers specifically to the elementary school and does not include the secondary school where problems and issues other than those mentioned here must be considered. The term *ability grouping*, as used here, refers to the practice of dividing pupils on a given grade level into class groups according to academic ability. The formation of "high," "average," and "low" groups is probably most common, although some larger schools have five or more levels of any single grade. Bases for classifying pupils into groups vary widely; very few schools now depend solely upon the I.Q. A combined basis of mental age and school achievement (as revealed on standardized tests and teachers' marks) is probably used most frequently, although some schools use a narrower base, such as the reading age.

Grouping children into classes on the basis of academic performance was used in some systems, among them Elizabeth, New Jersey and St. Louis, before the turn of the century. Detroit, however, in 1919 was probably the first system to put the plan into widespread use. During the

[8] Maurice F. Freehill, *Gifted Children* (New York, The Macmillan Company, 1961), pp. 192-193.

20's and 30's it grew in popularity, although it was never as widespread as some current statements imply. In the 40's and 50's the use of ability grouping declined sharply and Shane reported that, among thirty-five "educationally interesting schools," straight ability grouping was the least common approach to grouping.[9] In 1960 a survey of urban districts revealed that only 16.9 per cent had a basic policy of grouping according to ability in grades one through six, although 46.1 per cent of the respondents predicted an increased use of it in the future.[10]

From its inception, ability grouping has been the center of considerable controversy and the literature is rampant with statements from its advocates and critics. Strong criticisms of the plan are voiced in statements similar to the following.

There is our tendency in education to want to classify people into sheep and goats—to want to grade them, like eggs, or peas, or lumber. This is not limited to teachers, unfortunately. There are whole groups of people in our society who, for reasons that are essentially ugly, wish to see people classified and their potentialities limited. The fact that this kind of thing is urged in the name of the early identification of talent does not make it legitimate. . . . The early identification of talent, which certainly is necessary, is not a matter of finding out who are the sheep and who are the goats in our society. . . . What we require is a version of education, and a view of our society, that foster perpetual self-discovery and self-fulfillment. Our tendency to use the schools as a giant screening device is precisely contradictory to this idea.[11]

An opposite viewpoint is expressed as follows: "Homogeneous grouping . . . makes it possible to challenge each child. A challenge soon loses its motivating force for the pupil who can never meet it with success or for the pupil who finds it too easy. Neither child continues to work at his best level. And not only the child, but society at large, is the ultimate loser."[12]

Unfortunately research does not throw much light on the subject. This is not because attempts have not been made. Over the past forty-five years, numerous studies have investigated the problem. Studies, however, have differed so widely in statistical design, control of variables, size of sample, and duration of experiment that it is almost impossible to draw

[9] Harold G. Shane, "Grouping Practices Seem to Favor Composite Plan," *Nation's Schools*, Vol. 49 (May, 1952), pp. 72-73.

[10] Stuart E. Dean, *Elementary School Administration and Organization* (Washington, D. C., U. S. Department of Health, Education, and Welfare, Office of Education, 1960), pp. 69-71.

[11] Arthur W. Foshay, "A Modest Proposal," *Educational Leadership*, Vol. 18 (May, 1961), p. 513.

[12] Douglas E. Lawson, "An Analysis of Historic and Philosophic Considerations for Homogeneous Grouping," *Educational Administration and Supervision*, Vol. 43 (May, 1957), pp. 268-269.

any conclusive results. It is comparatively easy to find a study that "proves" almost any conclusion one wishes to draw about ability grouping. In general, contradictory evidence and opinion center about the following basic questions.

DOES ABILITY GROUPING AFFECT ACADEMIC ACHIEVEMENT? The evidence is more contradictory on this point than any other. Some studies have found that academic achievement was increased when children were placed in ability groups. Others concluded just the opposite. Some claimed that the abler children benefitted from being grouped together. Others discovered that, if ability grouping favored any level, it was the slow-learning children who profited. The following summaries of research reveal these contradictions.

There is no evidence that ability grouping, taken by itself, leads to improved mastery of subject matter.

Even if we take the most favorable position, which some investigators hold, that there is a slight balance of evidence in favor of ability grouping, the difference is minuscule and bears no relation whatever to the optimistic popular expectation of a signal change.

Again, even if we posit the greatest advantage from grouping that the data could possibly support, that advantage has rarely gone to the ablest group, on whose behalf the current movement is largely sponsored. The anticipated sharp rise of the high group as soon as it was "set free" has generally failed to appear.

If any one group has at all consistently gained from grouping it has been the low group. There is also substantial evidence that special programs for the mentally retarded are beneficial.[13]

The evidence, of limited value . . . slightly favors ability grouping in regard to academic achievement, with dull children seeming to profit more than bright children in this regard.[14]

Ability grouping in itself does not produce improved achievement in children. Improved achievement seems rather to result from the manipulation of other complex factors; curriculum adaptation, teaching methods, materials, ability of the teacher to relate to children and other subtle variables.

Contrary to statements in previous summaries of the research on the effects of ability grouping on children's achievement . . . more recent research evidence seems to indicate that ability grouping actually may be detrimental to children in the average and lower ability groups. These children appear to suffer from the deprivation of intellectual stimulation when brighter children are removed from the class. Conversely the brighter children did not appear

[13] Fred T. Wilhelms and Dorothy Westby-Gibson, "Grouping: Research Offers Leads," *Educational Leadership*, Vol. 18 (April, 1961), p. 411.

[14] John I. Goodlad, "Classroom Organization," *Encyclopedia of Educational Research*, 3rd ed., Chester W. Harris, ed. (New York, The Macmillan Company, 1960), p. 224.

to suffer when left with the average and lower ability students, at least through the elementary school.[15]

Despite the apparent logic of the contention that a teacher can achieve better results when confronted with a group which is relatively similar in learning ability, the available research on grouping practices does not provide consistent support for this contention.[16]

Altho contradictory findings have come from the many studies, a summary of the evidence slightly favors ability grouping as contrasted with heterogeneous grouping in academic learning. Standard tests of academic achievement, particularly where adaptations of standards, materials, and methods are made, show that pupils make slightly larger gains under ability grouping. The evidence for ability grouping indicates greatest relative effectiveness in academic learning for dull children, next greatest for average children, and least for bright children. This conclusion must be regarded as tentative.[17]

One conclusion emerges clearly from the above summaries. *There is no substantial and conclusive evidence to indicate that, in the elementary school, ability grouping per se improves the academic achievement of learners or any specific type of learners.* Those who advocate or institute ability grouping on the basis of academic gain apparently do so in ignorance or with disregard of the currently conflicting evidence.

DOES ABILITY GROUPING REDUCE THE RANGE OF INDIVIDUAL DIFFERENCES WITHIN THE GROUP? On this point, there is considerably more agreement than on the previous one. Most educators agree that, because of the wide range of intra-individual differences in each student, ability grouping does not reduce the range of variability except in the single criterion used as the basis for grouping. The following statements support this conclusion.

Ability grouping in elementary schools especially is woefully inadequate in reducing to any great extent academic differences of more than one variable.[18]

One investigator after another has uncovered roughly the same facts: Suppose we take a total population of children at any grade level; record for each not only his I. Q. and M. A. but also data on, say, eight or ten other variables—reading speed and comprehension, arithmetic reasoning and computation, and so on. Now divide these children into three levels *by any criterion or combination index you care to choose.* . . . How much will you reduce the total

[15] Maurice J. Eash, "Grouping: What Have We Learned?" *Educational Leadership*, Vol. 18 (April, 1961), p. 430.

[16] Miriam L. Goldberg and A. Harry Passow, "The Effects of Ability Grouping," *Education*, Vol. 82 (April, 1962), p. 486.

[17] J. Wayne Wrightstone, *Class Organization for Instruction*, What Research Says to the Teacher (Washington, D. C., Department of Classroom Teachers, American Educational Research Association of the National Education Association, 1957), p. 8.

[18] Maurice J. Eash, *op. cit.*, p. 432.

variability within each group? by two thirds? by half? No, you will be lucky if you reduce it by one-fifth. The layman and the unsophisticated teacher may —and do—continue to think of each subgroup as "homogeneous"; the expert knows it is still rampantly heterogeneous, concealing tremendous ranges on all but the one variable chosen as the basis for division.[19]

Is student variability materially reduced through ability grouping? When a broad range of human characteristics is considered, the answer is "not much." . . . Research suggests the following generalizations concerning the extent to which ability grouping reduces variability in achievement: (a) Ability grouping only imperceptibly reduces student variability when a broad range of academic, intellectual, physical, and social traits is considered. (b) When students of a given grade level are divided into A and B classes, or A, B, and C classes according to general ability, variability in school achievement is reduced about 7 and 17 percent, respectively. (c) When this kind of grouping is accompanied by vertical regrouping so that bright and slow students advance on separate promotional tracks, attainment variability is reduced about ten percent more. One kind of frequently advocated ability grouping—segregating the bright and the slow from the average group on the basis of a general ability criterion such as IQ—falls far short of achieving the virtues claimed for it.[20]

DOES ABILITY GROUPING THREATEN THE MENTAL HEALTH AND SELF-CONCEPT OF PUPILS? As Wrightstone says, "The data regarding the effects of ability grouping upon the personal characteristics of pupils are so inadequate or subjective in character that no valid conclusions can be drawn."[21] However, the mere fact that some, if not necessarily all, studies reveal that pupils' mental health is endangered by ability grouping should be of grave concern to conscientious teachers. One such study reported that twenty-five of thirty children in a "high" group explained their placements in such responses as, "I'm smart," "I work hard," "We're smarter," or, "We can work a little faster." Conversely, fourteen of the eighteen children in the lowest ability group revealed negative self-concepts through such remarks as, "I am not so smart," "I can't think good," "Most of us are lazy," or, "I'm too dumb."[22] Byers comments upon the effects of ability grouping on the self-concept as follows:

The effect on the self-concept of all children involved in homogeneous grouping is especially interesting. Children who are not in the gifted sections evidence feelings of worthlessness and sometimes of rejection. In a society that has often been enriched by ideas, inventions, and innovations from people who are not intellectually gifted, should we discourage children who are not en-

[19] Fred T. Wilhelms and Dorothy Westby-Gibson, *op. cit.*, p. 411.
[20] John I. Goodlad, *op. cit.*, p. 224.
[21] J. Wayne Wrightstone, *op. cit.*, p. 8.
[22] Maxine Mann, "What Does Ability Grouping Do to the Self-Concept?" *Childhood Education*, Vol. 36 (April, 1960), p. 360.

dowed with unusual intellectual powers? Should the school follow placement policies that limit the aspirations that these children set for themselves?[23]

Is ABILITY GROUPING UNDEMOCRATIC? It was pointed out in Chapter 6 that the low academic achiever is frequently from a low socio-economic, culturally and experientially deprived subculture. Thus, many argue that grouping upon the basis of academic achievement results in an undemocratic class system within the school. Luchins and Luchins[24] claimed the existence of such a class system as a result of their study of ability grouping and Bettelheim points to the serious danger of replacing the "white color elite with an even more securely established and more up-to-date elite—the white-collar elite."[25] He adds,

The younger the child, the more his school achievement and his attitude toward school and learning reflect parental attitudes and home background. In the early grades the child is strictly the product of his home, for the school has barely begun to exercise its full influence. It is usually only in senior high school that the young adult can free himself sufficiently from handicaps in his home background to give full play to his native talents. If children are grouped before high school, instead of equalizing differences in home background, the school will only add to them the agony of intellectual differences.[26]

Eash agrees with this viewpoint.

Grouping practices which separate students on the basis of ability as determined by group IQ or standardized tests reduce the likelihood that students will be exposed to a broader range of ethnic and cultural differences in the society.

Pressures to institute certain grouping practices in our schools represent pervasive social problems in our culture. Educators need to be doubly alert that the schools are not utilizing grouping practices which assist in maintaining and promoting social and racial biases which militate against the general education objectives, equal educational opportunity and the development of each person as an individual.[27]

There are, of course, those who take exactly the opposite point of view and contend that equality does not necessarily mean sameness. Lawson argues that,

Homogeneous grouping actually is an attempt to recognize each child's democratic right to an education that he can handle, to an education that will help

[23] Loretta Byers, "Ability Grouping—Help or Hindrance to Social and Emotional Growth," *School Review*, Vol. 69 (Winter, 1961), p. 455.

[24] Abraham S. and Edith H. Luchins, "Children's Attitudes Toward Homogeneous Grouping," *Journal of Genetic Psychology*, Vol. 72 (March, 1948), pp. 3-9.

[25] Bruno Bettelheim, "Segregation: New Style," *School Review*, Vol. 66 (Autumn, 1958), p. 264.

[26] *Ibid.*, p. 261.

[27] Maurice J. Eash, *op. cit.*, p. 431.

him individually to achieve his own maximum of self-realization, happiness, and effective growth. Homogeneous grouping is the very antithesis of an autocratic regimentation and an imposed uniformity.

Intelligent clinical studies of children show that some need one dietary regimen while others need a different prescription. The same fact is true in educational prescription. No one accuses the medical prescriptionist of being undemocratic! The very heart of democracy in education is in the determination to measure each child's weaknesses and strengths—and to see that the requirements and the opportunities are consistently tailored to his needs. Properly conducted and with adequately skilled guidance, homogeneous grouping is a step in this direction.[28]

It should be pointed out here that "individual prescription" does not necessarily imply ability grouping. It may mean just the opposite. Arguments that stress the frustrations of the slow in competing with the bright or the unfairness of holding the superior back in favor of the average or slow are based upon the traditional lock-step, single-textbook, mass teaching, identical assignment, narrow curriculum concept of the classroom only. This point is discussed further in the next section.

DOES ABILITY GROUPING FOSTER OR HAMPER THE DEVELOPMENT OF CREATIVITY? The previous chapter discussed the growing interest in all aspects of creativity. Recent research has demonstrated clearly that the creative individual is not necessarily the high academic achiever or the one who scores highest on standardized intelligence tests. Consequently many educators are concerned that grouping according to achievement or intelligence, as now determined by available instruments, may ignore, penalize, or stigmatize the independent and creative thinker whose talents are so badly needed today.

WHAT ARE TEACHERS' OPINIONS CONCERNING ABILITY GROUPING? In general, the evidence appears to indicate that a number of teachers favor ability grouping. A recent poll[29] revealed that 57.6 per cent of elementary teachers approved of ability grouping, 33.1 per cent disapproved, and 9.3 per cent were undecided. These results agree generally with those of earlier surveys. What are some of the possible reasons why some teachers prefer this method of grouping?

In the first place, it is entirely possible that many teachers have great faith in the ability of evaluative techniques and guidance procedures to place a child in a group of similar abilities. The trust of these teachers is exceeded only by their professional naviete.

Secondly, some teachers may favor ability grouping because it permits them to ignore the fact of individual differences. This is, of course, the

[28] Douglas E. Lawson, *op. cit.*, p. 266.
[29] "Teacher Opinion Poll," *NEA Journal*, Vol. 50 (April, 1961), p. 62.

serious weakness of the graded school. It deludes teachers into thinking in terms of a single group, rather than according to individuals. If every grade is further subdivided into "fast," "average," and "slow," there is even greater danger that the teacher will direct his instruction toward *a group* instead of toward twenty-five or thirty individuals. Thus, the possibility exists that ability grouping may actually make *less*, not greater, provision for individual differences. This danger is suggested in the following statement: "The myth [of homogeneity] can be a dangerous one, leading teachers to impose a stereotype upon a group and, by teaching to an assumed *type*, make *less* provision for the unique individuals than they would in classes they knew to be heterogenous.[30] Is it possible then, that some teachers prefer ability grouping because it is "easier" in that they can teach to a group instead of to individuals, without too much damage to their consciences?

Thirdly, some psychologists suggest that certain teachers prefer ability grouping because it contributes to their success needs and job satisfactions. In a typical situation where high, average, and low groups are rotated each year among teachers, each teacher may anticipate a reasonable degree of success for two out of three years. The third year? Well, any teacher can suffer through that as long as he is consoled with the thought that next year he'll again be blessed with the top group.

That such an attitude is grossly unfair to children to whom this nation has guaranteed equal educational opportunities should be obvious and needs no further comment here.

INTERCLASS GROUPING IS A MODIFIED FORM OF ABILITY GROUPING. Interclass or cross-class grouping classifies children according to ability in one or more curricular areas only, such as reading or arithmetic. In some systems, the regrouping is on a single grade level. In others, an attempt is made to group together regardless of grade level. Although this plan avoids the rigid stratification of total ability grouping, in general it is open to the same criticisms as ability grouping and departmentalization, discussed later in this section.

In summary, it can be concluded that agreement is far from unanimous concerning the advantages and disadvantages of ability grouping. Undoubtedly, it is being used with varying degrees of success in some school systems. Some have reinstituted it as a result of community pressures and national concern for a tightening up of the school program. Others have resorted to it in a sincere attempt to provide an adequate educational program for all. That it may fail to do this has been suggested throughout our discussion. That many look with favor upon alternative grouping plans is evident.

[30] Fred T. Wilhelms and Dorothy Westby-Gibson, *op. cit.*, p. 412.

WHAT ARE THE ALTERNATIVES TO ABILITY GROUPING? In the graded school, many prefer grouping according to social balance rather than academic ability. One popular basis for social grouping is the chronological age, defended by such statements as the following: "Since chronological age is the only common predictable characteristic about a given group of children and since it is the basis on which they are admitted to school, it is the best basis for grouping *most* children.[31]

Other schools group upon the broad base of over-all social maturity, of which the chronological age is only one indication. Still others are experimenting with classifying children according to sociometric choices. In this plan, children are asked in June to name children with whom they would or would not like to be placed the following year. These choices are observed insofar as possible in determining the composition of class groups.

A deliberate attempt to achieve heterogeneity is made by some schools. Classifying children purely by chance (in alphabetical order or by pulling names out of the hat) will achieve the desired heterogeneity, according to some. Others follow a system of planned heterogeneity in which clusters or small groups of children of widely varying abilities and interests are joined together in a single class.

Other alternatives are discussed later in this section.

Departmentalization

The present discussion of this controversial topic refers only to departmentalizing grades one through six. It does not pertain to the secondary school where additional problems and issues must be considered.

Departmentalization in the elementary school is, at the moment, as controversial as ability grouping. The term has been defined as follows: "An arrangement whereby each instructor teaches only one or two subjects in which he is a specialist; either the teacher moves from room to room to teach the various classes or the pupils shift from room to room during the successive periods of the school day.[32]

The opposite type of organization is the one-teacher-per-class plan known generally as the self-contained classroom. It has been defined as follows: "The self-contained classroom plan is a type of curricular organization which allows one group of students and one teacher to be together for a major portion of the school day in the elementary school. . . ."[33]

[31] Warren A. Ketcham, "How Should We Look at Levels—From Child Growth and Development," *Childhood Education*, Vol. 32 (December, 1955), p. 159.

[32] Carter V. Good, editor, *Dictionary of Education*, 2nd ed. (New York, McGraw-Hill Book Company, Inc., 1959), p. 163.

[33] Association for Supervision and Curriculum Development, *The Self-Contained Classroom*, Edith Roach Snyder, ed. (Washington, D. C., Association for Supervision and Curriculum Development of the National Education Association, 1960), p. 1.

It should be pointed out at the beginning of this discussion that, as Miel[34] suggests, the term *self-contained classroom* may be a misnomer. It is not an "isolation ward" (to use Miel's expression), in which a single teacher and group of pupils rely entirely upon their own resources. Rather, it is an arrangement that permits one teacher to assume the major responsibility for guiding the learning experiences of a group, while at the same time drawing freely upon other school and community resources and personnel whenever it is beneficial to the pupils to do so.

Departmentalization was introduced around the turn of the century, grew in popularity during the early decades and subsequently declined. Dunn reveals the declining trend in her study of 104 city school systems from 1920 to 1950.

1920-1929—Departmentalization ranged from five per cent in the primary grades (1-3) to thirty-seven percent in grade six.

1930-1939—Departmentalization ranged from seven percent in the primary grades to thirty-three percent in grade six.

1940-1949—Departmentalization ranged from three percent in the primary grades to eighteen percent in grade six.[35]

Today, according to a recent survey,

For grades 1 through 6 more than three-quarters of the elementary schools throughout the Nation use the one-teacher-per-classroom type of instructional organization. Slightly less than 10 percent of the schools use partial departmentalization. Complete departmentalization is negligible.[36]

A similar survey of 806 city schools reported that 44 per cent were departmentalized in one subject or more, with the most frequently departmentalized subjects being (1) music, (2) physical education, (3) art, (4) arithmetic, (5) science, (6) reading, (7) social studies, (8) library, (9) English, and (10) Language Arts. It was also noted that "Few subjects other than music, physical education and art were departmentalized below grade four."[37]

Simply stated, the present controversy centers about two diametrically opposite points of view. On the one hand, there are those who firmly believe that "because of the increasing accumulation and importance of modern knowledge it is no longer possible for the traditionally trained

[34] Alice Miel, "The Self-Contained Classroom: An Assessment," *Teachers College Record*, Vol. 59 (February, 1958), pp. 282-291.

[35] Mary Dunn, "Should There Be Any Set Type of Elementary School Organization?" *Elementary School Journal*, Vol. 53 (December, 1952), p. 202.

[36] Stuart E. Dean, *op. cit.*, pp. 29-30.

[37] Roland E. Barnes, "A Survey of Status and Trends in Departmentalization in City Elementary Schools," *Journal of Educational Research*, Vol. 55 (March, 1962), p. 292.

elementary school teacher to be capable of teaching all subjects to all children with equal skill and effectiveness"; on the other hand some believe "that the advancing science of human growth and development indicates that it is more important for a child of elementary school age to have a close contact with a single teacher who will be in a position to understand him and to provide for his individual differences in ability, maturation, and potential."[38] Let us examine the advantages claimed by each viewpoint.

WHAT ADVANTAGES ARE CLAIMED FOR A DEPARTMENTALIZED ORGANIZATION IN THE ELEMENTARY SCHOOL? The chief advantage repeatedly claimed is that it produces greater instructional efficiency by requiring teachers to teach only in one or two fields of specialization. According to some, the rapidly expanding horizons of knowledge in all areas, the addition of new content to the elementary curriculum, and the present concern over the development of high-level talent demand a departmentalized or specialized instructional staff. It is interesting to note, however, that thus far research has failed to demonstrate the superiority of departmentalization as far as academic achievement is concerned. Many studies over the years such as those of Stewart,[39] Vernon,[40] Hosley,[41] and Woods[42] have revealed either that academic gain was greater in a nondepartmentalized organization or that the difference between the two plans was negligible.

A second advantage claimed is that departmentalization or partial departmentalization in the elementary school facilitates articulation with the secondary school. Its proponents point to the abrupt transition made by the pupil from a one-teacher elementary class to a complex secondary school organization, and claim that some type of earlier departmentalization would ease this transition. The following statement points up the weakness of this argument. An excuse

. . . often offered for departmentalizing the elementary school is that junior high schools are departmentalized and elementary schools had better fellow suit to "get the children ready" for junior high schools. One of us recently

[38] Stuart E. Dean, *op. cit.,* pp. 28-29.

[39] Alfred W. Stewart, *A Comparison of Departmental and Grade Teaching* (unpublished Doctoral Dissertation, Ohio State University, 1927).

[40] Chester B. Vernon, *A Comparative Study of the Results Secured in Platoon and Conventional Elementary Schools* (unpublished Doctoral Dissertation, University of Southern California, 1935).

[41] Charles Thomas Hosley, *Learning Outcomes of Sixth Grade Pupils Under Alternate Grade Organization Patterns* (unpublished Doctoral Dissertation, Stanford University, 1954).

[42] Roy C. Woods, "Relative Merits of Departmental and Nondepartmental Elementary Schools," *Peabody Journal of Education,* Vol. 37 (November, 1959), pp. 164-169.

heard a school official defend departmentalization on the ground that the junior high schools will not modify their organization to the extent of undepartmentalizing the seventh and eighth grades. Therefore, he said, the elementary schools should departmentalize in the upper grades to "prepare" the children, even though departmentalization might not be the best arrangement for them. This line of reasoning, followed to its logical and ridiculous conclusion, would end only with the departmentalization of the kindergarten.[43]

A third advantage is concerned with the fair distribution of teaching talent. In every elementary school there are a few superior teachers. In a nondepartmentalized organization, the fortunate pupils may enjoy the exclusive services of these teachers for an entire year. The less fortunate may never meet them. In a departmentalized plan, it is possible to distribute the superior teachers over a wider pupil population.

WHAT ARE THE ADVANTAGES CLAIMED FOR THE SELF-CONTAINED CLASS-ROOM? The greatest benefit claimed for the self-contained classroom is the improved teacher-pupil relationship. Working with a single group of children over a prolonged period of time offers the teacher greater insight and understanding of their needs, abilities, and interests. As far as the pupil is concerned, the immature youngster needs the steady guidance and supervision of one teacher rather than being forced to adjust to six or more teacher personalities and classroom standards. The point is made by Miel as follows:

It is very important that a child have the help of a sensitive, accepting adult in assessing his strengths and weaknesses and in setting his aspiration level with respect to various facets of intellectual, physical, and social achievement. It is important that an adult who matters as much to a child as does a teacher have a chance to know the child as a total operating individual, not just as a learner of arithmetic, a reader, a speller, or a singer.

In a departmentalized setup it is hard for a child to qualify with the teacher of arithmetic if he is poor in that area, even though he may be adequate or even gifted in art or writing. To balance success and failure in one's school life, and to make constructive use of both, require guidance during the growing years by a sympathetic teacher who knows each pupil well and who has responsibility for few enough children to be able to care about each member of his class as a complete, learning person. The self-contained classroom gives the teacher opportunity to provide the kind of teacher-pupil relationships which foster mental health.[44]

Secondly, the self-contained classroom offers greater opportunity for the establishment of wholesome group relationships. According to Miel,

---

[43] Lawrence O. Lobdell and William J. Van Ness, "The Self-contained Classroom in the Elementary School," *Elementary School Journal*, Vol. 63 (January, 1963), p. 215.
[44] Alice Miel, *op. cit.*, p. 284.

". . . it is difficult for a group to build a healthy, supportive esprit de corps when the status leadership changes every hour or so and, with it, expectations, standards, rules, and preferences change. . . . Later on, when the children are older, they can much more easily take on the task of responding to differences in leadership."[45]

Thirdly, the nondepartmentalized administrative organization lends itself more easily to the establishment and utilization of a rich and exciting classroom intellectual environment (as described in Chapter 6).

Fourth, the flexibility of scheduling possible in the self-contained classroom is an advantage when dealing with the ephemeral interests, limited attention spans, spontaneous concerns, and varied abilities of elementary school youngsters.

Fifth, the flexible scheduling of the self-contained classroom permits time for cooperative planning and group evaluation sessions.

Sixth, it is possible that the self-contained classroom permits greater attention to the development of wholesome value judgments, social skills, and social attitudes than when the entire day is allocated to academic areas, as it may be in a departmentalized plan.

Seventh, the self-contained classroom permits (but does not guarantee) the functional integration of learning experiences.

Eighth, the self-contained classroom may promote stronger home-school relationships than the departmentalized plan. A teacher may know, and work more closely, with the fifty parents of pupils in a single class than he can with the two hundred or more parents of the children he may teach in a departmentalized set-up. It is also true that parents who can identify with a single teacher may feel closer to the school than those who must contact six or seven teachers to discover "how Johnny is doing in school." (Perhaps this is one of the reasons why Parent-Teacher Organizations are generally more active and more prevalent in elementary schools than in secondary schools.) Also, the parent-teacher conference which is replacing written report cards in many systems (see Chapter 11) is beyond the realm of practicality in the departmentalized organization.

THE DUAL PROGRESS PLAN IS A CURRENT PLAN FOR DEPARTMENTALIZING THE ELEMENTARY SCHOOL. Considerable publicity has recently been given to the Dual Progress Plan, originated by George B. Stoddard. According to this plan, the program is divided into the following curricular areas: Language Arts-Social Studies; Mathematics; Science; Health and Physical Education; Arts and Crafts; Music; and Foreign Languages. Each of these is taught by a specialist. Children are ability-grouped on grade levels for

[45] *Ibid.*, p. 284.

a half day's instruction in the "cultural imperatives," of language arts-social studies and physical education. For the other half of the day, pupils are ability-grouped, regardless of grade levels, for instruction in the "cultural electives" of science, mathematics, arts and crafts, music, and foreign languages.[46] Since the plan employs both ability grouping and departmentalization, the preceding statements of this chapter would seem to apply to it as well.

Multigrade Grouping

Multigrade or interage grouping is "a plan whereby children classified in one of two or three sequential grades are assigned to a single class comprising two or more grade levels."[47] Thus, instead of having thirty fourth-graders or thirty nine-year-olds in a single class, a teacher may have ten fourth-graders, ten fifth-graders, and ten sixth-graders. Each of these pupils may be working on several grade levels. A youngster, for instance, may be in grade four for reading, grade five for arithmetic, and grade six for social studies. According to one advocate, the plan provides maximum opportunity "to meet the individual needs of all boys and girls, by combining the flexibility of the old country school, the facilities of a modern city school and the know how of present day research."[48]

There is little doubt that the plan permits greater flexibility than the regular graded school while, at the same time, retaining the traditional grade levels. Another interesting feature is that, in some systems, only a portion of the group leaves the teacher at the end of any year. For instance, a teacher of a fourth-fifth-sixth grade group, each June may lose his sixth-graders and each September welcome a new fourth-grade group. Thus, it is necessary for the teacher to become acquainted with only about ten new pupils each year instead of an entirely new class. This plan, also, enables the teacher to work closely with each child over a three-year rather than a one-year span (which has many advantages and some disadvantages). Another claimed advantage is that the increased range no longer permits a teacher to succumb to the comfortable illusion that he is teaching to a single level of ability. He is, therefore, forced to recognize and provide for the widely varying abilities that confront him. The following is a summary of the advantages of the plan as seen in one situation.

[46] George B. Stoddard, *The Dual Progress Plan* (New York, Harper & Row, Publishers, Inc., 1961), p. 5.

[47] "Elementary School Organization, Purposes, Patterns, Perspective," *The National Elementary Principal*, Vol. 41 (December, 1961), p. 83.

[48] Wesley H. Carlson, "Interage Grouping," *Educational Leadership*, Vol. 15 (March, 1958), p. 363.

1. Older children seem to gain from helping younger children.

2. Younger children seem to learn from older.

3. Wider range of experiences and interests stimulates all.

4. Teacher attitude when faced with three grades seems to include a do-something-about-it-attitude.

5. Peer rivalry may to some extent be replaced by friendly acceptance of difference when the grade level loses its significance through spread of ability and interests.

6. Children gain the advantage of experiencing being in the younger, middle and older group on successive years rather than always having to view the situation from one position year after year.[49]

Nongraded Grouping

Since the 1950's there have been various attempts to replace the graded elementary school with a nongraded organization. Because of various modifications and conflicting definitions, it is difficult to determine the exact number of schools now using this plan in one form or another, although Goodlad estimates that ". . . there may well be close to 1,000 nongraded schools in existence in the United States as of 1962."[50]

The most common form of the nongraded school is undoubtedly the *primary unit* which commonly includes the first three grades, with or without the kindergarten. There are many types of nongraded primary units in existence at the present time. One of the best known units is the Milwaukee Primary School which was started in one school in January, 1942 and has since been adopted on a voluntary basis in 114 of 116 Milwaukee elementary schools.[51] After kindergarten, the pupil enters the first semester of the Primary School and is labeled simply as P^1. The designations of P^1 to P^8 simply indicate the number of semesters the child has been enrolled in the primary school. They do not designate the academic progress. Placement of each pupil is made according to over-all maturity and his specific needs.

As a result, most primary school classes above P^1 include several semester groupings, such as P^{3-4} or P^{4-5-6}. . . .

The total length of time a child spends in the primary school depends upon his abilities, accomplishments, and readiness for advancement to grade four.

---

[49] J. H. Hull, "Multigrade Teaching," *Nation's Schools*, Vol. 62 (July, 1958), p. 35. Copyright 1958, The Modern Hospital Publishing Co., Inc., Chicago. All rights reserved.

[50] John I. Goodlad, "Individual Differences and Vertical Organization of the School, *Individualizing Instruction*, Nelson B. Henry, ed., Sixty-first Yearbook, National Society for the Study of Education (Chicago, University of Chicago Press, 1962), p. 228.

[51] Florence C. Kelly, "Ungraded Primary School," *Educational Leadership*, Vol. 18 (November, 1960), pp. 79-80.

The range is from four to eight semesters. For most children, the work requires six semesters.[52]

Another type of primary unit is that which groups the children largely upon the basis of their progress in reading. Goodlad and Anderson describe this type of program as it operates in Park Forest, Illinois.

In Park Forest, children are assigned to the Ungraded Primary School after one year in kindergarten. Since all of the Park Forest schools are relatively large, with at least two or three beginning primary class groups each September, there usually are between six and ten primary classrooms in each building. All are labeled "Primary, Miss (Jones)." Parent-teacher conferences and interim prose reports are used to report progress, and no numerical or alphabetical marks are employed. At the end of the first year, the child receives a printed or mimeographed "promotion letter" which states simply that the child has completed one year in primary and is reassigned to primary school. In cases where the child has made so little progress that the necessity for a fourth year in the program seems quite possible, a supplementary statement to that effect may be included in the promotion letter. Although this latter procedure has certain disadvantages, it precludes the possibility of misunderstanding and seems to be appreciated by the parents. . . .

Similar reports are given the parents at the end of the second year. At the end of the third year, parents of those who are ready for fourth grade receive a letter or report describing the child's assignment to a fourth-grade class. The relatively few children who need another year are simply reassigned to Primary School by means of a letter or report similar to those received the two previous years. . . .

Class assignments are based largely upon reading readiness and progress, the theory being that division into slow, typical, and advanced reading groups simplifies the teaching task in the early school years. Although this is a form of ability grouping, experience seems to indicate that the groups have a fairly normal ability range and are essentially heterogeneous except for the reading factor. Each teacher usually divides her class into three reading groups representing the three reading levels.

Whenever a child progresses so well that he no longer fits into the most advanced reading group in his class, the teacher confers with the principal, and a study is made of the desirability of changing his class assignment to another primary teacher. Although reading progress is a dominant factor in these discussions, the principal and teachers involved are also very careful to analyze the social, emotional, and general academic effects of the proposed transfer. Usually the transfer would be made to a class in which the *middle* reading group is working at the child's present level; this is to prevent the necessity for another transfer in the event the child reaches a "plateau" period (he can then be changed to a lower group in the same room) or continues to spurt ahead (in which case he can move to the top group, again in the same

[52] *Ibid.*, p. 80.

room). If a transfer seems desirable, it is made immediately, since there is no semester schedule to follow. Almost always, a parent conference involving the principal is arranged to explain the transfer. The same procedure, in reverse, is followed for children who lag behind.[53]

Another type of primary unit abolishes grade levels in favor of levels of achievement in one particular field, such as reading or arithmetic. In a typical plan, the reading program of the first three grades is arranged in a carefully graded sequence of as few as ten and as many as thirty-two levels. Each level is carefully defined in terms of standards of achievement and reading materials covered. Classes are formed consisting of several levels. Thus, the child progresses at his own rate through the first three or four years of school according to perhaps thirty-two narrow steps instead of the three or four broader steps he formerly took. The following statements are interesting reactions to this plan.

The idea of further subdividing already closely graded instruction so that groups of learners can be guided through it more efficiently is most fully developed in some of the plans for the ungraded primary. Levels are set up to correspond to sequentially arranged materials, usually textbooks in a reading series, through which abler learners move more rapidly and the less able more slowly.

Ironically, the ungraded school thus defined becomes a school of many levels. How much can be covered how quickly—this criterion of progress combines quantity and rate to carry the old conception of the curriculum to a new point of impoverishment. The boundaries of the narrowed program close in even more tightly on all learners. . . .[54]

. . . one is struck by the lack of "fit" between many so-called primary units and the criteria of individuality, continuous pupil progress, and flexibility these units presumably are to serve. Many plans organized into arbitrary subject-matter levels appear more graded than the "graded" schemes which they presumably replaced.[55]

Summary

In this section we have examined briefly some of the more common administrative plans devised to meet the problem of individual differences. It should be fairly obvious that some are more promising than others. In general, however, many of them suffer from a common weakness: *they are based upon a very limited concept of the learner and the learning*

---

[53] John I. Goodlad and Robert H. Anderson, *The Nongraded Elementary School* (New York, Harcourt, Brace and World, Inc., 1959), pp. 72-73.

[54] Alexander Frazier, "Needed: A New Vocabulary for Individual Differences," *Elementary School Journal*, Vol. 61 (February, 1961), p. 263.

[55] John I. Goodlad, *op. cit.*, p. 235.

process. Some, for instance, attempt to provide for individual differences solely by attempting to eliminate them, or at least to reduce the range in any single group. That the complexity and intravariability of each person makes this relatively impossible has already been discussed. As Parker and Russell say, "The more modern, detailed studies of children seem to suggest that homogeneous grouping of two children is impossible, much less that of thirty or thirty-five youngsters. The general school population is not divisible into three or four ready-made groups."[56]

Furthermore, in the opinion of many, the attempt to reduce the range of differences among individuals is not only impractical but distinctly undesirable. The strength of a democracy lies in the diverse talents and contributions of its population. Instead of seeking to submerge or reduce human differences, we should not merely recognize and accept them, but go further and capitalize upon them, encourage them, and promote them.

Other administrative plans are impractical because they are based upon a very narrow concept of the learning process. Some, for instance, attempt to provide for varied abilities by varying only the rate of learning, on the theory that the able learner is a fast learner. Thus, in some plans (such as the early multiple-track plans and the current levels plan of nongrading) a single program of content is laid out which all children are expected to "cover," but at different rates of speed. The fallacy of this principle is obvious. As Frazier says, "Rate is one dimension of learning, but only one of many,"[57] and plans that take into consideration only this one aspect of learning, can hardly be said to be providing adequately for individual differences.

Still other plans vary only the *amount* of learning required of pupils on the theory that the able learner differs only in that he can learn *more* than his less capable peers. This, too, obviously is based upon a limited concept of learning that does not recognize that "more and less" is only one of the countless ways in which mental and academic abilities vary among the human population.

The conclusion is obvious and meets with general agreement today. No administrative plan *per se* can make adequate provision for the individual differences of pupils. No administrative plan, *in itself*, regardless of how elaborate it is, can improve the quality of learning of each individual child. *This is the job and the responsibility of the classroom teacher.* Now, it should not be inferred from this statement that the administrative organization is not important and that, after all is said and done, one plan is as good as another. This is completely false! For al-

[56] J. Cecil Parker and David H. Russell, "Ways of Providing for Individual Differences," *Educational Leadership*, Vol. 11 (December, 1953), p. 169.
[57] Alexander Frazier, *op. cit.*, p. 261.

though the administrative pattern cannot do the job, it can, and does, greatly facilitate or handicap the teacher's efforts in this direction. This leaves the teacher with two all-important obligations.

In the first place, he should have a knowledge of the various administrative plans now proposed for the elementary school. He should be able to appraise objectively the values and limitations of each. He should be fully aware of the extent to which each proposal supports the goals of elementary education in our present democratic society. He should look with interest upon any experimentation and research that offers promise for an improved school organization. Last but not least, he should support strongly in his local community a school organization that, in his best professional judgment, offers greatest promise for a quality education for each and every individual child. By the same token, he should resist strongly the pressures of those who desire something other than that for the youth of this nation.

Secondly, regardless of the administrative organization in which he works, the classroom teacher must adapt his instructional techniques and procedures to the various pupil differences that confront him daily in the classroom. Suggestions for doing this are contained in the following section.

INSTRUCTIONAL PROVISIONS FOR INDIVIDUAL DIFFERENCES

THE ATTITUDE AND KNOWLEDGE OF THE TEACHER ARE ALL-IMPORTANT. It was previously stated that there is an approximate four-year range of mental age in a typical first grade, and that this range increases on every grade level. In spite of this, certain teachers go along in a comfortable rut firmly believing that they are teaching a single grade level. Goodlad, for instance, reports that a sizable number of the thousands of teachers he queried, did not realize that less than 20 per cent of children enrolled in fourth grade are not at this level in all subjects as measured on standardized tests.[58] Ignorance or disregard of individual differences causes a teacher to err in three common ways, according to Burton.[59]

In the first place, teachers may stubbornly and persistently continue to aim their teaching at a single grade level. The fact that they may, in reality, be directing their efforts to only a handful of pupils apparently bothers them not at all.

The second error is to devote a disproportionate amount of time and effort to the pupils at either extreme. Very often, conscientious teachers spend more than a fair amount of time with the slower pupils. The more

[58] John I. Goodlad, *op. cit.*, p. 217.
[59] William H. Burton, *op. cit.*, p. 239.

able are, therefore, neglected or left to shift for themselves. Or, of course, the opposite is true with some teachers who concentrate on the upper extreme and ignore the slower pupils as long as they don't make any trouble.

The third error is made by the teacher who "understands only those pupils in the class who approximate his own speed or slowness of thought, his temperament, his breadth or narrowness of view" and heaven help those pupils "whose minds, temperaments, and reactions differ from his."[60] Teachers guilty of this error frequently neglect the lower socio-economic child or, as current research reveals, the creative, independent, individualistic, and nonconforming individual. The teacher's understanding of, and attitude toward, his individual pupils is paramount. Nothing, but nothing, replaces or supersedes it.

THE SIZE OF THE CLASS AFFECTS PROVISIONS FOR INDIVIDUAL DIFFERENCES. There is no conclusive research on the most desirable class size in the elementary school. Obviously, if identical teaching procedures are used, it makes little difference if the class has fifteen or fifty members. However, in order to adapt and modify instruction according to the needs of individuals, most authorities agree that the size of the elementary class should not exceed twenty-five pupils. Unfortunately, many public school classes exceed this figure today, for a recent survey reveals the following data.

The median urban elementary-school class contains 30 pupils, with a range from 15 or fewer to 56 or more . . .

Of some 113,164 classes in the 50 largest cities . . . 92.1 percent contain more than 25 pupils each; 65.8 percent, more than 30 pupils each; 23.2 percent, more than 35 pupils each; and in 3.2 percent of these classes each teacher is responsible for more than 40 pupils.

In all urban elementary schools combined, 121,958 pupils are in classes of more than 45 each; 488,752 are in classes of more than 40 each; and 2,652,672 pupils are in classes of 36 or more.[61]

Although these facts are discouraging, there is occasion for some optimism when one realizes that, approximately one hundred years ago, the *average* class size in certain cities was: Buffalo, 46; Cincinnati, 49; St. Louis, 50; Cleveland, 54; Philadelphia, 55; Boston, 57; and Chicago,

[60] *Ibid.*

[61] National Education Association, Research Division, *Class Size in the Elementary Schools in 50 Large Urban School Districts, 1961-1962* (Washington, D. C., National Education Association, October, 1962). National Education Association, Research Division, *Class Size in Urban Elementary Schools, 1962* (Washington, D. C., National Education Association, October, 1962), pp. 5, 11.

78.[62] Apparently, we are moving in the right direction. We just need to move with a little more speed.

AN ABUNDANCE AND VARIETY OF LEARNING AIDS AND MATERIALS ARE ESSENTIAL. This point is discussed at length in Chapters 6 and 10. The only point that needs to be reiterated here is a flat statement that *no* teacher, even if he is a genius, is able to meet the varied needs of his pupils without an adequate supply of varied learning aids. As Wiles states, "The richness of our collection of materials is one of the best measures of the extent to which we try to care for individual differences."[63]

SPECIALIZED RESOURCES AND PERSONNEL SHOULD BE AVAILABLE TO THE CLASSROOM TEACHER. It was stated earlier that no classroom should be an isolation ward. Every elementary classroom, regardless of how self-contained it is, should be enriched by specialized resources. In many schools, these are furnished by the services of staff personnel who operate either as special teachers or consultants, with the latter frequently considered more desirable (see Chapter 5). In others, specialized curricular school centers such as the library, art studio, science center, or skills laboratory are available for use by teacher and pupils. In still others, community personnel are used extensively to enrich the classroom program. In others, classroom teachers may serve as teacher-consultants (see Chapter 8) to provide guidance and advice in their particular fields of strength to other members of the staff. Through these, and other methods, the classroom teacher may coordinate and channel many specialized services toward the enrichment of a learning program for all pupils.

Provided all of these factors are present, the competent teacher may provide effectively for varied pupil abilities through the following techniques.

Grouping

In addition to providing more adequately for varied abilities and interests, grouping within the classroom is an invaluable technique for developing positive social relationships and skills of democratic group action. Intraclassroom groups may be formed according to a variety of purposes. Some of the most common are the following.

Grouping according to specific need. This is the most common basis for the formation of reading, arithmetic, spelling and other skill groups. Essentially, such groups may be of three general types. Probably the most common type is that used in the typical basal reading program in which

---

[62] John McGrath and Leo E. Buehring, "100 Years of School Plant Design," *Nation's Schools*, Vol. 59 (January, 1957), p. 50.

[63] Kimball Wiles, *Teaching for Better Schools* (Englewood Cliffs, N. J., Prentice-Hall, Inc., 1952), p. 253.

Reading groups are usually formed on a basis of common need.

approximately three to five groups operate continuously throughout the year. Such groups are usually formed upon the basis of (1) standardized test scores, (2) reading inventories, and (3) teacher judgment. In most instances the teacher makes the group assignments although some advocate a policy in which children ". . . would elect to join a certain group when they are introduced to the kind of material and the activity of each group."[64] To safeguard the effectiveness of these groups, the following suggestions should be observed.

1. Group placement should be flexible. Too frequently, teachers establish the pattern of their reading groups early in the year and never deviate from it. Psychologists tell us that children possess varying growth profiles and it is perfectly possible that a child who begins the year in one reading group will need to be reclassified several times as the year goes by. A careful reappraisal of each group about every six weeks should help to guarantee proper placement for each individual.

2. Group placement should avoid the dangers of stigmatization and competition. Let us face it, some children are more capable than others. Children know this and it is futile to try to conceal or disguise the fact. On the other hand, there is no need to emphasize it either. There are many subtle ways to lessen the comparison between groups. One is to

[64] Nellie C. Morrison, "Instead of Ability Grouping—What?" *Childhood Education*, Vol. 36 (April, 1960), p. 373.

avoid labeling them as first, second, or third groups but to designate them instead according to the name of their basal reader (the *Good Times Together* group, for instance) or by an individual member (John's group). Incidentally, can we do away with the "bluebirds" and "canaries" labels which are pretty silly and childish for today's sophisticated youngsters. If teaching in a system that uses multiple basal reading series, it usually is a good idea to use a different series with each group. This enables each group to share reading experiences with others in the class and avoids the situation in which youngsters say, "Oh, you're just starting that book? We finished that a long time ago."

A second type of skill or need grouping is grouping in depth and is probably used most frequently in arithmetic. Morton describes it as follows:

The plan . . . provides that the entire class take up each new topic at the same time. As a new topic is presented, the teacher, of course, may vary the plan of instruction according to the abilities of the pupils. Some pupils need more experience with concrete and semiconcrete materials than do others. The teacher shrewdly decides when any pupil is ready to move from the concrete to the semiconcrete, and from the semiconcrete to the abstract. Some pupils, the faster learners, go quickly from the concrete to the abstract. Others require more time to make this important transition. A few may require much time. But no one can be said to have really learned arithmetic until he has taken this step. . . .

After a unit of work has been completed, a carefully prepared diagnostic test is given. This test should indicate precisely where the deficiencies of individual pupils lie. The items of the test should be keyed to the pages in the textbook on which specific topics and phases of topics were developed. After the test has been scored, the teacher has information which can be used for temporarily dividing the class into three groups . . .

1. Those who need another chance to learn; these are the slower learners.

2. Those who have mastered the topic fairly well but who can profit from some extra practice and supplementary exercises. These exercises should be designed to extend and deepen understanding for average learners.

3. Those who excel. These pupils should have new and more difficult materials which are designed to stimulate and challenge, materials which will add further insight and result in a higher level of skill.

It is rarely if ever true that a pupil who is revealed to be a slow learner on one test will be classified as one who excels on another test. However, it not infrequently happens that pupils move back and forth between the slow and the average groups or between the average and the superior groups. The decision as to the group to which a pupil belongs after each test is, of course, left to the teacher.[65]

[65] Robert L. Morton, "Arithmetic," *Providing for Individual Differences in the Elementary School*, Norma E. Cutts and Nicholas Moseley, eds. (Englewood Cliffs, N. J., Prentice-Hall, Inc., 1960), pp. 205-208.

This method of flexible depth grouping is also used frequently in spelling. The teacher administers a pretest at the beginning of each spelling unit to the entire class and, upon the basis of the results, groups the children for developmental instruction.

Both types of need grouping are used by competent teachers with the choice determined by the individual situation. Thus far, research has failed to demonstrate the superiority of one method over the other.

A third type of need grouping is the small remedial group which may work daily with the class but also have a second daily session with the teacher. A unique type of remedial grouping is used with considerable success by Mrs. D. Every week or so, Mrs. D announces to her fifth grade that she will hold a remedial "clinic" or "hospital" group during the last half hour of each day of the following week on a specific skill. One week the group may work on changing common fractions to decimal fractions, another week on practice in skimming reference material, another on rules for adding suffixes and prefixes, and so on. When the topic is announced, children who feel they need extra work on that particular area voluntarily join the group. The only stipulation made is that no one may join or leave the group once it has been formed. This is, of course, to insure a necessary continuity of instruction. Over the years, Mrs. D has found this procedure to be an excellent means of providing additional instruction for those who need it. She finds that children are well aware of their weaknesses and are grateful for the extra opportunity to work on them. Since all membership is voluntary, there is no feeling of stigma attached to the group. Indeed, she finds that children look forward eagerly to the announcement of the area of the next sessions, and joke with their classmates, "Well, I guess I'll go to the clinic this week," or, "See you in the 'hospital' next week!"

Grouping according to a specific task. Group and committee work is begun in the kindergarten, with a certain group of children responsible for feeding the goldfish or collecting the crayons. Its use is expanded continually on each succeeding level until, in the intermediate and upper grades, entire units are developed through group work. There is no better method of developing social responsibility, social integration, respect for each other, qualities of leadership, communication skills, research skills, and democratic principles than through the wise utilization of this type of grouping. The basis for forming the groups varies, although they are most frequently and usually most successfully formed according to the expressed interests of the group—those who want to work on clothing in one group, those on food in another, and so forth. Occasionally the groups are formed successfully on the basis of sociometric choices. A

Committee work helps to develop social responsibilities and desirable interpersonal relationships.

third, and less common method, is for the class to elect or the teacher appoint group chairmen who, in turn, select the members.

Considering the potential values of group work in the elementary school, it is extremely unfortunate that it occasionally deteriorates into a shambles of confusion, chaos, and complete waste of time. To avoid this possibility, the following suggestions are offered.

1. The most successful elementary school groups usually consist of four or five members. Groups of a larger size are harder for young children to manage, and tend to be dominated by the more vocal children with a subsequent neglect of other members.

2. The assignment must be clear and specific. Before the group starts to work, each member must know specifically what the group, as well as he individually, is expected to accomplish in the designated work time.

3. Reference materials should be clearly designated and available. Books and supplementary materials should be placed on a nearby table or shelf, easily available to the group. Many teachers code the materials according to levels of difficulty and suggest, "The books with the yellow

markers will help this group," and, "The books with the blue markers are best for those children who are in John's reading group."

4. Standards for group work should be formulated cooperatively by teacher and pupils. Initial planning sessions should develop the standards of work and conduct expected of each group chairman and member. These can be placed on a chart or chalkboard where they may be referred to constantly.

5. The progress of the groups should be evaluated and appraised continuously. At the close of each work session, the wise teacher encourages a group evaluation session. "Are you satisfied with what we accomplished today?" "Did we meet any problems?" "How could these have been avoided?" "What shall we keep in mind for tomorrow?" These and other questions will help to insure the success of group work.

6. Elementary school work groups need continual supervision from the teacher. Unfortunately some teachers literally turn children loose in group work and then proceed to mark papers or do some other job completely removed from the children. Obviously, nothing is accomplished by the pupils. Committee work is a relatively new experience for elementary school youngsters, and the teacher must guide and supervise the daily progress of each group. A few minutes visit with each group, sitting down and talking over problems, goals, etc., is a valuable aid to the success of group enterprises with young children.

7. If the results of the group's efforts are to be presented as an oral report to the class, the teacher should preview the group's material and delivery. This is to prevent the group from presenting a report from which the audience may gain nothing but misinformation and poor listening habits.

Grouping according to immediate problems. These are the common buzz groups formed for a very short duration to fulfill an immediate purpose. Hock suggests that they be used to ". . . provide opportunities for rapid sharing of homework assignments, for exchange of ideas and experiences, for formulation of problems and questions, for discussion of controversy and differences."[66]

One of the most beneficial uses of buzz groups is the analysis of social behavior and attitudes. Miss F's class, for instance, had engaged in endless bickering with the other sixth grade over the use of the baseball diamond for days, until their differences almost culminated in a free-for-all fight. Miss F returned to the classroom with her pupils and faced them with the following assignment.

"All of you know we have been having playground trouble with the

[66] Louise E. Hock, "Classroom Grouping for Effective Learning," *Educational Leadership*, Vol. 18 (April, 1961), p. 421.

other sixth grade and so far we haven't been able to solve the problem. I am going to ask you to meet in groups of five each for the next ten minutes. During that time I would like you to answer two questions: (1) Exactly what is the cause of trouble between the other class and us? and (2) What can we do to solve the problem? After you have had ten minutes to discuss these two questions, each group will have an opportunity to suggest its answers to the class. Then we'll see what agreements we can reach."

Such a technique is a splendid method for helping children to analyze their own conduct. It is equally valuable in developing a sense of responsibility for individual and group action. Last, but not least, it is a wonderfully efficient and time-saving technique to elicit and capitalize upon the thoughts and suggestions of each single individual.

Grouping according to companionate instruction purposes. For centuries, teachers have known that he who teaches others, teaches himself. A promising, but rather infrequently used, type of grouping is to group two or more children together into a teaching-learning team. Frequently called buddy teaching, this technique employs the services of the abler children to help the slower ones. This does *not* mean a mere exploitation of the one or two ablest children in the room. *All* children may serve as teachers or learners with each other at one time or another. A slow academic learner may occasionally instruct other children in a constructional activity. Another may supervise a group that is working on a wall mural. Another may supervise a dramatic production. In a class of twenty-five or thirty youngsters, there are limitless possibilities of grouping and regrouping so that children may learn from each other. Children can frequently understand and communicate with each other more effectively than they can with the most skillful teacher. Also, such grouping helps to develop understandings of the limitations and strengths all of us possess.

Grouping according to a common interest. Small hobby clubs are found in many elementary classrooms. Many teachers schedule one period a week for these clubs so that children may have an opportunity to meet with others of similar interests.

In summary, it should be stated that grouping within the classroom is an effective means of adapting instruction to varied pupil abilities, when it is done by an intelligent teacher to serve a specific purpose for specific pupils. Mere subgrouping for its own sake is not, of course, any more of a guarantee of effective learning than any of the administrative plans discussed in the previous section. As Wrightstone says, "It must be emphasized that grouping, *per se*, does not automatically provide better learning or improved instruction. To be effective, it must have purpose

Hobby clubs are found in many elementary classrooms.

and meaning for both the classroom teacher and the child. When there is real understanding of the *why* of grouping, it becomes an effective aid to better teaching."[67]

Independent Study

Working with children in groups obviously requires other members of the class to work independently. Making provision for these children has been a concern of the teacher since the days of the one-room schoolhouse. Originally, independent work was labeled "busy work" or "seat work" since its chief purpose was to keep the nonreciting group quiet and busy. Such assignments as copying all the three-letter words, or all the words beginning with *A*, in one's reader achieved this purpose admirably.

Today, independent study is not considered merely as a necessary evil that accompanies group work. To the contrary, depending upon the type, independent study can serve several important purposes and produce many educationally desirable values.

[67] J. Wayne Wrightstone, *op. cit.*, p. 14.

BROADLY SPEAKING, INDEPENDENT WORK MAY BE CONSIDERED ACCORDING TO TWO BASIC TYPES. The first is the daily assignment which ordinarily consists of questions, problems, or exercises in the textbook, workbook, duplicated sheet, or written on the chalkboard. The purpose of this short, specific assignment is generally to (1) reinforce through practice a previously developed skill, (2) extend or enrich a concept or understanding developed during a previous discussion, (3) provide a basis for the teacher's diagnosis of specific learning gains, (4) develop positive study habits, or (5) introduce a new unit of work or area of study.

In order to realize the values of this type of independent work, the following basic principles should be carefully observed.

1. The purpose of the assignment should be made clear to children. Assignments such as "Read from pages 62 to 66 for tomorrow" should be strictly avoided because they present no problem to be solved nor any purpose for reading.

2. All directions should be made clear *before* work on the assignment is begun. How many teachers have assigned independent work only to discover that their time with another group was constantly interrupted by children who did not hear or did not understand the directions?

3. All necessary materials should be available to children to avoid interruption of the group lesson as well as time-wasting by the independent workers.

4. The assignment should be adaptable, in length and difficulty, to the varying abilities of children. Even the shortest and simplest assignment can make some provision for individual differences. Instructing certain children to do the first six problems, others the first ten, and others all fifteen is the most common way of adjusting the assignment. Including a few additional harder bonus exercises for those who wish to try them is another. Ingenious teachers utilize many other techniques to adapt the ordinary daily assignment to the varying ability levels of the children.

5. Varied types of assignments can be utilized to advantage. A conscientious teacher will make every effort to avoid letting assignments fall into a drearily monotonous routine. This is the chief criticism of workbooks. A good workbook, when properly used, is a valuable learning aid. But, like everything else, it is worse than useless when overused or abused. Some weary children spend most of their schoolday doing endless pages of exercises in reading, arithmetic, social studies, language, and other types of workbooks. Workbook assignments, paper-and-pencil assignments, chalkboard assignments, reading assignments, and others should be intermingled to capitalize upon the values of independent work and prevent its becoming sheer drudgery.

6. The assignment should be integrated with other learning activities. It has already been stated that assignments can be profitably used as initia-

tors, outcomes, or extensions of class learning experiences. They should never be isolated from the daily on-going work of the classroom.

7. Assignments should be checked carefully. If the assignment is used for diagnostic purposes, it should be carefully checked by the classroom teacher. On the other hand, some research has revealed the values of having pupils check their own assignments. Self-checking can be a definite learning experience under certain conditions. Having pupils check each other's work is an extremely questionable procedure. It has little or no educational value and may promote undesirable social and moral attitudes or habits.

THE LONG-RANGE PROJECT OR ASSIGNMENT OFFERS VALUABLE ENRICH-MENT OPPORTUNITIES. The purposes and values of this type of independent work are quite different from those of the daily assignment. These are the assignments that may consume several days or weeks, and may necessitate the use of numerous materials and references. They are the activities through which the teacher may make the classroom an exciting and intellectually challenging place for *all* youngsters because they are the jobs that develop the capabilities and explore the interests of each individual, as he strives for goals and follows interests, independent of his classmates. A few examples of worthwhile independent enrichment activities are listed below. All can be done independently by an individual or small group, while the teacher devotes his time to working with others.

Expressional Activities
1. Painting pictures at desk, easel, or art table.
2. Experimenting with new media and forms of two-dimensional or three-dimensional art.
3. Illustrating favorite stories, plays, poems, etc.
4. Making puppets, stage, and scenery for puppet show.
5. Making murals and other large-scale art work.
6. Making lantern slides, "movies," "filmstrips," etc. to be shown to class.
7. Block printing drapes, table pads, greeting cards, gift wrapping papers, etc.
8. Making dioramas and panoramas.
9. Working in clay or plasticene.
10. Making and illustrating booklets on any area or unit of work.
11. Creative writing—poems, stories, plays, TV scripts, etc.
12. Making and illustrating class booklet for gift for school library, another class, etc.
13. Writing biographies of famous personalities in government, science, literature, arts, etc.
14. Writing diaries and logs of historical personages or events.

CHILDREN CAN WORK INDEPENDENTLY.

15. Seasonal activities—making Christmas gifts, wrapping paper, cards, etc.

16. Composing songs—words, music, or both.

17. Preparing bulletin board display on unit of work or current news happenings.

18. Creating dances.

19. Writing and assembling class or school newspaper.

20. Compiling a notebook or card catalogue of new vocabulary words.

21. Making models, miniatures, etc.

22. Writing autobiographies, diaries, etc.

Work or Study Activities

1. Making or using maps, globes, graphs, tables, etc.

2. Observing and caring for living things in classroom.

3. Preparing bibliography on unit of study for individual or class use.

4. Cataloguing reference materials.

5. Reference reading—utilizing encyclopedia, dictionaries, atlas, and numerous supplementary texts.

6. Research and writing for individual or committee report.

7. Viewing filmstrips and other visual aids.

8. Conducting individual science experiments.

9. Observing, collecting, and recording data.

10. Interviewing.

Recreational-Appreciational Activities

1. Recreational reading.

2. Playing games of educational value—those that involve vocabulary building, spelling, counting, arithmetical skills, etc.

3. Exploring hobbies.

4. Making or solving puzzles—jigsaw, crossword, mathematical, etc.

5. Listening to records in music corner.

Constructional Activities

1. Constructing model, project, etc. in connection with unit of work.

2. Building containers or houses for pets kept in the classroom.

3. Weaving, sewing, basketry, leather work, and numerous craft activities.

There is little doubt that the long-range, independent project is one of the most valuable methods of providing for individual differences through a varied and enriched program. Wise and constant use of such assignments invalidates any criticism that the fast are held back by the slow or that the slow are frustrated trying to keep up with the others, regardless of the range of abilities present in the group.

Thus far, we have discussed independent assignments that are ordinarily completed in the classroom under the supervision of the teacher. A somewhat different type is examined below.

Homework

In any discussion of homework, it is necessary to keep in mind that the term has different meanings for different people. Strang[68] has suggested that the term really implies a continuum, with the mechanical, required type of assignment at one extreme, and the creative, individualized, and often voluntary type at the other. Let us consider briefly both types.

The Traditional Concept of Homework. Jacobs defines this as follows:

In the traditional concept of homework, the teacher prescribed what the child should do with a segment of time at home. Usually the assignment was a definite amount of subject matter to be covered, as, for example, spelling words to be studied, arithmetic problems to be solved, or pages in history or geography to be read. This assignment was uniformly prescribed for all the class. It frequently was given without consideration of individual abilities, other out-of-school responsibilities, home conditions for study, or the health and well-being of the youngsters.[69]

Fortunately, the use of this type of homework assignment has declined steadily in the elementary school since the mid-thirties, for three major reasons.

In the first place, schools responded to the pressures of parents, which had begun early in the century, against the long hours of home study imposed upon even very young children.

Secondly, changing theories of education inevitably resulted in a reevaluation of the homework policy. As Jacobs says,

As teaching practices changed, there naturally came to be some modifications of the concept of homework previously held. Thoughtful teachers began to question the wisdom of uniform home assignments that overlooked individual differences. They wondered if children were really learning good study habits. They asked if the homework really did make students more competent in the skills and knowledge prescribed. They thought about the child's need for free time to play, to explore individual interests, to engage in worthwhile

---

[68] Ruth M. Strang, "Homework and Guided Study," *Encyclopedia of Educational Research*, 3rd ed., Chester W. Harris, ed. (New York, The Macmillan Company, 1960), p. 677.

[69] Reprinted by permission of the Association for Childhood Education International, 3615 Wisconsin Avenue, N.W., Washington 16, D. C. "What About Homework?" by Leland B. Jacobs. From *Childhood Education*, October, 1954, Vol. 31, No. 2, p. 75.

community activities. They began to see that the usual homework assignments superficially took formal school content into the home but did not adequately utilize the home-community stimulation to explore, to know. They began to see certain pressures resulting from the ordeal of homework as having undesirable social-emotional effects upon boys and girls.[70]

Thirdly, research generally failed to support such values claimed for traditional homework as (1) It contributes to academic achievement, (2) It develops worthwhile habits of independent study, and (3) It contributes to the development of mental discipline.

There appears to be unanimous agreement among educators that, "research, dealing specifically with homework and directed study, is both limited and inadequate."[71] However, reviews of research to date, with some exception,[72] agree that, in general, research does not support the above-listed claimed values. Such statements as the following reveal consistency on this point.

Although many opinions exist on the effect of homework upon scholastic success, there has been little research on the subject. The many intangible factors involved have prevented exact and consistent measurement of changes and relationships.

Recognizing the limitations of even the most carefully controlled experiments, we can present only tentative conclusions. In the elementary school the observed values of a traditional type of homework do not justify assigning it. Homework done voluntarily produced about as good achievement as compulsory homework.[73]

. . . it is apparent that additional research evidence is needed on the whole question of homework. Certainly there is no conclusive evidence from achievement test results or other achievement records to justify the persisting faith of many persons in the merits of routine homework.[74]

In the nineteen forties and fifties, therefore, it was generally conceded that traditional homework did not realize the values claimed for it. In addition, many claimed the following negative concomitants.

1. It frequently promoted cheating or copying by the pupils.

2. It frequently represented the parents', not the child's, work.

3. It produced a negative attitude among pupils toward the school.

[70] *Ibid.,* p. 76.

[71] Ruth Strang, *Guided Study and Homework,* What Research Says to the Teacher (Washington, D.C., Department of Classroom Teachers, American Educational Research Association of the National Education Association, 1955), p. 2.

[72] Avram Goldstein, "Does Homework Help? A Review of Research," *Elementary School Journal,* Vol. 60 (January, 1960), pp. 212-224.

[73] Ruth Strang, *op. cit.,* pp. 19-20.

[74] Esther J. Swenson and others, "Research on Homework," *Journal of Education,* Vol. 137 (March, 1955), p. 22.

4. It limited the time available to children for the development of worthwhile leisure time interests and hobbies.

5. It subjected children to a rigorous time schedule in which most of their waking hours were rigidly budgeted.

6. It was injurious to pupils' physical and mental health.

7. It required of young children a longer working day than that of some adults. (How many parents bring work home from the office or factory every night?)

8. It placed a heavy burden of checking daily assignments upon the teacher.

The Modern Concept of Homework. Today, there is some evidence of a recurring interest in homework. A recent poll[75] of elementary teachers indicates that 83.5 per cent favor homework for elementary school pupils. It is hoped, however, that by "homework" these teachers had in mind a modern type of activity, the objectives of which are:

1. To stimulate voluntary effort, initiative, independence, responsibility, and self-direction. . . .

2. To encourage a carry-over of worthwhile school activities into permanent leisure interests. . . .

3. To enrich the school experience thru related home activities. . . .

4. To reinforce school learning by providing the necessary practice, integration, and application.[76]

Basic characteristics of homework designed to achieve these objectives are:

1. It may occasionally be required but is more often voluntary. To adopt a policy of regularly assigned homework is to believe in homework for homework's sake. On the other hand, an arbitrary policy of no homework does not take into consideration the needs of an individual situation. There may occasionally be values in requiring all pupils to complete an assigned task during out-of-school hours. Certainly there are infinite values in making the instructional program so interesting and so challenging that children will voluntarily extend and enrich learnings developed within the classroom.

2. It should usually consist of primary research activities that can better be done outside the schoolroom. The traditional type of homework assignment merely consisted of routine tasks, most of which would have been far better accomplished in the classroom. Homework may be a truly educational experience if it utilizes resources and experiences not

75 "Teacher Opinion Poll—Elementary School Homework," *NEA Journal*, Vol. 50 (September, 1961), p. 53.
76 Ruth Strang, *op. cit.*, p. 12.

easily attained in the school. Listening to TV and radio broadcasts, interviewing people, visiting local spots of interest, consulting newspapers and periodicals, observing and recording data on living plants and animals, are types of homework that may have functional value for children of all ages.

3. It should take into full consideration the pupil's home environment. Assignments that require the use of encyclopedias, dictionaries, and other reference tools should not be made unless the teacher is sure that these are available to the pupils.

4. It should be integrated with the on-going work of the classroom. Homework should not be considered as an extra superimposed upon the regular class work. Rather, it should be part of the continuous, progressive, total program. Assignments should emerge from the classroom lesson and, ideally, should be planned and formulated cooperatively by pupils and teacher.

An excellent type of homework assignment frequently emerges from questions that arise during class discussion. Frequently, during a discussion children ask questions that are interesting and thought provoking but are too tangential to warrant class exploration at that particular moment. On the other hand, they certainly should not be ignored. Many teachers list such questions on the chalkboard as they arise with a casual comment to the effect that, "That's a good question but it is not closely related to our problem. Shall we write it on the board so that we don't forget it and maybe we'll have time to answer it." At the close of the period or the day, the teacher and pupils together may examine the questions and determine if any of them might profitably be answered at home, on a voluntary or required basis, either by the entire class or certain individuals.

It seems unnecessary to state that homework can be integrated with the total program only through a careful follow-through on the part of the teacher. Written assignments should be checked the following day, either by the pupils themselves, or by the teacher, depending upon their purposes. Even casual suggestions such as "See if you can remember to bring in an important news item for our news board" should be followed through the following day to develop a sense of responsibility in pupils and also to achieve the academic purpose for which the assignment was made.

5. It should never be used as punishment. The negative effects of using homework as a disciplinary device should be evident, and need no explanation here.

6. It should never be used for testing purposes. Again, the impracticality and dangers of using homework for purposes of testing and grading should be evident to all teachers.

7. It should help to strengthen home-school relationships. Someone has said that homework is the school's most direct entry into the home. In many school systems this is probably true and every attempt should be made to make homework, when used, a vital bond between home and school. Unreasonably difficult and time-consuming homework assignments are poor public relations as well as poor educational devices. Unreasonable demands to "measure the floor area of your dining room," "bring in an empty oatmeal box tomorrow," or "ask your father to show you the gas meter in your house" are not appreciated by harassed parents who don't have a dining room, don't eat oatmeal, and prefer electricity to gas.

Equally threatening to good public relations is the dictatorial attitude that the child's education is the job of the school, not the home. Conscientious parents are interested in what their children are studying in school. They want to be of assistance when and how they can. The school has a definite responsibility to educate parents concerning (1) the purposes of homework, (2) the desirable types of homework, and (3) the valuable experiences parents can and should provide for their children. Many schools accomplish this through general meetings or study-group discussions. Others develop brochures, newsletters, or use such pamphlets as *What Every Parent Should Know About Homework*[77] to enlist the desirable cooperation of parents.

In summary, today's informed elementary teacher is neither for nor against homework. He is completely opposed to some types and interpretations of homework. He sees definite value in some types, in some situations, for some purposes, and for some pupils. The following criteria should be helpful in appraising the values of homework.

Do the assignments stem directly from class work?

Are the assignments varied according to each student's needs?

Does the student understand the assignment? Does he know just what he is to do and when he is supposed to finish?

Will the student have the necessary tools for his work? If, for instance, the assignment is to watch a television program, does the teacher make some alternate assignment for those not having television sets?

Are some of the assignments voluntary and others obligatory?

Are the assignments interesting to the student?

Do some of the assignments help to direct the student's interest toward new intellectual activities?

[77] Division of Press and Radio Relations, *What Every Parent Should Know About Homework* (Washington, D. C., National Education Association, n. d.).

Do some of the assignments help the student to understand his world, to take more interest in his home and his parents' work and problems, and to understand and feel pride in his neighbors and his community?

Does the plan for giving assignments allow for flexibility in the student's program? Can he skip his work occasionally in an emergency and make up for it afterward?[78]

Individualized Instruction

In general, there are three broad types of individualized instruction now in use in the elementary school. The first of these includes the modifications of the early "individualized-contract-plans" in which children progress through a series of job sheets under the guidance of the teacher. The second involves the use of auto-instructional devices, discussed in the following chapter. The third is a type of individualized program, used most frequently today in reading.

Described briefly, the individualized reading program is an attempt to direct instruction in reading toward the unique skills, interests, and abilities of each individual pupil. The key characteristics are *seeking, self-selection*, and *pacing*. Instead of organizing the class into basal reading groups, each child chooses the material he wishes to read. Instruction is on an individual basis. An individual record is kept of each child. Children occasionally share their reading interests with other members of the class, but there is no comparison between individuals nor no attempt to regulate reading progress or interests according to the needs of a group.

Although research has yielded no conclusive evidence to date, many of the advocates of the individualized program claim that it yields important values, among which are the following:

1. It enables each child to progress according to his specific ability.

2. It avoids unfavorable comparison and stigmatization of the slower learner.

3. It offers repeated opportunity for a one-to-one relationship between pupil and teacher.

4. It develops wide reading interests.

5. It capitalizes upon intrinsic motivation in that the child chooses his own materials.

6. It develops the individual's reading skills as the needs arise.

7. It provides greater opportunity for the genuine sharing of reading experiences among all pupils.

8. It encourages responsible self-direction.

[78] National Education Association, Research Division, *Homework* (Washington, D. C., National Education Association, January, 1958), p. 8.

9. It utilizes broader methods of evaluation.

10. It offers numerous enrichment opportunities for all pupils, including the academically talented.

SUMMARY

Provision for differences among learners has long been, and is, a primary concern of conscientious teachers and administrators. Shortly after the graded school was established in the mid-nineteenth century, it was criticized by educators because of its frequent neglect of the individual pupil. Numerous attempts have been made since that time to eliminate this inherent weakness. This chapter has examined many of these according to two major classifications, (1) those that attempt to provide for individual differences through an administrative plan or organizational pattern, and (2) those that recognize individual differences through the employment of certain classroom instructional procedures and techniques.

Among the first group, one of the most controversial issues today is that of ability grouping. There is some evidence that this method of classifying children may be increasing somewhat, although not a few educators are opposed to it because (1) research has failed to demonstrate the advantages claimed for it and (2) it may sacrifice certain educational and democratic ideals basic to our concept of educational opportunity for all pupils.

Another controversial issue examined in the present chapter was that of the departmentalized organization versus the self-contained classroom in the elementary school. Again, it was stated that research is inconclusive and opinion far from unanimous. On the whole, however, the advantages of the self-contained classroom for young children appear to outweigh the disadvantages.

Other present-day organizational patterns include multigrade grouping and the nongraded school, both of which were discussed briefly.

It was stated that, in general, most administrative plans failed, *in themselves,* to make adequate provision for individual differences because they were based upon a limited concept of the learner or the learning process. Adequate provision can be made only in the classroom by the teacher. However, administrative patterns either help or handicap the teacher's efforts. For this reason, the classroom teacher should know the values of each proposed organizational plan and should support those that, in his best judgment, are most compatible with the goals of American elementary education.

The second section of the chapter was devoted to a discussion of the classroom procedures and techniques employed by competent teachers in an effort to differentiate instruction according to pupil needs. Although there is a countless number of techniques through which this objective may be achieved, this chapter discussed in detail four primary methods, (1) grouping within the classroom, (2) independent study within the classroom, (3) independent study at home, and (4) individualized instruction.

ADDITIONAL LEARNING EXPERIENCES

Topics for Thought and Discussion

1. Would you prefer to teach a "high," "average," "low," or heterogeneous group? Can you analyze the reasons for your answer?

2. Did you attend an elementary school in which pupils were grouped according to academic ability? What was your private opinion of the pupils in the "high" group and the "low" group? Do you think your opinion was typical of that of the general school pupil population?

3. Some schools group according to academic ability but label the classes in such a manner as to disguise the fact. Furthermore, they refuse to tell parents which is the high group, the low group, etc. What is your opinion of this practice?

4. Are teachers' marks of academic achievement influenced by pupil attitude and behavior?

5. Are you in favor of college "honors" programs? Are there basic differences between these programs and ability grouping in the elementary school?

6. What do you think accounts for the current revival of interest in some quarters in ability grouping and departmentalization?

7. Many of our problems today stem from the fact that we are trying to implement a twentieth century philosophy through a nineteenth century school organizational pattern. What is the solution to this square peg in a round hole dilemma? Is it the abandonment of the graded school for a more up-to-date organizational pattern?

8. Were you ever accelerated or retained in a grade in the elementary school? Do you remember what the effect was on your self-concept? On your scholastic achievement?

9. A noted educator with thirty or more years of experience recently said, "In many respects, I feel that in education we are in a 'this is where I came in' stage." What did he mean by this statement?

10. A fourteen year old boy from a very poor home environment, with an approximate IQ of 105, is a serious behavior problem in a sixth grade class. The teacher says he is completely unmanageable and that he should be placed in "some sort of a special class." Is this the solution? If your answer is Yes, what type of class do you suggest? Did the school contribute at all to this boy's problems? In what respects?

11. Do you think that a teacher of academically gifted children should himself be academically gifted?

12. Some people have pointed out the irony of the fact that, in many colleges and universities, courses in the education of the intellectually gifted are taught by members of the Special Education department, whose interest and experience have been primarily in the area of mental retardation. What is your reaction to this statement? Who, in your opinion, should teach such a course? Why?

13. Do you think that it is advantageous or necessary for a teacher of atypical children to have had some experience in teaching "normal" children? Why?

14. What different factors and purposes must be considered in the secondary school that might alter the picture from the elementary school as far as ability grouping and/or departmentalization are concerned?

15. Recently pupils in a third grade class were given a home assignment to prepare a scrapbook about Abraham Lincoln and bring it to class to share with the group on Lincoln's Birthday. Bobby, a child of slightly less than average academic ability, brought to class a very elaborate scrapbook obviously made, for the most part, by his parents. How would you handle this situation? What would you say to Bobby? Would you talk with his parents? What would you say?

Projects and Activities

1. If possible, visit an elementary school in which pupils are grouped according to academic ability. Study carefully the socio-economic and/or racial population of at least one high group and one low group. Is there a difference of distribution of these factors between the two groups? What are the implications of your study?

2. Ask permission to observe in a primary class and an upper grade class. What types of intraclass grouping do you find in each group? To what extent, and in what curricular areas, is this type of in-class grouping practiced in each class? Do you think your findings are typical of general practice? Why?

3. Talk to several parents. Are they in favor of regular homework for elementary school youngsters? What reasons do they give for their opinions?

4. Try to locate, from your instructor or state department, a school near you that is organized on a nongraded pattern in either the primary grades or in all grades. Ask permission to visit for a day. What essential differences do you notice between this school and a traditional graded school? Talk with children and teachers. Do they like the nongraded pattern? Why?

5. Prepare a set of illustrations with accompanying narration entitled "What Every Elementary Teacher Should Know About Homework" which could be presented at a faculty institute.

6. Prepare a research paper on the early (late nineteenth century and early twentieth century) plans to individualize instruction. What factors contributed to the growth of popularity of these plans and, after a time, to their decrease in popularity?

7. Study the legislation of your state concerning education for the handicapped. For what types of handicapped individuals is public school legislation in your state mandatory?

8. Investigate the legislative provisions in your state for education of the academically gifted and also the teacher certification requirements for teachers of these children. How does your state compare with neighboring states in these matters?

9. Prepare a paper on *What Research Says About Nonpromotion (Retardation) in the Elementary School.*

10. Can you find any studies that indicate that pupil self-checking of assignments may be educationally valuable? What degree of agreement do you find?

11. Visit a special class or school (day or residential) for the physically handicapped, mentally retarded, or socially and emotionally disturbed. In what respects is the educational program similar to that of a regular public school? In what respects is it different?

12. Describe and react to the Dual Progress Plan. Read the book on it by Stoddard for further information.

Selected Bibliography

Association for Childhood Education International, *Grouping . . . problems and satisfactions.* Washington, D. C., 1953, 1954.

Children Can Work Independently, Constance Carr, ed. and Frances Hamilton, coordinator. Washington, D. C., Association for Childhood Education International, 1952.

"Elementary Education: Issues and Prospects." *Educational Leadership,* Vol. 18 (November, 1960).

"Elementary School Organization . . . Purposes, Patterns, Perspective." *National Elementary Principal,* Vol. 41 (December, 1961).

GOODLAD, John I., "Classroom Organization," in Chester W. Harris, ed., *Encyclopedia of Educational Research,* 3rd ed. New York, The Macmillan Company, 1960.

————, and ANDERSON, Robert H., *The Nongraded Elementary School.* New York, Harcourt, Brace & World, Inc., 1959.

"Grouping." *NEA Journal,* Vol. 48 (September, 1959).

"Grouping: Promising Approaches." *Educational Leadership,* Vol. 18 (April, 1961).

National Society for the Study of Education, *Individualizing Instruction,* Nelson B. Henry, ed. Sixty-first Yearbook, Part I. Chicago, University of Chicago Press, 1962.

National Society for the Study of Education, *The Grouping of Pupils*, Guy M. Whipple, ed. Thirty-fifth Yearbook, Part I. Chicago, University of Chicago Press, 1936.

Providing for Individual Differences in the Elementary School, Norma E. Cutts, and Nicholas Moseley, eds. Englewood Cliffs, N. J., Prentice-Hall, Inc., 1960.

STRANG, Ruth M., *Guided Study and Homework*. What Research Says to the Teacher, No. 8. Department of Classroom Teachers, American Educational Research Association of the National Education Association. Washington, D. C., 1955.

——, "Homework and Guided Study," in Chester W. Harris ed., *Encyclopedia of Educational Research*, 3rd ed. New York, The Macmillan Company, 1960.

The Self-Contained Classroom, Edith Roach Snyder, ed. Washington, D. C., Association for Supervision and Curriculum Development, 1960.

"Trends in Meeting Individual Differences." *Educational Leadership*, Vol. 15 (December, 1957).

WRIGHTSTONE, J. Wayne, *Class Organization for Instruction*. Department of Classroom Teachers, American Educational Research Association of the National Education Association. Washington, D. C., 1957.

CHAPTER **10**

Using Instructional Materials and Aids

A PEDAGOGICAL RIP VAN WINKLE, awakening from a deep professional sleep, would be amazed at many of the innovations in modern educational practice. Changes in schoolroom design, instructional methodology, curriculum content, teacher-pupil relationships, teacher competencies, and school-community relationships would be among those readily apparent. Perhaps superseding all of these, however, would be the revolution in the use of instructional tools and materials. The talk and chalk era of education is a thing of the past—to which we can add—thank goodness! Compared to his counterpart of yesteryear who relied solely upon a textbook and writing slate, the modern elementary teacher has at his disposal innumerable instructional tools. Books, periodicals, pictures, maps, globes, films, flannel boards, photographic equipment, filmstrips, displays, auto-instructional devices, television, and numerous other learning resources are readily available to many of today's teachers. No single one of these is inherently "good" or "bad" for the education of children. Nor is any one of them a panacea for all educational problems. None is designed nor intended to be a substitute for the teacher. To the contrary, the value of all such aids depends largely upon their careful selection and use. Research has demonstrated fairly conclusively that certain carefully selected materials, when properly used, can motivate, clarify, supplement, reinforce, and enrich teaching and learning. It is equally true that even the most expensive and best materials, when inappropriately or ineffectually used, or when gathering dust in an obscure storage closet, are merely a waste of children's and teachers' time and taxpayers' money. With this thought in mind, the following section examines the basic principles underlying the use of multisensory aids in the modern educational program.

THE MULTIMEDIA CONCEPT AND THE CURRICULUM

MANY FACTORS HAVE CONTRIBUTED TO THE CURRENT EMPHASIS ON THE CLASSROOM USE OF MULTILEARNING AIDS. Widespread social, technological, and educational changes have promoted the increasing acceptance of the multimedia concept. Among the most important factors are the following:

1. *Expansion in school population.* Over the years, the increasing importance of education for all children and the enactment of child labor legislation have resulted in a steadily increasing number of children attending school for an ever-lengthening period. In recent years, the well-known population explosion has made the problem more acute than ever. There are no signs that it will diminish in the foreseeable future. The rapidly expanding school population has forced educators to search for newer and better means of educating larger numbers of pupils.

2. *Variability of school population.* Not only is the school population greater, it is also more varied than ever before. There was a time when children who could not meet academic standards left school at an early age. This is no longer true. Compulsory attendance laws force children of widely varying abilities to attend school until they are sixteen or older. In addition, (as stated in the previous chapter) the public school has steadily expanded its program to provide for many types of exceptional children—the physically handicapped, mentally retarded, and socially or emotionally maladjusted. The school population grows steadily more heterogeneous, and ways must be found to meet the great variety of needs and abilities it possesses.

3. *The influence of two World Wars.* Much of the stimulus for using a variety of teaching aids has stemmed from the experimentation and successful use of such devices by the armed forces during both World Wars. With huge numbers of men to be educated and trained, the military searched for new, effective media of communication. Through experimentation, it was discovered that certain media, for example, mock-ups, films, and filmstrips, could convey a message to some personnel more effectively and in less time than traditional teaching methods.

4. *The unprecedented expansion of knowledge.* The explosion of knowledge is as well-known as the population explosion. Both have had, and will continue to have, a terrific impact on the school program. Both demand a careful reevaluation of the traditional program. The great strides being taken every day in the discovery and restructuring of knowledge make it necessary for the teacher to utilize numerous resources in screening, selecting, and imparting information to children.

5. *The national concern for a top-quality educational program.* Recent international events have emphasized the importance of a top-drawer educational program in every school in the country. Certainly, effective teaching aids and devices will occupy a larger portion of this program than has been true in the past.

6. *A new concept of the learning process.* Never have educators been more convinced of the truth of the old cliche, "Teaching is not telling and learning is not listening!" Vital, concrete, and meaningful experiencing is a requisite of learning as we now define it, and this can be gained only from a variety of aids and resources.

7. *The National Defense Education Act.* All of the above factors contributed to the passage in 1958 of the National Defense Education Act which, in turn, has provided a strong stimulus to the exploration of varied communication media and their educational possibilities. Title III of the NDEA provides that the government will subsidize the purchase of laboratory or other special equipment to improve instruction in certain curriculum areas (foreign language, mathematics, and science). Title VII authorizes federal support of research and experimentation concerning the more effective use of television, radio, motion pictures and related media for educational purposes.

THE SOLE PURPOSE OF USING MANY AND VARIED INSTRUCTIONAL AIDS IS TO IMPROVE THE QUALITY OF THE EDUCATIONAL PROCESS. Learning is, of course, contingent upon communication. One of the greatest obstacles, however, to communication and hence to learning is verbalism, defined as ". . . the student's use of words without knowing their true meaning or without having a perceptual basis for understanding."[1] Children may read, write, and talk about latitude parallels, monsoons, the War of the Roses, subjects and predicates, the Cradle of Civilization, addends and subtrahends, magnetic poles, the sound barrier, or any other subject without real understanding. Knowledge, however, that is gained, not by words alone, but by varied sensory experiences such as seeing, hearing, and touching, is usually more accurate, more meaningful, and more readily retained. To improve the quality of education by making learning more concrete and meaningful is, therefore, a primary reason for today's emphasis upon many different teaching aids. The point is made as follows:

A major difficulty in classroom communication springs from an emphasis upon verbal approaches to learning. Student learning outside of school may be real and firsthand. But the emphasis inside school is frequently upon more abstract learning through text materials. . . . This method of learning poses difficulties for large numbers of students who presently attend our schools. Our greatest

[1] James W. Brown, Richard B. Lewis, and Fred F. Harcleroad, *A-V Instruction, Materials and Methods* (New York, McGraw-Hill Book Co., Inc., 1959), p. 9.

intellectual resource, organized knowledge, is available for their personal development and the improvement of society only when a high percentage of
students can learn and apply it. In presenting this knowledge verbally, to be
mastered or memorized as an end in itself, teachers may never help students
realize its value in meeting their own life problems. The shortcomings of
exclusively verbal teaching are perhaps the most serious of the difficulties
facing any teacher and one of the main reasons supporting the development
and proper use of audio-visual materials.[2]

Not only can knowledge be made more meaningful through the use of
multimedia, it can also be more easily adapted to pupil abilities and needs.
The preceding chapter emphasized the wide range of learning abilities
found in the typical classroom. Obviously this range can be better met
through a wide variety of instructional tools than by reliance only upon
one or two resources. As Sands says,

The evidently great differences in learning ability among the taught can be at
least partly offset by a corresponding variety of teaching materials. Some
pupils learn better with verbal tools than with visual or auditory, some not so
well. All learn at their own tempo, and all, whatever we do, will end at
different levels. It follows that teachers need proficiency in using all the kinds
of instructional methods available to modern education. But that is a counsel
of perfection, for no two teachers are alike in either ability or personality,
and their uses of communicative devices will perforce differ as the teachers
do. The audio-visual idea provides an unlimited variety of approaches, and,
ideally, this variety ought to be used in every subject area as a means to help
teaching be freely individual.[3]

In summary, the multimedia approach is widely accepted today because it (1) helps to make learning a vital, meaningful, and first-hand
experience and (2) helps to provide a wide range of learning experiences
suited to learners of greatly varying abilities. It is, in short, an integral,
vital, and necessary component of what we believe today constitutes
sound educational practice.

THERE ARE STILL SOME TEACHERS WHO RESIST USING MANY OF THE IN-
STRUCTIONAL AIDS NOW AVAILABLE. Although educational theory has long
accepted the multimedia concept, it is not as readily accepted in classroom
practice, and, according to one reference, "There is evidence which says
that teachers pay lip service to the value of audio-visual aids but not
much beyond this."[4] Why is this true?

---

[2] *Ibid.*

[3] Lester B. Sands, *Audio-Visual Procedures in Teaching* (New York, The Ronald
Press Company, 1956), p. 11. Copyright © 1956, The Ronald Press Company.

[4] Hideya Kumata and Malcolm S. MacLean, Jr., "Education and the Problems of the
New Media in the United States of America," *Communication Media and the School,*
1960 Yearbook of Education, George Z. F. Bereday and Joseph A. Lauwerys, eds.,
(New York, Harcourt, Brace & World, Inc., 1960), p. 286.

In the first place, many teachers resist the use of new instructional media simply because of laziness, apathy, and a fairly human distrust of anything new. These teachers have taught and were taught for years, relying solely upon a chalkboard, textbook, and perhaps a few pictures. No one has yet convinced them of the need for change.

Another hard core of resistance comes from those teachers who hold one or more of the common misconceptions concerning the use of newer instructional media. A common misconception is the EQUIPMENT (always in capital letters) bugbear. Say "audio-visual" to some teachers and they immediately envision a lot of heavy, expensive, elaborate equipment all of which is difficult to get and more difficult to operate. Small wonder such teachers have a "no, thank you—not for me" attitude toward the multisensory concept.

A second misconception is the frosting on the cake idea. To these teachers, many of the devices are "extras" or "treats" to be offered to children. They see them as interest-catching devices, but not as essentials to learning. This is, of course, a hang-over from the traditional entertainment concept of some of the media, particularly films and television. Until such teachers understand the *instructional* rather than the *entertainment* value of the newer devices, they will never consider them an integral part of their program.

Perhaps the most formidable misconception of the multimedia concept is the teacher substitute fallacy. Many teachers are threatened by the newer media (particularly television and auto-instructional devices) because they think they will be replaced or forced into a subordinate role. This is not true. No reputable educators advocate substituting a machine for a teacher. Nor do they envision the teacher's role as merely a "mechanical maid to a mechanical aid."[5] The varied learning aids now available to the teacher do not, when used properly, eliminate or lessen the teacher's importance. Of this we can be sure.

However, there is no doubt that the use of many learning materials *modifies* or *changes* the teacher's role to some extent. As many have pointed out, the chief classroom role of the teacher in the past was as a purveyor of knowledge. He was the chief source from which his pupils derived information. Today, this is no longer true. Children learn, outside and inside of school, from a variety of sources. The classroom teacher can no longer consider his role as simply imparting information. Instead, he must learn how to capitalize upon, integrate, extend, and utilize the knowledge children gain from media outside the schoolroom (and research tells us that in many cases it is considerable). Then too, the teacher must learn how to direct, manage, and coordinate the various resources

[5] Edgar Dale, "No Room for Amateurs," *Audiovisual Instruction*, Vol. 6 (May, 1961), p. 192.

within the classroom in order to produce the most effective results. Thus, the teacher becomes a coordinator, a manager, an integrator, a director, an organizer of many learning resources rather than acting as a sole provider of information. One author summarizes the change in role as follows:

. . . the traditional media will survive and the new media, although increasingly used, cannot be used to an unlimited extent. The able teacher will not be subjugated by them and will never degenerate into a mere custodian of machines. Yet his role has been subtly changed, and it seems probable that it will continue for some time to change in the same direction. . . . A new attitude on the part of the teacher is called for. He is less alone in his teaching than he once was; he is forced to cooperate more and more with . . . 'background' teachers. He is also *seen* to be less alone, and more as one, even if the leading one, among several. From the pupil's standpoint the foci of attention are more numerous, but most have clearly not much to do with the teacher, who is constantly obliged to adopt this standpoint. It is now more difficult for a teacher to pose as a fount of wisdom and easier to demonstrate a humbler approach to knowledge. One surely cannot doubt which is preferable.[6]

Is this changed role less important? Is it easier? On the contrary, it demands highly skilled teachers with certain specific competencies. What are these?

THE CLASSROOM TEACHER SHOULD BE FAMILIAR WITH THE BASIC PROCEDURES UNDERLYING EFFECTIVE USE OF ALL LEARNING MEDIA. In brief, these are (1) preparation, (2) presentation, (3) follow-up, and (4) evaluation.

Preparation. This involves a three-step process, the first of which is the careful selection of the most appropriate device for a specific purpose. It was stated previously that no one aid will serve all purposes, and it is a pointless argument to debate which is "best" for an elementary school program. The primary criterion of the selection of any learning aid is how well it will fulfill the specific purpose. Is a visual device called for that will permit on-going discussion and pupil participation? Then perhaps a filmstrip or set of slides is the answer. Is a primary purpose to refine listening skills? Then the radio or a recording is called for. Is the purpose to recreate as nearly as possible a direct experience, for instance, a visit to a foreign land? If so, a sound film would be desirable. *No medium can be all things to all people*, and the careful selection of a device according to a specific purpose is one of the chief responsibilities of the teacher.

Other criteria for the wise selection of media include (1) maturity and

---

[6] W. R. Lee, "Mass Media and the Pupil-Teacher Relationship," *Communication Media and the School*, op. cit., pp. 103-104.

experience of the learners, (2) economy of time and money, and, of course, (3) availability.

Once the resource has been selected, the second step in the preparatory process is for the teacher to become thoroughly acquainted with it *before using it in class*. When possible, as in the case of most display materials and such projected materials as filmstrips and slides, this means a careful previewing by the teacher. When this is not always possible, as in the case of some rented sound films, television and radio programs, the teacher must make a conscientious attempt to become thoroughly familiar with the resource by reading any literature pertaining to it that may be available.

The third phase of the preparatory period involves acquainting children with the device they are about to use. Children should understand what they are to see and hear, and why. They can be motivated to look for answers to certain questions. Various individuals or small groups may be assigned specific problems to be answered. Standards of listening or viewing should be established. The relationship of the experience with previous work should be explained. Creative teachers will find numerous ways to prepare children in order that they derive maximum benefit from the experience. Exposing them cold to a new medium or experience is pointless and automatically detracts from the potential value.

Presentation. This step is examined more thoroughly in connection with each category of materials discussed later in the chapter. Here it is important only to stress the relationship of desirable physical conditions upon the effective use of all aids. If children can't see, if they can't hear, if they are seated uncomfortably, if they are overcrowded, if the room is poorly ventilated, the best learning device in the world loses its effectiveness, as many a teacher has learned from bitter experience.

Follow-up. Is the film, picture, recording, or whatever an isolated incident in the day or is it an integral part of the total learning experience? Are children given an opportunity for a thorough follow-up discussion? Are they encouraged to ask questions and give reactions? Does a follow-up assignment—to confirm a point, seek a further clarification, or compare a viewpoint—often emerge naturally from the experience?

All golfers are aware of the importance of the followthrough to a good game. In golf it is often *what happens after you hit the ball* that is important. The same thing is true here. It is what the teacher and children do *after* the film has been shown, the recording heard, the television program viewed which may determine to a considerable extent the ultimate value of the experience.

Evaluation. Teacher and pupils alike will make constant evaluations of their learning resources. Did the tape recording suit our purposes? Was the filmstrip interesting? Was the model accurate in detail? Could another medium be used more effectively? Was the resource worth the time and money it cost? These and other questions are necessary to evaluate the effectiveness of any learning aid. Very often, after a class evaluation, the teacher will make notes of the pupils' and his own reactions on his lesson plan or on a 3 x 5 card which can then be used for future planning and selection of appropriate materials.

THE CLASSROOM TEACHER SHOULD BE FAMILIAR WITH THE OPERATION AND MAINTENANCE OF EQUIPMENT. The degree to which teachers assume this responsibility varies with the school system. In those schools that employ a supervisor or coordinator of instructional materials, this person or his trained corps of pupils or lay aides or both together may assume full responsibility for the operation and maintenance of all materials. Thus, the teacher may have to operate only the equipment that is a permanent part of his classroom such as the record player or overhead projector. In other schools, however, teachers are required to operate all equipment or teach some of their older pupils to do it. If such teachers are fearful or unwilling to learn the basic operational principles of each piece of equipment, obviously it is rarely used. This is inexcusable. Most of the modern audio-visual equipment is sturdy, reasonably light, portable, and fairly simple to operate. If the taxpayers are willing to buy it, certainly the teachers should be willing to learn how to use it.

THE CLASSROOM TEACHER SHOULD BE FAMILIAR WITH THE TECHNIQUES FOR, AND THE ADVANTAGES OF, PRODUCING HAND-MADE INSTRUCTIONAL MATERIALS. Thus far, our discussion has seemed to emphasize the teacher's familiarity with commercially distributed resources and equipment. But these are only part of the picture and perhaps not even the most important part. A vast wealth of teaching possibilities is open to the teacher who is acquainted with the production of many learning aids. Various types of pictorial and display materials have, of course, been produced by capable teachers and their pupils for many years. Today, this range of possibilities has been widened to include filmstrips, numerous types of slides, radio programs and recordings, television programs, and sound films. Furthermore, none of these require an unreasonable expenditure of time or money.

The home-made aids have two distinct advantages over the commercial materials. They can more readily be integrated with the specific content and purposes of the topic under study, and they provide valuable creative experiences for children. A summary of the reasons why teachers should produce many of their learning aids has been stated as follows: "(1) They can produce materials which correlate better with their instructional goals; (2) it will give them a better knowledge of the material content; (3) teachers will develop abilities to discriminate, select, and evaluate; (4) new techniques will be learned; (5) ego and pride will be satisfied; (6) saving of money."[7]

In summary, the modern elementary teacher has a definite responsibility to understand the basic principles underlying the multimedia concept of education, as well as an obligation to be thoroughly familiar with techniques for selecting, using, and producing specific aids for specific purposes. To assist him in this important task, the basic categories of instructional materials now in popular use are examined in the following sections.

PRINTED MATERIALS

Textbooks. Of the wide variety of instructional aids now available, there is no doubt that printed materials are still used more than any other category. Within this category, the textbook still dominates. On the whole, there is considerable agreement that modern textbooks are greatly improved over those of the past on two major counts. In the first place, their physical format is infinitely improved. In general, children's textbooks are attractively and colorfully illustrated; the type is clear and easy to read; they are of a convenient size; and they have attractive and durable covers. Secondly, considerable effort has been directed in recent years toward improving the content of textbooks. Great emphasis is placed upon accuracy of material, clarity of expression, suitable vocabulary, and interesting writing style. Then too, the inclusion of many excellent study guide questions and suggestions for pupil activities and supplementary exercises makes the textbook a valuable teaching tool for the teacher.

The teacher may also find, in the future, that the growing interest in paper-back textbooks may be a boon. Paper-backs are cheaper and are not expected to last as long as the hard-back texts, which may be a distinct advantage in some fields in this day of rapidly changing curriculum content.

Although the textbooks themselves have improved greatly, unfortunately the teacher's use of them frequently has not. Textbook teaching is still found in many classrooms. Too many teachers admit that they follow the textbook. Too many children are told, day after day, to read the next five pages for tomorrow. In these classrooms, the textbook is the organizer, the determiner, of the learning situation and the teacher is but a docile follower. This is poor teaching today; it has always been poor teaching. There can be little disagreement with Burton who says, "It

[7] Robert E. Ness, "Producing Your Own Materials," *Educational Screen and Audio-Visual Guide*, Vol. 41 (May, 1962), p. 254.

would be difficult to devise an educational practice so grossly ineffective, so certainly calculated to interfere with learning as a page assignment to a single text followed by a formal verbal quiz."[8]

The specific weaknesses of reliance upon, and adherence to, a single textbook have been enumerated as follows:

1. It is deadly to the good student to follow textbook reading with a discussion in which no new material is introduced.

2. It is impossible to find a single text suited to the interests and abilities of all the students in a group.

3. It does not encourage the development of initiative and self-direction to assign students three or four pages in a textbook.

4. It limits the scope of the course and does not encourage students to work up to their maximum ability.

5. It encourages belief in the infallibility of the printed page and reliance upon a single authority.

6. It provides little opportunity for students to compare and evaluate different points of view and develop critical-mindedness.

7. It encourages bad reading habits in students and rote memorization.

8. It tends to routinize procedure—so many pages to be read, followed by recitation and a quiz on what was read.[9]

What are some valid uses of a textbook? Certainly there are many and it would be impossible to list them all. As examples, textbooks can be used to great advantage:

1. To motivate a unit of study.

2. To serve as the common base for a group discussion or assignment, i. e., finding answers to specific questions.

3. To provide a skeletal or factual account of a particular situation or incident.

4. To provide practice in certain critical reading skills, i. e., locating information, using the index or table of contents, reading to grasp the main idea, reading for specific details, adjusting the rate of reading to a specific purpose, etc.

5. To confirm information obtained from direct experience (discovery, experimentation, visitation, interviewing, etc.).

6. To introduce a new skill or process.

[8] William H. Burton, "Implications for Organization of Instruction and Instructional Adjuncts," *Learning and Instruction,* Forty-ninth Yearbook, National Society for the Study of Education, Part I, Nelson B. Henry, ed. (Chicago, University of Chicago Press, 1950), p. 227.

[9] "Education for Social Competence," by I. James Quillen and Lavone A. Hanna. Copyright 1948, 1961, by Scott, Foresman and Company, Chicago, p. 242.

7. To provide opportunities for skill reinforcement, particularly in arithmetic.

8. To provide a common basis for the orderly building of vocabulary and skills, as in the basal reading program.

Supplementary references. These include books, encyclopedia, atlases, almanacs, periodicals, newspapers, pamphlets, and all other types of printed references that are valuable in providing depth and enrichment to any area of study. As many of these as possible should be kept in the classroom library corner, the importance of which was emphasized in Chapter 6. In addition, the school, public, or traveling library will be happy in many situations to supply such materials upon the teacher's request.

DISPLAY MATERIALS

Flat pictures. An extensive collection of flat pictures is found in every competent teacher's classroom. Such a collection is kept carefully in a steel filing cabinet or in a home-made box or crate if a regular file is not available. It consists of pictures purchased from various commercial houses, as well as those clipped from advertisements, newspapers, and such magazines as *Life, Look,* the *National Geographic,* and *Scientific American.* In most classrooms, the picture file represents an accumulation of many years because conscientious elementary teachers are continually searching for pictures that will add interest and meaning to their teaching. This is all to the good. It is equally important, however, that the file be continually brought up to date, and materials that are out-of-date, dog-eared, or no longer pertinent be discarded. There is a great deal of difference between a collector and a hoarder; the picture file resembling the famous closet of Fibber McGee is of little use to anyone.

There are two main uses of flat pictures in the classroom. They can be used in the opaque projector or can be used in various display areas, particularly the bulletin board. For both of these uses it is important that the picture be mounted on cardboard, oaktag, construction paper, or some sort of durable backing. The old saying, "If a picture is worth saving, it is worth mounting," is as true today as it ever was. Mounted pictures are more attractive for display purposes, easier to file and keep from year to year, and much more suitable for use in the opaque propector. Then too, most mounted pictures can be lettered with a title or legend that easily identifies the picture and gives it meaning for children.

Many elementary teachers make the picture collection an educational activity by involving pupils in collecting, selecting, mounting, lettering, and filing pictures. In the intermediate or upper grades this can easily be an on-going project all year, assumed weekly by small groups or individual pupils. It is a vast help to the teacher, and helps to give pupils a feeling of responsibility for the cooperative management of the classroom.

Bulletin board. The types and values of tackboards in the elementary classroom were discussed in Chapter 6.

Flannel and magnetic boards. A popular device found in many elementary classrooms is the flannel or magnetic board, which can be purchased or made by the teacher. A simple flannel board may be made by covering a piece of cardboard, masonite, composition board, plywood, or old card table top with a very cheap flannel material. Cheap flannel is particularly desirable since it has more nap and objects will adhere to it more easily. If a flannel with considerable nap is used, small objects of paper, balsa wood, felt, or flannel will adhere without any difficulty, particularly if the board is tilted slightly backward when in use. Larger areas of paper, a 9 x 12 picture, for instance, need to be backed with flannel, felt, wool, suede, blotter paper, sponge, or sandpaper to adhere to the flannel surface.

A simple magnetic board may be made from a piece of sheet metal, or a piece of cardboard, composition board, or plywood backed with a sheet of metal, a piece of steel chicken wire, or a piece of wire mesh of the type used by plasterers. Satisfactory magnets of different strengths may be purchased from any hobby shop. These may simply be placed on the face of any sheet to hold it on the board, or they may be fastened permanently on the back of small, three-dimensional objects, if they are used on the magnetic board.

Several combinations of these boards can be used to advantage. A combination flannel and magnetic board is easily made, using one side for the magnetic surface and covering the other side with flannel. A combination chalkboard, magnetic board, and flannel board can be purchased for a relatively modest sum of money. It can also be made by the teacher, for considerably less money, from a piece of plywood painted on one side with chalkboard paint and backed with metal or wire, and covered on the other side with flannel.

The chief advantage of the flannel or magnetic board is its manipulative quality. Pictures, cut-outs, letters, and objects can be prepared in advance and freely manipulated on the board's surface. Thus, the board lends itself particularly well to such activities as (1) developing quantitative concepts (fractions, units of measure, etc.), (2) story-telling, (3) motivating creative writing or other creative activities, and (4) illustrating a sequence of events in social studies or science.

Dioramas and Panoramas. The panorama is a display, made in a cardboard box, packing crate, or some sort of a frame and base. It is usually

**Flannel or magnetic boards are found in many
classrooms.**

treated as a miniature stage-setting and is a popular project with some
teachers and pupils.

The diorama is similar to the panorama except that some attempt is
made to convey an impression of depth through background scenery. It
also consists of a display box or frame serving as a miniature stage. Attached to the back of the box is a curved piece of paper, oaktag, or other
sturdy material cut in a half-moon shape upon which scenery is painted.
An attempt is made to blend the foreground with the background and
thus gain a perspective and depth impression not possible in the ordinary
panorama. For correct proportion, the height and depth of the diorama
should be one-half the width.

Dioramas and panoramas may constitute valuable creative activities
for children and can be used to illustrate stories or poems. Unless meticulous attention is paid to detail, they are usually less valuable than some
other media in conveying accurate concepts in social studies or science.
A miniature shoebox scene of the defeat of the Spanish Armada, for instance, consisting of toothpick ships poised precariously on cardboard

waves, may have value as a creative activity but is probably not very helpful in developing an accurate concept of this historical event.

This is not true, of course, of the excellent life-size dioramas found in many museums which are completely accurate and successfully convey an impression of reality to the viewer.

Templates and mock-ups. A template is a blow-up of a person, place, or object on cardboard, plywood, or other stiff board. It may be painted, colored, or may be only an outline. Templates may be made of practically anything from an Indian brave to a silkworm. They furnish creative opportunities for children and generally enhance the eye-appeal of any display or bulletin board exhibit. Templates of maps and geometric figures such as squares, circles, and trapezoids, may serve a variety of functions in any elementary classroom.

A mock-up is a model or replica in which proportion has been disregarded. In other words, in a mock-up certain details are purposely blown-up out of proportion while others are omitted entirely or in part. Thus is attention directed toward the specific features or processes under study. Mock-ups can be stationary; they can contain movable parts; they can be made of wood, cardboard, plasticene, chicken wire covered with paper toweling, papier-mâché, or any other available material. They are excellent for calling attention to certain items under study, but the fact that they are simplified and distorted should always be explained to pupils.

PROJECTED MATERIALS

The overhead projector. One of the most versatile pieces of projection equipment for the elementary teacher is the overhead projector. Many classrooms are now furnished with this projector, which can be purchased for approximately two or three hundred dollars. It can be moved easily on a table with casters. Some companies have models that may be folded into a case that is about the size of that for an average record player. If a permanent possession in the classroom, the overhead projector may be built into the teacher's desk or a table so that it is ready for use at all times.

The overhead projector has many advantages. In the first place, it permits the teacher or user to face the group he is addressing. Secondly, it does not require a darkened room as do some other types of projection equipment.

Probably the greatest advantage of the overhead projector, however, is its versatility. Many models come equipped with an acetate roll which can be marked with a grease pencil, plain or colored. The roll can be rolled along to permit continuous writing for a period of about two hours. Furthermore, the pencil marks may be erased easily with a soft

**The overhead projector is a versatile piece of
equipment for the elementary school teacher.**

clean cloth, thus permitting continued reuse of the acetate surface. Used
in this manner, the overhead projector is preferred by some teachers to
the ordinary chalkboard because of the ease of writing or illustrating it
offers to the user, and because it can be easily seen by all viewers. This
last value is important particularly when large groups of pupils are
involved.

One of the most effective uses of the overhead projector is projection
of transparencies. These may be made on acetate sheets with grease pencil
or India ink. They may be colored with colored grease pencils or
colored inks. A variation of the ordinary transparency is a set of overlays used to illustrate sequence. For instance, a basic outline map on
a transparency may be overlaid with a consecutive sequence of brightly
colored transparent overlays, depicting such things as rainfall, population, and elevation. Also, if the teacher has access to a photo-copying
machine, transparencies may be made of any picture or page of a book
in a matter of seconds.

Transparencies made for use in the overhead projector may also be
used for more permanent display purposes. Backed with white paper,

and placed within simple frames, a set of vividly colored transparencies can make a most effective and attractive bulletin board display.

Lastly, the overhead projector may be used to view many different types of objects either opaque or transparent. Opaque objects or figures appear as silhouettes when projected on the screen, while objects or pictures that permit light to pass through will yield a brightly colored image.

The opaque projector. The country cousin of projection equipment is the opaque projector. With this versatile machine, teachers can project flat pictures, book or magazine pages, examples of student work, three-dimensional objects, transparencies, and just about any kind of opaque materials that can be fitted on the table of the projector.

The opaque projector is also very valuable in making large-scale reproductions. Small pictures, maps, graphs, diagrams, etc. may be projected on the chalkboard or on a large piece of paper to the desired size. The projected outlines may then be traced. This is the easiest and quickest way to make large-scale maps, templates, etc. and many teachers use the opaque projector as much for this purpose as for any other.

For group viewing, the opaque projector has a few serious disadvantages. It is not inexpensive, for the usual cost may range from three hundred dollars up. It cannot be used satisfactorily unless the room is almost completely dark which presents a problem to those teachers who do not have black-out curtains at their windows. It is rather a bulky piece of equipment and cannot easily be carried from place to place. Most schools, however, have solved this problem by installing it on a table with rollers or casters.

In general, although the opaque projector has some major limitations, its versatility makes it a desirable and popular piece of equipment in most elementary schools.

Filmstrips and slides. Frequently called a "headful in a handful," the filmstrip is probably the most widely used projected visual aid found in the elementary classroom. Most teachers are well acquainted with filmstrips, and their advantages:

1. They permit the user to regulate the speed of operation, thus permitting as much pupil participation, questions, and comments as desired.

2. They are inexpensive, averaging about six dollars. This means that most schools or school systems may maintain their own filmstrip library and do not have to depend solely on rentals.

3. They are available on a wide variety of topics, and maturity levels of pupils ranging from kindergarten through college.

The filmstrip projector is a popular and versatile instructional aid.

4. They are contained in very small containers (about 1 inch) which makes them easy to store and transport.

5. They are available in many topics in either black and white or in color.

6. They require only a slightly darkened room and can thus be shown in most ordinary classrooms.

7. They present a subject in a fixed sequential order of frames, which means that individual frames cannot be lost or misplaced.

8. The filmstrip projector is lightweight, portable, easy to operate, and relatively inexpensive. There are several types of projectors now on the market. A heavy-duty combination filmstrip and slide projector, suitable for school use, costs in the neighborhood of about one hundred fifty dollars. A sound filmstrip-slide projector, which combines a record player and a projector into one piece of equipment, can be purchased for a little over two hundred dollars. Projectors that provide for the automatic advance of frames are more expensive than those that are manually operated. In most school situations, however, the manually-operated machine is often preferred since the automatic advance for many lessons negates one of the chief advantages of this medium—that the speed can be regulated according to the purpose and needs of the group.

In general, the filmstrip has only three serious limitations. First, its fixed sequence is a disadvantage when teachers want to use only certain frames. Obviously, when this is the case, slides are preferable to the filmstrip. Secondly, both the filmstrip and slides are *still media* and usually do not create the degree of realism found in a moving picture. Thirdly, filmstrips may be easily damaged and are difficult to repair. The perforations along the sides of the strip may be ripped if the filmstrip is misused or threaded incorrectly, and if there is much damage, they are almost impossible to repair. However, the fact that they are so inexpensive compensates to some degree for this limitation which, in fact, is not very serious when the strips are cared for properly.

How may the filmstrip be used in an elementary classroom? As Cypher says, "There is no 'always' when using filmstrips—one does not always use a filmstrip *after* a motion picture; one does not always read aloud the captions; one does not always use a filmstrip for slowly paced, controlled viewing; one does not always use a filmstrip for summarization purposes."[10]

The variety of uses for a filmstrip is infinite. It may be used to motivate a unit of study or to summarize. It may be used by a pupil committee as part of a report to the class. It may be used to find the answers to specific questions, or to test or teach specific skills.

Because the filmstrip lends itself so well to pupil participation, this advantage should be capitalized upon as frequently as possible. Pupils can help to set up and operate the equipment. They can read the captions and supplement them with a discussion of their own experiences and knowledge. They can ask questions and make mental notes of points to be explored further through follow-up experiences. In all, the filmstrip permits a high degree of pupil contribution and interaction and this, without doubt, is one of its greatest strengths. The wise teacher will certainly capitalize upon it. The point is well made by Cypher as follows:

A filmstrip can stimulate interest, present facts, show a series of scenes of foreign places or people, outline the steps to take in some scientific process, indicate what to do under certain conditions, etc. But . . . the mere showing of such a series of pictures is not "teaching with pictures." There must be discussion; there must be time to weigh and talk about evidence shown; there must be explanation for some of the facts given; there should be analysis of details presented. In other words, there should be an opportunity to consider and talk about the relationship of the visualized presentation to the subject content or scope of an area of study. Unless we do this, the use of visualized

[10] Irene F. Cypher, "Filmstrips," *Educational Screen and Audio Visual Guide*, Vol. 40 (May, 1961), p. 236.

materials can be meaningless and add little if anything to the study of any subject.[11]

There are many types of slides that can be used to advantage in the elementary classroom. Those that can be used on the overhead projector have previously been mentioned. Perhaps the most popular slides are the 2" x 2", 35mm transparencies which are similar to the filmstrip except, of course, the frames are separate. These have, in general, the same advantages as the filmstrip with the added advantage that they can be shown in the order and quantity desired. Sets of 2" x 2" slides can be purchased on a variety of subjects or they can be made by the teacher and pupils. Today, in many schools, a teacher may requisition the purchase of an inexpensive camera for permanent use in his classroom. By having this immediately available, the teacher can snap pictures of classroom activities or exhibits that can be developed into the popular 2" x 2" slides.

For a time, the older 3¼" x 4" lantern slide declined in popularity, but its use is increasing again today because it does have some advantages over the smaller transparencies. Because it has a larger surface, it can present more detail which is an important consideration when viewing maps, diagrams, and detailed drawings.

Probably the greatest advantage of the 3¼" x 4" slide is that it lends itself to a variety of creative activities of children. Pupils can make many different types of slides. The simplest is the silhouette slide in which silhouetted figures are fastened between two pieces of clear glass, plastic, or cellophane. If glass slides are used, they should be purchased from a commercial supply company (for about 3 or 4 cents each) because the glass is thinner and clearer than ordinary window pane glass.

Clear glass can also be used for India ink or colored ink slides. Ink may be applied directly to the glass which may then be bound along the edges with tape to make the slide easier and safer to handle and harder to break. When desired, a cover of clear glass can be placed directly on top of the painted slide and the edges of both bound together with tape. Painted slides project a bright and attractive image when projected on the screen. Painting on glass, however, with satisfactory results is fairly difficult for young children, and these slides are usually recommended for upper elementary grade pupils.

More adaptable than the clear glass slides are the frosted glass slides. Pieces of 3¼" x 4" frosted glass can be purchased for approximately fifteen cents each. Clear glass can be frosted by children or teacher, however, by wetting two pieces of glass, placing a small amount of

[11] Irene F. Cypher, "Filmstrips," *Educational Screen and Audio Visual Guide*, Vol. 40 (January, 1961), p. 31.

The lantern slide projector is a valuable instructional aid.

grinding compound (carborundum) between them and rubbing them together until the surfaces on both pieces are frosted. Frosted glass will take ordinary pencil and colored marking pencils, and these slides can easily be made by fairly young children. The drawing should, of course, be made on paper first and then traced on the frosted glass. Frosted glass slides can be washed with steel wool pads and reused indefinitely. Again, for safety of handling and permanent storage, it is advisable to bind the edges with tape.

Slides may also be made on plastic or cellophane. The plastic is used in about the same way as frosted glass and many feel it is superior because it is unbreakable. Cellophane slides will take ink or are particularly suitable for projecting typewritten materials.

Films. Over the past several years, the sound motion picture has proven to be one of the teacher's most valuable instructional tools. It can effectively remove the limitations of time and space placed on the typical classroom learning situation. It can transport the learner to any era or any location in a matter of seconds. It can literally bring the entire world into the classroom. The specific contributions the correctly used film can make to teaching and learning are:

1. It brings the outside world into the classroom. Through motion, sound, and color it can bring into the classroom the world, cities, processes, and events for leisurely study.

2. It helps to bring unseen realms to the classroom. Through time-lapse photography and microphotography the flowering of a plant, the growth of tissues, or the flight of a bullet can be studied with ease.

3. It can recreate and dramatize the past. Historical events and great personalities of the past can be brought dramatically into the classroom through the medium of the motion-picture film. This can be of great value to the teacher in providing an illusion of reality to many aspects of history and to create student interest in further reading and research. The film is not a substitute for written material on history but it can be a great motivation.

4. It can be a substitute for a field trip. Trips into the community to see the world at work and play are features of any good instructional program. However, many times the distance and the time involved deter extensive use of field trips. The film can be a very effective substitute and in many instances can prove to be more effective. The film focuses the attention on important things to be seen and every student has an equal opportunity to see them—no one is standing in front of him and no disturbing noises prevent his hearing the guide.[12]

Many research studies have attempted to identify the specific influence of films on learning. It is, of course, extremely difficult, and dangerous, to draw conclusions concerning the specific contributions of an isolated film showing, or even a series of films, upon learning. The following, however, are general conclusions on which there appears to be agreement, with examples of statements supporting them.

1. Films can teach factual information.

Films can teach factual information effectively over a wide range of subject-matter content, age ranges, abilities, and conditions of use.[13]

. . . research supports the fact that using carefully selected teaching films results in the more effective learning of factual information.[14]

[12] Amo De Bernardis, *The Use of Instructional Materials* (New York, Appleton-Century-Crofts, 1960), pp. 51-52.
[13] Charles F. Hoban and E. B. Van Ormer, *Instructional Film Research, 1918-1950*, Technical Report No. SDC 269-7-19 (Port Washington, N. Y., U. S. Naval Special Devices Center, Instructional Film Research Program, Pennsylvania State University, 1950).
[14] Walter Arno Wittich and Charles Francis Schuller, *Audiovisual Materials: Their Nature and Use*, 3rd ed. (New York, Harper & Row, Publishers, Inc., 1962), p. 383.

2. Films can teach motor skills.

Films can be used in teaching perceptual motor skills, such as the construction of the reed mat, handwriting performance, athletic skills, and the teaching of lathe operators.[15]

3. Films are helpful in developing complex concepts.

Films can be used in developing concepts such as inferring one fact from another, comprehension of complex processes, and so on.[16]

An often made criticism is that the new media may be successful in aiding acquisition of factual knowledge but may be unsuccessful in developing conceptual thinking, critical ability, or inference drawing. The limited research done with this facet of learning does not substantiate these criticisms. Films are successful in aiding conceptual learning. In some instances, films have been more successful than conventional methods in getting across rather difficult concepts.[17]

4. Films can increase the retention of information.

Research studies which measure by delayed or duplicate-form tests the retention of information learned from films consistently show that films are superior to verbal materials.[18]

Loss or forgetting of what has been learned does not seem to be any greater for film than for any other method of teaching. Although loss is tied up with the nature of presentation and type of subject-matter, film research has shown that what is taught over film may be retained for long periods of time without appreciable loss.[19]

5. Films can increase interest.

The fact that . . . pupils so consistently mention the clarity and understandability of films as learning devices leads to the observation that pupil interest is enhanced because the sound film is a realistic way of learning, like that used in out-of-school situations.[20]

6. Films can strengthen reading interests.

. . . research evidence establishes the fact that the regular use of teaching films produces in pupils the desire, interest, and readiness both for more reading and for more comprehensible reading.[21]

Many teachers have wondered whether the introduction of newer media, particularly television, would lessen the role of the motion picture. There appears to be no evidence to this effect. On the contrary, the number of educational films available to schools continues to expand

[15] Charles F. Hoban and E. B. Van Ormer, *op. cit.*
[16] *Ibid.*
[17] Hideya Kumata and Malcolm S. MacLean, Jr., *op. cit.*, p. 282.
[18] Walter Arno Wittich and Charles Francis Schuller, *op. cit.*, p. 383.
[19] Hideya Kumata and Malcolm S. MacLean, Jr., *op. cit.*, p. 282.
[20] Walter Arno Wittich and Charles Francis Schuller, *op. cit.*, p. 381.
[21] *Ibid.*, p. 385.

rapidly and in 1955 a survey reported that the number of elementary teachers who made frequent use of sound films had increased to 35 per cent as compared to 15 per cent in 1946.[22]

There are many different types of films suitable for classroom use which may be classified in a variety of ways. Wittich and Schuller classify all sound films into two broad categories, (1) basic teaching films and (2) supplementary teaching films. The basic teaching film is, as its name implies, usually developed for the purpose of teaching a skill, concept, or process in a specific curriculum area. Supplementary teaching films are made available to the schools through various industrial, governmental, or other agencies and are used to enrich or supplement the curriculum. They include (1) documentary films, (2) sponsored films (to advertise or tell the story of a business or industrial concern), and (3) entertainment films.[23]

Correct classroom use of films follows the general procedure of effective usage stated earlier, (1) preparation, (2) presentation, (3) follow-up, and (4) evaluation. Specific guides to effective film usage are well stated in the following:

1. Steps should be taken to see that the members of the class are *ready* to see the film.

   a. They feel that the film will help them with a problem or question which has already come up. They know with a degree of definiteness why they want to see this film, what specifically they are going to look and listen for.

   b. They know what to expect to see and hear when the film is shown.

   c. Parts of the film, both pictures and sound, objects, persons, words, etc. which are likely not to be comprehended or will probably be misunderstood are clarified in so far as possible.

2. Steps should be taken to make sure that room and viewing and listening conditions will be as favorable as possible before the film is shown. (Remember that the film is a seeing-and-listening experience. It is not a "give-and-take" discussion, it is not a question-and-answer period; it is different and should be approached differently from the way in which one participates in other classroom experiences.)

   a. Make sure ahead of time that the film to be shown is free of defects which might interrupt the viewing by the class.

   b. Make sure that the film is on the projector already focused and that the projection equipment is ready to start projection without delay of any sort.

---

[22] "Audio-Visual Education in Urban School Districts, 1953-1954," *NEA Research Bulletin*, Vol. 33 (October, 1955), p. 116.

[23] Walter Arno Wittich and Charles Francis Schuller, *op. cit.*, pp. 372-380.

c. There should be no delay to rearrange desks or chairs or to move a screen into position.

d. Make sure that needs of individuals in the class have been taken care of so that they will not have to disturb the others during the projection.

e. Make sure that the class will not be distracted by visitors during the projection. (It is well to attach a small notice on the outside of the room, e. g., "Class viewing motion picture. Please do not disturb until lights go on.") Remember that learners cannot "attend" to two learning situations at the same time . . .

f. Make sure that seeing conditions are the best possible.

g. Make sure that listening conditions are the best possible.

h. Film should be projected without distraction of any sort by instructor or others. (When silent films are used it is well to have the instructor or some other person prepared to present appropriate commentary while projection is in progress.)

3. Evaluation of the film experience should begin immediately following the viewing of the film.

a. Normal classroom conditions, light, etc., should be restored immediately.

b. Projectionists should refrain from any manipulation, such as rewinding the film, taking down the projector, etc., until after the class has discussed the film.

c. Class members should be encouraged first to identify the specific help this film provided on the problem at hand.

d. Ample opportunity should be provided for a discussion of the film in relation to the problem at hand. Care should be taken to "keep on the subject," or reasonably close to it. It is at this point that progress on a unit of learning already begun is slowed considerably by a tendency to go off on a tangent to discuss some interesting but distracting and, for the moment, irrelevant part of the motion picture. Efficient classroom use of the film media will studiously avoid such sidetracking.

4. Provision should be made for reshowing of all or part of the film material just viewed and discussed. There is considerable evidence to indicate that such reshowing should be regularly practiced for all films which are properly associated with the ongoing work of the class. Reshowing not only assures more complete comprehension but provides for a desirable degree of "overlearning."

5. Ample provision should be made for integration of the film experience in follow-up activities of the class and of individual students.

a. Make sure that individuals have been encouraged to re-evaluate previous conclusions in the light of new experiences gained through the film showing.

b. Encourage pertinent new inquiries which may have been stimulated by the film.

   c. Encourage critical evaluation of film experience through checking with other sources and authorities.

   d. Encourage attempts to apply new knowledge gained by film experiences.[24]

Thus far, we have been discussing the 16mm film, either silent or sound, black-and-white or color. Perhaps some mention should be made, however, of the current interest in the 8mm film for school use. This film has long been popular for home use but has met with only a limited reception in the schoolroom. Today, some audio-visual experts predict a sharp rise in the school use of these "paper-backs of the film industry" in the very near future. This prediction is supported by such factors as (1) whereas the 16mm film is prohibitively expensive for many schools to buy (and some even to rent), the 8mm film is considerably cheaper and schools could therefore develop their own film libraries with ready accessibility to all teachers, (2) the 16mm projector is still an expensive piece of equipment to buy and a relatively complicated one to operate compared to the 8mm projector, and (3) it is comparatively easy and inexpensive to make an 8mm film of school activities which can serve a variety of purposes such as enriching the curriculum, enabling children to evaluate their past performances, providing an exciting creative experience for children, explaining the school program to parents and community, providing a permanent record of outstanding school events, or demonstrating effective instructional techniques to groups of teachers.

AUDITORY MATERIALS

Radio. In the 1920's and 1930's, there was considerable interest and research directed toward the possibilities of educational radio. However, with the advent of television it looked for a while as though radio was going to disappear from the scene entirely. This has apparently not happened, for many schools throughout the country tune in regularly on various educational networks, such as the Empire State FM School of the Air (New York State), the Wisconsin School of the Air, and the Texas School of the Air. In addition, certain cities, such as Philadelphia, have conducted for years system-wide broadcasts on a variety of topics which have been effectively utilized by all schools.

There is little doubt that radio is uniquely suited to certain purposes:

1. To teach listening skills.
2. To provide children with an on-the-spot awareness of current scientific, historical, political, and social events of significance.

[24] A. J. Foy Cross and Irene F. Cypher, *Audio-Visual Education* (New York, Thomas Y. Crowell Company, 1961), pp. 65-67.

3. To strengthen appreciation of music.
4. To bring into the classroom numerous resource people.
5. To teach modern languages.
6. To encourage creativity and appreciation by encouraging children to create their own mental images rather than merely view the visual images created by another.

In general, the consensus of opinion appears to be that (1) radio is a valuable educational tool in its own right and is not simply the poor man's TV, (2) it can do many things as well as other media and can do certain things better than any other, and (3) it realizes its fullest value when used cooperatively with other media rather than in isolation. This last point is well stated as follows:

It appears by now that radio's greatest value is in service *in conjunction with other media.* . . . What is important is not what *radio* can do but what it can *help do.* . . . Radio . . . is best when used in conjunction with such other procedures and materials as teachers' efforts, maps, books, pamphlets, group discussions, etc. . . . The concept needed, it would appear, is one which we might call the "concert," almost the "symphony," approach. There are times for solos, indeed. But for the great burden of education today, an orchestration of media can best bring results. It is in that role, rather than as a "solo instrument," that radio seems at its best.[25]

Recordings. The production of worthwhile disk recordings for schoolroom use has increased greatly in recent years. Such recordings have practically all of the values of radio plus the fact that they can be auditioned by the teacher and used at the exact time they are needed. In the past, most records were of the 78 rpm type. These had the disadvantages of having a fairly short playing time, were breakable, and were fairly cumbersome to store. Much more satisfactory are the 45 rpm, 33⅓ rpm, and 16 rpm unbreakable records now available on a wide variety of subjects. Musical recordings are, of course, very numerous and in many schools an extensive collection forms the backbone of the music appreciation program. Recordings of famous voices, Franklin Roosevelt, Winston Churchill, etc., or narrated events are valuable in recreating the past for children. Literary recordings of plays, stories, etc. can be used to great advantage in the elementary classroom. In addition, those schools with foreign language programs find disk recordings to be exceedingly valuable instructional aids.

[25] Harry J. Skornia, "Educational Radio: Its Past and Its Future," *Educational Television, The Next Ten Years* (Stanford, California, Stanford University, Institute for Communication Research, 1962), pp. 367-368.

Ideally, every elementary classroom should be equipped with a three or four speed record player, preferably with one or more sets of earphones to permit individual listening. This is far from an unrealistic dream, because a satisfactory machine can be purchased for somewhat over a hundred dollars. This is money well spent when one considers the variety of uses to which the record player may be put. One or two machines in a building are simply not sufficient. In the first place, the player is invariably in use in another classroom when a teacher wants to use it and secondly, with children, custodians, or teachers constantly toting it from one part of the building to another, half the time the player is unavailable because it is in need of repair.

Today, no one has to sell the elementary teacher on the values of the tape recorder. It is very easy to operate. Even a primary grade youngster can learn to use it without much difficulty. It is relatively inexpensive. A good model can be purchased for one hundred fifty to one hundred eighty dollars. It is so versatile it is difficult to mention all its possible uses. Most teachers find that it is particularly valuable for:

1. Offering children a variety of musical, literary, dramatic, scientific, and historical experiences now available on prerecorded tapes which may be purchased or borrowed from many sources. Particularly promising also is the expansion of tape-dubbing services of certain schools or universities. These centers maintain extensive collections of master tapes and, either for no cost or a very small expense, will duplicate any recording on a blank tape. Some centers will furnish the blank tape, at a certain fee, while others request the schools to forward their own blank tapes. With the ever-growing number of libraries of tape collections plus these duplicating services, it is easy to see how the elementary teacher may put his tape recorder to very good use.

2. Preserving on tape any classroom or school activity.

3. Duplicating valuable radio programs, disk recordings, etc., for classroom use.

4. Evaluating numerous types of language experiences. Panel discussions, oral reports, play rehearsals, class discussions, etc., can be taped and played to encourage children's critical evaluations of their own performances.

5. Speech correction activities. Children with articulatory disorders frequently cannot "hear" themselves speak. Taping a record of such a pupil's reading or speaking is invaluable in helping him to become conscious of his difficulty and in motivating him to correct it.

6. Strengthening listening skills.

7. Standardizing directions, etc., for any testing situation.

8. Preparing narrations for pupil-made slidefilms or filmstrips.

9. Making available to a class certain speeches, lectures, or interviews

with famous people or community personnel who could not visit the class in person.

10. Preserving records of pupil or pupil-parent conferences for further counseling purposes.

11. Teaching foreign languages.

Most commercial tape recorders record and play at either 3¾ or 7½ IPS (inches per second). When speech is desired, the slower speed is adequate and thus increases the amount of tape time available. For musical reproduction, the 7½ IPS is necessary. Generally speaking, the faster the tape passes through the machine, the higher the quality of reproduction.

Monoral tape is used for most ordinary purposes. This has two tracks, located on the dull side of the tape. This permits the user to record for the full length of the tape, flip the tape over (without rewinding) and record through a second time, thus doubling the recording and play-back time. On certain models, it is not necessary to turn over the tape, for a button can be pushed which reverses the direction of the tape and the machine continues to record.

Criteria for selecting a tape recorder include the following:

1. *Simplicity*. Is the recorder easy to operate? Can the tape be threaded quickly and easily?
2. *Portability*. Is the equipment easily transported? Is it designed to be portable? This is important if the equipment is to be used by a number of teachers.
3. *Quality of recording*. Is the quality of the recording high enough to meet all of the needs of the school: speech, music, broadcast, and so on?
4. *Service*. Are service and repair available locally?[26]

EDUCATIONAL TELEVISION

As every teacher knows, there is far from unanimous agreement on the role of television in education. It has been criticized by such strong statements as, "Under the impact of television I can contemplate a time in America when people can neither read nor write, but will be no better than forms of plant life," and it is as "dangerous to culture as the atom bomb is to civilization."[27] It has been completely ignored or rejected by some school systems. Many teachers fear and distrust it. On the other hand, many of its advocates consider it the greatest boon to education since the printing press, and claim that it is the most effective resource yet developed for teaching and learning.

[26] Amo De Bernardis, *op. cit.*, p. 71.
[27] Quoted by Charles A. Siepmann, *Television and Education in the United States* (Paris, UNESCO, 1952), p. 12.

Undoubtedly these differences of opinion will continue to exist for years to come. In general, however, the range of controversy seems to be narrowing; both its critics and advocates appear to be more temperate in their claims. Also, of one thing we can be certain.

IN SPITE OF MIXED REACTIONS, THE USE OF EDUCATIONAL TELEVISION IS STEADILY INCREASING. There are nearly eighty educational television stations now on the air, whereas ten years ago there were none. There are more than four hundred closed-circuit ETV systems in regular operation that are used for elementary to college and university teaching.[28] Several hundred research studies have been conducted on the efficacy of television as a learning medium. Moreover, there appear to be clear indications that this growth will accelerate in the future. One reference states,

Apparently, an even more explosive period of growth lies ahead. At least 40 new stations are in some stage of preparation. Several hundred educational institutions are now making plans for extending the use of closed-circuit television. Following the lead of Alabama, Oklahoma, Florida, North Carolina, and Texas, nearly a dozen states are planning state-wide educational television networks. In the Middle West and in New England, plans are being drawn for regional networks. A national "live" network, connecting educational stations by cable or microwave may not be far in the future. The possibility of an educational communications satellite, instantaneously relaying programs for national and hemispheric coverage, is a foreseeable reality. . . .

More and more schools and colleges are indicating that instructional television is part of their future plans. A large number of school officials believe that, ten years from now, television will carry some part of the teaching of the great majority of school children in this nation, and that it will be used increasingly for direct instruction in the large colleges and universities. It is also expected that television will make available at home to students of whatever age, a large part of the college curriculum. Thus education may become easily available at any time in life.

The growing proportion of leisure time in our society, and the increasing complexity of the knowledge a citizen must have about the world in which he lives, point to a constantly growing need for educational television broadcasting services in the community. By the same token, the population explosion and the rising costs of buildings and services, as well as the generally greater demands for educational quality, suggest a constantly growing need for direct instructional television in the schools. A medium with so much potential, with so many needs to meet, and so many plans being made for it, is likely to continue to grow for a long period of time.[29]

[28] National Educational Television and Radio Center, *Current Developments in Educational Television* (Washington, D. C., January, 1963), pp. 3, 8.

[29] "Recommendations—By the Television Advisory Panel of the United States Office of Education, Department of Health, Education, and Welfare," *Educational Television, The Next Ten Years, op. cit.*, pp. 2-3.

THERE IS GENERAL ACCEPTANCE OF THE ENRICHMENT ROLE OF TELEVISION. The controversy just mentioned concerning the role of educational television does not usually apply to it as an enrichment medium. Its value in this respect is generally accepted. No one will deny that certain commercial programs, or certain programs aimed directly for school consumption, have an enrichment and supplementary value. Millions of school children saw the flight of America's first astronaught, the presidential inauguration, and similar programs on television sets installed in schools throughout the country. The value of this type of experience is unquestioned by any sane educator.

Where the controversy *does* lie, however, is on the role of television *as a direct instructional tool*. This is more accurately called *instructional television*. It can be transmitted to the school or classroom through open-circuit (broadcast) or through closed-circuit utilizing cable transmission. In any case, it represents an attempt to delegate part (seldom more than this in the elementary school) of the school's instructional responsibility to the teacher on television rather than to the "live" teacher in the classroom. What are the major concerns and questions of teachers concerning instructional television?

WILL INSTRUCTIONAL TELEVISION REPLACE THE CLASSROOM TEACHER? This has previously been answered and there is little need for reiteration here. Those responsible educators who advocate the use of instructional television do not do so because it is an economical means of saving teachers' salaries, but rather because it is a means of improving the educational program. After all, only the most irresponsible would advocate improving education by getting rid of teachers!

True, the teacher's role may be changed by extensive use of television. This point was made earlier in the chapter. But it will not be lessened nor eliminated. Of this there can be no reasonable doubt.

WHAT ARE THE ADVANTAGES CLAIMED FOR INSTRUCTIONAL TELEVISION? These are usually considered to be:

1. Providing a high-quality of instruction for children. Instruction by television may be superior in many ways to ordinary classroom instruction for two good reasons. In the first place, only the highly-skilled, exceptionally capable teacher is chosen as the television teacher. Secondly, the television teacher has much more time to plan, and facilities to draw upon, to perfect a single lesson than does the classroom teacher who teaches a full day's schedule.

Instructional television procedures make possible the provision of more time for teacher planning, emphasizing the importance of content selection, organization, and the utilization of visuals to bring meaning to abstract ideas. As one teacher said, "There is no other situation where the teacher has so much time to plan lessons and create visuals for the lesson. This is the most satisfying part of teaching on television."[30]

2. Distributing superior quality of instruction to a large number of schools. This is an especially important consideration for those under-privileged or rural schools that cannot otherwise afford the equipment, visual materials, laboratories, and expert teachers televised instruction may offer them.

3. Improving the quality of instruction. Television may help to im-prove the instructional procedures of those teachers who teach on tele-vision as well as those who view the televised lesson. By means of kine-scopes the television teacher may view and evaluate his own performance, which should provide a strong means of professional growth. Then too, the classroom teacher has the opportunity of watching a master teacher at work, an opportunity denied to him under ordinary circumstances (see Chapter 12). Such an opportunity should certainly help to strengthen his teaching competence. As Asheim reports, "One of the major impacts of educational television may be on teaching method. Teaching by tele-vision is different from other teaching; it imposes a sharper discipline upon method; it increases the use of a variety of devices as teaching aids; it introduces innovations that can affect all teaching, in the classroom as well as on the screen."[31]

4. Offering unique educational experiences. The television camera can do things a live classroom teacher simply cannot do. It can enable all children in the group to look through a microscope at the same time. It can give children an intimate close-up view of any process or object. It can peer into inaccessible places. It can combine the teacher's presentation with films, filmstrips, and other visuals to an extent and with an ease just not possible in the ordinary classroom situation.

5. Offering possibilities for patterns of instruction different from the traditional one teacher per class type. Television makes it possible to teach larger groups when this is educationally desirable. It makes it pos-sible to differentiate instruction according to the needs of several groups. It may make it possible for the classroom teacher to spend more time with certain individuals or small groups.

WHAT ARE THE LIMITATIONS OF INSTRUCTIONAL TELEVISION? Undoubt-edly, the most serious limitation and the one that makes many educators question the ultimate value of instructional television is the lack of face-to-face interaction between teacher and learner. The television teacher

[30] William M. Brish, "Closed Circuit Television for Science—U. S. A.," *Communica-tion Media and the School, op. cit.*, pp. 220-221.
[31] Lester Asheim, "A Survey of Informed Opinion on Television's Future Place in Education," *Educational Television, The Next Ten Years, op. cit.*, p. 26.

does not see the reaction—amusement, agreement, perplexity, or confusion—of his pupils. He does not give children an opportunity to ask questions, nor can he stimulate a two-way discussion. He cannot go back to clarify a point someone missed. In short, he can distill information but most educators agree that this one-way process is not all that is necessary to learning. True, there have been experimental attempts to overcome this major limitation through push-button reaction panels, supplementary pick-up cameras, and various audio talk-back systems. But these, so far, would seem to be poor substitutes for the classroom teacher who knows his pupils, knows the local situation, and enjoys a steady two-way communication with his pupils.

Not only does this face-to-face relationship permit the two-way communication usually considered essential to most types of learning, but it also gives the pupil what he often needs most, a sympathetic friend, a counselor, a helper with his problems. The television teacher is an impersonal image on a screen. The live teacher is, particularly with young children, a parent surrogate to whom the pupil can turn for advice, help, and understanding. Is there any room for disagreement with the following? "The student wants to be known by his teacher, and he wants to know that he is known; this kind of personal relationship, built up through time, is as important as a brilliantly conceived and planned lecture crammed with facts. Information-acquisition is not enough in education, and there is danger that educational television lends itself to nothing more than this."[32]

HOW DO STUDENTS FEEL ABOUT INSTRUCTIONAL TELEVISION? Considerable research has been directed toward the attitudes of learners of all ages toward instruction via television. As one would expect, attitudes were influenced by the students' liking for the subject or for the television or classroom teacher. One group of students, for instance, reported nearly 100 per cent that they liked their TV science class better than their regular class, but more than 50 per cent preferred their regular social studies class to the TV class.[33] In general, however, it appears that students' liking for instructional television follows a U-shaped curve, according to age. Elementary children are fairly enthusiastic about it, high school and college students less so, with adult students often appearing to be the most enthusiastic of all.

HOW DO TEACHERS FEEL ABOUT INSTRUCTIONAL TELEVISION? The attitudes of teachers seem to parallel somewhat those of students. Again, ele-

---

[32] *Ibid.*, p. 18.
[33] Jefferson County Schools, *Project Report: Jefferson County Television Elementary Schools, 1957-1960* (Louisville, Ky., Jefferson County Board of Education, 1960).

mentary teachers, once their distrust and suspicion are alleviated, appear to be receptive and ". . . come to like and depend on television as one part of their teaching resources."[34] Secondary school teachers are apparently less receptive and ". . . the real center of teacher resistance to instructional television is in the colleges."[35] One may speculate on the reasons for the differences in attitudes among students and teachers but pertinent to our discussion only is the fact that, apparently, if television is going to make a large-scale impact on the educational scene, it will apparently begin in the elementary school.

Is INSTRUCTIONAL TELEVISION AS EFFECTIVE AS "LIVE" TEACHING? When all is said and done, this is the real, the vital, the important question, the crux of the whole matter. What is the answer to date?

Several hundred research studies have attempted to compare the success of instructional television with the traditional classroom pattern. The results of most of these can be summarized in one strongly supported conclusion: *there is no significant difference*. In other words, pupils apparently learn as much, but no more, in a TV class as in a conventional classroom. One review of research states the point as follows: "The conclusion is that the average student is likely to learn about as much from a TV class as from ordinary classroom methods; in some cases he will learn more and in some less, but the over-all verdict has been, 'no significant difference.' "[36]

This conclusion, however, refers only to gross academic gain and leaves many important questions to be answered before we can finally determine the role of television in education. Questions yet to be answered conclusively by research include: Is television more effective with one age level of learner than with another? What influence does the novelty effect have on the measured learning gain? What specific aspects of learning can best be developed by television? By the classroom teacher? How can the values of both be combined to the best advantage of the learner? In other words, as Tanner points out, the crucial need at the moment is, not to discover whether televised instruction is better or worse than classroom teaching, but to find out "What types of learning outcomes can be derived through instructional television that cannot be derived through direct classroom instruction? What types of learning outcomes can be derived through direct classroom instruction that cannot be derived through instructional television?"[37]

[34] Wilbur Schramm, "Learning from Instructional Television," *Review of Educational Research*, Vol. 32 (April, 1962), p. 162.

[35] *Ibid.*, p. 163.

[36] *Ibid.*, p. 156.

[37] Daniel Tanner, "Needed Research in Instructional Television," *School Review*, Vol. 69 (Autumn, 1961), p. 313.

The answers to these two questions will determine the future of instructional television. We can only hope that they are found in the not-too-distant future.

AUTO-INSTRUCTIONAL DEVICES

As with television, self-teaching devices are currently the center of considerable controversy. What are the most pertinent questions today's educators are asking about these new media?

WHAT ARE AUTO-INSTRUCTIONAL DEVICES? All devices fall into two broad classifications, (1) the mechanical devices popularly known as *teaching machines* and (2) the printed devices which are usually programmed textbooks, although they may be series of cards. Within these broad classifications, there are numerous types, makes, and models. However, all self-teaching devices have the following basic characteristics:

1. They present subject matter in the form of a series of small, sequential, carefully graded steps which may range from several hundred to more than twenty thousand. This arrangement of content is called a *program* and is described as follows:

The subject matter to be taught is composed into a *program*. The program may be of several physical forms. It may be a book; it may be in the form of tapes or strips of paper; it may be a series of microfilmed slides; it may be auditory material to be used with a tape recorder. It consists of a series of items, referred to as *frames*. A frame is a unit of the program that requires a response of the student. The material in the frame builds cumulatively. Appropriate to the paradigm of differentiation, the program builds in small steps. The information required to answer a given item is contained in that item or in preceding items, or in both.[38]

In general, there are two basic types of programs. The *linear program* of Skinner, Holland, and others consists of an inflexible sequence of small, carefully constructed, interlocking steps the student must master in the prescribed order. The *branching program* of Crowder, and others, starts the student on a linear type program until he either makes a mistake or gives a response that indicates he knows the immediate forthcoming subject matter. If he makes a mistake, he will branch out along a new route, retracing steps he has obviously not mastered. On the other hand, if he indicates that he knows the forthcoming subject matter, he will be routed ahead since he obviously doesn't need this material. Naturally, there are many arguments as to the merits of both types of programs, although "There seems to be a general trend toward increased variety

[38] Edward J. Green, *The Learning Process and Programmed Instruction* (New York, Holt, Rinehart and Winston, Inc., 1962), p. 117.

in programming procedures, with the rapid disappearance of the branching-linear dichotomy."[39]

2. The student receives an immediate notification of the correctness of his response either by turning a page, pressing a button, pushing back a slide, etc.

3. They permit the student to work at his own pace.

WHAT IS THE HISTORY OF AUTO-INSTRUCTIONAL DEVICES? The first teaching machine was developed by Pressey in 1926. At that time it was generally considered to be a testing machine although Pressey consistently maintained it could teach as well. However, for one reason or another, it attracted little attention and it was not until the 1950's that it captured the whole-hearted interest of the educational world. The self-instructional concept is based upon the psychological principles that (1) learning is the conditioning of behavior and (2) behavior is most effectively conditioned through *reinforcement* and *reward*. Demonstrated first on rats and pigeons with pellets of food, the teaching machine offers the student reinforcement and satisfaction through the immediate notification of the correctness of his response. Probst explains it as follows:

It has long been recognized that for new material to be firmly remembered by students it is important to reinforce it. To have students repeat material to the teacher, either in speech or in writing, is one means of reinforcement. But it bores the students who are not reciting. Another attempt to reinforce material is to give some kind of reward for learning. But up to the present the reward has usually been different from learning itself. Examples are good grades, the respect of the teacher or other students, or a privilege, or a simple pleasure, like candy. What programed learning set out to achieve was reinforcement by a reward intrinsic to learning. With those who learn the most, the pleasure of learning has proved the most effective reward. Programed learning makes this reward available to all students, not just the superior students.[40]

WHAT ARE THE ADVANTAGES OF AUTO-INSTRUCTIONAL DEVICES? Advocates of the new media cite several.

1. Learning is reinforced by immediate confirmation of the student's response. Very often the teaching machine is likened to an automatic tutor which checks the student's work every inch of the way and permits him to continue to advanced work only when he has mastered the necessary preliminary stages.

[39] Harry F. Silberman, "Self-Teaching Devices and Programmed Materials," *Review of Educational Research*, Vol. 32 (April, 1962), p. 188.

[40] George E. Probst, "Programmed Learning in the Schools: Tasks for 1962," Report of Conference held by Thomas Alva Edison Foundation and Grolier Incorporated, January 13-14, 1962, *Science Teacher*, Vol. 29 (October, 1962), p. 34.

The values of auto-instructional devices are currently being investigated.

2. With a self-instructional device, none of the deterrents to learning are present as they may be with a human (but we must add, incompetent) teacher. Such deterrents as the teacher's sarcasm, disparagement, and ridicule as well as peer rivalry and competition are eliminated by the impersonality of the machine or programmed text.

3. Self-instructional devices permit learners to proceed at their own rates. This is a major advantage, cited frequently in this age of concern to provide a high-quality education for children of widely varying abilities.

4. Self-instructional devices highlight the importance of presenting a carefully planned, well-organized, and meticulously graded sequence of material to the learner. As a matter of fact, some claim that one of the greatest benefits to be derived from auto-instruction to date has been the emphasis upon careful organization and sequence of subject matter. Good teachers have always known this, of course. But if all teachers can learn it from the present interest in auto-instructional devices, education will have taken a great stride forward.

WHAT ARE THE DISADVANTAGES OF AUTO-INSTRUCTIONAL DEVICES?

1. Since the heart of the concept is the program, any self-instructional device is only as good as the program. Good programming is an exceptionally difficult and time-consuming task. The steps should be so carefully arranged as to elicit the correct responses, or else the entire point is lost. On the other hand, this does not mean that just any series of "easy" questions will suffice. As Holland explains,

Not every item designed to produce a low error rate is necessarily effective in teaching. The poorly informed programmer often writes items which can be easily answered without the student's learning what that item is supposed to teach. This misses the point of behavioral control required in good programming. The answer to an item must be one which can be given by the student only after he has gone through the behavior the programmer intends to teach, whether that behavior is simply reading other parts of the item, deducing the answer, inducing a principle, or any of a variety of other tasks.[41]

The importance and difficulty of good programming raise many questions. Who is to do the programming, the subject matter specialist or the classroom teacher or both? How soon will good programs be available on the variety of subjects taught in the elementary school? Can programs be developed that will teach important personal-social-moral trait learnings? Is the typical classroom teacher or school administrator equipped to evaluate the quality of a program in the same sense that he evaluates a textbook or other learning aid? What criteria should be used? These, and many other questions concerning programming, must be answered before auto-instructional devices become standard equipment in all elementary classrooms.

2. Although its advocates claim that it individualizes instruction, critics of the self-instructional device claim exactly the opposite. They point out that in the linear program instruction is individualized by *rate* only, which is only one dimension of learning, as stated in the preceding chapter. As a matter of fact, say the critics, linear programming forces every student to plod through an identical, inflexible sequence of tiny steps, which is really the antithesis of individualizing instruction.

3. Just as its advocates claim the impersonality of the device as an advantage, so its critics claim it as a limitation. If teacher sarcasm and ridicule are deterrents to learning, and undoubtedly they are, by the same token, teacher praise and encouragement must be stimulants to learning, and undoubtedly they are. No machine can give the child an encouraging glance; a friendly, "Never mind—you'll do better next time," or an enthusiastic, "You did a wonderful job today!"

[41] James G. Holland, "Evaluating Teaching Machines and Programs," *Teachers College Record*, Vol. 63 (October, 1961), p. 58.

Then too, as Fitzgerald points out, there is something about the impersonality of a mechanical teacher that is repugnant to many Americans who would agree strongly with his statement, "I find the thought of millions of children spending hours each day with millions of machines in millions of separate cubicles an appalling prospect."[42]

4. Finally, many object to the basic principle of the self-instructional devices, that all knowledge of mankind may be fed into a machine and come out in nice, neat, little steps and that all the student has to do is to master each of these, one at a time, in order to become a wise and learned person. Fitzgerald says it very well,

. . . the single-answer approach to education remains objectionable in principle. This approach assumes that our knowledge of the world is a fixed and orderly body of facts and conclusions. It implies a concept of reality wrapped up in separate little packages and tied with string, stacked neatly on the shelves of a vast warehouse. But the task of intelligence is more than that of a warehouse employee picking stock down the aisles. . . . Education is also inquiry, insight, emergence, the development of a critical faculty and an intuition of the web of interdependent hypotheses and inferences, the structure of abstractions about the seen and the unseen that comprises our understanding of the physical world. Learning is also exploring, conceptualizing, experimenting, interacting, valuing.[43]

WHAT IS THE FUTURE OF AUTO-INSTRUCTIONAL DEVICES? There are few educators today who still dismiss these devices as a passing fad. But exactly how prominent a role they will play in the future has yet to be determined. It is possible that they may offer a real potential for the improvement of the educational process. But how, where, when, and for how many that potential can best be incorporated into classroom practice is yet unanswered. Thus far, research that has attempted to compare the effects of programmed instruction with traditional classroom patterns has resulted in the familiar "no significant difference." One summary states,

Beyond demonstrating that a carefully written set of materials will teach if a student will spend enough time studying them, we have little unequivocal evidence for principles of programmed instruction. Comparisons between programmed and conventional instruction, however, generally show that programs are at least as good as conventional procedures and certainly better than no instruction at all.[44]

[42] H. T. Fitzgerald, "Teaching Machines: A Demurrer," *School Review*, Vol. 70 (Autumn, 1962), p. 256.
[43] *Ibid.*, pp. 251-252.
[44] Harry F. Silberman, *op. cit.*, p. 187.

Concerning the results of research in this field upon the total educative process, the same author states,

It is to be expected that the heightened research activity in programmed instruction will lead toward more carefully written, empirically developed textbooks; toward instruction that is more directly contingent on frequent testing; toward a greater relative emphasis on development of instructional materials, in contrast to the presentation of those materials; toward a greater effort devoted to the maintenance or retention of learning, in contrast to its acquisition; and toward a greater emphasis on specifying the behavioral goals of education. The programming research signals a shift in emphasis toward placing a greater burden of responsibility for learning on the quality of the instructional materials.[45]

THE INSTRUCTIONAL MATERIALS CENTER

The number and variety of teaching materials available in this technological age make the establishment of a Materials Center in the elementary school a necessity. Such a center is organized and maintained by a specialist usually designated as the Supervisor or Coordinator of Instructional Materials. Depending upon the size of the school and the extensiveness of the collection, he may serve in either a full-time or part-time capacity. If part-time, he may divide his time among two or more schools or with other teaching duties. In general, the Instructional Materials Center and Personnel provide the following services to the elementary school teacher.

1. Establish and maintain a service program. The type of program will, of course, depend upon the specific school. However, the following are generally considered to be basic to the success of a worthwhile multimedia program.

a. Equipment storage room.
b. Materials files designed to the sizes of various materials, for instance filmstrips and mounted pictures.
c. Preview room.
d. Graphics room with full stock of art supplies: construction paper, pens, ink, etc.
e. Projection equipment:
   16mm sound projectors
   Slide and filmstrip projectors
   Overhead projectors
   Lantern slide projector
   Opaque projector
f. Additional equipment:
   Tape recorders
   Easels

[45] *Ibid.*, p. 188.

Flannel and magnetic boards
Wall screens and portable screens
Rolling projection tables
Public address system
Portable display boards

g. Projection crew. A small group of older, capable elementary school children can be utilized as a service corps for the school. This does not relieve the classroom teacher from being familiar with the operation of each piece of equipment in order to assist, or help out in case of difficulty.

2. Provide a resource center to serve the needs of all teachers. The purchasing of materials and equipment is frequently the responsibility of a faculty committee with the Instructional Materials Coordinator serving as chairman. All materials should be kept in the Center, with a catalogue made available to each teacher. It is usually a good idea to make the catalogue in loose-leaf form to permit additions and changes.

Materials may be circulated on a check-out system, developed by the coordinator and suited to the needs of the school. It should always be kept in mind that the availability of equipment and materials is the most important single factor in the development of a successful program. The schedule and check-out system the coordinator uses must be systematic and accurate, but also flexible enough to anticipate unforeseen emergencies.

3. Provide and supervise a center for the adequate production of materials. Many transparencies, mock-ups, etc., can be more conveniently made in the Materials Center than in the classroom, if the center is planned with this function in mind.

4. Acquaint teachers with new materials. Through displaying and circulating new books, publishers' catalogues, etc., the coordinator may keep the faculty informed of new materials constantly being made available. Of the several hundred sources of teaching materials now available, the following are typical of those that are kept up-to-date through annual publication or through periodic revisions and supplements.

Coronet Films. Coronet Building, Chicago, Illinois.

Educational Film Guide. H. W. Wilson Company, 950 University Avenue, New York 52, New York.

Educational Films. Audio-Visual Center, Division of University Relations, Florida State University, Tallahassee, Florida.

Educational Films, Slides, Filmstrips. Pennsylvania State University, University Park, Pennsylvania.

Educational Filmstrip Catalogue. Society for Visual Education, Inc., 1345 Diversey Parkway, Chicago 14, Illinois.

Educational Music Guide. Capitol Records Distributing Corporation, 1750 Vine Street, Hollywood 28, California.

Educators Grade Guide to Free Teaching Aids. Educators Progress Service, Randolph, Wisconsin.

Educators Guide to Free Films. Educators Progress Service, Randolph, Wisconsin.

Educators Guide to Free Filmstrips. Educators Progress Service, Randolph, Wisconsin.

Educators Guide to Free Tapes, Scripts, Transcriptions. Educators Progress Service, Randolph, Wisconsin.

Educators Guide to Free Science Materials. Educators Progress Service, Randolph, Wisconsin.

Educators Index of Free Materials. Educators Progress Service, Randolph, Wisconsin.

Film Catalogue. Film Associates of California, 11014 Santa Monica Boulevard, Los Angeles, California.

Filmstrip Catalogue. Society for Visual Education, Inc., 1345 Diversey Parkway, Chicago 14, Illinois.

Filmstrip Guide. H. W. Wilson Company, 950 University Avenue, New York 52, New York.

Free and Inexpensive Learning Materials. Division of Surveys and Field Services, George Peabody College for Teachers, Nashville 5, Tennessee.

Free Loan Motion Pictures. Association Films, Inc., 347 Madison Avenue, New York 17, New York.

National Tape Recording Catalogue. National Education Association, 1201 Sixteenth Street, N. W., Washington, D. C.

Text-Films. McGraw-Hill Company, 330 West 42nd Street, New York 36, New York.

U. S. Government Films for Public Educational Use. U. S. Department of Health, Education, and Welfare, Office of Education, Washington, D. C.

5. Evaluate the multimedia program. Suggested guidelines for the evaluation of the school-wide program by the materials coordinator, principal, and faculty are:

Can all teachers satisfactorily operate the basic audiovisual equipment?

Are audiovisual materials used in the regular classroom as part of the regular teaching situation whenever possible? Do teachers, with darkened rooms, use their rooms for all films and filmstrips?

Are teachers teaching with AV materials or just showing films, displaying study prints or playing recordings?

How well acquainted are teachers with the content of the material before presenting it to the class? . . .

Are teachers using instructional films in social studies only or in other subject areas also?

Are individual teachers using a variety of materials rather than settling on one kind of material only?

Do teachers stimulate the pupils' thinking by asking questions which the film or recording will answer?

Are the follow-up activities appropriate to clinch ideas and make the material remembered longer? Is total or partial reshowing of materials practiced when teachers feel that reshowing will materially aid pupil learning? . . .

Is an in-service training program carried on to assist teachers in:
   a. Proper ordering procedures?
   b. Utilization of materials?
   c. Operation of equipment?

Are all teachers making use of educational trips as an aid to developing better pupil understanding? . . .

Are the faculty members aware of their audiovisual representative and how he can be of service to them?

Are there magazines dealing with audiovisual instruction in your school?

Do you have a student organization used to facilitate delivery of audiovisual materials and equipment to the classroom?

Are audiovisual materials used in PTA meetings or with out-of-school groups to help interpret the school program?[46]

SUMMARY

Our present technological age offers the teacher many materials and devices with which he may enrich, clarify, extend, or supplement his teaching. None of these will do the job alone. None is "best" for all purposes. None is a substitute for the teacher. None is the answer to all educational problems. But a great many, when properly used, can increase the effectiveness of the total teaching-learning situation.

This chapter examined several basic categories of materials, generally applicable to the school-wide program. For suggestions for teaching materials in specific curricular areas, the reader should consult Chapter 6.

Printed materials were examined briefly with emphasis placed upon the correct use of the textbook.

Display materials included those that can be purchased as well as those that can be made by teacher and pupils. Flat pictures, flannel and mag-

[46] Ben Gumm, "How to Evaluate Your AV Program," *Educational Screen and Audiovisual Guide*, Vol. 40 (May, 1961), pp. 228-229.

netic boards, dioramas and panoramas, templates, and mock-ups were suggested as valuable aids in this category.

Many of the most popular teaching aids are projected materials. The popularity of the overhead projector is steadily growing, for its versatility makes it a valuable piece of equipment in any classroom. The ever-popular filmstrips and slides also offer a wide variety of possibilities to the creative teacher, both in producing and showing them. Included in this category also, were films and the unique contributions they may make to the school program.

The two major types of auditory materials discussed were (1) educational radio, and (2) recordings.

The controversial role of instructional television was examined in the next section. Questions frequently asked by teachers formed the basis of the discussion and included: (1) Will instructional television replace the classroom teacher? (2) What are the advantages claimed for instructional television? (3) What are the limitations of instructional television? (4) How do students feel about instructional television? (5) How do teachers feel about instructional television? and (6) Is instructional television as effective as "live" teaching?

The equally controversial issues of auto-instructional devices, both mechanical devices (teaching machines) and printed devices (programmed texts, sets of cards, etc.) were also examined. As with television, the exact role of these media in education to date is uncertain. They have advantages and limitations, which is, of course, also true of all other media.

With both television and auto-instructional devices, it was pointed out that research has thus far shown "no significant difference" in the results obtained by them when compared with those of conventional teaching. However, most educators believe that this type of research has now served its purpose. What is now needed is research that will discover the specific and unique contribution each medium can make, when integrated into the total program by a creative and competent elementary school teacher.

The last section was devoted to a discussion of the Instructional Materials Center in the elementary school.

ADDITIONAL LEARNING EXPERIENCES

Topics for Thought and Discussion

1. Some states require at least one course in audio-visual techniques for an elementary teaching certificate. Are you in favor of such a requirement? Why?

2. Does your state specify a course in this area for elementary certification?

3. Would you like to be a television teacher? Why?

4. Does a successful television teacher need different competencies than a regular classroom teacher?

5. Do you personally favor instructional television or do you prefer a "live" teacher? Why?

6. Have you ever enrolled in a college course via instructional television? Did you learn more or less than you would have from a similar course taught in the conventional classroom manner? Why?

7. To what extent do you think the current interest in auto-instructional devices has been promoted by manufacturers and publishers who see in these devices a vast new potential sales market?

8. To what extent do you think the current interest in auto-instructional devices is influenced by the typical American's fondness for gimmicks or gadgets?

9. Someone has said that there is nothing that educational television can do that a good film can't do better. Do you agree?

10. Do you feel reasonably well prepared to operate a filmstrip projector? An opaque projector? A sound film projector? A slide projector? If a course in audiovisual techniques is not part of your preservice education, where and how will you acquire this technical know-how?

11. What are the best available sources in your town or county (or the district in which you teach or plan to teach) for obtaining worthwhile visual aids at a minimum fee?

Projects and Activities

1. Make a flannel or magnetic board you can use in teaching. Consider carefully such factors as desirable size, choice of materials, storability, ease of handling and versatility before constructing this teaching aid.

2. Examine several programmed texts. What is your opinion of these compared to conventional texts?

3. Make a survey (as extensive as is practical) through a brief questionnaire directed to elementary school principals on the extent to which auto-instructional devices are currently used in your state or county. Try to find out (a) what types of devices are used, (b) on what grade levels, and (c) in what curricular areas? Also include two questions that will enable you to chart a trend concerning the increasing use or decreasing use of these devices, according to your study. Such questions might be (1) Do you contemplate using these devices to a greater extent in your school in the near future? and (2) Do you contemplate using these devices to a lesser extent in the near future? Why?

4. Construct a mock-up that could be used to demonstrate a basic scientific principle to primary grade children.

5. Make a set of overlay transparencies to be used in an overhead projector in connection with an elementary school social studies or science unit of your choice.

6. Prepare an annotated bibliography of available teaching aids for a social studies or science unit of your choice.

7. Make a set of lantern slides that may be used in teaching a social studies or science unit of your choice.

8. Prepare a set of flannel board cut-outs you could use in connection with a story-telling experience in the kindergarten or first grade.

9. Construct a role-playing situation in which a school faculty reacts to a question from the superintendent concerning the advisability of teaching science by instructional television during the coming year.

10. Interview a small sample of elementary school teachers. In the past month how many of them have used at least one filmstrip in their classroom? A sound film? An opaque projector? A set of slides? An overhead projector? A tape recorder? A radio program? What are your conclusions?

Selected Bibliography

Audio-Visual Materials of Instruction, Nelson B. Henry, ed. Forty-eighth Yearbook, National Society for the Study of Education, Part I. Chicago, University of Chicago Press, 1949.

Automatic Teaching: The State of the Art, Eugene Galanter, ed. New York, John Wiley & Sons, Inc., 1959.

DeBernardis, Amo, *The Use of Instructional Materials*. New York, Appleton-Century-Crofts, 1960.

Brown, James W., Lewis, Richard B., and Harcleroad, Fred F., *A-V Instruction, Materials and Methods*. New York, McGraw-Hill Book Co., Inc., 1959.

Cassirer, Henry R., *Television Teaching Today*. Paris, UNESCO, 1960.

Communication Media and the School, George Z. F. Bereday, and Joseph A. Lauwerys, eds. The Yearbook of Education, 1960. New York, Harcourt, Brace & World, Inc., 1960.

Costello, Lawrence F., and Gordon, George N., *Teach With Television*. New York, Hastings House, Publishers, 1961.

Cross, A. J. Foy, and Cypher, Irene F., *Audio-Visual Education*. New York, Thomas Y. Crowell Company, 1961.

Dale, Edgar, *Audio-Visual Methods in Teaching*, rev. ed. New York, Holt, Rinehart and Winston, Inc., 1954.

East, Marjorie, and Dale, Edgar, *Display for Learning*. New York, Holt, Rinehart and Winston, Inc., 1952.

Educational Television, the Next Ten Years. Stanford, Calif., Stanford University Institute for Communication Research, 1962.

Fry, Edward, *Teaching Machines and Programmed Instructions*. New York, McGraw-Hill Book Co., Inc., 1963.

GREEN, Edward J., *The Learning Process and Programmed Instruction.* New York, Holt, Rinehart and Winston, Inc., 1962.

"Instructional Materials: Educational Media and Technology." *Review of Educational Research,* Vol. 32 (April, 1962).

"Instructional Materials." *Review of Educational Research,* Vol. 26 (April, 1956).

KINDER, James S., *Audio-Visual Materials and Techniques,* 2nd ed. New York, American Book Company, 1959.

LEWIS, Philip, *Educational Television Guidebook.* New York, McGraw-Hill Book Co., Inc., 1961.

LUMSDAINE, A. A., and GLASER, Robert, *Teaching Machines and Programmed Learning.* Washington, D. C., National Education Association, Department of Audio-Visual Instruction, 1960.

Mass Media and Education, Nelson B. Henry, ed., Fifty-third Yearbook, National Society for the Study of Education, Part II. Chicago, University of Chicago Press, 1954.

MINOR, Ed, *Simplified Techniques for Preparing Visual Instructional Materials.* New York, McGraw-Hill Book Co., Inc., 1962.

SANDS, Lester B., *Audio-Visual Procedures in Teaching.* New York, The Ronald Press Company, 1956.

SIEPMANN, Charles A., *Television and Education in the United States.* Paris, UNESCO, 1952.

TARBET, Donald G., *Television and Our Schools.* New York, The Ronald Press Company, 1961.

TROW, William Clark, *Teacher and Technology.* New York, Appleton-Century-Crofts, 1963.

WILLEY, Roy D., and YOUNG, Helen Ann, *Radio in Elementary Education.* New York, D. C. Heath & Company, 1948.

WITTICH, Walter Arno, and SCHULLER, Charles Francis, *Audiovisual Materials: Their Nature and Use,* 3rd ed. New York, Harper & Row, Publishers, Inc., 1962.

CHAPTER 11

Appraising Pupil Growth

THERE IS PROBABLY no professional responsibility approached more gingerly by many teachers than that of evaluating pupil abilities, achievements, and personality. Some regard evaluation as a highly technical field, laid with explosive mines of statistics and formulas, and well-posted by specialists with warnings of "Classroom Teachers—Keep Out!" Others think of it merely as a clerical job, boring and time consuming. Still others regard it as yet another extra imposed upon the overworked and long-suffering teacher. Actually, worthwhile evaluation is none of these. True, a comprehensive evaluation program serves certain administrative, guidance, and research functions, the responsibilities for which may be frequently delegated to specialized personnel. But these functions overlap and are subservient to the major purpose of evaluation, namely, the *instructional* function. This is the function most pertinent and most important to the classroom teacher. *Evaluation is an integral part of teaching.* Without it, any type of teaching becomes a trial-and-error, catch-as-catch-can process. Although recognizing, therefore, the multipurposes of evaluation and the important responsibilities of specialized functionaries, the emphasis in this chapter is upon evaluation *as an indispensable instructional tool and responsibility of the classroom teacher.*

First, a brief definition of major terms. The early years of the twentieth century were marked by an increasing interest in *testing*, which is exactly what the name implies. Growing concern over the quality and equality of education in the nation's schools resulted in numerous attempts to develop effective tests of academic performance. By approximately 1920, the limitations of tests were generally recognized and other instruments such at rating scales, check lists, and score cards became popular. Thus, testing was expanded to the broader and more pupil-centered concept of *measurement* which was an attempt to express in *quantitative* terms a defined pupil characteristic. The still broader concept of *evaluation* evolved gradually in succeeding years. Evaluation uses tests and other measuring instruments but employs *qualitative* techniques to appraise interests, attitudes, appreciations, and other aspects of the individual's total growth. The distinction between evaluation and earlier forms of measurement is made by one source as follows:

Modern evaluation differs from older forms of appraisal in several ways. First, it attempts to measure a comprehensive range of objectives of the modern school curriculum rather than subject-matter achievement only. Second, it uses a variety of techniques of appraisal, such as achievement, attitude, personality, and character tests. Included also are rating scales, questionnaires, judgment scales of products, interviews, controlled-observation techniques, sociometric techniques, and anecdotal records. Third, modern evaluation includes integrating and interpreting these various indices of behavior into an inclusive portrait of an individual or an educational situation.[1]

The following section examines the basic characteristics of a modern program of effective evaluation.

CHARACTERISTICS OF EFFECTIVE EVALUATION

EFFECTIVE EVALUATION IS KEYED TO THE EDUCATIONAL OBJECTIVES OF THE LOCAL SITUATION. It should be obvious that effective evaluation is irrevocably related to the objectives of the school. Inconsistencies between the two indicate either that (1) the verbalized statement of goals does not represent the true objectives of the staff or (2) the staff is disinterested or incapable of determining its success in achieving stated objectives. To illustrate, a school staff prepares a comprehensive list of worthwhile objectives related to the total growth of its pupils. Its evaluation program, however, consists almost entirely of one or two standardized achievement tests designed to determine mastery of informational facts and skills. Only two conclusions can be drawn. One, the staff has verbalized but never really accepted its statement of broad educational objectives. Two, the staff does believe in its objectives but is completely uninformed as to the techniques, procedures, and instruments it might use to determine its attainment of them.

It is, of course, extremely difficult to evaluate an educational objective such as "to develop skills of critical reading." This broad objective, however, can be broken down into subobjectives, one of which might be "to develop the ability to locate information." This, in turn, can be identified in terms of specific pupil behaviors such as "uses the index of a book,"

---

[1] J. Wayne Wrightstone, Joseph Justman, and Irving Robbins, *Evaluation in Modern Education* (New York, American Book Company, 1956), p. 3.

"uses the table of contents," and "uses a variety of reference tools." Once these have been stated, it becomes fairly easy to decide upon appropriate evaluation techniques to appraise them. In this case, such techniques might include tests, self-rating forms, teacher-observation, and others.

EFFECTIVE EVALUATION IS A CONTINUOUS, ON-GOING PROCESS. Since learning and growth are continuous processes, it follows that the evaluation of them must be continuous. The modern concept of evaluation emphasizes its importance in diagnosing pupil needs and in indicating appropriate instructional techniques. This is a continuous and cyclic process. It is far different from the earlier interest in measuring only the end results of instruction. Evaluation as an on-going process is not confined to end-of-semester tests nor bringing records up to date once a year.

EFFECTIVE EVALUATION IS SYSTEMATICALLY PLANNED ACCORDING TO LONG RANGE GOALS. The most worthwhile results will be realized from an evaluation program carefully organized over a several year period. Many recommend that basic techniques be determined and used consistently over a five or ten year period. Using various forms of one test is, for instance, usually more desirable in appraising growth than using completely different tests every year. Obviously, however, changes should be made as new and better instruments are developed. Also, although the basic framework may remain constant, some flexibility is desirable to permit the teacher's using additional or supplementary instruments demanded by an immediate situation.

EFFECTIVE EVALUATION IS THE COOPERATIVE RESPONSIBILITY OF MANY INDIVIDUALS. As Morgan states, "Democratic principles imply that all persons involved in the evaluative process are affected by it and should share fully in it. Those affected by judgments or decisions should understand and participate in making them. . . . Teachers, pupils, parents, and others affected by evaluation should participate in the planning and action involved."[2]

It is fairly clear that we are moving rapidly away from the concept of evaluation as the responsibility of only the administrative or testing staff. The team approach is almost universally accepted today as a necessary requisite of effective evaluation and guidance.

EFFECTIVE EVALUATION EMPLOYS A VARIETY OF INSTRUMENTS AND TECHNIQUES. The assessment of human growth is an extremely difficult and complex task. It can not be done by employing one or two instruments, regardless of how worthwhile they may be. Over the years, many instruments have been developed to help do the job. Some are highly technical

[2] H. Gerthon Morgan, "What is Effective Evaluation?" *NEA Journal*, Vol. 48 (November, 1959), p. 16.

and should be utilized only by personnel with specialized training. Many others may be used, or adapted for use, by the classroom teacher. Those usually recommended are examined in the following section.

EVALUATIVE TECHNIQUES AND INSTRUMENTS

Standardized Tests

During the past several decades, much time, effort, and money have been devoted to the construction of standardized tests to measure various abilities and personal qualities. Today, these instruments comprise an important part of the evaluation programs of many schools. Their use has increased since 1955 by about 10 million annually, and, at present, there are over 150 million tests administered annually to elementary and high school pupils. In addition there are more than 2 million college entrance and scholarship tests administered annually. The growing dependence of schools upon standardized tests causes considerable concern among some educators who worry about putting the cart before the horse or letting the tail wag the dog. They point, with some justification, to such possible dangers of overdependence upon tests as (1) standardization and control of the curriculum by test makers, (2) premature and rigid classification of pupils, (3) disproportionate amount of class time devoted to testing, (4) neglect of some of the most important but nonmeasurable outcomes of education, and (5) submergence of the individual in a mass of impersonal statistical data. (This brings to mind the popular story about the phenomenal rise of the office boy to corporation president because someone stepped on his IBM card with golf shoes!) Seriously, however, Ramsey points to the possible danger of an overemphasis upon testing to ". . . reduce the individual student to an ignominious set of numerals which can be 'treated' in statistical fashion. . . . As a companion service to closed systems of instruction and automated tutoring devices, testing and electronic analysis and computation could administer the final *coup de grace* to individual integrity of students."[3]

These dangers are real and clear. They cannot be avoided by closing our eyes to them. Nor is it wise or practical to abandon testing. As Tyler says, "Tests are here to stay and their uses will increase."[4] The only possible solution is the correct use and interpretation of tests.

STANDARDIZED TESTS ARE VALUABLE EDUCATIONAL TOOLS WHEN USED CORRECTLY. Many of the dangers cited above are not inherent in the tests

[3] Curtis Paul Ramsey, "Testing in Tomorrow's Schools," *Educational Leadership*, Vol. 17 (May 1960), p. 508.
[4] Ralph W. Tyler, "What Testing Does to Teachers and Students," *Proceedings, 1959 Invitational Conference on Testing Problems* (Princeton, N. J., Educational Testing Service, 1960), p. 16.

themselves, but result rather from their misuse and abuse. The almost universal agreement on this point is indicated in statements similar to the following.

There is general agreement that current deficiencies in educational measurement are more the result of inadequate or improper use of test results than of inadequate test instruments. (This can be said without implying that currently available tests are beyond serious criticism.)[5]

Unless school administrators, teachers, and counselors understand the meaning and the implications of test results and unless full and wise use is made of the scores, the giving of larger numbers of tests may be mostly a waste of time, detracting from instruction and contributing to feelings of insecurity on the part of the pupil and his parents. The crux of the matter is in the understanding and the use of tests.[6]

Over the years, it is neither the publisher nor the critic who most effectively determines the quality of tests; rather it is the test user. . . . There is no Good Housekeeping seal of approval in the field of test publication; there is no substitute for professionally competent and conscientious judgment on the part of the test user. Test publishers have important professional obligations; test users have parallel responsibilities.[7]

It is impossible to mention all the misuses of standardized tests. One of the most insidious is to use them as a basis for teacher evaluation. Chapter 2 examined the invalidity of judging teacher effectiveness upon the basis of standardized tests of pupil performance and there is no need for repetition here. It is sufficient to state only that standardized achievement tests are *not* designed to indicate teaching competency; should *not* be interpreted in this light; and, if so interpreted, will inevitably result in negative attitudes, insecurity, and unethical practices upon the part of teachers.

The fallacy of using test results to make rigid classifications among pupils or to counsel authoritatively concerning curriculum and occupational choices is also to be avoided if tests are to serve properly the purposes for which they are intended.

It is also unfortunate that test results are frequently used to make comparisons between schools. It is difficult to see how published rankings

[5] Robert L. Ebel and Robert E. Hill, Jr., "Development and Applications of Tests of Educational Achievement," *Review of Educational Research,* Vol. 29 (February, 1959), p. 49.

[6] Arthur E. Traxler, "Educational Measurement: An Aid to School Administration," *School Review,* Vol. 68 (Summer, 1960), p. 197.

[7] Alexander G. Wesman, "The Obligations of the Test User," *Proceedings, 1955 Invitational Conference on Testing Problems* (Princeton, N. J., Educational Testing Service, 1956), p. 61.

of all schools in a system according to standardized achievement test scores can result in anything but community misunderstanding, poor public relations, and below-zero teacher morale.

We have mentioned only briefly some of the most common misuses of testing results. There are many others, any or all of which may result in the educational pitfalls cited previously as causing grave concern in some educational circles.

STANDARDIZED TESTS MAY PERFORM SEVERAL VALUABLE FUNCTIONS. The primary purpose of tests has been stated as follows: "The main function of standardized tests is to help school personnel acquire more precise and dependable information about their pupils so that the effectiveness of their instruction and guidance may be enhanced."[8]

Subsumed under this major function are the following purposes:

1. To help estimate the pupil's learning potential.
2. To convey fairly accurate data concerning the pupil's grasp of certain academic knowledges, powers, and skills.
3. To indicate specific areas of strength and difficulty.
4. To indicate pupil growth in a particular area over a certain period of time.
5. To assist the teacher in appraising the pupil's readiness for a new learning experience.
6. To provide cumulative data concerning the pupil's developmental history.
7. To assist the teacher and guidance worker in personal, academic, and vocational counseling.
8. To assist the teacher in gauging the correct level of instruction.
9. To assist the teacher and administrator in gaining a generalized picture of a class or school group.

STANDARDIZED TESTS MAY BE GROUPED ACCORDING TO A VARIETY OF CLASSIFICATIONS. Test scores have little or no meaning unless one knows the *type* of test. The IQ, for instance, obtained from one test may mean something vastly different from the IQ derived from another test. Durost emphasizes the importance of knowing the type of test in the following statement.

Intelligence tests differ enough one from another that it is not practical or reasonable to talk about the IQ; one must refer to an IQ derived on a specific test. Thus, one speaks of an Otis IQ, a Terman-McNemar IQ, a Kuhlmann-Anderson IQ, a Stanford-Binet IQ, a Pintner Non-Language IQ, or a California Mental Maturity Test IQ, fully recognizing that without this further defini-

[8] Arthur E. Traxler, "Standardized Tests," *NEA Journal*, Vol. 48 (November, 1959), p. 18.

tion one cannot truly comprehend the significance of the intelligence measure derived.[9]

There are generally considered to be three major categories of standardized tests, when grouped according to the traits they are designed to measure. Thus, a standardized test may be used to determine. (1) aptitudes, (2) achievement, and (3) personality.

The most common aptitude tests are those designed to determine *intelligence*, today more accurately defined as *scholastic aptitude*. They are defined as follows: "An intelligence test is a carefully selected series of problem situations for the solution of which varying amounts of mental ability or skill are required; the score on such a test is then interpreted by referring the pupil's measured ability to some standard of comparison or norm."[10]

Scholastic aptitude tests vary in the type of scores they produce. Some may yield a single score of the M. A. (Mental Age) or I. Q. (Intelligence Quotient). Some may yield two subscores for language and nonlanguage skills or for verbal and quantitative aptitudes. Others may yield a profile of scores in certain mental abilities such as perceptual speed, reasoning, quantitative skill, and others.

Many naive teachers think that the scholastic aptitude tests measure innate learning ability. This is not true. Today, no informed person denies the influence of environment, motivation, and schooling upon these tests. As a matter of fact, many claim that the influence is so great that there is relatively little difference between scholastic aptitude and achievement tests. This is an exaggeration for, although there is considerable overlapping, as Traxler points out, scholastic aptitude tests are ". . . so designed that they contain questions not directly dependent upon school learning" while the achievement tests ". . . are specifically planned to measure what is learned in school."[11]

There is little doubt that scholastic aptitude tests, in spite of their limitations, constitute a worthwhile part of the modern school's evaluation program. Some authorities recommend that scholastic aptitude tests be administered annually to reduce chances of errors. In general, it would seem that a minimal testing program would include such tests every two or three years if they are to provide any service at all to the educational program.

[9] Walter N. Durost, "What Constitutes a Minimal Testing Program for Elementary and Junior High School," *Test Service Notebook, No. 1*, rev. (New York, Harcourt, Brace & World, Inc., 1956), pp. 1-2.
[10] *Ibid.*, p. 1.
[11] Arthur E. Traxler, *op. cit.*, p. 19.

Another type of aptitude test is the special aptitude test used to determine aptitude in such fields as art and music. Also in this category are the many reading readiness tests now available.

Undoubtedly the most frequently used standardized tests are *achievement* tests. Indeed, in some systems, the annual or semiannual administration of achievement tests represents more than 90 per cent of the entire testing program. Such tests may be designed to measure achievement in a particular academic field or they may be general batteries covering almost all curricular fields.

Personality tests may be classified as projective or nonprojective techniques. The projective instruments (such as the well-known Rorschach test) are time-consuming and complex instruments which should be administered, scored, and interpreted only by a person with specialized training. This is an important point that cannot be stressed too strongly. Much harm, and no good, can come from the uninformed classroom teacher rushing into a field where occasionally even angels fear to tread.

The structured tests of personality are not really tests as such in that they have no right or wrong answers. They are inventories of interests (reading, television, sports, hobbies, etc.), likes, and dislikes. Some of these should be administered by the specialist although others may be used by classroom teachers. Here, also, extreme caution should be exercised concerning the use and interpretation of results. Today, there is increasing concern that the use of such tests, particularly by teachers who fancy themselves armchair psychologists, may lead to the "discovery" of imaginary abnormalities in many pupils. This, of course, becomes particularly serious when such data are listed on permanent records that may follow a pupil from elementary school all the way through graduate school. One psychologist lists the following trends concerning the use and interpretation of these instruments.

Psychologists are much more critical than they were, and do not take on faith everything that is published purporting to measure personality. . . .

Concepts about the dimensions of personality are undergoing radical changes even among statisticians. We are beginning to see objections raised to the unidimensional profile of personality presentation, and tendencies in favor of multi-dimensional approaches.

More and more do we find criticism of all types of instruments for independent use for personality appraisal. When such instruments are used, they are used to supplement rather than replace interview, observational, and other techniques.

More and more do we find recommendation of the case study and observational techniques by qualified psychologists rather than reliance on test scores or formulae for personality appraisal. . . .

More and more do we find multi-discipline approaches to the study of personality. Simple approaches are becoming suspect. . . .[12]

There are, of course, ways to classify tests other than by the traits they determine. For instance, all tests are either *group* or *individual* tests. The first, as its name indicates, is usually a paper-and-pencil test administered to a group of pupils. The individual test is administered only to a single pupil at a time, often by a person who has more specialized training than the classroom teacher. As a rule, individual tests, except with young children, are administered (1) when the results of a group test deviate widely from the teacher's judgment of an individual pupil or (2) when the behavior or performance of a pupil warrants intensive, concentrated study.

Then too, tests may be classified according to the method of response. *Verbal* tests depend largely upon language facility in following directions and arriving at answers. *Nonverbal* tests substitute puzzles, mazes, pictorial materials, numbers, special forms, and three-dimensional objects for the written word. Directions may be written or presented in pantomine by the teacher or tester. *Performance* tests may require the testee to arrange blocks according to a certain design, complete a picture puzzle, repeat orally a series of numbers, or something similar.

It is worth repeating that, particularly with scholastic aptitude tests, it is imperative to know the type of test, whether it is verbal or nonverbal, group or individual. Unless this is done, an untold amount of harm may result. The author remembers one case in which an eighth grade boy who was seriously handicapped in reading had two IQs on his record. One was 85 which was achieved on a verbal group test. The other was 117 achieved on an individual performance test. The following year the boy was transferred to a large junior-high school that grouped pupils homogeneously strictly according to IQ (the invalidity of this practice needs no comment here). The sending school recorded on his transfer card only the higher IQ, on the grounds that it was the most recent and most accurate. The name of the test yielding the score was, of course, recorded opposite the score. The receiving school ignored the type of test and placed the boy in a class of very able academic children. His reading handicap prevented him from keeping up with the work (which was almost 100 per cent verbal) and he failed miserably in every subject. The teacher accused him of being lazy. He retaliated with impudence, truancy, and disobedience. Things went from bad to worse and, as soon as he reached the legal age limit, he left school entirely.

---

[12] Morris Krugman, "Changing Methods of Appraising Personality," *Proceedings, 1956 Invitational Conference on Testing Problems* (Princeton, N. J., Educational Testing Service, 1957), pp. 56-57.

Who was to blame in this unfortunate situation? Almost everyone except the pupil himself. The sending school should have recorded all data needed to help the child, not just the most recent. The receiving school should have interpreted the IQ properly. The teachers should have checked the records against their own judgments and observations of the boy. The moral of this true tragedy of errors is, of course, that apparently only the innocent suffer from the errors of the guilty.

THERE ARE CERTAIN ESSENTIAL CRITERIA BY WHICH TO JUDGE A STANDARD-IZED TEST. Equally as important as knowing the type of test is determining its value for a particular situation. The most important criterion for the selection of a standardized test is *validity*. A test is valid to the degree that it measures *what it purports to measure*. A test, for instance, may propose to measure certain quantitative skills and understandings. But it may be designed so that, in reality, it measures reading comprehension and vocabulary. Such a test is obviously not valid. To reiterate, a test is valid only to the degree that it measures the trait it purports to measure and to the degree to which it is used in the situation for which it was designed.

A second criterion, *reliability*, indicates the degree to which the instrument consistently measures the same trait. A test may be reliable but not valid. If, for instance, in the illustration above the test consistently measured reading comprehension and vocabulary it would be reliable but not valid. On the other hand, a valid test is also reliable in that it consistently measures what it purports to measure.

Objectivity is a third criterion. Standardized tests should be such that they may be scored objectively, thus eliminating the influence of bias or personal judgment of the scorer.

The ease of *administrability* is another important factor to consider when selecting a test. Time-consuming and elaborate tests that necessitate lengthy directions or complicated marking and folding procedures are not suitable for elementary school youngsters.

Scorability or ease of scoring is an important criterion, as any teacher will readily concede.

In many systems, *economy* is an important consideration when selecting tests. Also, the *utility* of the test for a particular situation should be carefully weighed. Is one comprehensive test preferable to several specialized instruments? Which tests meet our objectives? Answers to these and other questions will indicate the usefulness of a test in a specific situation.

INFORMATION CONCERNING STANDARDIZED TESTS MAY BE SECURED FROM SEVERAL SOURCES. Every school should have a file of publisher's catalogs and other advertising material in the central office. It should be the starting point for the teacher or administrator seeking a particular type of test. Extremely valuable, also, are the *Mental Measurements Yearbooks*,[13] edited by Buros. To date, there have been five such yearbooks published, the latest in 1958. They contain unbiased reviews by reputable educators of available tests and are an excellent means of discovering the quantity and quality of available instruments.

A recent publication, also edited by Buros, is a comprehensive bibliography of tests in print for use in education, psychology, and industry.[14] Helpful also are reviews of tests in such periodicals as *Educational and Psychological Measurement*, although sometimes these are more helpful to the specialist than to the classroom teacher.

After the choice has been narrowed to a few possibilities, a specimen test set may be secured from the publisher for approximately fifty cents. This contains a copy of the test, a scoring key, and a manual of directions. Careful study of the specimen set should yield the desired information and enable the individual to decide on the most helpful test for his particular needs.

THE CLASSROOM TEACHER PLAYS AN IMPORTANT ROLE IN THE STANDARD-IZED TEST PROGRAM. The point has been previously made that the classroom teacher shares responsibility in the testing program with such specialized personnel as the psychometrist, psychologist, guidance worker, or testing director. The specific responsibilities of the classroom teacher usually fall into the following categories.

1. *Determining the testing program.* It is extremely unfortunate that in some systems teachers may have very little to say about the testing program. Such a policy is woefully shortsighted for teachers cannot be expected to understand, appreciate, or support a testing program that springs like the goddess, Athene, full grown from the head of the administrative staff. Wise administrators recognize this fact and designate the planning of the testing program as a cooperative responsibility of the staff. In some smaller schools, the entire staff serves as a committee to determine the testing program. In system-wide programs, a committee of teacher-representatives works with the administrative and guidance staff to plan the over-all program.

Then too, the classroom teacher participates in determining the testing program through his requests for additional or supplementary tests. In most systems, teachers are given the privilege of requesting tests, over and above those used in the basic testing program, as they are needed. For example, in one system "The Bureau of Educational Testing makes

---

[13] *Mental Measurements Yearbooks*, Oscar K. Buros, ed. (Highland Park, N. J., The Gryphon Press, 1938, 1941, 1949, 1953, 1958).

[14] *Tests in Print*, Oscar K. Buros, ed. (Highland Park, N. J., The Gryphon Press, 1961).

available to teachers various kinds of group and individual tests for measuring improvement in some particular skill or for diagnosing individual
or group needs. During the school year these tests may be ordered by
teachers, with approval of their principal, at a time when they best fit
into the instructional program of the classroom."[15]

2. *Preparing for the test.* In general, the teacher has three major responsibilities in this area. First, he must prepare his pupils for the test.
How this is done depends largely upon the age and experience of the
group. Two cautions should be observed. Pupils should not be prepared
for the test at the risk of inducing anxieties harmful to mental health as
well as test performance. Studies of children's anxieties[16] reveal that test
anxiety is by no means an uncommon phenomenon among elementary
school children. Every effort must be made to avoid overemphasizing the
importance of the test to the extent that children become unduly anxious
and worried about its results.

Also, advance preparations should not be made of the type or kind
that will skew test results. Many conscientious teachers do not realize
that they are guilty in this respect. A very few may foolishly and un-
ethically prepare children to the point where the test results may be inaccurate. General guidelines concerning the ethics of preparing children
to take standardized achievement tests have been formulated by one
author, some of which are the following:

It is acceptable and proper to explain to pupils, well before the day a standardized achievement test is given, something about the purposes and general
form of the test. . . .

It is acceptable and proper to familiarize pupils with the mechanics of a
standardized achievement test before the actual testing begins, through the
use of practice exercises. . . .

It is acceptable and proper to try to bring about optimum motivation of
the pupils for the taking of a standardized achievement test. . . .

It is acceptable and proper in giving a machine-scored test to pass around
a sample well-marked answer sheet before the test is begun, and to point out
the possibility that the pupils will lower their test scores if they don't try to
mark their answer sheets like the sample. . . .

It is not acceptable and proper for a teacher to coach pupils on the subject
matter of a specific standardized test. . . .

It is not acceptable and proper to give one form of a standardized test a few
days or weeks before a second form of the test is to be given as a district-wide
survey. . . .

[15] Vivian Cord and Jacob Epstein, "A Team Approach to Testing," *NEA Journal,*
Vol. 48 (November, 1959), p. 24.
[16] Seymour B. Sarason and others, *Anxiety in Elementary School Children* (New
York, John Wiley and Sons, Inc., 1960).

It is not acceptable and proper to make individual pupils overanxious and tense concerning the outcome of a standardized achievement test, nor to set impossible goals for a class. . . .[17]

It seems unnecessary to belabor this point. In addition to being un-ethical, the teacher who overprepares pupils for a standardized test is dishonest and unfair to his pupils. How can a test fulfill its function as a valuable instructional tool if the teacher, deliberately or not, has skewed its results?

A second type of preparation requires attention to certain mechanics. Securing proper materials (well-sharpened pencils, a Testing—Do Not Disturb sign for the classroom door, etc.) and careful consideration of the physical conditions (seating, lighting, etc.) are attended to by the conscientious teacher prior to the test administration.

A third type involves the teacher's self-preparation (if he is to administer the test). Careful study of the manual is an absolute *must*. The reasons should be obvious and should not need to be spelled out to any intelligent teacher.

3. *Administering the test.* In some systems, specialized personnel administer all standardized group or individual tests. There are, however, some advantages to the classroom teacher administering group tests to his class, particularly in the lower grades where the presence of a stranger may adversely influence pupil performance. In administering tests, scrupulous care must be taken to follow instructions exactly. Altering time limits, giving additional help or directions, reading directions or items orally (unless directed to do so) may negate the results of the test. On the other hand, it is important that good rapport exist between pupils and teacher, and that they understand why the teacher may suddenly become less helpful than usual. The importance of the teacher's being helpful but not too helpful is emphasized in the following statement.

One of the most difficult aspects of test administration for the teacher is that of "doing enough but not too much" in helping children to understand the test. The teacher's role as an impersonal examiner is an unnatural one for her. In her eagerness to help children understand the test, the teacher may be tempted to reword the directions. Such rewording not only violates the requirement of standard conditions but it often reduces the effectiveness of communication to the child.[18]

[17] Anton Thompson, "Tentative Guidelines for Proper and Improper Practices with Standardized Achievement Tests," *California Journal of Educational Research*, Vol. 9 (September, 1958), pp. 159-166.

[18] Theodore L. Torgerson and Georgia Sachs Adams, *Measurement and Evaluation for the Elementary School Teacher* (New York, Holt, Rinehart and Winston, Inc., 1954), p. 400.

4. *Scoring and Recording Scores.* The importance of scoring a test carefully and accurately should be obvious to all teachers. Yet many studies reveal that an appalling number of errors are made by scorers. One such study reports that 28 per cent of achievement tests in a set scored by teachers contained scoring errors. In some cases, the errors resulted in final scores of more than three grade equivalents higher or lower than the true score.[19]

One way to eliminate this problem is to have the test scored by machine. If this is not possible, most authorities recommend an assembly-line procedure in preference to single-teacher scoring. A group of teachers may form an assembly line, each scoring one page or one subtest and then passing the test booklet to the next in line. This procedure is less time-consuming, more efficient, less subject to errors, and more impersonal than one teacher's scoring all tests for his class. If several teachers are not available, a teacher will find it easier and more time saving to score the first page or subtest in all booklets, then the next subtest, then the next, rather than scoring a complete booklet one at a time.

Whether a group of teachers or a single individual scores a test set, some provision should be made for spot checking by a person other than the scorer. This may seem like an unnecessary task to some teachers unless they stop to realize that all of the time, work, and energy that have gone into constructing, selecting, and administering a test are wasted if it is not scored accurately.

Another area in which some teachers may be careless is in computing the final scores or in transferring the scores from the test booklets to the pupils' record cards. A glaring example of this is offered by Wesman. "Every one of us, I dare say, has seen impossible scores reported on answer sheets, in personnel files or on cumulative record cards. I recall, for example, a set of records . . . which contained half a dozen or so IQs of 400 and over, twice that many in the 300's and as for IQs of 200 or so, they were quite routine."[20] Surely such a statement should fill every teacher with a firm resolve to score, and to record scores, as accurately as is humanly possible.

5. *Interpreting and using test results.* It has been stated repeatedly that the value of tests lies in their correct interpretation and use. It is obviously impossible to include here all of the many cautions that should be observed in this respect. We can, however, mention a few of the most important.

[19] Beeman N. Phillips and Garrett Weathers, "Analysis of Errors Made in Scoring Standardized Tests," *Educational and Psychological Measurement*, Vol. 18 (Autumn, 1958), pp. 563-567.

[20] Alexander G. Wesman, *op. cit.*, p. 64.

Every effort should be made to avoid attaching undue significance to *a precise score*. The score reveals only how the pupil performed in a particular area, determined by a particular test, at a particular time, and in a particular situation. At another time, on another test, the results may be quite different. This is particularly important when interpreting the results of scholastic aptitude tests, for it is well known that the IQ may vary fifteen or more points from one testing to another. Results of an extensive longitudinal study of young children, for instance, reveal that changes in IQ may have been previously underestimated for the average change of IQ in children from three to ten years of age was 17.9 IQ points, with 62 per cent of them changing more than 15 points.[21]

Similar caution, although to a somewhat lesser degree, should be exercised when viewing exact scores on achievement tests. The child whose total grade equivalent score is 3.8 is not necessarily "ahead" of the pupil who makes 3.6. It is to avoid this type of misinterpretation that some newer tests yield final results in broad bands or ranges of performance rather than a precise numerical score.

Secondly, the teacher must keep in mind the various factors that may influence a test score. Environmental factors are very important and have not yet been completely eliminated, even by the so-called *culture-free tests*. Personality factors, motivations, and physical conditions under which the test was taken all influence the final score and must be considered when that score is studied.

A third caution relates to the understanding and interpretation of the term *norm*. The term has been defined as follows: "A norm is usually the average or typical value of a particular psychological characteristic measured in a specified homogeneous population. . . . A norm is a statement of present achievement of the group and not a universal standard of accomplishment."[22]

Unfortunately, many teachers and administrators still insist on using the norm as the standard of achievement toward which they should strive, in spite of repeated admonitions that it represents only the *average* performance of a group. The following excellent statement by Rivlin emphasizes the point.

The table of norms does not set the goal for any class, since it reflects nothing more than the average attainment of large groups of students, bright and dull, eager and apathetic, well-taught and incompetently taught, in well equipped schools and in impoverished schools, etc. The national norms indi-

[21] Lester W. Sontag, Charles T. Baker, and Virginia L. Nelson, *Mental Growth and Personality Development: A Longitudinal Study.* (Lafayette, Ind., Child Development Publications, 1958).

[22] J. Wayne Wrightstone, Joseph Justman, Irving Robbins, *op. cit.*, p. 69.

cate what *average* (i. e., mediocre) students achieve when they attend *average* (i. e., mediocre) schools and are taught by *average* (i. e., mediocre) teachers. No teacher who is dissatisfied with mediocrity can accept norms as indicating the goals towards which he and his class must strive. On the other hand, under less favorable conditions, use of the norms as standards may set goals far beyond anything which these boys and girls can hope to achieve.[23]

Ramsey agrees with the statement,

Reliable test publishers have insisted that their test norms are not standards of achievement to which all schools should necessarily aim their instructional programs. Administrators and teachers less sophisticated in the ways of appraisal and statistics, however, have continued to use national norms—in achievement tests particularly—as a criterion of excellence. To surpass national norms in the "Spring administration" of a test is cause for glee in the individual classroom, pride in the principal's newsletter, and the source of a public relations "release" from the superintendent's office to the local press. Everyone is hoodwinked by the same myth—that norms are a standard for measuring achievement, when no other factors are considered.[24]

It is important also to remember that norms are derived from specific populations. In order to interpret and use them as a basis for comparison, therefore, it is imperative to know something about the population from which they were derived. The following suggestions should help to understand and use norms properly.

If we want to use the publisher's norms provided for any test, our first question should be: What is this norms group supposed to represent? For instance, is it supposed to be a sample of all 4th graders in the nation? all the public high school students of a given state who have completed a course in American history? all entering female freshmen in New England teachers' colleges? all male independent secondary school students who have completed two years of algebra?

Norms provide a specific *comparison group*, in relation to which test performance may be meaningfully described. Therefore, whatever the norms group is intended to represent, its characteristics should be clearly defined so that we can judge whether the norms given in the manual will be useful in interpreting scores for the population we want to test. (Incidentally, one of these characteristics should be the time of testing. The distribution of scores for 4th graders tested in the spring may not look like the distribution of scores for 4th graders tested in the fall). . . .

. . . for many purposes local or other specified norms will be much more useful than "national" norms. Local norms will generally have to be developed

[23] Harry N. Rivlin, "The Teacher's Role in Achievement Testing," *Test Service Notebook, #9* (Harcourt, Brace, & World, Inc., 1949), p. 2.

[24] Curtis Paul Ramsey, *op. cit.,* p. 507.

by the test user himself. (Some test manuals offer specific directions for compiling local norms.)[25]

Another common misinterpretation related to the use of the *norm* is to assume the score is a reliable measure of the pupil's over-all performance. For instance, Randy, a fifth-grader, scores 8.1 on a standardized arithmetic test. His teacher mistakenly interprets this to mean that Randy is doing eighth grade arithmetic. This is not what the score means at all. It means that Randy made on this particular test the same number of errors as the average eighth-grader of the norm group. This is far different from saying Randy is doing eighth-grade work, for Randy may not have the maturity, academic background, experience, or over-all knowledge needed to perform consistently at an eighth-grade level.

Teachers should also be cautioned against considering the test score apart from the total evaluation program, the curriculum or both. It was stated on page 452 that an effective evaluation program employs numerous and varied techniques. The standardized test is but one of these. It must be viewed in conjunction with other factors if it is to have meaning and value. As Daly says, the test score

. . . can be viewed and interpreted soundly only in relation to the total picture, which includes the child's scholastic record, his home environment, his developmental history, his classroom behavior, his health record, his past performance on similar standardized tests, and teachers' reports and observations. All these together can reveal much about a youngster, shed light on his problem, and offer a guide to planning.[26]

It is particularly important, also, that achievement test scores be interpreted in their relationship to the local curriculum. Traxler states, "A published achievement test prepared by an outside agency seldom, if ever, perfectly fits the curriculum of a particular school. In interpreting test results, differences between the objectives and content of standardized tests and the objectives and content of the curriculum of the school must be taken into account."[27]

The possible lack of relationship between the achievement test and the curriculum is also emphasized by Rivlin.

The emphasis which the standardized test places on topics that are generally taught throughout the country runs counter to the teacher's attempt to adjust the curriculum to meet the specific needs of the individual boys and girls in

[25] Educational Testing Service, *Selecting an Achievement Test* (Princeton, N. J., Educational Testing Service, 1961), pp. 9-10.

[26] William C. Daly, "Test Scores: Fragment of a Picture," *Elementary School Journal,* Vol. 60 (October, 1959), p. 44.

[27] Arthur E. Traxler, "Educational Measurement: An Aid to School Administration," *School Review,* Vol. 68 (Summer, 1960), p. 202.

his classes. The more freely the teacher adjusts the curriculum to his specific class, the more vital may schooling become to his students—but the lower may be their scores on a standardized test that is based on subject matter which a specific school regards as outdated.[28]

A final caution concerns the danger of using test results to decide whether a pupil is, or is not, working up to his intellectual capacity. Two of the most misunderstood words in current educational literature are *underachiever* and *overachiever*. What is an underachiever? One whose aptitude and achievement test scores don't exactly match? This traditional, narrow, and test-oriented concept is not accepted by most educators today, as evidenced from the following statements.

Traditional concepts of underachievement and overachievement based on a comparison of achievement with an intelligence quotient score or with a score on a test of scholastic aptitude no longer make sense.[29]

The business of comparing a child's performance with some vague "potential" based on scores of general intelligence tests is virtually outmoded. To say that a child is or is not working up to his ability when that ability is only a score on an intelligence test suggests erroneously that the test score is a highly stable measure of some over-all potential that can be mustered for use in any subject at any time.[30]

Today's broader concept of the underachiever is based upon a comparison of his daily performance with information obtained from a wide variety of sources over an extended period of time. Once identified, what does the teacher do about this problem? Does he consistently condone or tolerate inferior work? Does he tighten up with pressures, threats, and additional assignments? Does he recognize that no human being, adult or child, always works up to the limit of his ability? Does he recognize that academic performance varies, depending on many factors? And most of all, does he seek to find the cause of the underachievement? The present investigations into creativity and intelligence suggest that there are many dimensions of intelligence, many of which are not measurable by available standardized instruments. As Torrance says, out of this research, ". . . a new concept of underachievement must be fashioned, a concept in which overachievement has no place, a concept which supplies its own challenge."[31]

[28] Harry N. Rivlin, *op. cit.*, p. 2.

[29] E. Paul Torrance, "Who is the Underachiever?" *NEA Journal*, Vol. 51 (November, 1962), p. 15.

[30] John W. M. Rothney, *Evaluating and Reporting Pupil Progress*, What Research Says to the Teacher (Washington, D. C., Department of Classroom Teachers, American Educational Research Association of the National Education Association, 1955), pp. 11-12.

[31] E. Paul Torrance, *op. cit.*, p. 17.

6. *Communicating test results to parents.* The question of whether or not parents should be informed of standardized test scores does not meet with universal agreement among teachers. A recent poll reveals that 9.3 per cent of elementary teachers thought it should be standard practice to tell parents their children's IQ scores, 22.8 per cent thought it was all right in most cases, 49.7 per cent thought they should be told only in unusual cases, 15.1 per cent said it should be standard practice not to tell them, and 3.1 per cent were undecided. Concerning achievement test scores, 31.7 per cent thought it should be standard practice to tell parents, 41.7 per cent thought it was all right in most cases, 21.0 per cent thought they should be told only in unusual cases, 4.6 per cent said it should be standard practice not to tell them, and 1.0 per cent were undecided.[32]

There are, of course, many pros and cons on this issue. All teachers recognize that parents are interested in, and responsible for, the welfare and guidance of their children. All teachers should agree that the school is obligated to give parents whatever information and assistance it can to help them in this task. On the other hand, the point has been made that many teachers and administrators misinterpret and misuse test results. If this is true of those in the profession, how much truer is it of the layman? An IQ, a grade-equivalent score, or an age-equivalent score can be a dangerous piece of information in many situations. And, although conscientious teachers and counselors may try hard to put the score into proper perspective, there is still grave danger of misunderstanding. What is the solution?

As with many other problems, there is no exact rule that applies to all situations. In what terms and to what degree test scores should be communicated to parents depend largely upon the considered, expert, professional judgment of each individual teacher. In general, however, teachers should be guided by the following points of agreement among authorities:

a. There is no doubt that parents have a right to be informed of their child's test performance.

b. The school has an obligation to communicate this information in clear, nontechnical, and direct terminology. (In some schools this is required either by a state or local ruling.)

c. Such information may be conveyed more meaningfully in a face-to-face conference rather than in writing.

d. There are two general ways of minimizing the possibility of parental misinterpretation of scores. The first is for the school to report *general* indications of performance, rather than exact scores, to parents.

[32] Teacher Opinion Poll, "Telling IQ and Achievement Scores," *NEA Journal,* Vol. 51 (March, 1962), p. 92.

This is particularly true with the IQ score. The IQ may be stated in terms such as "very high" or "above average" rather than as a precise score. Or, as Noll recommends, "Instead of saying that a child's IQ is 115 one learns that it is more accurate and just as useful to say that it is highly probable that his IQ is between 105 and 125, or that there is a 50-50 probability that his IQ is between 110 and 120."[33]

General statements are also recommended for communicating achievement test scores. These may, for instance, be expressed in percentile terms, or perhaps graphed on a profile chart, which is clear and understandable but avoids mention of exact scores.

It should be clearly understood that general statements are recommended, not in an attempt to be secretive or deceptive, but conversely, to be as accurate and helpful as possible.

A second way to minimize possible misinterpretation is through a continuing program of parent education. This can be done through room conferences, PTA meetings, or written communications and colored filmstrips similar to those obtainable from the National Education Association entitled, *Your Child's Intelligence*.[34]

e. A pupil's test score should *never* be discussed with a parent other than his own. Occasionally inexperienced teachers fall into a trap of making comparisons between certain children in the room to a parent, thus conveying information to one parent about another's child. The serious consequences of such a practice should be evident.

Teacher-Made Tests

Use. Teacher-constructed tests and examinations assume increasing importance as one proceeds up the elementary school grade ladder. For obvious reasons, tests are rarely, if ever, used in the primary grades. In the intermediate grades, pupils may be introduced to short tests in spelling and arithmetic, and these are expanded to include most curriculum areas in the fifth and sixth grades.

Certainly these tests have an important place in the total evaluation program, although care should be taken not to use them in isolation in appraising and reporting academic growth. Daily assignments, class contributions, and the continuous, on-going, total performance of pupils should provide a broad base for assessing academic performance. Test results are but a part of this base.

Teacher-made tests can be invaluable instructional tools. They can provide an excellent basis for pupil self-evaluation and also help a teacher

[33] Victor H. Noll, *Introduction to Educational Measurement* (Boston, Houghton Mifflin Company, 1957), pp. 9-10.

[34] National Education Association, *Your Child's Intelligence* (Washington, D. C., National Education Association, n. d.).

to appraise his instructional strengths and limitations. They can diagnose academic ailments and indicate remedies in the following specific ways.

1. They can be used to locate specific pupils who are having difficulty. Upon the basis of test results, the teacher may determine the pupils who need regrouping, reteaching, individual tutoring, or some other type of remedial help.

2. They may indicate areas of general difficulty. From the results of an arithmetic test, Miss Q made the following item analysis.

Problem Number	Number of Incorrect Answers
1	2
2	5
3	1
4	16
5	19
6	7
7	6
8	2
9	3
10	2

It is obvious at a glance that problems 4 and 5 were missed by a large proportion of the class. Both of these involved the addition of fractions with unlike denominators. It was clear to Miss Q that she had not taught this skill successfully and that reteaching was in order.

3. They can specify the type of error. In a third grade test of column addition, Mrs. D discovered the following errors.

a.	14	b.	14	c.	14
	21		21		21
	18		18		18
	43		413		71

An analysis of the above reveals that the first and second errors were caused by failure to carry and the third by carrying the wrong digit. It became clear to Mrs. D that some of her pupils were experiencing difficulty with harder addition, not because they didn't know their basic facts or because they were careless, but because they didn't understand the concept of carrying. Her course of action now became clear.

Construction. Construction of worthwhile tests is a difficult and time-consuming task. There is, of course, little need for these tests to be constructed as carefully as standardized tests. On the other hand, unless some attempt is made at careful construction, the tests are not worth the paper they are written on. Detailed advice on test construction may be found in several of the excellent references listed in the bibliography at the close of the chapter. For our purposes, three major suggestions are sufficient.

1. The tests should be keyed to the immediate objectives of the specific learning situation. The discrepancy between educational objectives and teacher-made tests is noticeable in many classrooms. Teachers *say* they are teaching for broad understandings and problem-solving skills, but they *test* for mere memorization of facts or manipulation of skills. *The type and content of the test should be determined by what the teacher has tried to teach and hopes that his pupils have learned.*

2. Every attempt must be made to avoid ambiguity in wording test items. Torgerson and Adams suggest the following helpful techniques.

(1) Ask other teachers to read over test materials, to call attention to poor test items, and to make suggestions for improvement.

(2) Ask the children to indicate the questions which do not seem clear to them, and to underscore words they do not understand.

(3) Administer the test as a pretest to find out which questions the children can answer correctly before they have had instruction in the unit of work. These will not function as a measure of growth.

(4) After a test is given, check how many children missed each question— either by having the children raise their hands or by tallying incorrect responses to each question from the test papers.[35]

3. The maturity and verbal ability of pupils must be considered carefully when deciding upon the length and type of test. Many, many a youngster has failed a social studies, a science, or an arithmetic test, not because he didn't know the subject matter, but because he couldn't read or write as proficiently as his classmates.

Type. Educators have argued for years over the relative merits of various types of examinations. Today, most agree that there is no "best" type, for all have advantages and disadvantages that are, in turn, influenced by the purpose, construction, interpretation, and use of scores.

The *essay* test was used almost exclusively in the nineteenth century. Early twentieth-century emphasis upon accurate measurement took a dim view of the subjective nature of this test and consequently it almost disappeared from the scene. Recently, however, it has regained its former respectable status, particularly *if it is designed to serve an instructional rather than administrative function.* The following is a brief summary of the advantages and disadvantages of the essay test *as an instructional tool of the elementary school teacher.*

[35] Theodore L. Torgerson and Georgia Sachs Adams, *op. cit.*, p. 226.

Advantages	*Disadvantages*
1. Offers opportunity for the functional use of writing, problem-solving and organizational skills.	1. May be too time-consuming for young children.
2. Can indicate mastery of broad understandings and concepts.	2. May require verbal and organizational skills (handwriting, summarizing, outlining, capitalization, punctuation, spelling, etc.) not yet mastered by elementary school pupils.
3. Can encourage depth of knowledge.	
4. Can encourage the development and exercise of skills of creative thinking.	3. May not locate *specific* areas of pupil weaknesses and strengths.
	4. Difficult to score objectively.

The *objective* test was introduced into schools and colleges in the 1920's and gained widespread popularity because of its much-publicized "objectivity." Basic forms of this test used most frequently in the elementary school include (1) the simple recall or short answer item that can be worded as an incomplete statement or as a direct question, (2) the true-false, yes-no item, (3) matching items, and (4) multiple-choice items.

Throughout the 1940's and 1950's the values of the objective test were practically unchallenged. Today, however, many questions are being raised about its limitations and many people are concerned about the almost total dependence of some schools (as well as other institutions) upon objective testing. Such objections usually deal with the ambiguity of the items, the tendency to strait jacket pupils' powers of independent and creative thinking as well as organizational and integrational skills, and the possible bias against depth of knowledge and human individuality.

In essence, the advantages and disadvantages of objective tests can be summarized as follows:

Advantages	*Disadvantages*
1. Does not penalize the immature pupil who has not yet developed writing and organizational skills required by the essay type test.	1. May emphasize memorization and factual knowledge.
	2. May permit guessing.
2. Easily scored (by pupils or teacher).	3. Items may be ambiguous.
3. May be used for self-evaluation by the pupils.	4. Provides no opportunity for the development and exercise of writing and organizational skills.
4. May be used as a teaching device before or after the unit of study.	5. May restrict pupils' independent and creative thinking powers.

The *problem* test is the third type used in the elementry school and is very valuable for the testing of critical thinking skills. It may be either an essay or objective test or it may require pupils to interpret, use, or construct a map, graph, diagram, or pictorial representation.

Scoring. One of the advantages of the objective test listed above is that it frequently may be scored by pupils. Research has indicated that, under certain conditions, self-scoring can be a valuable instructional technique. It can reinforce learnings, help pupils to understand their mistakes, and afford the teacher a valuable opportunity to clarify areas of confusion.

These values can be realized only if children score their own papers. Exchanging papers for scoring purposes is completely useless educationally and it may produce many undesirable social habits, attitudes, and interpersonal relationships.

It should be repeated that self-scoring is desirable only when tests are used for instructional purposes. Pupils should never score their own tests if the results are used primarily for such administrative purposes as reporting, recording, or classifying children for instruction.

Rating Scales and Checklists

There are three different types of rating scales or checklists that may be used to appraise pupil development in any grade in the elementary school. The first involves *teacher rating* of pupils. The teacher may rate or check the existence of certain traits and attitudes among pupils on either commercial instruments or on locally-designed forms. Sometimes the teacher uses a rating scale or checklist to help him study the child's behavior more deeply, and in this capacity it may have value. The form, as an accurate or objective evaluative instrument, however, has many limitations. Rothney says,

Often classroom teachers indicate a pupil's development by checking or putting a symbol after a word or short description of some aspect of personality. Thus, the teacher may be asked to check whether a child's "citizenship" is excellent, good, fair, or poor. He may be asked to indicate which of a number of briefly defined characteristics placed in supposed order of excellence best describes the behavior of the pupil as he has observed it. Rating and checking of this kind is likely to be a compilation of errors, for the procedure is a relic of the dark ages of psychology. The procedure would be discarded if it did not *seem* to accomplish its purpose in a very short time.

Actually such ratings may be definitely harmful since research has shown that among their other limitations they (a) suggest that certain characteristics are equally desirable in equal amounts for all individuals at all times; (b) encourage generalization about a pupil's characteristics beyond what was actually observed by the rater; (c) encourage the making of comparisons of pupils who are quite different and who have had unequal environmental opportunities;

(d) assume that teachers can observe behavior, such as cooperation, sort it into units on a scale, and allot values to it; (e) suffer from "halo" effect, that is, the teacher who rates a pupil high in one characteristic tends to rate him high in others or vice versa; and (f) usually suffer from inadequate definition of the terms to be rated so that what is satisfactory to one person may be very unsatisfactory to another. . . . Research on individual differences suggests that it is unrealistic and unwise to try to place pupils on the same scale without considering their unique circumstances and situations. Perhaps as our knowledge of individual differences increases, the common rating scale or checklist will become obsolete.[36]

It is, perhaps, not fair to ascribe equal limitations to all types of checklists because some are certainly better than others, and recent research has eliminated some of the glaring weaknesses of the earlier instruments.

A second type is the *self-rating scale* which can be used with pupils. Often teachers find this is an effective means of directing a pupil toward a thoughtful analysis of his behavior. Many times it is helpful to compare the pupil's self-rating with the teacher's rating of him. If, for instance, a checklist is part of the report card, the teacher may duplicate this on paper and ask the pupil to rate himself. His rating can then be compared to the teacher's report card rating in a short private conference. This technique helps (1) the pupil to develop self-direction and self-knowledge, (2) the teacher to understand the pupil's self-concept, and (3) the pupil to interpret his record card to his parents.

The third type includes the variety of instruments used to determine pupils' ratings and opinions of each other. Popular types are the *acceptance scales* on which children indicate their reactions to classmates or the *reputation tests* on which the pupil indicates the name of a classmate fitting a certain description.

Personal Documents

Autobiographies. Autobiographies written by children in the upper grades can be functional language experiences as well as indicators of personality development. Some autobiographies are entirely unstructured in that children are simply given an opportunity to write a story about themselves. Others are more structured in that pupils are asked to include answers to such questions as (1) Who have been the most important people in your life? (2) What are your pleasantest memories? (3) What was the worst thing that ever happened to you? (4) What changes would you make in your life if you could?

Other types of personal writing may be motivated through suggested

[36] John W. M. Rothney, *op. cit.*, pp. 15-17.

titles such as "My Longest Day," "A Moment I'll Never Forget," or "A Look into My Future."

There is little doubt that personal writing can be very revealing. It may be particularly helpful to the teacher in understanding the resistant or noncommunicative or introspective youngster. Care must be taken, of course, to place the document in proper perspective, remembering always the lively imaginations and exaggeration tendencies of young children.

Diaries, logs, time charts. These are often very valuable in acquainting the teacher with pupils out-of-school activities. They may also help the student to evaluate the worth of his leisure time activities as well as to budget his time more wisely.

Expressional and Interpretational Activities

It was said earlier that most projective techniques should be used by personnel with specialized training. The principle of these techniques, however, may be used by the classroom teacher, often with worthwhile results. Wrightstone defines the projective approach as follows: "Projective technics have come into prominence over the past two decades. The projective approach to the study of personality is indirect, in that the person is not asked questions about himself, but is asked to respond to various stimuli and his responses are interpreted as indicating significant personality trends."[37]

It should be fairly easy to see how the teacher may adapt this approach to his informal study of pupil personality. Children's creative efforts (stories, poems, dramatics, painting, finger-painting, and clay work); completing stories, sentences, or pictures; interpreting abstract forms such as cloud pictures; role playing; informal play with tops and puppets; and picture or music interpretation may be meaningful to the perceptive teacher when placed within the total framework of his knowledge of his pupils.

Conferences and Interviews

Every experienced teacher knows the value of sitting down informally with a pupil and just talking things over. Such conferences can be very helpful and revealing to the teacher, *provided he is a good listener.* Many a teacher is in love with the sound of his own voice and insists on monopolizing the conversation. Delivering a lecture is not the purpose of this type of conference. Two important prerequisities of successful confer-

---

[37] J. Wayne Wrightstone and others, "Educational Measurements," *Review of Educational Research*, Vol. 26 (June, 1956), p. 276.

encing are (1) the pupil should be permitted to talk freely and fully, without fear of punishment or retaliation, and (2) a state of rapport exists between pupil and teacher. Unless these are present, the conference is doomed to dismal failure.

It is worth noting that a successful conference may yield to the teacher information, not only about the pupil, but about himself. The teacher may well keep in mind the story, told by A. J. Cross,

> . . . about a small redhead named Jerry, whose misbehavior every day stirred turmoil in the classroom. The teacher kept him after school one day and they both worked quietly at their desks. Afterward, she asked him to help clean erasers. As they worked together, they chatted in an easy and friendly way.
> "Jerry," she said finally, "I wish you would be this way during class time."
> "Ain't it funny?" the boy reflected: "I was just thinking the same thing about you."[38]

Records

Anecdotal records. Anecdotal records can constitute one of the teacher's most important techniques for observing and understanding pupil behavior. Simply defined, they are short, concise recordings of pupil behavior in a variety of situations, as observed by the teacher. Entries are frequently called thumbnail sketches because they are brief, terse, descriptive statements of a pupil's behavior. At the time of recording, no attempt should be made to interpret the behavior. As time goes on, however, a pattern of behavior may emerge from repeated observations, which will enable the teacher to make an interpretation, or to suggest or take a course of action. An efficient method of organizing anecdotal records is according to three parallel columns, as illustrated on pages 478 to 480.

General guidelines to be observed in maintaining anecdotal records include the following:

1. It is impractical and unnecessary to keep anecdotal records on all pupils. It is usually wise for the teacher to begin such records for two or three pupils whose behavior appears to warrant concentrated study. Later, if necessary, the number of records may be increased. It should be remembered, however, that problem behavior is not necessarily disruptive and aggressive (see Chapter 3). The teacher should make every effort to avoid concentrating on these children to the neglect of the quiet, withdrawn, introverted personality.

2. The period of time over which the record is kept depends upon the judgment of the teacher. It may be begun at any time and terminated

---

[38] Mildred S. Fenner, "Editor's Notebook," *NEA Journal*, Vol. 51 (September, 1962), p. 64.

at any time, either because it has served its purpose, or because it appears that nothing may be gained from additional recordings.

3. Behavior should be recorded as objectively as possible. "Lazy," "spiteful," "dirty-minded," or "silly" are biased words that will not permit the teacher to make an accurate interpretation of the total behavioral pattern at a later date.

4. The day and time of the incident should be recorded.

5. Behavioral incidents of two types are usually recorded and may be determined by the purpose of the record. The teacher may wish to record *typical* behavior. If the purpose is to ascertain a typical behavioral pattern, it may help to make systematic recordings each day at 9:30 A. M., 11:30 A. M., and 2:30 P. M., for instance. On the other hand, the teacher may want to study *nontypical* behavior for certain reasons. The example on pages 478 to 480 is a condensation of this type of record kept over a two-month period. It illustrates the tremendous value of careful study and careful recording of pupil behavior by a perceptive teacher.

Cumulative records. In earlier days, the pupil's entire school record was often maintained on a 3 x 5 card file in the principal's office. Today, this has been replaced by a comprehensive record, usually in the form of a file folder. Such forms may be ordered from a commercial company or designed by a local school system to meet its specific needs. Such records are not mere bookkeeping devices. Their purposes have been stated as follows:

(a) to enable teachers to get acquainted quickly with new pupils, (b) to identify scholastic strengths and weaknesses of individual pupils and to plan a program to fit the pupil, (c) to identify problems of personal or social adjustment that a pupil faces, (d) to provide comprehensive and continuous data for counseling with the pupil, and (e) to serve as a source of information in a conference with a parent.[39]

In general, the cumulative record folder should represent a comprehensive inventory of the pupil's academic, mental, physical, and social-emotional development. It should include (1) name and vital statistics of child, (2) physical and mental history, (3) yearly record of academic achievement, (4) all standardized test data, (5) pertinent personal data such as socio-economic level of family, record of interests, out-of-school activities, and hobbies, and (6) selected samples of pupil's work. This last item should be carefully screened to avoid the folder's becoming too cumbersome. However, a few carefully selected samples of work each year may be very illuminating in appraising the pupil's long-range growth.

[39] J. Wayne Wrightstone and others, *op. cit.*, p. 225.

TABLE 11.1

Anecdotal Record

NAME: EUGENE H.   AGE: TEN   GRADE: FIVE

Date	Observation	Comment	Action
January 10 10 A.M.	Failed weekly spelling test. Appeared close to tears while papers were being checked.	Gene's work seems to have deteriorated steadily in the past few weeks. He was such an excellent student at the beginning of the year.	
January 12 2 P.M.	Daydreamed through most of the social studies lesson.	Appears disinterested in class work. Quite a change from his usual performance.	
January 13 11 A.M.	Asked to be excused from physical education class. Said he felt too tired to play in the gym.		Have watched Gene carefully to see if he is having trouble with any other children in the class. Watched him walk home from school as far as I could. He walked with several of his friends, with no apparent signs of discord.
January 14	Asked to be excused to go to the lavatory three times this morning.	Have noticed this frequently in recent weeks. Is it possible he is trying to get out of work?	
January 17 3 P.M.	Fell asleep over his library book.	Is Gene getting enough rest at home?	

Date	Observation	Comment
January 22 3:30 P.M.	Asked to be excused seven times to go to the lavatory or to get a drink today.	
January 27 10:30 A.M.	Stared out of window during most of science period.	Talked with Gene after school about his poor work. Said he will try to do better. Asked about frequent trips to lavatory. Said they were necessary and that he was not trying to get out of work.
January 28 3:30 P.M.	Left room several times today to go to lavatory or to get a drink.	No improvement noticed after our talk yesterday.
February 4 11 A.M.	Asked to be excused from physical education. Said he was "just tired."	Is it possible Gene is not well? I can't think of any other reason for his changed behavior.
February 7 3 P.M.	Did not complete his science project. Said he "didn't feel like doing it."	
February 11 4 P.M.		Just had a conference with Mrs. H about Gene. Told her he seemed tired and listless and that his work was slipping. Mentioned his frequent trips to the lavatory and drinking fountain. Mrs. H said she noticed some of this at home but didn't think it was very important. Promised to discuss it with Mr. H.

TABLE 11.1 (Continued)

Anecdotal Record

NAME: EUGENE H.   AGE: TEN   GRADE: FIVE

Date	Observation	Comment	Action
February 12 9 A.M.	Received note from Mrs. H. She is taking Gene to the family doctor tonight for a check-up.		
February 15 Noon	Mrs. H phoned. Gene is in the hospital for observation. His illness has been diagnosed as diabetes.		
March 18 9 A.M.	Gene returned to school today. Looks fine. Received a lovely note from Mrs. H thanking me for calling their attention to his illness.		

Class folders. It is difficult to see how any elementary school teacher can get along without a file of class folders. These are different from the official cumulative records in that they are kept and used in the classroom by the pupil and teacher. They may be kept in a file drawer, in a large sturdy cardboard carton, or occasionally in pupils' desks. They are receptacles for all types of work, such as pictures, daily assignments, corrected test papers, creative writing efforts, and graphs showing weekly progress in spelling. At the close of a six or eight week period, the folders form an excellent basis for evaluation of progress by both teacher and pupil. They may also be used, with extremely valuable results, as the basis for teacher-parent conferences. If written report cards are used, the accumulation of significant work may be sent home with the card. In general, it is wise to accumulate work samples only over a several week period. Much of the work may then be discarded or taken home by pupils, once it has served its purpose. Exceptions should be made, of course, for very significant items which should be kept in the class folder throughout the year or transferred to the administrative cumulative record folder or to the teacher's private file.

It has been the author's experience that this folder, when carefully kept, can be one of the most valuable records of pupil growth used by the teacher. It is much more meaningful, revealing, comprehensive, and accurate than the small record book kept by some teachers which contains merely a conglomeration of numbers or letters. The limitations of this type of evaluation are further discussed in the following section.

METHODS OF REPORTING PUPIL PROGRESS TO PARENTS

CHANGING METHODS OF REPORTING REFLECT BASIC CHANGES IN EDUCATIONAL PHILOSOPHY. In probably no other area of educational practice is there less consistency than in the matter of reporting pupil progress to parents. At the moment, there are an infinite number and variety of methods in use, and it is difficult to find the same report card used in any two school systems. Furthermore, even within one system, the type of card often varies according to the school, and even within the school the method may vary according to the grade level. It is not uncommon to find three entirely different instruments or methods operating simultaneously within a single school. Multiply this by the number of schools or systems in the country, and one gets some idea of the present state of inconsistency and indecision in this area. The lack of consistency, however, is not due to mere whim but to a tendency of report cards to reflect the educational philosophy of the individual system. As that philosophy has evolved over the present century, reporting methods have changed accordingly.

In general, the basic changes in educational philosophy and the corresponding trends in reporting methods may be summarized briefly as in Table 11.2 below.

TABLE 11.2

Philosophic Emphases	Reporting Trends
1. Expanding scope of school's responsibility with emphasis upon the physical, mental, and social-emotional development of the child.	Increased comprehensiveness of card, utilizing Narrative statements Check-lists and rating scales Profile charts etc. Supplementing card with samples of pupils' work, home visits, etc.
2. Recognition of individual differences.	Elimination of competitive features—numerical and alphabetical ratings, class standings, honor rolls, etc. Emphasis upon diagnostic features of reporting.
3. Refinement of evaluation and guidance procedures.	Elimination of pseudo scientific ratings such as numerical and alphabetical grades. Increasing emphasis upon pupil self-evaluation. Synthesizing reporting data from a wide variety of data.
4. Growing importance of positive home-school relationships.	Emphasis upon two-way communication rather than one-way reporting. Emphasis upon cooperative development and evaluation of reporting method.

CERTAIN BASIC TYPES OF REPORTING METHODS HAVE DEVELOPED OVER THE YEARS. The changing philosophic emphases and reporting trends have, in general, produced certain basic types of cards that have evolved gradually but steadily since the nineteenth century. It should be understood that no single pure type was ever used by all schools at any one time. Variations, combinations, and modifications were, and are, used simultaneously throughout the country. However, at the risk of oversimplification, the climb toward improved reporting methods is illustrated in Figure 11.1 below.

Single, comprehensive ratings. Nineteenth century methods of reporting to parents frequently consisted of small cards that, by color or legend, reported that the pupil rated excellent, good, fair, or failing in over-all scholarship and deportment.

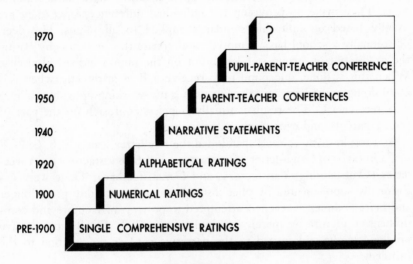

1970	?
1960	PUPIL-PARENT-TEACHER CONFERENCE
1950	PARENT-TEACHER CONFERENCES
1940	NARRATIVE STATEMENTS
1920	ALPHABETICAL RATINGS
1900	NUMERICAL RATINGS
PRE-1900	SINGLE COMPREHENSIVE RATINGS

FIGURE 11.1

The trend toward improved reporting practices.

Numerical ratings. Interest in objective measurement as well as an attempt to portray a more comprehensive picture of the pupil's performance paved the way toward numerical ratings. The impossibility and ambiguity of rating an individual 72 in reading, 69 in arithmetic, and 81 in language gradually became apparent to many educators. Numerical ratings were consequently succeeded by letter marks in most schools.

Alphabetical ratings. In this type of card, each letter is usually defined in terms of a judgment such as "excellent," "very good," "average," or in terms of numerical equivalents such as A = 91-100, B = 81-90, and so forth. Generally speaking, letter ratings are popular with many parents and some teachers. Parents like them because they think they understand them and are used to them. Uninformed or lackadaisical teachers like them because they place a relatively light bookkeeping burden upon them. Then too, they make a wonderful screen behind which a superficial teacher may hide. A father recently complained, "My son received a D in arithmetic. I went to the school to find out the trouble and to see if I could help him. When I asked the teacher why Ned received a D on his report card, she took out her record book and showed me a lot of little D's. All the little D's added up to a final D on the report card. But I still want to know, Why did my son receive a D in arithmetic?" Thus, can a lazy or incompetent teacher evade her responsibilities toward pupil and parent through reliance upon meaningless grades.

To most intelligent educators, alphabetical ratings have serious limitations. They make no provision for individual differences since they are usually based on inflexible standards applied to all pupils. However, occasionally a school has attempted to eliminate this weakness by basing the grade, not on group standards, but on the pupil's individual ability. When this is done, one pupil may receive a B in arithmetic whereas a child doing much better work (but who is not working up to his ability) may receive a C. The result is usually hopeless confusion on the part of pupils, parents, and even teachers themselves.

As a result, many schools abandoned the five-letter scale (A, B, C, D, E or F) in favor of a two-letter (*S* atisfactory and *U* nsatisfactory) or three-letter (*O* utstanding, *S* atisfactory, and *U* nsatisfactory). These were occasionally supplemented by checklists or scales that steadily grew longer and more complex as teachers attempted to portray an accurate and comprehensive picture by merely manipulating symbols. Finally, many gave up the struggle and turned to the narrative card as the solution to the problem.

Narrative statements. There is little doubt that, in theory, the narrative statement is an improvement over the earlier use of letters or numbers. It can be defended from a sound educational point of view in that (1) it eliminates the competitive aspects of marks, either alphabetical or numerical, (2) it presents a comprehensive picture of the child's total growth, and (3) it serves a diagnostic and remedial function in that it can report specific strengths and limitations as well as suggestions for parental action.

Unfortunately, the narrative card is more valuable in theory than in practice, except in the hands of a very capable, conscientious teacher. If this is not the case, the narrative card can deteriorate into a vague, rambling statement equally unpopular with parents and teachers. Parents complain that it is not "concrete" and that it is full of educational jargon that means nothing to them. Indifferent and inexperienced teachers complain that it is time-consuming and virtually impossible to make the card clear, definite, constructive, and helpful.

Parent-teacher conferences. Many educators, after struggling for years to develop an adequate printed card, decided that the only satisfactory method of reporting to parents was through face-to-face conferences.

There is little doubt that direct communication among the two or three individuals most responsible for, and most interested in, the pupil's welfare represents a vast improvement over any type of written report. Here again, however, as with all other methods of evaluation, its worth depends largely upon how it is used. The best method in the world becomes worthless in the hands of an inefficient teacher or administrator. Many of the references listed in the bibliography contain helpful suggestions for insuring the worth of the parent-teacher conference. A brief statement of the elementary principles of successful conferencing contains the following suggestions.

1. Make careful preparation.
2. Insure privacy.
3. Have an informal setting.
4. Set a time limit.
5. Overlook parents' critical remarks.
6. Establish rapport.
7. Encourage the parent to talk.
8. Listen attentively.
9. Begin on a positive note.
10. Develop attitude of mutual cooperation.
11. Delay making definite suggestions.
12. Let suggestions come from parents.
13. Build on parents' suggestions.
14. Summarize points covered.
15. Make plans together.
16. End on a note of continuing cooperation.
17. Make notes after parent leaves.[40]

Today, the parent-teacher conference is used most frequently in combination with some method of written report card. A survey of urban school districts reports that "less than 1 per cent make reports exclusively by conference," but that "more than three-fourths of the districts report pupil progress in elementary school by means of both parent conferences and report cards." The survey concludes, "The trend at all levels is away from reporting by card only and toward reporting by card plus a conference with the parents."[41]

[40] U. S. Office of Education, Division of State and Local School Systems, *Reporting Pupil Progress to Parents*, Education Briefs, No. 34 (Washington, D. C., Department of Health, Education, and Welfare, Office of Education, December, 1956), p. 18, mimeographed.

[41] "Reporting to Parents," *NEA Research Bulletin*, Vol. 39 (February, 1961), pp. 24.

Parent-pupil-teacher conferences. One of the most serious limitations of the parent-teacher conference is its frequent neglect of the person most concerned, the child. Today, some schools are strengthening this form of reporting by adopting the triangular conference which includes parents, pupil, and teacher. Such a conference can direct the pupil toward self-evaluation and can also help the parent and teacher to understand better the pupil's view of his situation. It is, of course, occasionally desirable *not* to include the child for fairly obvious reasons. When this is the case, a private conference between parent and teacher may be held, with or without the pupil's knowledge. In general, however, some schools have recently moved toward the triangular conference as their standard method of reporting progress. This may, of course, be supplemented by, or combined with, any type of written report.

Thus, we come to the 1960's in our climb toward improved methods of reporting. What does the future hold? Who knows? One thing, however, is certain. The present amount of variance among reporting methods indicates that no perfect, or even wholly adequate, method has yet been found. As we continue to learn more about how to appraise pupil progress, we will continue to perfect our methods of reporting our knowledge to parents. As to what form this will take, who, at the moment, can say?

REGARDLESS OF THE METHOD, THE TEACHER HAS CERTAIN BASIC OBLIGA-TIONS IN REPORTING PUPIL PROGRESS TO PARENTS. It was said previously that any valuable method of reporting becomes worthless when used by an incompetent teacher. To a lesser extent, the opposite may also be true. Only a miracle could turn a poor report card into a good one, but every capable teacher can compensate somewhat for the limitations of the reporting method he is required to use. The following suggestions are offered:

1. Secure data for the report card from a variety of evaluative methods and sources. In the preceding section, several evaluative techniques for appraising the total growth of the pupil were suggested. Information from all of these should be weighed, synthesized, and condensed for reporting purposes. This is a far different job from simply transferring the average of marks in a record book to a report card.

2. Make the report card as comprehensive and revealing as possible. Many ingenious teachers find ways to supplement the scant information conveyed through a numerical or alphabetical rating. Some include a narrative statement in a space provided for it on the card. Others attach a written note to the card. Others make phone calls. One particularly capable teacher makes a functional language experience out of having her pupils summarize their work in various curricular areas at the close

of each marking period. These summaries are written (individually or as a cooperative class project), mimeographed, and sent home with the report cards. Thus, parents receive a clear picture of the type of work on which the pupil received his grades.

3. Make the tone of the report positive and constructive. Harsh, critical, negative statements should be avoided at all costs. This does not mean that the report should be evasive or untruthful. It simply means that the report card was never purposed as a vehicle for airing grievances, criticizing pupils, and telling parents they are at fault.

4. Make the language of the report clear, nontechnical, and direct. "Pedaguese" has no place on report cards. Parents don't understand it and strongly suspect (with some justification) that teachers do not either. Anything that is important enough to be said is important enough to be said clearly.

5. Utilize the report card as a self-evaluative instrument for pupils. It has already been suggested that the contents of the class folders be examined cooperatively at the close of each marking period by pupil and teacher. In some instances, the report card mark may be decided by both upon this evidence. In other situations, the pupil may be asked to prepare a scratch copy of his report card and compare it with that marked by the teacher. The very least that should be done is for the teacher and pupil to read and discuss the card *together* before it is taken or sent home. The idea of perfunctorily distributing cards to the entire class two minutes before dismissal, with no opportunity for individual consultation, belongs to the dark ages of education. May it never return!

6. Make some provision for two-way communication. Many printed cards today provide some space for parental comments. Then too, the teacher is always free to include with the card a mimeographed form on which parents are asked to note suggestions or comments. Some teachers also include a short note stating that they will be available certain hours the following week should any parent desire a conference. There are numerous ways of letting parents know that their suggestions and assistance are appreciated. And never was there a person who did not appreciate being appreciated.

SUMMARY

As teachers become increasingly responsible for determining the goals, methods, and materials of education, they must become correspondingly more competent in evaluating the success of their efforts. Although recognizing that evaluation has several functions and is the cooperative responsibility of many persons, this chapter emphasized it as an instructional tool of the classroom teacher.

In order to fulfill his responsibilities in this area, it is necessary, first of all, that the teacher recognize the basic characteristics of an effective evaluation program. These were mentioned in the first section. Effective evaluation is (1) keyed to the educational objectives of the local situation, (2) continuous and on-going, (3) systematically planned according to long-range goals, (4) cooperatively developed by all vital personnel, and (5) dependent upon a variety of procedures and instruments.

The second section was devoted to an examination of the basic methods of evaluation used in the modern elementary school. The first of these was standardized tests, which were recognized to be valuable and indispensable educational tools when properly used and interpreted. Major emphasis was placed upon the classroom teacher's specific responsibilities in the standardized testing program, i .e., (1) determining the testing program, (2) making advance preparations for the standardized test, (3) administering the test, (4) scoring and recording scores, (5) interpreting and using test results, and (6) communicating test results to parents.

Teacher-made tests were considered briefly as to their (1) use, (2) construction, (3) type, and (4) scoring. Again, the value of such tests was recognized although teachers were cautioned against using them as the sole basis for evaluating pupils' academic performance.

Other evaluative methods examined were (1) rating scales and checklists, (2) personal documents, (3) expressional and interpretational activities, (4) conferences and interviews, and (5) basic types of records.

The last section was concerned with the evolution of methods of reporting pupil progress to parents. It was pointed out that, over the twentieth century, changing educational philosophies were mirrored in reporting methods. Basic methods included (1) single, comprehensive ratings, (2) numerical ratings, (3) alphabetical ratings, (4) narrative statements, (5) parent-teacher conferences, and (6) pupil-parent-teacher conferences. It is important to remember that no "pure" type ever completely dominated the educational scene, however, for modifications and combinations were, and are, used in an almost bewildering number and variety.

What form will the report card of the future take? It is difficult to say. The only thing we do know is that, as we earnestly try to refine our techniques of evaluating pupil progress, so will we continue to improve our methods of reporting this progress to parents.

ADDITIONAL LEARNING EXPERIENCES

Topics for Thought and Discussion

1. Do you think that the increasing emphasis upon testing, particularly in the secondary school, is putting pressures upon pupils and causing anxieties

that should be of serious concern to teachers? Is some of this increasing emphasis filtering down to the elementary school?

2. Were you ever informed of your own IQ? How did this knowledge affect your vocational goals? Your academic motivations? Your self-concept?

3. Did you suffer from test anxiety when you were a student in the elementary school?

4. If you were a parent, would you want to know your child's IQ? Why?

5. Can you think of any situation today in which there may be a real danger of test makers controlling the curriculum?

6. What is your opinion of a state-wide or nation-wide testing program for elementary schools?

7. What type of report card do you think is most popular with parents, as a general rule? Why?

8. To what extent do you think teachers' grades are influenced by their knowledge of pupils' IQ's?

9. The serious problem caused by the misuse and misinterpretation of psychological test data by some teachers has led some principals and school guidance counselors to maintain files of confidential pupil data to which teachers may not have access. Is this a good idea?

10. Someone has said that there is a possibility that the profession has oversold the public on what tests can do and underemphasized what they cannot do. Do you agree with this statement?

11. Are teachers generally as careful about the handling of confidential information as members of other professions?

12. A teacher recently took a set of confidential pupil records home to work on them during the evening. She accidentally left them on the bus. Another passenger picked them up and they were eventually circulated widely through the community. To prevent such an occurrence, should teachers be forbidden to take such materials out of the school building?

13. Should student teachers be allowed access to pupils' confidential records?

14. Should a single type of report card be used for an entire elementary school or should different types be used for primary and upper grades? Why?

Projects and Activities

1. Read and give a report on *The Brain Watchers* by Martin L. Gross. (New York, Random House, 1962).

2. You have been asked to serve on a panel to discuss the topic, "Standardized Testing: Educational Boon or Bane!" What viewpoint will you express? With what literature or research will you support your viewpoint?

3. Study the objectives of the unit on Electricity and Magnetism outlined in Chapter 7. Suggest specific evaluative techniques that could be used to evaluate the attainment of each objective.

4. If possible, maintain an anecdotal record of an elementary school child over a several week period. Write a summary statement, based upon the patterns of behavior revealed, for a narrative report card to be sent to his parents. Do you think the anecdotal record helped you to observe and report behavior more objectively and more analytically? Why?

5. Talk with a school psychologist or psychiatrist. To what extent does he consider the misuse and misinterpretation of psychological test data by teachers to be a serious problem? What solution does he suggest? Compare his opinions with those of an elementary school principal. A teacher. A parent.

6. Demonstrate, through role playing, a successful parent-teacher conference. A parent-teacher-pupil conference.

7. Prepare a research paper on "The Academic Underachiever in the Elementary School." Be sure to discuss (1) how an underachiever is identified, (2) possible causes of underachievement, and (3) a suggested program to alleviate the problem.

8. If possible, ask a group of fifth or sixth graders to write a short personal document entitled, "How I Feel on Report Card Day," or "How I Feel When I Take a Test," or a similar title. Does such writing give you any insight into children's behavior and attitudes? What does it reveal about the presence of test anxiety or grade anxiety among elementary school pupils?

9. Interview several parents. Are they in favor of the school's reporting pupil progress through parent-teacher conferences? What advantages do they see in this method? What disadvantages?

10. Talk with several elementary teachers who use letter grades on report cards. Are they satisfied with this method of reporting? How do they manipulate the symbols so as to provide for individual differences among pupils?

11. From the *Mental Measurements Yearbooks* locate a recommended test of each of the following types.
    A general scholastic aptitude test.
    A reading readiness test.
    A general academic achievement test.
    A paper and pencil personality inventory.
    A group scholastic aptitude test.
    A performance test.
    An achievement test in one curricular field.
    Secure a specimen test set of each test. Give an analytical report to your college class, describing the function, format, standardization procedures, norms group, scoring techniques, etc. of each test you have examined.

12. Read and give a report on *The Tyranny of Testing* by Banesh Hoffman (New York, The Crowell-Collier Press, 1962).

Selected Bibliography

AHMANN, J. S., and others, *Evaluating Elementary School Pupils*. Boston, Allyn and Bacon, Inc., 1960.

———, and GLOCK, Marvin D., *Evaluating Pupil Growth*, 2nd ed. Boston, Allyn and Bacon, Inc., 1963.

ANASTASI, Anne, *Psychological Testing*, 2nd ed. New York, The Macmillan Company, 1961.

BARON, Denis, and BERNARD, Harold W., *Evaluation Techniques for Classroom Teachers*. New York, McGraw-Hill Book Co., Inc., 1958.

BRADFIELD, James M., and MOREDOCK, H. Stewart, *Measurement and Evaluation in Education*. New York, The Macmillan Company, 1957.

D'EVELYN, Katherine E., *Individual Parent-Teacher Conferences*, 7th ed. New York, Bureau of Publications, Teachers College, Columbia University, 1959.

"Educational and Psychological Testing." *Review of Educational Research*, Vol. 29 (February, 1959).

Educational Testing Service, *Making the Classroom Test: A Guide for Teachers*. Princeton, N. J., 1961.

ELSBREE, Willard S., *Pupil Progress in the Elementary School, No. 5*. New York, Bureau of Publications, Teachers College, Columbia University, 1949.

GREENE, Harry A., JORGENSEN, Albert N., and GERBERICH, J. Raymond, *Measurement and Evaluation in the Elementary School*, rev. ed. New York, Longmans, Green and Company, 1953.

NOLL, Victor H., *Introduction to Educational Measurement*. Boston, Houghton Mifflin Company, 1957.

ODELL, C. W., *How to Improve Classroom Testing*. Dubuque, Iowa, William C. Brown Company, Publishers, 1953.

"Reporting." *NEA Journal*, Vol. 48 (December, 1959).

ROTHNEY, John W. M., *Evaluating and Reporting Pupil Progress*. What Research Says to the Teacher No. 7. Department of Classroom Teachers, American Educational Research Association, of the National Educational Association. Washington, D. C., 1955.

SHANE, Harold G., and McSWAIN, Eldridge T., *Evaluation and the Elementary School Curriculum*, rev. ed. New York, Holt, Rinehart and Winston, Inc., 1958.

STRANG, Ruth, *Reporting to Parents*. New York, Bureau of Publications, Teachers College, Columbia University, 1952.

"Testing and Evaluation." *NEA Journal*, Vol. 48 (November, 1959).

THOMAS, R. Murray, *Judging Student Progress*. New York, Longmans, Green and Company, 1954.

THORNDIKE, Robert L., *The Concepts of Over-and Under-achievement*. New York, Bureau of Publications, Teachers College, Columbia University, 1963.

———, and HAGEN, Elizabeth, *Measurement and Evaluation in Psychology and Education*. New York, John Wiley & Sons, Inc., 1955.

TORGERSON, Theodore L., and ADAMS, Georgia Sachs, *Measurement and Evaluation for the Elementary School Teacher*. New York, Holt, Rinehart and Winston, Inc., 1954.

VERNON, P. E., *Intelligence and Attainment Tests*. New York, Philosophical Library Inc., 1961.

WILLEY, Roy D., *Guidance in Elementary Education*, rev. ed. New York, Harper & Row, Publishers, Inc., 1960.

WRIGHTSTONE, J. Wayne, and others, "Educational Measurements." *Review of Educational Research*, Vol. 26 (June, 1956).

——, JUSTMAN, Joseph, and ROBBINS, Irving, *Evaluation in Modern Education*. New York, American Book Company, 1956.

PART IV

GROWING ON THE JOB

CHAPTER 12

Growing Personally and Professionally

CONTINUING PERSONAL and professional growth accounts for the difference between the teacher who has had twenty years of experience and the teacher who has had one year of experience twenty times.

The intelligent teacher realizes that his professional preparation is never really completed. Certainly it is not when he receives the Baccalaureate degree, regardless of how superior his undergraduate education may be. Neither is it complete when he finally struggles through that difficult first year of teaching, nor when he attains tenure or permanent certification. Throughout his entire professional career the intelligent, competent, and professional teacher is constantly raising his intellectual, cultural, and professional sights. He realizes all too clearly that no one ever really stands still in his field; he either goes forward or backward. And the short-sighted teacher who thinks that he has nothing more to learn about teaching, whether he has taught one year or half a lifetime, is going backward with the speed of sound.

Continued growth is necessary in all professions and desirable in all occupations. It is absolutely imperative in good teaching. As one source states,

It is axiomatic in the professional, business and industrial fields that those persons who are involved continue to study and to grow. The doctor who does not continue to study soon becomes antiquated in his field. The man who was an expert mechanic on the Model T Ford can do little with a modern automobile unless he has continued to study the new developments. The bankers hold regular courses for in-service education so as to be able to meet the new demands and follow the new laws. Likewise with teachers. . . .

No school and no faculty is static. Staff members either are striving to improve the program of their school or an increasingly poorer job of teaching is being done and the youth that the school is set up to serve are thereby being penalized.[1]

Conditions that demand that all teachers engage in a consciously-directed and continuing program of personal and professional growth are examined in the following section.

NEEDS AND PURPOSES OF CONTINUING TEACHER GROWTH

Basic factors necessitating continual teacher growth are considered in this section to be: (1) the ever-changing content, techniques, and materials of instruction, (2) the limitations of preservice preparation, (3) the lack of certain built-in stimulants to self-improvement in teaching, and (4) the expanding role of the teacher.

EDUCATION IS NOT STATIC. We are living today in a period of unprecedented change. Cultural changes, social advancements, technological developments, and international relationships inevitably affect every aspect of the school program. Chapter 8 examined a few of the new trends in curriculum content at the present time. The drastic changes in the content and grade placement of mathematics, the indefinite future of foreign languages in the elementary school, the increased emphasis upon a broader science program in all grades, the concern with creativity in all areas, the attention to previously neglected areas of international education, and the emphasis upon linguistics are only some of the new curriculum issues under careful scrutiny at present. It is difficult to see how any teacher today can be effective in the classroom who has not kept abreast of the changing form and content of the elementary school curriculum.

The expanding horizons of knowledge are as important in our field as in any other. In recent years research has added considerably to knowledge of the learning process and of child growth and development. Many teachers are aware of the crucial need to be continually informed in these vital areas. This is evidenced by the fact that child study and psychology of learning are among the most popular choices of topics among teachers for workshops, courses, conferences, or other types of in-service educational activities.

Then too, the materials of instruction are constantly changed and improved. Excellent new textbooks, reference books, globes, maps, audio-visual aids, learning kits, auto-instructional devices, and others appear

[1] School Board of Austin, Texas, "Why In-Service Education?" *Educational Leadership*, Vol. 9 (October, 1951), pp. 9-10.

on the market every day. How can any teacher do a good job unless he keeps informed of current developments in this area?

The educational program is, of course, determined to a great extent by the local community. As it changes, so does the school change and so must the teacher change. Wiles offers the following example.

In some New York City schools, the number of Puerto Rican students has increased rapidly. Although the teachers had the skills and attitudes necessary for good teaching in a community with a high percentage of first-generation American students, they knew far too little about the simple agrarian culture from which these Puerto Ricans had suddenly been transferred to the confusion of polyglot New York. Wide-awake supervision established in-service experience designed to give greater understanding of the background of the Puerto Rican youth and the problems they faced in transferring to New York, thus increasing the ability of the teacher to do the job confronting him.[2]

There is no need to belabor this point. Social, cultural, and technological developments result in changes in the content and method of education. These, in turn, demand the continuing professional self-improvement of the teacher. As the Red Queen said to Alice, ". . . it takes all the running you can do, to keep in the same place!"

THE PRESERVICE PREPARATION OF THE TEACHER IS, EVEN AT ITS BEST, INCOMPLETE. In recent years great strides have been taken to improve the quality of preservice education for elementary teachers. A major improvement, of course, has been the lengthening, in most states, of the period of preparation from one or two years to four years. This will, in all probability, be increased to five or six within the foreseeable future. Another area of improvement has resulted from the more desirable balance between general education and professional education now evidenced in the better programs. Then too, professional education has been strengthened in many schools through the inclusion of prolonged professional laboratory experiences which offer the prospective teacher the opportunity to work with children in a variety of school and community situations.

Regardless of the excellence of the program, however, it is a serious mistake for a teacher to think that his preservice education can, or should, equip him to handle completely every facet of teaching. For instance, a first-year teacher recently complained because his professional courses in college had failed to tell him how to handle the problem he now faced of an epileptic pupil in the classroom. Such an attitude is ridiculous for

[2] Kimball Wiles, *Supervision for Better Schools: The Role of the Official Leader in Program Development,* 2nd ed. (Englewood Cliffs, N. J., Prentice-Hall, Inc., 1955), p. 261.

every teacher should recognize that professional courses must and should deal with basic principles, methods, techniques, and procedures that have wide applicability. They cannot prepare a teacher to meet every specific situation he will encounter in his individual classroom for, as Hass says, "Each new pupil and each new combination of pupils creates problems which could not have been anticipated in the most enlightened preservice courses."[3]

Neither can preservice education, even through a superior internship plan, give the future teacher full responsibility for a class of children over a prolonged period of time. Rarely can it include wide experiences in working with parents, community members, and professional colleagues. Frequently it cannot offer the opportunity to understand fully the individual differences among a group of children. Nor does it always offer the opportunity to apply sound and modern principles of learning and teaching to a practical classroom situation.

The intelligent teacher recognizes these and other limitations of his preservice preparation. He realizes that completion of the initial requirements for teaching is, in actuality, only the starting point of his professional education and that it cannot preclude the need for a continuous program of self-improvement and professional growth.

CERTAIN INHERENT STIMULI TO PROFESSIONAL GROWTH ARE NOT AS CHARACTERISTIC OF TEACHING AS OF SOME OTHER PROFESSIONS. Since continued growth is an absolute necessity to teaching competence, it is unfortunate that it is not automatically stimulated by the nature of the activity itself. As a matter of fact, there are certain conditions peculiar to teaching that may operate *against* self-growth unless the teacher recognizes them and makes a voluntary and deliberate attempt to compensate for them.

One of the most natural stimuli to an individual's self-improvement and self-evaluation is the opportunity to compare one's performance with that of his colleagues. In many professions, the individual works side-by-side with one's coworkers. In the courtroom, in the office, in the clinic, in the laboratory, or in the operating room the professional worker has the opportunity to improve by (1) observing the work of his colleagues and (2) evaluating his own performance accordingly. There is little doubt that such an opportunity is a vital incentive to professional growth. Unfortunately it is an opportunity that, in the conventional teaching situation, is denied to the classroom teacher. He enters his own classroom each morning and closes the door behind him. Almost never does he have the opportunity to observe others teach and to compare his own per-

---

[3] C. Glenn Hass, "In-Service Education Today," *In-Service Education*, Fifty-sixth Yearbook, National Society for the Study of Education, Part I, Nelson B. Henry, ed. (Chicago, University of Chicago Press, 1957), p. 29.

formance with that of others. True, he meets his coworkers in a variety of professional situations and undoubtedly grows from these contacts. But the stimulation of observing and working side-by-side with one's colleagues is an avenue of professional growth seldom open to the classroom teacher. It may be, therefore, comparatively easy for the mediocre teacher to delude himself into thinking he is doing a good job simply because *he rarely has an opportunity to use the teaching of others as a yardstick against which to measure his own performance.* (Incidentally, the fact that this opportunity is offered in television teaching or in team teaching is one of the major advantages claimed for these organizational patterns.)

Another automatic stimulant to professional growth frequently denied to the teacher is a critical clientele. A doctor who fails to keep up with the newest developments in medicine, or who grows lax and careless in his work, may soon lose his practice. The same is true of a lawyer. But the teacher has a captive clientele. A class of children is usually not as critical nor as demanding of consistently high performance as an adult clientele which pays directly for the service it receives. It is true that children are often astute and reliable judges of good teaching (see Chapter 2). They are also honest, as many a teacher has learned to his dismay. But children are also realists who can frequently learn to live with a bad situation. Faced with a captive clientele, which may neither want nor dare to complain, the teacher may find it fairly easy to slide into a rut of second-quality teaching. One way, of course, to avoid this possibility is to solicit anonymous pupil evaluations of certain lessons, techniques, examinations, activities, or assignments. Unsigned written evaluations by pupils may be real eye openers in helping the teacher to improve phases of his teaching.

Permanent and life certification, tenure, and automatic salary increments are other conditions peculiar to teaching that do not automatically stimulate continuing self-growth. This does not necessarily mean that they should be eliminated. It does mean, however, that the ultimate responsibility for growth must rest squarely upon the individual teacher. Growth and improvement must be motivated by the teacher's dedication to his profession, rather than by the fear of losing his job or suffering a loss of salary.

What point is made here? Simply that, although continued growth is vitally necessary to good teaching, it is not automatically stimulated by certain built-in factors frequently found in other professions. Obviously this fact places a great responsibility upon the individual teacher to recognize, and side-step, the pitfalls of smugness, laziness, and apathy that may threaten his professional self-improvement.

THE EXPANDING ROLE OF THE TEACHER HAS EMPHASIZED THE IMPORTANCE OF CONTINUED GROWTH. It has been stated repeatedly in previous chapters that the teacher's responsibilities extend far beyond the classroom walls. Spears traces this expanding role in relationship to two important twentieth century movements, namely (1) supervision and (2) curriculum improvement. He claims that in earlier days the distinctions between teachers, supervisors, and curriculum workers were clearly marked. Teachers stayed in the classroom and did as specialists or administrators told them to do. Supervisors looked after and judged teachers and their techniques. Curriculum workers busied themselves with the production of courses of study, materials of instruction, and teachers' guides. Gradually, however, both supervisors and curriculum workers realized the importance of the teacher's becoming a full-fledged member of the team rather than a water boy carrying out others' instructions. According to Spears, "Supervision turned off its penetrating classroom spotlight and sought to entice the teacher to step out of the classroom into cooperative group endeavors. At the same time the curriculum expert invited the teacher to participate in cooperative curriculum development."[4]

The democratizing of supervision and the cooperative approach to curriculum improvement were, of course, only two of the movements that contributed to the teacher's expanding role. As recruitment procedures became more selective, as preservice programs were lengthened and improved, as professional associations grew stronger, the teacher's scope of responsibility steadily increased, with corresponding demands for continually raising the standards of competence.

THE TEACHER'S PROGRAM OF SELF-IMPROVEMENT IS GUIDED BY SEVERAL SPECIFIC PURPOSES. In general, the teacher's inservice growth is directed toward the following:

1. *To realize personal and professional improvement.* It has already been stated that every intelligent teacher feels the need to raise his intellectual, cultural, and professional sights. Knowledge begets knowledge and the more the intelligent individual learns, the more he realizes there is to learn. There is a thrill to learning, a thrill to achieving knowledge, a thrill to pushing back one's boundaries of ignorance, a thrill that the intelligent person never stops seeking. Julian Huxley is reported to have once said, "Isn't it wonderful to *know!*" The intelligent teacher understands and appreciates this feeling. Whether in the field of the humanities, the arts, the natural sciences, the social sciences, or professional areas, the competent teacher charts himself a steady course of cultural,

---

[4] Harold Spears, *Improving the Supervision of Instruction* (Englewood Cliffs, N. J., Prentice-Hall, Inc., 1953), p. 351.

intellectual, and professional improvement. Barnes emphasizes its importance in the following excellent statement.

The person in teaching, or inclined to enter teaching, must never forget that education is basically an intellectual pursuit. If study, mental activity, and critical thinking are foreign to one's nature, he should adjust his occupational sights. Try as he may, a teacher cannot escape the academic and the intellectual pursuits. . . . A constant quest for knowledge is the golden thread of a teacher's professional and personal development. . . . Amiable mental midgets are not needed in our classrooms. We need men and women who love knowledge and seek to develop that love in others.[5]

2. *To achieve professional advancement.* Undoubtedly many teachers engage in in-service growth activities to secure professional advancement. Such advancement may be in the form of another position for which an advanced graduate degree, additional courses, or other inservice educational experiences are required. Such positions as school principal, curriculum specialist, guidance worker, supervisor, supervising teacher for student teachers, instructor in a laboratory school, or faculty member in a school of education may interest the elementary teacher who seeks professional advancement.

Another type of advancement is represented by moving up on the salary schedule. Many systems recognize the teacher's participation in in-service educational activities either through supplementary salary increments or through a differentiated salary scale. The activity most commonly recognized by school boards is participation in college courses. There are, however, numerous other in-service growth activities recognized by some school boards as equivalents to college credits. According to one survey, these include a wide variety such as travel, summer school teaching, exchange teaching, demonstration teaching, supervision of practice teaching, study groups, lectures, institutes, NEA activities, coaching school, civic federation courses, private study, nature study camp, organization leadership, community leadership, work on extracurricular programs, teaching courses for local teachers, officer or committee work in teachers associations, reading educational books and magazines, delivering educational addresses, reviewing texts, group study of professional books, industry forums, correspondence study, and reporting on educational books.[6]

There are, of course, many different opinions on the wisdom of recognizing in-service educational activities by advancement on the salary

[5] John B. Barnes, *Educational Research for Classroom Teachers* (New York, G. P. Putnam's Sons, 1960), pp. 21-22.

[6] "Equivalents for College Credits Recognized as Meeting Professional Growth Requirements of Salary Schedules in Cities Over 30,000 Population," *Educational Research Circular #1* (January, 1950), pp. 1-35.

scale. Naturally such activities are of most value when they are voluntary and intrinsically motivated, and there is no denying the statement,
"There is no way to force the teacher to learn and to grow."[7] On the
other hand, every realist admits that there are a few teachers in any
system who would refuse to participate in any type of growth activity
unless it was required or rewarded by financial gain. Those who argue
for the practice claim that it is better for teachers to be motivated
toward such activities by financial gain than not to be motivated at all.

Those who take an opposite stand emphasize the extremely intricate
system of accounting necessitated by relating professional growth to
salary. Take, for instance, the one item of travel. What travel should
be recognized? For what salary advance? How far must the traveler go?
Is travel equally broadening to all individuals? What is meant by "travel"?
Is visiting a friend a few hundred miles away considered to be travel?
Who decides?

A more serious disadvantage of relating growth to salary is that it may
result in mere credit-chasing, one of the more serious blights on the
educational scene today. Credit-chasers take additional courses or engage
in activities not because they want to improve, but only because they are
interested in salary advance. Much harm, and no good, is the inevitable
result. The individuals themselves don't improve an iota; they lower the
morale of the serious participants; and, particularly in college courses,
they may depress standards of academic performance.

Spears points to the possible dangers of connecting growth and salary
in the following statement,

We should predict that within ten or twenty years the intricate accounting
systems will kill the spirit of systematic teacher growth on the job, unless the
present tendency is curbed. The spirit of any supervisory or in-service program must be the participant's enthusiastic desire to improve the learning for
the child. It cannot be credit chasing for the sake of financial remuneration. . . .

Those school systems that require a specified amount of in-service activity
must beware of the old educational curse of credit chasing. If motivated by
credit accumulation, the in-service program is apt to be dominated not by
pressing instructional matters but by the pressing need of credit accumulation. It is quite possible that the in-service course or activity that is convenient may take precedence over that which is more meaningful.[8]

There seems to be no clear-cut answer to the problem although there
is some indication that the practice is decreasing, at least with regard to

[7] Clark E. Moustakas, *The Alive and Growing Teacher* (New York, Philosophical
Library, Inc., 1959), p. 25.

[8] Harold Spears, *op. cit.*, pp. 359-380.

rewarding every specific growth activity with some salary compensation. Perhaps as teachers become more competent, more professional, and more convinced of the need for continued growth, the practice may disappear. Whether or not this is an idealistic dream, only time will tell.

3. *To widen one's circle of professional and social contacts.* The point was made previously that, for a major portion of the school day, the elementary teacher has little contact with his professional colleagues. Many teachers report that the opportunity to make stimulating professional and social contacts is one of the chief values of participation in in-service educational activities. Travel, committee work, attending conferences, attending college courses, and joining professional associations are some of the activities ideally suited to this purpose.

4. *To maintain physical and mental health.* The strenuous and confining phases of teaching can be overcome or minimized by the teacher who realizes the values of deliberately striving for personal and professional improvement. Advanced study; travel; attendance at concerts, lectures, plays, and art exhibits; interest in sports and hobbies; a well-rounded reading program; and participation in community affairs and adult social groups are beneficial to the mental and physical health of all adults. They are absolutely necessary, and must be sought deliberately, by the teacher who does not normally encounter them in the course of his everyday work.

In connection with this point, it is important to remember that throughout this entire discussion we are concerned with the teacher's *personal* and *professional* growth. As a matter of fact, it is pointless and often impossible to distinguish between these two areas. Practically anything, from a hobby of collecting antiques to reading a good book, that contributes to the wholesome, healthful, cultural, social, or intellectual enrichment of the teacher will also contribute to his professional growth and the improvement of his classroom performance. There can be little argument with the following:

Personal and professional growth are so interrelated that it is hard to tell where one ends and the other begins. The "whole teacher" comes to school just as does the "whole child." The steps you take to develop your personal interests, to enrich your life and enlarge your horizons through new experiences, and to expand your contacts with persons in your community can make a professional contribution to the growth of boys and girls that is often more significant than the new methods which you might learn in a college class or in a teachers' institute.[9]

[9] Margaret G. McKim, Carl W. Hansen, and William L. Carter, *Learning to Teach in the Elementary School* (New York, The Macmillan Company, 1959), p. 542.

THERE ARE TWO MAJOR AVENUES THROUGH WHICH TEACHER GROWTH MAY BE PROMOTED. The teacher's in-service growth has been defined by a discussion group of the National Education Association as

. . . those processes and techniques (following preservice growth), formal and informal, for credit or noncredit through which an individual (including all school personnel) secures growth which leads to his development academically, personally, socially, and professionally, and which leads to excellence in group participation both for himself and for those he leads.[10]

It is obvious that this broad definition includes a wide variety of activities. In general, however, these may be classified into two major categories although, admittedly, the distinction between the two is not hard and fast. For our purposes, we will examine in the remainder of the chapter possibilities of teacher growth through (1) participation in the activities of a formal, planned, and structured in-service program and (2) certain selected activities that are usually voluntary and frequently individualized.

PARTICIPATION IN A STRUCTURED IN-SERVICE EDUCATIONAL PROGRAM

The idea of requiring or strongly encouraging the teacher to participate in certain educational activities sponsored by the local, county, or state system is certainly not new. Over the years, however, the purpose and nature of the program have changed considerably. In the nineteenth century and early years of the present century, the major purpose of the "in-service training program" (as it was then called) was to remove, as far as possible, the glaring deficiencies of very young, incompetent, and poorly prepared teachers. To achieve this purpose, the program was usually planned by adminstrators. In-service training was something done *to* teachers in the desperate hope that it would result in improved classroom practice. Gradually, as administration and supervision became more democratic and teachers became more competent and better educated, the focus of the program changed from training teachers to complete staff involvement.

TODAY, THE IN-SERVICE EDUCATIONAL PROGRAM IS THE COOPERATIVE RESPONSIBILITY OF MANY INDIVIDUALS. Who is involved in the planned program of in-service education and what is his role?

The teacher. Basic to the success of the entire program is the teacher's attitude. This attitude should consist of (1) a dedication to teaching, (2) a desire to improve, and (3) an ability to evaluate oneself objectively.

[10] Linn Sheets, "What's Happening in Teacher Education?" *Journal of Teacher Education*, Vol. 12 (March, 1961), p. 122.

The first is self-evident. In order to grow professionally, the teacher must have a deep, abiding, and dedicated interest in teaching. As Hass says, "To be professional, teachers need to have a profound conviction of the worth of their work. For this feeling to exist, the individual must have a sense of greatness of his profession, of its significance for society, and its power to benefit boys and girls."[11]

The desire to improve is next in importance. Does the teacher genuinely want to increase his effectiveness or is he content to jog along, year after year, in low gear?

Thirdly, does the teacher have the ability to evaluate himself objectively? There is some evidence that teachers and student teachers lack this ability to a serious degree. They either do not see their limitations or refuse to admit them. In order to improve, it is imperative that the teacher be capable of recognizing his strengths and limitations. Does he feel threatened by suggestions for improvement? Does he feel that an in-service educational program implies a criticism of his competency? Is he afraid of change? Answers to these and similar questions will mark the difference between the success or failure of any program.

The administrator and supervisor. Along with the teacher, the superintendent, supervisor, and principal are undoubtedly key figures in the in-service program. In the first place, does the administrator regard in-service growth as something necessary for the teacher only? Or does he participate in numerous activities himself, aware of the fact that he, as much as a teacher, needs constant stimulus to professional growth. Another responsibility of the administrator is the fostering of a school climate conducive to growth, self-evaluation, experimentation, and change. The point is made by Mason as follows:

Professional improvement requires an atmosphere in which teachers feel they have the support, confidence, and respect of their principal. They need to feel that their individual differences are recognized and respected; that each is encouraged to make a contribution in his own way; that they are free to try out their own ideas and make mistakes.[12]

Obviously, also, the leadership and initiative the administrator displays in making decisions, suggesting activities, and arranging necessary details of scheduling are vital to the success of the program.

The community. Does the community and its representatives on the school board recognize the need for continuing professional growth? Does it support suitable activities with necessary funds and a reasonable

---

[11] C. Glenn Hass, *op. cit.*, p. 31.
[12] Barbara T. Mason, "The Principal's Role in In-Service Education," *National Elementary Principal*, Vol. 41 (February, 1962), p. 21.

amount of release time for the participants? Does it recognize that teacher growth depends, to a large extent, upon teacher morale? And does it attempt to bolster that morale through a program of cooperation with, and loyalty to, the school and its teachers?

The community and general public should realize that nothing is less conducive to teacher improvement and educational advancement than a continual program of carping criticism and hostile attack. One of the most insidious results of the current open season on teachers is the what's-the-use attitude it produces in the target. Even the most conscientious teacher may eventually give up trying to grow and improve when his efforts are rewarded only by criticism from the community and general public. The extent to which the community supports the in-service program financially, and even more important, through encouragement, recognition, and loyalty, is vital to its over-all success.

The state and county departments of education and professional associations. Leadership in sponsoring various types of in-service activities as well as furnishing consultant and specialized services are important functions assumed by these divisions in the in-service educational program.

The teacher education institution. In recent years, the teacher education institutions have assumed an increasing responsibility for the in-service education of teachers. Obviously, the first responsibility of these institutions in this field is to offer their students the type of preservice education that will be a stimulus to continuing intellectual and professional growth. An experimental and creative attitude, an intellectual curiosity, a love for teaching, and a quest for knowledge, if developed in a superior preservice program, will lay a firm foundation for the in-service program.

The first step toward effective in-service education rests in preservice teacher education programs. The attitude toward learning, toward change, toward experimentation which is created in the student before he completes his preservice preparation has an important impact upon his attitude toward in-service education and continued growth when he is placed in a job. The fledgling teacher who comes from his teacher preparation well grounded in subject matter and methodology and with a real urge to continue learning and to experiment is already on the way to successful in-service growth.[13]

A carefully planned follow-up of recent graduates is now a part of many teacher education institutions. In some schools, faculty are employed whose major responsibility is to visit recent graduates on the job to offer advice and guidance. Others periodically send to graduates bulletins and

[13] Lyle W. Ashby, "Today's Challenge to In-Service Education," *Educational Leadership*, Vol. 15 (February, 1958), p. 271.

pamphlets dealing with specific areas of elementary education. Still others hold conferences or workshops on campus to which all recent graduates and their principals are invited. A strong and dynamic follow-up program is one of the most positive steps teacher education institutions have taken in recent years to upgrade the quality of in-service performance.

Probably the most common channel of participation in in-service programs by the college is the offering of extension and summer courses. On or off campus, most schools of education today offer courses that may be taken by the teacher for personal enrichment and professional improvement, for an advanced degree (see following section), for salary increments, or to meet certification or tenure requirements.

The type of extension course varies considerably. Some are regular college courses, scheduled on or off campus, in which teachers may enroll. Some are courses specially designed for the faculty of a school or school system. Some are intended only for persons in a particular position (for example, principal, third-grade teacher, supervising teacher, science consultant). Some are offered for college credit; some are not. Some meet for an entire college term while many consist only of a half-dozen or so meetings. Many of those designed for a specified group are planned and conducted cooperatively by college faculty, local system personnel, and members of the county or state departments of education. Some are held during the regular school year; many are held during the summer. In some attendance is voluntary while in others it is required by the local school system. Some provide opportunities for observation of, and limited participation in, laboratory or demonstration classes. Some are organized to meet a specific need, such as curriculum revision, revision of report cards, or development of needed instructional aids.

Although varying widely in purpose and design, there is little doubt that college courses for teachers are today probably the most common instrument of promoting teacher growth on the job.

CERTAIN BASIC ACTIVITIES ARE COMMON TO MOST IN-SERVICE EDUCATIONAL PROGRAMS. These include the following:

Teachers' Institute. The institute is probably the oldest type of activity planned by a school system to stimulate the professional growth of its staff. It is still fairly common today, although radically changed in purpose and pattern. Richey points out that, in the decades prior to the Civil War, when the competency and training of public school teachers were extremely low, in-service programs were needed that

. . . should be directed toward the correction of the most obvious defects of teachers, i. e., inadequate command of subject matter to be taught and lack of professional skill; that they should take into account the needs of the inexperienced and entirely untrained teacher; that they should be inexpensively operated; and that they should involve large numbers of teachers.[14]

The early institute was designed to meet these conditions. All teachers were called together for one or more days prior to the opening of the school year and instructed, for the most part, in the subject matter they were expected to teach their pupils. Gradually, as teachers became better informed, the emphasis was placed upon professional skills and techniques rather than the subject matter to be taught although, as is true today, it is difficult to separate the two entirely.

Although its popularity is waning, the institute is still held by some systems, usually prior to the opening of the school year, although not always. Its general pattern follows that described below.

The programs of the one-day institutes were similar in pattern. They began with a general session at which time a speaker addressed the teachers. The presentation was usually inspirational in nature and on a broad educational topic. Services provided by the county superintendent of schools were explained in general or section meeting. In some instances new materials available from the county superintendent's office, such as, courses of study, audio-visual catalogues, or other curriculum materials were distributed. County teachers' associations held meetings during certain institute sessions.[15]

Workshops. Systems that have abandoned the traditional pattern of the institute have either substituted or supplemented it with the workshop. Almost without exception, the workshop ranks first among the techniques favored by teachers for in-service growth. It is characterized by active participation of small groups directed toward such practical purposes as:

To develop a philosophy of education for the district

To sharpen the objectives of education for the community

To reach common agreements on the philosophy and objectives as the basis for planning curriculum experiences

To evaluate classroom organization and procedures in relation to the agreements reached on the philosophy and objectives of education for the community

To work on instructional programs related to the particular grade they are teaching

To prepare instructional materials for use in classrooms

[14] Herman G. Richey, "Growth of the Modern Conception of In-Service Education," *In-Service Education,* Fifty-sixth Yearbook, National Society for the Study of Education, Part I, Nelson B. Henry, ed. (Chicago, University of Chicago Press, 1957), pp. 38-39.

[15] Esther Nelson, "In-Service Education Programs in California Counties," *California Journal of Elementary Education,* Vol. 25 (August, 1956), p. 25.

To deepen insights in relation to the characteristics of growth and development of children

To deepen insights into the causes of children's behavior

To become better acquainted with the resources of the community

To coordinate the curriculum on a district-wide basis

To provide continuity of curriculum experiences for children and youth

To observe educational theory translated into the realities of classroom life.[16]

It is difficult to trace any definite pattern for the scheduling of workshops. In many systems, one day to one week at the beginning of the school year may be devoted to a series of workshops. These may be continued for several days spaced at intervals during the year. Growing in popularity is the trend toward lengthening the school year for teachers, thus allowing from five to twenty days at the beginning or close of the school year for workshops and other activities directed toward curriculum improvement and other important matters.

Although teachers appear to favor the workshop over other techniques of the planned in-service program, few have been fortunate enough to escape at least one sorry experience with it. Unfortunately this is because many of the so-called workshops are run by incompetent or inexperienced leaders and are not workshops in any sense of the word. A workshop is a specific type of learning experience with a clear-cut purpose and pattern that must be understood by those in charge in order to be effective. This is important and must be understood clearly in order for the workshop to be successful. (For further reading on the purposes, patterns, techniques, and outcomes of successful workshops read *The Workshop Way of Learning* by Earl C. Kelley, New York, Harper & Row, 1951 and *Workshops for Teachers* by Mary A. O'Rourke and William H. Burton, New York, Appleton-Century-Crofts, 1957.)

Teachers' handbooks. These serve a dual function. They are extremely valuable in orienting teachers, particularly those new to the system, to the organizational routines of the school and the educational resources of the community. They are also a stimulus to the professional growth of those teachers who assist in writing and preparing them.

Demonstration lessons and clinics. It was stated earlier that few classroom teachers enjoy the opportunity to observe their colleagues in action. Perhaps this is why demonstration lessons always have been and still are popular with teachers. The technique is not new. As early as the nineteenth century, an outstanding teacher was employed by Henry Barnard

[16] Bernard J. Lonsdale and Lorene Marshall, "In-Service Education Programs in Selected California School Districts," *California Journal of Elementary Education*, Vol. 25 (August, 1956), p. 38.

". . . to travel from meeting to meeting in a covered wagon, with his class of twelve children, to give demonstration lessons of what was then approved of as good teaching."[17]

When done correctly, the demonstration lesson may have considerable value for both the demonstrator and the observers. The careful planning, thorough knowledge, and professional skill demanded by a worthwhile demonstration lesson can provide a real challenge to the teacher offering the demonstration. Also, the invitation to teach a lesson before a group is a distinct professional compliment and morale-builder, appreciated by many teachers.

In order to have optimum value for the observers, every attempt must be made to make the demonstration as realistic as possible. Demonstration lessons that are spectacular shows are of no value to anyone, certainly not to the teacher who risks a nervous breakdown in presenting them to an audience that fully realizes their artificiality. In attempting to approximate an actual classroom situation, the following cautions should be observed: (1) The demonstration should be conducted in a classroom with which children are familiar rather than on a stage or in a large auditorium, (2) The size of the observing group should be kept to a reasonable minimum to avoid overpowering the pupils, (3) The lesson should never, never be rehearsed in any way, shape, or form, (4) The pupil group should not be artificially selected, and (5) Children should not have been previously intimidated by the impending visit of the group.

Demonstration lessons conducted in clinic situations have greatest value and meaning for the observer. This means that, preceding the lesson, a discussion should be held to explain certain purposes and techniques the group will later observe. A similar discussion should be held following the lesson, in which questions and reactions from the entire group may be voiced freely.

Many systems utilize their own teaching staff to offer demonstration lessons to groups of their colleagues. Others encourage or require their teachers to visit laboratory schools of nearby universities. In other situations, college faculty, state department personnel, or representatives from commercial firms may be invited to give demonstrations to various local groups. Also, such lessons are usually a popular item on the agenda of any educational convention or professional meeting.

Interclass visitation. Another opportunity to observe colleagues at work is offered through interclass visitation. Some school faculties work together so harmoniously that it is possible to establish a program whereby each teacher may visit the classrooms of several of his colleagues to

[17] A. S. Barr, William H. Burton, and Leo J. Brueckner, *Supervision* (New York, Appleton-Century-Crofts, 1938), p. 685.

observe them teach. This may be valuable for experienced teachers as well as inexperienced teachers, although it is more common with the latter. Interclass visitation may be extended throughout the system, of course, or may involve a cooperative arrangement among several systems. Although comparable to demonstration lessons, interclass visitation may actually be the more valuable since it is usually more informal, more realistic, and offers an opportunity to observe longer than the duration of a single lesson.

Study groups and teachers' councils. Many of the teacher's responsibilities discussed in previous chapters such as curriculum improvement, structuring a satisfactory testing program, and revising reporting techniques are often implemented through various types of study groups and teacher committees.

Faculty meetings. Functional faculty meetings have long been recognized as a primary channel for in-service improvement. As stated in Chapter 5, teachers generally view their role as receivers rather than planners in this area. There is little doubt, however, that the responsibility teachers assume in planning, contributing to, and participating in faculty meetings is directly related to the values such meetings have for continuing teacher growth.

Use of television, filmstrips, films, and tapes. Some systems are taking advantage of these new media in an attempt to promote in-service growth. Demonstration lessons by expert teachers may be televised or filmed and shown to groups of teachers. Also, educational talks, panels, and discussions may be carried to all schools in a system via closed circuit television. The use to which the Atlanta, Georgia school system is currently putting these media in stimulating teacher growth is described as follows:

Teachers and supervisors sometimes use WETV to explain new methods and processes or to give fresh looks at older techniques. New types of science equipment have been demonstrated by science teachers. So have new trends and new curriculum guides in the teaching of science. Before Christmas holidays, art teachers showed how to make both traditional and modern Christmas decorations. When a new curriculum guide in high-school English was distributed during preplanning week, committee members explained how to use the guide to high-school teachers of English all over the city as they watched the television screen, guide in hand. These TV programs have achieved a balanced pattern, having included arithmetic, art, English, reading, and science. . . .

In the offing is a mobile video tape unit, which promises infinite possibilities for inservice training. This unit, housed in a bus or van, will be a traveling TV studio with video tape recorder and television cameras. Believing that excellent teaching goes on in Atlanta schools, administrators plan to film and record some of these activities for other teachers to share. Good laboratory lessons in foreign languages, in science, in techniques of reading, and in many other aspects of study can be filmed and taped for the inspiration of other teachers. Possibilities of this mobile video tape unit are almost unlimited as one envisions creative teaching in many subject areas being shared by teachers all over the city.[18]

In this section we have examined briefly the major techniques comprising a structured program of in-service professional growth. Participation by the teacher may be required or encouraged by the administration. In any case, it is generally expected.

The activities discussed in the following section are equally valuable, but are generally dependent almost entirely upon the initiative and motivation of the individual teacher.

SELF-DIRECTED GROWTH ACTIVITIES

Graduate Study

Used in its present context, graduate study refers to "formal study pursued after receiving the bachelor's or first professional degree, usually for the purpose of obtaining a higher degree."[19]

The present discussion is directed to those present or future elementary school teachers who are interested in extending their formal college education beyond the baccalaureate degree, on either a full or part-time basis.

The ever-growing recognition of the fact that teaching is a difficult and complex task has resulted in a steadily lengthening period of preparation. As stated in Chapter 1, forty-five states today require the Bachelor's Degree for the initial standard elementary teaching certificate. Several states require the Master's Degree or its equivalent in semester hours of college credit, plus a certain number of years of teaching experience, for elementary teachers to attain the permanent or life certificate (see Chapter 1).

In order to realize intellectual, cultural, and professional improvement; in order to meet ever-rising standards of certification; and in order to secure professional advancement, an increasing number of elementary teachers are enrolling in graduate study. This steady increase is evidenced by the fact that in 1931, .6 per cent of elementary school teachers held the Master's Degree; by 1956, this figure had climbed to 12.9 per cent; and by 1960 it had reached 15 per cent.

[18] Catherine McKee, "Teachers Improve Their Skills through On-the-Job Training," *The Clearing House*, Vol. 36 (January, 1962), p. 261.
[19] *Dictionary of Education*, 2nd ed., Carter V. Good, ed. (New York, McGraw-Hill Book Co., Inc., 1959), p. 531.

In view of the ever-increasing interest of elementary school teachers, this discussion examines some of the questions most frequently asked by those who are contemplating graduate study. The discussion is equally applicable to students who plan to pursue a five year preservice program and to students who plan to teach and engage in part-time graduate study.

WHAT ARE THE ADMISSION REQUIREMENTS TO GRADUATE SCHOOL? In general, it is safe to say that the trend among graduate schools is toward the adoption of broad, flexible admission requirements. This does not mean a relaxing of standards. It does mean that most graduate schools attempt to appraise a broad profile of the individual rather than adhering to rigid, narrow standards of admission. It should also be remembered that many graduate schools of education distinguish between admission to the graduate school or division, and admission to a graduate program leading to a degree. Requirements for the first are usually more liberal than for the second. The distinction, when made, is usually explained carefully in the graduate catalogue.

In general, admission requirements to a graduate division, school, or degree program include a combination of the following:

1. The Bachelor's Degree from an approved or accredited undergraduate institution.

2. Evidence of scholastic ability. All creditable graduate institutions require some evidence of the candidate's scholastic ability, although it may be secured from a variety of sources. Some require a general undergraduate average of B or its equivalent. Some are interested primarily in the academic average of the junior and senior years. Some are concerned with the average in the major field. Some are interested in the undergraduate's class standing.

In the case of marginal undergraduate academic performance, some schools are willing to grant conditional admission, or delayed matriculation, to a student whose other qualifications appear to promise success in graduate study. In any case, although previous academic performance is always a major factor, it is usually balanced with many others. One reference, stressing the importance of interest and motivation to success in graduate study and the need to look carefully at all academic and personal aspects of the applying candidate, states that, until the attitudes and characteristics that determine failure or success in graduate study are more consistently identified, ". . . even the C student should not automatically eliminate himself from the possibility of graduate study."[20]

3. A qualifying examination may be required of all applicants for admission, or it may be required only to supplement a marginal under-

[20] *A Guide to Graduate Study*, 2nd ed., Frederick W. Ness, ed. (Washington, D. C., American Council on Education, 1960), p. 20.

graduate record. An institution may administer its own qualifying examination, or it may use a standardized instrument, usually the *Graduate Record Examinations*, the *Miller Analogies Test*, or the *National Teachers Examinations*.

The *Graduate Record Examinations* (GRE) may be administered by the institution, or may be offered at various testing centers throughout the country. It consists of two tests. The general *Aptitude Test* is a 150 minute test that yields scores on (1) verbal ability and (2) quantitative ability. The *Advanced Test* is a three-hour test offered in a specific field. There is not an advanced test in elementary education, as such, although the advanced test in education covers various aspects of the field, including elementary education. A school that uses the GRE may require the candidate to take either the aptitude or advanced test, or both.

Information concerning the administration of the *Graduate Record Examinations* is available from Educational Testing Service, Princeton, New Jersey.

The *Miller Analogies Test* (MAT) is a fifty-minute test of information and reasoning ability based on verbal analogies. It is published by the Psychological Corporation. Information concerning its administration may be obtained from the Psychological Corporation, 304 East 45th Street, New York 17, New York.

The *National Teacher Examinations* (NTE) consist of two parts. The first is a slightly longer than three hour battery of Common Examinations designed to measure certain general knowledges and abilities of teachers. The battery consists of five discrete tests in (1) Professional Information, (2) English Expression, (3) Social Studies, Literature, and Fine Arts, (4) Science and Mathematics, and (5) Nonverbal Reasoning.

The second part consists of one or two optional tests in thirteen specific teaching fields. Two of these are designed for those interested in elementary education. The *Education in the Elementary School* option is designed for teachers in grades one through eight. The *Early Childhood Education* option is designed for teachers of kindergarten through third grade. Information concerning the administration of the *National Teacher Examinations* may be secured from Educational Testing Service, Princeton, New Jersey.

4. Letters of recommendation are requested by some graduate schools of education. Some schools require letters testifying to the candidate's teaching competence; others desire letters of personal and character reference. Still others request letters from faculty or administrative personnel of the applicant's undergraduate institution.

5. A personal interview may be required by some schools prior to admission to graduate study. Where this is not practical, the candidate may be required to submit evidence of personal qualifications, interests,

and background through a questionnaire, autobiography, or some other type of personal document.

WHAT FACTORS SHOULD BE CONSIDERED IN SELECTING A GRADUATE SCHOOL? Almost all individuals who contemplate graduate study are faced with some realistic considerations in selecting a school. This is particularly true of the teacher who intends to do graduate work on a part-time basis. Practical factors such as (1) location of school, (2) availability of extension centers, (3) variety of programs offered, (4) tuition, and (5) residence requirements determine to some degree the selection of school. The individual, however, who selects the school entirely upon these factors will inevitably live to regret it. Graduate study is a serious undertaking which places heavy demands upon the individual's time, finances, and personal life. It should not be undertaken lightly at any institution that happens to be cheapest or nearest to the person's home.

Within a flexible framework of practical considerations, several factors should influence the selection of a graduate school. Undoubtedly the first of these is the quality of the faculty. Faculty who are outstanding in their fields, who have made real contributions to education, who have earned the respect of colleagues and students, and whose reputations are well known and respected are the best indication of a high-quality graduate institution.

Then, too, the quality of alumni is indicative of the quality of the institution. If, for instance, the individual discovers that several of his undergraduate instructors, whom he particularly admires, were prepared at a certain institution, this may be a fairly reliable indication that the school, or at least that particular program, is of high scholastic quality.

It is unfortunate that few students embarking upon graduate study are sophisticated enough to consider carefully the physical facilities of the school because these may determine in large measure the worth of the graduate program. The size and extensiveness of the library collection, for instance, are very important. Also, the hours during which the library is open may be very important, particularly to the part-time student. To the elementary education major, the extent to which such facilities as a well-equipped and forward-looking laboratory school, reading clinic, psychological center, speech and hearing clinic, or nursery school are available to, and used by, graduate students may be very important.

A major factor influencing the selection of a graduate institution is the type of program it offers. Although an unbelievable variety exists among schools, the following generalizations can safely be made.

WHAT TYPE OF GRADUATE PROGRAM IS AVAILABLE TO THE PRESENT OR FUTURE ELEMENTARY SCHOOL TEACHER? In general, three types of graduate programs are available for those interested in elementary education.

The first is the program leading to the Master's Degree. This is normally a one-year full college program, requiring the completion of from twenty-four to thirty-six semester hours of course credit. The most typical number is probably thirty hours. In general, the Masters program may be completed in one year of full-time study. For part-time students, the minimum period is usually two winters and a summer, or two winters and two summers. The Master's Degree awarded upon the completion of the program may be one of several types, although the most common are the Master of Arts (MA), Master of Science (MS), Master of Arts in Education (MA in Ed.), Master of Science in Education (MS in Ed.), and Master of Education (Ed. M). Originally, certain distinctions were made among these degrees, but these have become so blurred that it is hard to make any general statement to this effect today. As Henry says, "The significant fact is that a program leading to the M. A. degree in one institution may be virtually identical with the Ed. M. program in another institution, or with a program leading to the M. S. in Ed. in still other institutions."[21]

Program requirements are, of course, detailed carefully in the institutions' graduate catalogues. In general, they specify intensive study in a major field, some work in one or more related fields, and some provision for free electives. Independent study and research are stressed in the majority of programs. These may, however, be provided for in specific courses and term assignments and do not necessarily require a thesis. Although writing a thesis is optional in many schools, it is required on the Masters level by a steadily decreasing number of institutions.

A relatively new type of graduate program in education is the *sixth year* program, offered for the first time in the mid-thirties and introduced on a fairly wide-scale basis only during the fifties. This program consists of an additional full college year of study (approximately thirty semester hours of credit) beyond the Master's Degree, and not leading to the Doctor's Degree. Its functions, purposes, or aims are considered to be:

(a) to provide the student with the additional specialized education needed beyond the master's degree for the following school positions—superintendent, principal, supervisor, counselor, subject matter consultant, and other specialized personnel; (b) to prepare more effective and competent classroom teachers; (c) to offer a program for those educational workers who need education beyond the master's degree but not at the doctoral level; and (d) to give the

---

[21] Nelson B. Henry, "Summary of Reports Received from Eighty-Five Institutions," *Graduate Study in Education*, Fiftieth Yearbook, National Society for the Study of Education, Part I, Nelson B. Henry, ed. (Chicago, University of Chicago Press, 1951), pp. 354-355.

student a greater depth of professional and academic training not possible at the master's level.[22]

A survey of forty-eight institutions offering a sixth year program revealed that school administration is the most common field of specialization, with elementary teaching, secondary teaching, and supervision following in that order.[23]

Various degrees, diplomas, or certificates are awarded upon the completion of a sixth year program. These include the Diploma of Advanced Study, Advanced Master of Education. Advanced Post Graduate Certificate, Specialist in Education Degree, Post Master's Certificate, Certificate of Advanced Graduate Specialization, Certificate of Advanced Study, Advanced Master of Arts, and Professional Diploma.[24] Of these, the Specialist in Education is probably used most frequently.

The third type of graduate program is, of course, the doctoral program. This may be completed in approximately three to five years of full-time study, or its equivalent in part-time study. Although it is possible to secure the Doctor's Degree solely through part-time study in some institutions, many schools have residence requirements requiring the doctoral candidate to take at least a part of the program in residence. Specific requirements of each graduate program as well as over-all institutional requirements are carefully detailed in the graduate school's catalogue, and should be painstakingly studied by the individual desirous of earning the Doctor's Degree.

Research and Experimentation

The ever-growing lag between classroom practice and educational research has been long lamented by educators. There are many reasons for the dichotomy between these two fields, one of which is that, in the past, workers in either field rarely ventured across into the other. Educational researchers stayed in their ivory towers and seldom looked, or cared, to see if the results of their work found their way into the classroom. Teachers, on the other hand, considered themselves as practitioners, far removed from the theoretical and experimental world of the researcher.

In recent years, a serious struggle has been made to bring these two groups closer together. Some progress has been made, but much more

[22] Robert H. Koenker, "Sixth-Year Programs in Teacher Education: A Survey," *Journal of Teacher Education*, Vol. 9 (March, 1958), p. 21.

[23] *Ibid*.

[24] John O. Goodman, "Summary of a Study of Professional Education in Selected Universities Beyond the Master's Degree and Not Leading to the Doctor's Degree," *Education*, Vol. 73 (June, 1953), pp. 645-651.

needs to be accomplished. If education is ever to advance beyond the theory stage, the classroom teacher definitely must cultivate more than a nodding acquaintance with the research in his field. Two avenues are open to him.

Every teacher should be an intelligent consumer of research. If he is sincerely interested in improving his professional skills, the teacher must know where to find research, how to interpret the study, how to evaluate its quality and significance, and what the implications are for his own individual situation. Most graduate programs and some high-quality undergraduate programs attempt to lay the basic foundation of the student's acquaintance with significant research through formal course work. Away from the college campus and in the elementary school classroom, the individual teacher should attempt to build on this foundation by keeping abreast of research findings insofar as possible. Basic sources of research that should be periodically consulted by every teacher include the following:

Encyclopedia of Educational Research, Third ed., Chester W. Harris, ed. (New York, The Macmillan Company, 1960).

Handbook of Research on Teaching, N. L. Gage, ed. American Educational Research Association, National Education Association (Chicago, Rand McNally and Company, 1963).

Journal of Educational Research (Madison, Wisconsin, Dembar Publications, Inc., monthly).

NEA Research Bulletin, Research Division, National Education Association (Washington, D. C., National Education Association, quarterly).

Review of Educational Research, American Educational Research Association (Washington, D. C., National Education Association, bi-monthly).

What Research Says to the Teacher, Department of Classroom Teachers and American Educational Research Association (Washington, D. C., National Education Association). Series of pamphlets on assorted topics.

It is not enough, however, for the teacher to be a consumer of the research of others. Today, there is considerable emphasis upon the values and importance of applied research, commonly called action research in education. This is, simply stated, the application of scientific methods of investigation to the solution of actual classroom practices. A more detailed definition is offered by Corey as follows:

Action research in education is research undertaken by practitioners in order that they may improve their practices. The people who actually teach children, supervise teachers, or administer school systems attempt to solve their practical problems by using the methods of science. They accumulate evidence to define their problems more sharply. They draw on all of the experience available to them for action hypotheses that give promise of enabling them to ameliorate or eliminate the difficulties of their day-to-day work. They test out

these promising procedures on the job and accumulate evidence of their effectiveness. They try to generalize as carefully as possible in order that their
research may contribute to the solution of future problems or to the elimination of future difficulties.[25]

Two questions are usually asked in connection with the definition of
action research. First, how does it differ from pure or basic or fundamental research? According to Corey, the major difference is one of
motivation. Those engaged in fundamental research are primarily interested in adding to the general store of scientific knowledge, applicable
to other population groups and situations similar to those studied. The
action researcher is, on the other hand, directly and almost solely concerned with improving his own professional performance. Corey states,

Probably the major difference between action research and traditional educational research arises from the motivation of the investigators. In fundamental
research the basic aim is to conduct an inquiry that will result in generalizations of broad applicability. . . .

Those who engage in action research do so primarily because they wish to
improve their own practices. Action research is conducted in the heat of
combat, so to speak. It is conducted by teachers or supervisors or administrators in order that they may know, on the basis of relatively objective evidence,
whether or not they are accomplishing the things they hope to accomplish.

The differences in methodology between traditional research and action
research are minor. Each investigator attempts to define the problem being
studied with precision, to derive his hypotheses from as rich a background of
information related to the problem as possible, to design an inquiry so that it
will result in a genuine test of the hypotheses, to use facts or evidence rather
than subjective impressions throughout the research procedure, and to generalize cautiously and tentatively from the evidence collected. The conditions
under which the two investigators carry out their inquiries, however, may differ appreciably. The traditional investigator in education tries to control a
situation so that many of the variables involved in real teaching or supervising
or administering are ruled out by definition or by the use of laboratory techniques. This practice results in a more definitive test of the stated hypotheses.
But precision is gained at the expense of the relevance of the findings. People
engaged in action research conduct their inquiries in the complicated psycho-
sociological climate of on-going school activities. Because of the multiplicity of
variables involved, the research is often lacking in precision. The results, however, have meaning for practice because they derive from an inquiry carried
out in a real situation.[26]

The second question concerning the definition of action research is,
How does it differ from the everyday attempt of the conscientious teacher

[25] Stephen M. Corey, *Action Research to Improve School Practices* (New York,
Bureau of Publications, Teachers College, Columbia University, 1953), p. 141.
[26] *Ibid.*, pp. 142-143.

to improve his classroom practice? Unfortunately, many attempts by teachers to improve their teaching, although well motivated, consist of trial-and-error, stumbling-in-the-dark techniques. Seldom is a problem clearly defined, seldom are data secured systematically, and seldom is an attempt made to evaluate results carefully. Thus, although the desire to improve is unquestionably commendable, the results are often unreliable and dependent entirely upon individual judgment as to whether *this way* was better than *that way*.

Even worse, are the teachers who do not attempt to improve their classroom situation by any method, scientific or otherwise. The difference between the teacher who lopes along, day after day, in a comfortable rut and the teacher who approaches his problems with the fresh spirit of scientific inquiry and research is, of course, infinite. Barnes comments upon the inability and reluctance of some teachers to attack their problems systematically in the following statement.

The ability to identify, clearly delimit, analyze, and outline an approach toward the solution of problems, however, is rare among teachers. They have difficulty in the systematic development of a study approach and plan. Why? First, many teachers fail to recognize that their profession requires constant analysis and reflection. The workbook, pre-cooked lesson plans, single textbook, crowded teaching schedules, choreboy activities, seem to dull the intellectual edge of many who man the nation's classrooms.

Second, teachers who fail in their ability to identify and study teaching and learning problems are generally those who inquire and question least. Problems emerge out of critical inquiry and the subsequent search for better ways of promoting learning. Some teachers seem to lose the eager quest for knowledge when they sign a contract to teach.

Third, many teachers are not able to apply scientific thinking to professional problems. There is entirely too much "telling" and not enough "asking" in teacher preparation programs. Such "telling" is found both in the subject matter courses and in the professional education courses. The tragedy is compounded since many teachers teach as they were taught.[27]

Another minor difference between the ordinary, daily, common sense, trial-and-error method and action research is that the former is usually, although not always, done on an individual basis. In other words, the teacher tries one method after another until he finds one that seems to be an improvement. The innovation is then incorporated into his daily program. But many times this is done without anyone else's knowledge. Certainly the results are rarely known by other teachers. Action research, on the other hand, may be done by an individual teacher but it is probably more frequently done by a group or team. Also, its results are usually made available to other members of the staff. Thus, the teacher

[27] John B. Barnes, *op. cit.*, pp. 172-173.

enjoys the added advantage of working as a member of a professional group in the scientific attempt to improve the educational program of his local situation.

What types of problems may be attacked through action research? The number and variety are inexhaustible. Such questions as the following may provide an impetus to scientific investigation by a school staff: Does ability grouping in our school foster pupil cliques according to socio-economic status, race, or nationality? What effect does the use of a competitive grading system have upon academic achievement and peer relationships? Does nonpromotion have a negative effect upon our pupils' self-concepts? How can we utilize parent participation in revising our present report cards? and What are some practical and efficient methods of handling certain noninstructional duties such as collecting milk and lunch money, and taking attendance?

Another opportunity for the classroom teacher to engage in experimentation and research is in connection with the many new curriculum projects now in progress. Formerly, such experimentation was confined largely to selected laboratory schools. The present intensive experimentation, however, in all curriculum areas is using many public schools as pilot centers to try out new content, new methods, and new materials. Teachers who volunteer or are selected to participate in these projects, either on a local or national basis, usually find that they offer a challenge and added dimension to their regular classroom work.

The value of placing research-oriented teachers in the classroom cannot be overestimated. Education will advance in this country in direct proportion to the extent to which classroom teachers approach their problems and task with a desire for improvement, an intellectual curiosity, and an ability to apply scientific methods to everyday problems.

Recreational and Professional Reading

Every elementary teacher is a teacher of reading. Every elementary teacher claims, as one of his major objectives, to stimulate children's interest in reading. It is extremely ironic, therefore, that teachers have long been known to be something less than avid readers. This is true of both recreational and professional reading.

Several studies have emphasized the fact that the amount and level of teachers' leisure-time reading are not noticeably different from those of the general public. A recent study, for instance, of the magazine reading habits of present and prospective teachers makes the following discouraging observation.

. . . these teachers and prospective teachers apparently are reading essentially non-scholarly magazines. Escape reading predominates. Journals of political comment, of ideas, or of such difficulty—however conceived—that the reader would have to struggle for understanding are conspicuously absent. To the extent that periodical reading reflects a desire for knowledge, these education students show little interest in the realm of ideas, whether it be literature, art, science, or politics.[28]

The picture is, if anything, even worse in regard to professional reading. This is true in spite of the fact that statements similar to the following appear in various sources repeatedly. "No other single means of in-service education offers greater opportunities for the teacher to keep abreast of new developments and trends in the profession than those afforded by a carefully planned program of professional reading."[29]

Teachers, of course, tend to excuse their lack of professional reading on many grounds. The most popular is always "not enough time." Certainly teachers are busy and the problem of time cannot be dismissed lightly. But this is certainly not the entire reason for, ironically, the busiest people usually have the most time for self-improvement. One serious reason, voiced less frequently than some others, may be the lack of availability of professional books and periodicals. Some teachers live and teach a considerable distance from any public or university library that has a worthwhile collection of professional references. Building an extensive personal library is a commendable but expensive undertaking. The only satisfactory solution appears to be the establishment of a decent professional library in every school or, in certain urban centers, in every school system.

There are very few educators who would disagree with the statement by Wiles, "A strong professional library is a basic element of a good in-service training program."[30] Apparently this sentiment is still in the realm of educational theory, however, for there is some evidence to indicate that many elementary schools have little or nothing that resembles a professional library. A study by the author[31] of 424 elementary schools, distributed over all fifty states, reveals that, in general, elementary school professional collections leave much to be desired. Of the total number of principals replying, 326, or 76.9 per cent, reported that their schools contained a collection of professional books *and* periodicals. The number of books ranged from five to five hundred, with the median number of volumes between forty-six and fifty, representing a total expenditure of

[28] Bruce Balow, "Magazine Reading Among Teachers and Prospective Teachers," *Journal of Teacher Education*, Vol. 12 (March, 1961), p. 58.

[29] Marie A. Mehl, Hubert H. Mills, and Harl R. Douglass, *Teaching in Elementary School*, 2nd ed. (New York, The Ronald Press Company, 1958), p. 471.

[30] Kimball Wiles, *op. cit.*, pp. 262-263.

[31] Dorothy G. Petersen, "The Teacher's Professional Reading," *Elementary School Journal*, Vol. 63 (October, 1962), pp. 1-5.

approximately two hundred fifty dollars. The median number of volumes added each year was five, indicating an annual expenditure for professional books of approximately twenty-five dollars. Furthermore, only 50 per cent of the principals reported that books were purchased from a regular budgetary allocation. The others reported that books were donated by members of the staff or were purchased with funds received from the PTA, school projects (paper sales, peanut sales, entertainment, etc.) library fines, or class gifts.

Of the 424 schools surveyed, 39, or 9.2 per cent, reported that their schools had no collection of *either* professional books *or* periodicals. Some of these schools reported that they were forty or fifty miles away from the nearest professional collection, and even that was not adequate for their needs. How in the world are teachers in these schools expected to read professional literature?

In spite of the lip service given to the importance of professional reading by teachers, therefore, there is some evidence to indicate that it is not encouraged or financially supported by school systems to the extent that it should be, or to an extent equal with other forms of in-service growth.

It is perfectly obvious that, if teachers are expected to read, they must have something to read. The American Association of School Librarians recommends a professional book collection in every school of from two hundred to one thousand titles and minimum annual expenditure for the professional collection from two hundred dollars to eight hundred dollars.[32] There are several available guides to selecting worthwhile professional books. Book reviews appear regularly in most educational periodicals. The *Education Index* is an invaluable guide to current professional literature. The *Elementary School Journal* in each issue lists selected references in various elementary fields. *Educational Leadership* lists significant books for teachers as do the *Instructor, Grade Teacher, Nation's Schools*, and numerous others. The *NEA Journal* each May lists the sixty best books on education published during the year. These and other sources should be consulted carefully by an elementary school staff as it starts or strengthens its collection of professional books.

Professional periodicals are certainly as valuable as books. The following periodicals[33] are among those most helpful for elementary teachers.

[32] American Association of School Librarians, *Standards for School Library Programs* (Chicago, American Library Association, 1960), p. 86.

[33] The bibliographic information and annotations for all the periodicals contained in this list have been secured from an excellent bibliography entitled *Recommended Materials for a Professional Library in the School*, compiled by the Committee on Professional Materials of the Michigan Association of School Librarians, Rose S. Vincent, chairman, (Ann Arbor, Michigan, Edwards Brothers, Inc., 1962), pp. 79-96.

A generous number of these, in the school's or individual's professional library, should certainly help to keep the teacher informed of current developments in elementary education.

The Arithmetic Teacher, National Council of Teachers of Mathematics, 1201 16th St., N. W., Washington 6, D. C., $7.00 (monthly, O-My) . . . Concerned with the teaching of mathematics in grades K-8. Special features include information on investigations and research, teaching and curriculum problems, testing and evaluation, teaching aids and devices, and reviews.

Art Education, The National Art Education Association, NEA, 1201 16th St., N. W., Washington 6, D. C., $3.00 (monthly, O-Je) . . . Official journal of the National Art Education Association. Offers articles on art and techniques of teaching for art teachers of all levels. Reviews books and films, and reports on items of general interest in the fields of art and education.

Arts and Activities, (Formerly, *Jr. Arts and Activities*), Jones Publishing Company, 8150 N. Central Park Blvd., Skokie, Ill., $6.00 (monthly, S-Je) . . . A professional magazine of creative arts and activities for the classroom teacher. It offers the advice and guidance of the nation's top art educators in modern methods of using creative art activities.

Childhood Education, Association for Childhood Education International, 3615 Wisconsin Avenue, N. W., Washington 16, D. C., $4.50 (monthly, S-My) . . . Official journal of the Association for Childhood Education International. A magazine written for those concerned with children two to twelve years of age. Emphasizes problems of child development as well as classroom methods and procedures, and aims to stimulate thinking rather than advocate fixed practices.

Education, Bobbs-Merrill Co., Inc., 1720 E. 38th St., Indianapolis 6, Ind., $5.00 (monthly, S-My) . . . An independent general educational magazine of particular value to principals and supervisors. Each issue features the current thought and trends on one specific area, e. g., music education, reading, science, exceptional child. Different editor, specialist in the field, for each issue. Quality of articles and issues varies widely.

The Education Digest, The Education Digest, 416 Longshore Drive, Ann Arbor, Mich., $5.00 (monthly, S-My) . . . A magazine resembling the *Reader's Digest* in size and plan, giving digests of articles from educational journals in all areas. Especially useful in libraries with limited number of educational journals. Articles well chosen. Useful survey of current educational developments and discussions.

Educational Leadership, Association for Supervision and Curriculum Development, 1201 16th Street, N. W., Washington 6, D. C., $4.50 (monthly, O-My) . . . Official journal of the Association for Supervision and Curriculum Development, NEA. Its focus is in the curriculum area; its main object is the general improvement of instruction and supervision at elementary, junior high and senior high levels. Each issue develops a theme. Reviews and regular departments are included.

Educational Screen and Audio-Visual Guide, Educational Screen, Inc., 2000 Lincoln Park West Bldg., Chicago 14, Ill., $4.00 (monthly) . . . Contains descriptions of new A-V equipment, materials. Reports on problems, practices, and developments in uses of A-V aids in schools.

Elementary English, National Council of Teachers of English, 508 S. 6th Street, Champaign, Ill., $4.00 (monthly, O-My) . . . Official publication of the National Council of Teachers of English. Articles on teaching elementary language arts, sketches of authors of children's books, reviews of books for children. Also practical helps, summaries of educational developments.

The Elementary School Journal, University of Chicago Press, 5750 Ellis Avenue, Chicago 37, Ill., $4.50 (monthly, O-My) . . . A journal of professional discussion of the problems of education on the elementary level and emphasizing instruction, administration and social change.

Elementary School Science Bulletin, National Science Teachers Association, 1201 16th St., N. W., Washington 6, D. C., $1.00 (8 issues) . . . Eight page bulletin for elementary teachers. Articles prepared by teachers, educators, and leading scientists. Reports on new developments, studies, book listings, and references.

Exceptional Children, Council for Exceptional Children, NEA, 1201 16th Street N. W., Washington 6, D. C., $5.00 (monthly, S-My) . . . The official organ of the Council, NEA. A monthly journal for all who are interested in the education of the handicapped and the gifted. Carries carefully selected articles, current literature, classroom hints, opinions on controversial questions and news items.

Grade Teacher, Grade Teacher, Leroy Avenue, Darien, Conn., $5.00 (monthly, S-Je) . . . An up-to-date professional magazine for elementary teachers. Specializes in authoritative practical classroom help prepared by leading educational experts. Saves teachers hours of research and preparation.

The Instructor, The Instructor, Dansville, N. Y., $6.00 (monthly, S-Je) . . . "The Magazine for Better Teaching." An outstanding professional magazine for elementary teachers that provides classroom-tested suggestions and aids, adapted to the months of the school year. Each issue presents specific classroom plans, devices, and practices; pictorial materials, stories, plays, poems, science experiments, social studies, health and safety units.

Journal of Education, Boston University, School of Education, 332 Bay State Road, Boston 15, Mass., $3.00 (bi-monthly, O-Ap) . . . Each issue is on a single topic with the whole number written by one or two authors. Topics are concerned with both elementary and secondary schools.

Journal of Educational Psychology, American Psychological Assn., Inc., 1333 16th St., N. W., Washington 6, D. C., $10.00 (bi-monthly, O-Ag). (Subscriptions are available on a January-December basis only.) . . . Scholarly studies of learning and teaching; measurement of psychological development, psychology of school subjects, methods of instruction, school adjustment.

Journal of Educational Research, Dembar Publications, Inc., Box 1605, Madison 3, Wis., $7.50 (monthly, S-My) . . . Contains reports of systematic studies of all phases of school education, and at all levels, by both practitioners and university specialists.

The Journal of Experimental Education, Dembar Publications, Inc., Box 1605, Madison 3, Wis., $7.50 (quarterly) . . . A technical publication for technical workers, carrying reports of carefully designed experimental studies in the field of education. Good source for statistics, examples of various methods, and research techniques as they relate to all levels of education. Summarizations and interpretations given.

The Modern Language Journal, National Federation of Modern Language Teachers Assn., 7144 Washington Avenue, St. Louis 30, Mo., $4.00 (monthly, O-My) . . . Contains articles on methods of theory of interest to teachers from elementary grades through college. Evaluative reviews of books. Notes on audio-visual materials. Should be available in all schools that teach modern languages.

Music Educators Journal, Music Educators National Conference. NEA, 1201 16th St., N. W., Washington 6, D. C., $3.50 (bi-monthly, S-Je) . . . The official spokesman for the music education field. A reliable and up-to-date information source concerning trends, activities, publications, materials at all levels, preschool through college. Contributors are leaders in general and in music education.

NEA Journal, National Education Association, 1201 16th St., N. W., Washington 6, D. C., $10.00 (monthly, S-My) . . . Official organ of the National Education Association. Articles by experts on education and other subjects describe and evaluate new ideas and developments in educational practice and philosophy and provide guidance for classroom activities.

NEA Research Bulletin, Research Division, National Education Association, 1201 16th St., Washington 6, D. C., $2.00 (quarterly) . . . A professional journal summarizing the Division's major studies which present new and original research data, or intensive review, analysis, and new presentation of exisitng research.

The National Elementary Principal, Department of Elementary School Principals, NEA, 1201 16th St., N. W., Washington 6, D. C., $8.00 (bi-monthly, S-Je) . . . Official magazine of the Department of Elementary School Principals, NEA. Each issue centers around a specific facet of elementary education, e. g., school health program; music education; arithmetic. Also includes book reviews and local, state and national news of elementary principals' associations.

The Nation's Schools, Circulation Department, 1050 Merchandise Mart, Chicago 54, Ill., $4.00 (monthly) . . . Devoted to practices, problems and theories of school buildings, equipment and administration. Designed for school superintendents, their assistants, school business officials, and architects.

The PTA Magazine (Formerly, *National Parent-Teacher*), National Congress of Parents and Teachers, 700 Rush St., Chicago 11, Ill., $1.50 (monthly, S-Je) . . . Official magazine of the National Congress of Parents and Teachers for the advancement of schools, education and understanding of the child and his environment. Articles of general interest on the child, his relationships at home, school and the psychological aspects of his development. Has regular section of book reviews, and evaluation of movies and television programs.

The Reading Teacher, International Reading Association (IRA), 5454 South Shore Drive, Room 707-709, Chicago 15, Ill., $4.50 (6 times a year, S-My) . . . Official publication of International Reading Association. Each issue centers around one theme—an aspect or phase of the instruction of reading. Also contains current trends in teaching methods, and book lists for children's pleasure reading.

Review of Educational Research, American Educational Research Association, NEA, 1201 16th St., N. W., Washington 6, D. C., $7.00 (bi-monthly, O-Je) . . . Each issue is devoted to a major educational topic, such as educational and psychological testing, technical and vocational education, mental and physical health, etc. Articles treat different aspects of topic, each reviewing literature on that aspect appearing since the topic was treated in the *Review*, each containing a thorough and comprehensive bibliography.

Safety Education, National Safety Council, 425 North Michigan Ave., Chicago 11, Ill., $3.75 (monthly, S-My) . . . A magazine written by educators for teachers and school administrators. It offers methods and programs in safety education and deals with problems in accident prevention in the school, such as in the vocational shop, in the gymnasium and on the playground.

School and Society, Society for the Advancement of Education, Inc., 1834 Broadway, New York 23, N. Y., $7.50 (bi-weekly, S-Je) . . . Aims at a comprehensive coverage of the entire field of education, including educational controversies, special conference reports, profiles of leading educators, research in all phases of education, international and comparative education, educational literature and reviews.

School Arts, School Arts, Printers Building, 44 Portland Street, Worcester 8, Mass., $6.00 (monthly, S-Je) . . . Illustrates and describes creative art, drawing and handwork. Treats drawing, design, poster, cut paper, illustration, projects, plays and puppets. A standard reference and instruction magazine for art teachers in all school levels.

School Life, Superintendent of Documents, U. S. Government Printing Office, Washington 25, D. C., $1.75 (monthly, S-My; bi-monthly, N. F.) . . . Summarizes in detail the major publications of the Office of Education, and reports on its service activities, presents pertinent statistics, reviews legislation, and offers additional information useful to educators.

The Science Teacher, National Science Teachers Association, NEA, 1201 16th St., N. W., Washington 6, D. C., $6.00 membership dues, or $8.00 for library subscription including subscription to *Elementary School Bulletin* (monthly, 8 issues) . . . Excellent publication of the Association for the teacher of science, elementary through high school. Includes classroom procedures, developments in all scientific areas, reviews of materials, and other features.

Social Education, National Council of Social Studies, NEA, 1201 16th Street, N. W., Washington 6, D. C., $5.00 (monthly, O-My) . . . Official organ of National Council of Social Studies, in collaboration with the American Historical Association. Discusses the significance of social studies in education, articles on history, and current events, and suggestions for presenting social studies topics. For social studies teachers at all levels.

The Social Studies, McKinley Publishing Company, 890 N. 19th Street, Philadelphia 30, Pa., $5.00 (monthly, O-Ap) . . . Practical and pertinent articles covering all phases of the social studies for teachers and administrators.

If books and periodicals are made available to the school staff, their use can be encouraged through such techniques as (1) displaying new materials in a central location, (2) posting on the faculty bulletin board published reviews of current books and articles, (3) posting on the faculty bulletin board reviews by teachers of books or articles they have particularly enjoyed, (4) devoting a portion of a faculty meeting to the review and discussion of a current book or article, (5) making the purchase of all professional books and periodicals the responsibility of a teachers' committee, (6) organizing informal and voluntary discussion groups, (7) housing the professional collection in a central place with maximum availability for the faculty at all times, (8) distributing to staff members several times a year reading bulletins recommending articles, in various journals or books, of particular interest (an excellent program of this type is that conducted in the Rochester, Minnesota Public Schools), and (9) making the collection available to teachers throughout the summer months when their time is not at a premium.

Professional Writing

This usually represents an extension or culmination of various other channels of in-service growth. After one has studied, conducted research, experimented, or read extensively he may desire to make an additional contribution to the profession through writing. It is difficult to enumerate all of the values one may derive from writing professionally. It is, of course, an undertaking that develops self-discipline, perseverance, and the refinement of all one's expressional language skills. It requires intensive reading and study in order to put into proper focus one's own ideas and experiences. It can be a vital impetus to continued growth as one receives comments, suggestions, and reactions from professional colleagues. It can satisfy a genuine need for service and contribution as one offers to others the results of his own experience and efforts.

The writer is not the only one who benefits. Teachers throughout the country are interested in reading ideas and suggestions from other teachers. Teachers want to read about new units that have been successful; about new techniques for efficient classroom management; about new methods, content, and materials with appeal for children; about others' ideas on major educational issues; and about many other subjects from fellow teachers. The classroom teacher who writes professionally is not only extending his own professional growth, but he is making a genuine contribution to the in-service education of his colleagues.

All of the periodicals listed on the preceding pages, and many others, welcome contributions from classroom teachers. Any issue will usually contain information as to the person and address to whom manuscripts should be mailed. Manuscripts should be neatly typed, double-spaced, on plain white paper. Correct form for footnotes and bibliography, when included, should be carefully observed.

The values of professional writing are many. According to one author,

It can guide you to lead the life of an intellectual. And that is precisely what every educator should be. One cannot help but grow when one sees new ideas, reads, and keeps in touch with new trends. Such a practice is bound to accelerate one's adequacy both as a teacher and as a scholar. Then, too, it will improve a person's morale to see his ideas run parallel with those of other educators. All of this will make him more satisfied with the job he is doing, or will inspire him to improve if he is not satisfied. What is more, if he learns to share ideas through writing about them, all schools will benefit.[34]

Recreational Activities

Chapter 2 emphasized physical and mental fitness as a factor necessary for effective teaching. In the first section of the present chapter, it was stated that one of the needs and purposes of continuing teacher growth is to maintain physical and mental health. It was further mentioned that the teacher's personal growth was just as important as his professional growth and that, as a matter of fact, the two could never be entirely separated. Unfortunately, some conscientious teachers do try to separate them, with occasional disastrous results. There is some evidence that points to the fact that mental and emotional maladjustment is higher among teachers than among similar professional groups and also that, as a group, teachers tend to devote less time to hobbies and other leisure time activities than do other similar groups. It does not seem to be too far-fetched to conclude that there may be some relationship between these two facts. Many teachers are extremely conscientious. They are hard working and dedicated to their profession and vitally concerned about the total health and welfare of their pupils. This is all fine. But they should also be concerned about their own total health and welfare. And

[34] Sister Mary Xavier, "Write for Self-Improvement," *The Clearing House*, Vol. 36 (January, 1962), p. 268.

there is no better way to do this than to develop some interesting hobbies and worthwhile leisure time activities. Travel, reading, bowling, bridge, tennis, swimming, oil painting, gardening, golf—the list is endless—are valuable and necessary to the teacher's health and personal-professional growth. They should not be neglected.

Exchange Teaching

Studying, living, and working in a foreign country has long been recognized as a valuable means of extending one's cultural and professional horizons. Today, under private and government sponsored programs, a wide variety of opportunities exist for the teacher to study or teach abroad. By far the most extensive program is the Mutual Educational and Cultural Exchange Act of 1961 (the Fulbright-Hayes Act) through which opportunities to teach or study in another country are provided each year to several thousand elementary and secondary school teachers. These opportunities are of the following types:[35]

1. *Interchange of teaching positions with Canada, Sweden, and the United Kingdom.* In this type, the American teacher receives a leave of absence with pay and receives his own salary while teaching abroad. The same is true of the foreign teacher with whom he exchanges positions. The teacher may, or may not, be responsible for transportation costs, depending upon the host country.

2. *Interchange of teaching positions with other countries.* The American teacher receives a leave of absence and, while abroad, receives a maintenance allowance payable in the currency of the host country. Round-trip transportation fare is provided for the teacher but not for his dependents. Under this plan, interchanges are arranged with Argentina, Australia, Austria, Belgium-Luxembourg, Chile, Denmark, Federal Republic of Germany, the Netherlands, New Zealand, Norway, Peru, and Uruguay.

3. *One-way foreign assignments for American teachers.* The American teacher receives a leave of absence and, while abroad, receives a maintenance allowance in the currency of the host country or in American currency. The amount of the award varies, depending upon the living costs of the host country. Round-trip transportation fare is provided for the teacher but not for his dependents. Under this plan, teaching opportunities are offered in Austria, Brazil, Chile, Cyprus, Denmark, Ecuador, Finland, Federal Republic of Germany, Greece, Iceland, India, Iran, Italy, Japan, Pakistan, Paraguay, Peru, Sweden, Turkey, and United Kingdom

[35] U. S. Department of Health, Education and Welfare, "1964-65 Teacher Exchange Opportunities," Bulletin 1964, No. 6 (Washington, D. C., 1963), pp. 5-7.

Dependencies. Additional opportunities may soon become available in such countries as Bolivia, Cambodia, Costa Rica, Guinea, Haiti, Honduras, Indonesia, Laos, Liberia, Libya, Martinique, Morocco, Nicaragua, Nigeria, Somalia, Tunisia, and Vietnam.

4. *Grants to attend seminars abroad.* These opportunities vary as to country and the qualifications of the teacher.

5. *One-way assignments in the United States for foreign teachers.* A limited number of one-way assignments for teachers from certain countries is available for teaching opportunities in American secondary schools and junior colleges.

The basic application requirements for participation in these programs are as follows:

1. *Citizenship:* U. S. citizenship, either by birth or naturalization.

2. *Educational Training:* At least a bachelor's degree or its equivalent. Additional graduate work, preferably a master's degree, is desirable.

3. *Educational Experience:* At least 3 years of successful, full-time teaching, preferably in the subject field and at the level of the position for which application is made. Elementary and secondary school teachers and college teachers holding the rank of instructor or assistant professor are eligible to apply. . . .

4. *Health:* Evidence of good physical health, moral character, emotional stability, maturity, and adaptability.

5. *School Approval:* Endorsement by the applicant's school authority of the type of exchange plan . . . in effect with the country of choice.

6. *Foreign Language:* Facility in reading, writing, and speaking the language of the host country is a requisite for some exchanges and a definite asset for all.

7. *Related Factors:* Veterans and persons under 50 years of age are usually given preference. Teachers who have previously served satisfactorily under the program are eligible for a second grant in a subsequent program year, provided they apply to go to a country other than the one for which the first grant was awarded. In most cases, however, preference will be given to those applicants who have not been the recipients of previous grants.[36]

Applications for participation in the program during any academic year should be submitted by October 15 of the preceding academic year to:

> Teacher Exchange Section
> Bureau of International Education
> Office of Education
> U. S. Department of Health, Education, and Welfare
> Washington 25, D. C.

There is no doubt that the opportunity to teach and study abroad is one of the most valuable means of in-service teacher growth. In addition

[36] *Ibid.*, pp. 4-5.

to a personal benefit to the teacher, exchange teaching also offers a two-fold benefit to the school system, ". . . the teacher from outside brings different experiences with him to share with his hosts; and the teacher who goes away brings back new ideas. In each case the school system learns new ways of doing things and learns them in a practical way through direct experiences."[37]

True, exchange teaching may provide some problems regarding such things as salaries, certification, and retirement benefits but these are more than compensated for by the values it brings to the individual teacher, the school system, and the nation.

SUMMARY

To the young person just entering college, the completion of his preservice preparation seems to be in the far distant future and seldom does he look beyond that point. Sooner or later, however, he realizes that his preservice preparation represents only the first faltering step in his long journey toward becoming an educated citizen and a competent teacher.

The first section of this chapter examined the needs and purposes of continued personal and professional growth throughout the teacher's entire career. It was stated that growth is desirable in all fields; certain factors in teaching make it an absolute necessity. Those factors that emphasize the need for the teacher's embarking upon a deliberate program of improvement include (1) the ever-changing nature of education, (2) the limitations of even the best preservice preparation, (3) the absence in teaching of certain automatic stimulants to growth found in some other fields, and (4) the ever-expanding role of the teacher.

To the teacher interested in continuing his education, two avenues are open. The first of these is the structured in-service educational program, offered by the school system and in which the teacher is required or strongly urged to participate. In general, it is safe to say that all systems have some type of program although there are wide differences in quality. Techniques fairly common in most programs include (1) teachers' institutes, (2) workshops, (3) teachers' handbooks, (4) demonstration lessons and clinics, (5) interclass visitation, (6) study groups and teachers' councils, (7) faculty meetings, and (8) the use of modern mass communication media such as television, radio, films, and filmstrips.

In addition to participating in a structured program, the alert teacher may grow professionally through voluntarily engaging in many self-directed activities. Of these, none is more important than graduate study.

[37] National Education Association Research Division, "Inservice Education of Teachers," *NEA Research Memo, 1960-62* (Washington, D. C., National Education Association, August, 1960), p. 12.

In recent years, interest in graduate study has accelerated throughout the country, as an increasing number of individuals participate in formal college study beyond the baccalaureate degree, on a full or part-time basis. The discussion of this chapter attempted to answer some of the basic questions usually asked by in-service or prospective teachers contemplating graduate study.

In addition to graduate study, five voluntary activities offering promise for continuing growth are (1) experimentation and research, (2) recreational and professional reading, (3) professional writing, (4) recreational activities, and (5) teaching and/or studying abroad. Each of these was examined briefly in the remainder of the chapter.

ADDITIONAL LEARNING EXPERIENCES

Topics for Thought and Discussion

1. Do you intend to study for an advanced degree after you receive the Bachelor's Degree? Why? When?

2. Do you think a five year period of preservice education will eventually be required for elementary teachers in your state? Upon what trends or factors do you base your opinion?

3. If your state offers permanent or life certification, how much study beyond the Bachelor's Degree is required?

4. In what areas do you think your preservice education has been strongest? Weakest?

5. What do you think is the solution to the widespread problem of credit-chasing among teachers?

6. Do you approve of relating teacher growth to salary adjustments? Why?

7. Do you think that, in general, tenure and permanent certification are deterrents to teacher growth?

8. With how many of the professional periodicals listed on pages 524 to 528 are you familiar? To which ones do you, or will you when you become a teacher, subscribe?

9. How many professional books do you now have in your personal library? On the average, how many professional books do you think a teacher should purchase a year?

10. What are your ultimate professional goals?

11. Would you like to be on the staff of a demonstration or laboratory school? Why?

12. How many books have you read in the last year?

13. What magazines do you read regularly? Newspapers?

14. Must teachers themselves be readers in order to stimulate a love of reading in children?

15. Approximately how many teachers have you had who asked for anonymous pupil evaluations of their teaching? Were those who did, generally above or below the average caliber of teacher you have known? To what extent do you think they used, and profited by, the pupils' evaluations?

Projects and Activities

1. One study reports that, on the average, teachers who had been teaching twenty or thirty years had had opportunity to observe another teaching only three or four times. Make a similar study of a group of experienced elementary teachers. How many times, in their total teaching careers, have they had an opportunity to observe another teacher teach? What are your conclusions?

2. Talk with a school superintendent or elementary school principal about the in-service growth program in his system. What techniques are used? To what extent does the community support the concept of continuing teacher growth? What major problems are involved?

3. Ask a member of your state education association to speak to your college class on the association's contributions to the in-service growth of teachers in your state. What activities in this area, other than the common ones of publishing a state organ and conducting an annual convention, does your state association sponsor?

4. Talk with the Dean or the Chairman of the Education Department in your college. In what ways does your college assume a leadership role in the in-service education program of school systems in your state?

5. Ask permission to examine the professional library of one or more nearby elementary schools. Examine and evaluate each collection according to the recommendations for a professional library contained in the *Standards for School Library Programs* of the American Association of School Librarians.

6. If you are teaching or working with children in any capacity, ask for written, unsigned evaluations of a lesson you have taught or an activity you have sponsored. How helpful and how revealing do you find these evaluations? In what specific respects can you improve your performance accordingly?

7. Talk with, or write to, a member of your state department of education. In what specific ways does the state department play a leadership role in the in-service improvement of teachers in the state? Compare its activities in this area with those of the state education association (see project 3).

8. You are an elementary school principal. Outline a program through which you will attempt to stimulate the professional reading of your staff. Ask several experienced elementary teachers or members of your college class to evaluate your proposed program. Do they think it is practical and workable? Or idealistic?

9. Write a review of at least one professional book included in the most recent May issue of the *NEA Journal*'s list of outstanding books in education.

10. Write a review of 6 to 12 of the educational periodicals listed on pages 524 to 528. Include such information as (1) special features of interest to elementary school teachers, (2) general type of article, and (3) special group, if any, for whom the periodical would have greatest interest.

11. Talk with the Director of Teacher Education in your college. Does your college have a planned follow-up program of its graduates? What techniques does it use? If possible, ask some recent graduates for their evaluation of the program. Do they think it has real value in aiding their professional growth?

Selected Bibliography

ARCHER, Clifford P., "Inservice Education," in Chester W. Harris, ed., *Encyclopedia of Educational Research*, 3rd ed. New York, The Macmillan Company, 1960.

BARNES, John B., *Educational Research for Classroom Teachers*. New York, G. P. Putnam's Sons, 1960.

BERELSON, Bernard, *Graduate Education in the United States*. New York, McGraw-Hill Book Co. Inc., 1960.

BRUCE, William F., and HOLDEN, John A. Jr., *The Teacher's Personal Development*. New York, Holt, Rinehart and Winston, Inc., 1957.

COREY, Stephen M., *Action Research to Improve School Practices*. New York, Bureau of Publications, Teachers College, Columbia University, 1953.

"Continuing Education for the Teaching Profession." *Educational Leadership*, Vol. 15 (February, 1958).

"Continuing Growth for the Teacher." *Educational Leadership*, Vol. 20 (November, 1962).

GOOD, Carter V., *Introduction to Educational Research*, rev. ed. New York, Appleton-Century-Crofts, 1963.

Great Teachers, Houston Peterson, ed. New Brunswick, N. J., Rutgers University Press, 1946.

HENRY, Nelson B., *Graduate Study in Education*. Fiftieth Yearbook, National Society for the Study of Education, Part I. Chicago, University of Chicago Press, 1951.

———, *In-service Education*, Fifty-sixth Yearbook, National Society for the Study of Education, Part I. Chicago, University of Chicago Press, 1957.

KEARNEY, Nolan C., *A Teacher's Professional Guide*. Englewood Cliffs, N. J., Prentice-Hall, Inc., 1958.

KELLEY, Earl C., *The Workshop Way of Learning*. New York, Harper & Row, Publishers, Inc., 1951.

MOUSTAKAS, Clark E., *The Alive and Growing Teacher*. New York, Philosophical Library, Inc., 1959.

NEA Research Division, *Inservice Education of Teachers.* NEA Research Memo, 1960-62. Washington, D. C., National Education Association, August, 1960.

O'Rourke, Mary A., and Burton, William H., *Workshops for Teachers.* New York, Appleton-Century-Crofts, 1957.

Shumsky, Abraham, *The Action Research Way of Learning.* New York, Bureau of Publications, Teachers College, Columbia University, 1958.

Stinnett, T. M., and Huggett, Albert J., *Professional Problems of Teachers,* 2nd ed. New York, The Macmillan Company, 1963.

U. S. Department of Health, Education, and Welfare, Office of Education, *What Some School Systems Are Doing to Promote Teacher Growth.* Education Briefs, No. 33. Washington, D. C., August, 1956.

CHAPTER **13**

Meeting Persistent Problems

IN ALL WALKS OF LIFE there appear to be a fortunate few who, judging by the apparent ease of their accomplishments, avoid the pitfalls and problems that plague their colleagues. These few pacesetters may be gifted with rare insight, possess unusual abilities, or simply be blessed with good fortune. A more probable explanation of their success is that they have learned how to side-step the common problems of their chosen profession by profiting from the experiences of others. It is comparatively easy to learn from one's own mistakes. It is more difficult, but equally valuable, to learn from those of others.

Every occupation, every profession, every career presents frustrations to those who would master it. Whether these frustrations are regarded as unavoidable problems, inherent deterrents, or mettle-testing challenges depends, of course, upon many factors. But the fact remains that, in all fields, there are certain obstacles that hinder, to varying degrees, the worker's effectivenesses and satisfactions.

Elementary school teaching is no exception. It, too, presents certain problems. Over the past few years, the author has attempted to determine these by asking several hundred teachers the question, "What do you consider to be the most serious problems or handicaps that prevent you from attaining greater teaching effectiveness?" Answers were separated into two categories according to (1) problems reported by first-year teachers and (2) problems reported by experienced teachers (those with five or more years of teaching). Table 13.1 on page 528 reveals the six problems mentioned most often by each group, in order of frequency.

An examination of the above lists reveals a somewhat surprising consistency between the two categories. Furthermore, this consistency is also revealed in an examination of current literature. Numerous studies that have been made of teachers' problems reveal that certain problems

537

TABLE 13.1

Problems Reported by Inexperienced Teachers	*Problems Reported by Experienced Teachers*
1. Discipline	1. Lack of home-school cooperation
2. Getting a good start	2. Overcrowded classrooms
3. Providing for a wide range of pupil abilities	3. Providing for a wide range of pupil abilities
4. Lack of teaching supplies, resources, and equipment	4. Excessive noninstructional duties
5. Lack of home-school cooperation	5. Discipline
6. Excessive noninstructional duties	6. Lack of teaching supplies, resources, and equipment

appear repeatedly. It may be concluded, therefore, that, according to teachers' reports, there are certain persistent problems generally associated with elementary school teaching. The remainder of this chapter is devoted to an analysis of these problems with suggested possible solutions. Some, of course, have been discussed in detail in earlier chapters. The brief examination of these in this chapter, therefore, is in the nature of a summary and reiteration of what has been said previously. Others are examined in more detail. Since the order of frequency varied between the two lists, the following sections are not arranged in order of importance.

Getting a Good Start

"Well begun, half done" is an old cliche particularly appropriate to teaching. A good first day, a smooth first week, can, and frequently does, make the difference between teaching success and failure. Problems met by first-year teachers in trying to make a successful beginning were indicated in such comments as the following:

In this system there is absolutely no provision for the orientation of new teachers. The principal and superintendent take it for granted that new teachers know what to do. They couldn't be more mistaken.

I could have used some guidance in planning the daily activities. It is so hard when you don't know the school nor your pupils.

My biggest problem in the beginning was feeling my way with everything and everybody—pupils, materials, principal, parents, etc.

Getting started on the right foot was, and still is, my biggest problem!

I needed much help on classroom organization at the beginning of the year— rules within the class, time allotments for various subjects, how to plan with children, etc.

Obviously, the degree of seriousness of this problem depends on many factors. It depends upon the provisions the school system has made for the orientation of new teachers. This may vary from a very thorough orientation period of several weeks to absolutely nothing. It depends upon the supervisory and administrative assistance available to the teacher. It depends upon the teacher-preparing institution and whether it has attempted to provide its students with observation and participation experiences during the opening weeks of the school year as part of their preservice preparation. But, more than all else, it depends upon the beginning teacher himself and how carefully he has familiarized himself with his situation and how conscientiously he has planned and organized his work. To help him in these tasks, the following discussion is organized according to the major areas of (1) getting ready for the opening of school and (2) the first day of school.

Getting ready. Prior to the opening session, the beginning teacher will find it extremely valuable to:

1. Become acquainted with the community. The more knowledge the new teacher has of his school's community and parents, the more he will be helped in getting to know his pupils. Visiting homes, walking or riding through the neighborhood, chatting with local storekeepers and business people, will provide invaluable information to him. Webber makes the following suggestions:

. . . let's assume you are a newcomer. Your principal probably has a map of your school district and can certainly tell you· its boundaries. You can walk down one street and up the next, wondering if the tow-head on the bike, and the carrot-top running alongside, will be in your room. You may want to stop them and ask.

Or you may want to get out your list of names and addresses, make a few phone calls, and start meeting parents. The temptation, of course, will be to choose the parents who live in the charming house with the delft-blue door—but you may get more needed insight by climbing a dark stair to the second-floor apartment where a small boy amuses himself with TV while his mother works.

If you are to teach in a sprawling district, you may need to board a bus or go by car to cover your territory. Here the names of the main streets and the location of shopping centers may be the most important things to learn.

If you have time, a more extensive and personal parent-relations project can be undertaken, such as serving tea and cookies to the mothers right in the classroom a day or so before school is to open. Substitute lemonade for tea, and small sons and daughters will be glad to tag along. Postal card invitations are the thing for affairs like this—inexpensive, informal, and friendly. And there's no reason, of course, why this kind of a party can't be given after school starts.

Rural areas take different treatment—especially if you yourself are completely urban. Better take a go-see trip yourself and learn the difference between a harrow and a combine, a Black Angus and a Jersey. But don't ask your questions of the busy farmer in the field. Do make a friend of the county agent. He'll be invaluable as a source of information; he can help you see a rolling field of wheat or an eroded hillside in terms of their socio-economic relationships to your pupils.[1]

2. Become acquainted with the school building. An hour's tour through an empty building will help the teacher to orient himself to the location of playgrounds, offices, special rooms, auditorium, and other important areas.

3. Become familiar with important school procedures, policies, and routines. Most schools have organization bulletins or teachers' handbooks which will give the new teacher the vital information he needs regarding these points. If such bulletins are not available, the teacher may secure the information through a conference with the principal or an experienced teacher. The checklist on pages 541 to 542 will help him to know what information he needs to start the school year successfully.

4. Prepare the classroom for the opening day. First impressions are important and the pupils' first impression of their classroom is often a lasting one. A few hours spent in making the classroom inviting, attractive, and interesting to pupils when they first arrive will pay great dividends. An attractive bulletin board display will help to arouse interest in a beginning social studies or science unit. Pictures of pets, current news events, sports, hobbies, or summer activities will serve as stimuli to oral or written language experiences. An acquarium or a small collection of leaves or shells may motivate the need for some research and study. A table or shelf of new library books and a tempting display of attractive book jackets will suggest possibilities for spare-time reading. A few flowers or green plants will help to initiate a discussion of room responsibilities and committees.

In addition, of course, certain books and supplies need to be secured and ready for use, as indicated in the checklist on pages 541 to 542.

5. Study the cumulative records of the incoming pupils. The new teacher will find it helpful to study whatever records are available of the pupils assigned to him. There may be some who do not advocate this practice, on the grounds that it will prejudice the teacher before he meets his pupils. This is sheer nonsense. As a matter of fact, it is difficult to see how the teacher can begin grouping in his classroom, can prepare suitable assignments, or can write lesson plans unless he has some knowledge of

[1] Grace Cramer Webber, "Start Off on the Right Foot," *NEA Journal*, Vol. 45 (September, 1956), p. 353.

his pupils' abilities and needs. If the teacher is a true professional, any advance information he can secure about his pupils will be to his and their advantage, never to their disadvantage.

6. Study curriculum guides and textbooks. It is difficult to see how any teacher may make long-range plans unless he is familiar with whatever curriculum guides, textbooks, and basic supplementary references are available.

In summary, the following checklist should help the beginning teacher to test his readiness for the opening of the school year.

ARE YOU READY?

DO YOU KNOW:

THE LOCATION OF:
Medical suite or nurse's room?
Stockroom?
Auditorium?
All-purpose room?
Playrooms?
Gymnasium?
Library?
Main office?
Instructional materials center?
Cafeteria and kitchen?

THE NAMES OF:
Custodians?
Secretary or clerk?
Specialized staff personnel?
Supervisory and administrative personnel?
Nurse?
Cafeteria helpers?
School traffic policeman?

THE REGULATIONS FOR:
Reporting attendance and keeping a class register?
Fire and air raid drills?
Scheduling use of playground, lunchroom, gymnasium, all-purpose room, instructional materials center, skills laboratory, art studio, etc.?
Admitting and dismissing pupils?
Teacher absence?
Requisitioning supplies?
Teacher arrival and leaving?
Collecting milk money, lunch money, etc.?
School policy on opening exercises—inspirational reading, flag salute, etc.?
Excusing children early from class?
Securing medical attention or first-aid for pupils?

Teachers' nonclass duties—lunch duty, bus patrol, playground supervision, etc.?

Taking class field trips and excursions?

Providing for substitute in case of teacher absence?

THE ALL-SCHOOL SCHEDULE FOR:

Playground periods?

Gymnasium periods?

Lunch periods?

Special classes?

Auditorium assembly?

Faculty meetings?

DO YOU HAVE:

Class list of pupils?

Plan book—containing detailed plans for first few days and beginnings of long-range plans?

Organizational bulletin or teachers' handbook (if it exists)?

Equipment for opening exercises—flag, etc.?

Necessary forms for:

Reporting daily attendance?

Requisitioning supplies?

Collecting lunch or milk orders?

Minimum playground equipment—large rubber ball, softball, bat, jumping rope, etc.?

Chromatic pitch pipe?

Minimum art supplies?

General supplies—paper, sharpened pencils, thumb tacks, paper clips, scotch tape?

Textbooks?

HAVE YOU:

Studied available curriculum guides and courses of study?

Arranged your classroom to attract and please the children?

Studied whatever pupil records are available?

Planned the first few days in meticulous detail?

The First Day of School. The following is a humorous account of his first day of teaching by the author of a recent delightful book entitled, *Never Tease a Dinosaur.*[2]

... no matter how great his courage, how thorough his training, how varied his pre-teaching experiences, one day early in September our teacher will be confronted by his first class.

[2] From *Never Tease a Dinosaur* by Joseph F. Hannan. Copyright © 1961, 1962 by Joseph F. Hannan. Reprinted by permission of Holt, Rinehart and Winston, Inc., pp. 9-12.

In addition to his schooling he will have had the advice of other teachers which consists of, "Keep them busy and they won't give you any trouble."

His relatives will have made dire predictions betraying their deep-seated and ofttimes justifiable lack of confidence in his ability. His friends will have made him a present of *The Blackboard Jungle*, which, unfortunately for his peace of mind, he has had time to read.

It's no wonder he starts as the warning bell rings and the clean, well-mannered children begin to file into the room. A look at their anxious-to-please expressions should have settled his nerves immediately, but our teacher is seeing nothing at all. Ashen-faced, he has managed to stand erect by clinging to his desk, which has become his fortress and which, incidentally, hides his trembling knees.

Remembering the admonition to "keep them busy" he plunges into his new task. His voice is a strained croak as he speaks his first words to his class.

"Take out your spelling books."

The children exchange puzzled glances and shift uncomfortably in their seats.

Prepared for such defiance by his reading of *The Blackboard Jungle*, he raises his voice. "You heard me. I'll have no insubordination. Get our your Spelling books!"

Again his orders are met by an uncomfortable shuffling of feet.

Incensed and beginning to panic, he starts to repeat his order for the third time, when one boy, braver than the rest, raises his hand.

"Well," glares our teacher.

"Sir, we don't have any Spelling books, we don't have any books. You didn't give them out yet."

"Oh! Oh! Well, all right then. Well, well, well (panic is mounting.) Well, everyone write a composition on 'What I Did This Summer'."

A few children stir but most just sit eying the teacher until the brave boy raises his hand again.

"Sir, we don't have any paper. The teacher usually gives out paper."

"Oh, oh, oh, yes. Here you"—he points to the brave one—"go to the closet, get out a package of paper and give it out."

(He assigns someone to the job because his trembling legs won't carry him as far as the closet.)

As the paper is being distributed to the children a boy and girl enter the room. Anxious to show that he is alert and will tolerate no violation of school rules, he is prompt in his decision, "You two go to the office, you're late." In a few minutes they return bearing a note.

Dear Mr. Hannan:

It is only 5 minutes to 9. School starts at 9 o'clock when the opening bell rings. Please admit these students.

The Principal

At 9:10 our teacher calls a halt to the compositions. "Hey," the kids chorus, "we didn't have time to finish."

"Never mind," he growls, "finish it for homework. Now get out the Arithmetic books."

"Hey," calls the brave boy, "you didn't give us books yet." Now our teacher feels that his authority and judgment are being questioned.

"Listen you," he says, "don't you know better than to call a teacher, 'hey'? Haven't your teachers and parents taught you common politeness? You're to call me by my name, not 'hey'."

"But sir . . ."

"Never mind, go to the office. I know your type. I won't stand for insubordination." As the boy starts to leave the room the class begins to revolt.

In unison they scream, "You never told us your name."

"Well," he snaps right back, "if you weren't so insubordinate I would have told you long ago."

"What's insubordinate?" asks a little girl.

"Be quiet and copy my name."

He writes shakily and slowly and the children start dutifully to copy. "I want that copied one thousand times while I'm giving out books." As our insecure hero stumbles around distributing the forgotten books he sneaks a glance at the clock: 9:35.

"My God, I won't last till noon let alone work at this job for a lifetime," he thinks. . . .

A clanging bell is the final nerve-cracking straw.

"FIRE DRILL," screams our hero rushing aimlessly around. "Everyone remain absolutely calm. No talking! REMAIN CALM! FOLLOW ME! NO TALKING! I WON'T STAND FOR INSUBORDINATION. NO TALK-ING!"

"Sir," says the brave little boy. "Sir," he says. "Mr. Hannan," he says. "Mr. Hannan, this isn't a fire drill. That's the lunch bell. Don't worry, Mr. Hannan, I'll take the class to the lunchroom. You just go and sit down awhile. I'll see to everything. . . ."

After lunch the whole character of that class changed. They well knew he wasn't to be trifled with and they got right down to work. In no time at all they organized a system for passing and collecting papers. They reminded him politely that he had forgotten to salute the flag and do morning prayers that day. They told him that this was required by state law and offered to set up a rotating system to relieve him of this administrative responsibility. They explained about the attendance sheet and how important it was to keep it accurately. Fire and air raid drill procedures were carefully outlined to him. They also taught him to admit when he was wrong, to say "I don't know" when he didn't know and to apologize to those falsely accused, just as if they were grown-up people.

Don't think it was all one-sided. He taught them something too. He taught them to look up "insubordinate" in the dictionary. He taught them a new method of subtraction which he invented on the spot. Most important he taught them that teachers can make mistakes just like any other person.

It is hoped that the suggestions already offered will help to protect the reader from a similar experience. In addition, the following should guarantee a smooth opening day. It should be understood, of course, that all suggestions are, of necessity, very general and should be modified according to the individual situation and the grade level.

1. *General*
    a. Arrive early enough to greet children as they enter the room. If children enter gradually, circulate around the room, socialize informally with groups and individuals. Try to learn as many names as possible.
    b. Conduct opening exercises according to school policy.
    c. Check attendance according to class list. Report absentees to office as directed. Introduce yourself. Write name on board.
    d. Take care of other necessary routines—lunch money, etc.
    e. Begin to establish the exact type of firm, friendly pupil-teacher relationship you hope to maintain throughout the year. Avoid being too permissive or too harsh. Anticipate and begin to establish cooperatively necessary classroom routines for sharpening pencils, distributing and collecting supplies, entering and leaving the room, etc. These can be written on the chalkboard, transferred to a wall chart, and added to as the need arises.
    f. End both morning and afternoon sessions on a pleasant note by reading a story, reading poetry, group singing, etc. (As soon as children leave the room, morning or afternoon, the first question they will be asked by peers and parents is, "How did you like your new teacher?" Be sure their answer will be a positive one!)
    g. Avoid making drastic changes in furniture arrangements, etc. Children feel secure with the familiar. You have the rest of the year to introduce innovations.
    h. Don't be discouraged or upset if the day doesn't go exactly as you planned. Remember you are working with people—and they are always unpredictable!
2. *Informal Language Period.*
    a. In a get acquainted session, encourage children to talk about themselves. Tell some interesting facts about yourself.
    b. Discuss current news happenings, or summer activities, or subjects related to bulletin board displays.
    c. Make future plans for the classroom, "What can we do to make our room more interesting and attractive?" (This can open the door for many art projects—making curtains, making pictures, making wall panels or murals, etc.)
    d. Open discussion of plans for the year. "What did you study last year? Do you have any ideas about what you would like to study this year?" etc.
3. *Reading.*
    Form reading groups according to personnel and level of reading material indicated by previous study of pupils' records.

4. *Arithmetic.*

Administer a short diagnostic test on material you think children have mastered. Use textbooks, workbooks, curriculum guides, etc., to determine items for the test. The results will help you to establish groupings and also provide the basis for future work. Explain purpose of the test (to help you know what arithmetic they have learned) to children. Avoid referring to it as a test.

5. *Physical education.*

Outdoor or indoor game according to weather and school regulations. Encourage children to choose a familiar game in preference to teaching a new one.

6. *Science and/or social studies.*

Review discussion of previous year's work. Motivate interest in first unit with filmstrip, pictures, etc., where feasible. (A common error of beginning teachers is to avoid starting a new unit during the first few days or week of school. This stalling for time can lead to boredom and apathy on the part of the pupils. Most of them have been eagerly awaiting the opening of school. Why not capitalize upon their anticipation and eagerness? What can be gained by waiting?)

Discipline

Problems related to pupil behavior were reported by both experienced and inexperienced teachers, although the frequency was greater with the latter. Such comments as the following are indicative of the concern of many teachers.

My biggest problem? DISCIPLINE!

I did not initiate firm, consistent discipline right at the start. I discovered my mistake when it was almost too late to correct it.

I have often wondered if I have good control over my class compared to other third grades.

Discipline—it was discussed briefly in our college courses but more attention should be given to it.

Effective discipline of children. Pupils know that a teacher is limited in her methods of administering discipline and will even tell the teacher this.

Children's behavior and attitude. I miss the classroom atmosphere of another community where children are taught at home to be quiet, receptive, and anxious to learn. Here, a large part of every teacher's energy goes into police work and breaking down resistance to learning.

Discipline—the children lack self-control and the desire to develop it. It is rather obvious that many children have very little, if any, parental supervision.

Discipline of the two or three who disturb the class by loud talking, clowning, and doing anything to get attention.

For a detailed discussion of this problem, the reader is referred to Chapter 3. The following list summarizes the major aids to positive classroom discipline mentioned in the earlier discussion.

BASIC AIDS TO POSITIVE CLASSROOM DISCIPLINE

1. Remember the basic four *F*'s underlying good classroom discipline and healthful pupil-teacher rapport—*Fairness, Friendliness, Firmness,* and *Fun* (sense of humor).
2. Establish necessary routines and rules of classroom management early in the year.
3. Provide a healthful physical environment. (One study reports that 65 per cent of disciplinary incidents encountered by a group of student teachers were in categories of (a) discipline arising out of a defective physical setting, and (b) failure to cope with routine disturbances.[3]
4. Create a challenging and interesting classroom intellectual environment.
5. Look for the underlying *causes* of poor discipline. Remember that multiple-causative factors are operative in most instances.
6. Consult whatever specialized help is available.
7. Remember that disciplining is teaching. It is not time wasted to teach a child to be a socially desirable citizen. It is an important part of your job.
8. Spend considerable time in planning interesting lessons and preparing or securing worthwhile multisensory aids. It will be time well spent.
9. Keep in mind the two basic key words of effective discipline—*persistency* and *consistency.*
10. Use punishment only as a last resort.
11. Develop standards of classroom behavior cooperatively with pupils.
12. Be sure that you are not placing unrealistic demands upon children.
13. Remember that the ultimate goal of all discipline is self-discipline.
14. Remember that your pupils are entitled to the same courtesy, kindness, thoughtfulness, and consideration you extend to your friends.
15. Examine yourself. Are you unfair to place all of the blame on children? Osborn suggests the following checkup for the teacher with problem pupils.

(1) Why am I teaching anyway?
   What needs does teaching satisfy for me? Do I overpressure children? Is their success, my success—their failure, my failure?

[3] Edwin J. Swineford, "Discipline—A Basic Problem of the Beginning Teacher," *The Clearing House,* Vol. 36 (February, 1962), pp. 350-352.

(2) What is my philosophy?

What is your own philosophy? Ask yourself, "What *really* counts?

(3) Is what really counts significant?

I knew one teacher who wanted all the children to place their pencils on the desks with the erasers pointed in the same direction. I've known a few kindergarten teachers who were unhappy when even the slightest paint was spilled, and they felt they had "problem" children. Instead, the children had a compulsive teacher. Often these problems are real problems—but they are teacher problems and unfortunately are insignificant "tempests in the proverbial teapot."

(4) What do children do that gives me real satisfaction?

You should find many positive answers to this question. If you have trouble with this question, seriously review question one.

(5) What do the children do that upsets me?

In many ways, this question is the most significant one in our checklist. Do not forget to consider things which cause "minor upsets." Little problems, like small bills, really can add up. In a number of cases, the child does not have the problem—rather, the teacher has a problem which she must learn to handle.

(6) Am I tired or upset?

Unless care is taken, the tired teacher makes her own problem situations. At this time even minor problems can assume major proportions.

A word of warning: Be honest with yourself and take care with your checkup. Answering the above questions may provide some "answers" to that problem child.[4]

Oversized Classes

Many teachers complain bitterly about oversized classes on two counts. First, a large number of pupils does not permit adequate attention to individual differences. The following comments reveal teachers' concern with this problem.

Large class size. This year I have thirty-six pupils and cannot give the individual help I would like to.

Far too many children to do individual work. It is difficult to keep the discussion from being dominated by only a few vocal ones.

The class is too large. I have fifty-five kindergartners (twenty-eight in the morning and twenty-seven in the afternoon). I can't give them enough individual attention.

Number of children prevents as complete a program of individual help as I would like to give.

Certainly it is to these teachers' credit that they desire to give individual attention to their pupils. Grouping, differentiated assignments, long-range projects, and other techniques suggested in Chapter 9 will certainly help. Another solution is, of course, the reduction of class size.

[4] D. Keith Osborn, "Checkup," *Grade Teacher*, Vol. 80 (November, 1962), p. 145.

As stated on page 380, there has been a steady trend in this direction for the past several decades, but the average-size class still exceeeds a total of twenty-five, considered a desirable maximum by most educators. This, however, is a long-range goal that will be realized only when the American public is willing to support financially a quality educational program in each individual school and classroom. Heffernan states the point very well.

Obviously the solution lies in the reduction of enrollments to a teachable class size of 25 to 30 children. But this means the employment of more teachers, building more classrooms, increasing maintenance personnel. School business experts supply us with fantastic figures concerning what it would cost a city school district to reduce the class load of teachers by even one or two children. No one can question the fact that teachable-sized classes will result in increased school budgets.

So the solution lies ultimately in how much our society values schools. How much do we, as a people, actually believe in youth? In the past decade, we have spent 78 billion dollars as the total cost of all education. During the same decade, we invested nearly twice as much, 151 billion, in tobacco, beverage alcohol and cosmetics. We spent 127 billion for recreation, and we spent another 110 billion for automobiles.

At the same time, general recognition is being expressed that the basic contest in the world today is the fight for knowledge—a race for minds. We are in a critical period in which we must look at the provisions we are making for education and know that *striving for excellence* is not enough; we must be willing, as a people, to provide the conditions which make the *attainment of excellence* possible.

We can be certain that the quality of education will not improve greatly until teachers have time enough to work with individual children in a situation freed from the pressure of large numbers in overcrowded classrooms.[5]

Secondly, oversized classes result in overcrowded classrooms, with a serious lack of space for a well-rounded elementary program. Again, there is a general trend toward the solution of this problem, for newer schools contain larger, more flexible, and better-planned classrooms than those of a few years ago (see Chapter 6).

This, however, unfortunately does not help the teacher in the older school building who reports the problem in such comments as:

Size of room and general layout are great problems and prevent my developing the kind of program I'd like. A larger room or differently shaped room would be helpful.

The room is impossible. I have forty children in a classroom which, according to our state building code, is adequate for fifteen. What shall I do?

[5] Helen Heffernan, "What is Your Biggest Roadblock to Good Teaching?" *Grade Teacher*, Vol. 77 (January, 1960), p. 24.

Small classroom plus large class equals my biggest problem.

Too small a room for first grade. Impossible to have construction work or any type of rhythms program.

This kindergarten room is ridiculous. When we have rhythms, skipping, running, hopping, etc., we fall over each other and everything else in the room.

The only practical solution to this problem lies in clever room planning. Let's start first with pupil desks and chairs.

Although movable furniture should be moved freely according to the activity, most teachers organize the room into some type of basic furniture arrangement. It was stated in Chapter 6 that the most space-consuming furniture arrangement is the traditional single rows of individual desks and chairs. One way to approach this problem is to substitute tables with a seating capacity of six to eight, for the individual tables and chairs. Another is to arrange desks and chairs into clusters, semicircles, open square, or similar groupings. Such arrangements will provide more floor space for activity work and will also promote an informal classroom environment.

What about the teacher's desk? This is a bulky piece of furniture and should be moved into an obscure corner where it will occupy less valuable space. One teacher went a step further and asked the custodian to remove it entirely and to furnish her with a pupil's desk which, together with a steel filing cabinet, was sufficient for her records and materials.

There are many other tricks teachers in old buildings may use to gain space. Big, old, space-extravagant cloakrooms can be relighted (if necessary) and converted into science experiment centers, classroom libraries, creative writing corners, art studios, or workrooms. Hallways can be used for large construction and art work. Granted, such arrangements are makeshift. They are considerably preferable to teaching children in cramped, overcrowded quarters that permit none of the variety and activity considered essential to a well-rounded elementary educational program.

Lack of Home-School Cooperation

This was a concern expressed by both experienced and inexperienced teachers, although for different reasons. The experienced teachers appeared to be critical of parents' lack of cooperation, understanding, and support with such statements as:

Handling parents who expect more from their children than the children are able to give. They push the child until he becomes nervous and withdrawn.

Lack of parental cooperation.

Failure of parents to recognize that a mark or grade is *not* the most important thing in their child's education. If you don't teach them anything but give them a good mark, you are a good teacher.

Lack of concern of parents of those children who need to be "pushed" to produce according to their ability.

I have difficulty in getting parents to understand homework policy. We do not give homework as such but the parents want hours of assignments because they feel this is the only way to help their children.

These comments indicate two things. First, there is a very apparent need for a stronger program of parent and community education than many schools now have. If parents do not understand the school's philosophy, if they do not understand basic principles of child growth and learning, if they do not support a quality educational program, the need for a stronger and more consistent program of parent education becomes imperative. This need, and techniques for meeting it, were emphasized in Chapter 4.

Secondly, the apparent tendency of experienced teachers to criticize and blame parents for all pupil shortcomings suggests that they need to reexamine the meaning of the word *cooperation*. It does *not* mean what one third-grader said who, when asked to define the word, replied, "Cooperation means getting other people to do what you want them to do." Rather, cooperation is a two-way process involving mutual understanding and respect. It is an old joke in educational circles that, for all student deficiencies, the graduate school blames the college, the college blames the high school, the high school blames the elementary school, and the elementary school blames the parents. Several comments of experienced teachers indicate that there may be more truth than humor in this statement. If home and school are to work together, the teacher must begin by ceasing to place all blame upon the parents. After all, as someone has said, parents send to school the best children they have! And, in the large majority of cases, they are genuinely anxious to raise their children according to the best of their ability and knowledge. If the elementary school teacher realizes this, and tries to help and understand more than merely to criticize and find fault, his total role may be somewhat different than he anticipated, but this is not necessarily a problem.

Inexperienced teachers were much more fearful than critical of parents. They said:

Gaining the confidence of the parents of the most intelligent students. I felt they were suspicious of such a young, new teacher.

How do you talk with parents?

Fear of parent reaction caused me some sleepless nights. How I dreaded that first parent conference. However, the parents proved to be most gracious and I have almost overcome my initial insecurity.

My biggest problem was how to talk with parents. How can I be diplomatic and honest at the same time?

Time and experience, of course, are the natural solutions to this problem. In addition, many teacher-education institutions are now offering their students varied experiences that should help to minimize their initial insecurity. Role playing of parent-teacher conferences in psychology and education courses; home visitations, and attendance at PTA meetings during student teaching; and numerous types of community-centered experiences are some of the techniques forward-looking institutions have incorporated into their preservice programs to minimize this problem for the inexperienced teacher.

Lack of Teaching Supplies, Resources, and Equipment

This problem was expressed in such comments as the following:

The most serious problem is that of gathering written and A-V material for adequate and interesting social studies and science lessons. The school is lacking in texts and books for children to use as supplementary references.

I wish I could have more books for science and social studies.

. . . not being able to obtain needed supplies.

A new, extremely poorly equipped room with very few supplies makes all areas of teaching limited and difficult.

Textbooks. Either there are not enough or they are too outdated to be of much help.

Difficulty in obtaining reference materials and equipment quickly and inexpensively.

Teaching aids such as film strips, sound films, tape recorders, etc. are not accessible to all teachers. Much time has to be spent in seeking equipment.

The most obvious solution to this problem is to increase the school budget. But this, again, is a long-range goal dependent entirely upon the willingness of the American public to support a quality school program. In the meantime, several more immediate partial solutions lie within the hands of the teachers themselves.

First, many teachers complain that they do not have a sufficient *number* of texts and references, particularly in the social studies and science. What they probably mean is that they do not have a sufficient *variety* of texts and references. This is quite another problem but one that can be at least partially solved through wise purchasing. Purchasing thirty copies of a single text means essentially that the school is paying more than one hundred dollars for *one* book. Obviously, any single volume is limited in its scope and presentation. Five copies of six different texts cost no more. But they offer far, far greater depth and variety of material to teacher and pupils. The use of a single textbook is not only poor teaching (see Chapter 10), but it is also a very poor way of stretching the school dollar as far as it will go.

Secondly, much of the problem can be attributed, not so much to *lack* of materials, as to *inaccessibility* of materials. One teacher comments, "In our school, there seems to be no system for listing or otherwise making known what materials are available in other classrooms or in the school closets. The searching takes time from other more important tasks."

The answer to this facet of the problem lies in (1) central storage and (2) an efficient method of distribution. Both of these factors are extremely important and cannot be emphasized too strongly. Teachers are notorious hoarders. They tend to tuck away in their classrooms books or materials they may use only a few times a year. Obviously, this deprives other teachers. Central storage in which all books, supplies, and equipment are stored in a central instructional materials center and distributed to teachers on a loan basis is rapidly finding acceptance in most schools. Of course, its success depends heavily upon an efficient system of check-out and distribution. This can be the responsibility of the instructional materials coordinator, a faculty committee, or an employed lay person depending upon the individual situation. But it is high time that schools borrowed from industry the idea of a central depository where workers secure and return materials as their needs demand. Admittedly, this suggestion is unpopular with those teachers who like to guard jealously "their" books and supplies. But are these materials really "theirs" or are they the property of the entire school to be used to greatest advantage for all?

Thirdly, the problem can be lessened by providing teachers with a small petty cash fund to purchase a few supplies or books at the time the need arises. Basic equipment and supplies are, of course, purchased prior to the opening of the school years. But, as all teachers know, it is extremely difficult to anticipate all needs a year in advance. It has been the experience of the author that providing each teacher with a small cash fund ($25.00-$100.00) with which to purchase incidental art supplies, science equipment, and other items is a terrific morale-booster. The total sum involved is, in most cases, approximately one thousand dollars per school building. This is not a prohibitive sum for most schools. Furthermore, it is money well spent for there is no doubt that it will help to relieve teachers from the ever-present, nagging problem of no materials.

Excessive Noninstructional Duties

Evidence from many studies indicates that most teachers consider this to be one of the most serious deterrents to effective teaching. In our own study, the problem was reported in such statements as:

The lack of release time in the self-contained classroom for planning, correcting papers, etc. I feel that six continuous hours in the classroom each day (20 minutes for lunch) does not permit a teacher to operate at his or her maximum effectiveness.

The bookkeeping involved in running a classroom (taking attendance, collecting milk and ice cream money, etc.) all tend to subtract from the teaching day.

The little things (such as taking lunch orders) when I could be giving individual help.

Lunch duty, followed by playground duty.

Lunch duty. Lack of relaxation at noon lessens energy for afternoon teaching.

Too much clerical work.

The teacher has too many "outside jobs" that take time from her class, namely, banking; patrol, lunch, library, and bus duties; report cards; etc.

Keeping classroom register and other clerical work.

The abnormally high number of things such as lunch orders, collections, insurance, etc., etc., etc., which have to be done daily cut down on our time for lessons.

Taking care of picture money, insurance money, etc. takes too much time away from teaching, especially in the primary grades.

Is there any evidence to support the claims of teachers that a disproportionate amount of their time is spent in noninstructional duties? There is. According to one study, teachers ". . . spend 25 per cent of their time in school engaging in activities that are other than face-to-face instruction."[6] Another survey reports that the typical elementary teacher has an average work week of 48 hours and 30 minutes. Of this total, 29 hours, 30 minutes (60.8 per cent) is spent in class instruction. Eleven hours, 54 minutes (28.6 per cent) is spent in related instructional activities such as correcting papers, preparing materials, etc. Seven hours, 6 minutes (14.6 per cent) is spent in miscellaneous duties such as monitorial duties, meetings, records and reports, etc. Figure 13.1 on page 555 illustrates this division of time.

What can be done to alleviate the situation? First of all, it is important to remind teachers that their role extends far beyond the actual instruc-

[6] Fred Guggenheim, "Nonteaching Activities of Teachers in a Staff Utilization Study," *Journal of Educational Research*, Vol. 54 (May, 1961), p. 325.

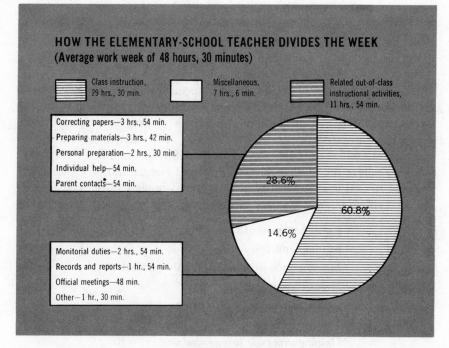

HOW THE ELEMENTARY-SCHOOL TEACHER DIVIDES THE WEEK
(Average work week of 48 hours, 30 minutes)

Class instruction,
29 hrs., 30 min.

Miscellaneous,
7 hrs., 6 min.

Related out-of-class
instructional activities,
11 hrs., 54 min.

Correcting papers—3 hrs., 54 min.
Preparing materials—3 hrs., 42 min.
Personal preparation—2 hrs., 30 min.
Individual help—54 min.
Parent contacts—54 min.

Monitorial duties—2 hrs., 54 min.
Records and reports—1 hr., 54 min.
Official meetings—48 min.
Other—1 hr., 30 min.

28.6%

60.8%

14.6%

FIGURE 13.1

Division of the week by the elementary school teacher. From "Time
Devoted to School Duties," *NEA Research Bulletin*, Vol. 40 (October,
1962), p. 86.

tional process. It is appalling to find some teachers labeling as "noninstructional" such tasks as writing lesson plans, conferencing with parents, attending professional meetings, and writing report cards. These are certainly not noninstructional in any sense of the word. They are closely related to the instructional process and it is difficult to see how teaching can be effective without them. True, they are time-consuming. But they are basic essentials to good teaching and it is impossible to understand how teachers could, or should, be relieved of them.

Because of the difficulty of distinguishing finely between "instructional" and "noninstructional" duties, amounts of time teachers report in each area may be somewhat misleading. However, even taking this into consideration, the evidence still indicates that many teachers do spend a considerable amount of time on duties that are only remotely, if at all, related to instruction. One of the most common of these is lunchroom, playground duty, or both. One study reports that only 12 per cent of urban districts provide duty-free lunch periods for elementary school teachers.[7] This startling low per cent indicates that most teachers are indeed justified in naming lack of release time during the day as one of their major problems or deterrents to greater effectiveness.

What are some possible solutions?

Some schools merely insist that all children go home for lunch. Others arrange for clerical, administrative, or special staff personnel to be in charge during the noon hour to free the teachers from spending the full day with children.[8] Still another solution is the current trend toward employing teacher-aides, paraprofessionals, instructional secretaries, or teacher assistants as they are variously called. Such aides may be employed solely to relieve the teacher of monitorial and clerical duties. Others have assumed related instructional tasks of a fairly simple nature. The following are typical tasks frequently assigned to nonprofessional personnel.

> Arranging materials for classes
>
> Reading and story-telling
>
> Managing the milk fund and other collections
>
> Housekeeping chores
>
> Arranging bulletin-board displays
>
> Keeping attendance and other class records
>
> Helping supervise playground and cafeteria
>
> Administering first aid
>
> Helping with wraps
>
> Supervising bus loading
>
> Helping on excursion trips
>
> Processing books and supplies
>
> Scoring objective tests
>
> Correcting papers
>
> Setting up and operating audio-visual aids
>
> Typing and cutting stencils for class use
>
> Helping in library
>
> Supervising study halls[9]

In general, it is difficult to evaluate the success of using teacher-aides because reports of different experiments vary widely. Some studies, for instance, report that the use of aides does not necessarily allow the teacher

---

[7] "Duty-Free Lunch Periods—a Break for Teachers," *NEA Research Bulletin*, Vol. 38 (December, 1960), p. 105.

[8] *Ibid.*

[9] Educational Research Service Circular, *Teacher-Aides: Current Practices and Experiments*, No. 5, 1960 (Washington, D. C., American Association of School Administrators and Research Division, National Education Association, July, 1960), p. 3.

more time for instruction and may even, in some cases, add to the teacher's responsibilities and duties. Roberts concluded that,

The real significance of this study is that noninstructional duties of teachers in this school system constitute a problem but its prevalence and crucial nature can be over-magnified. There are elements in the load of teachers that can be termed "noninstructional." Yet, it turns out to be quite difficult to project a major change in the roles of modern teachers by separating organizationally or personnel-wise, such duties from classroom teaching functions.[10]

The Yale-Fairfield Study of the use of teacher assistants in the elementary school reports quite different findings.

Substantial amounts of time were saved by teachers in clerical work, routine classroom activities, and certain easy instructional tasks. Minor amounts of time were saved in housekeeping, and supervision outside the classroom. Some additional time was required in planning. Because of the time saved and because of greater protection from interruptions, teachers were able to give more individual attention to pupils, use more specially prepared material, carry the instruction further in some subject areas, provide better for individual differences by better grouping, and spend more time on curriculum enrichment.[11]

It can only be concluded that the success of employing teacher assistants apparently varies widely according to the specific situation. Certainly, however, it would behoove any school system to study the possibilities of the plan to relieve teachers from excessive monitorial or clerical duties.

A slightly different approach to the problem has been taken by school systems that have employed part-time personnel solely for the purpose of relieving teachers of monitorial duties. In Pasadena, California, for instance, housewives who live near the school are employed for one hour a day for noontime duty in lunchrooms and playgrounds, with at least one certificated teacher on call at all times. In addition, local college students are employed to supervise playground activities after school hours.[12]

Another variation is the use of volunteer help to assist teachers in certain duties (see Chapter 4). This has been successful in some systems, although the degree, again, is dependent upon many factors in the local situation.

[10] Charles T. Roberts, *Elements Which Have Extended the Role of the Teacher and the Influence of These Elements on Teachers' Duties in One School System,* Ed. D. Dissertation, University of Texas, 1960. Dissertation Abstracts, Vol. 21, pp. 1825-1826.

[11] Clyde M. Hill and others, *Teacher Assistants, An Abridged Report.* The Yale-Fairfield Study of Elementary Teaching (New Haven, Conn., February, 1959), p. 42.

[12] "Can Your Teachers Have Duty-Free Lunch Hours?" *School Management,* Vol. 5 (April, 1961), p. 96.

It should be of some comfort also to the classroom teacher to realize that some states are moving toward legislation that prescribes a duty-free minimum lunch period for classroom teachers. Among the states that have such legislation are California, Illinois, Massachusetts, and Ohio.[13]

Thus far we have discussed mainly the out-of-class monitorial duties of teachers. But in-class noninstructional duties are also a problem. What can be done here?

Elementary school teachers complain most bitterly about the amount of class time devoted to collecting monies for such things as charity drives, school fund-raising projects, and lunch and milk orders. Again, some of these are essential while others are not. To see that a child has a suitable lunch or a glass of milk is often just as important as teaching him arithmetic. If these monies cannot be collected centrally, the elementary teacher, with a little efficiency and ingenuity, should be able to dispense with this responsibility in a few minutes. Some teachers capitalize upon the educational possibilities of such activities. Primary grade teachers may count the money, add up the number of people and tickets, and so on as a regular part of their daily arithmetic instruction. Intermediate and upper grade teachers rotate the responsibility among individuals and small groups with desirable educational outcomes.

There are other ways to reduce the problem. Some teachers organize such an efficient method of collecting essential monies that almost no time is taken from instruction. Mrs. N, for instance, at the beginning of the year, makes good-sized name cards for her class of first-graders. Every morning she lines these cards along the chalkboard ledge. As the children enter, those who do not want to buy lunch simply remove their cards and place them in a cardboard box. A glance at the names remaining on the ledge tells Mrs. N the total number who are buying lunch. The children then pay her, according to the order of their name cards on the ledge. There is almost no possibility for error and the whole process takes less than five minutes. With efficiency and ingenuity, it *is* possible for the elementary teacher to devise a scheme for collecting essential monies without serious loss of instructional time.

In quite another category, however, are other collections. There is no doubt that, in some schools, teachers have been exploited to become collectors for every conceivable kind of charity or fund-raising drive. It is the responsibility of every teacher and administrator to resist this practice in the strongest manner. Teachers should not be asked to be responsible for several hundred dollars belonging to one fund or another. There are no adequate facilities to keep such sums of money in the ordinary classroom. Nor should teachers be bookkeepers for various interests. Nor

[13] "Duty-Free Lunch Period—a Break for Teachers," *op. cit.*, p. 106.

should they be forced to give priority to tasks other than teaching children. There is no doubt that some of these collections are nonessential, noninstructional, and nonprofessional. They must be eliminated in order to allow the teacher to do the job for which he is prepared and for which he receives his salary.

Providing for a Wide Range of Pupil Abilities

This subject has been examined thoroughly in Chapter 9, and there is little that needs to be said here. Individuals *are* different. They always will be different. There is nothing that a teacher can, or should, do to change that fact. We can classify, assort, group, and pigeonhole children in any way we think best. But this does not reduce, to any perceptible degree, their distinctive differences and uniquenesses. As long as there are twenty-five children in a class there will be twenty-five different individuals in the group. Providing for each of these according to his unique potential is, not necessarily a problem, but an intensely challenging, interesting, and rewarding task for today's competent elementary school teacher.

SUMMARY

Every profession presents certain problems that produce frustrations and low morale and generally hinder the worker's effectiveness. Elementary school teaching is no exception. According to several hundred statements from teachers, the most persistent problems appear to be (1) getting a good start at the beginning of the year, (2) discipline, (3) oversized classes, (4) lack of home-school cooperation, (5) lack of teaching supplies, resources, and equipment, (6) excessive noninstructional duties, and (7) providing for a wide range of pupil abilities. There appears to be a high degree of consistency between the problems mentioned by experienced and inexperienced teachers. There is also consistency between the problems reported by this group and those mentioned in other surveys.

Some of the above problems have been discussed fully in other chapters. The discussion here, therefore, was in the nature of a brief summary and reiteration of earlier statements. Others were examined in more detail and suggestions for their solution were offered. Some solutions appear to be long-range; others are more immediate. Some depend ultimately upon the willingness of the American public to support a quality educational program while others lie in the hands of inventive and capable teachers. Some are genuine deterrents to good teaching but others are problems existing only in the attitudes and minds of unhappy teachers. Though some have existed for years, others appear to be nearing a solution in some school systems.

Everyone realizes that the elimination of all problems in any field is an unrealistic goal. At the same time, if the elementary school is to achieve its goal of providing a quality educational program for every child, every effort must be made to identify, and find solutions for, those problems that detract in any measure from the effectiveness of the elementary school teacher.

ADDITIONAL LEARNING EXPERIENCES

Topics for Thought and Discussion

1. What preservice experiences have you had that you think will help you to work positively and cooperatively with parents and community members?

2. Does your state have any legislative prescriptions concerning compulsory release time for elementary school teachers during the day? For secondary teachers?

3. Do you know of any school system that provides a petty cash fund through which teachers may be permitted to purchase incidental supplies and materials? How much is allocated to each teacher? What is the feeling of teachers concerning the value of this fund?

4. Do teachers tend to exaggerate the problem of noninstructional duties? The other problems mentioned in this chapter?

Projects and Activities

1. You have been appointed a member of a teachers' committee to develop an orientation handbook for beginning teachers. Outline the items you would include in such a publication. Consult the existing handbooks of several school districts for ideas and suggestions.

2. For sheer enjoyment read *Never Tease a Dinosaur* by Joseph F. Hannan (New York, Holt, Rinehart, and Winston, 1961). Does this humorous book contain some sound advice for elementary school teachers?

3. Demonstrate, through a scaled drawing or a model, how a clever furniture arrangement can compensate for lack of space in the classroom of traditional size.

4. Talk with an elementary school principal about the problem of availability of instructional materials. How does he try to insure the maximum use and availability of instructional materials?

5. Observe in an elementary classroom for an entire day. Make a time study of the teacher's activities. What per cent of his day is devoted to noninstructional duties? To direct instructional duties? To related instructional duties? How does your study compare with the per cents reported in this chapter? Could you make any suggestions to the teacher for the better use of his time?

6. Prepare a research paper on the use of teacher-aides in the elementary school. Summarize your findings as to (1) the extent of the practice, (2) the advantages, (3) the disadvantages, and (4) the possible future trends.

7. Prepare a research paper on team teaching in the elementary school. To what extent does this organizational pattern alleviate the problem of non-instructional duties discussed in this chapter?

8. Through a questionnaire, determine the problems mentioned most frequently by (1) beginning teachers, or (2) experienced teachers, as deterrents to their teaching effectiveness. How consistent are your findings with the problems mentioned in this chapter? With problems mentioned in other studies?

9. Ask a school principal to speak to your college class on any one of the problems mentioned in this chapter. Ask him to include in his discussion how he attempts to solve or minimize the problem in his school.

Selected Bibliography

Brown, Richard F., *Problems and Difficulties of Teachers*. Unpublished doctoral dissertation, University of Southern California, 1952.

Heffernan, Helen, "What is Your Biggest Roadblock to Good Teaching?" *Grade Teacher*, Vol. 77 (January, 1960).

Hilding, Arthur, *Limitations in the Elementary School Which Teachers Feel Tend to Retard Their Teaching Effectiveness*. Unpublished doctoral dissertation, Washington State College, 1953.

Metfessel, Newton S., and Shea, John T., "Fifty Often Overlooked Areas of Teacher Frustration." *American School Board Journal*, Vol. 142 (June, 1961).

Phillips, Margaret M., and Smith, Marjorie Carr, *Try These Answers*. New York, Harper and Row, Publishers, Inc., 1956.

Suggs, Mary F., *Persistent Problems of Teachers*. Unpublished doctoral dissertation, University of Indiana, 1955.

Index